Brief Contents

Property of BUENO CAMP
Aims Community College
South Campus, PR #106a

---

e **LearningCurve** activities and additional grammar exercises are available for the topics in this chapter. Visit **macmillanhighered.com/rrw**.

Real Reading and Writing

Susan Anker

with **Miriam Moore**
Lord Fairfax Community College

BUENO CAMP Property

According to the checkout agreement signed, I
consent to return this textbook **no later** than the
following date:

12/11/17

Bedford/St. Martin's
Boston ◆ New York

For Bedford/St. Martin's

Vice President, Editorial, Macmillan Higher Education Humanities: Edwin Hill
Editorial Director for English and Music: Karen S. Henry
Executive Editor: Vivian Garcia
Developmental Editor: Jill Gallagher
Production Editor: Annette Pagliaro Sweeney
Senior Production Supervisor: Dennis Conroy
Senior Marketing Manager: Christina Shea
Project Management: Matt Rosenquist, Graphic World, Inc.
Photo Researcher: Sheri Blaney
Director of Rights and Permissions: Hilary Newman
Senior Art Director: Anna Palchik
Text Design: Claire Seng-Niemoeller
Cover Design: William Boardman
Cover Art: © Klaus Vedfelt/Getty Images, © Reza Estakhrian/Getty Images, © Siri Stafford/
    Getty Images, © Yagi Studio/Getty Images, © Amos Chappel/Getty Images
Composition: Graphic World, Inc.
Printing and Binding: C.O.S. Printers Pte Ltd - Singapore

Manufactured in Singapore.
9   8   7   6
f   e   d   c   b

For information, write: Bedford/St. Martin's, 75 Arlington Street, Boston, MA 02116
    (617-399-4000)

ISBN 978-1-4576-6711-4 (Student Edition)

Acknowledgments

A note to students from Susan Anker

For the past twenty years or so, I have traveled the country talking to students about their goals and, more important, about the challenges they face on the way to achieving those goals. Students always tell me that they want good jobs and that they need a college degree to get those jobs. I designed *Real Reading and Writing* with those goals in mind—strengthening the writing, reading, and editing skills needed for success in college, at work, and in everyday life.

Here is something else: Good jobs require not only a college degree but also a college education: knowing not only how to read and write but how to think critically and learn effectively. So that is what I stress here, too. It is worth facing the challenges. All my best wishes to you in this course and in all your future endeavors.

A note to students from Miriam Moore

Since 1991, I have taught writing, grammar, reading, and ESL in a variety of places, including a university, an Intensive English program, two community colleges, and even a chicken processing plant! In each place, I have tried to share my love of words with students, and I have learned by listening to their words, their rhythms of speech, their questions, and their frustrations.

Words, and the ways we put them together, help us accomplish ordinary tasks and (as our skills improve) some incredible feats: getting a date, making a sale, convincing the boss to try a new idea, changing a law, or solving a long-standing problem. The words we use to read and write can also help us to think more creatively, more deeply, and more effectively. In *Real Reading and Writing*, I wanted to help you see the value of language skills like reading and writing, and the power of practicing them together. Sure, it takes time and attention to learn new words, understand them when you read, and master rules for combining and punctuating them accurately. But in the end, after working for these skills, you will begin to see **them** working **for you**. It will be worth the effort.

I applaud your decision to take this course, and I wish you every success.

Contents

▣ **LearningCurve** activities and additional grammar exercises are available for the topics in this chapter. Visit **macmillanhighered.com/rrw**.

ℯ **LearningCurve** activities and additional grammar exercises are available for the topics in this chapter. Visit **macmillanhighered.com/rrw**.

ⓔ **LearningCurve** activities and additional grammar exercises are available for the topics in this chapter. Visit **macmillanhighered.com/rrw**.

e **LearningCurve** activities and additional grammar exercises are available for the topics in this chapter.
Visit **macmillanhighered.com/rrw**.

Preface

Real Reading and Writing takes the core message of the Anker series—that good writing skills are both *essential* and *attainable*—and builds on it, providing substantive reading coverage integrated with the same quality writing instruction. The book provides both an engaging real-world context for reading and writing skills, as well as an abundance of exercises, activities, and discussion questions that challenge and foster student learning.

Real Reading and Writing reframes critical reading and writing skills for students who view them as boring, irrelevant, and impossible and instead presents these skills as potentially life-altering: eminently learnable and worthy of students' own best efforts. The book's goal is to teach students how to not only learn these skills, but also how to implement them in their college courses, jobs, and everyday lives.

Features

The integration of reading and writing is stressed throughout *Real Reading and Writing.* The authors continually emphasize the powerful interconnections that make reading and writing easier and more rewarding to learn in tandem. Activities, assignments, and readings have all been thoughtfully tailored to the integrated curriculum. The "Reading/Writing Workbook" section in each rhetorical mode chapter puts integrated reading and writing in context, highlighting two professional readings, as well as student paragraphs and essays. In addition, special attention is given to building vocabulary, an essential skill for students in both reading and writing.

Numerous models of student and professional writing address such real-world issues and concerns as answering challenging job interview questions, commuting to school, and dealing with academic dishonesty.

Four Basics boxes guide students to focus first on the most important elements of reading and writing. For example, the "Four Basics of Good Writing" stresses audience, purpose, a clear, definite main point, and support, while the "Four Basics of Annotation" focuses on vocabulary, finding the main point, identifying support, and making connections. In addition, each chapter in Part 2, "Reading and Writing Different Kinds of Paragraphs and Essays," begins with the four key points to remember about the particular type of writing being discussed, followed by models that are color-coded to show the four basics at work.

End-of-chapter writing guides give students step-by-step advice as they write and revise their papers.

In the Classroom sections offer concrete examples of writing that students are likely to encounter in their daily lives such as résumés, timelines, and online discussion boards.

A focus, initially, on the four most serious errors—fragments, run-ons, subject-verb agreement problems, and verb-tense problems—helps students avoid or fix the grammar mistakes that count against them most in college and the real world. Once students master these four topics and start building their editing skills, they are better prepared to tackle the grammar errors treated in later chapters.

"Find and Fix" boxes and end-of-chapter review charts visually summarize key information and make excellent review and reference tools.

[e] LaunchPad Solo for *Real Reading and Writing:* Throughout this textbook you will see icons in the margins indicating when additional online content is available through our LaunchPad Solo platform.

> **LearningCurve,** innovative adaptive online quizzes, allows students to learn at their own pace with a game-like interface that keeps them engaged. Quizzes are keyed to grammar instruction in the book. Instructors can also check in on each student's activity in an online gradebook.

> **Additional multiple-choice grammar exercises** offer students even more practice with their most challenging grammar concepts. The exercises are auto-gradable and report directly to the instructor's gradebook.

Support for Instructors and Students

Real Reading and Writing is accompanied by comprehensive teaching and learning support.

STUDENT RESOURCES

📖 Print   🖥 Online   💿 CD-ROM

Free with a New Print Text

🖥 **LaunchPad Solo for *Real Reading and Writing,*** at **macmillanhighered.com /rrw**, provides students with interactive and adaptive grammar exercises. Please see the inside back cover for more information on LaunchPad Solo. **Free** when packaged with the print text. Package ISBN: **978-1-319-00774-4**

🖥 ***Re:Writing 3,*** at **bedfordstmartins.com/rewriting**, gives students new open online resources with videos and interactive elements that engage them in new ways of writing. You'll find tutorials about using common digital writing tools, an interactive peer review game, Extreme Paragraph Makeover, and more—all for free and for fun.

📖 *The Bedford/St. Martin's Planner* includes everything that students need to plan and use their time effectively, with advice on preparing schedules and to-do lists plus blank schedules and calendars (monthly and weekly). The planner fits easily into a backpack or purse, so students can take it everywhere. **Free** when packaged with the print text. **ISBN: 978-0-312-57447-5**

Premium

📖 *The Bedford/St. Martin's Textbook Reader,* **Second Edition,** by Ellen Kuhl Repetto gives students practice in reading college textbooks across the curriculum. This brief collection of chapters from market-leading introductory college textbooks can be packaged inexpensively with *Real Reading and Writing.* Beginning with a chapter on college success, *The Bedford/St. Martin's Textbook Reader* also includes chapters from current texts on composition, mass communication, history, psychology, and environmental science. Comprehension questions and tips for reading success guide students in reading college-level materials efficiently and effectively. Package ISBN: **978-1-319-01166-6**

E-BOOK OPTIONS

🖥 *Real Reading and Writing* **e-book.** Available as a value-priced e-book and as either a CourseSmart e-book or in formats for use with computers, tablets, and e-readers—visit **macmillanhighered.com/rrw/formats** for more information.

FREE INSTRUCTOR RESOURCES

📖 **The Instructor's Annotated Edition of** *Real Reading and Writing* gives practical page-by-page advice on teaching with *Real Reading and Writing* and answers to exercises. It includes discussion prompts, strategies for teaching ESL students, ideas for additional classroom activities, suggestions for using other print and media resources, and cross-references useful to teachers at all levels of experience. **ISBN: 978-1-4576-8867-6**

🖥 *Instructor's Manual for Real Reading and Writing* provides helpful information and advice on teaching integrated reading and writing. It includes sample syllabi, reading level scores, tips on building students' critical thinking skills, resources for teaching non-native speakers and speakers of nonstandard dialects, ideas for assessing students' writing and progress, and up-to-date suggestions for using technology in the writing classroom and lab. Available for download; see **macmillanhighered.com/rrw/catalog**.

Testing Tool Kit: Writing and Grammar Test Bank CD-ROM allows instructors to create secure, customized tests and quizzes from a pool of nearly 2,000 questions covering 47 topics. It also includes 10 prebuilt diagnostic tests. **ISBN: 978-0-312-43032-0**

Teaching Developmental Reading: Historical, Theoretical, and Practical Background Readings, Second Edition, is a professional development resource edited by Sonya L. Armstrong, Norman A. Stahl, and Hunter R. Boylan. It offers a wealth of readings from the historical foundations of the developmental reading field to the latest scholarship. **ISBN: 978-1-4576-5895-2**

Teaching Developmental Writing: Background Readings, Fourth Edition, is a professional resource edited by Susan Naomi Bernstein, former co-chair of the Conference on Basic Writing. It offers essays on topics of interest to basic writing instructors, along with editorial apparatus pointing out practical applications for the classroom. **ISBN: 978-0-312-60251-2**

The Bedford Bibliography for Teachers of Basic Writing, Third Edition (also available online at **macmillanhighered.com/basicbib**), has been compiled by members of the Conference on Basic Writing under the general editorship of Gregory R. Glau and Chitralekha Duttagupta. This annotated list of books, articles, and periodicals was created specifically to help teachers of basic writing find valuable resources. **ISBN: 978-0-312-58154-1**

Ordering Information

To order any of these ancillaries for *Real Reading and Writing,* contact your local Bedford/St. Martin's sales representative; send an e-mail to **sales_support@ macmillan.com**; or visit our Web site at **macmillanhighered.com**.

Acknowledgments

Like every edition that preceded it, this book grew out of a collaboration with teachers and students across the country and with the talented staff of Bedford/ St. Martin's. I am grateful for everyone's thoughtful contributions.

REVIEWERS

I would like to thank the following instructors for their many good ideas and suggestions for this edition. Their insights were invaluable.

Andrea Berta, University of Texas at El Paso
Donna Beverly, Montgomery Community College
Annette Cole, Tarrant County College, Northeast Campus
Maryann Errico, Georgia Perimeter College
Heather Fullerton, Heald College
Kris Giere, Ivy Tech Community College of Indiana
Nicole Oechslin, Piedmont Virginia Community College
Carl Olds, University of Central Arkansas
Elaine Pascale, Suffolk University
Jamie Sadler, Richmond Community College

STUDENTS

Many current and former students have helped shape *Real Reading and Writing*, and I am grateful for all their contributions.

Among the students who provided paragraphs and essays for the book are Dora Garcia, Lauren Mack, Inez King, James Carnill, Ibrahim Alfaqeeh, Jasen Beverly, Lorenza Mattazi, Beth Trimmer, Said Ibrahim, Rui Dai, Caitlyn Prokop, Tyler Dashner, Jason Yilmaz, Shari Beck, and Dara Riesler.

CONTRIBUTORS

Art researcher Sheri Blaney, working with Martha Friedman, assisted with finding and obtaining permission for the many new, thought-provoking images included in the book.

Christine End, working with Kalina Ingham, successfully completed the large and essential task of clearing text permissions.

I am also deeply grateful to designer Claire Seng-Niemoeller, who freshened the look of the book's interior.

Finally, I would like to thank copyeditor Arthur Johnson for his careful attention to detail, good questions, and varied contributions to this book. Thanks also to Matt Rosenquist and the rest of the team at Graphic World for managing the project through to its finished form.

BEDFORD/ST. MARTIN'S

I have been extremely fortunate to work with the incredibly talented staff of Bedford/St. Martin's, whose perceptiveness, hard work, and dedication to everything they do are without parallel.

Thanks to Edwin Hill, Vice President, Editorial, Macmillan Higher Education Humanities. Editorial Assistants Brenna Cleeland, Jonathan Douglas, and Kathleen Wisneski have helped with innumerable tasks, from running review programs to assisting with manuscript preparation. We were very fortunate to have Annette Pagliaro Sweeney, Production Editor, shepherding *Real Reading and Writing* through production. Overseeing and thoughtfully contributing to all aspects of the design was Anna Palchik, Senior Art Director. Thanks to William Boardman for his work on the cover design. I must also extend tremendous gratitude to the sales and marketing team. Christina Shea, Senior Marketing Manager, has been a great advocate for all my books and has helped me to forge greater connections with the developmental market and to stay up to date on its needs. And I continue to be deeply thankful for the hard work and smarts of all the sales managers and representatives.

This book would not have reached its fullest potential without the input and attention it received, from the earliest stages of development, from executives and long-time friends in the Boston office: Joan Feinberg, former President of Bedford/St. Martin's; Denise Wydra, former Vice President, Editorial for Humanities, Bedford/St. Martin's; and Karen Henry, Editorial Director for English and Music. I value all of them more than I can say.

Thanks also to my editor, Jill Gallagher, for helping develop this edition. As he has in the past, to my great good fortune, my husband Jim Anker provides assurance, confidence, steadiness, and the best companionship throughout the projects and the years. His surname is supremely fitting.

—*Susan Anker*

In addition to the names already mentioned, I want to thank Alexis Walker, former Executive Editor for Developmental Studies at Bedford/St. Martin's, for asking me to be involved in this project. It was a delight to collaborate with Alexis and Martha Bustin, my initial contacts at Bedford/St. Martin's, and I am grateful for their trust in letting me work with Susan Anker's time-tested materials. I would also like to acknowledge Jill Gallagher, who walked me through the final stages of the book's development and conquered unforeseen glitches as we moved into production. Thanks also to the developmental English instructors across the Virginia Community College system whose expertise and insights on integrating reading and writing permeate my contributions to this text. In addition, Dr. Brenda Wiens, Associate Professor of Biology at Lord Fairfax Community College, provided invaluable information and helpful review for the "In the Classroom" section of Chapter 11.

Finally, I want to thank my family. My husband, Michael Moore, has been a blessing to me for many years in more ways than I could possibly list. He encourages me daily, and I am grateful. Mandy, Mallory, and Murray—my children—also supported me through this project. Their smiles, laughter, and willingness to let me monopolize the family computer made my work a pleasure. I love you all.

—Miriam Moore

Part 1
The Processes of Reading, Writing, and Critical Thinking

Understand Reading, Writing, and Critical Thinking

"If I had eight hours to chop down a tree, I'd spend six hours sharpening my ax."

—Abraham Lincoln

This book is all about sharpening your skills, just as President Lincoln sharpened his ax. Like him, you probably have a goal in mind. Perhaps you want to get a particular certificate or degree; on the other hand, maybe you are simply exploring and want to find out how education can help you build a different life. Whatever your goal is, college courses require a strong foundation in reading, writing, and thinking. This book can help you acquire that foundation.

In this chapter, you will learn about the four basics that characterize all good reading and writing. In Chapters 2–6, you will explore these four basics in more detail. In Chapters 7–14, you will see how these same basics apply to the patterns of writing and reading you may be asked to do in your college courses.

Four Basics of Reading and Writing

1	Good readers and writers follow a thoughtful process.
2	Good readers and writers pay attention to context—the audience, purpose, and topic.
3	Good writers make and support a point; good readers identify the point and the supporting details.
4	Good writers organize support effectively, and good readers identify organizational patterns.

The First Basic: Follow a Thoughtful Process

In this textbook, you will read many examples of good writing, both from professionals and from students like you. As you read these examples, it is important to remember that each piece is a finished **product**—the result of a **process** that involves work. Sometimes, it is easy to forget the work that goes into the words we see on the printed or electronic page.

The truth is that any task that includes reading or writing requires a process. Good reading involves a process of at least four stages, as does good writing:

The reading process

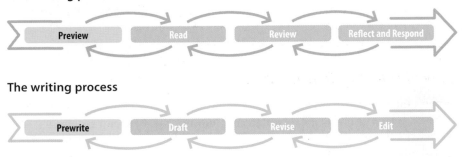

The writing process

Reading and Writing: Closely Linked Processes

Why work on the reading and writing processes at the same time? For the following reasons:

- The stages in each process require similar thinking: Good writers think like readers, and good readers think like writers.

- The processes often overlap. For example, when you preview a reading assignment, you will also write, crafting guiding questions and taking notes. Similarly, when you prewrite, you will also read what you have written, what others have written, and what your teacher has written as instruction or feedback.

- Both processes are **recursive**. That is, we may revisit any step or stage later in the process, as many times as needed. We do not march through all the steps in order, doing each step only once.

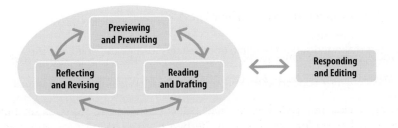

- Both processes require critical thinking—a careful and reasoned approach to making decisions, solving problems, and understanding complex issues. As you learn about the steps in the reading and writing process in Chapters 2–5, you will also learn strategies for thinking critically about your own reading and writing.

PRACTICE 1   **Reflect On Your Reading and Writing Process**

Think about a reading or writing assignment you were given in a previous class, perhaps in high school or an adult education program. What steps did you follow to complete that assignment? What was your goal for the assignment? Were you successful in accomplishing that goal? If so, what parts of the process were most important to your success? If not, what do you think you could have done differently?

Critical Thinking: Reflection

When you ask and answer questions like those in Practice 1, you are using a thinking strategy called **reflecting**. Reflecting means reviewing and analyzing an experience so that you can learn from it. In this book, you will have many chances to practice reflection.

Consider the following example. Jackie struggled with writing assignments in high school, and she failed her first college English course. Here's how Jackie answered the practice exercise:

> *My senior year in high school, I had to write a research paper about the march in Selma, Alabama in the 1960's. I Googled to find some information and I wrote the paper. I just wanted to pass. I worked for probably two hours on it, but I failed. There was so much red on that paper, I could hardly see what I wrote. I guess I just can't write. I have failed everything I've done for English classes since then. I will probably fail this class, too.*

When Jackie reflected on her experience, she saw only one lesson: failure. But her teacher encouraged her to think differently about the experience by considering these questions:

- What else was happening in your life at that time? Was it hard for you to focus on the paper? Why?
- Did you understand the instructions?
- Did you ask for help?
- Do you think you spent enough time on the project? How do you know?
- Did you understand what the teacher said about the paper?

In reflecting, Jackie realized that she had missed most of the classes on how to do research her senior year because she had been working long shifts at a restaurant. She failed primarily because she didn't understand the assignment, and she waited until much too late to start the project. She concluded that she could improve by making more time for writing papers, using a calendar to plan, and visiting the writing center at her college regularly to get help.

PRACTICE 2   Discover Resources

Working with your instructor, your college's Web site, or a classmate, find out what resources are available on your campus if you need help with the following:

_____ child care

_____ transportation

_____ making up missed classwork or tests

_____ getting class notes

_____ getting help with grammar, punctuation, and spelling

_____ finding a job

_____ planning a career

_____ planning a course schedule

PRACTICE 3   Explore a Course Syllabus

One resource that is available to students is a **course syllabus**. With a partner, study the syllabus for this course carefully. How can the information in the syllabus help you plan your work for the semester?

The Second Basic: Pay Attention to Context— the Audience, Purpose, and Topic

When we encounter a new word, situation, or idea, our brains process that new information more effectively if we can connect it to something familiar to us. In other words, we need to find a **context** for the new information. When we put a new word in context, we connect it to surrounding words and phrases so that it makes sense. In fact, the word *context* comes from a Latin word that means "joined together by weaving" or, more simply, "connected." The context for reading or writing involves three key elements.

The audience: As they are writing, good writers think about the audience and what that audience needs to know. If the audience changes, the writing will change as well. At the same time, good readers identify the writer's intended audience so that they can understand that writer better.

The purpose: A writer needs a reason to write. He might be writing to tell a story, to persuade an audience to do something, or to impress a girl. A writer who has a clear purpose is able to make effective choices as he or she moves through the writing process. Similarly, when readers understand a writer's purpose, they are better able to comprehend what they are reading.

The topic: Good writers think about a topic carefully, identifying what they know, what they need to know, and what they want to say about the topic. In the same way, to fully understand a reading passage, good readers identify the topic of the passage and make connections between their own experience and knowledge and what they are reading.

The following chart gives examples of common topics, audiences, and purposes you might encounter in college, at work, or in your everyday life.

Type of Writing/Topic (topics are highlighted)	Audience	Purpose
Your course syllabus for Algebra 1	Students	To explain the course requirements, expectations, and schedule
An e-mail from the head of your company's human resources department about a new insurance provider and co-pay changes	Fellow workers	To make sure all employees understand changes in their insurance policies and coverage
A Facebook post about the State of the Union address	Friends	To share an opinion
A newspaper article about a bank robbery in town	General public	To provide facts about a situation
A review of *Killzone Shadow Fall*, a new game for PlayStation 4	General public, perhaps teens and young adults in particular	To inform and entertain in describing a new product
A letter from a student opposing the school's proposal to begin classes two weeks earlier in August	The school board	To persuade the board to look at alternative scheduling ideas

PRACTICE 4	Identify Topic, Audience, and Purpose

Look at the following types of reading or writing. If possible, find an example of each type to read and consider. Identify the topic, audience, and purpose for each one.

Type of writing	Topic	Audience	Purpose
A handout you received in one of your classes			
A note to a teacher			
A letter from a company that provides a product or service to you, such as your phone, cable, or Internet service provider			
Your college's home page on the Internet			
The first chapter in a textbook for another course			
Chapter 6, "Practice Summarizing," in this textbook			
The Lizzie Bennet Diaries (www.lizziebennet.com)			
Any article in the *New York Times* (www.nytimes.com)			

The Third Basic: Writers Make and Support a Point, and Readers Identify the Point and Supporting Details

You just learned that a topic is part of the context for reading and writing. Good writers have something to say about the topic, and we call the combination of the topic and what the writer says about the topic the **main idea**.

In many ways, our human experience has prepared us to read and write main ideas from the time we begin to talk. Imagine a father walking with his young daughter. Each time the child sees something she recognizes, she names it: *doggy, flower, balloon*. The father not only confirms that his daughter has named the object correctly but also expands on her word:

> *The flower smells good.*

He might then expand the statement with details: *It smells like mommy's perfume. I like that smell*. In other words, the father has offered support for his statement about the world. In doing so, he has illustrated in a simple way the third basic of reading and writing: he said something about the topic (main idea), he gave details about his idea (support), and he offered a final observation (conclusion). These three simple parts (main idea, support, and conclusion) appear in all good writing, both paragraphs and essays.

As writers, we discover what we have to say and find the words to say it, thinking carefully about our audience and our purpose. As readers, we listen to and interpret what someone else says, and we respond to it. These activities of discovering, saying, listening, and interpreting work best when they are part of a process (the First Basic) and when they fit into a context (the Second Basic).

The Fourth Basic: Organize Support Effectively and Identify Organizational Patterns

Good writers know that they cannot drop ideas randomly into a piece of writing; if they do, their readers will not be able to follow their ideas. Instead, good writers arrange or organize their material in logical ways, and they make sure that one idea flows easily and naturally to the next. Skilled readers are familiar with the patterns that writers use to organize ideas, and they recognize the clues that link ideas together.

Let's consider an example:

> *The summer between tenth and eleventh grade, I spent some time at the pool and some at the beach. My mom knew someone at the local hospital. He got me a job as a candy striper, also known as a hospital assistant. Our school was competitive. We were supposed to do things in the summer to help us write our college essays later. I read a lot and volunteered at the local library. I wanted to be an ordinary teenager and hang out with my friends. There was a really popular guy from my school working at the same hospital in the cardiac lab. We had a great summer. He met me in the lounge for a Coke during break each day. We got back to school, and he acted cold and distant. He ignored me. He wouldn't even look at me when he was around his friends. My friends were great but generally not all that popular. At least overall I had a good mix of experiences—and learned the difference between a summer friend and a true one.*

In this short piece of writing, the writer is exploring summer memories. But her writing is not well organized: Her ideas jump suddenly from one place and idea to the next, because she has not found a **principle of organization** to follow.

Now compare that first version of the paragraph to this second version, written after the writer worked on organizing ideas, examples, and details into a logical flow that readers can easily follow:

> The summer between my tenth- and eleventh-grade years was a perfect blend of work and fun. I wanted to be an ordinary teenager and hang out with my friends at the pool and the beach. But my high school was competitive, and the guidance counselor there encouraged us to find summer activities that would look good on a college application. So I took books to the pool to read more on areas I was interested in, specifically health trends and media, and I worked one afternoon a week as a volunteer at our local library. I also got a job as a hospital assistant twice a week, doing filing and other small jobs for the cardiac lab. A guy from my school, who happened to be popular, also worked there in the summer. I was nervous at first because I didn't have many friends in the popular group. But he turned out to be nice, and he sat with me during breaks in the lounge, telling jokes and stories about his quirky family. Unfortunately, that blend of work and relaxation disappeared when school started again. Not only was I back in the classroom, but the popular guy ignored me completely when he got around his in-crowd friends again. Summer was definitely over. At least I had, overall, a good mix of fun and serious experiences. I gained some items for the college application, and I learned the difference between a summer friend and a true one.

In the second version, the writer expresses a main idea (*the summer was a perfect blend of work and fun*), and she has arranged the examples of both work and fun so that they make sense to a reader. We could draw a map of the paragraph to show how it is organized:

Main idea → Examples of fun → Examples of work → Example of work and fun blended → Conclusion: the end of the summer

PRACTICE 5   **Explore Paragraph Organization**

Look at the following set of sample sentences. These sentences address a topic, but they are not organized effectively. Discuss other possible arrangements with a partner. What organization do you think would work best, and why?

1. Over the past century, dystopian novels have been popular with both teens and adults.

2. A recent example is Suzanne Collins's novel *The Hunger Games* (2008), a young adult story about teenagers who are selected by the government and forced to fight to the death for the entertainment of the citizens of the powerful capital city.

3. Most dystopian stories encourage readers to question the motives of government or religious authorities, and they inspire readers to have the courage to escape or defy unjust systems of government.

4. An example of a dystopian story from early in the twentieth century is Aldous Huxley's classic *Brave New World* (1932). This novel describes a society where people are created in test tubes to have certain class characteristics. The members of the highest class, the alphas, make decisions for the rest of the society.

5. *Dystopia* is a word that combines the prefix *dys-*, meaning "not," and *utopia*, meaning "a perfect society." Dystopian stories focus on societies characterized by misery, poverty, abuse, and corruption.

6. An example of a dystopian story from later in the past century is Margaret Atwood's novel *The Handmaid's Tale* (1985), which describes government control by a fundamentalist religious group. In the story, some women serve as handmaids; their job is to provide children for powerful families who cannot have children themselves.

Grammar, Spelling, and Vocabulary

Some of you may be wondering where vocabulary, spelling, and grammar are in the list of basics. Isn't a good knowledge of grammar a basic part of being able to write and read well? Isn't a good vocabulary crucial to good writing and good reading? Yes, grammar and vocabulary *are* important. When you write for an academic audience, you need to write in ways that will make sense to that audience. An academic audience will expect writing to follow the conventions, or rules, of formal, academic English. Believe it or not, though, grammar skills and vocabulary knowledge will develop in the process of learning and practicing good reading and writing skills. Let's look again at those Four Basics of Reading and Writing and consider how they relate to learning grammar, spelling, and vocabulary:

Four Basics of Reading and Writing	How are Grammar, Spelling, and Vocabulary Integral to the Reading and Writing Processes?
1. Good readers and writers follow a thoughtful process.	• When they read, critical thinkers look up the meaning of words they don't know and consider the grammatical and vocabulary choices that authors have made. • When they write, critical thinkers take care in choosing the right words and spelling them correctly, and in observing grammatical conventions, so their language is free from errors that would distract their readers.

Continued

Four Basics of Reading and Writing	How are Grammar, Spelling, and Vocabulary Integral to the Reading and Writing Processes?
2. Good readers and writers pay attention to context—the audience, purpose, and topic.	Part of paying attention is asking questions, such as: • What vocabulary is appropriate to this situation? • How formal or informal can my spelling be? • How can I use correct grammar so that I can better achieve my purpose and communicate about my topic in the best and clearest way?
3. Good writers make and support a point; good readers identify the point and the supporting details.	Writers who know and apply the rules of grammar and who have a good vocabulary are better able to communicate their points. Readers appreciate this clarity.
4. Good writers organize support effectively, and good readers identify organizational patterns.	Knowledge of grammar, spelling, and vocabulary helps readers and writers to see patterns, transitions, and main and supporting points in what they read and write.

As we focus on the Four Basics of Reading and Writing, we will address grammar, spelling, and vocabulary as inseparable and mutually supportive elements in the processes of reading and writing.

The Four Basics: Put It All Together

Over the next four chapters, we will explore each stage in the processes of reading and writing in more detail, and you will have a chance to read what professional writers and students have said about the various stages. These readings are designed to help you turn the reflections you began in this chapter into a fully developed essay that illustrates all four basics of good writing. Each of the readings is followed by reflection questions. Spend time thinking and writing your responses to these questions, and be sure to share your thoughts with a classmate or your teacher. Consider getting a notebook or designating a folder on your laptop or tablet to record your reflections. When you are ready to write, you will find it helpful to have all your reflections in one place.

Chapter Reading

George Dorrill

Reading: A Personal History

George Dorrill is an English professor at Southeastern Louisiana University. The following essay was published in *The Voice* in 2003.

PHOTO BY RICHARD LOUTH, COURTESY OF GEORGE DORRILL

1   In the Sunday, June 16, 2002, New Orleans *Times-Picayune*, English professor John Biguenet writes:

> As I'm thinking about traveling, I'm realizing how important walking is to me when I go somewhere. I don't know of a better place on Earth to get lost than Venice. We found Peggy Guggenheim's[1] house that's open once a week by walking. On my first trip to Paris, we came upon Musée Rodin[2]. Finding both places were happy accidents. Every time I've anticipated seeing something, I've been disappointed, but turning a corner and discovering the unanticipated is the great pleasure of travel. . . . Only a walker moves slowly enough to catch the surprise in the corner of the eye.

2   My reading is like Professor Biguenet's walking. Most of the significant reading of my life has been by accident, rather than by assignment. I am a great disciple of Randall Jarrell's[3] dictum[4], "Read at whim." Let me give you a short history of my reading.

3   I had the lucky accident of being born into a family with a father who loved to read. Among my first memories of reading are the times my father read to my brother Sparky and me from his collection of Classics Comics. We would get on either side of him on his and Momma's double bed, and he would read to us as we looked at the pictures. My special favorites were the ones that told of adventures in exotic places, like *Under Two Flags, The Swiss Family Robinson*, and *Mysterious Island*. Later, I was to become a voracious reader of Classics Comics myself.

4   My father got his Classics Comics from his mother Mamie, who ran the newsstand in Orangeburg, South Carolina, my hometown. A near-yearly ritual at our house was the construction of a new bookcase to hold his burgeoning[5] collection of all kinds of reading material. In addition to the bookcases in the house, we had three war-surplus prefabricated plywood one-room buildings in our backyard where he stored stacks of magazines, among other things. I spent hours in those buildings reading old issues of *Popular Science, True*, and *Colliers*.

5   And there was another happy accident. How many kids have access to a family newsstand? One half of the newsstand was devoted to comic books, or funny books, as we called them, and that's where I spent most of my time. Here too, my

1. **Peggy Guggenheim:** 1898–1979, American art collector

2. **Musée Rodin:** a museum in Paris that exhibits the work of sculptor Auguste Rodin

3. **Randall Jarrell:** 1914–1965, American poet

4. **Dictum:** a saying or strong pronouncement

5. **Burgeoning:** growing or expanding quickly

favorites were ones that dealt with the experience of adventurers in exotic places: *Blackhawk*, who led an international squadron of jet fighters from an uncharted island in the remote Pacific; *Scrooge McDuck*, which featured him, his nephew Donald, and Donald's nephews Huey, Dewey, and Louie, who together went on quests of discovery and rediscovery, like their search for the golden fleece[6]. It may not have been Euripides[7], but it served me well at the time.

6   I did not confine my reading to comic books, however. I also haunted the shelves of the Orangeburg County Free Library, which was a three-block walk from the newsstand. There were no assignments here. I was coming on books by accident. My most vivid memory of a library book was another tale of adventure in an exotic place. I don't remember the title or the author, but I'll never forget the contents. Two boys who were somehow turned to ants and spent some time in an ant nest, fighting with their hosts against a rival nest of ants, wearing armor made of flax seeds. The power of the imagination, I was learning, had no limits.

7   I still remember the day when, having read all the books on the children's side of the library, I was permitted to move to the adult side. The first book I came on was *Shelters, Shacks, and Shanties* by Dan Beard, a guide for living in the woods, another passion of mine, though I was more adept[8] at reading about it than doing it.

8   In high school, the books I remember are the paperbacks, mostly science fiction, I got from the newsstand, rather than the texts assigned in school. I was still reading adventures set in exotic places, but now, the exotic places had moved from the earth to interstellar space. However, browsing in the library I learned that an exotic place could in fact be most any place I had never been—England, for example. I devoured Thomas Hardy's *Return of the Native* and Samuel Butler's *The Way of All Flesh*, as well as the novels of Graham Greene and Evelyn Waugh and the stories of G. K. Chesterton.

9   The single most important work I stumbled across in my high school years, however, was the autobiography of a man born "in the shadow of some French mountains on the borders of Spain," Thomas Merton, the son of a New Zealander father and an American mother. Merton was brought up in France and England, and moved to America after failing college in England. I still have a copy of *The Seven Storey Mountain* that is the same edition as the one I read when I was fifteen years old. It's a Signet Double Volume, a fifty-cent paperback with a lurid[9] cover typical of the late fifties. I don't know what attracted me to that book, the lurid cover or the peculiar spelling of *storey*, but it changed my life. I wanted to be like Merton. Merton had joined a Trappist[10] monastery; I too decided to become a Trappist monk. When I visited the Trappist monastery of Mepkin in low-country South Carolina my senior year, I was told I should go to college and study Latin first, as they expected that anyone planning to be a choir monk should know Latin. So I went away to college, and I've been in college more or less ever since. Why I am not in a monastery is another story.

10   It was in college that I came on another work, not so accidentally this time, that affected my life, George Orwell's essay "Why I Write." Orwell closes his essay with four motives for writing: sheer[11] egoism[12], esthetic[13] enthusiasm, historical

6. **Golden fleece:** in Greek mythology, a fleece (piece of wool from a sheep) made entirely of gold

7. **Euripides:** 484–406 BC, Greek writer of tragedies in the fifth century BC

8. **Adept:** skilled

9. **Lurid:** sensational or shocking

10. **Trappist:** an order or group of monks within the Catholic Church

11. **Sheer:** absolute or complete; not mixed with anything else

12. **Egoism:** selfishness; determining what is important by personal preferences and needs

13. **Esthetic (also spelled *aesthetic*):** related to beauty or a sense of beauty

impulse, and political purpose. Since I have copied Orwell's structure in this essay (an earlier version was entitled "Why I Read"), I will close this essay by giving my four great motives for reading. They are:

11   1. *Sheer pleasure.* At the beginning of this essay, I quoted Professor Biguenet saying, "Discovering the unanticipated is the great pleasure of travel." For me, discovering the unanticipated is the great pleasure of reading, also. There are other pleasures as well. The aesthetic pleasure of reading a well-written sentence or phrase can sometimes be overwhelming. There is also the hidden pleasure of living someone else's life vicariously[14], of traveling to places in the mind that you will never be able to go to in your "real" life. Emily Dickinson puts it well: "There is no frigate[15] like a book."

14. **Vicariously:** enjoyed through the experiences of others

15. **Frigate:** a type of ship

12   2. *Information.* Others may read for different purposes, but for me, a primary purpose is to obtain information. When I go to book sales, I always search all the nonfiction tables before I go to fiction. When I was in the third grade, my teacher Mrs. Jeter would sometimes send me out of class down to the library to read the encyclopedia because I had a tendency to talk overmuch in class. I gradually obtained a reputation for encyclopedic knowledge, a reputation I have kept to this day. It has served me in good stead. I can truthfully say that whatever success I have had in my life is due in no small part to reading.

13   3. *Spirituality.* As I've mentioned, the most influential book in my life was Thomas Merton's *The Seven Storey Mountain*, a spiritual autobiography. Having experienced Merton, at a book sale I now head first of all for the nonfiction table labeled "Religion." *Lectio Divina*, or spiritual reading, is an important part of Catholic spirituality and an important part of my spirituality.

14   4. *As an aid to writing.* Donald Murray has said that there are many readers who never become writers, but that there has been no good writer who was not first a strong reader. I am a devout[16] believer of this. Whatever success I have had as a writer is based on my extensive reading. Writing is too complicated to figure out: you just have to try to copy in your own writing what has pleased you in your reading, and hope for the best.

16. **Devout:** devoted and sincere; committed to

15   These are reasons why I read, but I don't always seek out reading with these ends in mind. Like Biguenet the traveler, I have had my greatest pleasures as a reader from my accidental encounters with literature. I need to take my time, to browse, to move slowly enough to "catch the (reading) surprise in the corner of my eye."

QUESTIONS FOR REFLECTION

1. Dorrill says he has discovered many unexpected and accidental pleasures while reading, just like Professor Biguenet discovered while walking. When have you found something you loved or enjoyed by accident? What were you doing at the time? How did your accidental discovery affect you?

2. In what ways did Dorrill have a typical childhood? In what ways was his childhood different from yours? Explain.

3. Why did Dorrill originally go to college? How did his plans change after he arrived?

4. What are the four reasons that Dorrill reads? Which of these reasons makes the most sense to you?

5. What do these quotes mean, and why does Dorrill include them in the essay?

    "Read at whim." (Randall Jarrell)

    "There is no frigate like a book." (Emily Dickinson)

6. How would you describe the types of books that have influenced Dorrill's life? Are they all similar? Explain.

SUGGESTIONS FOR WRITING

Think about your own experiences in reading and writing. What has shaped your personal reading and writing history? How do you think this course will change that history? Write a paragraph or essay explaining your answer.

Chapter Review

1. Choose five terms in bold from this chapter and define them in your own words.

    1. _____

    2. _____

    3. _____

    4. _____

    5. _____

2. What are the four basics of good reading and writing?

    1. Basic 1: _____

    _____

    _____

    _____

    _____

2.   Basic 2: _____

    _____

    _____

    _____

    _____

3.   Basic 3: _____

    _____

    _____

    _____

    _____

4.   Basic 4: _____

    _____

    _____

    _____

    _____

3. What are the four stages in the reading process?

    _____

4. What are the four stages in the writing process?

    _____

2

Begin Well:

Focus on Context and Audience

In Chapter 1, we learned that good writing and reading both result from a thoughtful process. In this chapter, you will learn about the first step in the reading process (previewing) and the first step in the writing process (prewriting).

Making Connections: Finding the Context

Preview to Find Audience, Purpose, and Topic in Reading

You saw in Chapter 1 that writers compose for a number of audiences (such as for a single person, a teacher, a group of friends or coworkers, or the general public) and for a variety of purposes (such as to explain or inform, to persuade, to illustrate, or to entertain). When you **preview** an assigned reading selection, ask yourself three important questions:

1. Who wrote this and why? (purpose)

2. For whom was it written? (audience)

3. What is it about? (topic)

You may not be able to identify the audience, topic, or purpose fully before you read, but you can **scan** (quickly glance over) the selection and make a reasonable guess based on what you see. What clues can you use?

- The source or location of publication (online magazine, newspaper, Facebook, class handout)
- The author(s)
- The title or subject line
- Definitions or comments in the margins (sidebars)
- Charts, graphics, or photos
- Words or phrases in bold
- Subtitles, headings, or captions
- A short summary or abstract (located in many scholarly publications)

PRACTICE 1   **Scan for Context Information**

Explore each of the reading examples listed below. Use scanning skills to find clues about the topic, audience, and purpose of each reading. Discuss your findings with a classmate.

Grammar Link Topics and audiences are both examples of **nouns** (see Chapter 15). A purpose, on the other hand, is stated as an **infinitive**, or "to" plus the basic form of the verb (see Chapter 25).

Reading Example	Topic	Audience	Purpose
www.suzanne collinsbooks.com			
One of the talks from TED (www.ted.com/ talks)			
Susan Adams's "The Weirdest Job Interview Questions and How to Handle Them" (Chapter 8, p. 142)			

Reading Example	Topic	Audience	Purpose
Samantha Levine-Finley's "Isn't It Time You Hit the Books?" (Chapter 9, p. 177)			

What can happen if we do not understand the context of what we are reading? Consider what occurred in 1938, when *The Mercury Theatre on the Air* broadcast an adaptation of the H. G. Wells novel *The War of the Worlds*. Directed by Orson Welles, the radio broadcast had the form of a news bulletin, and it told, in a realistic style, a story of the invasion of the earth by Martians. Unfortunately, some listeners did not catch the beginning of the program, which established the context of the piece as a fictional drama. These listeners mistakenly believed that an invasion was actually occurring, and the result was widespread panic and confusion.

Preview a Reading to Find a Personal Context

As we have seen, when you preview a reading to find the **rhetorical context,** you ask three basic questions:

1. Who wrote this and why? (purpose)
2. For whom was it written? (audience)
3. What is it about? (topic)

When you preview a reading to find a **personal context**, you ask different questions, ones designed to determine *your personal connections to the topic*:

1. Why am I reading this? (my purpose)
2. What do I know already about this topic? (my background and experience)
3. What is my attitude toward this topic? (my beliefs)

A personal context activates our brains so that we can more easily connect what we read to what we already know. A personal context also helps us understand our reactions to a reading, especially when our reactions involve memories or beliefs.

In Practice 1 above, you scanned several different readings for clues about their rhetorical context. Later in this chapter, you will read an essay about free-writing by Barbara DeMarco-Barrett (p. 30). One student, Chase, previewed the reading this way:

BETTMANN/CORBIS

Article	My purpose for reading	What I know about the topic	My attitude about the topic
Barbara DeMarco-Barrett's "Set Your Writing Free: Use This Technique to Spark Creativity and Loosen Your Inhibitions"	Honestly, I am reading because I have to. We might have a quiz. But I would like to know WHY we have to do freewriting. Nobody ever told me before.	Not much. We did something called freewriting in high school, but I was never sure why. If we did it and turned something in, we got 5 points on the grade rubric.	The teacher made us do freewriting, and I never did see the point, except it was good to be able to write without worrying about the rules.

PRACTICE 2   **Think about Personal Context**

Before you actually read Barbara Demarco-Barrett's essay, "Set Your Writing Free: Use This Technique to Spark Creativity and Loosen Your Inhibitions," find a personal context for the essay by completing the chart below. Are your responses similar to Chase's answers?

Article	My purpose for reading	What I know about the topic	My attitude about the topic
Barbara DeMarco-Barrett's "Set Your Writing Free: Use This Technique to Spark Creativity and Loosen Your Inhibitions"			

Preview by Asking Guiding Questions

Once you understand the rhetorical and personal context for what you are reading, you can develop a **guiding question** for your reading. A guiding question helps you identify what the writer will say about the topic and gives you a **purpose** for reading: you read to find an answer to the question. Guiding questions may come from the title, from subtitles or headings, or from background information supplied by the publisher or writer. Depending on the length of the assigned reading, you may have more than one guiding question. No matter the length, however, you should be able to find at least one guiding question for each reading.

PRACTICE 3   **Create Guiding Questions**

After scanning these essays for a rhetorical context, choose a guiding question for each one. The first one has been done for you.

Type of writing	Topic	Audience	Purpose	Guiding Question
Samantha Levine-Finley's "Isn't It Time You Hit the Books?" (Chapter 9, p. 177)	Study skills for college	College students	To explain how to be a good student	What are the steps to becoming a better student?
Taylor Mali's "Making Kids Work Hard" (Chapter 3, p. 42)				
Annie Murphy Paul's "Your Brain on Fiction" (Chapter 3, p. 44)				
Gail Godwin's "The Watcher at the Gates" (Chapter 4, p. 66)				

Begin Well in Writing: Prewriting

Prewrite to Find Audience, Purpose, and Topic

In the first stage of reading (previewing), readers use scanning clues to identify a rhetorical context for what they are reading. In the same way, in the first stage of writing, or prewriting, writers answer three important questions:

1. What is my purpose for writing?
2. Who is my audience for this paper?
3. Given my purpose and audience, what should the focus of my paper be?

In prewriting, writers find and explore ideas so that they can make a point and support it for an audience.

Prewrite by Narrowing Topics

For most of the writing you do in college, you will be assigned a topic. No matter what sort of topic you are assigned, you need to identify a personal context for the writing. A personal context includes your background knowledge, your experiences related to the topic, and your attitude toward the topic. Writers find these personal connections by **narrowing general topics** and practicing prewriting techniques.

To narrow a general topic, focus on the smaller parts of the topic until you find something that is both specific and interesting to you. Here are some ways to narrow a general topic.

DIVIDE IT INTO SMALLER CATEGORIES

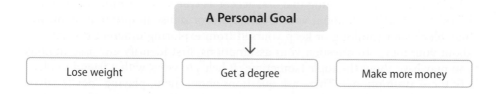

THINK OF SPECIFIC EXAMPLES FROM YOUR LIFE

GENERAL TOPIC   **Crime**

Stolen identities (how does it happen?)

When I had my wallet stolen by two kids (how? what happened?)

The e-mail scam that my grandmother lost money in (how did it work?)

GENERAL TOPIC   **Social media**

Twitter (which feeds do I follow regularly? what do I get from them?)

Facebook (what features are fun or useful? what feels like a waste of time?)

Google+ (is it just another Facebook, or is it truly different?)

THINK OF SPECIFIC EXAMPLES FROM CURRENT EVENTS

GENERAL TOPIC   **Job-creation ideas**

Tax breaks for businesses

Training of future entrepreneurs in growth areas, like solar or wind energy

A special fund for public projects that will employ many people

GENERAL TOPIC   **Heroism**

The guy who pulled a stranger from a burning car

The people who stopped a robbery downtown

Another way to narrow the topic in prewriting is to question your assumptions. An **assumption** is something that you accept as true without thinking about it. When you don't think about your assumptions or refuse to question them, you may block your thinking or keep yourself from exploring different possibilities about your topic. To question your assumptions, first identify any assumptions you may have about the topic (sometimes it helps to work with a friend to identify these assumptions). Then, ask questions about them, playing "devil's advocate"; in other words, imagine what someone with a different point of view might say. For example, imagine that your general topic is the pros and cons of letting kids play video games.

POSSIBLE ASSUMPTIONS	QUESTIONS
Video game pros: Kids get rewarded with good scores for staying focused. → Video games can teach some useful skills. →	Does staying focused on a video game mean that a kid will stay focused on homework or in class? Like what? How am I defining "useful"?
Video game cons: They make kids more violent. → They have no real educational value. →	Is there really any proof for that? What do experts say? Didn't my niece say that some video game helped her learn to read?

Next, ask yourself what assumptions and questions interest you the most. Then, focus on those interests.

You may need to work through these processes several times to find a narrow topic that will work for your assignment. Remember to review the rhetorical context for your paper as you finalize your topic: you need to focus on a topic that is specific enough for the length of writing required by your instructor. A single page (250 words) or a paragraph requires a more specific narrowed topic than an essay of more than one page.

Read the following examples of how a general topic was narrowed to a more specific topic for an essay and an even more specific topic for a paragraph.

General topic		Narrowed essay topic		Narrowed paragraph topic
Internships	→	How internships can help you get a job	→	One or two important things you can learn from an internship
Public service opportunities	→	Volunteering at a homeless shelter	→	My first impression of the homeless shelter
A personal goal	→	Getting healthy	→	Eating the right foods
A great vacation	→	A family camping trip	→	What I learned on our family camping trip to Michigan

PRACTICE 4   Narrow Topics

Look at the following assignments given to students Chelsea, Brian, and Dana. Use one of the four strategies listed above to narrow each topic to something that is specific and interesting to you.

- Chelsea's assignment for Student Development: Write a one-page essay describing a personal goal. Due: the day after tomorrow at the beginning of class.

  - General topic: _____
    _____
    _____

  - My narrow topic: _____
    _____

- Brian's assignment for Sociology: Write a six-page paper on a current influence on teens. Due: the final class session.

  - General topic: _____
    _____
    _____

  - My narrow topic: _____
    _____

- Dana's assignment for Sociology: Write an editorial for the school newspaper promoting an event on campus.

  - General topic: _____
    _____
    _____

  My narrow topic: _____
    _____

Use Prewriting Techniques

Once you have identified (or been assigned) a narrow topic, you can explore your personal connections to the topic with **prewriting techniques**. These techniques can give you ideas at any time during the writing process; they help you identify what you know about the topic, what interests you about the topic, and what you want to say about the topic. They can also help you discover if you want to learn more, read, or do research. No one uses all of the techniques; writers choose the ones that work best for them.

Prewriting techniques:

- Freewriting
- Listing/brainstorming
- Clustering/mapping
- Discussing

When prewriting, your goal is to come up with as many ideas as possible. Do not say, "Oh, that's stupid," or "That won't work." Instead, get your brain working by writing down all the possibilities.

A student, Chelsea Wilson, was assigned to write a short essay. She chose to write on the general topic of a personal goal, which she narrowed to "Getting a college degree." The following pages show how she used the four prewriting techniques to explore her topic.

FREEWRITING

Freewriting is like having a conversation with yourself, on paper. To freewrite, just start writing everything you can think of about your topic. Write nonstop for five minutes. Do not go back and cross anything out, and do not worry about using correct grammar or spelling; just write. Here is Chelsea's freewriting:

> So I know I want to get a college degree even though sometimes I wonder if I ever can make it because it's so hard with work and my two-year-old daughter and no money and a car that needs work. I can't take more than two courses at a time and even then I hardly get a chance to sleep if I want to do any of the assignments or study. But I have to think I'll get a better job because this one at the restaurant is driving me nuts and doesn't pay much so I have to work a lot with a boss I can't stand and still wonder how I'm gonna pay the bills. I know life can be better if I can just manage to become a nurse. I'll make more money and can live anywhere I want because everyplace needs nurses. I won't have to work at a job where I am not respected by anyone. I want respect, I know I'm hardworking and smart and good with people and deserve better than this. So does my daughter. No one in my family has ever graduated from college even though my sister took two courses, but then she stopped. I know I can do this, I just have to make a commitment to do it and not look away.

Tip If you are writing on a computer, try a kind of freewriting called "invisible writing." Turn the monitor off, or adjust the screen so that you cannot see what you are typing. Then, write quickly for five minutes without stopping. After five minutes, read what you have written. You may be surprised by the ideas that you can generate this way.

LISTING / BRAINSTORMING

Listing, or **brainstorming**, involves writing down all the ideas about your topic that you can think of. Write as many as you can in five minutes without stopping.

> GETTING A COLLEGE DEGREE
>
> want a better life for myself and my daughter
> want to be a nurse and help care for people
> make more money
> not have to work so many hours
> could live where I want in a nicer place
> good future and benefits like health insurance
> get respect
> proud of myself, achieve, show everyone
> be a professional, work in a clean place

CLUSTERING / MAPPING

Tip For online mapping tools, visit **http://bubbl.us**.

Clustering, also called **mapping,** is like listing except that you arrange your ideas visually. Start by writing your narrowed topic in the center. Then, write the questions "Why?" "What interests me?" and "What do I want to say?" around the narrowed topic. Using Chelsea's clustering above as a model, write three answers to each question. Keep branching out from the ideas until you feel you have fully explored your topic. Note that when Chelsea filled in "Why?" "What interests me?" and "What do I want to say?" she had lots of reasons and ideas that she could use in her writing assignment.

PRACTICE 5   **Practice Prewriting**

Practice two different prewriting techniques to explore one of the narrow topics you identified in Practice 4.

Prewriting: Ask Guiding Questions

Guiding questions are also an important part of your prewriting. Remember that the purpose of prewriting is to explore your personal context for a writing assignment: your background knowledge, your experiences, and your attitudes toward the topic. If you prewrite and then forget what you have written, your prewriting has not really helped you. In fact, prewriting requires reading: you must go back and read what you have written. In this case, you will create guiding questions to read your own prewriting.

Examples of guiding questions for prewriting:

- What do I think about _____?
- What do I hear myself saying here?
- What is the most important idea in my prewriting?
- Why do I react this way to the topic?
- What else do I want to know?
- What have I left out?

Let's look back at some of the prewriting Chelsea did. Chelsea decided to reread her freewriting, her brainstorming, and her clustering. In each case, she asked two guiding questions: what do I hear myself saying here, and what is the most important idea in my prewriting?

FREEWRITING:
> I hear myself saying that I don't really like my life right now; it's really hard.
> The most important thing is that I am determined to be a nurse.

BRAINSTORMING:
> I hear myself saying I WANT—I want something better than I have now.
> The most important thing is that I can get something better than I have now.

CLUSTERING:
> I hear myself saying that I really want this degree.
> The most important thing is that I have a lot of reasons to get this degree.

As Chelsea moves into the next phase of her writing, her guiding questions will help her focus and strengthen her ideas.

PRACTICE 6   **Create Guiding Questions for Prewriting**

Use two of the guiding questions listed above to review your prewriting from Practice 5. Discuss your answers with a classmate. Have you thought enough about the topic to move to the next phase of writing? Why or why not?

Chapter Reading

Barbara DeMarco-Barrett

Set Your Writing Free: Use This Technique to Spark Creativity and Loosen Your Inhibitions

Barbara DeMarco-Barrett is the author of *Pen on Fire: A Busy Woman's Guide to Igniting the Writer Within* (2004) and is the editor of *The ASJA Monthly*, the official publication for the American Society of Journalists and Authors. A writing instructor and radio personality, her work has appeared in *Writer's Digest*, *Poets & Writers*, and the *Los Angeles Times*, among others.

© MARLA HIRSCH COHEN, COURTESY OF BARBARA DEMARCO-BARRETT

1. **Insidious:** something which seems harmless but is actually very dangerous

1   While the blank page and the lack of time are both obstacles to writing, there's another, more insidious[1] threat to the beginning writer: perfectionism. For some reason, new writers believe they should be better than they are, that the words should flow perfectly from the start, that they should always have lots of ideas waiting to be used.

2   See if this sounds familiar: You sit down to write and as the words begin to flow, you start to judge them. You cross out words or delete them. You fuss with sentences before they've even been written, and then beat yourself up for not being good enough.

3   You need to learn to quiet that internal critic so you can be creative and allow whatever wants to come out to come out. Revision is critical—just not now. Once you have a draft, then it's time for revising—not before. This is where freewriting comes in.

4   Freewriting has been called many things: "writing practice," "stream-of-consciousness writing," "jumpstarting," but these are all essentially the same thing. Freewriting is the act of writing nonstop for a preplanned period of time. You don't stop to fix grammar, misspellings or sentence structure, or to reread what you're writing. You just keep your fingers moving.

5   And you don't need a computer or a room with a view. All you need is paper and a writing implement. A cheap old pen and notebook will do.

2. **Puritans:** members of a religious group in the 1600s who promoted strict moral behavior; anyone who follows a strict moral code

3. **Self-indulgent:** behavior which satisfies a person's desires or gives in to those desires

4. **Spontaneity:** the practice of doing things without planning, on the spur of the moment

5. **Languish:** become weak

6   The Puritans[2] may have considered freewriting self-indulgent[3], but it's a constructive kind of indulgence. Rather than writing with a specific end in mind (pleasing an editor or your writing group, making money), you freewrite to loosen up, to feel good. Freewriting sparks the spontaneity[4] and creativity that far too many people let languish[5] from disuse. Who would want to be a Puritan when you can let your imagination soar and discover the fun, beauty and playfulness of your own words?

7   When my son Travis was 4, I hosted a freewriting group. On Tuesday nights, women writers gathered around my kitchen table with notebooks and pens. To set the mood, I turned off the overhead light and switched on two lamps that sat on the counter. A candle flickered in the middle of the table and jazz played over the speakers. We drank green tea and chitchatted for a spell; then it was time to write. We each wrote a word or phrase on a slip of paper, folded it, and dropped it into a small heart-shaped tin used only for freewriting.

8   Someone then picked one or two slips of paper and said the words. For the first freewrite, we set the timer for five minutes. The timer is vital[6], as it serves as a sort of deadline that, paradoxically[7], allows you to forget about time.

9   On this particular evening, Sandy chose "lavender hour" and "not here," next to which the writer had written "all one sentence," meaning we had to write one long continuous sentence until the timer beeped, at which point we could use the imperious[8] period.

10   When you let go and practice freewriting a lot, over time you learn to stop thinking and trust the process, which is when your writing flows easily. Not all freewriting involves writing "all one sentence," but doing so encourages you to become loose and fluid. Freewriting is a superb inhibition[9] remover. When you don't stop to think about what you're writing, your concern about whether it's good or bad vanishes, and you begin to enjoy the process of writing for what it is: the laying of words on a page.

11   If you're working on a story or an essay, try freewriting with your characters or topic in mind. It doesn't matter whether you end up using what you write or not. Freewriting is about taking your writing to that loose, languid[10] place where anything goes.

Set Your Timer

12   On slips of paper, write evocative[11] words or phrases, fold them, and store them in a small container.

13   Then, alone or with someone, pick a time when you're relaxed and ready to have fun. Choose a word or two and set the timer for five minutes. Write whatever comes into your head. Disregard[12] your internal editor's opinions: "Tsk, tsk, dangling participle[13], misspelled words, tense change . . ."

14   Just write. And don't stop until the timer goes off. If you're with others, take turns reading aloud, without comment.

15   If you're alone, read it over silently—or aloud—then set the timer for a longer period, pick a few words, and have at it again.

16   Like most things in life, the main thing about starting to write is to stop dreaming and do it. Freewriting is a way to make this possible.

17   If you have trouble putting words on the page, use freewriting to get fired up. If you're stuck, freewrite.

18   If you want writing to be fun again, freewrite. Allow your subconscious to take you on vacation every day.

6. **Vital:** necessary

7. **Paradoxically:** resulting in the opposite of what we expect

8. **Imperious:** demanding or arrogant

9. **Inhibition:** something that restrains us or holds us back

10. **Languid:** slow, lacking in energy

11. **Evocative:** reminding us of places, people, or things

12. **Disregard:** ignore

13. **Dangling participle:** a grammar problem which can make writing confusing for a reader

QUESTIONS FOR REFLECTION

1. In the example preceding Practice 2, Chase said he had never under-stood the purpose of freewriting. What is the purpose of freewriting, according to DeMarco-Barrett?

2. In paragraph 6, DeMarco-Barrett says that freewriting involves "self-indulgence." What are some other activities that involve self-indulgence? How is freewriting similar to these activities?

3. In paragraph 10, DeMarco-Barrett describes the benefits of practicing freewriting over time. What are those benefits?

4. What do you think DeMarco-Barrett would say to someone who feels like a failure in writing? What would she say to you?

SUGGESTIONS FOR WRITING

Try a freewriting exercise as described by DeMarco-Barrett. Have each mem-ber of your class write a word or a phrase on a slip of paper. Shuffle these slips and draw one randomly from the pile. Set a timer for five minutes, and write for five minutes without stopping, following your thoughts wherever they take you. After you have finished, think about the value of freewriting. Can this technique help you improve your writing? Why or why not?

Chapter Review

1. Choose five terms in bold from this chapter and define them in your own words.

2. What is the first stage of the reading process? _____

3. What is the first stage of the writing process? _____

4. How can you discover the audience, purpose, and topic of a reading assign-ment? of a writing assignment?_____
   _____

5. How can you narrow a topic that is too broad or general? _____
   _____

6. What are some prewriting techniques? _____
   _____

7. How can you use prewriting techniques as part of the reading process? _____
   _____

8. What questions do you have for your instructor? _____
   _____

3

Read Well:

Annotate, Question, and Connect

In Chapter 2, we learned that in order to write or read effectively, we must begin well, with previewing and prewriting and a focus on context and audience. When we preview and prewrite, we explore the rhetorical context (the audience, purpose, and topic), as well as our personal context (our background, experiences, and goals) for the assignment. This chapter will focus on techniques for reading well: annotating, questioning, and making connections.

The Work of Reading

Have you ever "read" a paragraph or a page, only to realize that you have no idea what you just read? Reading works best when you read actively and **annotate** as you read. Annotating means making notes in the margins (or in a dedicated space in your notebook) as you read. Annotation is not the same as highlighting. When you highlight, you are not using language for yourself—you are merely adding color to language that is already there. You can highlight without thinking, but you cannot annotate without thinking.

In this chapter, we will explore and practice the Four Basics of Annotation.

Four Basics of Annotation

1 Pay attention to vocabulary using marginal notes, context clues, or a dictionary.

2 Find the main point.

3 Identify supporting details and organizational strategies.

4 Ask questions and make connections.

e Log in to **macmillanhighered .com/rrw** and look for LearningCurve > Vocabulary

The First Annotation Basic: Pay Attention to Vocabulary

Annotating a text involves making a note of vocabulary words that are new to you. As you do so, look for two things: the definition of the word as it is used in that particular context, and the **connotations** (attitudes and associations) that the word suggests.

For example, let's take a look at a sentence from Barbara DeMarco-Barrett's essay in Chapter 2:

> While the blank page and the lack of time are both obstacles to writing, there's another, more insidious threat to the beginning writer: perfectionism.

If you didn't know the meanings of the word *insidious*, you could use the footnote or a dictionary, or you could try to guess the meaning from context. You could tell, for example, that *insidious* is something negative because it is describing a threat. Also, the word *another* tells us that this threat is a type of obstacle, just like a *blank page* and a *lack of time*.

Here is how one student annotated this word in the margin of her text.

While the blank page and the lack of time are both obstacles to writing, there's another, more insidious threat to the beginning writer: perfectionism.	*Insidious: stealthy, deceptive because it doesn't appear harmful, but it actually is. Why is perfectionism insidious?*

Notice that this student has written not only a definition of *insidious* in her annotation, but also a good question about the word. When she looked up the word, she learned that it comes from a Latin word related to deception, plotting, and ambush. The connotations of *insidious* (attitudes and feelings associated with the word) are negative: people fear something insidious because it takes them by surprise. An insidious disease does not appear deadly when the first symptoms appear; in the same way, the desire to be perfect in writing may not seem like a significant problem, but that desire can shut down some writers before they have even begun. The student's annotations, which contained definitions and questions, helped her understand DeMarco-Barrett's essay more effectively.

Some students also find it helpful to write **synonyms** (words with similar meanings) or **antonyms** (words with opposite meanings) when they annotate. *Stealthy* and *treacherous* are synonyms for *insidious*, while *harmless* and *obvious* are antonyms.

> **PRACTICE 1**   **Annotate for Vocabulary**
>
> Read the following paragraph from Gail Godwin's essay "The Watcher at the Gates" (Chapter 4, p. 66). Annotate it, focusing on vocabulary that is new to you, figuring out meaning from context, and asking questions about words.

My Watcher has a wasteful penchant for 20 pound bond paper above and below the carbon of the first draft. "What's the good of writing out a whole page," he whispers begrudgingly, "if you just have to write it over again later? Get it perfect the first time!" My Watcher adores stopping in the middle of a morning's work to drive down to the library to check on the name of a flower or a World War II battle or a line of metaphysical poetry. "You can't possibly go on till you've got this right!" he admonishes. I go and get the car keys.

The Second Annotation Basic: Find the Main Point

Remember the four basics of good writing from Chapter 1? Every good piece of writing has a **main point** or **main idea**—what the writer wants to get across to the readers about the topic or the writer's position on that topic. When we read, we must identify the main idea. In a paragraph, the main idea is usually expressed in a *topic sentence*. In an essay, the main idea is usually expressed in a *thesis statement*.

THE MAIN POINT IN PARAGRAPHS

A **paragraph** is a group of sentences that make a single point and support it. A paragraph usually has three parts: the **topic sentence**, the **body**, and the **concluding sentence**.

Paragraph Part	Purpose of the Paragraph Part
1. The **topic sentence**	states the **main point**. The topic sentence is often the first sentence of the paragraph.
2. The **body**	supports (shows, explains, or proves) the main point with **supporting sentences** that contain facts and details.
3. The **concluding sentence**	reminds readers of the main point and often makes an observation.

Look at the following paragraph from Barbara DeMarco-Barrett's essay, "Set Your Writing Free: Use This Technique to Spark Creativity and Loosen Your Inhibitions," in Chapter 2 (p. 30). The main parts have been annotated for you.

The Puritans may have considered freewriting self-indulgent, but it's a constructive kind of indulgence. Rather than writing with a specific end in mind (pleasing an editor or your writing group, making money), you freewrite to loosen up, to feel good. Freewriting sparks the spontaneity and creativity that far too many people let languish from disuse. Who would want to be a Puritan when you can let your imagination soar and discover the fun, beauty and playfulness of your own words?

→ Topic sentence

— Body or support sentences

→ Conclusion

For more information and practice with paraphrasing, see Chapter 6.

When you annotate, mark the topic sentences of paragraphs by underlining them. Write out the main idea in your own words. When you write the main idea in your notes using your own words, you are **paraphrasing**. When you paraphrase the main idea, don't copy words or phrases from the original. Instead, explain the idea without looking back at the reading.

Here's how one student paraphrased the main idea from Barbara DeMarco-Barrett's essay, "Set Your Writing Free: Use This Technique to Spark Creativity and Loosen Your Inhibitions," above:

Freewriting helps us write better by allowing us to play with words and have fun with language.

PRACTICE 2   **Practice Annotating and Paraphrasing Main Ideas**

Annotate the following paragraphs. Find and underline the main idea in each paragraph, and then rewrite the main idea in your own words.

1.   Making a plan for your college studies is a good way to reach your academic goals. The first step to planning is answering this question: "What do I want to be?" If you have only a general idea—for example, "I would like to work in the health-care field"—break this large area into smaller, more specific subfields. These subfields might include working as a registered nurse, a nurse practitioner, or a physical therapist. The second step to planning is to meet with an academic adviser to talk about the classes you will need to take to get a degree or certificate in your chosen field. Then, map out the courses you will be taking over the next couple of semesters. Throughout the whole process, bear in mind the words of student mentor Ed Powell: "Those who fail to plan, plan to fail." A good plan boosts your chances of success in college and beyond.

Main Point: _____

_____

2. Networking is a way businesspeople build connections with others to get ahead. Building connections in college also is well worth the effort. One way to build connections is to get to know some of your classmates and to exchange names, phone numbers, and e-mail addresses with them. That way, if you cannot make it to a class, you will know someone who can tell you what you missed. You can also form study groups with these other students. Another way to build connections is to get to know your instructor. Make an appointment to visit your instructor during his or her office hours. When you go, ask questions about material you are not sure you understood in class or problems you have with other course material. You and your instructor will get the most out of these sessions if you bring examples of specific assignments that you are having trouble with.

Main Point: _____

_____

THE MAIN POINT IN ESSAYS

An **essay** is a group of paragraphs that work together to make a single point. In an essay, we call this point or main idea the **thesis**. The topic sentences of the paragraphs in the essay support the thesis of the essay. There are three parts to an essay: the **introduction**, the **body**, and the **conclusion**.

ESSAY PART	PURPOSE OF THE ESSAY PART
1. The **introduction**	provides background and hooks the reader's interest. Many writers state the thesis clearly in the introduction.
2. The **body**	supports the thesis. The topic sentences of the body paragraphs support the thesis of the essay.
3. The **conclusion**	reminds readers of the main point and makes an observation or application of the main point.

Did you notice that the three parts of an essay are similar to the three parts of a paragraph? When you are annotating, use the three parts of an essay or a paragraph to help you identify and confirm the thesis or topic sentence.

The thesis appears in the introduction of an essay. The thesis is supported by the topic sentence of each body paragraph and is emphasized again in the conclusion.

As you are annotating, double underline the thesis or main point of an essay. Make a note of the thesis in the margins of the essay, writing in your own words.

Hints for annotation: Identifying main ideas

- Don't stop when you have identified the topic. A topic is not a thesis. A thesis tells us what the writer says about the topic. To make sure you have identified the thesis and not just the topic, use this sentence starter to paraphrase the main idea:

     In other words, the writer is saying that _____

- A main point is often the answer to the guiding question you created when previewing the reading. Check your thesis: does it answer your guiding question?

- An essay can have only one main point. The topic sentences of the paragraphs support the main idea of the essay. Make sure you identify the thesis of the essay, not the topic sentence of one body paragraph.

- A main point or thesis may be stated in a single sentence that you can find in the reading. We call this the **stated main idea**. When the thesis is stated directly, you can underline it.

- A main point or thesis may not be stated directly. If a writer chooses NOT to state the main idea directly, we say that the main idea is **implied**.

The Third Annotation Basic: Identify Support and See How Support Is Organized

IDENTIFY SUPPORT

Every good piece of writing also includes support that is organized to show, explain, or prove the main idea. We usually identify two types of support: **primary (major) supporting details** and **secondary (minor) supporting details**. Notice how a student writer has annotated the following paragraph:

Topic sentence. He's saying that the history courses he took taught him important lessons about life. ←

First major supporting detail ←

> When I first enrolled in college, I thought that studying history was a waste of time. But after taking two world history classes, I have come to the conclusion that these courses count for far more than some credit hours in my college record. First, learning about historical events has helped me put important current events in perspective. *For instance, by studying*

the history of migration around the world, I have learned that immigration has been going on for hundreds of years. In addition, it is common in many countries, not just the United States. I have also learned about ways in which various societies have debated immigration, just as Americans are doing today. <u>Second, history courses have taught me about the power that individual people can have, even under very challenging circumstances.</u> *I was especially inspired by the story of Toussaint L'Ouverture, a former slave who, in the 1790s, led uprisings in the French colony of Saint-Domingue, transforming it into the independent nation of Haiti. Although L'Ouverture faced difficult odds, he persisted and achieved great things.* <u>The biggest benefit of taking history courses is that they have encouraged me to dig more deeply into subjects than I ever have before.</u> *For a paper about the lasting influence of Anne Frank, I drew on quotations from her famous diary, on biographies about her, and on essays written by noted historians. The research was fascinating, and I loved piecing together the various facts and insights to come to my own conclusions.* To sum up, I have become hooked on history, and I have a feeling that the lessons it teaches me will be relevant far beyond college.

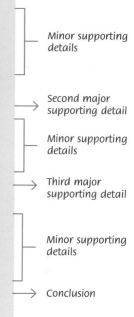

Minor supporting details

Second major supporting detail

Minor supporting details

Third major supporting detail

Minor supporting details

Conclusion

Here, the writer has given three major supporting points. These points, however, are not specific enough. For example, here is the second major supporting detail:

> . . . history courses have taught me about the power that individual people can have, even under very challenging circumstances.

The words "individual people" and "challenging circumstances" are general: they do not name specific people who lived at specific times in history. In the sentences that follow, the writer gives a specific example to provide readers with secondary or minor support. He mentions a specific person (Toussaint L'Ouverture) who lived at a specific time (1790s) and who participated in a specific event (the uprisings in the French colony of Saint-Domingue).

The topic sentence is the most general statement in a paragraph. Each of the major supporting details is slightly more specific, and each one gives an example or evidence related to the topic sentence. Finally, the minor supporting details are the most specific, and each of these illustrates a major supporting detail.

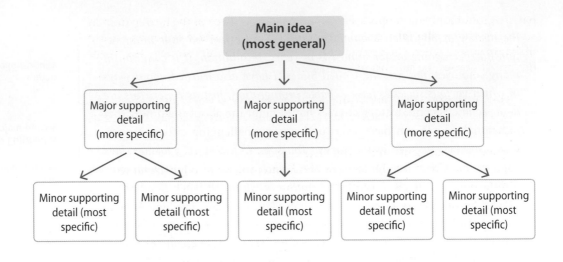

Identify Support

Use the paragraph on pages 38–39 to complete the following chart with the major and minor details.

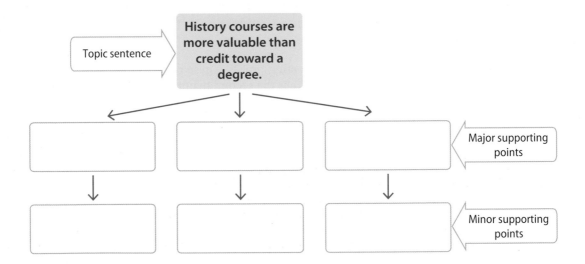

SEE HOW SUPPORT IS ORGANIZED

The support for a main idea is organized into an appropriate order. Order means the sequence in which a writer presents his ideas: what comes first, what comes next, and so on. In Chapters 7 through 15, we will look at several common patterns for organizing support. For now, let's look at three of the most common strategies: **time order** (also called **chronological order**), **space order**, and **order of importance**. When you annotate, you should identify the strategy the writer has used to order the support in a paragraph.

Time order presents supporting details according to when they happened: first to last (or last to first), or least recent to most recent (or most recent to least recent).

Space order presents supporting details according to the way that they appear visually: top to bottom (or bottom to top), near to far (or far to near), left to right (or right to left), or back to front (or front to back).

Order of importance presents supporting details according to their significance, interest, or surprise value. Most writers will save the most important point for last. The sample paragraph about history on pages 38–39 follows order of importance.

The Fourth Annotation Basic: Ask Questions and Make Connections

The last basic strategy for annotations is to **ask questions and make connections**. Good annotations not only pay attention to vocabulary and identify main points with supporting details, they also allow you as a reader to interact with the text, asking questions and connecting what the writer says to your own experiences. Consider the additional annotations one student added to his notes on Barbara DeMarco-Barrett's essay "Set Your Writing Free: Use This Technique to Spark Creativity and Loosen Your Inhibitions."

Topic Sentence. *Puritans—like the people who came here from England in the 1600s. They were really strict. *Constructive = Helpful, useful. *Self-indulgent = giving in to what you want to do.

So she's saying that it's a good thing to write without worrying about the results. That makes sense, but it's hard to do when you know you are going to get a grade.

    The Puritans may have considered freewriting self-indulgent, but it's a constructive kind of indulgence. Rather than writing with a specific end in mind (pleasing an editor or your writing group, making money), you freewrite to loosen up, to feel good. Freewriting sparks the spontaneity and creativity that far too many people let languish from disuse. Who would want to be a Puritan when you can let your imagination soar and discover the fun, beauty and playfulness of your own words?

*Languish = fade or get weak. My dad always says if you don't use it, you lose it.

?? I don't think my words are usually fun or playful. Is she talking to professional writers, or to everyone??

PRACTICE 4   **Annotate an Essay**

Now it's your turn. Read and annotate the following excerpt from Taylor Mali's book, *What Teachers Make* (2012). This chapter is called "Making Kids Work Hard." In your annotations, follow the Four Basics of Good Annotation:

1. Pay attention to vocabulary using marginal notes, context clues, or a dictionary.

2. Find the main point.

3. Identify supporting details and organizational strategies.

4. Ask questions and make connections.

Taylor Mali

Making Kids Work Hard from *What Teachers Make*

Taylor Mali (b. 1965) is an educator, a voiceover artist, a dedicated supporter of teachers and their work, and a slam poet. Slam poetry is a predominantly urban art form influenced by hip hop. Taylor Mali lives in New York City. © BEN HIDER/GETTY IMAGES ENTERTAINMENT

1   Whenever someone challenges me about what teachers make, my first answer is that teachers "make kids work harder than they ever thought they could." The most important thing a teacher can do is make students apply themselves. Some achieve it through gentle coaxing and encouragement while others use fear and intimidation. I would argue that both strategies are forms of love. Simply put, the best teachers are the ones you work your tail off for because in the end you just don't want them to think any less of you. You want and need their approval.

2   There's a story about President Nixon's secretary of state, Henry Kissinger, that I like to tell students. Kissinger asked an aide to produce a report. The aide submitted his report, but it was returned to him later that afternoon with a note from Kissinger that said: "I'm sorry. This is not good enough." The aide felt like he'd been busted because he knew Kissinger was right. So he sheepishly took it back and revised it. He made the report significantly better and resubmitted it, but it came back again with a similar note: "This is still not nearly good enough." Now the aide was scared! He canceled his plans for the

evening and stayed up all night working on the report. He caught careless errors he hadn't seen before and added a section of analysis that tied the whole thing together. He felt he had done his absolute best work, so instead of just submitting the report as he had done twice before, he made an appointment to deliver the report to Kissinger personally. "Mr. Secretary," he said, "I have written this report three times and twice you have sent it back saying it was not good enough. Sir, what I am handing you now is the absolute best I can do, so if it is still not good enough, then I am not the right person for the job." Kissinger thanked him, smiled, and took the report, adding, "Excellent. This time I will actually read it."

3   It was this story I was thinking of when I wrote the line in "What Teachers Make" about how teachers can make an A− seem like "a slap in the face." When you do not submit your absolute best work for evaluation, everyone loses. So an A− really can be an insult to a student who is capable of A+ work.

4   But the other part of that line is just as important: "I can make a C+ feel like a Congressional Medal of Honor." An outstanding teacher knows that when a struggling student truly applies himself and earns a C+ on an assignment, it is entirely appropriate to write underneath the grade: "Congratulations!"

5   In the long run the ability to work harder than you ever thought you could may be the most important thing a teacher can teach. The actual subject matter is not the real lesson you want your students to learn; the real lesson is learning how to keep going even when what you're learning is hard and confusing. When the student inevitably asks, "When are we ever going to need this in real life?" the answer is not what they expect: *never*.

6   These exact facts, figures, and problems? You'll probably never need them. The real lesson here is the diligence, cooperation, resilience, flexibility, critical thinking, and problem solving you are actively using today. You will use those skills every time life presents you with something difficult or unexpected: obstacles in your personal life, accidents and catastrophes, lost jobs and loved ones. Working through those challenges is what matters most. When I'm teaching kids to work harder than they ever thought they could? That is what they will need every day of their lives.

Check your annotations. After you have annotated, ask yourself these questions:

1. Have you identified the main point of the essay? the main point of each paragraph?
2. Have you identified the support for each paragraph?
3. Have you identified strategies for organizing?
4. Have you identified new vocabulary?
5. Have you asked questions or connected the essay to your own life?

Compare your annotations with those of a classmate. Discuss any differences, connections, or questions that you have.

Chapter Reading

Annie Murphy Paul

Your Brain on Fiction

Annie Murphy Paul is a journalist, author, and speaker. Her books include *Origins: How the Nine Months before Birth Shape the Rest of Our Lives* (2011) and *How to Be Brilliant* (2013). This essay was first published in the *New York Times.* © COURTESY OF ANNIE MURPHY PAUL

Practice your annotation skills further by working through this article by Annie Murphy Paul. Read through the article at least two times, annotating as you read and reflect.

1 Amid the squawks and pings of our digital devices, the old-fashioned virtues of reading novels can seem faded, even futile[1]. But new support for the value of fiction is arriving from an unexpected quarter: neuroscience[2].

2 Brain scans are revealing what happens in our heads when we read a detailed description, an evocative[3] metaphor[4] or an emotional exchange between characters. Stories, this research is showing, stimulate the brain and even change how we act in life.

3 Researchers have long known that the "classical" language regions, like Broca's area and Wernicke's area[5], are involved in how the brain interprets written words. What scientists have come to realize in the last few years is that narratives[6] activate many other parts of our brains as well, suggesting why the experience of reading can feel so alive. Words like "lavender," "cinnamon," and "soap," for example, elicit[7] a response not only from the language-processing areas of our brains, but also those devoted to dealing with smells.

4 In a 2006 study published in the journal *NeuroImage*, researchers in Spain asked participants to read words with strong odor associations, along with neutral words, while their brains were being scanned by a functional magnetic resonance imaging (fMRI) machine. When subjects looked at the Spanish words for "perfume" and "coffee," their primary olfactory cortex[8] lit up; when they saw the words that mean "chair" and "key," this region remained dark. The way the brain handles metaphors has also received extensive study; some scientists have contended[9] that figures of speech like "a rough day" are so familiar that they are treated simply as words and no more. Last month, however, a team of researchers from Emory University reported in *Brain & Language* that when subjects in their laboratory read a metaphor involving texture[10], the sensory cortex[11], responsible for perceiving texture through touch, became active. Metaphors like "The singer had a velvet voice" and "He had leathery hands" roused[12] the sensory cortex, while phrases matched for meaning, like "The singer had a pleasing voice" and "He had strong hands," did not.

1. **Futile:** useless, a waste of time
2. **Neuroscience:** the study of the brain and nervous system
3. **Evocative:** suggestive or reminding one of something
4. **Metaphor:** a word picture; one thing is said to be something else ("Love is a rose")
5. **Broca's area and Wernicke's area:** regions of the brain associated with language use
6. **Narratives:** stories
7. **Elicit:** bring out or produce

8. **Olfactory cortex:** the region of the brain associated with smelling

9. **Contended:** claimed or argued

10. **Texture:** the way something feels (rough, smooth, bumpy)
11. **Sensory cortex:** a region of the brain
12. **Roused:** activated or excited

5   Researchers have discovered that words describing motion also stimulate regions of the brain distinct from language-processing areas. In a study led by the cognitive scientist Véronique Boulenger, of the Laboratory of Language Dynamics in France, the brains of participants were scanned as they read sentences like "John grasped the object" and "Pablo kicked the ball." The scans revealed activity in the motor cortex, which coordinates the body's movements. What's more, this activity was concentrated in one part of the motor cortex when the movement described was arm-related and in another part when the movement concerned the leg.

6   The brain, it seems, does not make much of a distinction between reading about an experience and encountering it in real life; in each case, the same neurological regions are stimulated. Keith Oatley, an emeritus professor[13] of cognitive psychology at the University of Toronto (and a published novelist), has proposed that reading produces a vivid[14] simulation of reality, one that "runs on minds of readers just as computer simulations run on computers." Fiction—with its redolent[15] details, imaginative metaphors and attentive descriptions of people and their actions—offers an especially rich replica[16]. Indeed, in one respect novels go beyond simulating reality to give readers an experience unavailable off the page: the opportunity to enter fully into other people's thoughts and feelings.

13. Emeritus professor: retired from a position as professor

14. Vivid: bright and striking

15. Redolent: suggestive or reminding one of something

16. Replica: imitation

7   The novel, of course, is an unequaled medium for the exploration of human social and emotional life. And there is evidence that just as the brain responds to depictions of smells and textures and movements as if they were the real thing, so it treats the interactions among fictional characters as something like real-life social encounters.

8   Raymond Mar, a psychologist at York University in Canada, performed an analysis of 86 fMRI studies, published last year in the *Annual Review of Psychology*, and concluded that there was substantial[17] overlap in the brain networks used to understand stories and the networks used to navigate interactions with other individuals—in particular, interactions in which we're trying to figure out the thoughts and feelings of others. Scientists call this capacity[18] of the brain to construct a map of other people's intentions "theory of mind." Narratives offer a unique opportunity to engage this capacity, as we identify with characters' longings and frustrations, guess at their hidden motives, and track their encounters with friends and enemies, neighbors and lovers.

17. Substantial: significant or obvious; of a large amount

18. Capacity: ability

9   It is an exercise that hones[19] our real-life social skills, another body of research suggests. Dr. Oatley and Dr. Mar, in collaboration with several other scientists, reported in two studies, published in 2006 and 2009, that individuals who frequently read fiction seem to be better able to understand other people, empathize[20] with them, and see the world from their perspective. This relationship persisted[21] even after the researchers accounted for the possibility that more empathetic individuals might prefer reading novels. A 2010 study by Dr. Mar found a similar result in preschool-age children: the more stories they had read to them, the keener[22] their theory of mind—an effect that was also produced by watching movies but, curiously, not by watching television. (Dr. Mar has conjectured that because children often watch TV alone, but go to the movies with their

19. Hones: improves or sharpens

20. Empathize: share in someone else's feelings
21. Persisted: lasted or continued

22. Keener: sharper or more developed

parents, they may experience more "parent-children conversations about mental states" when it comes to films.)

10   Fiction, Dr. Oatley notes, "is a particularly useful simulation because negotiating the social world effectively is extremely tricky, requiring us to weigh up myriad[23] interacting instances of cause and effect. Just as computer simulations can help us get to grips with complex problems such as flying a plane or forecasting the weather, so novels, stories, and dramas can help us understand the complexities of social life."

11   These findings will affirm the experience of readers who have felt illuminated and instructed by a novel, who have found themselves comparing a plucky young woman to Elizabeth Bennet[24] or a tiresome pedant[25] to Edward Casaubon[26]. Reading great literature, it has long been averred[27], enlarges and improves us as human beings. Brain science shows this claim is truer than we imagined.

23. **Myriad:** many

24. **Elizabeth Bennet:** the main character in the novel *Pride and Prejudice*, by Jane Austen

25. **Pedant:** someone who shows off a great deal of learning

26. **Edward Casaubon:** a difficult character in George Eliot's novel *Middlemarch*.

27. **Averred:** claimed

QUESTIONS FOR REFLECTION

1. Using your annotations, describe what happens when our brains read fiction.

2. What evidence does neuroscience give us to suggest that our brains experience the world in different ways when we read?

3. What is a "theory of mind"? How do we develop it?

4. Have you ever read a story that reminded you of people or situations in your own life? Explain.

5. Paul uses several references to scientists and their research. How do these references help her achieve her purpose in this article?

6. This essay reports only on the value of reading fiction. Do you think other types of reading (handbooks, essays, news reports, social media) are also valuable? In what ways?

7. You may have found this reading challenging. Do you think this selection should be included in future editions of this textbook? Why or why not?

SUGGESTIONS FOR WRITING

1. Write a paragraph that considers this question: Can reading fiction be collaborative, or must it be the work of a single person? Use your own experiences and the ideas in Paul's essay to explain your answer.

2. Write a brief essay on this question: How do you think either Taylor Mali ("Making Kids Work Hard," this chapter, p. 42) or George Dorrill ("Reading: A Personal History," Chapter 1, p. 13) would respond to this essay by Annie Murphy Paul? To answer, choose either Mali or Dorrill,

and in your essay, consider how Paul's essay confirms, contradicts, expands on, or complicates the ideas presented by the writer you have chosen.

Chapter Review

1. Choose five terms in bold from this chapter and define them in your own words.

2. What is annotating, and what are the four basics of annotation? _____

   _____

   The four basics of annotation are:

   1. _____

   2. _____

      _____

   3. _____

      _____

   4. _____

3. What are the main parts of a paragraph?_____

   _____

   What are the main parts of an essay? _____

   _____

4. What are three ways to organize a paragraph? _____

   _____

4

Write Well:

Develop Your Topic, Thesis, and Support

In Chapter 3, we looked at the second stage of the reading process: doing the active work of reading, reading closely with a guiding question in mind, and annotating. In this chapter, we will explore the second stage of the writing process, known as drafting.

The Four Basics of the Drafting Process begin with the work you did in stage one, prewriting.

Four Basics of the Drafting Process

1. Write a preliminary main point (topic sentence or thesis statement).
2. Write support for the thesis.
3. Arrange support for the thesis.
4. Write an introduction and a conclusion.

Log in to **macmillanhighered .com/rrw** and look for LearningCurve > Topics and Main

Write a Preliminary Main Point

Before you begin writing a **draft** or a complete version of an assignment, review your prewriting, your instructions, and your topic. Remember that your goal is to find and develop

- a topic worth writing about, that interests you and that will interest your audience of readers;

- a topic that is neither too broad nor too narrow, but just right for the parameters of the assignment, in terms of content and length.

In Chapter 2, page 23, you learned how to narrow a topic for a paragraph or an essay. You also learned how to discover ideas about your topic using prewriting techniques.

Once you have explored your topic through prewriting, it is time to develop your **main idea**. Your prewriting helps you identify the audience, purpose, and topic for your assignment. When you read your prewriting carefully, you may also discover a potential **topic sentence** or **thesis statement**.

A main idea, as we have seen, is a comment or position about the topic you have chosen. To draft your preliminary topic sentence (for paragraphs) or thesis statement (for essays), use this basic formula as a starting point:

Narrowed topic   +   Main point/position   =   Topic sentence or thesis statement

The tutoring center has helped me improve my writing by offering friendly, one-on-one guidance.

When Chelsea Wilson looked over her prewriting about getting a college degree (see p. 27), she saw that several times she had mentioned wanting a better life than she has now. Chelsea shaped these ideas into the following topic sentence:

Narrowed topic   +   Main point/position   =   Topic sentence or thesis statement

Getting a nursing degree will make my life better financially, professionally, and emotionally.

A good topic sentence or thesis statement has the following four characteristics:

- It fits the size of the assignment.
- It states a single main point or position about a topic.
- It is specific.
- It is something you can show, explain, or prove.

It Fits the Size of the Assignment

As you develop a topic sentence or thesis statement, think carefully about the length of the assignment. Sometimes, a main-point statement can be the same for a paragraph or an essay. Often, however, a topic sentence for a paragraph is much narrower than a thesis statement for an essay, simply because a paragraph is shorter and allows less development of ideas.

Consider how one general topic could be narrowed into an essay topic and into an even more specific paragraph topic.

General topic	Narrowed essay topic	Narrowed paragraph topic
Internships →	How internships can help you get a job →	One or two important things you can learn from an internship

POSSIBLE THESIS STATEMENT (ESSAY)	The skills and connections you gain through a summer internship can help you get a good job after graduation.

[The essay would discuss several benefits of internships, describing the various skills they can teach and the professional connections they can offer to interns.]

POSSIBLE TOPIC SENTENCE (PARAGRAPH)	A summer internship is a good way to test whether a particular career is right for you.

[The paragraph would focus on one benefit of internships: they are a way to test out a career. The paragraph might go on to discuss signs that a certain type of work is or is not passing the test.]

PRACTICE 1   Write Topic Sentences and Thesis Statements

Using the following example as a guide, write a thesis statement for the narrowed essay topic and a topic sentence for the narrowed paragraph topic.

Example:

TOPIC: **Sports**

NARROWED FOR AN ESSAY: **Competition in school sports**

NARROWED FOR A PARAGRAPH: **User fees for school sports**

POSSIBLE THESIS STATEMENT (essay): *Competition in school sports has reached dangerous levels.*

POSSIBLE TOPIC SENTENCE (paragraph): *This year's user fees for participation in school sports are too high.*

1.   TOPIC: Public service opportunities

     NARROWED FOR AN ESSAY: Volunteering at a homeless shelter

     NARROWED FOR A PARAGRAPH: My first impression of the homeless shelter

POSSIBLE THESIS STATEMENT (essay): _____

_____

POSSIBLE TOPIC SENTENCE (paragraph): _____

_____

2.   TOPIC: A personal goal

NARROWED FOR AN ESSAY: Getting healthy

NARROWED FOR A PARAGRAPH: Eating the right foods

POSSIBLE THESIS STATEMENT (essay): _____

_____

POSSIBLE TOPIC SENTENCE (paragraph): _____

_____

3.   TOPIC: A great vacation

NARROWED FOR AN ESSAY: A family camping trip

NARROWED FOR A PARAGRAPH: A lesson I learned on our family camping trip

POSSIBLE THESIS STATEMENT (essay): _____

_____

POSSIBLE TOPIC SENTENCE (paragraph): _____

_____

Some topic sentences or thesis statements are too broad for either a short essay or a paragraph. A main idea that is too broad is impossible to show, explain, or prove within the space of a paragraph or short essay.

Too broad   Art is important.

[How could a writer possibly support such a broad concept in a paragraph or essay?]

Narrower   Art instruction for young children has surprising benefits.

A topic sentence or thesis statement that is too narrow leaves the writer with little to write about. There is little to show, explain, or prove.

Too narrow   Buy rechargeable batteries.

[OK, so now what?]

Broader   Choosing rechargeable batteries over conventional batteries is one action you can take to reduce your effect on the environment.

It Contains a Single Main Point or Position about a Topic

Your topic sentence or thesis statement should focus on only one main point. Two main points can split and weaken the focus of the writing.

MAIN IDEA WITH TWO MAIN POINTS

High schools <u>should sell healthy food instead of junk food</u>, and they <u>should start later in the morning</u>.

The two main points are underlined. Although both are good main points, together they split both the writer's and the readers' focus. The writer would need to give reasons to support each point, and the ideas are completely different.

MAIN IDEA WITH A SINGLE MAIN POINT

High schools <u>should sell healthy food instead of junk food</u>.

OR

High schools <u>should start later in the morning</u>.

It Is Specific

A good topic sentence or thesis statement gives readers specific information so that they know exactly what the writer's main point is.

General   Students are often overwhelmed.

[How are students overwhelmed?]

Specific   Working college students have to learn how to juggle many responsibilities.

One way to make sure your topic sentence or thesis statement is specific is to make it a preview of what you are planning to say in the rest of the paragraph or essay. Just be certain that every point you preview is closely related to your main idea.

PREVIEW: Working college students have to learn how to juggle many responsibilities: doing a good job at work, getting to class regularly and on time, being alert in class, and doing the homework assignments.

PREVIEW: I have a set routine every Saturday morning that includes sleeping late, going to the gym, and shopping for food.

It Is Something You Can Show, Explain, or Prove

If a main point is so obvious that it does not need support or if it states a simple fact, you will not have much to say about it.

Obvious	The Toyota Prius is a top-selling car.
	Many people like to take vacations in the summer.
Revised	Because of rising gas costs and concerns about the environmental impact of carbon emissions, the Toyota Prius is a top-selling car.
	The vast and incredible beauty of the Grand Canyon draws crowds of visitors each summer.
Fact	Employment of medical lab technicians is projected to increase by 14 percent between 2008 and 2018.
	Three hundred cities worldwide have bicycle-sharing programs.
Revised	Population growth and the creation of new types of medical tests mean the employment of lab technicians should increase by 14 percent between 2008 and 2018.
	Bicycle-sharing programs are popular, but funding them long-term can be challenging for cities with tight budgets.

PRACTICE 2   Revise Topic Sentences and Thesis Statements

Each of the following thesis statements has a problem: it is too broad or too narrow, it is not specific, it contains more than one idea, or it is a statement that cannot be shown, explained, or proven. For each thesis statement, identify the problem and revise the statement to make it a stronger thesis.

1.   My job is fun.

Problem: _____

Revision: _____

_____

_____

_____

2.   Pets can bring families together, and they require a lot of care.

   Problem: _____

   Revision: _____

   _____

   _____

   _____

3.   College is challenging.

   Problem: _____

   Revision: _____

   _____

4.   I take a bus to work.

   Problem: _____

   Revision: _____

   _____

   _____

   _____

5.   Technology is important.

   Problem: _____

   Revision: _____

   _____

   _____

   _____

PRACTICE 3   **Write Topic Sentences and Thesis Statements**

Choose one of the narrow topics you developed in Chapter 2, Practice 5
(p. 28). Write a main idea for a paragraph or an essay based on the topic
you chose. Once you have a preliminary version of your main idea, evaluate
it using the following checklist.

☐ It is a complete sentence.

☐ It fits the assignment.

☐ It includes my topic and the main point I want to make about the topic.

☐ It states only one main point.

☐ It is specific.

☐ It is something I can show, explain, or prove.

Write Support for the Thesis

The topic sentence or thesis statement anchors your writing so that you can find the major and minor details that will support your main idea. You have already learned about identifying major and minor details when you are reading. You can apply these same concepts to your writing.

e Log in to **macmillanhighered .com/rrw** and look for LearningCurve > Topic Sentences and Supporting Details

Basics of good support

- It relates directly to the main point. The purpose of support is to show, explain, or prove your main point.

- It considers your readers and what they will need to know.

- It gives readers enough specific details, particularly through examples, so that they can see what you mean.

To generate support for the main point of a paragraph or an essay, you can use one or more of the following strategies.

1. Use a prewriting technique (freewriting, listing, clustering, discussing) while thinking about your main point and your audience. Write for three to five minutes without stopping.

2. Use your reading notes. Are there examples or ideas from the readings that might help you support your point?

3. Circle the important words or phrases in your topic sentence (for a paragraph) or thesis statement (for an essay). Write as many specific examples of each word or phrase that you can think of.

Select the Best Primary Support

After you have generated possible support, review your ideas; then, select the best ones to use as primary support. Here you take control of your topic, shaping the way readers will see it and the main point you are making about it. These ideas are *yours,* and you need to sell them to your audience.

The following steps can help.

1. Carefully read the ideas you have generated.

2. Select three to five primary supporting points that will be clearest and most convincing to your readers, providing the best examples, facts, and

observations to support your main point. If you are writing a paragraph, these points will become the primary support for your topic sentence. If you are writing an essay, they will become topic sentences of the individual paragraphs that support your thesis statement.

3. Cross out ideas that are not closely related to your main point.

4. If you find that you have crossed out most of your ideas and do not have enough left to support your main point, use one of the three strategies from page 55 to find more.

Once you have selected your best primary supporting points, you need to flesh them out for your readers. Do this by adding secondary support: specific examples, facts, and observations.

PRACTICE 4　**Create Primary and Secondary Support**

Using one of the topic sentences or thesis statements you wrote above in Practice 1 or 2, create three to five primary (major) supporting points. Then include two or three secondary (minor) details to illustrate each of your major supporting details. You may use the example form below to guide you.

Primary Support Point #1:

　Supporting Details:

Primary Support Point #2:

　Supporting Details:

Primary Support Point #3:

　Supporting Details:

PRACTICE 5　**Write Support for the Thesis**

Using the main idea you developed for Practice 3 (pp. 54–55), write at least three primary supporting points with at least one secondary detail for each.

Arrange Support for the Thesis

Once you have selected strong support for your main idea, you must arrange the support in a logical order. In Chapter 3, you learned about three patterns of organization for support: time order (chronological), space order, and order of importance. Whether you are planning a paragraph or an essay, you will need to select the organization that best fits your support.

Planning Paragraphs

Earlier we looked at Chelsea's topic sentence (p. 49). Chelsea brainstormed to find supporting ideas for her main point and details to illustrate each of those ideas. When she thought about how to arrange her support, the only pattern that made sense to her was order of importance. If she had been describing the process of becoming a nurse, a time order arrangement would have made sense. But because she was writing about her reasons for wanting the nursing degree, Chelsea decided to arrange her ideas in order of importance, with the most important reason last. Here is the plan (or outline) that she made for her paragraph:

Topic Sentence: Getting a nursing degree will make my life better financially, professionally, and emotionally.

I. Primary Supporting Point #1: Nurses earn a good salary.

Supporting Details: Licensed professional nurses make an average of $40,000 per year, which is much more than I make now. With that salary, I could move to a better place with my daughter, and give her more, including more time.

II. Primary Supporting Point #2: Nursing is a respected profession with possibilities for advancement.

Supporting Details: Nurses help people who are sick and in need. Being an LPN can lead to additional education and becoming a registered nurse. Nurses are respected.

III. Primary Supporting Point #3: I will increase my self-esteem and my self-respect if I work hard to achieve this goal.

Supporting Details: I can be proud of myself and be a role model for my daughter. Knowing I can accomplish things will help me and my confidence.

Conclusion: Reaching my goal is important to me and is worth the work.

Planning Support in an Essay: Mapping and Outlining

In Chapter 3, you learned how to annotate an essay to show the main point and supporting details. We saw that one strategy for understanding a paragraph or an essay is to use annotations to make a map, such as the one on the next page, which follows time order:

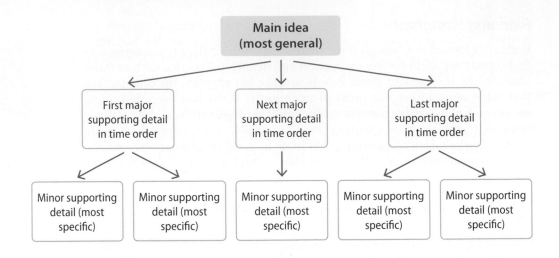

Maps can be used to make an informal plan for an essay. The introduction includes the thesis statement or main idea, and each body paragraph includes one major supporting detail. Many students enjoy sketching a map before they begin working on an essay.

Another strategy is to compose a formal outline. The outline below is for a typical five-paragraph essay in which three body paragraphs (built around three topic sentences) support a thesis statement. The thesis statement is included in an introductory paragraph; the fifth paragraph is the conclusion. However, essays may include more or fewer than five paragraphs, depending on the size and complexity of the topic.

Sample outline for a five-paragraph essay
Thesis statement (part of introductory paragraph 1)

    A. Topic sentence for support point 1 (paragraph 2)

        1. Supporting detail 1 for support point 1

        2. Supporting detail 2 for support point 1 (and so on)

    B. Topic sentence for support point 2 (paragraph 3)

        1. Supporting detail 1 for support point 2

        2. Supporting detail 2 for support point 2 (and so on)

    C. Topic sentence for support point 3 (paragraph 4)

        1. Supporting detail 1 for support point 3

        2. Supporting detail 2 for support point 3 (and so on)

Concluding paragraph (paragraph 5)

The example above is a "formal" outline form, with letters and numbers to distinguish between primary supporting and secondary supporting details.

Some instructors require this format. If you are making an outline just for yourself, you might choose to write a less formal outline, simply indenting the secondary supporting details under the primary support rather than using numbers and letters.

> **PRACTICE 6**   Plan a Paragraph or an Essay
>
> Using the topic sentence and support you developed in Practice 5 (p. 56), make a map or a formal outline to plan a paragraph or an essay.

Write an Introduction and a Conclusion

With your plan or outline in place, you are ready to write a draft of your paper. In addition to the support you have planned, a complete draft will include an introduction and a conclusion.

In a paragraph, the introductory sentence is often the topic sentence. But there are other ways to introduce a paragraph, and these same strategies can be expanded to write the introductory paragraph of an essay. As you consider how to introduce your paragraph or essay, remember the basics of a good introduction:

Basics of a good introduction

- It should catch the readers' attention.
- It should present the main point of the paragraph or essay.
- It should give the readers a clear idea of what the writing will cover.

Here are some common strategies writers use to introduce paragraphs and essays. In each example, the introductory sentence is in boldface. These are not the only ways to introduce paragraphs and essays, but they should give you some useful models.

Open with a Misconception

A misconception is an idea that is shared by many people but is not true. Because readers may identify with the misconception, it is a good way to begin a paragraph or an essay. The misconception only works, however, if your topic sentence or thesis challenges the misconception.

> **When I first enrolled in college, I thought that studying history was a waste of time.** But after taking two world history classes, I have come to the conclusion that these courses count for far more than some credit hours in my college record.

Open with a Quotation

A good, short quotation definitely gets people interested. It must lead naturally into your main point, however, and not be there just for effect. If you start with a quotation, make sure you tell the reader who the speaker is.

> **George Farquhar once said that necessity was the mother of invention, but we know that to be nonsense, really:** who needs an iPod that holds 10,000 songs? There is, however, one area of life in which technology keeps step with nature—the size of things. As we Americans are getting bigger (the Centers for Disease Control and Prevention in Atlanta estimate that roughly a third of Americans are overweight, with 20 percent of us qualifying as obese), so, too, is our stuff.
>
> —James Verini, "Supersize It"

Give an Example, or Tell a Story

People like stories, so opening an essay with a brief story or example often draws readers in.

> **Something snapped inside Jerry Sola during his evening commute through the Chicago suburbs two years ago.** When the driver in front of the fifty-one-year-old salesman suddenly slammed on his brakes, Sola got so incensed that he gunned his engine to cut in front of the man. Still steaming when both cars stopped at a red light, Sola grabbed a golf club from the backseat and got out.
>
> —Dianne Hales, "Why Are We So Angry?"

Start with a Surprising Fact or Idea

Surprises capture people's interest. The more unexpected and surprising something is, the more likely people are to notice it.

> Yes, money can buy happiness, but probably not in the way you imagined. **Spending it on yourself may not do much for your spirits, but spending it on others will make you happier, according to a report from a team of social psychologists in the new issue of *Science*.**
>
> —John Tierney, "Money Can Buy Happiness"

Offer a Strong Opinion or Position

The stronger the opinion, the more likely it is that your readers will pay attention. Don't write wimpy introductions. Make your point and shout it!

> Cedric "C. J." Mills. Isaiah Brooks. Tedric Maynor. Felicia Hines. Vinson Phillips. Kurt Anthony Bryant. Amuel Murph. Alfonso Williams. These names are forever inscribed on my private "Wall of Black Death." My wall contains the names of black people killed by other black people, along with those believed to have been killed by fellow blacks, in the Tampa Bay area since May. I will update the roster as new deaths are reported. More are sure to follow. I do not have answers as to how to stop blacks from killing their brethren. **But I do have an answer for catching some, if not all, of these murderers. Snitch.**

—Bill Maxwell "Start Snitching"

Ask a Question

A question needs an answer, so if you start your introduction with a question, your readers will need to read on to get the answer.

> **Have you ever noticed how many gym membership advertisements appear on television right after the New Year?** Many people overindulge through the holiday season, beginning with Halloween candy and ending with the last sip of eggnog on Christmas evening. On average, Americans gain seven pounds in that six-week period. That weight gain does not include the other forty-six weeks of the year when people typically overeat and quit going to the gym. Do not despair; there is hope! Instead of dreading the inevitable holiday weight gain and spending money on expensive exercise clubs, you can instead resign yourself to starting a new exercise routine at home. Exercise is the best way to combat the "battle of the bulge." One of the most effective ways to lose weight and get into shape is aerobic exercise. I am living proof that beginning a home workout regimen will become a positive, life-altering experience that quickly balances your physical and emotional health, has a maximum gain for minimum pain, and can lead you to improve other aspects of your life as well.

—Michele Wood, "My Home Exercise Program"

> **PRACTICE 7**   **Identify Strategies for Introductions**
>
> Explore the introductions used by Dorrill (Chapter 1, p. 13), DeMarco-Barrett (Chapter 2, p. 30), Mali (Chapter 3, p. 42), Paul (Chapter 3, p. 44), and Godwin (this chapter, p. 66). What strategies does each writer use?

Write a Conclusion

A good piece of writing gives a reader a sense of completion; it lets the reader know that you have made your point. A conclusion is often what the reader remembers most, so it is important to draft a conclusion that has as much energy as the rest of the paragraph or essay, if not more.

Basics of a good conclusion

- It refers back to the main point.
- It sums up what has been covered.
- It makes a further observation or application of the main idea (usually in an essay).

One of the best ways to end an essay or a paragraph is to refer directly to something in the introduction. If you began with a misconception, explain again why it isn't true. If you asked a question, answer it. If you used a quote, give another quote, perhaps by the same person. If you began with a story, tell the ending. Look again at two of the introductions you read earlier, and notice how the writers conclude their essays. Pay special attention to the text in boldface.

Hales's introduction

> **Something snapped inside Jerry Sola during his evening commute through the Chicago suburbs two years ago.** When the driver in front of the fifty-one-year-old salesman suddenly slammed on his brakes, Sola got so incensed that he gunned his engine to cut in front of the man. Still steaming when both cars stopped at a red light, Sola grabbed a golf club from the backseat and got out.

—Dianne Hales, "Why Are We So Angry?"

Hales's conclusion

> **Since his roadside epiphany, Jerry Sola has conscientiously worked to rein in his rage.** "I am a changed person," he says, "especially behind the wheel. I don't have to listen to the news on the car radio. Instead, I put on nice, soothing music. I force myself to smile at rude drivers. And if I feel myself getting angry, I ask a simple question: 'Why should I let a person I'm never going to see again control my mood and ruin my whole day?'"

—Dianne Hales, "Why Are We So Angry?"

Maxwell's introduction

> Cedric "C. J." Mills. Isaiah Brooks. Tedric Maynor. Felicia Hines. Vinson Phillips. Kurt Anthony Bryant. Amuel Murph. Alfonso Williams. These names are forever inscribed on my private "Wall of Black Death." My wall contains the names of black people killed by other black people, along with those believed to have been killed by fellow blacks, in the Tampa Bay area since May. I will update the roster as new deaths are reported. More are sure to follow. I do not have answers as to how to stop blacks from killing their brethren. **But I do have an answer for catching some, if not all, of these murderers. Snitch.**

—Bill Maxwell, "Start Snitching"

Maxwell's conclusion

> Because I regularly write about this issue, I receive a lot of hate mail from both blacks and whites. White letter-writers remind me that blacks are "animals" and "cause all of America's social problems." Black letter-writers see me as the "enemy of people" and a "sell-out" because I condemn blacks for killing one another without taking into account the nation's history of racism. To whites, I have nothing to say. **To blacks, I have one message: We need to start snitching. Only we can stop black-on-black murders. Until then, I will be adding names to the Wall of Black Death.**

—Bill Maxwell, "Start Snitching"

Relationship between Paragraphs and Essays

For more on the important features of writing, see the Four Basics of the Drafting Process on page 48.

Paragraph Form

Topic sentence

Although they are entering the job market in tough economic times, Millennials (those born between 1981 and 2000) have some important advantages in the workplace. First, having grown up in a fast-changing world, they value flexibility, independence, and collaboration.

Support 1

According to a report from the Boston College Center for Work and Family's Executive Briefing Series, Millennials seek flexibility in the workplace; meaning, for one thing, that they want the independence to find the most effective way to work. Additionally, younger people generally prefer to work collaboratively and to motivate others on their team; therefore, they hold the promise of being inspiring leaders.

Support 2

Second, Millennials are smart about using technology to make connections and succeed on the job. Most are accustomed to being in nearly constant contact with others via phones, laptops, or other devices. Millennials who use their electronic communication skills wisely will be comfortable keeping managers and colleagues up to date about projects. Also, Millennials' social media skills can be put to good use by employers looking for new ways to market products.

Support 3

Finally, the economy is creating more jobs that demand the flexibility, independence, and technological skills that Millennials are acquiring. For example, many jobs are being created in the health care field, where workers must not only exercise independence in decision making but must also be able to collaborate effectively. Additionally, many more companies need employees who know how to use social media and other electronic tools.

Concluding sentence

As long as they remain determined, Millennials have every reason to believe that they will achieve success.

Main Point: May be the same for a paragraph and an essay (as in this case). Or the main point of a paragraph may be narrower than one for an essay (see pp. 48–55).

Support for the Main Point

Facts, Details, or Examples to Back Up the Support Points: Usually, 1 to 3 sentences per support point for paragraphs and 3 to 8 sentences per support point for essays.

Conclusion

Essay Form

1

Fairly often, I hear older people saying that Millennials (those born between 1981 and 2000) are spoiled, self-centered individuals who have much less to contribute to the workplace than previous generations did. Based on my own experiences and research I must disagree. Although they are entering the job market in tough economic times, Millennials have some important advantages in the workplace.

Thesis statement

First, having grown up in a fast-changing world, they value flexibility, independence, and collaboration. Unlike their parents and grandparents, Millennials never knew a world without personal computers, and the youngest of them never knew a world without the Internet or ever-changing models of smart phones. They are used to rapid change, and most of them have learned to adapt to it. Consequently, Millennials, for the most part, expect workplaces to adapt to them. According to a report from the Boston College Center for Work and Family's Executive Briefing Series (EBS), Millennials seek flexibility in the workplace—for example, in when and where they work. This attitude

Topic sentence 1

2

does not mean that they are looking out for themselves alone. Instead, they want the independence to find the most effective and productive way to work. Additionally, according to the EBS report, Millennials are more likely than older workers to reject old-fashioned business hierarchies in which managers tell lower-ranking employees what to do, and there is no give-and-take. In general, younger people prefer to work collaboratively and to do what they can to motivate others on their team; therefore, they hold the promise of being inspiring leaders.

Second, Millennials are smart about using technology to make connections and succeed on the job. Most of them are accustomed to being in nearly constant contact with others via phones, laptops, or other devices. Although some people fear that such connectedness can be a distraction in the workplace, these technologies can be used productively and allow effective multitasking. For instance, over the course of a day, Millennials who have learned to use their electronic communication skills wisely will be comfort-

Topic sentence 2

Support paragraphs

3

able keeping managers and colleagues up to date about projects and responding to questions and requests as they arise. Furthermore, most Millennials are open to continuing such electronic exchanges during evenings and weekends if they feel they are collaborating with colleagues to meet an important goal. Also, many Millennials are skilled in using social media to reach out to and remain connected with others; in fact, some people refer to them as "the Facebook generation." Employers can put these skills to good use as they look for new ways to market their products and find new customers.

Finally, the economy is creating more jobs that demand the flexibility, independence, and technological skills that Millennials are acquiring. For example, many jobs are being created in the health care field, where workers, such as nurses and physician assistants, must not only exercise independence in decision making but must also be able to collaborate effectively. Additionally, many more companies need employees who know how to use social media and other elec-

Topic sentence 3

4

tronic tools for marketing purposes. Similarly, Millennials with social media skills may have an advantage in finding work in the marketing and advertising industries specifically. There is also always a need for independent-minded people to create new businesses and innovations. Thus, Millennials play a valuable role in helping the economy grow.

As long as they remain determined and confident, Millennials have every reason to believe that they will achieve career success. According to the EBS report and other sources, meaningful, challenging work is more important to this generation than having a high salary. In the long term, workers with those types of values will always be in demand.

Concluding paragraph

> **PRACTICE 8**   **Identify Strategies for a Conclusion**
>
> Explore the conclusions used by Dorrill (Chapter 1, p. 13), DeMarco-
> Barrett (Chapter 2, p. 30), Mali (Chapter 3, p. 42), Paul (Chapter 3, p. 44),
> and Godwin (below). What strategies does each writer use?

A Complete Draft

Follow your plan (outline or map) to write a draft of your paragraph or essay, using complete sentences in the introduction, the body, and the conclusion. As you write, you may want to add support or change the order. Many writers make such changes as they write their first complete draft.

Like the models on pages 64–65, your complete draft will contain a main idea, organized support, an introduction, and a conclusion. With a complete draft, you are ready to begin the final stages of the writing process: revising and editing (see Chapter 5).

Chapter Reading

Gail Godwin

The Watcher at the Gates

Gail Godwin is a writer of short stories, novels, and essays. She was born in Birmingham, Alabama, and now lives in Woodstock, New York. She has published thirteen novels, along with journals and essays about the practice and art of writing. PHOTO BY JOLANTA DROZD KAMINSKI

Read and annotate the following essay by Gail Godwin. When you have finished, compare your annotations with a classmate's.

1. **Restraining:** limiting or keeping one from action

2. **Freud:** (Sigmund) 1856–1939, Austrian psychiatrist and doctor; the founder of psychoanalysis

1   I first realized I was not the only writer who had a restraining[1] critic who lived inside me and sapped the juice from green inspirations when I was leafing through Freud's[2] *Interpretation of Dreams* a few years ago. Ironically, it was my "inner critic" who had sent me to Freud. I was writing a novel, and my heroine was in the middle of a dream, and then I lost faith in my own invention and rushed to "an authority" to check whether she could have such a dream. In the chapter on dream interpretation, I came upon the following passage that has

helped me free myself, in some measure, from my critic and has led to many pleasant and interesting exchanges with other writers.

2   Freud quotes Schiller[3], who is writing a letter to a friend. The friend complains of his lack of creative power. Schiller replies with an allegory[4]. He says it is not good if the intellect examines too closely the ideas pouring in at the gates. "In isolation, an idea may be quite insignificant, and venturesome in the extreme, but it may acquire importance from an idea which follows it. . . . In the case of a creative mind, it seems to me, the intellect has withdrawn its watchers from the gates, and the ideas rush in pell-mell[5], and only then does it review and inspect the multitude. You are ashamed or afraid of the momentary and passing madness which is found in all real creators, the longer or shorter duration of which distinguishes the thinking artist from the dreamer. . . . You reject too soon and discriminate[6] too severely."

3   So that's what I had: a Watcher at the Gates. I decided to get to know him better. I discussed him with other writers, who told me some of the quirks and habits of their Watchers, each of whom was as individual as his host, and all of whom seemed passionately dedicated to one goal: rejecting too soon and discriminating too severely.

4   It is amazing the lengths a Watcher will go to keep you from pursuing the flow of your imagination. Watchers are notorious[7] pencil sharpeners, ribbon changers, plant waterers, home repairers and abhorrers[8] of messy rooms or messy pages. They are compulsive looker-uppers. They are superstitious scaredy-cats. They cultivate self-important eccentricities[9] they think are suitable for "writers." And they'd rather die (and kill your inspiration with them) than risk making a fool of themselves.

5   My Watcher has a wasteful penchant[10] for 20 pound bond paper above and below the carbon of the first draft. "What's the good of writing out a whole page," he whispers begrudgingly, "if you just have to write it over again later? Get it perfect the first time!" My Watcher adores stopping in the middle of a morning's work to drive down to the library to check on the name of a flower or a World War II battle or a line of metaphysical[11] poetry. "You can't possibly go on till you've got this right!" he admonishes. I go and get the car keys.

6   Other Watchers have informed their writers that:

7   "Whenever you get a really good sentence you should stop in the middle of it and go on tomorrow. Otherwise you might run dry."

8   "Don't try and continue with your book till your dental appointment is over. When you're worried about your teeth, you can't think about art."

9   Another Watcher makes his owner pin his finished pages to a clothesline and read them through binoculars "to see how they look from a distance." Countless other Watchers demand "bribes" for taking the day off: lethal doses of caffeine, alcoholic doses of Scotch or vodka or wine.

---

3. **Schiller:** (Friedrich) 1759–1805, German poet and writer

4. **Allegory:** a story that is used to explain spiritual or abstract ideas

5. **Pell-mell:** in a confused or random order; jumbled together

6. **Discriminate:** to separate or focus on differences and distinctions

7. **Notorious:** well-known for a negative feature or habit

8. **Abhorrer:** someone who hates or cannot stand something

9. **Eccentricities:** odd or unusual behaviors

10. **Penchant:** preference or longing for something

11. **Metaphysical:** referring to a type of poetry from seventeenth-century England; highly intellectual and abstract

12. **Pacify:** make peace with; calm; make happy

10   There are various ways to outsmart, pacify[12], or coexist with your Watcher. Here are some I have tried, or my writer friends have tried, with success:

11   Look for situations when he's likely to be off-guard. Write too fast for him in an unexpected place, at an unexpected time. (Virginia Woolf captured the "diamonds in the dust heap" by writing at a "rapid haphazard gallop" in her diary.) Write when very tired. Write in purple ink on the back of a Master Charge statement. Write whatever comes into your mind while the kettle is boiling and make the steam whistle your deadline. (Deadlines are a great way to outdistance the Watcher.)

12   Disguise what you are writing. If your Watcher refuses to let you get on with your story or novel, write a "letter" instead, telling your "correspondent" what you are going to write in your story or chapter. Dash off a "review" of your own unfinished opus[13]. It will stand up like a bully to your Watcher the next time he throws obstacles in your path. If you write yourself a good one.

13. **Opus:** a composition

13   Get to know your Watcher. He's yours. Do a drawing of him (or her). Pin it to the wall of your study and turn it gently to the wall when necessary. Let your Watcher feel needed. Watchers are excellent critics after inspiration has been captured; they are dependable, sharp-eyed readers of things already set down. Keep your Watcher in shape and he'll have less time to keep you from shaping. If he's really ruining your whole working day, sit down, as Jung[14] did with his personal demons, and write him a letter. "Dear Watcher," I wrote, "What is it you're so afraid I'll do?" Then I held his pen for him, and he replied instantly with a candor[15] that has kept me from truly despising him.

14. **Jung:** (Carl) 1875–1961, Swiss psychiatrist

15. **Candor:** honesty

14   "Fail," he wrote back.

QUESTIONS FOR REFLECTION

1. What is a "Watcher"? Do you think you have one?

2. What does a Watcher like to do?

3. What advice does Godwin give so that writers can outsmart their watchers?

4. How do you think Godwin's Watcher would like a freewriting exercise? Explain.

5. Having read Barbara DeMarco-Barrett's essay "Set Your Writing Free: Use This Technique to Spark Creativity and Loosen Your Inhibitions," would you say that DeMarco-Barrett had a "watcher" in her writing career? If so, how did she deal with the watcher?

SUGGESTIONS FOR WRITING

1. Write a paragraph or an essay that considers this question: what does your watcher do to keep you from writing?

2. Why do you think writer's block is common among student writers? Think about your own experiences and the Godwin and DeMarco-Barrett essays.

Chapter Review

1. Choose five terms in bold from this chapter and define them in your own words.

2. What are the four basics of drafting?

   1. _____

   2. _____

   3. _____

   4. _____

3. What are four characteristics of a good topic sentence?

   1. _____

   2. _____

   3. _____

   4. _____

4. What are three characteristics of good support?

   1. _____

   _____

   2. _____

   _____

   3. _____

   _____

5. What are two strategies for planning a draft?

　　1. _____

　　2. _____

6. What are three features of a good introduction?

　　1. _____

　　2. _____

　　3. _____

7. What are three features of a good conclusion?

　　1. _____

　　2. _____

　　3. _____

　　_____

Finish Well:

Review, Revise, and Reflect

In Chapter 3, we learned that reading well means reading carefully and actively to identify the main idea, the major and minor supporting details, and the pattern of organization used to arrange the support. In Chapter 4, we saw that the work of writing means creating a topic sentence or thesis statement, generating support for that statement, arranging the support, and writing a complete version or draft of the assignment with an introduction and a conclusion.

Many student readers and writers stop at this point. They put the reading away and submit the writing. But the process isn't finished. If you do not finish the reading process by reflecting and responding, you may forget what you have read or have some lingering confusion about it. Similarly, if you do not finish the writing process by revising and editing, your work is probably not your best effort, and it may not get the results you desire.

Finish Well When Reading

Once you have read an assignment carefully, you should take time to pause, review, reflect, and respond. **Reviewing** means thinking about what you have read and restating the key points. **Reflecting** and **responding** mean telling not only what you have read but also your own thoughts, experiences, and questions.

Reviewing

There are four basic questions to ask yourself when you review after reading:

- What is the answer to your guiding question(s) for the reading?
- How would you state the main point of the reading in a single sentence?
- Do all of the major and minor supporting points you identified connect to that point?
- What organizational pattern(s) did the writer use to develop the support?

You can also review by using your annotations to make a map (p. 58) or an outline (p. 58) of your reading. If you have made an outline, make sure that the outline shows both the main idea and the major and minor supporting details. An outline or a map can help you check your comprehension: if you have correctly identified the thesis or topic sentence, then all of the major supporting points will relate directly to that thesis. The outline can also help you determine how the reading is organized.

PRACTICE 1   **Review Reading with Annotations**

Annotate Barbara DeMarco-Barrett's essay "Set Your Writing Free: Use This Technique to Spark Creativity and Loosen Your Inhibitions," in Chapter 2 (pp. 30–31) and use your annotations to complete the following outline and review your reading.

I.   Introduction (Paragraphs 1–3)

    A.   The author introduces _____ to writing, including blank pages, time, and perfectionism.

    B.   Thesis: DeMarco-Barrett says that _____

    _____

II.   Definition and Purpose of Freewriting (Paragraphs 4–6)

    A.   Main Idea (paragraph 4): The author says that _____

    _____

    B.   Main Idea (paragraph 5): The author says freewriting doesn't require fancy equipment.

    C.   Main Idea (paragraph 6): The author says that _____

    _____

    _____

III.   Description of Freewriting with a Group (Paragraphs 7–9)

    A.   Detail: _____

    B.   Detail: _____

    C.   Detail: _____

IV.   Benefits of Freewriting (Paragraph 10)

    Main Idea: DeMarco-Barrett says that _____

    _____

V.   Helpful Hints for Freewriting (Paragraphs 11–15)

    A.   Hint: _____

    B.   Hint: _____

    C.   Hint: _____

    D.   Hint: _____

    E.   Hint: _____

VI.   Conclusion: (Paragraphs 16–18)

    In these paragraphs, the author suggests freewriting as a way to find motivation, get past writer's block, and have fun.

Reflecting and Responding

In the final step of reading, you reflect and respond to what you have read. You do this by making connections and asking questions.

There are four basic questions to ask yourself when you reflect and respond to a reading:

- How does the reading connect with my course or career?
- How does the reading connect with other things I have read or seen?
- How does the reading connect with my life and experiences?
- How does the reading connect with my writing?

Each connection you make strengthens the context for your reading.

To help you focus these four basic questions, consider using these question frameworks. In each case, you will fill in the blanks with the author's name or the title of the selection.

To connect to the course:

Why did my teacher ask me to read _____?

How does the main point in _____ relate to this course?

To connect to other readings:

Where does _____ confirm or agree with what _____ says?

Where does _____ contradict or disagree with what _____ says?

How does _____ complicate or extend what _____ says?

To connect to your own experiences:

Where does _____ confirm or agree with my experiences?

Where does _____ contradict or disagree with my experiences?

How does _____ complicate or extend my experiences?

What questions would you ask _____ about the content of his/her work?

To connect to your writing:

What can I learn from _____?

What style or technique does _____ use that I can try?

What words did I learn from _____?

What questions would I ask _____ about the language or structure of his/her work?

> ### PRACTICE 2 Explore Reflection Questions in Reading
>
> 1. Look at the reflection questions that follow the chapter readings in Chapters 1, 2, 3, and 4. Which of the questions ask you to make connections with other readings? with your own experiences? with your writing?
> 2. How can you help yourself reflect, even when there are no questions to guide you?

Finish Well When Writing

Revising Your Writing

Once you have a complete first draft of your writing, it is important to take a break and then come back to complete the final steps: revising and editing.

Revising is making your ideas clearer, stronger, and more convincing. When you revise, you review your work from the reader's point of view (pp. 78–79). Does your work make the point you intended? Is it convincing? Is the meaning clear for readers? In contrast to revising, **editing** is finding and correcting mistakes in grammar, word usage, punctuation, and capitalization. We can describe editing as having a "word-level" focus, while revising has an "idea-level" or "meaning-level" focus.

Most writers find it difficult to revise and edit well at the same time, as each job requires you to read differently. To revise, read with a focus on meaning to find and solve problems with ideas. To edit, read with a focus on words to find and solve problems with grammar, spelling, and mechanics. The remainder of this chapter addresses strategies for revising. For editing help, use Chapters 15 through 32.

Tips for revising your writing

- Wait at least a few hours, if not a couple of days, before starting to revise.

- Listen to your draft. You can do this by reading aloud, recording your voice on a voice recorder, or by having a friend read the draft aloud to you. Parts that are difficult to follow when reading aloud may need to be revised.

- Make notes on your draft about things to change, based on your listening and critical reading.

- Get comments or feedback from a tutor, friend, or classmate.

- Use the revision checklist below.

CHECKLIST

Revising Your Writing

☐ If someone else just read my topic sentence or thesis statement, what would he or she think the paper is about? Would the main point make a lasting impression? What would I need to do to make it more interesting?

☐ Does each support point really relate to my main point? What more could I say about the topic so that someone else will see it my way? Is any of what I have written weak? If so, should I delete it?

☐ What about the way the ideas are arranged? Should I change the order so that the writing makes more sense or has more effect on a reader?

☐ What about the ending? Does it just droop and fade away? How could I make it better?

☐ If, before reading my paragraph or essay, someone knew nothing about the topic or disagreed with my position, would what I have written be enough for him or her to understand the material or be convinced by my argument?

When you get your friends or classmates to give you feedback, you are using **peer review**. Your instructor may give you time in class for peer review: you may exchange papers with a partner or in a small group. You may also take turns reading your work out loud. Peer review works best when you keep a few basics in mind.

Basics of useful feedback

- It is given in a positive way.
- It is specific.
- It may be given in writing or orally.
- It focuses on the reader's experience: the questions, feelings, and responses of the reader.

In other words, good peer review requires someone who goes through all four steps of the reading process: previewing, reading (annotating), reviewing, and reflecting/responding. Improving your reading skills makes you both a better peer reviewer and a more effective writer.

CHECKLIST

Questions for Peer Reviewers

- ☐ What is the main point?
- ☐ Can I do anything to make my opening more interesting?
- ☐ Do I have enough support for my main point? Where could I use more?
- ☐ Where could I use more details?
- ☐ Are there places where you have to stop and reread something to understand it? If so, where?
- ☐ Do I give my reader clues as to where a new point starts? Does one point "flow" smoothly to the next?
- ☐ What about my conclusion? Does it just fade out? How could I make my point more forcefully?
- ☐ Where else could the paper be better? What would you do if it were your paper?
- ☐ If you were going to be graded on this paper, would you turn it in as is? If not, why not?
- ☐ What other comments or suggestions do you have?

PRACTICE 3 Practice Peer Review

Read Chelsea Wilson's essay draft using the preceding checklist. Annotate her draft, following the guidelines for annotation, and make notes on your concerns or questions in the margins.

Chelsea Wilson

Professor Holmes

EN 099

September 14, 2014

The Benefits of Getting a College Degree

My goal is to get a college degree. I have been taking college courses for two years, and it has been difficult for me. Many times I have wondered if getting a college degree is really worth the struggle. However, there are many benefits of getting a college degree.

I can work as a nurse, something I have always wanted to do. As a nurse, I can make decent money: The average salary for a licensed practical nurse is $40,000 per year. That amount is substantially more than I make now working at a restaurant job that pays minimum wage and tips. With the economy so bad, people are tipping less. It has been hard to pay my bills, even though I work more than forty hours a week. Without a degree, I don't see how that situation will change. I have almost no time to see my daughter, who is in preschool.

I didn't get serious about getting a degree until I became a mother. Then, I realized I wanted more for my daughter than I had growing up. I also wanted to have time to raise her properly and keep her safe. She is a good girl, but she sees crime and violence around her. I want to get her away from danger, and I want to show her that there are better ways to live. Getting a college degree will help me do that.

The most important benefit of getting a college degree is that it will show me that I can achieve something hard. My life is moving in a good direction, and I am proud of myself. My daughter will be proud of me, too. I want to be a good role model for her as she grows up.

Because of these benefits, I want to get a college degree. It pays well, it will give my daughter and me a better life, and I will be proud of myself.

Strategies for Revision

Once you have reread your work and received feedback from your classmates, you are ready to revise. Most writers find it helpful to address three areas in revision: unity, detail, and coherence.

REVISE FOR UNITY

Unity in writing means that all the points you make are related to your main point; they are *unified* in support of it. As you draft a paragraph or an essay, you may detour from your main point without even being aware of it, as the writer of the following paragraph did with the underlined sentences. The diagram after the paragraph shows what happens when readers read the paragraph.

First, double-underline the main point in the paragraph that follows to help you see where the writer got off-track. Then, underline the detour.

> If you want to drive like an elderly person, use a cell phone while driving. A group of researchers from the University of Utah tested the reaction times of two groups of people—those between the ages of sixty-five to seventy-four and those who were eighteen to twenty-five—in a variety of driving tasks. All tasks were done with hands-free cell phones. That part of the study surprised me because I thought the main problem was using only one hand to drive. I hardly ever drive with two hands, even when I'm not talking to anyone. Among other results, braking time for both groups slowed by 18 percent. A related result is that the number of rear-end collisions doubled. The study determined that the younger drivers were paying as much—or more—attention to their phone conversations as they were to what was going on around them on the road. The elderly drivers also experienced longer reaction times and more accidents, pushing most of them into the category of dangerous driver. This study makes a good case for turning off the phone when you buckle up.

Detours weaken your writing because readers' focus is shifted from your main point. See the diagram on page 79 showing how a detour from the main point can break up your paragraph. As you revise, check to make sure your paragraph or essay has unity.

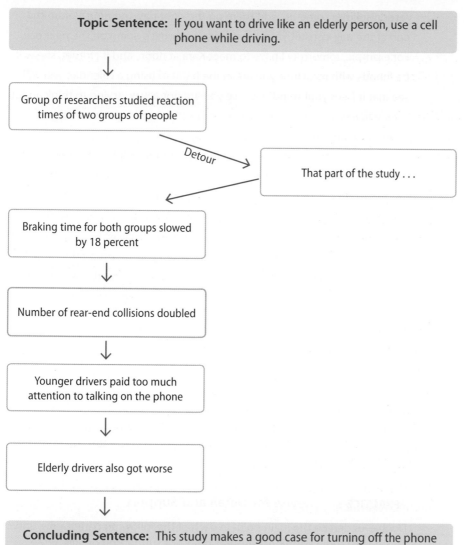

Topic Sentence: If you want to drive like an elderly person, use a cell phone while driving.

↓

Group of researchers studied reaction times of two groups of people

Detour →

That part of the study . . .

Braking time for both groups slowed by 18 percent

↓

Number of rear-end collisions doubled

↓

Younger drivers paid too much attention to talking on the phone

↓

Elderly drivers also got worse

↓

Concluding Sentence: This study makes a good case for turning off the phone when you buckle up.

PRACTICE 4   **Revise for Unity**

Each of the following paragraphs contains a sentence that detours from the main point. First, double-underline the main point. Then, underline the detour in each paragraph.

1. One way to manage time is to keep a print or electronic calendar or schedule. It should have an hour-by-hour breakdown of the day and evening, with space for you to write next to the time. As appointments or

responsibilities come up, add them on the right day and time. Before the end of the day, consult your calendar to see what's going on the next day. For example, tomorrow I have to meet Kara at noon, and if I forget, she will be furious with me. Once you are in the habit of using a calendar, you will see that it frees your mind because you are not always trying to think about what you're supposed to do, where you're supposed to be, or what you might have forgotten.

2. As you use a calendar to manage your time, think about how long certain activities will take. A common mistake is to underestimate the time needed to do something, even something simple. For example, when you are planning the time needed to get money from the cash machine, remember that a line of people may be ahead of you. Last week in the line I met a woman I went to high school with. When you are estimating time for a more complex activity, such as reading a chapter in a textbook, block out more time than you think you will need. If you finish in less time than you have allotted, so much the better.

REVISE FOR DETAIL AND SUPPORT

When you revise a paper, look carefully at the support you have developed. Will readers have enough **detail**—that is, will they have enough information to understand and be convinced by the main point?

In the margin or between the lines of your draft (which should be double-spaced), note ideas that seem weak or unclear. As you revise, build up your support by adding more details.

PRACTICE 5 Revise for Detail and Support

Double-underline the main point in each of the following paragraphs, and add at least three additional support points or supporting details. Write them in the spaces provided under each paragraph, and indicate where they should go in the paragraph by writing in a caret (∧) and the number.

Example: **Sojourner Truth was a brave woman who helped educate people about the evils of slavery.** She was a slave herself in New York. 1
2 After she had a religious vision, she traveled from place to place giving speeches about how terrible it was to be a slave. 3 But even after the Emancipation Proclamation was signed in 1863, slave owners did not follow the laws. Sojourner Truth was active in the Civil War, nursing soldiers and continuing to give speeches. She was active in the fight for racial equality until her death in 1883.

1. *and was not allowed to learn to read or write.*

2. *Sojourner Truth ran away from her owner because of his cruelty.*

3. *Although she was beaten for her beliefs, she continued her work*
   and was part of the force that caused Abraham Lincoln to sign the
   Emancipation Proclamation freeing the slaves.

1.   Sports fans can turn from normal people into destructive maniacs. After big wins, a team's fans sometimes riot. Police have to be brought in. Even in school sports, parents of the players can become violent. People get so involved watching the game that they lose control of themselves and are dangerous.

    1. _____
    2. _____
    3. _____

2.   If a friend is going through a hard time, try to be as supportive as you can. For one thing, ask if you can help out with any errands or chores. Also, find a time when you can get together in a quiet, non-stressful place. Here, the two of you can talk about the friend's difficulties or just spend time visiting. Let the friend decide how the time is spent. Just knowing that you are there for him or her will mean a lot.

    1. _____
    2. _____
    3. _____

REVISE FOR COHERENCE

Coherence in writing means that all your support connects to form a whole. In other words, you have provided enough "glue" for readers to see how one point leads to another.

A good way to improve coherence is to use **transitions**—words, phrases, and sentences that connect your ideas so that your writing moves smoothly from one point to the next. The table on pages 82–83 shows some common transitions and what they are used for.

Here are two paragraphs, one that does not use transitions and one that does. Read them and notice how much easier the second paragraph is to follow because of the underlined transitions.

No transitions

It is not difficult to get organized—it takes discipline to stay organized. All you need to do is follow a few simple ideas. You must decide what your priorities are and do these tasks first. You should ask yourself every day: What is the most important task I have to accomplish? Make the time to do it. To be organized, you need a personal system for keeping track of things. Making lists, keeping records, and using a schedule help you remember what tasks you need to do. It is a good idea not to let belongings and obligations stack up. Get rid of possessions you do not need, put items away every time you are done using them, and do not take on more responsibilities than you can handle. Getting organized is not a mystery; it is just good sense.

Transitions added

It is not difficult to get organized—<u>even though</u> it takes discipline to stay organized. All you need to do is follow a few simple ideas. You must decide what your priorities are and do these tasks first. <u>For example</u>, you should ask yourself every day: What is the most important task I have to accomplish? <u>Then</u>, make the time to do it. To be organized, you <u>also</u> need a personal system for keeping track of things. Making lists, keeping records, and using a schedule help you remember what tasks you need to do. <u>Finally</u>, it is a good idea not to let belongings and obligations stack up. Get rid of possessions you do not need, put items away every time you are done using them, and do not take on more responsibilities than you can handle. Getting organized is not a mystery; it is just good sense.

Transition words can be prepositions, coordinating conjunctions, conjunctive adverbs, adjectives, or subordinating conjunctions. See Chapter 17 for information about these types of words.

Common Transitional Words and Phrases

Indicating Space

above	below	near	to the right
across	beside	next to	to the side
at the bottom	beyond	opposite	under
at the top	farther/further	over	where
behind	inside	to the left	

Indicating Time

after	before	finally	later
as	during	first	meanwhile
at last	eventually	last	next ▶

Indicating Time (*continued*)

now	since	then	while
second	soon	when	

Indicating Importance

above all	in fact	more important	most important
best	in particular	most	worst
especially			

Signaling Examples

for example	for instance	for one thing	one reason

Signaling Additions

additionally	and	as well as	in addition
also	another	furthermore	moreover

Signaling Contrast

although	however	nevertheless	still
but	in contrast	on the other hand	yet
even though	instead		

Signaling Causes or Results

as a result	finally	so	therefore
because			

PRACTICE 6   Add Transition Words

Read the following paragraphs. In each blank, add a transition that would smoothly connect the ideas. In each case, there is more than one correct answer.

Example: LifeGem, a Chicago company, has announced that it can turn cremated human ashes into high-quality diamonds. __*After*__ cremation, the ashes are heated to convert their carbon to graphite. __*Then*__ , a lab wraps the graphite around a tiny diamond piece and again heats it and pressurizes it. __*After*__ about a week of crystallizing, the result is a

diamond. _Because of_ the time and labor involved, this process can cost as much as $20,000. _Although_ the idea is very creative, many people will think it is also very weird.

1.   Frida Kahlo (1907–1954) is one of Mexico's most famous artists. From an early age, she had an eye for color and detail. _____ , it was not until she was seriously injured in a traffic accident that she devoted herself to painting. _____ her recovery, she went to work on what would become the first of many self-portraits. _____ , she married the famous muralist Diego Rivera. _____ Rivera was unfaithful to Kahlo, their marriage was difficult. _____ , Kahlo continued to develop as an artist and produce great work. Rivera may have summed up Kahlo's paintings the best, describing them as "acid and tender, hard as steel and delicate and fine as a butterfly's wing, lovable as a beautiful smile, and profound and cruel as the bitterness of life."

2.   Many fast-food restaurants are adding healthier foods to their menus. _____ , several kinds of salads are now on most menus. These salads offer fresh vegetables and roasted, rather than fried, chicken. _____ , be careful of the dressings, which can be very high in calories. _____ , avoid the huge soft drinks that have large amounts of sugar. _____ , skip the french fries. They are high in fat and calories and do not have much nutritional value.

In Practice 3 above, you read and commented on Chelsea's first draft. Read Chelsea's revised draft below. Compare the changes that you suggested above with those that she made.

Identifying information

Title, centered

First line indented

Details

Chelsea Wilson
Professor Holmes
EN 099
September 28, 2014
                    The Benefits of Getting a College Degree
        I have been taking college courses for two years, and it has been difficult for me. I have a full-time job, a young daughter, and a car that breaks down often. Many times as I have sat, late at night, struggling to stay awake to do homework or to study, I have wondered if getting

Added details

▶

Thesis statement

a college degree is really worth the struggle. That is when I remind myself why getting a degree is so important: It will benefit every aspect of my life.

Topic sentence / Support point 1

One benefit of getting a degree is that I can work as a nurse, something I have always wanted to do. Even as a child, I enjoyed helping my mother care for my grandmother or take care of my younger brothers and sisters when they were sick. I enjoy helping others, and

Added transition

Supporting details

nursing will allow me to do so while making good money. The average salary for a licensed practical nurse is $40,000 per year, substantially more than I make now working at a restaurant. Without a degree, I don't see how that situation will change. Meanwhile, I have almost no time to spend with my daughter.

Topic sentence / Support point 2

Another benefit of getting a college degree is that it will allow me to be a better mother. In fact, I didn't get serious about getting a degree until I became a mother. Then, I realized I wanted more for

Added transitions

my daughter than I had had: a safer place to live, a bigger apartment, some nice clothes, and birthday presents. I also wanted to have time

Supporting details

to raise her properly and keep her safe. She is a good girl, but she sees crime and violence around her. I want to get her away from danger, and I want to show her that there are better ways to live. The job opportunities I will have with a college degree will enable me to do those things.

Topic sentence / Support point 3

The most important benefit of getting a college degree is that it will show me that I can achieve something hard. In the past, I have often given up and taken the easy way, which has led to nothing good.

Added details

The easy way has led to a hard life. Now, however, working toward a goal has moved my life in a good direction. I have confidence and self-

Supporting details

respect. I can honestly say that I am proud of myself, and my daughter will be proud of me, too. I will be a good role model as she grows up, not only for her but also for her friends. She will go to college, just like her mother.

Conclusion

So why am I working so hard to get a degree? I am doing it because I see in that degree the kind of life I want to live on this earth and the kind of human being I want to be. Achieving that vision is worth all the struggles.

Conclusion strengthened with an observation

CHECKLIST

Evaluating Your Revised Essay

☐ My thesis statement is confident, and my main point is clear.

☐ My ideas are detailed and specific and are organized logically.

☐ My ideas flow smoothly from one to the next.

☐ This essay fulfills the original assignment.

☐ I am ready to turn in this essay for a grade.

☐ This essay is the best I can do.

Important note: After you have revised your writing to make the ideas clear and strong, you need to edit it to eliminate any distracting or confusing errors in grammar, word use, punctuation, and capitalization. When you are ready to edit your writing, turn to Part 3, the beginning of the editing chapters.

Chapter Reading

Donald M. Murray

The Maker's Eye

Donald Murray (1924–2006) was a columnist for the *Boston Globe*, a long-time professor of English at the University of New Hampshire, an influential writing teacher, and the author of many books on the art of writing, including *The Craft of Revision* (1998) and *My Twice-Lived Life: A Memoir* (2001). This selection is from *The Writer*, October 1973.

COURTESY OF THE POYNTER INSTITUTE

Read and annotate Murray's essay, using your reading skills. After you have finished, review the essay by answering these four basic questions:

- What is the answer to your guiding question(s) for the reading?
- How would you state the main point of the reading in a single sentence?
- Do all of the major and minor supporting points you identified connect to that point?
- What organizational pattern(s) did the writer use to develop the support?

Reflect and respond to Murray's essay by writing six reflection questions using the frameworks for reflection on pages 73–74. Share your questions with a classmate, and discuss your answers together.

1. **Constructively:** in a helpful way

1   The writer must learn to read critically but constructively[1], to cut what is bad, to reveal what is good. Eleanor Estes, the children's book author, explains: "The

writer must survey his work critically, coolly, as though he were a stranger to it. He must be willing to prune[2], expertly and hard-heartedly. At the end of each revision, a manuscript may look . . . worked over, torn apart, pinned together, added to, deleted from, words changed and words changed back. Yet the book must maintain its original freshness and spontaneity."

2   Most readers underestimate the amount of rewriting it usually takes to produce spontaneous[3] reading. This is a great disadvantage to the student writer, who sees only a finished product and never watches the craftsman who takes the necessary step back, studies the work carefully, returns to the task, steps back, returns, steps back, again and again. Anthony Burgess, one of the most prolific[4] writers in the English-speaking world, admits, "I might revise a page twenty times." Roald Dahl, the popular children's writer, states, "By the time I'm nearing the end of a story, the first part will have been reread and altered and corrected at least 150 times. . . . Good writing is essentially rewriting. I am positive of this."

3   Rewriting isn't virtuous[5]. It isn't something that ought to be done. It is simply something that most writers find they have to do to discover what they have to say and how to say it. It is a condition of the writer's life.

4   There are, however, a few writers who do little formal rewriting, primarily because they have the capacity and experience to create and review a large number of invisible drafts in their minds before they approach the page. And some writers slowly produce finished pages, performing all the tasks of revision simultaneously[6], page by page, rather than draft by draft. But it is still possible to see the sequence followed by most writers most of the time in rereading their own work.

5   Most writers scan their drafts first, reading as quickly as possible to catch the larger problems of subject and form, and then move in closer and closer as they read and write, reread and rewrite.

6   The first thing writers look for in their drafts is *information*. They know that a good piece of writing is built from specific, accurate, and interesting information. The writer must have an abundance of information from which to construct a readable piece of writing.

7   Next writers look for *meaning* in the information. The specifics must build to a pattern of significance. Each piece of specific information must carry the reader toward meaning.

8   Writers reading their own drafts are aware of *audience*. They put themselves in the reader's situation and make sure that they deliver information which a reader wants to know or needs to know in a manner which is easily digested. Writers try to be sure that they anticipate[7] and answer the questions a critical reader will ask when reading the piece of writing.

9   Writers make sure that the *form* is appropriate to the subject and the audience. Form, or genre, is the vehicle which carries meaning to the reader, but form cannot be selected until the writer has adequate information to discover its significance and an audience which needs or wants that meaning.

10   Once writers are sure the form is appropriate, they must then look at the *structure*, the order of what they have written. Good writing is built on a solid framework of logic, argument, narrative[8], or motivation which runs through the entire piece of writing and holds it together. This is the time when many writers

2. **Prune:** trim or cut back

3. **Spontaneous:** unplanned, natural, or without effort

4. **Prolific:** writing or producing a lot

5. **Virtuous:** morally good

6. **Simultaneously:** at the same time

7. **Anticipate:** expect or think about before it actually happens

8. **Narrative:** a story told in time order

find it most effective to outline as a way of visualizing the hidden spine by which the piece of writing is supported.

11   The element on which writers spend a majority of their time is *development*. Each section of a piece of writing must be adequately developed. It must give readers enough information so that they are satisfied. How much information is enough? That's as difficult as asking how much garlic belongs in a salad. It must be done to taste, but most beginning writers underdevelop[9], underestimating the reader's hunger for more information.

9. Underdevelop: fail to provide enough details to make the point effectively

10. Dimension: size

11. Proportion: relationship between the sizes or lengths

12   As writers solve development problems, they often have to consider questions of *dimension*[10]. There must be a pleasing and effective proportion[11] among all the parts of the piece of writing. There is a continual process of subtracting and adding to keep the piece of writing in balance.

13   Finally, writers have to listen to their own voices. *Voice* is the force which drives a piece of writing forward. It is an expression of the writer's authority and concern. It is what is between the words on the page, what glues the piece of writing together. A good piece of writing is always marked by a consistent, individual voice.

14   As writers read and reread, write and rewrite, they move closer and closer to the page until they are doing line-by-line editing. Writers read their own pages with infinite care. Each sentence, each line, each clause, each phrase, each word, each mark of punctuation, each section of white space between the type has to contribute to the clarification of meaning.

15   Slowly the writer moves from word to word, looking through language to see the subject. As a word is changed, cut, or added, as a construction is rearranged, all the words used before that moment, and all those that follow that moment must be considered and reconsidered.

16   Writers often read aloud at this stage of the editing process, muttering or whispering to themselves, calling on the ear's experience with language. Does this sound right—or that? Writers edit, shifting back and forth from eye to page to ear to page. I find I must do this careful editing in short runs, no more than fifteen or twenty minutes at a stretch, or I become too kind with myself. I begin to see what I hope is on the page, not what actually is on the page.

12. Tedious: long and boring

17   This sounds tedious[12] if you haven't done it, but actually it is fun. Making something right is immensely satisfying, for writers begin to learn what they are writing about by writing. Language leads them to meaning, and there is the joy of discovery, of understanding, of making meaning clear as the writer employs the technical skills of language.

13. Connotation: suggested meaning, an idea or feeling associated with a word

14. Denotation: the dictionary definition of a word

18   Words have double meanings, even triple and quadruple meanings. Each word has its own potential of connotation[13] and denotation[14]. And when writers rub one word against the other, they are often rewarded with a sudden insight, an unexpected clarification[15].

15. Clarification: understanding or explanation, when something becomes clear

19   The maker's eye moves back and forth from word to phrase to sentence to paragraph to sentence to phrase to word. The maker's eye sees the need for variety and balance, for a firmer structure, for a more appropriate form. It peers into

the interior of the paragraph, looking for coherence, unity, and emphasis, which make meaning clear.

20   I learned something about this process when my first bifocals were prescribed. I had ordered a larger section of the reading portion of the glass because of my work, but even so, I could not contain my eyes within this new limit of vision. And I still find myself taking off my glasses and bending my nose toward the page, for my eyes unconsciously flick back and forth across the page, back to another page, forward to still another, as I try to see each evolving line in relation to every other line.

21   When does this process end? Most writers agree with the great Russian writer Tolstoy, who said, "I scarcely ever reread my published writings, if by chance I come across a page, it always strikes me: all this must be rewritten; this is how I should have written it."

22   The maker's eye is never satisfied, for each word has the potential to ignite[16] new meaning. This article has been twice written all the way through the writing process [. . .]. Now it is to be republished in a book. The editors made a few small suggestions, and then I read it with my maker's eye. Now it has been re-edited, re-revised, re-read, and re-re-edited, for each piece of writing to the writer is full of potential and alternatives.

16. **Ignite:** spark or create

23   A piece of writing is never finished. It is delivered to a deadline, torn out of the typewriter on demand, sent off with a sense of accomplishment and shame and pride and frustration. If only there were a couple more days, time for just another run at it, perhaps then . . .

My six reflection questions:

1. _____

2. _____

3. _____

4. _____

5. _____

6. _____

Chapter Review

1. Choose five terms in bold from this chapter and define them in your own words.

2. What are four questions to ask when you review a reading?

   1. _____

   2. _____

   3. _____

      _____

   4. _____

3. What are four questions to ask when you reflect and respond to a reading?

   1. _____

   2. _____

   3. _____

   4. _____

4. Why is it important to take a break before you revise?

   _____

   _____

   _____

   _____

5. What are Four Basics of Good Peer Review?

   1. _____

   2. _____

   3. _____

   4. _____

      _____

6. Why is reading important in the peer review process?

   _____

   _____

   _____

   _____

7. What are three areas to focus on in revision?

   1. _____

   2. _____

   3. _____

Practice Summarizing

A **summary** is a condensed or shortened version of something—often, a longer piece of writing, a movie or play, a situation, or an event. An **analytical summary** is a paragraph that presents the main ideas, support, and organizational pattern of a longer piece of writing (or text), stripping the information to essential elements. A summary is a logical final step in the reading process: it expresses what you have learned about the important features of the text, but in your own words.

Four Basics of a Good Summary

> **1** It has a topic sentence that states the title of the selection, the author, and the main idea.
>
> **2** It includes the major supporting details, with references to the author and descriptive verbs.
>
> **3** It concludes with the author's final observations or recommendations.
>
> **4** It is written in your own words and presents information without opinion or comments.

Here are two sample summaries with the first three basics highlighted:

1 In her essay "The Benefits of Getting a College Degree," Chelsea Wilson explains three reasons that a college degree will make her life better. **2** First, she suggests that a degree in nursing will allow her to have a well-paid job in a field she has always respected. Another reason the author identifies is that a college degree will help her be a more effective mother for her daughter. Finally, the author shows that a college degree will give her the confidence and sense of achievement that comes from having finished something difficult. **3** Wilson concludes that the challenges and hard work of college will be worth it when she has finally earned the degree.

1 In her essay "The Watcher at the Gates," Gail Godwin explains strategies for dealing with writer's block. **2** First, Godwin explains that most writers have a critical voice, which she calls a "Watcher at the Gates," that may interfere with the writing process. She illustrates the ways that this critical voice will keep writers from actually writing, from insisting on a certain type of paper to insisting on perfection or a certain look for the writing. Godwin explains, however, that the "Watcher" can be outsmarted, and she gives several examples of strategies for getting past writer's block, including changing the place, time, or materials of writing. She even suggests writing the "Watcher" a letter if he interferes too much. **3** In the end, Godwin suggests that a Watcher has a role to play in helping writers evaluate their work, but the writer needs to control the Watcher's voice.

You may notice that nothing is highlighted in blue and labeled with a four. The fourth basic reminds us to write in our own words, but without inserting our own opinions. The summary writers have not added personal comments on the essays they have summarized, so these summaries illustrate all four basics.

Summaries: A Result of Both Reading and Writing Together

A good summary requires a combination of both the reading and the writing processes. The first step to writing a good summary is careful reading. Let's review the stages in the reading process as they relate to writing a summary.

Preview We learned in Chapter 2 that we need to know the rhetorical context for what we read and write. In other words, we need to identify the audience and purpose of the reading that we will summarize. If we know the audience and purpose, it is easier to identify the author's main point (thesis) and the major supporting details. But we also need to know who will be reading the summary and why; in other words, we need to identify our audience and our purpose for writing the summary. Although most academic summaries are written for a teacher, your job will be easier if you imagine a reader who has not read the original essay or source. Your purpose in the summary is to give this reader a clear picture of what the reading says and how it is organized, in a condensed form.

Read (Annotate) We learned in Chapter 3 how to identify the main point and the major supporting points. As you read to summarize, take notes as you identify the main point in each paragraph (or section). Make a chart (see next page) or an outline (see pp. 57–59) to help you "map" the essay as you read. Use one row on the chart (or one point on the outline) for each major supporting detail in the source. Write your notes in complete sentences.

The chart below contains notes about Chelsea's essay, which is summarized on page 91.

Main idea: The writer says that getting a college degree will make her life better for three reasons.	
Section/paragraph	**Main idea/topic sentence**
Paragraph 2	A degree in nursing will allow her to have a well-paid job in a field she has always respected.
Paragraph 3	A college degree will help her be a more effective mother for her daughter.
Paragraph 4	A college degree will give her the confidence and sense of achievement that comes from having finished something difficult.
Paragraph 5	The challenges and hard work of college will be worth it when she has finally earned the degree.

When you write a summary, you also pay attention to the strategies the writer has used to develop the main point and organize the support. We learned about three possible patterns of organization in Chapter 3: time order, space order, and order of importance. In later chapters, we will learn other strategies that writers can use, including comparison, contrast, definition, and classification. Spotting these strategies will help you organize your summary. For example, notice that Chelsea's essay uses reasons arranged in order of importance. The summary of Chelsea's essay reflects that same structure. The summary presents three reasons in order of importance, and it uses appropriate transitions: "first," "another reason," and "finally."

Review In Chapter 5, we learned the four basic questions for reviewing a reading:

- What is the answer to your guiding question(s) for the reading?
- How would you state the main point of the reading in a single sentence?
- Do all of the major and minor supporting points you identified connect to that point?
- What organizational pattern(s) did the writer use to develop the support?

If you are satisfied with your answers to these questions, based on your annotations, then you are ready to draft a summary.

Drafting the Summary

Write your draft, referring back to your notes (annotations, map, or outline). Your first sentence should include the author's full name, the title of the article or essay (in quotation marks), and the main idea of the essay. Then, write sentences that explain each of the major supporting details, making sure that you introduce those ideas with a reference to the author (by last name, if it is a professional writer, or by a word like "author" or "writer") and a strong descriptive verb. Make sure that your last sentence captures the author's conclusion or comment, but don't add any comments of your own.

Descriptive verbs for a summary

Verbs followed by a complete idea (to introduce what the writer says)	Verbs followed by a noun or nouns (to introduce what the writer does, or the strategies the writer uses)
argues (that)	analyzes
asks (that)	classifies
asserts (that)	compares
claims (that)	contrasts
demands (that)	defines
denies (that)	describes
explains (that)	evaluates
implies (that)	exemplifies
points out (that)	expresses
suggests (that)	illustrates
	synthesizes

PRACTICE 1   **Recognize Descriptive Verbs in Summaries**

Circle the references to the author and underline the descriptive verbs in the sample summaries on pages 91–92.

WRITING IN YOUR OWN WORDS: PARAPHRASING

Your summary must also be written in your own words. It is easy to think that you are using your own words when you are actually using some of the author's words, especially when you have identified the main idea and the major supporting points from the original source. Taking a specific sentence (such as the thesis or a major supporting detail) and putting it into your own words is called **paraphrasing**. Paraphrasing is an important skill that you must practice when you are summarizing. Here are three tips to help you effectively paraphrase key points for your summary.

Tip 1: Do not copy the main idea (thesis) or major supporting details (topic sentences) when you make your map or chart.

Tip 2: Think about what the writer says for each point, cover the source, and imagine you are explaining that point to one of your friends. Remember that the purpose of a summary is to make the author's ideas clear to someone who hasn't read the original essay. Begin your explanation this way: "In other words, the writer is saying that . . ." Write your explanation on your map or chart without looking back at the original.

Tip 3: Avoid cut-and-paste paraphrases. A **cut-and-paste paraphrase** copies the original and then just changes one or two words. For example, here is Chelsea's thesis followed by a cut-and-paste paraphrase. The parts that are the same are highlighted.

Original:

"That is why I remind myself why getting a college degree is so important: It will benefit every aspect of my life."

Cut-and-paste paraphrase:

Chelsea says that she reminds herself why getting a college degree is important: it will benefit every part of her life.

Do you see how close the sentence structure and language are to the original? As a result, the cut-and-paste paraphrase is not acceptable. Now compare this to an appropriate paraphrase:

In her essay "The Benefits of Getting a College Degree," Chelsea Wilson explains three reasons that a college degree will make her life better.

While some of the individual words are the same in this paraphrase, the writer has not borrowed Chelsea Wilson's structure or longer strings of words.

PRACTICE 2   Recognize Effective Paraphrases

Meghan plans to summarize the essay by Shari Beck on pages 289–290. Look at her essay chart. Determine which of her statements are correctly paraphrased and which are not correctly paraphrased. If there is a problem with a statement, rewrite it to make a correct paraphrase.

Main idea: *The writer says that there are several reasons we shouldn't bring social media into college classrooms.*

Section/paragraph	Main idea/topic sentence
Paragraph 3	*She says that the first reason is the distraction factor.* Acceptable? Yes _____ No _____ Revision: _____
Paragraph 4	*She also says she is against social media in education because students' postings on Facebook or Twitter might compromise their privacy.* Acceptable? Yes _____ No _____ Revision: _____
Paragraph 5	*She says the most important reason for being cautious about social media in the classroom is that it might make it a lot easier for students to give away answers unfairly or even plagiarize.* Acceptable? Yes _____ No _____ Revision: _____
Paragraph 6	*She concludes that the disadvantages of this initiative far outweigh any benefits.* Acceptable? Yes _____ No _____ Revision: _____

PRACTICE 3   Write a Summary: Shari Beck, "A Classroom Distraction—and Worse"

Use the corrected chart from Practice 2 above to write a draft summary of Shari Beck's essay "A Classroom Distraction—and Worse" (p. 289).

PRACTICE 4   Write a Summary: Barbara DeMarco-Barrett, "Set Your Writing Free: Use This Technique to Spark Creativity and Loosen Your Inhibitions"

Use your outline from Practice 1 in Chapter 5 (pp. 72–73) of Barbara DeMarco-Barrett's "Set Your Writing Free: Use This Technique to Spark Creativity and Loosen Your Inhibitions" to write a draft summary of the essay.

REVISING A SUMMARY

In Chapter 5, you learned how to revise by checking for unity, coherence, and details and support in your paragraph. We focus on the same issues when we revise a summary.

Unity: Is the topic sentence clear? Does it accurately reflect the main idea of the source?

Coherence: Does the arrangement of the major details show the organization of the primary support in the original essay? Are there logical transitions to connect your ideas?

Details and Support: Are all the major supporting points included in the summary? Have you avoided adding the minor supporting details and your own opinions or comments?

PRACTICE 5   Review and Revise a Summary

With a partner, review your summaries of the essays "A Classroom Distraction—and Worse" and "Set Your Writing Free: Use This Technique to Spark Creativity and Loosen Your Inhibitions." Discuss problems with unity, coherence, and details and support. Read the summaries aloud and make notes. Then, revise your summaries.

PRACTICE 6   Evaluate a Summary

A student wrote the following summary of Taylor Mali's essay "Making Kids Work Hard" (Chapter 3, pp. 42–43). Answer the following questions about the draft summary:

1. Does it have an effective topic sentence? Does it accurately capture Mali's main point?

2. Are each of the supporting sentences effective? Do they accurately capture Mali's main ideas without including minor details?

3. Is the summary written entirely in the writer's own words? If not, which sentence(s) is problematic?

4. Are there effective transitions throughout the summary?

    In his essay "Making Kids Work Hard," Taylor Mali shows that one great lesson a teacher gives students is hard work. He says students work really hard for good teachers because they want and need their approval. Mali uses a story about an aide to Henry Kissinger to illustrate the point. Kissinger wouldn't even read the aide's report until the third time he submitted it, because Kissinger knew the aide wasn't doing his best work. Mali says that grades can mean different things to students, and sometimes a student who gets a C+ has really done hard work. Mali says that it's the hard work, work that is harder than what you thought you could do, that is the best lesson a teacher teaches.

Chapter Review

1. What are the four basics of a good summary?

    1. _____

       _____

    2. _____

       _____

    3. _____

    4. _____

       _____

2. Who is the audience for a summary?

    _____

    _____

3. How does a chart or outline help a reader prepare to write a summary?

    _____

    _____

    _____

4. What are three examples of descriptive verbs for a summary? _____

    _____

    _____

    _____

    _____

5. What is a paraphrase? _____

    _____

6. What is a cut-and-paste paraphrase? _____

    _____

7. How can you avoid a cut-and-paste paraphrase in a summary? _____

_____

_____

_____

_____

_____

_____

_____

8. What are three things to check when you revise a summary?

• _____

_____

• _____

_____

_____

• _____

_____

_____

Part 2
Reading and Writing Different Kinds of Paragraphs and Essays

Narration and Description:

Texts That Tell a Story

Understand What Narration Is

Narration is writing that tells the story of an event or an experience.

Four Basics of Good Narration

1 It reveals something of importance to the writer (the main point).

2 It includes all the major events of the story (primary support).

3 It brings the story to life with details about the major events (secondary support).

4 It presents the events in a clear order, usually according to when they happened.

In the following paragraph, the numbers and colors correspond to the Four Basics of Good Narration.

1 Last year, a writing assignment that I hated produced the best writing I have done. 2 When my English teacher told us that our assignment would be to do a few hours of community service and write about it, I was furious. 3 I am a single mother, I work full-time, and I am going to school: Isn't that enough? 2 The next day, I spoke to my teacher during her office hours and told her that I was already so busy that I could hardly make time for homework, never mind housework. My own life was too full to help with anyone else's life. 3 She said that she understood perfectly and that the majority of her students had lives as full as mine. Then, she explained that the service assignment was just for four hours and that other students had enjoyed both doing the assignment and writing about their experiences. She said they were all surprised and that I would be, too. 2 After talking with her, I decided to accept my fate. The next week, I went to the Community Service Club, and

4 Events in time order

4 Events in time order

was set up to spend a few hours at an adult day-care center near where I live. A few weeks later, I went to the Creative Care Center in Cocoa Beach, not knowing what to expect. **3** I found friendly, approachable people who had so many stories to tell about their long, full lives. **2** The next thing I knew, I was taking notes because I was interested in these people: **3** their marriages, life during the Depression, the wars they fought in, their children, their joys and sorrows. I felt as if I was experiencing everything they lived while they shared their history with me. **2** When it came time to write about my experience, I had more than enough to write about: **3** I wrote the stories of the many wonderful elderly people I had talked with. **2** I got an A on the paper, and beyond that accomplishment, I made friends whom I will visit on my own, not because of an assignment, but because I value them.

You can use narration in many practical situations.

College	In a lab course, you are asked to tell what happened in an experiment.
Work	Something goes wrong at work, and you are asked to explain to your boss—in writing—what happened.
Everyday life	In a letter of complaint about service you received, you need to tell what happened that upset you.

In college, the word *narration* may not appear in your writing and reading assignments. Instead, an assignment may ask you to *describe* events, report what happened, or retell what happened. In addition, you may be asked to read accounts, reports, case histories, or case studies. All of these tasks require you to understand how to read or write narration and description.

Narration in the Classroom: Timelines

Dwayne is taking American History. He earned a D on the first test. The instructor said that Dwayne's answer to the essay was disorganized and lacked support. Dwayne feels overwhelmed: how can he learn so many dates and events?

After learning the Four Basics of Good Narration, Dwayne began to think differently about the material. He knew that his history textbook followed chronological order, but he had never really paid attention to the chapter titles and headings. As he skimmed the chapter covering the years before the Civil War, he saw some headings he recognized, including "The Compromise of 1850" and "The Election of 1860." Other headings covered events that occurred between those years. Dwayne realized that this chapter showed the Four Basics of Good Narration: it used the events of history to focus on one main idea—the South's decision to leave the Union. The headings in the chapter illustrated the major events that relate to the main idea. Details appeared in the text to describe the major events, which appeared in time order.

Dwayne didn't need to focus on every detail; he needed to organize his learning around the major events in the chapter. Dwayne created a timeline. Each major event became a point on his timeline. Here is a section of the timeline:

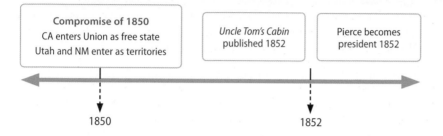

Once Dwayne completed his timeline, he knew how to focus his studies: he first learned the major events leading to the war and then practiced arranging the main events on the timeline to make sure he understood the order correctly. He also used his chapter headings to predict possible essay questions for the next test. By organizing his notes and his thinking, Dwayne was able to prepare for and succeed on the next test.

APPLY WHAT YOU HAVE LEARNED

1. Look at the table of contents from a textbook you are using this term. Can you find examples of time order? If so, how do the titles, subtitles, and highlights from the text support the narration? How could an understanding of narration help you study this text more effectively?

2. How could a timeline help you read a textbook, short story, or newspaper article more effectively? How could a timeline help you in prewriting for a narration assignment?

Main Point in Narration

In narration, the **main point** is what is important about the story—for the writer and the readers. To help you identify the main point when you are reading a narration, complete the following sentence:

What is important to the writer about this story is that . . .

To help you write a main point when you are drafting a narration, complete the following sentence:

What is important to me about this story is that . . .

The topic sentence (paragraph) or thesis statement (essay) usually includes the topic and the main point the writer wants to make about the topic. Let's look at a topic sentence first.

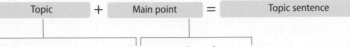

My first day at my new job was nearly a disaster.

Remember that the topic for an essay can be a little broader than one for a paragraph.

Over the course of my summer internship, I became a more confident and skilled worker.

Whereas the topic sentence focuses on just one workday, the thesis statement considers a season-long internship.

PRACTICE 1   Identify Main Points in Narration

1. Look back at the sample paragraph on page 103. Complete the diagram below to illustrate the parts of the topic sentence.

2. Look at the paragraph by Dora Garcia on page 114. Complete the diagram below to illustrate the parts of her topic sentence.

3. Look at the student essay by Lauren Mack on pages 115–116. Identify the thesis statement, and complete the diagram below to illustrate her main point.

Support in Narration

In narration, **support** demonstrates the main point—what's important about the story.

The paragraph and essay models on pages 108–109 use the topic sentence (paragraph) and thesis statement (essay) from the Main Point in Narration section of this chapter. (The thesis statement has been revised slightly.) Both models include the support used in all narration writing: major events backed up by details about the events. In the essay model, however, the major support points (events) are topic sentences for individual paragraphs.

Choosing Major Events

When you tell a story to a friend, you can include events that are not essential to the story. When you are writing a narration, however, you need to give more careful thought to which events to include, selecting only those that most clearly demonstrate your main point.

PRACTICE 2   **Write Main Ideas and Choose Major Support**

For each of the following topics, write a main idea. Write at least three events that will help you show your main idea. (For help writing the main idea, see the examples in Practice 1, p. 106.)

1.   Topic: A strange, embarrassing, or funny experience

    Main idea: _____

    Major supporting details (events): _____

    _____

    _____

    _____

2.   Topic: A lesson I learned

    Main idea:

    Major supporting details (events): _____

    _____

    _____

    _____

Paragraphs vs. Essays in Narration

For more on the important features of narration, see the Four Basics of Good Narration on page 103.

Paragraph Form

Main Point: Often narrower for a paragraph than for an essay: while the topic sentence (paragraph) is focused on just one workday, the thesis statement (essay) considers a season-long internship.

Major Events Supporting the Main Point

Details about the Events: Usually 1 to 3 sentences per event for paragraphs and 3 to 8 sentences per event for essays.

Conclusion

- **Topic sentence** — My first day at my new job was nearly a disaster. First, a traffic jam from highway construction caused me to be a half hour late.
- **Support 1 (first major event)** — I had left myself plenty of time for the commute, but because of the traffic backup, it took me nearly an hour to travel seven miles. At one point, I tried a detour to avoid traffic, but I ended up getting lost. By the time I finally pulled into the employee parking lot, I was already full of stress.
- **Support 2 (second major event)** — After I arrived in the office, I discovered that I would have to fill in for a sick worker whose job I was not familiar with. I had been trained in accounts payable, while my sick colleague worked in accounts receivable. Although I had some understanding of his job, I was worried about making mistakes and had to ask coworkers a lot of questions, which took a lot of time. For example, I estimate that I spent a half hour on a billing procedure that would take an experienced worker five minutes.
- **Support 3 (third major event)** — Near the end of the day, my computer broke down, erasing two documents that I had been working on. One was a small set of file labels, but the other was a detailed summary of the day's billings. At this point, I wanted to put my head down on my desk and cry. Seeing my distress, my supervisor came by and kindly said, "You have had a long, hard day and done great work. Why don't you go home and make a fresh start tomorrow?"
- **Concluding sentence** — I was grateful for her kindness, and I came around to thinking that if I could handle this type of day on the new job, I could handle just about any day.

Think Critically As You Write Narration

Ask Yourself

- Would someone who is unfamiliar with this story be able to follow it and relate to it?
- Have I provided enough detail to bring each event to life?

1

Several of my friends question whether summer internships are really worthwhile, especially if the pay is low or nonexistent. However, the right internship definitely pays off professionally in the long run even if it doesn't financially in the short run. The pr~~o~~ **Thesis statement** my own summer marketing internship, which made me a far more confident and skilled worker.

During the first two weeks of the inter~~n~~ **Topic sentence 1 (first major event)** received thorough training in every part of my j example, my immediate supervisor spent three full days going over everything I would need to do to help with e-mail campaigns, online marketing efforts, and other promotions. She even had me draft a promotional e-mail for a new product and gave me feedback about how to make the message clearer and more appealing. I also spent a lot of time with other staffers, who taught me everything from how to use the photocopier and printers to how to pull together marketing and sales materials for executive meetings. Most impressive, the president of the company took some time out of a busy afternoon to answer my questions about how he got started in his career and what he sees as the

2

keys to success in the marketing field. As I explained **Topic sentence 2 (second major event)** to a friend, I got a real "insider's view" of t~~he~~ and its leadership.

Next, I got hands-on experience with listening to customers and addressing their needs. Specifically, I sat in on meetings with new clients and listened to them describe products and services they would like the company's help in promoting. They also discussed the message they would like to get across about their businesses. After the meetings, I sat in on brainstorming sessions with other staffers in which we came up with as many ideas as we could about campaigns to address the clients' needs. At first, I didn't think anyone would care about my ideas, but others listened to them respectfully and even ended up including some of them in the marketing plans that were sent back to the clients. Later, I learned that some of my ideas **Topic sentence 3 (third major event)** would be included in the actual ~~marketing~~ campaigns.

By summer's end, I had advanced my skills so much that I was asked to return next summer. My supervisor told me that she was pleased not only with

3

all I had learned about marketing but also with the responsibility I took for every aspect of my job. I did not roll my eyes about having to make photocopies or help at the reception desk, nor did I seem intimidated by bigger, more meaningful tasks. Although I'm not guaranteed a full-time job at the company after graduation, I think my chances are good. Even if I don't end up working there long term, I am very grateful for how the job has helped me grow.

In the end, the greatest benefit of the internship might be the confidence it gave me. I have learned that no matter how challenging the task before me—at work or in real life—I can succeed at it by getting the right information and input on anything unfamiliar, working effectively with others, and truly dedicating myself to doing my best. My time this past summer was definitely well spent.

Concluding paragraph

109

Descriptive Details about the Events in Narration

In narration, writers want readers to **visualize** (see) the story and to understand why each event is important. In other words, writers want readers to share their point of view and to see the same message in the story. To accomplish that, writers include details and examples with the major events that allow readers to understand those events more clearly.

> **PRACTICE 3**   **Read for Descriptive Detail in Narration**
>
> The major events and minor support from the sample paragraph on page 108 are reprinted here. Each major event is underlined. In the minor supporting sentences, circle the key words (repetitions and transitions) that connect the details to the major event, and put brackets around new information that helps you understand the major event more fully. The first one has been done for you.

First, a traffic jam from highway construction caused me to be a half hour late. I had left myself plenty of time for the commute, but because of the traffic backup, it took me nearly [an hour to travel seven miles]. At one point, I tried [a detour] to avoid traffic, but I ended up [getting lost]. By the time I finally pulled into the employee parking lot, I was already [full of stress].

1. After I arrived in the office, I discovered that I would have to fill in for a sick worker whose job I was not familiar with. I had been trained in accounts payable, while my sick colleague worked in accounts receivable. Although I had some understanding of his job, I was worried about making mistakes and had to ask coworkers a lot of questions, which took a lot of time. For example, I estimate that I spent a half hour on a billing procedure that would take an experienced worker five minutes.

2. Near the end of the day, my computer broke down, erasing two documents that I had been working on. One was a small set of file labels, but the other was a detailed summary of the day's billings. At this point, I wanted to put my head down on my desk and cry.

PRACTICE 4   **Write Descriptive Details in Narration**

Choose one of your main ideas from Practice 2. For each major event, write two details that will help a reader visualize the story.

Example:

Main Idea: *After a horrible fight with my sister, I learned the value of staying calm.*

Major Event: *We disagreed about who was going to have the family party.*

  Detail: *Even though we both work, she said she was too busy and I would have to do it.*

Major Event: *She made me so mad I started yelling at her, and I got nasty.*

  Detail: *I brought up times in the past when she had tried to pass responsibilities off on me, and I told her I was sick of being the one who did everything.*

Major Event: *I hung up on her, and now we are not talking.*

  Detail: *I feel bad, and I know I will have to call her sooner or later because she is my sister. I do love her, even though she is a pain sometimes.*

Main Idea: _____

Major Event: _____

  Detail: _____

_____

Major Event: _____

  Detail: _____

_____

Major Event: _____

  Detail: _____

_____

Organization in Narration

Narration usually presents events in the order in which they happened; this is known as **time (chronological) order**. As shown in the paragraph and essay models on pages 108–109, a narration starts at the beginning of the story and describes events as they unfold.

For more information on using and punctuating these transitions, see Chapters 17 and 24.

We learned in Chapter 5 that **transitions** help move readers from one event to the next. Good writers use transitions wisely to help readers follow the development of the story. Readers, in turn, use transitions to follow the narration accurately.

Conjunctive Adverbials	Subordinating Conjunctions	Prepositions	Adjectives
at last	after	after	final
eventually	as	before	first
finally	before	since	last
first	once		next
later	when		second
meanwhile	while		
next			
now			
soon			
then			

PRACTICE 5   Use Transitions in Narration

Read the paragraph that follows and fill in the blanks with time transitions. You are not limited to the ones listed in the preceding box.

Some historians believe that as many as four hundred women disguised themselves as men so that they could serve in the U.S. Civil War (1861–1865). One of the best known of these women was Sarah Emma Edmonds. _____ the war began, Edmonds, an opponent of slavery, felt driven to join the Union Army, which fought for the free states. _____ President Abraham Lincoln asked for army volunteers, she disguised herself as a man, took the name Frank Thompson, and enlisted in the infantry. _____ her military service, Edmonds worked as a male nurse and a messenger. _____ serving as a nurse, she learned that the Union general needed someone to spy on the Confederates. _____ extensive training, Edmonds took on this duty and, disguised as a slave, went behind enemy lines. Here, she learned about the Confederates' military strengths and weaknesses. _____, she returned to the Union side and went back to work as a nurse. In 1863, Edmonds left the army after developing malaria. She was worried that hospital workers would discover that she was a woman. As a result of her departure, "Frank Thompson" was listed as a deserter. In later years, Edmonds, under her real name, worked to get a veteran's pension and to get the desertion charge removed from her record. _____, in 1884, a special act of Congress granted her both of these wishes.

Read and Analyze Narration

Student Narration Paragraph: "Beowulf and Me," Dora Garcia

Preview ▷ Read ▷ Review ▷ Reflect and Respond

- What do you expect to read, based on the title?
- What is your guiding question for reading this paragraph?

Preview ▷ **Read** ▷ Review ▷ Reflect and Respond

Guidelines for Reading and Annotating Narration

Read and annotate this paragraph using the guidelines:

1. Pay attention to vocabulary using marginal notes, context clues, or a dictionary. (Note especially any detail that shows how something looks, sounds, smells, tastes, or feels.)

2. Find the main point and underline it. (In a narration, the main point shows why the story is important to the writer.)

3. Identify supporting details and organizational strategies. Number the major events in the story; these are the major supporting details. Circle transitions, key repetitions, and other clues that help a reader follow the chronological order of the story.

4. Ask questions and make connections. Remember to connect the story to your own experiences and other things you have read.

Dora Garcia

Beowulf and Me

1   I was seventeen years old going into eleventh grade, and my goal was to get out of ESL classes into a regular English class. Getting out of ESL was a difficult challenge for me as a Spanish speaker. I tried hard and worked hard. I came up with the idea to ask my ESL teacher to give me extra work so that I could accomplish this goal. My teacher was thrilled to see how motivated I was. Mrs. Doughty, one of my ESL teachers, helped me accomplish my goal by giving me projects and extra work for extra credit. She even stayed after school to give me extra help. I will never forget her. At the end of the year, she told me that I was ready to move into regular English. I was extremely excited, and I could feel the butterflies in my stomach. Finally, I was going to be in a regular English class, joining all my friends who had been there for me since I first moved to Virginia. I was ready for my first assignment in my Regular English class; it was to read about Beowulf. What an amazing story! I will never forget reading about a monster named Grendel, imagining the swamp he lived in and the brave man Beowulf who would hunt him down. I could relate to Beowulf because I too was eager to defeat my monster, "English." It was awesome to imagine what I was reading in the story and to fully understand what the characters were saying, in English; I will never forget this story. I will always remember what victory felt like when we wrote an essay about the story, and I earned a B+ grade. That grade reflected my hard work, and it made me very proud of myself. Now I know that hard work pays off, no matter what monster I am facing.

| Preview | Read | **Review** | Reflect and Respond |

Review your reading. Make sure you can answer these questions:

1. What is Garcia's main point?
2. What are the major events in her story?
3. Does her paragraph illustrate the Four Basics of Good Narration? Explain.

| Preview | Read | Review | **Reflect and Respond** |

1. When have you overcome a challenge and enjoyed success? Explain.
2. If you could talk to Dora Garcia, what questions would you ask her?
3. Garcia identifies in some way with the hero, Beowulf, because he persevered and accomplished a goal. Do you have a story or a hero who inspires you? Explain.

Student Narration Essay: "Gel Pens," Lauren Mack

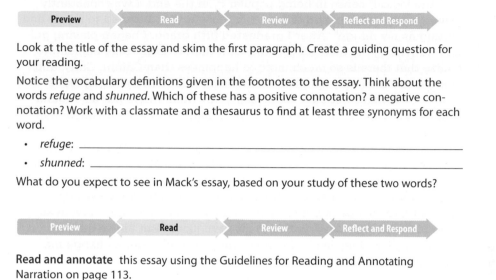

Look at the title of the essay and skim the first paragraph. Create a guiding question for your reading.

Notice the vocabulary definitions given in the footnotes to the essay. Think about the words *refuge* and *shunned*. Which of these has a positive connotation? a negative connotation? Work with a classmate and a thesaurus to find at least three synonyms for each word.

- *refuge*: _____
- *shunned*: _____

What do you expect to see in Mack's essay, based on your study of these two words?

Read and annotate this essay using the Guidelines for Reading and Annotating Narration on page 113.

Lauren Mack

Gel Pens

1   I was in fifth grade. Everything was new and interesting; our elementary school had just been redone, and I had a new teacher and a whole new class. And more than anything, I wanted to be cool. The way I saw it, once I was cool, I'd be popular; and once I was popular, I'd have lots of friends, which, of course, was the key to juvenile[1] happiness. So on the first day of school, I pulled the boldest move of my elementary career. Rather than sitting with my old friends, who I knew were friendly and nice, I sat with the popular girls, Caitlin, Carly, and Maggie. It was my ticket to fame, I thought, because these girls could help me become the person I wanted to be. But I'd never been so wrong.

2   And so all year, I sat with Caitlin, Carly, and Maggie, and throughout that entire year, I was the odd girl out. What stands out more than anything from fifth grade were these gel pens. I remember the girls had this fantastic collection of gel pens in all different colors; sparkly greens and pinks and blues, and they were the greatest things that a fifth grader could fathom[2] and they were all right in front of me—except I couldn't use them. I wasn't cool enough to use these gel pens and, to me, this was absolutely heartbreaking.

3   Looking back, it's strange to think that, throughout an entire year of being shunned[3] and neglected by these girls, it was a collection of pens

1. **Juvenile:** an adjective referring to young people

2. **Fathom:** to understand or discover

3. **Shunned:** avoided

4. Logical: based on reasoning

5. Refuge: a place of escape or relief

6. Disciples: a follower or student of someone or something

7. Crafting: to exercise skill in making something

that made me come to my senses about what I was doing wrong. What was the logical[4] sense in being popular if, in the end, I was constantly feeling jealous, upset, and left out? To answer this, I turned to music and writing as my refuge[5]. After I graduated fifth grade, I began playing guitar and writing my own songs. And with that, it didn't take me long to realize that there is so much more to happiness than Caitlin, Carly, and Maggie and their silly gel pens. In breaking free from the disciples[6] of "cool," I felt that I not only set myself apart from others but also found something I hadn't found at all that year: happiness and satisfaction in myself.

4 These days, I refuse to adjust myself to meet the standards of others. Instead, I invest my time working on the things that have molded me into the person I am today. I am a musician: I write my songs about people, but not for them. I am an artist: I create my works from my own imagination, not from the person next to me. I am a writer: I express my ideas and opinions by crafting[7] words to my own liking. But above all, I am my own person: People can influence me, but they cannot change me, regardless of how many gel pens they may have.

| Preview | Read | **Review** | Reflect and Respond |

- Make sure you can answer your guiding question.
- Identify and paraphrase the main point in this essay.
- Write to Improve Reading: Using your annotations, write a summary of the essay. Make sure that the summary captures the main point and the major supporting ideas in your own words. Use strong descriptive verbs in each sentence (see p. 94).

| Preview | Read | Review | **Reflect and Respond** |

1. Why do you suppose Mack chose to make the gel pens an important part of her essay? What appeal did they have for her apart from their "sparkly greens and pinks and blues"?

2. Mack discusses how making music and writing helped her become a more satisfied and independent person. Would any further details about her music and writing have helped you as a reader better understand Mack and the changes she went through? If so, explain the types of details you would like her to have included.

3. Make Connections: In the final paragraph, Mack writes, "People can influence me, but they cannot change me." Mack's statement invites a question: what can change people in a deep and lasting way?

Reading/Writing Workbook: Narration

Professional Essay: "Fish Cheeks," Amy Tan

Preview

1. Ask Questions: Skim the essay title, the information about the author, and the first paragraph. Write a guiding question for your reading.

2. Make Connections: Can you remember yourself at age fourteen? What things did you long for when you were that age?

Read and annotate this essay carefully, using the Guidelines for Reading and Annotating Narration on page 113.

Amy Tan

Fish Cheeks

Amy Tan was born in Oakland, California, in 1952, several years after her mother and father emigrated from China. She studied at San Jose City College and later at San Jose State University, receiving a B.A. with a double major in English and linguistics. In 1973, she earned an M.A. in linguistics from San Jose State University. In 1989, Tan published her first novel, *The Joy Luck Club*, which was nominated for the National Book Award and the National Book Critics Circle Award. Tan's other books include *The Kitchen God's Wife* (1991), *The Hundred Secret Senses* (1995), and *Saving Fish from Drowning* (2005). Her short stories and essays have been published in the *Atlantic, Grand Street, Harper's*, the *New Yorker*, and other publications.

   In the following essay, Tan uses narration to describe an experience that taught her an important lesson. © WIREIMAGE/GETTY

1   I fell in love with the minister's son the winter I turned fourteen. He was not Chinese, but as white as Mary in the manger. For Christmas I prayed for this blond-haired boy, Robert, and a slim new American nose.

2   When I found out that my parents had invited the minister's family over for Christmas dinner, I cried. What would Robert think of our shabby Chinese Christmas? What would he think of our noisy Chinese relatives who lacked proper American manners? What terrible disappointment would he feel upon seeing not a roasted turkey and sweet potatoes but Chinese food?

3   On Christmas Eve I saw that my mother had outdone herself in creating a strange menu. She was pulling black veins out of the backs of fleshy prawns[1]. The kitchen was littered with appalling[2] mounds of raw food: A slimy rock cod with

1. **Prawns:** shrimp or shrimp-like creatures
2. **Appalling:** horrifying

bulging eyes that pleaded not to be thrown into a pan of hot oil. Tofu, which looked like stacked wedges of rubbery white sponges. A bowl soaking dried fungus back to life. A plate of squid, their backs crisscrossed with knife markings so they resembled bicycle tires.

3. Clamor: noise

4   And then they arrived—the minister's family and all my relatives in a clamor[3] of doorbells and rumpled Christmas packages. Robert grunted hello, and I pretended he was not worthy of existence.

5   Dinner threw me deeper into despair. My relatives licked the ends of their chopsticks and reached across the table, dipping them into the dozen or so plates of food. Robert and his family waited patiently for platters to be passed to them.

4. Murmured: spoke in low tones

My relatives murmured[4] with pleasure when my mother brought out the whole steamed fish. Robert grimaced. Then my father poked his chopsticks just below the fish eye and plucked out the soft meat. "Amy, your favorite," he said, offering me the tender fish cheek. I wanted to disappear.

5. Belched: burped

6   At the end of the meal my father leaned back and belched[5] loudly, thanking my mother for her fine cooking. "It's a polite Chinese custom to show you are satisfied," explained my father to our astonished guests. Robert was looking down at his plate with a reddened face. The minister managed to muster up a quiet burp. I was stunned into silence for the rest of the night.

7   After everyone had gone, my mother said to me, "You want to be the same as American girls on the outside." She handed me an early gift. It was a miniskirt in beige tweed. "But inside you must always be Chinese. You must be proud you are different. Your only shame is to have shame."

8   And even though I didn't agree with her then, I knew that she understood how much I had suffered during the evening's dinner. It wasn't until many years later—long after I had gotten over my crush on Robert—that I was able to fully appreciate her lesson and the true purpose behind our particular menu. For Christmas Eve that year, she had chosen all my favorite foods.

CHECK COMPREHENSION

1. Why did Tan cry when she found out the minister's family was coming to dinner?

2. Why is the essay called "Fish Cheeks"?

MAKE INFERENCES

When we use the information given by a writer to make a logical conclusion, we are making an **inference**. Sometimes, a writer does not state an idea directly; instead, the writer gives clues that a reader can use to **infer** (determine through logical reasoning) that idea. Use information from Tan's essay to make inferences that answer these questions:

1. How did Tan feel about being Chinese when she was fourteen? How do you know?

2. How does Tan feel about her Chinese heritage now? How do you know?

> **WRITE TO IMPROVE READING**   **Summarize**

Using the guidelines from Chapter 6 and your annotations, write a summary of Tan's essay. Remember that your summary will include the **main point** and **major supporting details**, written in your own words. Think about Tan's purpose as you draft your summary. Don't forget that a summary includes references to the author throughout, along with strong descriptive verbs.

Build Vocabulary: Descriptive Words

Good narrations include descriptions that appeal to the readers' senses: sight, smell, taste, touch, and sound. Look at paragraph 3 in Tan's essay. Notice how many specific words Tan uses to create a visual image for her readers: "black veins," "slimy rock cod with bulging eyes," and "stacked wedges of rubbery white sponges." Can you find other words that Tan has used to give a visual image? What words help the reader hear the story? (For additional practice with descriptive words, see Chapter 21.)

Understand Strategies Used in Narration: Using Dialogue

One way a writer can help a reader "hear" the events of the story is to include dialogue. Dialogue occurs when we quote what a person said. Dialogue is usually marked with quotation marks. (For more information about quotation marks, see Chapter 30.)

> **PRACTICE**

1. Find each place in Tan's essay where she uses dialogue. Who is speaking? How do you know?

2. Why did Tan decide to include these examples of dialogue? How do they help her make her point?

3. Based on Tan's use of dialogue, what can you infer about the punctuation rules for dialogue? Consider the use of commas, periods, and capital letters.

Know P/Q: How to Paraphrase and Quote

In each workbook section in Chapters 7–14, there is a **paraphrase/quote (P/Q) assignment**. A P/Q assignment asks you to answer a specific question in a paragraph that includes a paraphrase or a quotation from the reading. Before you complete your first P/Q assignment, review the key parts of a good paraphrase:

- It has a signal phrase that names the author/speaker and uses a strong descriptive verb.
- It covers the idea or concept of the original without borrowing language or strings of words.
- It is usually followed by a citation, which is the page number in parentheses.

For more information on paraphrasing, see Chapter 6.

Let's look at an example: Signal phrase   Paraphrase

Amy Tan suggests that she was not happy with her obvious Asian features, and at the age of fourteen, she wanted to be more American, with a blond boyfriend and an attractive nose (117).   Citation

PRACTICE   Paraphrase

In her essay, Tan describes important words her mother said to her. Look at these quotes from Tan's mother, and paraphrase each one. Remember the characteristics of a good paraphrase: it explains the original concept without copying words or phrases. Make sure that you cover the original quote while you are writing so that you avoid a **cut-and-paste paraphrase** (see Chapter 6, p. 95).

1. Tan's mother says, "You want to be the same as American girls on the outside" (118).

    Paraphrase: She says that _____(118).

2. She also says, "But inside you must always be Chinese. You must be proud you are different" (118).

    Paraphrase: She says that _____(118).

3. Tan's mother says, "Your only shame is to have shame" (118).

    Paraphrase: She says that _____(118).

RESPOND IN WRITING

1. Amy Tan says, "For Christmas I prayed for this blond-haired boy, Robert, and a slim new American nose" (117). Write a paragraph about a time you felt different from others. Did you want to change, like Tan did, or did you have a different reaction? Tell about your experience in a paragraph or an essay.

2. Have you ever been embarrassed by your family or by others close to you? Write about the experience, and describe what you learned from it.

3. P/Q Assignment: Paraphrase the lesson that Amy Tan's mother taught her, making sure you have a signal phrase and a citation. Use your paraphrase to introduce a paragraph that answers these questions: Why do you think it took Tan so long to understand the lesson? Would you have understood this lesson when you were fourteen? Why or why not?

Professional Essay: "Chili Cheese Dogs, My Father, and Me," Pat Conroy

Preview

1. Ask Questions: Skim the essay title, the information about the author, and the first paragraph. Write a guiding question for your reading.
2. Make Connections: Is there a specific food that you associate with a person from your childhood? Describe that food and the memories that it brings to you.

Read and annotate the essay carefully, using the Guidelines for Reading and Annotating Narration on page 113. Pay attention to the Four Basics of Good Narration: an important point, major supporting details, minor details that bring the story to life, and an organizational strategy (in this case, time order). Highlight or number supporting details as you read, and circle Conroy's transition words.

Pat Conroy

Chili Cheese Dogs, My Father, and Me

The writing of Pat Conroy (b. 1945) draws heavily on his life experiences. *The Water Is Wide* (1972) recounts his days teaching at a one-room school in South Carolina. *The Great Santini* (1976) describes the difficulty of growing up with a strict military father. Several of Conroy's books have been made into movies. The most famous of these films is *The Prince of Tides* (1991), which was based on Conroy's 1986 novel of the same name. His most recent books include *The Pat Conroy Cookbook: Recipes of My Life* (2005), a mix of food writing and memoir; the novel *South of Broad* (2009); *My Reading Life* (2010), in which Conroy explores the role of books in his life; and *The Death of Santini* (2013), a memoir recounting Conroy's complicated and evolving relationship with his father after the publication of *The Great Santini*.

In the following essay, Conroy uses narration to tell a story about two important relationships—with food and with his father—and how they came together. © AP PHOTO/LOU KRASKY

1   When I was growing up and lived at my grandmother's house in Atlanta, my mother would take us after church to The Varsity, an institution with more religious significance to me than any cathedral in the city. Its food was celebratory, fresh, and cleansing to the soul. It still remains one of my favorite restaurants in the world.

1. Deviated: changed

2   I had then what I order now—a habit that has not deviated[1] since my sixth birthday in 1951, when my grandmother, Stanny, ordered for me what she considered the picture-perfect Varsity meal: a chili cheese hot dog, onion rings, and a soft drink called "The Big Orange."

3   On that occasion, when my family had finished the meal, my mother lit six candles on a cupcake she had made, and Stanny, Papa Jack, my mother, and my sister Carol sang "Happy Birthday" as I blushed with pleasure and surprise. I put

2. Consumption: using; eating (in the case of food)

together for the first time that the consumption[2] of food and celebration was a natural and fitting combination. It was also the first time I realized that no one in my family could carry a tune.

4   When my father returned home from the Korean War, he refused to believe that The Varsity—or the American South, for that matter—could produce a hot

3. Partisan: one who takes sides

dog worthy of consumption. My Chicago-born father was a fierce partisan[3] of his hometown, and he promised me that he would take me to eat a real "red hot" after we attended my first White Sox game.

5   That summer, we stayed with my dad's parents on the South Side of Chicago. There, I met the South Side Irish for the first time on their own turf. My uncles

spent the summer teasing me about being a southern hick as they played endless games of pinochle[4] with my father. Then, my father took me for the sacramental[5] rite of passage: my first major league baseball game. We watched the White Sox beat the despised Yankees.

6   After the game, my father drove my Uncle Willie and me to a place called Superdawg to get a red hot. He insisted that the Superdawg sold the best red hots in the city. When my father handed me the first red hot I had ever eaten, he said, "This will make you forget The Varsity for all time." That summer, I learned that geography itself was one of the great formative[6] shapers of identity. The red hot was delicious, but in my lifetime I will never forsake[7] the pleasure of The Varsity chili cheese dog.

7   When my father was dying of colon cancer in 1998, he would spend his days with me at home on Fripp Island, South Carolina, then go back to Beaufort at night to stay with my sister Kathy, who is a nurse and was in charge of his medications. Since I was responsible for his daily lunch, I told him I would cook him anything he wanted as long as I could find it in a South Carolina supermarket.

8   "Anything, pal?" my father asked.

9   "Anything," I said.

10   Thus, the last days between a hard-core Marine and his edgy son, who had spent his career writing about horrific father-son relationships, became our best days as we found ourselves united by the glorious subject of food.

11   My father was a simple man with simple tastes, but he was well-traveled, and he began telling me his life story as we spent our long hours together. The first meal he ordered was an egg sandwich, a meal I had never heard of but one that kept him alive during the Depression[8]. He told me, "You put a fried egg on two slices of white bread which has been spread with ketchup."

12   "It sounds repulsive[9]," I said.

13   "It's delicious," he replied.

14   When Dad spoke of his service in Korea, I fixed him kimchi (spicy pickled vegetables), and when he talked about his yearlong duty on an aircraft carrier on the Mediterranean, I made spaghetti carbonara[10] or gazpacho[11]. But most of the time, I made him elaborate sandwiches: salami or baloney tiered high with lettuce, tomatoes, and red onions. The more elaborate I made them, the more my father loved them.

15   He surprised me one day by asking me to make him some red hots, done "the Chicago way, pal." That day, I called Superdawg and was surprised that it was still in business. A very pleasant woman told me to dress the red hots with relish, mustard, onion, and hot peppers with a pickle on the side. "If you put ketchup on it, just throw it in the trash," she added.

4. **Pinochle:** a card game popular in the mid-1900s

5. **Sacramental:** sacred

6. **Formative:** giving form to

7. **Forsake:** to give up

8. **Depression:** a serious economic downturn lasting from 1929 until the late 1930s

9. **Repulsive:** disgusting

10. **Spaghetti carbonara:** pasta with a sauce of cream, eggs, and bacon

11. **Gazpacho:** a cold vegetable soup from Spain

12. Descent: a way down; a passage down to

13. Bill Cosby: the actor who played a wise, kind father in a 1980s TV comedy

16 The following week, he surprised me again by ordering up some chili cheese dogs, "just like they make at The Varsity in Atlanta." So I called The Varsity and learned step by step how to make one of their scrumptious chili cheese dogs.

17 When my father began his quick, slippery descent[12] into death, my brothers and sisters drove from all directions to sit six-hour shifts at his bedside. We learned that watching a fighter pilot die is not an easy thing. One morning, I arrived for my shift and heard screaming coming from the house. I raced inside and found Carol yelling at Dad: "Dad, you've got to tell me you're proud of me. You've got to do it before you die."

18 I walked Carol out of the bedroom and sat her down on the sofa. "That's Don Conroy in there, Carol—not Bill Cosby[13]," I said. "You've got to learn how to translate Dad. He says it, but in his own way."

19 Two weeks before my father died, he presented me with a gift of infinite price. I made him the last chili cheese dog from The Varsity's recipe that he would ever eat. When he finished, I took the plate back to the kitchen and was shocked to hear him say, "I think the chili cheese dog is the best red hot I've ever eaten."

20 There is a translation to all of this, and here is how it reads: In the last days of his life, my father was telling me how much he loved me, his oldest son, and he was doing it with food.

CHECK COMPREHENSION

Determine whether the following statements are true or false, based on this essay.

1. Conroy's father was born and raised in the South.

2. Conroy's essay is more about the way his father expressed love than it is about hot dogs.

3. Conroy's sister Carol got angry at her father because he was yelling at her.

4. It was difficult for Conroy's father to express his feelings in words.

MAKE INFERENCES

As you will recall, when we use the information given by a writer to make a logical conclusion, we are making an inference. Sometimes, a writer does not state an idea directly; instead, the writer gives clues that a reader can use to infer (determine through logical reasoning) that idea. Use information from Conroy's essay to make inferences that answer these questions:

1. What kind of relationship did Conroy have with his father before 1998?

2. What did Conroy learn about his father that he did not know already?

> **WRITE TO IMPROVE READING**   Summarize
>
> Using the guidelines from Chapter 6 and your annotations, write a summary of Conroy's essay. Remember that your summary will include the main point and major supporting details, written in your own words.

Build Vocabulary: Descriptive Words

Like Amy Tan, Pat Conroy uses specific details to appeal to his readers' senses, especially taste and sight. What examples can you find of details that show taste or sight?

Conroy says he learned that "geography itself was one of the great formative shapers of identity." What do you think he means? What geographical locations appear in the story? What vocabulary (specifically food words) is connected with each of these locations?

Conroy uses the words *formative* and *repulsive* in his narration. What similarity do you notice in these words? Both words end in a **suffix**. A suffix is a set of letters added to the end of a word. When we add a suffix to a word, we often create a new but related word that is a different part of speech. We can add the suffix *-ive* to verbs to create adjectives:

create + -ive = creative

repulse + -ive = repulsive

response + -ive = responsive

conclude + -ive = conclusive

Here are some other common suffixes that indicate that a word is an adjective. Can you find examples of adjectives with these suffixes in the narrations by Conroy and Tan?

-ious/-ous: _____

-al: _____

-ible/-able: _____

Understand Strategies Used in Narration: Using Dialogue

Like Tan, Conroy uses dialogue to help the reader "hear" the story.

PRACTICE

1. What can we learn about Conroy's father by hearing him speak in dialogue? Explain.

2. Why does Conroy create paragraphs with only one line of dialogue? (See paras. 8–9 and 12–13.)

3. In paragraph 17, the readers hear from Conroy's sister Carol, who has not been a part of the story until this point. Why does Conroy introduce her voice here? How does this dialogue support his main idea?

RESPOND IN WRITING

1. Write a paragraph that tells about a time when a particular food played a role during a family celebration, such as a birthday or a holiday. Like Conroy, include details about family members and your own response to the celebration.

2. In what way has geography been a "formative shaper" of your identity? Write a paragraph or an essay that tells the story of how your relationship with a particular place has made you who you are.

Extend and Connect: Write Your Own Narration

1. Both Tan and Conroy show how relationships with parents can change. In an essay, trace your relationship with a parent or another significant adult in your life. How has it changed and developed over time? What lesson have you learned?

2. Tan and Conroy both learned to understand how their parents showed love. Love might not always be best expressed through words; sometimes, love can be demonstrated through a shared activity such as eating. What other ways can love be expressed? Write a narration essay to explain how love has been expressed to you.

3. Write a narration response essay. A narration response essay tells a story that is "framed" or introduced by another writer's words or ideas. Consider the following quotes from Conroy and Tan. Summarize either Tan or Conroy, as appropriate, and use one of these quotes (or a paraphrase) as an introduction to your own story. If you paraphrase, remember that you must explain the main idea of the passage without borrowing phrases or strings of words from the original. Don't just cut and paste.

a. Pat Conroy says, "Then, my father took me for the sacramental rite of passage: my first major league baseball game" (123). (Write the story of an important "rite of passage" from your childhood.)

b. When Amy Tan's father offered her the fish cheek, she said she "wanted to disappear" (118). (Write about a time when a family member's behavior caused you shame.)

c. Amy Tan's mother said to her, "You must be proud you are different" (118). (Write about a time when your difference—or that of your family—brought you a feeling of pride.)

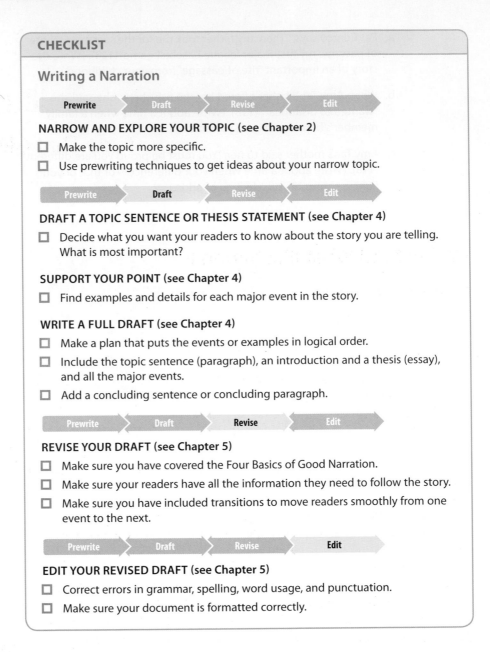

CHECKLIST

Writing a Narration

| Prewrite | Draft | Revise | Edit |

NARROW AND EXPLORE YOUR TOPIC (see Chapter 2)

☐ Make the topic more specific.

☐ Use prewriting techniques to get ideas about your narrow topic.

| Prewrite | **Draft** | Revise | Edit |

DRAFT A TOPIC SENTENCE OR THESIS STATEMENT (see Chapter 4)

☐ Decide what you want your readers to know about the story you are telling. What is most important?

SUPPORT YOUR POINT (see Chapter 4)

☐ Find examples and details for each major event in the story.

WRITE A FULL DRAFT (see Chapter 4)

☐ Make a plan that puts the events or examples in logical order.

☐ Include the topic sentence (paragraph), an introduction and a thesis (essay), and all the major events.

☐ Add a concluding sentence or concluding paragraph.

| Prewrite | Draft | **Revise** | Edit |

REVISE YOUR DRAFT (see Chapter 5)

☐ Make sure you have covered the Four Basics of Good Narration.

☐ Make sure your readers have all the information they need to follow the story.

☐ Make sure you have included transitions to move readers smoothly from one event to the next.

| Prewrite | Draft | Revise | **Edit** |

EDIT YOUR REVISED DRAFT (see Chapter 5)

☐ Correct errors in grammar, spelling, word usage, and punctuation.

☐ Make sure your document is formatted correctly.

8

Illustration:
Texts That Give Examples

Understand What Illustration Is

Illustration is writing that uses examples to support a point.

Four Basics of Good Illustration

1 It has a point.

2 It gives specific examples that show, explain, or prove the point.

3 It gives details to support the examples.

4 It uses enough examples to get the point across to the reader.

In the following paragraph, the numbers and colors correspond to the Four Basics of Good Illustration.

1 Many people would like to serve their communities or help with causes that they believe in, but they do not have much time and do not know what to do. Now, the Internet provides people with ways to help that do not take much time or money. 2 Web sites now make it convenient to donate online. With a few clicks, an organization of your choice can receive your donation or money from a sponsoring advertiser. For example, if you are interested in helping rescue unwanted and abandoned animals, you can go to www.theanimalrescuesite.com. 3 When you click as instructed, a sponsoring advertiser will make a donation to help provide food and care for the 27 million animals in shelters. Also, a portion of any money you spend in the site's online store will go to providing animal care. 2 If you want to help fight world hunger, go to www.thehungersite.com 3 and click daily to have sponsor fees directed to hungry people in more than seventy countries via the Mercy Corps, Feeding America, and Millennium Promise. Each year,

4 Enough examples provided

4 Enough examples provided

hundreds of millions of cups of food are distributed to one billion hungry people around the world. **2** Other examples of click-to-give sites are www.thechildhealthsite.com, www.theliteracysite.com, and www.breastcancersite.com. **3** Like the animal-rescue and hunger sites, these other sites have click-to-give links, online stores that direct a percentage of sales income to charity, and links to help you learn about causes you are interested in. One hundred percent of the sponsors' donations go to the charities, and you can give with a click every single day. Since I have found out about these sites, I go to at least one of them every day. **1** I have learned a lot about various problems, and every day I feel as if I have helped a little.

It is hard to explain anything without using examples, so you use illustration in almost every communication situation.

College	An exam question asks you to explain and give examples of a concept.
Work	Your boss asks you to tell her what office equipment needs to be replaced and why.
Everyday life	You complain to your landlord that the building superintendent is not doing his job. The landlord asks for examples.

In college, the words *illustration* and *illustrate* may not appear in assignments. Instead, you may be asked to *give examples* of something or to *be specific* about something. In addition, you may be asked to *find examples* or *instances* of something when you are reading. Regardless of how an assignment is worded, good readers and writers find and use specific examples in order to be clear and effective.

Illustration in the Classroom: Résumés

Jason is taking a student development course called College and Career Success Skills at his community college. The instructor asked the students to prepare a résumé for a mock job interview. Jason's goal is to get a degree in landscape design and business management so that he can own his own landscaping company. While in school, he hopes to continue working with landscaping companies to improve his understanding of the business. Jason knew that a résumé includes previous work experience in time order, so he submitted the following section as part of his résumé:

Work Experience
2011–present   A and G Landscaping, assistant
2010–2011   Intern, Martin High School Landscaping Division
2008–2010   Self-employed, lawn cutting and maintenance

The instructor returned the draft of the résumé with two comments:

Jason, what do you want a potential employer to know about you, based on your work history? Can you add any details to the Work Experience section of your résumé to help you make this point?

Jason's instructor was asking Jason to apply the Four Basics of Good Illustration. First, he needed to use his résumé to make a point: he was experienced in many aspects of landscaping. His work history showed three good examples of experience, but he needed to give details to support the examples so that his examples would be strong enough to make his point to an employer.

Jason submitted the following revision to his instructor:

Work History

2011–present	**Assistant, A and G Landscaping**
	Managed site crew (mowing, trimming, planting, mulching, and fertilizing)
	Completed paperwork for client review
	Managed/maintained equipment for site crew
	Assisted manager with site review process
2010–2011	**Intern, Martin High School Landscaping Division**
	Worked with Martin High School crew to maintain football fields, soccer field, baseball fields, and track area
2008–2010	**Self-employed, Lawn Care and Maintenance**
	Cut and maintained lawns (watering, trimming, fertilizing) for fifteen clients

Jason and his instructor agreed that the second version was much better at providing the specific examples and details that would support Jason's main goal.

APPLY WHAT YOU HAVE LEARNED

1. Explore your résumé. Each section of a résumé (education, work experience, activities and community service, awards and accomplishments, references) helps a prospective employer understand who you are. What do the examples in your résumé say about you? What details do you need to add?

2. Explore a textbook. Many textbooks, including this one, use examples to make points clear. Identify supporting examples in a textbook. How do those examples support the point of the chapter? What would happen if the examples were removed? Explain.

Paragraphs vs. Essays in Illustration

For more on the important features of illustration, see the Four Basics of Good Illustration on page 129.

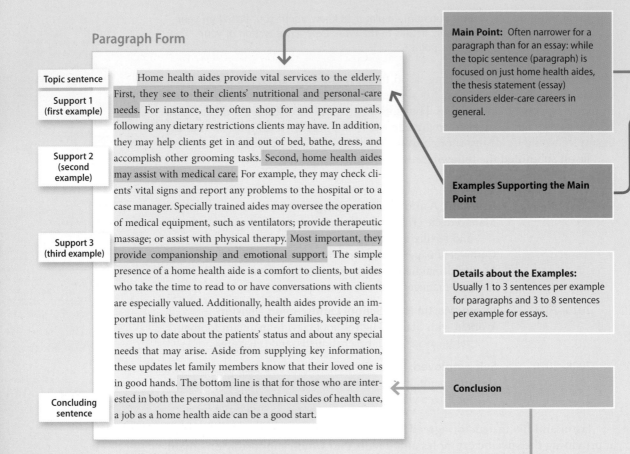

Paragraph Form

Topic sentence

Support 1 (first example)

Support 2 (second example)

Support 3 (third example)

Concluding sentence

Home health aides provide vital services to the elderly. First, they see to their clients' nutritional and personal-care needs. For instance, they often shop for and prepare meals, following any dietary restrictions clients may have. In addition, they may help clients get in and out of bed, bathe, dress, and accomplish other grooming tasks. Second, home health aides may assist with medical care. For example, they may check clients' vital signs and report any problems to the hospital or to a case manager. Specially trained aides may oversee the operation of medical equipment, such as ventilators; provide therapeutic massage; or assist with physical therapy. Most important, they provide companionship and emotional support. The simple presence of a home health aide is a comfort to clients, but aides who take the time to read to or have conversations with clients are especially valued. Additionally, health aides provide an important link between patients and their families, keeping relatives up to date about the patients' status and about any special needs that may arise. Aside from supplying key information, these updates let family members know that their loved one is in good hands. The bottom line is that for those who are interested in both the personal and the technical sides of health care, a job as a home health aide can be a good start.

Main Point: Often narrower for a paragraph than for an essay: while the topic sentence (paragraph) is focused on just home health aides, the thesis statement (essay) considers elder-care careers in general.

Examples Supporting the Main Point

Details about the Examples: Usually 1 to 3 sentences per example for paragraphs and 3 to 8 sentences per example for essays.

Conclusion

Think Critically As You Write Illustration

Ask Yourself

- Is each of my current examples clearly related to the main point?
- If my paragraph or essay feels "thin," might I find relevant new examples to enrich it? (For more on generating ideas, see pp. 26–29.)

Essay Form

1

During these difficult economic times, many students are looking to pursue careers in expanding fields with good long-term prospects. One they should seriously consider is elder care. Because the U.S. population is aging, demand for workers who specialize in the health of the elderly is increasing rapidly. *[Thesis statement]*

One set of workers in great demand consists of physical therapists, who help elderly patients improve their mobility and retain their independence. *[Topic sentence 1 (first example)]* Some of these therapists are based at hospitals or nursing facilities, others at clinics or private offices. Regardless of where they work, they provide a variety of services to elderly patients, from helping stroke sufferers relearn how to walk and perform other daily activities to showing others how to live a more active life. Physical therapists can also help patients injured in falls reduce their reliance on painkillers, which can become less effective over time and in certain cases even addictive. According to the U.S. Department of Labor, employment of physical therapists will grow by 30 percent

2

over the next ten years, largely because of the increasing number of elderly Americans.

Also in demand are nutritionists who specialize in older people's dietary needs. *[Topic sentence 2 (second example)]* These professionals may plan meals and provide nutrition advice at hospitals, nursing homes, and other institutions, or they may counsel individual patients on how to eat more healthfully or on how to prepare meals that meet certain dietary restrictions. For instance, elderly patients suffering from heart disease may need to eat foods that are low in salt and saturated fat. Other patients might have to avoid foods that interfere with the absorption of certain medications. Although the market for nutritionists is not expected to grow as quickly as that for physical therapists, it is projected to rise steadily as the population continues to age.

The highest-demand workers are those who provide at-home health care to the elderly. *[Topic sentence 3 (third example)]* One subset of these workers consists of home nurses, who often provide follow-up care after patients are released from a hospital or other medical facility. These nurses help

3

patients transition from an institutional setting while making sure they continue to receive high-quality care. For instance, they track patients' vital signs, administer and monitor medications, and carry out specific tasks required to manage particular diseases. Another subset of home health workers is made up of home health aides, who assist nurses and other professionals with medical care, see to clients' nutritional and personal-care needs, and provide companionship and emotional support. Both home health aides and nurses provide an important link between patients and their families, keeping relatives up to date about the patients' status and about any special needs that may arise. In addition to supplying key information, these updates let family members know that their loved one is in good hands. Because of home health care workers' vital role in serving the expanding elderly population, their employment is expected to grow significantly: on average, 30 to 40 percent over the next ten years.

4

Given the growing demand for elder-care workers, people pursuing these professions stand an excellent chance of getting jobs with good long-term outlooks. *[Concluding paragraph]* Based on what I have learned about these professions, the best candidates are those who have a strong interest in health or medicine, a willingness to work hard to get the necessary qualifications, and, perhaps most important, an ability to connect with and truly care for others.

Main Point in Illustration

In illustration, the main point is the message that the writer wants the readers to receive and understand. To discover a writer's main point or to draft your own main point, complete the following sentence:

What readers need to know about this topic is that . . .

The topic sentence (in a paragraph) or thesis statement (in an essay) usually includes the topic and the main point the writer wants to make about the topic. Let's look at a topic sentence first.

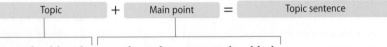

Home health aides provide vital services to the elderly.

Remember that the thesis statement for an essay can be a little broader than a paragraph topic.

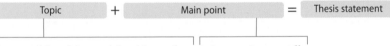

Demand for elder-care health workers is increasing rapidly.

Whereas the topic sentence focuses on just home health aides, the thesis statement considers elder-care careers in general.

PRACTICE 1   **Identify Main Points in Illustration**

1. Complete the diagram below using the sample paragraph on page 129.

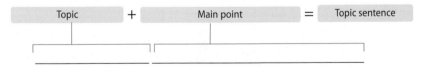

2. Complete the diagram below using Inez King's paragraph on page 139.

Support in Illustration

The paragraph and essay models on pages 132–133 use the topic sentence (paragraph) and thesis statement (essay) from the Main Point in Illustration section of this chapter. Both models include the **support** used in all illustration writing: examples backed up by details about the examples. In the essay model, however, the major support points (examples) are topic sentences for individual paragraphs.

PRACTICE 2   **Write Supporting Points for Illustration**

Read the following main points, and give three examples you might use to support each one.

Example: My boss's cheapness is unprofessional.

makes us bring in our own calculators

makes us use old, rusted paper clips

will not replace burned-out lightbulbs

1. My (friend, sister, brother, husband, wife—choose one) has some admirable traits.

2. This weekend is particularly busy.

PRACTICE 3   **Identify Minor Details in Illustration**

The major and minor supporting details from the sample paragraph on page 129 are listed below. For each one, underline the major support. Circle the transition words or repetitions that connect the minor details to the major support. Then put brackets around new details that help the reader understand the major support. The first one has been done for you.

Example: First, they see to their clients' nutritional and personal-care needs. For instance, they often [shop for and prepare meals], following any dietary restrictions clients may have. In addition, they may [help clients get in and out of bed, bathe, dress, and accomplish other grooming tasks].

1. Second, home health aides may assist with medical care. For example, they may check clients' vital signs and report any problems to the hospital or to a case manager. Specially trained aides may oversee the operation of medical equipment, such as ventilators; provide therapeutic massage; or assist with physical therapy.

2. Most important, they provide companionship and emotional support. The simple presence of a home health aide is a comfort to clients, but aides who take the time to read to or have conversations with clients are especially valued. Additionally, health aides provide an important link between patients and their families, keeping relatives up to date about the patients' status and about any special needs that may arise. Aside from supplying key information, these updates let family members know that their loved one is in good hands.

PRACTICE 4	**Write Details about the Examples**

In the spaces provided, copy your main points and examples from Practice 2. Then, for each example, write a detail that further shows, explains, or proves what you mean.

Example:

Main point: My boss's cheapness is unprofessional.

Example: *makes us bring in our own calculators*

  Detail: *Some people do not have a calculator.*

Example: *makes us use old, rusted paper clips*

  Detail: *They leave rust marks on important documents.*

Example: *will not replace burned-out lightbulbs*

  Detail: *The dim light leads to more errors.*

1. Main point: _____

   Example: _____

    Detail: _____

Example: _____

Detail: _____

Example: _____

Detail: _____

2. Main point: _____

Example: _____

Detail: _____

Example: _____

Detail: _____

Example: _____

Detail: _____

Organization in Illustration

Illustration often uses **order of importance**, saving the most powerful example for last. This strategy is used in the paragraph and essay models on pages 132–133. Sometimes, the examples are given according to when they happened. In those cases, writers are using **time order** to organize.

Transitions in illustration let readers know that the writer is introducing an example or moving from one example to another.

Common Transitions in Illustration

Conjunctive Adverbials	Adjectives	Nouns
also	additional	(one, another) example
finally	another	
first, second, next, etc.	last	(one, another) instance
for example	next	
for instance	one	
for one thing/for another thing	the least _____	
	the most _____	
in addition		
moreover		

For information on using and punctuating these transitions, see Chapters 17 and 24.

| PRACTICE 5 | **Identify Transitions in Illustration** |

1. Circle the transitions in the sample paragraph on page 129. What pattern of organization does this paragraph follow? How do you know?

2. Circle the transitions in the paragraph by Inez King on page 139. What pattern of organization does this paragraph follow? How do you know?

3. After you complete Practice 6 below, determine what pattern of organization the paragraph follows. How do you know?

| PRACTICE 6 | **Use Transitions in Illustration** |

Read the paragraph that follows, and fill in the blanks with transitions.

Greek myths include many heroes, such as the great warriors Achilles and Herakles. _____ , the myths describe several monsters that tested the heroes' strength. _____ of these frightening creatures was the Hydra, a water serpent with many heads. When a warrior cut off one of these heads, two or more would sprout up in its place. _____ _____ of these mythical monsters was the Gorgons, three sisters who had snakes for hair. Any person who looked into the Gorgons' eyes would turn to stone. _____ terrifying monster was Cerberus, a three-headed dog with snapping jaws. He guarded the gates to the underworld, keeping the living from entering and the dead from leaving. Fortunately, some heroes' cleverness equaled the monsters' hideousness. _____ , Herakles discovered that by applying a torch to the wounds of the Hydra, he could prevent the creature from growing more heads. _____ , Orpheus, a famous mythical musician, soothed Cerberus by plucking the strings of a lyre. In this way, Orpheus got past the beast and entered the underworld, from which he hoped to rescue his wife.

Read and Analyze Illustration

Student Illustration Paragraph: "Empathy," Inez King

| Preview | Read | Review | Reflect and Respond |

- Skim the title and the first sentence. What do you think the reading will be about?
- Make Connections: What is the context (audience and purpose) for this paragraph? How do you know?

- Make Connections: When have you felt empathy before?
- Ask Questions: Create a guiding question for your reading.

Preview → **Read** → Review → Reflect and Respond

Guidelines for Reading and Annotating Illustration

Read and annotate this paragraph using these guidelines:

1. Pay attention to vocabulary using marginal notes, context clues, or a dictionary.
2. Find the main point and underline it. (In an illustration, the main point is the general idea that all of the examples illustrate.)
3. Identify supporting details and organizational strategies. Number each supporting example (major support). Note how the examples are organized by circling the transition words.
4. Ask questions and make connections. Remember to connect the paragraph or essay to your own experiences and other things you have read.

Inez King

Empathy

1   When I first learned the word *empathy*, I couldn't connect my life with the word. Now that I have studied the definition, however, I can recall times when I probably displayed "empathy." While watching the movie *The Color Purple*, without warning, I was crying my eyes out and laughing at the same time. I cried when Sophia was physically attacked and jailed for standing up for her beliefs. I rejoiced when Ms. Celie battled with Mr. Albert and rose above her past. In fact, the same emotions I experienced while viewing *The Color Purple* occur each time I read a Danielle Steel novel. Each novel draws me into the emotional lives of every character to the point where I feel their joy, anger, and pain. Not only have I experienced "empathy" vicariously through movies and novels, but also through a personal experience. I recall the tragic death of my neighbor. No words could have comforted his wife during her struggle with the loss. I felt her pain and heartbreak, and I could not help but think this could easily happen to me. In the end, "empathy" took a silent approach with me; it ignited tears of sadness and sparked my feelings.

Preview → Read → **Review** → Reflect and Respond

In Chapter 6, you learned how to paraphrase main ideas in order to write a summary. Use your annotations to write a short summary of this paragraph. Remember that a good summary captures the main idea and major supporting details in your own words. The summary refers to the author and uses strong descriptive verbs. When you have completed your summary, share your work with a classmate.

1. Does this paragraph follow the Four Basics of Good Illustration? Explain.
2. Is there any place in the paragraph where you would like more information? Explain.
3. What makes King's examples effective in this paragraph?

Student Illustration Essay: "You," James Carnill

- Look at the title of the selection. What do you think this essay will be about?
- Read the first paragraph of the essay. What is the context (author and purpose) for this essay? How might the context help you understand the essay better?
- Create a guiding question for your reading of the essay.

Read and annotate this essay using the Guidelines for Reading and Annotating Illustration on page 139.

James Carnill

You

1   Technology has transformed our generation from social beings into more egocentric people. In his commencement speech titled "This Is Water," David Foster Wallace makes a valid statement: "It's a matter of my hardwired default setting, which is to be deeply and literally self-centered." Technology only strengthens this setting, because its features, more often than not, cater to the consumer. We love to be catered to, everything with *us* in mind. We think about *ourselves* constantly; how we look, how we dress, and what phone we have are all a part of *our* image, and *we* want to be the best. Having the newest phone means everything to *us*, but does it matter to anyone else?

2   Handheld technology grows increasingly more powerful as the days go by. Facebook gets faster, pictures are captured more quickly, and calls are dialed faster. But that Facebook post, it's about what *you* just did. That picture is of *you*, utilizing the front-facing camera for *#Selfie*Sunday. That call is placed to vent to your friend about "some twit" that just cut *you* off. It's all about *you*. *You* then wait for likes on the post, *you* wait for someone to comment on the photo of *you*, and *you* all wish that person who cut *you* off would get into a fiery explosion down the road. The Facebook post is "liked," and then *you* think *you*

are liked. The picture comments are, usually, all positive, making *you* feel good. The "twit" *you* labeled that way makes *you* feel better about *your* driving. All of these actions boost our self-esteem for our own benefit. Doing these things makes *us* feel better, while doing very little to promote the common good.

3   In reference to social media, our generation has used these as platforms to promote themselves, but not to their full potential. Most of these services are offered to promote productivity and help the user. Instead, the users, mostly of our generation, have manipulated the apps to favor themselves. With every update we demand it to point to us, and when the update is released, it usually features more things to not only aid the consumer, but also help them exemplify their existence to other users.

4   As a generation, we never become detached from technology. Always on this, constantly on that, tweeting every two minutes, posting every four, and uploading throughout the day. Facebook's main user base is in our generation, the current youth. We post the most; we look at our own wall, adorned with creations from ourselves. It's all about *us*, updating where *we* are, what *we* are doing, and how great of a time *we* are having. It makes others feel good for us, but bad for themselves. Although I love seeing your pictures from Turks and Caicos, I'd rather have been there, of course *I* would. *I* want to be there; you shouldn't have gone, because *I* should have. It's a vicious cycle of *me, Me, ME*!

5   Maybe we should ignore ourselves just a little and become more versed in the interests of those around us. The people who we love and care for should be getting more attention. We need to take a step away from the technology; it is a move worth taking. We need to get away from ourselves sometimes, and get away from our image. We need to break free of our egotistical ways and technologies; we need to be more willing to see those around us, and not just ourselves.

Preview	Read	**Review**	Reflect and Respond

In Chapter 6, you learned how to paraphrase main ideas in order to write a summary. Using those guidelines and your annotations, write a summary of Carnill's essay. When you have completed your summary, share your work with a classmate.

Preview	Read	Review	**Reflect and Respond**

1. One of the Four Basics of Good Illustration is that the writing gives enough examples to get the point across to the reader. Do you think Carnill has given enough examples to make his point effectively? Are you convinced by his examples? Why or why not?

2. Carnill uses the pronoun "we" in the first paragraph, but he shifts to "you" in the second. How does his choice of pronoun affect your understanding of the essay? What does it tell you about his audience?

3. Carnill refers to a speech by David Foster Wallace. Explore this speech (you can listen to the speech or find the full text online). How does Carnill's essay support what David Foster Wallace says?

4. What is Carnill's conclusion? Do you agree with him?

5. Can you find examples of technology or social media use that contradict Carnill's thesis? Explain.

Reading/Writing Workbook: Illustration

Professional Essay: "The Weirdest Job Interview Questions and How to Handle Them," Susan Adams

Preview

1. Skim the title and the information about the author. What can you learn about the context (author, purpose, and topic) for this essay?

2. What is the strangest question you have ever been asked in a job interview? If you were Jason (see p. 130), what questions might you expect during an interview with a landscaping company?

3. Create a guiding question for your reading, based on your preview of the selection.

Read and annotate the essay carefully, using the Guidelines for Reading and Annotating Illustration on page 139.

Susan Adams

The Weirdest Job Interview Questions and How to Handle Them

Susan Adams is a senior editor at *Forbes*, a major publisher of business news. Since joining *Forbes* in 1995, Adams has written about a wide variety of subjects, including the art and auction market. Previously, she was a reporter for the *MacNeil/Lehrer NewsHour*. Adams holds a B.A. from Brown University and a J.D. from Yale University Law School.

Every week, Adams writes an advice column for Forbes.com, and the following is one of those columns. In it, she gives examples of some of the stranger questions that come up in job interviews. PHOTO BY © SETH DAVID COHEN

1   I once interviewed for a job with a documentary producer who made boring if well-meaning films for public TV. By way of preparation, I studied up on the producer's projects and gave a lot of thought to how my interests and experience dovetailed[1] with his. Our chat went swimmingly[2] until he asked me a question that caught me completely off guard: "Who is your favorite comedian?"

2   Wait a second, I thought. Comedy is the opposite of what this guy does. My mind did backflips while I desperately searched for a comedian who might be a favorite of a tweedy, bearded liberal Democrat. After maybe 30 seconds too long, I blurted out my personal favorite: David Alan Grier, an African-American funnyman on the weekly Fox TV show *In Living Color*. My potential boss looked at me blankly as I babbled about how much I liked Grier's characters, especially Antoine Merriweather, one of the two gay reviewers in the brilliantly hilarious sketch "Men on Film."

3   Wrong answer. I had derailed the interview. My potential employer asked me a few more perfunctory[3] questions and then saw me to the door.

4   We all prepare studiously[4] for job interviews, doing our homework about our potential employers and compiling short but detailed stories to illustrate our accomplishments, but how in the world do we prep for an off-the-wall interview question?

5   Glassdoor.com, a three-year-old Sausalito, California, Web site that bills itself as "the TripAdvisor for careers," has compiled a list of "top oddball interview questions" for two years running. Glassdoor gets its information directly from employees who work at 120,000 companies.

6   Crazy as it sounds, an interviewer at Schlumberger, the giant Houston oilfield services provider, once asked some poor job applicant, "What was your best *MacGyver* moment?," referring to a 1980s action-adventure TV show. At Goldman Sachs, the question was, "If you were shrunk to the size of a pencil and put in a blender, how would you get out?" At Deloitte, "How many ridges [are there] around a quarter?" At AT&T, "If you were a superhero, which superhero would you be?" And at Boston Consulting: "How many hair salons are there in Japan?"

7   No matter where you apply for work, there is a chance you could get a question from left field. According to Rusty Rueff—a consultant at Glassdoor who is the author of *Talent Force: A New Manifesto for the Human Side of Business* and former head of human resources at PepsiCo and Electronic Arts—most job applicants are woefully[5] unprepared for off-the-wall questions. "Ninety percent of people don't know how to deal with them," he says. Like me, they freeze and their minds go blank.

8   To deal with that, Rueff advises, first you have to realize that the interviewer isn't trying to make you look stupid, as stupid as the question may seem. For instance, the *MacGyver* question is meant as an invitation to talk about how you

1. **Dovetailed:** matched
2. **Swimmingly:** smoothly; well

3. **Perfunctory:** quick
4. **Studiously:** thoroughly; carefully

5. **Woefully:** seriously; regrettably

got out of a tough jam. "They're not looking for you to tell about the time you took out your ballpoint and did a tracheotomy[6]," Rueff notes. Rather, you can probably extract an answer from one of the achievement stories you prepared in advance.

9   With a question like "How many hair salons are there in Japan," the interviewer is giving you an opportunity to demonstrate your thought processes. Rueff says you should think out loud, like the contestants on *Who Wants to Be a Millionaire?* You might start by saying, We'd have to know the population of Japan, and then we'd have to figure out what percentage of them get their hair done and how often. Rueff says it's fine to pull out a pen and paper and start doing some calculations right there in the interview.

10   Connie Thanasoulis-Cerrachio, a career services consultant at Vault.com, agrees with Rueff. "These are called case interview questions," she says. Another example, which may seem equally impossible to answer: Why are manhole covers round?

11   In fact the manhole cover question, and "How would you move Mt. Fuji?," were brought to light in a 2003 book, *How Would You Move Mount Fuji? Microsoft's Cult of the Puzzle: How the World's Smartest Company Selects the Most Creative Thinkers.* Microsoft's grueling[7] interview process often includes such problem-solving and logic questions. Just start thinking through the question, out loud, Thanasoulis-Cerrachio advises. "I would say, a round manhole cover could keep the framework of the tunnel stronger, because a round frame is much stronger than a square frame," she suggests. In fact, there are several reasons, including the fact that a round lid can't fall into the hole the way a square one can and the fact that it can be rolled.

12   Business schools teach students how to deal with case interview questions, and Vault has even put out a book on the subject, *Vault Guide to the Case Interview.*

13   Other weird-seeming questions, like "If you were a brick in a wall, which brick would you be and why," or "If you could be any animal, what would you be and why," are really just invitations to show a side of your personality. Thanasoulis-Cerrachio says a friend who is chief executive of a market research company used to ask applicants what kind of car they would be. "She wanted someone fast, who thought quickly," Thanasoulis-Cerrachio says. "She wanted someone who wanted to be a Maserati[8], not a Bentley[9]." For the brick question, Thanasoulis-Cerrachio advises saying something like, "I would want to be a foundational brick because I'm a solid person. You can build on my experience and I will never let you down."

14   According to Rueff and Thanasoulis-Cerrachio, my comedian question was also a behavioral question, a test of my personality. "You gave a fine answer," says Rueff. Maybe. But I didn't get the job.

6. **Tracheotomy:** a cut made into the throat to open a blocked airway

7. **Grueling:** difficult; tiring

8. **Maserati:** a fast Italian sports car
9. **Bentley:** a British luxury car known more for elegance than speed

CHECK COMPREHENSION

1. What question was the author asked during her job interview in paragraph 1? How did the interview end?

2. How does Rusty Rueff advise applicants to handle strange questions?

3. According to Adams, why do employers ask these strange questions?

MAKE INFERENCES

You learned in Chapter 7 that an inference is a logical conclusion we make based on the evidence provided in the reading. Consider what Adams says in her essay to determine whether the following statements are true or false.

1. We cannot really prepare for the strange questions we may get in a job interview.

2. Most employers have one right answer that they are looking for when they ask a strange question.

WRITE TO IMPROVE READING   Summarize

Using the guidelines from Chapter 6 and your annotations, write a summary of Adams's essay. Remember that your summary will include the main point and major supporting details, written in your own words. When you have finished, compare your summary with a classmate's version.

Build Vocabulary: The Language of Specificity

Study the vocabulary words footnoted throughout Adam's essay. What do the following words have in common?

swimmingly

studiously

woefully

These words are examples of **adverbs**, or words that describe an action. Many adverbs end with an *-ly* suffix, as these examples do. Adverbs help a writer make the meaning of an action more specific. For example, notice that the writer here says that people "prepare studiously" for interviews. Why is "prepare studiously" more specific than just "prepare"?

PRACTICE

- Find three additional examples of adverbs in the essay that make the writer's meaning more specific:

  _____

  _____

  _____

What do these two vocabulary words have in common?

Maserati

Bentley

These two words are examples of **proper nouns**. A proper noun is a name, and it is always capitalized. A proper name is always more specific than other nouns, because it names something specific. When you are working with illustration, proper nouns make the writing as specific as possible.

PRACTICE

- Would Susan Adams's essay be as effective if she had said "fast car" instead of "Maserati"? if she had said "expensive car" instead of "Bentley"? Explain.

- Look at each of the following nonspecific nouns. Find a specific proper noun that Adams uses with or instead of the nonspecific one in her essay. The first one is done for you.

  - An African-American comedian _David Alan Grier_

  - Online site about careers and interviews

  - A consultant

  - A communications company

  - A software company

  - A career-services consultant

Understand Strategies Used in Illustration: Hypothetical Examples

In paragraph 6, Adams lists five examples of interview questions. Each of these questions is a real example; the question was used by an actual company in an actual interview. Sometimes, writers don't have real examples. Instead, they create hypothetical instances: examples which could be possible but aren't associated with an actual event. Adams uses a hypothetical example in paragraph 9 to illustrate one way to answer the question about hair salons in Japan.

- What is one clue that the example is hypothetical?
- Should an entire illustration essay rely on hypothetical examples? Why or why not?

RESPOND IN WRITING

1. Write about your own experiences with job interviews, giving examples of anything you found challenging—the stress of preparing for the interview, questions or awkward moments during the interview, and so on. If you were able to address these challenges in any way, explain how. (If you have not had many job interviews, write about the experiences of a friend or relative.)

2. Adams discusses how unusual interview questions can provide useful information. Come up with at least three odd interview questions, and explain how each one would provide an employer with helpful information.

Professional Essay: "Why Are We So Angry?" Dianne Hales

Preview

1. Skim the title and the information about the author. What can you learn about the context (audience, purpose, and topic) for this essay?

2. What makes you angry? How do you express your anger? Has your anger ever gotten you in trouble?

3. Create a guiding question for your reading.

Read and annotate this essay carefully, using the Guidelines for Reading and Annotating Illustration on page 139.

Dianne Hales

Why Are We So Angry?

Dianne Hales specializes in writing about mental health, fitness, and other issues related to the body and mind. A former contributing editor for *Parade* magazine, she has also written several college-level health textbooks. In her critically acclaimed book *Just Like a Woman* (2000), she examined assumptions about the biological differences between women and men. Most recently, she authored *La Bella Lingua: My Love Affair with Italian, the World's Most Enchanting Language* (2009). Both the American Psychiatric Association and the American Psychological Association have presented Hales with awards for excellence in writing. In addition, she has earned an Exceptional Media Merit Award (EMMA) from the National Women's Political Caucus for health reporting. She lives in Marin County, California.

In the following article, Hales uses vivid examples to illustrate the "rage" phenomenon. She reports on the causes and results of the apparent increase in out-of-control anger—and explains what can be done to relieve the problem. PHOTO BY JULIA ANN HALES

1   Something snapped inside Jerry Sola during his evening commute through the Chicago suburbs two years ago. When the driver in front of the fifty-one-year-old salesman suddenly slammed on his brakes, Sola got so incensed[1] that he gunned his engine to cut in front of the man. Still steaming when both cars stopped at a red light, Sola grabbed a golf club from the backseat and got out.

2   "I was just about to smash his windshield or do him some damage," the brawny, 6-foot-1 former police officer recalls. "Then it hit me: 'What in God's name am I doing? I'm really a nice, helpful guy. What if I killed a man, went to jail, and destroyed two families over a crazy, trivial thing?' I got back into my car and drove away."

3   Like Sola, more and more Americans are feeling pushed to the breaking point. The American Automobile Association's Foundation for Traffic Safety says incidents of violently aggressive driving—which some dub[2] "mad driver disease"—rose 7 percent a year in the 1990s. Airlines are reporting more outbursts of sky rage. And sideline rage has become widespread: A Pennsylvania kids' football game ended in a brawl involving more than one hundred coaches, players, parents, and fans. In a particularly tragic incident that captured national attention, a Massachusetts father—angered over rough play during his son's hockey practice—beat another father to death as their children watched.

4   No one seems immune[3] to the anger epidemic. Women fly off the handle just as often as men, though they're less likely to get physical. The young and the infamous, such as musicians Sean "Puffy" Combs and Courtney Love—both sentenced to anger-management classes for violent outbursts—may seem more

1. **Incensed:** angered

2. **Dub:** to call

3. **Immune:** protected against

volatile[4], but even senior citizens have erupted into "line rage" and pushed ahead of others simply because they felt they had "waited long enough" in their lives.

5   "People no longer hold themselves accountable[5] for their bad behavior," says Doris Wilde Helmering, a therapist and author of *Sense Ability*. "They blame anyone and everything for their anger."

6   ***It's a mad, mad world.***   Violent outbursts are just as likely to occur in leafy suburbs as in crowded cities, and even idyllic[6] vacation spots are not immune. "Everyone everywhere seems to be hotter under the collar these days," observes Sybil Evans, a conflict-resolution expert in New York City, who singles out three primary culprits[7]: time, technology, and tension. "Americans are working longer hours than anyone else in the world. The cell phones and pagers that were supposed to make our lives easier have put us on call 24/7/365. Since we're always running, we're tense and low on patience. And the less patience we have, the less we monitor what we say to people and how we treat them."

7   Ironically[8], the recent boom times may have brought out the worst in some people. "Never have so many with so much been so unhappy," observes Leslie Charles, author of *Why Is Everyone So Cranky?* "There are more of us than ever, all wanting the same space, goods, services, or attention. Everyone thinks, 'Me first. I don't have time to be polite.' We've lost not only our civility but our tolerance for inconvenience."

8   The sheer complexity of our lives also has shortened our collective fuse. We rely on computers that crash, drive on roads that gridlock, place calls to machines that put us on endless hold. "It's not any one thing but lots of little things that make people feel like they don't have control of their lives," says Jane Middleton-Moz, a therapist and author. "A sense of helplessness is what triggers rage. It's why people end up kicking ATM machines."

9   ***Getting a grip.***   When his lawn mower wouldn't start, a St. Louis man got so angry that he picked it up by the handle, smashed it against the patio, and tore off each of its wheels. Playing golf, he sometimes became so enraged that he threw his clubs 50 feet up the fairway and into the trees and had to get someone to retrieve them. In anger-therapy sessions with Doris Wilde Helmering, he learned that such outbursts accomplish nothing. "Venting" may make you feel better—but only for a moment.

10   "Catharsis[9] is worse than useless," says Brad Bushman, a psychology professor at Iowa State University whose research has shown that letting anger out makes people more aggressive, not less. "Many people think of anger as the psychological equivalent of the steam in a pressure cooker: It has to be released, or it will explode. That's not true. The people who react by hitting, kicking, screaming, and swearing just feel more angry."

4. **Volatile:** explosive

5. **Accountable:** responsible

6. **Idyllic:** peaceful

7. **Culprits:** guilty ones

8. **Ironically:** opposite to what is or might be expected

9. **Catharsis:** release of emotional tension

10. **Equanimity:** balance: to call

11. **Chronic:** habitual

11   Over time, temper tantrums sabotage physical health as well as psychological equanimity[10]. By churning out stress hormones like adrenaline, chronic[11] anger revs the body into a state of combat readiness, multiplying the risk for stroke and heart attack—even in healthy individuals. In one study by Duke University researchers, young women with "*Jerry Springer Show*–type anger," who tended to slam doors, curse, and throw things in a fury, had higher cholesterol levels than those who reacted more calmly.

12   *How do you tame a toxic temper?* The first step is to figure out what's really making you angry. Usually the rude sales clerk is the final straw that unleashes bottled-up fury over a more difficult issue, such as a divorce or a domineering boss. Next, monitor yourself for early signs of exhaustion or overload. While stress alone doesn't cause a blow-up, it makes you more vulnerable[12] to overreacting.

12. **Vulnerable:** open to damage or attack

13   When you feel yourself getting angry, control your tongue and your brain. "Like any feeling, anger lasts only about three seconds," says Doris Wilde Helmering. "What keeps it going is your negative thinking." As long as you focus on who or what irritated you—like the oaf who rammed that grocery cart into your heels—you'll stay angry. "Once you come to understand that you're driving your own anger with your thoughts," adds Helmering, "you can stop it."

13. **Epiphany:** a sudden understanding of something

14   Since his roadside epiphany[13], Jerry Sola has conscientiously worked to rein in his rage. "I am a changed person," he says, "especially behind the wheel. I don't listen to the news on the car radio. Instead, I put on nice, soothing music. I force myself to smile at rude drivers. And if I feel myself getting angry, I ask a simple question: 'Why should I let a person I'm never going to see again control my mood and ruin my whole day?'"

CHECK COMPREHENSION

1. According to Hales, why do angry outbursts seem to be increasing?

2. Do experts think it is a good idea to release anger in a fit of screaming or by throwing things?

3. What are three steps that Hales recommends for controlling anger?

MAKE INFERENCES

1. Based on the sources of increased stress and anger listed in paragraph 6, do you think the anger issue exists worldwide? Explain.

2. Is it possible for our society to reduce its overall level of anger? Explain.

WRITE TO IMPROVE READING   **Summarize**

Using the guidelines from Chapter 6 and your annotations, write a summary of Hale's essay. Remember that your summary will include the main point and major supporting details, written in your own words. When you have finished, share your summary with a classmate.

Explore Grammar: Commas after Introductory Dependent Clauses

Look at the following sentence from the essay:

> When the driver in front of the fifty-one-year-old salesman suddenly slammed on his brakes, Sola got so incensed that he gunned his engine to cut in front of the man.

Did you notice the comma after the word "brakes"? This sentence begins with a **dependent clause**. A dependent clause begins with a dependent word, and it has a subject and a verb. Look at the dependent clause, which is underlined below:

Dependent word   Subject

When the driver in front of the fifty-one-year-old salesman suddenly

Verb —— slammed on his brakes, Sola got so incensed that he gunned his engine

to cut in front of the man.

When a sentence begins with a dependent clause, the dependent clause is followed by a **comma**. (For more on dependent words, dependent clauses, and commas, see Chapters 17 and 24.)

PRACTICE

Add commas after the dependent clauses in the following sentences. When you have finished, check your work by looking back at the essay.

1. Since we're always running we're tense and low on patience.

2. When his lawn mower wouldn't start a St. Louis man got so angry that he picked it up by the handle, smashed it against the patio, and tore off each of its wheels.

3. When you feel yourself getting angry control your tongue and your brain.

4. If I feel myself getting angry I ask a simple question.

Understand Strategies Used in Illustration: Providing Credentials

Many of the specific names used by both Adams and Hales are names of **experts**. When the writers introduce an expert, they also include the expert's **credentials**. Credentials explain *why* someone qualifies as an expert.

For each of the following experts mentioned in Hales's essay, find and list the expert's credentials. The first one has been done for you.

- Sybil Evans *conflict-resolution expert in New York City*
- Leslie Charles
- Jane Middleton-Moz
- Brad Bushman
- Doris Wilde Helmering

  Why do the writers need to include the credentials of the authorities or experts that they quote?

  Do you find these experts convincing? Why or why not?

  Would Hales's examples have worked as well if she had cited one of the following as her experts? Why or why not?

  Oprah Winfrey, Tim Tebow, Mariah Carey, Bill Gates, Jeb Bush

Know P/Q: Quoting Someone Else's Words

When you **quote**, you copy exactly what the author says, without changing anything, and you show that you have copied by using quotation marks at the beginning and the end of the copied material. You also show the source of the quote in a signal phrase. A **signal phrase** introduces the quote and shows the reader that you have copied the information from another writer. A signal phrase uses words like *say, explain,* or *tell.* Finally, the quote is usually followed by a page number, or **citation**, in parentheses, if there is one available. This is basic MLA (Modern Language Association) format for citations. There are also other styles of citation used by scholars and writers. For more information about MLA style, see Chapter 14.

Let's look at an example.

Quotation marks   Citation
→ Signal phrase

Dianne Hales says, "No one seems immune to the anger epidemic" (148).

Can you identify the signal phrase, quotation marks, and citation in the following example?

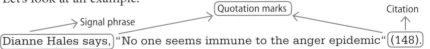

Quotation marks
Signal phrase

Hales suggests, "Like Sola, more and more Americans are feeling pushed to the breaking point" (148).

Citation

PRACTICE   Paraphrasing

The following four sentences are paraphrases from Dianne Hales's essay. For each paraphrase, find the original quote and copy it in the space provided, along with a signal phrase. The first one has been done for you.

Paraphrase	Quote
Example **Dianne Hales suggests that location isn't a factor in determining where dangerous displays of anger occur: suburban neighborhoods to crowded urban areas to resorts or other vacation destinations (148).**	*Dianne Hales says, "Violent outbursts are just as likely to occur in leafy suburbs as in crowded cities, and even idyllic vacation spots are not immune" (148).*
1. The writer explains that economic prosperity may have actually pushed people toward ugly or violent displays of anger, as unlikely as that may sound (149). (Hint: para. 7)	
2. Hales also says that as a society, we have filled our lives with so many things—things which inevitably don't act the way we expect them to—that we tend to get angry much more quickly (149). (Hint: para. 8)	
3. According to the writer, repeated displays of anger can damage us not only physically but also emotionally and psychologically (149). (Hint: para. 11)	
4. In order to improve our anger management, Hales advises that we watch ourselves carefully to see if there are warning signals, such as being extraordinarily tired or busy (149). (Hint: para. 12)	

Once you have filled in the quotes above, check your work:

1. Do you have a signal phrase?

2. Do you have a citation?

3. Do you have beginning and ending quotation marks?

4. Did you copy exactly? To check the accuracy of your quotes, do a quick word count. First, look at the original sentences in Hales's essay. How many words are in each? Now check your quotes above. How many words are in each? If the number of words in a quote does not match the number of words in the original, look back to see what word(s) you may have left out.

PRACTICE   **Paraphrases Versus Quotes**

Writers use both paraphrases and quotes to introduce other writers' words or ideas. How are paraphrases and quotes similar? How are they different? Complete the following chart.

	Paraphrase	**Quote**
How is it introduced?		
What punctuation do you use with the signal phrase?		
What other punctuation do you use?		
Is the language borrowed from the original source?		

RESPOND IN WRITING

1. Find one piece of advice in Hales's essay that makes sense to you. In a paragraph, explain how you might apply that advice in your own life, giving at least two specific examples. Quote the advice from Hales in the paragraph, making sure that it is properly copied, punctuated, and cited.

2. Do you think our society is becoming angrier? Develop your answer in a paragraph with at least three examples, making sure that at least one of your examples comes from Hales's essay. Use a quotation that is copied accurately and cited correctly.

Extend and Connect: Write Your Own Illustration

1. Susan Adams suggests that job interviewers ask specific questions in order to understand an applicant's creativity and logical thinking. Imagine an employer who knows that a job is very stressful. The interviewer wants to discover how applicants handle stress and whether they lose control of their anger. What questions might the interviewer ask to find this information? Explain, using specific examples.

2. James Carnill suggests that our use of technology makes us self-centered. How does technology use relate to anger? Does being self-centered make us more likely to explode in anger? Write an essay in which you give examples of anger related to technology.

3. Do you think students on your campus have problems managing anger? Before you answer this question, consider people on your campus who might qualify as experts on this question. Interview at least three people, making sure to note each person's credentials. Develop your answer in an essay, using specific examples and quotes from the people you interviewed.

4. Inez King gives examples of empathy in her paragraph on page 139. Can technology help people develop empathy, or is it more likely to make people self-centered, as suggested by James Carnill? Write an essay that explores the relationship between technology and empathy, providing specific examples to support your thesis.

CHECKLIST

Writing an Illustration

| Prewrite | Draft | Revise | Edit |

NARROW AND EXPLORE YOUR TOPIC (see Chapter 2)
- ☐ Make the topic more specific.
- ☐ Use prewriting techniques to get ideas about your narrow topic.

| Prewrite | **Draft** | Revise | Edit |

DRAFT A TOPIC SENTENCE OR THESIS STATEMENT (see Chapter 4)
- ☐ Decide what you want your readers to know about the topic.

SUPPORT YOUR POINT (see Chapter 4)
- ☐ Find examples and details that will illustrate your main idea.

WRITE A FULL DRAFT (see Chapter 4)
- ☐ Make a plan that puts the examples in logical order.
- ☐ Include the topic sentence (paragraph), an introduction and a thesis (essay), and enough examples to make your point.
- ☐ Add a concluding sentence or concluding paragraph.

| Prewrite | Draft | **Revise** | Edit |

REVISE YOUR DRAFT (see Chapter 5)
- ☐ Make sure you have covered the Four Basics of Good Illustration.
- ☐ Make sure your readers have all the information they need to connect the examples to the point.
- ☐ Make sure you have included transitions to move readers smoothly from one example to the next.

| Prewrite | Draft | Revise | **Edit** |

EDIT YOUR REVISED DRAFT (see Chapter 5)
- ☐ Correct errors in grammar, spelling, word usage, and punctuation.
- ☐ Make sure your document is formatted correctly.

9

Process Analysis:

Texts That Present a Sequence of Steps

Understand What Process Analysis Is

Process analysis either explains how to do something (so that your readers can do it) or explains how something works (so that your readers can understand it).

Four Basics of Good Process Analysis

> **1** It tells readers what process the writer wants them to know about and makes a point about it.
>
> **2** It presents the essential steps in the process.
>
> **3** It explains the steps in detail.
>
> **4** It presents the steps in a logical order (usually time order).

In the following paragraph, the numbers and colors correspond to the Four Basics of Good Process Analysis.

The poet Dana Gioia once said, "Art delights, instructs, consoles. It educates our emotions." **1** Closely observing paintings, sculpture, and other forms of visual art is a great way to have the type of experience that Gioia describes, and following a few basic steps will help you get the most from the experience. **2** First, choose an art exhibit that interests you. **3** You can find listings for exhibits on local museums' Web sites or in the arts section of a newspaper. Links on the Web sites or articles in a newspaper may give you more information about the exhibits, the artists featured in them, and the types of work to be displayed. **2** Second, go to the museum with an open mind and, ideally, with a friend. **3** While moving through the exhibit, take time to examine each work carefully. As you do so, ask yourself questions: What is my eye most drawn to, and why? What questions does this work raise for me, and

4 Time order is used.

4   Time order is used.

how does it make me feel? How would I describe it to someone over the phone? Ask your friend the same questions, and consider the responses. You might also consult an exhibit brochure for information about the featured artists and their works. **2** Finally, keep your exploration going after you have left the museum. **3** Go out for coffee or a meal with your friend. Trade more of your thoughts and ideas about the artwork, and discuss your overall impressions. If you are especially interested in any of the artists or their works, you might look for additional information or images on the Internet, or you might consult books at the library. Throughout the whole experience, put aside the common belief that only artists or cultural experts "get" art. The artist Eugène Delacroix described paintings as "a bridge between the soul of the artist and that of the spectator." Trust your ability to cross that bridge and come to new understandings.

You use process analysis in many situations.

College	In a science course, you explain photosynthesis.
Work	You write instructions to explain how to operate something (the copier, the fax machine).
Everyday life	You write out a recipe for an aunt.

When you are reading and writing in your college classes, you may be asked to *describe* a process, to *discover* how something works, or to *explain* the stages in a process. All of these assignments involve process analysis.

Process Analysis in the Classroom: Diagramming a Sequence of Steps

Clarisse is taking an introductory anatomy and physiology class. She is currently studying the circulatory system. She has memorized the major chambers of the heart and the valves which connect them, but her instructor told students they would have to *trace the pathway* followed by blood from the time it enters the heart until it exits. Clarisse realizes she will need to study more than the names on the diagram.

Clarisse went back to her text, looking for help to explain the process. Underneath the diagram of the heart, she found a paragraph that began this way:

> The circulatory system is a cycle that keeps the body supplied with oxygen-rich blood. First, oxygen-poor blood enters the right atrium of the heart through the superior and inferior venae cavae. The blood exits the right atrium through the tricuspid valve into the right ventricle. Next, the right ventricle . . .

Clarisse recognized the basics of process analysis. First, she saw the main point: "The circulatory system is a cycle that keeps the body supplied with oxygen-rich blood." She also saw that the major steps corresponded to the structures she had memorized before, while the details for each major support step included the entry and exit points and the changes to the blood during each step. The steps were presented in chronological order, and she could follow the steps using transition words: *first, next, then*. Using her annotations from the text, Clarisse made the following **cycle diagram** based on her reading:

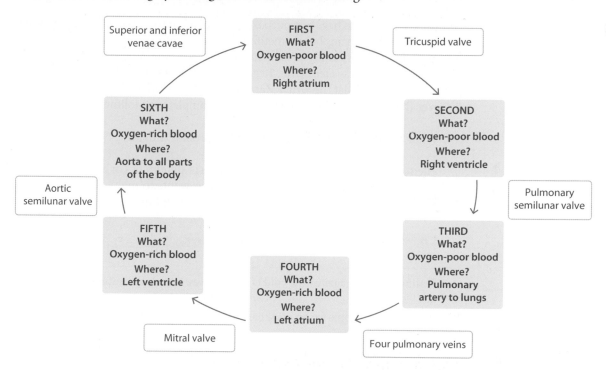

Once Clarisse saw how the process worked, she was able to study more effectively. To review, she made a blank diagram and filled in the different steps of the process. She also studied a diagram of the heart that she had labeled and, using her finger to point to each structure in the process, reviewed each step out loud. Finally, she practiced writing about the process, making sure that she used transition words to make each step clear.

APPLY WHAT YOU HAVE LEARNED

1. Look back at Chapters 2, 3, 4, and 5 of this textbook. How do these chapters work together to describe a process? What are the major steps in the process? What details does each chapter add to help you understand the process? Can you create a diagram or flow chart to show your understanding of the process of reading or writing?

2. Study another textbook you are currently using. Identify two or three examples of process writing in each one. Does the text use diagrams

or charts to help readers understand the processes involved? If not, what strategies would you recommend to a student who is using that textbook for a class?

Main Point in Process Analysis

A process analysis can have two purposes: to explain or to instruct. An **explanatory process analysis** explains how something works *so that readers can understand*. An **instructional process analysis** explains how to do something *so that readers can actually try the process themselves*. Regardless of the purpose, the main point in a process analysis is what the writer wants the reader to know about the process. To discover the main point in a process analysis, complete the following sentence:

What the readers need to know about this process is that . . .

The topic sentence (in a paragraph) or thesis statement (in an essay) usually includes the topic and the main point the writer wants to make about the topic. Here is an example of a topic sentence for a paragraph:

Process	+	Main point	=	Topic sentence

Sealing windows against the cold is an easy way to reduce heating bills.

Remember that the topic for an essay can be a little broader than one for a paragraph.

Process	+	Main point	=	Thesis statement

Improving a home's energy efficiency can actually be done fairly easily, significantly lowering energy bills.

Whereas the topic sentence focuses on just one method to improve energy efficiency, the thesis statement sets up a discussion of multiple methods.

> **PRACTICE 1**   **Identify Main Ideas in Process Analysis**
>
> 1. Look at the sample paragraph on pages 157–158 and complete the diagram below.

Process	+	Main point	=	Topic sentence

2. Look at the paragraph by Ibrahim Alfaqeeh on page 167 and complete the diagram below.

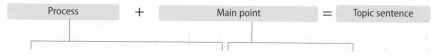

| Process | + | Main point | = | Topic sentence |

Support in Process Analysis

The paragraph and essay models on pages 162–163 use the topic sentence (paragraph) and thesis statement (essay) from the Main Point in Process Analysis section of this chapter. Both models include the **support** used in all writing about processes: the steps in the process backed up by details about these steps. In the essay model, however, the major support points (steps) are topic sentences for individual paragraphs.

PRACTICE 2   Identify Secondary Support in Process Analysis

Each of the steps (major support) from the sample paragraph on page 162 is listed below. For each step, underline the major support step, and circle any transitions or repetitions that tie the details to that step. Then, put brackets around the details that expand or clarify the major support step. The first one has been done for you.

Example: First, make sure the inside window frames are clean and clear of dust. Often, it is enough [to wipe the frames with a soft, dry cloth]. However, if the frames are especially dirty, [clean them thoroughly with a damp cloth], and then [dry them with paper towels or a blow dryer].

1. Next, apply two-sided adhesive tape on all four sides of the window frame. Begin by peeling the cover from one side of the adhesive. Then, affix this side of the tape to the frame. After you have taped all four sides of the frame, remove the front side of the adhesive cover.

2. Finally, attach the plastic sheeting to the tape. Start by measuring your window and cutting the plastic so that it fits. Next, apply the plastic to the tape, starting at the top of the window and working your way down. When the plastic is fully attached, seal it over the window by running a blow dryer over the plastic from top to bottom.

Paragraphs vs. Essays in Process Analysis

For more on the important features of process analysis, see the Four Basics of Good Process Analysis on page 157.

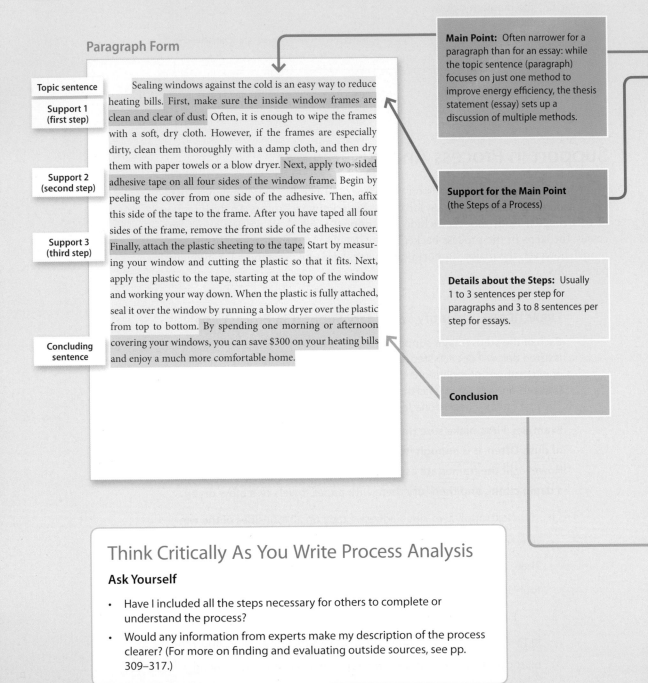

Paragraph Form

Topic sentence	Sealing windows against the cold is an easy way to reduce heating bills.
Support 1 (first step)	First, make sure the inside window frames are clean and clear of dust. Often, it is enough to wipe the frames with a soft, dry cloth. However, if the frames are especially dirty, clean them thoroughly with a damp cloth, and then dry them with paper towels or a blow dryer.
Support 2 (second step)	Next, apply two-sided adhesive tape on all four sides of the window frame. Begin by peeling the cover from one side of the adhesive. Then, affix this side of the tape to the frame. After you have taped all four sides of the frame, remove the front side of the adhesive cover.
Support 3 (third step)	Finally, attach the plastic sheeting to the tape. Start by measuring your window and cutting the plastic so that it fits. Next, apply the plastic to the tape, starting at the top of the window and working your way down. When the plastic is fully attached, seal it over the window by running a blow dryer over the plastic from top to bottom.
Concluding sentence	By spending one morning or afternoon covering your windows, you can save $300 on your heating bills and enjoy a much more comfortable home.

Main Point: Often narrower for a paragraph than for an essay: while the topic sentence (paragraph) focuses on just one method to improve energy efficiency, the thesis statement (essay) sets up a discussion of multiple methods.

Support for the Main Point (the Steps of a Process)

Details about the Steps: Usually 1 to 3 sentences per step for paragraphs and 3 to 8 sentences per step for essays.

Conclusion

Think Critically As You Write Process Analysis

Ask Yourself

- Have I included all the steps necessary for others to complete or understand the process?

- Would any information from experts make my description of the process clearer? (For more on finding and evaluating outside sources, see pp. 309–317.)

1

Many people are intimidated by the work necessary to make their homes more energy efficient; they do not see it as a do-it-yourself job. However, improving a home's energy efficiency can actually be done fairly easily, significantly lowering utility bills.

Thesis statement

First, seal air leaks around windows and doors. To seal air leaks around windows, apply caulk [to] window frames and walls. Also, if you have [old-fash]ioned windows that are not weather-proof, cover them with plastic before the cold temperatures set in. This process involves affixing two-sided adhesive tape to the window frames and then attaching plastic sheeting, which is sealed with the use of a blow dryer. Next, look for drafty spots around doors. Many air leaks at the top or sides of doors can be sealed with adhesive-backed foam strips. Leaks under doors can be stopped with foam draft guards. Alternatively, a rolled-up blanket, rug, or towel can keep the cold from coming in. All of these measures can save up to $60 [a sea]son on heating bills.

**Topic sentence 1
(first step)**

Second, install water-saving shower heads and faucet aerators. These fixtures are inexpensive and are

**Topic sentence 2
(second step)**

2

available in most hardware stores. Also, they are easy to install. First, unscrew the old shower or faucet head. Then, follow the package instructions for affixing the new shower head or aerator. In some cases, you might have to use pipe tape or a rubber washer to ensure a good seal. After this step, run the water to make sure there are no leaks. If you find any leaks, use pliers to tighten the seal. In time, you will discover that the new shower heads and aerators will cut your water [use] and the cost of water heating by up to 50 perce[nt].

Finally, look for other places where energy efficiency could be increased. One simple improvement is to replace traditional light bulbs with compact fluorescent bulbs, which use up to 80 percent less energy. Also, make sure your insulation is as good as it can be. Many utilities now offer free assessments of home insulation, identifying places where it is missing or inadequate. In some cases, any necessary insulation improvements may be subsidized by the utilities or by government agencies. It is well worth considering such improvements, which, in the case of poorly insulated homes, can save thousands of dollars a year,

**Topic sentence 3
(third step)**

3

quickly covering any costs. Although some people prefer to have professionals blow insulating foam into their walls, it is not difficult to add insulation to attics, where a large amount of heat can be lost during cold months.

Concluding paragraph

Taking even one of these steps can make a significant financial difference in your life and also reduce your impact on the environment. My advice, though, is to improve your home's energy efficiency as much as possible, even if it means doing just a little at a time. The long-term payoff is too big to pass up.

| PRACTICE 3 | Write Topic Sentences, Major Support, and Secondary Support (Details) in Process Analysis |

For each topic below, write a topic sentence and three or four steps in the process (major support).

1. The writing process

   Topic sentence: _____

   a. Step 1: _____

   b. Step 2: _____

   c. Step 3: _____

   d. Step 4: _____

2. Shopping for _____ (a specific family member or friend)

   Topic sentence: _____

   a. Step 1: _____

   b. Step 2: _____

   c. Step 3: _____

   d. Step 4: _____

3. Planning/training for _____ (an event, a meeting, a competition)

   Topic sentence: _____

   a. Step 1: _____

   b. Step 2: _____

   c. Step 3: _____

   d. Step 4: _____

4. Operating a _____

   Topic sentence: _____

   a. Step 1: _____

   b. Step 2: _____

c. Step 3: _____

d. Step 4: _____

5. A traditional _____ meal

Topic sentence: _____

a. Step 1: _____

b. Step 2: _____

c. Step 3: _____

d. Step 4: _____

PRACTICE 4   **Add Details in Process Analysis**

Choose one of the topics from Practice 3. Add details to each step. Use additional paper if you need to add more steps.

Topic: _____

Step 1: _____

   Detail: _____

Step 2: _____

   Detail: _____

Step 3: _____

   Detail: _____

Step 4: _____

   Detail: _____

Organization in Process Analysis

Process analysis is usually organized by **time order** because it explains the steps of the process in the order in which they occur. This is the strategy used in the paragraph and essay models on pages 162–163.

   Transitions move readers smoothly from one step to the next.

Common Transitions in Process Analysis

Conjunctive Adverbials	Adjective + Noun Pairs	Subordinating Conjunctions	Prepositions
eventually	the first (second, third, etc.) step	after	after
finally		as	before
first, second, next, etc.	the next (last) stage	before	during
later		now that	
meanwhile		once	
next		since	
then		when	
		while	

For more information on using and punctuating these transitions, see Chapters 17 and 24.

PRACTICE 5   Use Transitions in Process Analysis

Read the paragraph that follows, and fill in the blanks with transitions.

Scientists have discovered that, like something from a zombie movie, a mind-controlling fungus attacks certain carpenter ants. _____, as if following the fungus's orders, the ants help their invader reproduce. The process begins when an ant is infected. _____, the ant begins to act strangely. For instance, instead of staying in its home high in the trees, it drops to the forest floor. _____ wandering, it searches for a cool, moist place. _____ the zombie-ant finds the right place, it clamps its jaws to a leaf and dies. _____, the fungus within the ant grows until it bursts from the insect's head, and more ants are infected. By studying this process, researchers may find better ways to control the spread of carpenter ants.

Read and Analyze Process Analysis

Student Process Paragraph: "Weddings in Saudi Arabia," Ibrahim Alfaqeeh

Preview	Read	Review	Reflect and Respond

- Skim the title and the first sentence. What do you think the reading will be about?
- What is the context (audience and purpose) for this paragraph? How do you know?
- What are the steps required for planning a wedding in your culture or tradition?
- Create a guiding question for your reading.

Preview → Read → Review → Reflect and Respond

Guidelines for Reading and Annotating Process Analysis

Read and annotate this paragraph using these guidelines:

1. Pay attention to vocabulary using marginal notes, context clues, or a dictionary.
2. Find the main point and underline it. (In process analysis, the main point is what the writer wants the readers to know about the process.)
3. Identify supporting details and organizational strategies. Number each major step in the process. Circle the transition words. If necessary, make a flow chart to illustrate the steps in the process.
4. Ask questions and make connections. Remember to connect the paragraph or essay to your own experiences and other things you have read.

Ibrahim Alfaqeeh

Weddings in Saudi Arabia

1   A wedding in Saudi Arabia is mostly traditional. If a Saudi man wants to get married, he has to follow these difficult steps. First, he has to ask his mother to look for a girl. Indeed, the ways that the mother chooses a girl include noticing a girl at another wedding or finding a girl through relatives or other social connections. Second, if his mother finds the girl that she thinks is the perfect one for him, he and his father go to the girl's father in order to ask for her hand. Third, both the fathers and the mothers agree on the price of the dowry[1]. Specifically, the dowry ranges from 40,000 SAR[2], which is $11,000, to 100,000 SAR, which is $27,000, and the groom only will pay the price they agree on. Moreover, the groom pays for the dress, a stylist for hair and makeup, gold and diamonds, perfumes, and some gifts for the bride, while the bride doesn't spend anything on the groom, not even a little tiny gift. Fourth, the groom should pay to rent the hall for the celebration and all the staff. Although both the bride's and groom's families have their own maids, they require at least six additional people for the wedding. Finally, the people celebrate the wedding from 6:00 in the evening until 4:00 in the morning. In conclusion, because a traditional Saudi wedding is so difficult, I plan to get married in a casual way, and my mother won't choose my future wife, so that I can both save money and choose the girl that I want.

1. **Dowry:** the money and gifts offered by a groom to the family of the bride; can also be the money and belongings a woman brings to a marriage
2. **SAR:** Saudi Arabia riyal

> Preview > Read > **Review** > Reflect and Respond >

Review your reading. Make sure you can answer these questions:

1. Answer your guiding question.
2. In your own words, what is the main point of the paragraph?
3. What are the major steps in the process of getting married in Saudi Arabia?
4. Has the writer demonstrated the Four Basics of Good Process Analysis? Explain.

> Preview > Read > Review > **Reflect and Respond** >

1. How does this writer's description of planning a marriage connect with your own experiences?
2. What surprised you most about the process of planning a marriage in Saudi Arabia?
3. If you could talk to this writer, what questions would you ask him?
4. What might be the advantages of an arranged marriage? the disadvantages?

Student Process Essay: "My Pilgrimage," Jasen Beverly

> **Preview** > Read > Review > Reflect and Respond >

1. Look at the title of the selection. What is a pilgrimage? Where do people traditionally go to make a pilgrimage? What does the title suggest to you about the piece?
2. After reading the essay title, read the first paragraph quickly. What expectations or questions arise about the essay?
3. Read the first paragraph of the essay again. What is the context (author and purpose) for this essay? How might the context help you understand the essay better?
4. Create a guiding question for your reading of the essay.
5. Build Vocabulary
   a. Skim the vocabulary in the footnotes of the reading. What can you learn about the setting of the essay (location)? What words in the vocabulary set are related to the title? Explain.
   b. Two of the vocabulary words relate to habits of the mind: *ponder* and *reminisce*. Before you begin reading, do a quick search of an online dictionary and thesaurus to explore these two words.
      • What are some synonyms for each word?
      • How are these two words related to the habits of reflection and reading that you discovered in Chapters 2, 3, 4, and 5? Explain.

> Preview > **Read** > Review > Reflect and Respond >

Read and annotate this essay using the Guidelines for Reading and Annotating Process Analysis on page 167.

Jasen Beverly

My Pilgrimage

1   I'm tired and scared as hell. I've been running from this thing for who knows how long, but now I'm trapped. I crouch into a fetal position as the monster approaches me. With a closer look, I realize it's my best friend trying to kill me. He lifts his arm and cocks the gun back. Without words, he pulls the trigger.

2   The sound of a newly received instant message wakes me up. It's only 6:30 in the morning, so I'm hesitant to check the instant message. Minutes later, I roll over and reach for my phone. I slowly wipe the crust from my eyes and begin to read, "Wakey, wakey, eggs and bakey . . . skoo time!" reads the IM from my Mexican friend. I slide my phone open and reply with a quick "aiight," before I proceed to pass out again. Just as I begin to reconnect with my dream, at about 6:45, I'm interrupted once more. This time, it is a loud repeated banging at my bedroom door.

3   Without thoughts or words, I roll out of bed, grab my cloth and towel, and head for the bathroom. Upon reaching the bathroom, I hop into the shower. When my shower ends, I am forced to rush through both the grooming and dressing processes because there is a massive cold front sweeping through my apartment. This cold front is caused by a lack of heat in the apartment. This, in turn, is caused by what I like to call "hard times."

4   By 7:20, all is well, and I am ready to begin my pilgrimage[1] to Bunker Hill Community College for my first day of college. I leave my apartment with my hoodie unzipped, backpack half on, while trying fast to detangle my headphones for use. As I walk down the street, the frigid air begins to take its toll. My whole face is stinging as if it was being poked, the air circulating inside my shirt. I immediately slip my headphones into my pocket and zip my hoodie. I tie my hood tightly around my eyes. My hood cuts off my peripheral[2] vision but keeps all unwanted air off my face. Now I finish untangling my headphones and plug them into my phone. I quickly browse my list of albums before choosing one to listen to. This morning, I choose John Legend's *Once Again*. The music is soothing; it puts me in the zone as I continue the short trek to the bus stop.

5   While waiting patiently at the bus stop, I begin to ponder[3]. My first thought is, "How much longer will I be here waiting for the bus?" Next, I ask myself, "Am I even going to be able to sit when I get on the bus?" As this thought leaves my head, I see a bus coming down Columbia Road.

6   I enter the bus, tap my Charlie Card[4] on the target area, and begin to walk away. Shortly after, a stranger taps me on my leg as I walk by. When I look back, he is pointing to the fare box. I walk back and notice

1. **Pilgrimage:** a long journey, often made to some sacred place as an act of religious devotion

2. **Peripheral:** to the sides of a person's main line of sight

3. **Ponder:** to think about

4. **Charlie Card:** a plastic pass card used to pay fares on Boston's public transportation

the driver saying something. I'm not able to make out what he is saying because I have my headphones on. My card must not have been processed correctly. I re-tap my card on the target area. This time, I wait for it to register before walking away. I spot a seat in the back of the bus, so I fill it. Once I sit, I look around at the other people on the bus. I feel as if everyone is looking at me, so I close my eyes and let the music soothe my mind. When the bus pulls into Andrew Station, I stand and exit the bus. I walk down the stairs and wait for the train to arrive.

7   When it arrives, it is packed with an uncountable number of business-people taking a trip to the Financial District. In fact, it is so packed that I prefer to wait for the next train. While waiting, I begin to think about all of the businesspeople. I ask myself, "How long did they have to attend college to put themselves into the position they're in now?" As the next train pulls into the station, I notice it is much like the last, but this time I squeeze myself into the middle of the car. Luckily for me, Downtown Crossing, my stop, is only three stops away.

8   Upon reaching Downtown Crossing at 7:45, I exit the train and begin to watch as people dart down the long corridor in hopes of catching the train. This becomes the highlight of the morning as I watch the doors slam in people's faces. There's no explaining the humor of watching people who have tried so hard, panting angrily as the train leaves without them. After this joyous moment, I proceed to transfer from the Red Line to the Orange Line.

9   Standing on the Orange Line platform, I recognize a few familiar faces. They belong to students of Charlestown High School. I laugh, knowing that school for them began at 7:20. Then I begin to reminisce[5] about my own CHS experiences. I think about all my suspension hearings, the work I refused to do, and how easy it was to get by doing the bare minimum. Only the cold draft of the approaching train brings me back to reality.

10   I step on the train and position myself against the door. I could sit, but I figure it is too short a ride to get comfortable. One by one, the stops come and go: State, Haymarket, and then North Station. The train seems to be on an effortless glide as it starts to move toward Community College.

11   My stomach begins to churn[6] as I start the last phase of my pilgrimage. The last phase consists of walking out of the train station, down the walkway, and into Bunker Hill Community College. I compare this walk to the walk death row inmates take before they are executed. As I take this walk, I begin to ask myself, "What the ---- are you doing here?" Within seconds, my sensible half answers, "You're here so that you don't have to live like the rest of your family. The rest of your friends are in school, and Lord knows half of them aren't half as smart as you. Lastly, we already paid for this, so get it done." With BHCC right in front of me, I take a deep breath and end this pilgrimage by entering the Mecca[7] that will start me on the path of reaching my pinnacle.[8]

5. Reminisce: to think back or recollect

6. Churn: to stir powerfully

7. Mecca: a place that many people want to visit; a center of activity (Mecca is an Islamic holy city in Saudi Arabia)

8. Pinnacle: the highest point or achievement

Preview ⟩ Read ⟩ **Review** ⟩ Reflect and Respond

In Chapter 6, you learned how to paraphrase main ideas in order to write a summary. Use your annotations to write a short summary of this essay. Remember that a good summary captures the main idea and major supporting details in your own words. The summary refers to the author and uses strong descriptive verbs.

Preview ⟩ Read ⟩ Review ⟩ **Reflect and Respond**

1. When you previewed this essay, you read the first paragraph. What effect does the nightmare in the first paragraph have on the rest of the essay?

2. One of the Four Basics of Good Process Analysis is that the writing presents details in step-by-step order. How does Beverly use transition words to show time order in this piece? What else does he do to help the reader follow the steps of his "pilgrimage"?

3. Some students may be wondering why this essay is classified as a process analysis instead of a narrative. How would you answer that question? How does the main verb tense of this essay (present, not past) influence your understanding of the essay?

4. Write a paragraph about a short, everyday kind of trip you often take. Following Beverly's example, give a description of each step of the trip.

5. Expand your analysis of a trip or a commute into an essay. What makes this trip meaningful, memorable, or important to you? What do you see, think about, or feel during each stage of the journey?

Reading/Writing Workbook: Process Analysis

Professional Essay: "How to Boost Your Willpower,"
Tara Parker-Pope

Preview

1. Skim the title and the information about the author. What can you learn about the context (author, purpose, and topic) for this essay?

2. Make Connections: What is an area in which you have wished for more willpower? Where do you need willpower right now in relation to your reading and writing skills?

3. Ask Questions: Create a guiding question for your reading, based on your preview of the selection.

4. Use Vocabulary Notes Strategically: In the information about the author, Tara Parker-Pope talks about her approach to scientific research. Look carefully at the words defined for you on pages 172–173. Which of the words suggests a focus on scientific research? Why?

5. Predict: Skim the essay by reading just the first sentence in each paragraph. Predict at least three topics that will be discussed in the reading, based on your skimming.

Read and annotate this essay carefully, using the Guidelines for Reading and Annotating Process Analysis on page 167.

Tara Parker-Pope

How to Boost Your Willpower

Tara Parker-Pope is an award-winning columnist and the author of several books. She wrote for the *Wall Street Journal* for fourteen years as a weekly consumer health columnist before moving to the *New York Times* in 2007. Her writing often interprets medical research in a way that is easy to understand for her readers, a process that she says is important to her as a writer: "I also think that as reporters, we should never take anything at face value.... That's what you have to do with any kind of scientific research—ask what is really being asked here, and how much is really being answered." © NBC NEWSWIRE VIA GETTY IMAGES

1   Every day, we are tested. Whether it's a cookie tempting us from our diets or a warm bed coaxing us to sleep late, we are forced to decide between what we want to do and what we ought to do.

2   The ability to resist our impulses is commonly described as self-control or willpower. The elusive[1] forces behind a person's willpower have been the subject of increasing scrutiny[2] by the scientific community trying to understand why some people overeat or abuse drugs and alcohol. What researchers are finding is that willpower is essentially a mental muscle, and certain physical and mental forces can weaken or strengthen our self-control.

3   Studies now show that self-control is a limited resource that may be strengthened by the foods we eat. Laughter and conjuring up[3] powerful memories may also help boost a person's self-control. And, some research suggests, we can improve self-control through practice, testing ourselves on small tasks in order to strengthen our willpower for bigger challenges.

4   "Learning self-control produces a wide range of positive outcomes," said Roy Baumeister, a psychology professor at Florida State University who wrote about the issue in this month's *Current Directions in Psychological Science*. "Kids do better in school, people do better at work. Look at just about any major category of problem that people are suffering from and odds are pretty good that self-control is implicated[4] in some way."

5   Last month, Dr. Baumeister reported on laboratory studies that showed a relationship between self-control and blood glucose levels. In one study, participants watched a video, but some were asked to suppress[5] smiles and other facial reactions. After the film, blood glucose levels had dropped among those who had

1. **Elusive:** difficult to find or achieve
2. **Scrutiny:** a close, searching look or investigation

3. **Conjuring up:** bringing to mind

4. **Implicated:** shown to be involved

5. **Suppress:** to prevent or inhibit

exerted[6] self-control to stifle[7] their reactions, but stayed the same among the film watchers who were free to react, according to the report in *Personality and Social Psychology Review.*

6   The video watchers were later given a concentration test in which they were asked to identify the color in which words were displayed. The word "red," for instance, might appear in blue ink. The video watchers who had stifled their responses did the worst on the test, suggesting that their self-control had already been depleted[8] by the film challenge.

7   But the researchers also found that restoring glucose levels appears to replenish[9] self-control. Study subjects who drank sugar-sweetened lemonade, which raises glucose levels quickly, performed better on self-control tests than those who drank artificially sweetened beverages, which have no effect on glucose.

8   The findings make sense because it's long been known that glucose fuels many brain functions. Having a bite to eat appears to help boost a person's willpower, and may explain why smokers trying to quit or students trying to focus on studying often turn to food to sustain[10] themselves.

9   Consuming sugary drinks or snacks isn't practical advice for a dieter struggling with willpower. However, the research does help explain why dieters who eat several small meals a day appear to do better at sticking to a diet than dieters who skip meals. "You need the energy from food to have the willpower to exert self-control in order to succeed on your diet," said Dr. Baumeister.

10   Kathleen Vohs, professor of marketing at the University of Minnesota, says that in lab studies, self-control is boosted when people conjure up powerful memories of the things they value in life. Laughter and positive thoughts also help people perform better on self-control tasks. Dr. Vohs notes that self-control problems occur because people are caught up "in the moment" and are distracted from their long-term goals.

11   "You want to look good in a bikini next summer but you're looking at a piece of chocolate cake now," said Dr. Vohs. "When we get people to think about values we move them to the long-term state, and that cools off the tempting stimuli[11]."

12   Finally, some research suggests that people struggling with self-control should start small. A few studies show that people who were instructed for two weeks to make small changes like improving their posture[12] or brushing their teeth with their opposite hand improved their scores on laboratory tests of self-control. The data aren't conclusive[13], but they do suggest that the quest for self-improvement should start small. A vow to stop swearing, to make the bed every day, or to give up just one food may be a way to strengthen your self-control, giving you more willpower reserves for bigger challenges later.

---

6. **Exerted:** put forth or employed

7. **Stifle:** to keep in or hold back

8. **Depleted:** used up

9. **Replenish:** to fill again or resupply

10. **Sustain:** to strengthen or support

11. **Stimuli:** things that cause us to act or respond

12. **Posture:** position of a person's body

13. **Conclusive:** serving to prove

14. **Arbitrary:** coming about by chance, rather than by reason or need

13   "Learning to bring your behavior under control even with arbitrary[14] rules does build character in that it makes you better able to achieve the things you want to achieve later on," said Dr. Baumeister. "Self-control is a limited resource. People make all these different New Year's resolutions, but they are all pulling off from the same pool of your willpower. It's better to make one resolution and stick to it than make five."

CHECK COMPREHENSION

1. What process does Parker-Pope analyze?

2. What are the three steps in the process?

3. Are the three major steps in any particular order? Explain.

4. What is her main point?

MAKE INFERENCES

Based on your reading, determine whether the following statements are true or false.

1. People who struggle with self-control can improve with practice.

2. People who do not have strong self-control are very likely to focus on long-term goals.

3. Students who eat snacks while studying and before taking tests are more likely to succeed.

WRITE TO IMPROVE READING   Summarize

Using your answers from the preceding Check Comprehension questions, the guidelines from Chapter 6 and your annotations, write a summary of Parker-Pope's essay. Remember that your summary will include the main point and major supporting details, written in your own words.

Explore Grammar: Active and Passive Verbs

Look at the verbs in the following sentence:

The video watchers were later given a concentration test in which they were asked to identify the color in which words were displayed.

These verbs are passive: they include a form of the verb "be" and the past participle of the main verb. In a passive verb, the subject is not doing the main action. Instead, the subject is receiving the action of the verb. In this sentence, the video watchers aren't giving the test; they are receiving the test. The person giving the test is not mentioned. The writer could have included the person who gave the test:

For more on passives, see Chapter 19

> The <u>researchers</u> <u>gave</u> the video watchers a concentration tes*t*.

Here, the verb is active, and the person doing the action is the subject of the sentence.

PRACTICE

1. In writing about science, many authors use passive verbs. Why do you think they make this choice?

2. Find additional examples of passive in Tara Parker-Pope's essay.

3. Most stylebooks tell students to avoid the passive. What happens if a writer uses the passive all the time?

Understand Strategies Used in Process Analysis: Giving Expert Opinions

In this essay, Tara Parker-Pope expands on a strategy that you have seen before: giving expert opinions. Parker-Pope not only **cites** (refers to) experts but also explains some of the specific scientific studies that the experts conducted. Consider each of the experts listed below, and answer the questions that follow:

Dr. Roy Baumeister

1. What are Dr. Baumeister's credentials? (Remember, credentials are the qualifications that allow us to call someone an expert.)

2. Where and when did he publish the results of his study?

3. What did he learn?

Dr. Kathleen Vohs

1. What are Dr. Vohs's credentials?

2. Do we know where or when she published results from a study?

3. Do we know what she learned from her studies? Explain.

Finally, consider paragraph 12. The author mentions "a few studies," but does not name the researchers, publication information, or procedures of these studies. Why do you think she decided not to include that information?

Know P/Q: Paraphrase

In describing the work of Dr. Baumeister, Parker-Pope explains the actual study that he conducted to explore the relationship between glucose in the blood and a person's ability to exercise self-control. She describes this experiment in paragraphs 5–6.

Asked to paraphrase the description of the study, one student wrote the following:

> Dr. Baumeister reported on laboratory experiments that showed a connection between self-control and blood glucose levels. In one study, participants saw a video, but some were asked not to smile or show other facial reactions. After the video, blood glucose levels had fallen among those who had used self-control to hide their reactions, but stayed the same among the film viewers who were free to express emotions. The watchers were next given a concentration test in which they had to identify the color in which words were shown. The word "red," for instance, might appear in a different color ink.

1. Is this an effective paraphrase? Why or why not?

2. With your partner, discuss ways to improve the paraphrase to make sure that it does not plagiarize the original source.

RESPOND IN WRITING   **P/Q Assignment**

1. Choose one of the strategies or steps recommended by Parker-Pope. Write a paraphrase of that strategy carefully. How could you use that strategy to help you face a challenge in your life, large or small, for which you need self-control? In a paragraph, identify your challenge and list at least three steps for facing that challenge. Use your paraphrase from this reading, properly cited, in your paragraph.

2. The article says that "the quest for self-improvement should start small" (173). Paraphrase this concept. Do you see yourself as being on a "quest for self-improvement"? Answer this question in a paragraph that focuses on a goal you have set for yourself, as well as the steps that you are taking to achieve that goal. Include your paraphrase from Parker-Pope, properly cited, in your response.

Professional Essay: "Isn't It Time You Hit the Books?" Samantha Levine-Finley

Preview

1. Skim the title and the information about the author. What can you learn about the context (author, purpose, and topic) for this essay?

2. What does the expression "hit the books" suggest to you?

3. Create a guiding question for your reading, based on your preview of the selection.

4. Predict: Read the first two sentences and then stop. What do you think will happen?

Read and annotate the essay carefully, using the Guidelines for Reading and Annotating Process Analysis on page 167.

Samantha Levine-Finley

Isn't It Time You Hit the Books?

 The author of the essay "Isn't It Time You Hit the Books?," Samantha Levine-Finley, has worked as a reporter for several publications, including the *Houston Chronicle*, where she covered topics relating to national politics, and *U.S. News & World Report*, where she contributed to the "Education" and "Nation & World" sections. This article was originally published in *U.S. News & World Report*'s America's Best Colleges 2008.
COURTESY OF SAMANTHA LEVINE-FINLEY

1   It was freshman year, and Angie Trevino thought she'd ace her microeconomics class at the University of Oklahoma. An older student had told her she could skip the lectures—the required discussion sessions would cover all the course material. So Trevino gladly slept in on lecture days and faithfully attended the discussions. "I was doing fairly well—I got high grades on tests and quizzes. I went in and took the final and thought I did great," she says. When she ended up with a B, she was shocked. "It was because my professor didn't see my face in the lecture," she says. "It was a rude awakening."

2   Now a graduating senior, Trevino, 22, realizes she got bum advice. "In high school, I was so monitored[1] to go to class, it was hard to miss," she says. "In college, you are responsible for your own actions and can't blame problems on someone else. It doesn't work like that."

3   Disappointing grades are just one hint that the approach many students took during high school won't work in college. The answer for new students is to step up their academic game. So, in addition to a "things to do" list, here are a few "things to be" that can help your transition to college.

4   *Be there.* "You will get an experience in the classroom that you will not get from a book," says Gavin Sands, 22, a graduating senior from Elon University in North Carolina. Skipping class may seem tempting, especially those introductory classes that can have several hundred students in them. The professors are unlikely to take attendance or even learn most students' names. But Trevino says class is great for meeting people, feeling connected to campus, and getting those crucial[2] snippets[3] of advice that professors mete[4] out to help with exams.

1. **Monitored:** watched over and guided

2. **Crucial:** important
3. **Snippets:** pieces
4. **Mete:** give

5. **Spiraling:** spinning out of control
6. **Moxie:** courage, nerve

5   *Be willing to talk to teachers.* Stress, confusion, and a low grade here or there are all part of college. Talking to a professor or adviser can keep those problems from spiraling[5]. But talking up takes moxie[6]. "If you are shy, it might be intimidating, but you have to put yourself out there," says Heath Thompson, 19, a sophomore at the University of Oklahoma. Sands thought "professors were going to be crazy, ridiculous, intense academic scholars, and I would be racing to keep up with them. But when I got here, I was amazed that they were real people and approachable."

6   You won't be wasting anyone's time. Professors are usually required to maintain[7] a certain number of office hours per week to see students, says Alice Lanning, who teaches a freshman-year experience class, also at Oklahoma. The problem is when "students don't take advantage of these office hours until the end of the semester, and the grades are scary." Her advice? Visit each professor at least once during the first month of school. "Ask what the professor is looking for and how to get the most out of class," Lanning says. That's especially critical because you'll have fewer exams and graded papers than in high school, so rebounding[8] from a bad grade is tough.

7. **Maintain:** preserve, keep

8. **Rebounding:** bouncing back or returning

9. **Extension:** more time to finish an assignment

7   Trevino recalled a time when she had a family problem and needed an extension[9] on a project in her business communications class. She had already talked with the professor several times about career and academic issues. When the problem came up, Trevino says, the professor's reaction blew her away. "He gave me an extension because he felt that he knew me and could trust me."

10. **Salvation:** something that saves you from risk, harm, or danger

8   *Be a syllabus-ologist.* The syllabus can be your salvation[10]. Professors hand out these precious pages at the start of each semester. The syllabus outlines the material required for the class, all assignments, and the dates that papers are due and exams are held. "You have to keep track of things because there is not going to be anyone handing you a reminder note before you leave for home or writing everything on the board," says Sands. Her solution: Go through each syllabus immediately, highlight all the quizzes, tests, and assignments, and put them in a day planner. "If you know you have three big projects due around the same time," she says, "you can think about it early on."

11. **Analytical:** logical, reasonable, able to understand how things or ideas can be broken down into smaller parts and how those parts relate to the whole

12. **Baffled:** confused

9   *Be deep.* College-level assignments require a questioning attitude, analytical[11] abilities, and a level of organization beyond anything you came across in high school. College-level writing assignments also demand higher-order thinking. Independent and creative thinking is key. Sands says she was baffled[12] at first in a class that focused on how to ask questions and do research. "I couldn't understand why you would ask a question you couldn't find an

answer to," she says. "But that wasn't the point. It was to find something that hasn't been asked a million times before. I struggled with that for weeks." As for writing the papers themselves, Ian Brasg, 18, a sophomore at Princeton, accidentally learned many ways to annoy professors. "Random, fancy-sounding adjectives may not make a paper better," he says. And in a paper about the philosopher Descartes[13], Brasg's grade suffered because he inconsistently[14] capitalized certain words. "To the professor, it showed a lack of preparation," he says.

10   One sure way to stay on track with college papers is to give yourself enough time to write a couple of drafts before you hand them in. Some professors require students to rewrite their papers so they can see where they're doing well and where they need to do more work. It gets ugly, but it helps. "There is a point when the students will hate me, and I will hate them because we are handing things back and forth," Carol Zoref, a writing instructor at Sarah Lawrence College, says. "And then this amazing thing happens: They all get much better at it. They have a kind of fearlessness. If they can put themselves through that, there will be a big payoff."

11   *Be a good manager.* The important thing is to manage your day and not waste time. Pay attention to how your time is spent and manage it to fit your preferences and habits and your various responsibilities. Time management methods vary according to the individual.

12   If time management methods differ among students, so do study styles. Sands stays organized using three-ring binders with dividers, loose-leaf paper, and pencil pouches in the front (high-tech approaches work, too). Trevino cheats her brain by writing due dates for assignments as earlier than they really are. Finding your own way to work, but also time for fun, is key, Thompson says. "You can't study every day of the week, and you can't play video games every day of the week," he says. "Balancing things is the most important part."

13   *Be cool.* Colleges know that students, especially those who were successful in high school, might resist seeking help, says Steven Lestition, dean of Mathey College, one of five residential colleges at Princeton. Get over it! "If nobody had that problem, the resources wouldn't be there," Trevino says. "If you are embarrassed or shy about getting help, weigh your options. Are you more worried about hurting your pride or your grade point average?"

14   *Tip:* All-nighters should be rare; same with end-of-semester cram sessions. Plugging away as assignments come in is the best way to get the most out of college.

13. **Descartes:** French philosopher and mathematician René Descartes (1596–1650), who has been called the "Father of Modern Philosophy"

14. **inconsistently:** not reliably, regularly, or predictably

CHECK COMPREHENSION

1. Which of the following would be the best alternative title for this essay?

    a. "How to Be a More Successful College Student"

    b. "College Students Cannot Manage Their Time"

    c. "Today's Students Need Extra Help in College"

    d. "Transition from High School to College Proves Impossible for Some"

2. According to Levine, one good way to write college papers is to

    a. use the strict, five-paragraph essay form.

    b. find as many sources as possible in your college library and online.

    c. give yourself enough time to write multiple drafts of your essays.

    d. understand that your professors are pressed for time.

MAKE INFERENCES

Consider the following advice for college freshmen. Based on your understanding of this reading, is this advice wise or unwise?

- If your instructor permits up to six absences without a grade penalty, you should plan to take them all.

- You should keep a laminated copy of your syllabus at the front of your notebook.

- Professors don't want to hear about your life or your stress, so don't tell them if you are having problems at home.

- If you were able to write A papers in high school, you will be able to write A papers in college without changing your work habits.

WRITE TO IMPROVE READING   Summarize

Using your answers to these questions and your annotations, write a summary of this essay, following the guidelines from Chapter 6.

1. What is the writer's main point? What is it that she wants readers to know about this process?

2. What specific steps does the writer mention?

3. What is the writer's conclusion?

Explore Grammar: Commas and Appositives

Like Tara Parker-Pope and other writers in this textbook, Levine-Finley includes quotations from people she has interviewed for her paper. Those quoted include students, professors, and a dean (an academic official who oversees a department within a college or university). Notice how Levine-Finley introduces one of the students:

> "You will get an experience in the classroom that you will not get from a book," says Gavin Sands, 22, a graduating senior from Elon University in North Carolina.

Pay attention to the commas in this sentence: there is a comma after the quotation (before the signal phrase), and there are commas after the student's name and the student's age. We use commas to mark extra information in the sentence. Specifically, we use commas to mark an **appositive**. An appositive follows a noun and gives an explanation of the noun (or renames the noun). In this sentence, the appositive "graduating senior" explains who Gavin Sands is. When Levine-Finley uses the appositive, she is showing her readers *why* she is quoting Gavin Sands: he is a graduating senior, so he has a lot of experience with studying.

For more information on commas, see Chapter 28.

> "You will get an experience in the classroom that you will not get from a book," says Gavin Sands, 22, a graduating senior from Elon University in North Carolina.
> —Appositive

PRACTICE

1. Find four other places where Levine-Finley uses commas to mark appositives.

2. When does the author include the age of the speaker with the appositive?

Understand Strategies Used in Process Analysis: Audience Awareness

Writers are aware of their audiences, and they choose words and examples that will be effective for their intended readers. Tara Parker-Pope, for example, writes for educated readers of the *New York Times*. As a result, she uses vocabulary such as "elusive" and "scrutiny," and she follows more formal expectations for writing by using third person pronouns (he, she, they) instead of second person pronouns (you, your). Consider how Levine-Finley's writing choices reflect her audience as you answer the following questions.

PRACTICE

1. Who is the intended audience for this essay? How do you know?

2. Levine-Finley presents the steps in her process as "things to be," not "things to do." Why might this approach appeal to her target audience?

3. Levine-Finley selected a number of quotes for this essay. How do you think her audience influenced her selection of quotes? Explain.

RESPOND IN WRITING

1. This essay begins with the story of a student who received bad advice and followed it. One way to write a humorous process analysis is to give bad advice intentionally. Write an essay in which you explain how to be a bad student, how to get fired from a job, or how to become a couch potato.

2. Interview some of your classmates to discover what they have learned about being successful in college. Write your own process analysis essay, using quotes from classmates as supporting details for the steps in the process. Use appositives to introduce the classmates you quote.

Extend and Connect: Write Your Own Process Analysis

1. Tara Parker-Pope makes several suggestions for improving self-control and willpower. How do her ideas support the recommendations in Samantha Levine-Finley's article? Choose one of Levine-Finley's steps, and write a process analysis explaining how to improve self-control or willpower in that area. Paraphrase or quote Parker-Pope in your essay, and cite your reference correctly.

2. One of Levine-Finley's steps is talking with teachers. Write a process analysis essay that explains how a shy student can approach and talk to a professor.

3. Several of the authors in this textbook write about adjusting to new cultures. What would be the most important steps a person might need to take to adjust to your community? In an essay, write a guide to the process of "fitting in" in your community, school, or workplace.

CHECKLIST

Writing a Process Analysis

Prewrite > Draft > Revise > Edit

NARROW AND EXPLORE YOUR TOPIC (see Chapter 2)

- ☐ Make the topic more specific.
- ☐ Use prewriting techniques to get ideas about your narrow topic and the steps you need to explain to your readers.
- ☐ Make sure your topic can be covered in the space given.

Prewrite > **Draft** > Revise > Edit

DRAFT A TOPIC SENTENCE OR THESIS STATEMENT (see Chapter 4)

- ☐ Decide what you want your readers to know about the process you are describing.

SUPPORT YOUR POINT (see Chapter 4)

- ☐ Include all the steps in the process, and explain the steps in detail.

WRITE A FULL DRAFT (see Chapter 4)

- ☐ Make a plan that puts the steps in logical order.
- ☐ Include the topic sentence (paragraph), an introduction and a thesis (essay), and all the supporting steps.
- ☐ Add a concluding sentence or concluding paragraph.

Prewrite > Draft > **Revise** > Edit

REVISE YOUR DRAFT (see Chapter 5)

- ☐ Make sure you have covered the Four Basics of Good Process Analysis.
- ☐ Reread to make sure all steps are present.
- ☐ Get feedback from peers.
- ☐ Make sure you have included transitions to move readers smoothly from one step to the next.

Prewrite > Draft > Revise > **Edit**

EDIT YOUR REVISED DRAFT (see Chapter 5)

- ☐ Correct errors in grammar, spelling, word usage, and punctuation.
- ☐ Make sure your document is formatted correctly.

10

Classification:

Texts That Analyze Through Grouping

Understand What Classification Is

Classification is writing that organizes, or sorts, people or items into categories. It uses an **organizing principle**: *how* the people or items are sorted. The organizing principle is directly related to the purpose for classifying. For example, you might sort clean laundry (your purpose) using one of the following organizing principles: by ownership (yours, your roommate's) or by where it goes (the bedroom, the bathroom).

Four Basics of Good Classification

1. It makes sense of a group of people or items by organizing them into categories.
2. It has a purpose for sorting the people or items.
3. It categorizes using a single organizing principle.
4. It gives detailed explanations or examples of what fits into each category.

In the following paragraph, the numbers and colors correspond to the Four Basics of Good Classification.

1 In researching careers I might pursue, I have learned that there are three major types of workers, **2** each having different strengths and preferences. **3** The first type of worker is a big-picture person, who likes to look toward the future and think of new businesses, products, and services. **4** Big-picture people might also identify ways to make their workplaces more successful and productive. Often, they hold leadership positions, achieving their goals by assigning specific projects and tasks to others. Big-picture people may be drawn to starting their own businesses. Or they might manage or become a consultant for an existing business. **3** The second type of worker is a detail person, who focuses on the smaller picture, whether it be a floor plan in a construction project, a spreadsheet showing a business's revenue and expenses, or data from a scientific experiment. **4** Detail people take pride in understanding all the ins and outs of a task and doing everything carefully and well. Some detail people prefer to work with their hands, doing such things as carpentry or electrical wiring. Others prefer office jobs, such as accounting or clerical work. Detail people may also be drawn to technical careers, such as scientific research or engineering. **3** The third type of worker is a people person, who gets a lot of satisfaction from reaching out to others and helping meet their needs. **4** A people person has good social skills and likes to get out in the world to use them. Therefore, this type of worker is unlikely to be happy sitting behind a desk. A successful people person often shares qualities of the other types of workers; for example, he or she may show leadership potential. In addition, his or her job may require careful attention to detail. Good jobs for a people person include teaching, sales, nursing, and other health-care positions. Having evaluated my own strengths and preferences, I believe that I am equal parts big-picture person and people person. I am happy to see that I have many career options.

You use classification anytime you want to organize people or items.

College	In a criminal justice course, you are asked to discuss the most common types of chronic offenders.
Work	For a sales presentation, you classify the kinds of products your company produces.
Everyday life	You classify your typical monthly expenses to make a budget.

In your college reading and writing assignments, you may not see the word *classification*. Instead, you might be given a reading about *the types or kinds of something*. You might also be asked to discuss *how something is organized* or *what the categories of something are*.

Classification in the Classroom: Learning Specialized Words by Grouping Them into Categories

Karla is taking a course called Medical Terminology, and she is struggling to memorize the hundreds of terms and word parts included in her textbook. How can an understanding of classification help her?

After learning the Four Basics of Good Classification, Karla began to think differently about the chapter in her text on the cardiovascular system. She noticed that the authors of her book used different sizes and colors for headings and subheadings. She wondered whether those different colors and sizes might be an example of classification. When she looked at the section called Pathology (in large blue type), she saw at least ten subheadings underneath that heading. These subheadings were in smaller black type, and they included words like "diseases of the arteries," "diseases of the blood," and "diseases of the heart muscle."

Karla's textbook was using classification *to make sense of a complicated subject* by organizing it into smaller categories. *The purpose* of the classification was to help students memorize nearly seventy new words. All of the cardiovascular diseases were *organized according to a single principle*: which structure of the heart they affected. There were at least *three examples* in each category.

Once Karla understood the way the authors were classifying diseases, she began to study differently. She no longer memorized words individually; instead, she practiced sorting them into categories. She color-coded her flashcards, based on her classification system. Karla also used a graphic organizer to show the structure of the classification system. By organizing her thinking, she was better able to learn the new vocabulary.

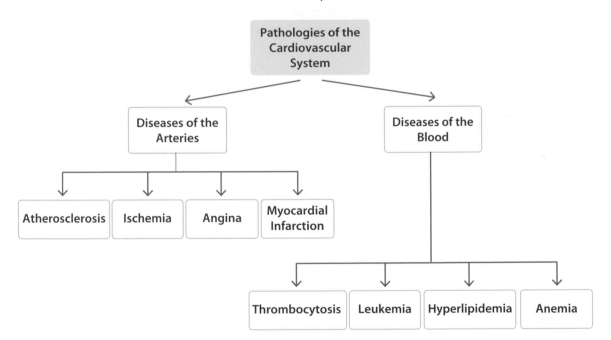

APPLY WHAT YOU HAVE LEARNED

1. Look at the table of contents from a textbook you are using this term. Can you find examples of organization by classification? If so, how do the titles, subtitles, and highlights from the text support the classification? How could an understanding of classification help you study this text more effectively?

2. Chapters 7 through 14 of *Real Reading and Writing* classify writing into eight different categories. How does the organization of this text illustrate the Four Basics of Good Classification? What is the single organizing principle of this classification?

Main Point in Classification

The main point in classification uses a single organizing principle to sort items in a way that serves a purpose. The categories help a writer achieve his purpose.

To identify or draft an organizing principle for a classification assignment, complete one of the following sentences:

The writer's purpose for classifying this topic is to explain that . . .

I can best explain my topic for my readers by sorting according to _____.

In classification, the main point may or may not state the organizing principle directly. Look at the following examples:

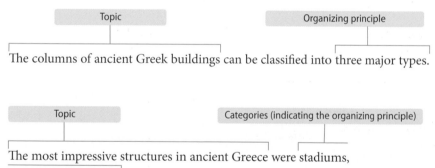

In both of these examples, the organizing principle is the type of things—columns in the first case and buildings in the second. In the second example, the words "type of building" are not stated directly. Instead, the categories themselves—stadiums, theaters, and temples—make the organizing principle clear.

The first sentence is the topic sentence for the paragraph that appears on page 190. The second example is the thesis statement for the essay on page 191. The thesis is broader than the topic sentence: the latter focuses on just one part of Greek buildings (the columns), while the thesis considers the entire structure.

Make sure that the categories in your classification serve your purpose. In the thesis statement on page 191, the categories serve the purpose of presenting the impressive structures in ancient Greece.

> **PRACTICE 1**   **Identify Main Parts of a Classification Paragraph**
>
> Sometimes it helps to think of classification in terms of a graph or chart. The chart below shows the major parts of the classification paragraph on page 184. Following this example, complete the blank chart to show the main parts of the student classification by Lorenza Mattazi on page 194.

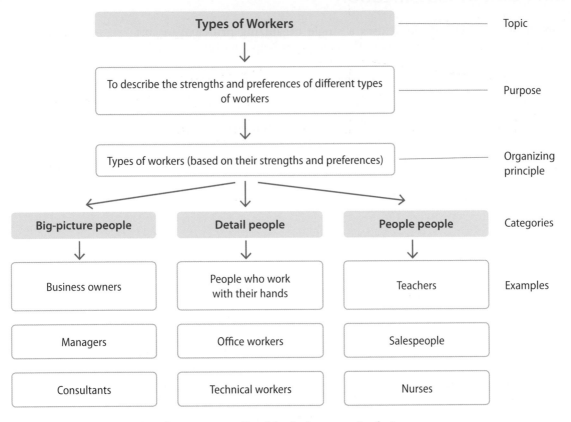

See the corresponding blank chart on the facing page.

Support and Details in Classification

The paragraph and essay models on pages 190–191 use the topic sentence (paragraph) and thesis statement (essay) from the Main Point in Classification section of this chapter. Both models include the **support** used in all classification writing: categories backed up by explanations or examples of each category. In the essay model, however, the major support points (categories) are topic sentences for individual paragraphs.

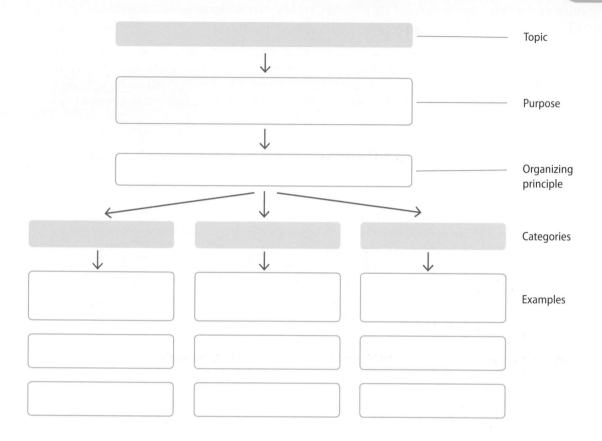

Topic

Purpose

Organizing
principle

Categories

Examples

The main supporting details in classification are the categories that the writer sets up. Within each category, the writer may choose different ways to provide secondary support. In the essay on page 191, for example, the major supporting details are stadiums, theaters, and temples, and the writer has chosen to use a **description** of each type of structure as secondary support. A writer may also choose to **define** each category or **illustrate** each category with examples. Description, illustration, and definition (see the workbook section of this chapter) are all strategies for providing supporting details for the categories in a classification paragraph or essay.

PRACTICE 2   **Identify Support and Details in Classification**

Look back at the sample paragraph at the beginning of this chapter (pp. 184–185). Which strategy or strategies does the writer use to give details about each category? Explain.

☐ Description   ☐ Definition   ☐ Illustration (example)

Paragraphs vs. Essays in Classification

For more on the important features of classification, see the Four Basics of Good Classification on page 184.

Paragraph Form

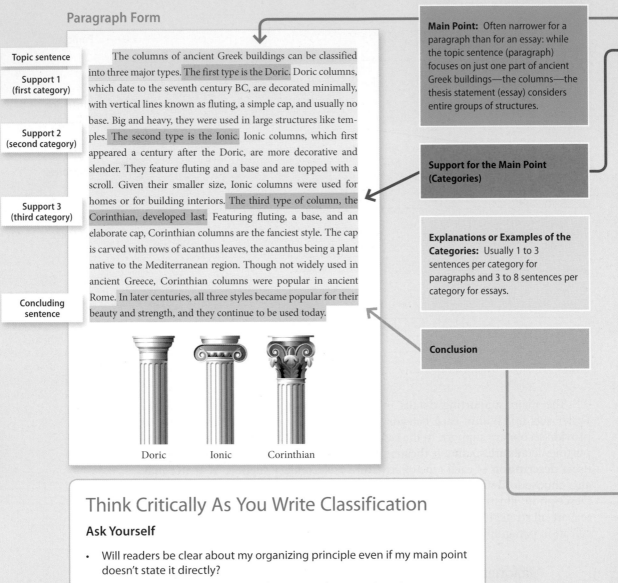

Topic sentence

Support 1 (first category)

Support 2 (second category)

Support 3 (third category)

Concluding sentence

The columns of ancient Greek buildings can be classified into three major types. The first type is the Doric. Doric columns, which date to the seventh century BC, are decorated minimally, with vertical lines known as fluting, a simple cap, and usually no base. Big and heavy, they were used in large structures like temples. The second type is the Ionic. Ionic columns, which first appeared a century after the Doric, are more decorative and slender. They feature fluting and a base and are topped with a scroll. Given their smaller size, Ionic columns were used for homes or for building interiors. The third type of column, the Corinthian, developed last. Featuring fluting, a base, and an elaborate cap, Corinthian columns are the fanciest style. The cap is carved with rows of acanthus leaves, the acanthus being a plant native to the Mediterranean region. Though not widely used in ancient Greece, Corinthian columns were popular in ancient Rome. In later centuries, all three styles became popular for their beauty and strength, and they continue to be used today.

Doric   Ionic   Corinthian

Main Point: Often narrower for a paragraph than for an essay: while the topic sentence (paragraph) focuses on just one part of ancient Greek buildings—the columns—the thesis statement (essay) considers entire groups of structures.

Support for the Main Point (Categories)

Explanations or Examples of the Categories: Usually 1 to 3 sentences per category for paragraphs and 3 to 8 sentences per category for essays.

Conclusion

Think Critically As You Write Classification

Ask Yourself

- Will readers be clear about my organizing principle even if my main point doesn't state it directly?

- Do the categories that make up the support for my main point go with my organizing principle? If not, does it make sense to rethink the categories, the organizing principle, or both?

- Are all the explanations or examples for each category relevant?

190

1

Ancient Greek civilization produced a wealth of architectural wonders that were both bea[utiful and] lasting. The most impressive structures were stadiums, theaters, and temples.

Thesis statement

The stadiums were designed to hold thousands of spectators. These open-air spaces were set int[o hillsides] so that the seating, often stone benches, wou[ld rise] from the central space, giving all spectators a decent view. One of the most famous stadiums, built in Delphi in the fifth century BC, seated audiences of about 7,000 people. Many stadiums featured ornamental details such as dramatic arches, and some of the more sophisticated examples included heated bathhouses with heated floors. Most often, the stadiums hosted sporting events, such as foot races. A common racin[g event] was the "stade," equaling one length of the st[adium.]

Topic sentence 1 (first category)

Another type of structure, the theater, was also a popular public gathering place. Like stadiums, the theaters were open-air sites that were set into hillsides. But instead of sports, they featured plays, musical performances, poetry readings, and other cultural events. In the typical Greek theater, a central performance area

Topic sentence 2 (second category)

2

was surrounded by semicircular seating, which was often broken into different sections. Wooden, and later stone, stages were set up in the central area, and in front of the stage was a space used for singing and dancing. This space was known as the "orchestra." Among the most famous ancient Greek theaters is the one at Epidaurus, built in the fourth century BC and seating up to 14,000 people. Performances still take place there.

The most beautiful structures were the te[mples,] with their grand entrances and large open [spaces.] Temples were rectangular in shape, and their outer walls as well as some interior spaces were supported by columns. Their main structures were typically made of limestone or marble, while their roofs might be constructed of terra-cotta or marble tiles. Temples were created to serve as "homes" for particular gods or goddesses, who were represented by statues. People left food or other offerings to these gods or goddesses to stay in their good graces, and communities often held festivals and other celebrations in their honor. Temples tended to be built in either the Doric or the Ionic style, with Doric temples featuring simple, heavy columns

Topic sentence 3 (third category)

3

and Ionic temples featuring slightly more ornate columns. The most famous temple, in the Doric style, is the Parthenon in Athens.

Turning to the present day, many modern stadiums, theaters, and columned civic buildings show the influence of ancient Greek buildings. Recognizing the lasting strength and beauty of these old structures, architects and designers continue to return to them for inspiration. I predict that this inspiration will last at least a thousand more years.

Concluding paragraph

191

PRACTICE 3   **Create Support and Details in Classification**

In the items that follow, you are given a topic and a purpose for sorting. Choose three categories that fit your purpose, and then add at least one detail (a definition, an example, or a description) for each category.

1. Topic: Movies

   Purpose: To choose what to see with the family

   Category: _____

       Detail: _____

   Category: _____

       Detail: _____

   Category: _____

       Detail: _____

2. Topic: College courses

   Purpose: To choose classes for the next term

   Category: _____

       Detail: _____

   Category: _____

       Detail: _____

   Category: _____

       Detail: _____

3. Topic: Items on my laptop (or phone or flash drive)

   Purpose: To organize my devices and delete things I don't need

   Category: _____

       Detail: _____

   Category: _____

       Detail: _____

   Category: _____

       Detail: _____

Organization in Classification

Classification can be organized in different ways (**time order**, **space order**, or **order of importance**) depending on its purpose.

Purpose	Likely Organization
to explain changes or events over time	time
to describe the arrangement of people/items in physical space	space
to discuss parts of an issue or problem, or types of people or things	importance

Order of importance is used in the essay model on page 191.

As you write your classification, use **transitions** to move your readers smoothly from one category to another.

Common Transitions in Classification

Adjective + Noun	Conjunctive Adverbials
one kind	first, second, next, etc.
another type	for example
the next category	for instance
the final/last type	

For more information on using and punctuating transitions, see Chapters 17 and 24.

PRACTICE 4   Use Transitions in Classification

Read the paragraph that follows and fill in the blanks with transitions. You are not limited to the ones listed in the preceding box.

Every day, I get three kinds of e-mail: work, personal, and junk. The _____ of e-mail, work, I have to read carefully and promptly. Sometimes, the messages are important ones directed to me, but mostly they are group messages about meetings, policies, or procedures. _____ _____, it seems as if the procedure for leaving the building during a fire alarm is always changing. _____ _____ of e-mail, personal, is from friends or my mother. These I read when I get a chance, but I read them quickly and delete any that are jokes or messages that have to be sent to ten friends for good luck. _____

_____ of e-mail is the most common and most annoying: junk. I get at least thirty junk e-mails a day, advertising all kinds of things that I do not want, such as life insurance or baby products. Even when I reply asking that the company stop sending me these messages, they keep coming. Sometimes, I wish e-mail did not exist.

Read and Analyze Classification

Student Classification Paragraph: "All My Music," Lorenza Mattazi

| **Preview** | Read | Review | Reflect and Respond |

- What do you expect to read, based on the title?
- What is your guiding question for reading this paragraph?

| Preview | **Read** | Review | Reflect and Respond |

Guidelines for Reading and Annotating Classification

Read and annotate this paragraph using these guidelines:

1. Pay attention to vocabulary using marginal notes, context clues, or a dictionary.
2. Find the main point and underline it. Remember that the main point shows the writer's purpose for classifying the topic.
3. Identify supporting details and organizational strategies. Number each category and note the examples in each. If the writer has included definitions of the categories, put an asterisk (*) by each one.
4. Ask questions and make connections. Remember to connect the categories to your own experiences and other things you have read.

Lorenza Mattazi

All My Music

1   From the time I was young, I have always loved music, all kinds of music. My first experience of music was the opera that both of my parents always had playing in our house. I learned to understand the drama and emotion of operas. My parents both spoke Italian, and they told me the stories of the operas and translated the words sung in Italian to English so that I could understand. Because hearing opera made my parents happy, and they taught me about it, I loved it, too. Many of my friends

think I am weird when I say I love opera, but to me it is very emotional and beautiful. When I was in my early teens, I found rock music and listened to it no matter what I was doing. I like music with words that tell a story that I can relate to. In that way, rock can be like opera, with stories that everyone can relate to, about love, heartbreak, happiness, and pain. The best rock has powerful guitars and bass, and a good, strong drumbeat. I love it when I can feel the bass in my chest. Rock has good energy and power. Now, I love rap music, too, not the rap with words that are violent or disrespectful of women, but the rest. The words are poetry, and the energy is so high that I feel as if I just have to move my body to the beat. That rhythm is so steady. I have even written some rap, which my friends say is really good. Maybe I will try to get it published, even on something like Helium, or I could start a blog. I will always love music because it is a good way to communicate feelings and stories, and it makes people feel good.

Preview	Read	**Review**	Reflect and Respond

Review your reading. Make sure you can answer these questions:

1. What is Mattazi's main point?
2. What are the major categories in the paragraph?
3. Does the paragraph illustrate the Four Basics of Good Classification? Explain.

Preview	Read	Review	**Reflect and Respond**

1. Which strategy or strategies from among description, illustration, and definition does Mattazi use to develop the secondary details in the paragraph?
2. Would the paragraph be more effective with different details (names of specific composers, artists, operas, or songs)? Explain.
3. Mattazi finds that music communicates stories and emotion. What besides story and emotion can draw you to certain styles of music? Explain.

Student Classification Essay: "Birth Order," Beth Trimmer

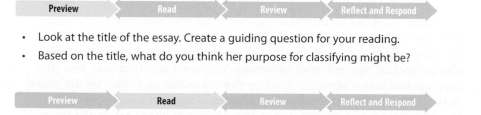

Preview	Read	Review	Reflect and Respond

- Look at the title of the essay. Create a guiding question for your reading.
- Based on the title, what do you think her purpose for classifying might be?

Preview	**Read**	Review	Reflect and Respond

Read and annotate this essay using the Guidelines for Reading and Annotating Classification on page 194.

Beth Trimmer

Birth Order

1   Birth order is one way to gain an understanding of friends, family members, co-workers, and others. Birth order has an effect on personality, though it does not explain everything about human behavior and personality. A person's character is also affected by factors such as heritage[1], upbringing, family size, education, religion, and geographic location, among others. Birth order is not a precise or exact science, but it does give a fascinating possible explanation for why people are the way they are. A family with three children can illustrate some typical characteristics of the firstborn, middle, and youngest child.

2   Firstborn children are the perfectionists. Firstborns may be more highly motivated to achieve than their younger siblings and may be drawn to professions that attract many high achievers, such as medicine, law, or science. The firstborn child is usually the one who has the most family attention given to him or her, if only because for a while there are no other children. Firstborns often exhibit precision, powerful concentration, and mental discipline. They are also typically reliable, well organized, cooperative, assertive, energetic, logical, and ambitious. They are natural leaders and people-pleasers. The firstborn child often feels more family pressure to behave well, and may experience more parental discipline. In school, firstborn children are more likely to participate in class and to achieve high grades. They are also more likely to attend college than their younger siblings.

3   Next are the middle-born children, the mysterious middle, whose general characteristics are the most diverse and contradictory of all birth orders. Some middle children are loners: quiet, shy, impatient, and tightly wound. Others, however, are outgoing, friendly, and gregarious[2]. Most are attention-seeking, competitive, rebellious, and peacemaking. In families, middle children are the ones who can get lost and feel misunderstood or overlooked in favor of older or younger siblings. Middle children are competitive mainly with other siblings, especially the older ones, who seem to them to get more attention. Sometimes, middle children feel that life is unfair.

4   Finally comes the youngest child, the baby, who often gets lots of attention. They are often charming and a bit manipulative[3], as well as affectionate, uncomplicated, and sometimes a bit absent-minded. They are more carefree than their older siblings and, though charming, can also be critical, spoiled, and impatient. Youngest children may feel that they are not taken seriously, first by their families and then by the world at large. Some negative traits may be immaturity and secretiveness. More positive traits, in addition to those already cited, can make them

1. **Heritage:** the traditions, achievements, beliefs, etc., that are part of the history of a group or nation

2. **Gregarious:** enjoying the company of other people

3. **Manipulative:** to change by artful or unfair means so as to serve one's purpose

risk-takers, idealists[4], humorous, and hardworking. Popular fields for youngest children are journalism, advertising, the arts, and sales.

5   The types of birth orders and their characteristics are general personality traits and may not apply to all children. Certainly, families are different, and many factors influence how children grow and develop. Birth order may help explain why children are the way they are, and what they have to do to prove they are unique. Birth order offers one way to understand people and, if nothing else, it is interesting to consider and compare traits with other people.

4. **Idealist:** a person that places ideals before practical considerations

Preview > Read > **Review** > Reflect and Respond

Review your reading. Make sure you can answer these questions:

1. What is the answer to your guiding question?

2. Can you identify the main point of this essay?

3. Write to Improve Reading: Using your annotations, write a summary of the essay. Make sure that the summary captures the main point and the major supporting ideas in your own words. Use strong descriptive verbs in each sentence (see p. 94).

Preview > Read > Review > **Reflect and Respond**

1. What strategies does Trimmer use to develop each of her categories? Do you think she provides enough information in each category? Explain.

2. How does Trimmer move from one category to the next? What transitions does she use?

3. Do any of the descriptions in her categories seem contradictory? Explain.

4. Trimmer suggests that birth order cannot explain all of a child's behavior and personality. What other factors might influence a child's personality and social habits?

Reading/Writing Workbook: Classification

Professional Essay: "The Ways We Lie," Stephanie Ericsson

Preview

1. Skim the key features of this essay (title and subheadings). What features of a good classification can you see before you begin to read?

2. Consider your experience with lies and deception. When have you told a lie? To whom did you tell it, and why? What was the outcome?

3. Build Vocabulary: In studying classification, you have learned that an organizing principle is essential to making sense of something through categories. Classifying vocabulary is an excellent strategy for learning that vocabulary more effectively. You can classify new vocabulary according to:

   • parts of speech (noun, verb, adjective, adverb)

   • connotation (positive, negative, neutral)

   • subject matter (science, literature, history, psychology)

   • level of formality (academic, formal, informal, slang)

   • workplace association (mechanics, real estate, hospital, church)

4. Skim the vocabulary notes with this essay. What organizing principle could help you make sense of these vocabulary words? Why?

Read and annotate the essay carefully, using the Guidelines for Reading and Annotating Classification on page 194. Remember to underline and paraphrase the stated main idea (if there is one), circle key transition words and phrases, and ask questions or make connections as you read.

Stephanie Ericsson

The Ways We Lie

Stephanie Ericsson was born in 1953 and raised in San Francisco. She has lived in a variety of places, including New York, Los Angeles, London, Mexico, the Spanish island of Ibiza, and Minnesota, where she currently resides. Ericsson's life took a major turn when her husband died suddenly when she was two months pregnant. She began a journal to help her cope with the grief and loss, and she later used her writing to help others with similar struggles. An excerpt from her journal appeared in the *Utne Reader,* and her writings were later published in a book titled *Companion through the Darkness: Inner Dialogues on Grief* (1993). About her book, Ericsson writes, "It belongs to those who have had the blinders ripped from their eyes, who suddenly see the lies of our lives and the truths of existence for what they are."

In "The Ways We Lie," which also appeared in the *Utne Reader* and is taken from her follow-up work, *Companion into the Dawn: Inner Dialogues on Loving* (1994), Ericsson continues her search for truth by examining and classifying our daily lies.

1   The bank called today, and I told them my deposit was in the mail, even though I hadn't written a check yet. It'd been a rough day. The baby I'm pregnant with decided to do aerobics on my lungs for two hours, our three-year-old daughter painted the living-room couch with lipstick, the IRS put me on hold for an hour, and I was late to a business meeting because I was tired.

2   I told my client that the traffic had been bad. When my partner came home, his haggard[1] face told me his day hadn't gone any better than mine, so

1. **Haggard:** drawn, worn out

when he asked, "How was your day?" I said, "Oh, fine," knowing that one more straw might break his back. A friend called and wanted to take me to lunch. I said I was busy. Four lies in the course of a day, none of which I felt the least bit guilty about.

3   We lie. We all do. We exaggerate, we minimize[2], we avoid confrontation[3], we spare people's feelings, we conveniently forget, we keep secrets, we justify lying to the big-guy institutions. Like most people, I indulge[4] in small falsehoods and still think of myself as an honest person. Sure I lie, but it doesn't hurt anything. Or does it?

4   I once tried going a whole week without telling a lie, and it was paralyzing. I discovered that telling the truth all the time is nearly impossible. It means living with some serious consequences: The bank charges me $60 in overdraft fees, my partner keels over[5] when I tell him about my travails[6], my client fires me for telling her I didn't feel like being on time, and my friend takes it personally when I say I'm not hungry. There must be some merit to lying.

5   But if I justify lying, what makes me any different from slick politicians or the corporate robbers who raided the S&L industry? Saying it's OK to lie one way and not another is hedging[7]. I cannot seem to escape the voice deep inside me that tells me: When someone lies, someone loses.

6   What far-reaching consequences will I, or others, pay as a result of my lie? Will someone's trust be destroyed? Will someone else pay *my* penance[8] because I ducked out? We must consider the *meaning of our actions.* Deception, lies, capital crimes, and misdemeanors[9] all carry meanings. *Webster's* definition of *lie* is specific:

1.   a false statement or action especially made with the intent to deceive;
2.   anything that gives or is meant to give a false impression.

7   A definition like this implies that there are many, many ways to tell a lie. Here are just a few.

The White Lie

8   The white lie assumes that the truth will cause more damage than a simple, harmless untruth. Telling a friend he looks great when he looks like hell can be based on a decision that the friend needs a compliment more than a frank[10] opinion. But, in effect, it is the liar deciding what is best for the lied to. Ultimately, it is a vote of no confidence. It is an act of subtle arrogance[11] for anyone to decide what is best for someone else.

9   Yet not all circumstances are quite so cut and dried. Take, for instance, the sergeant in Vietnam who knew one of his men was killed in action but listed

---

2. **Minimize:** to reduce
3. **Confrontation:** an argumentative meeting
4. **Indulge:** to become involved in

5. **Keels over:** falls over
6. **Travails:** painful efforts; tribulations

7. **Hedging:** avoiding the question

8. **Penance:** a penalty to make up for an action
9. **Misdemeanors:** minor violations of rules

10. **Frank:** honest; direct
11. **Arrogance:** belief in one's superiority

him as missing so that the man's family would receive indefinite compensation instead of the lump-sum pittance[12] the military gives widows and children. His intent was honorable. Yet for twenty years this family kept their hopes alive, unable to move on to a new life.

Facades

10   We all put up facades[13] to one degree or another. When I put on a suit to go to see a client, I feel as though I am putting on another face, obeying the expectation that serious businesspeople wear suits rather than sweatpants. But I'm a writer. Normally, I get up, get the kid off to school, and sit at my computer in my pajamas until four in the afternoon. When I answer the phone, the caller thinks I'm wearing a suit (although the UPS man knows better).

11   But facades can be destructive because they are used to seduce others into an illusion. For instance, I recently realized that a former friend was a liar. He presented himself with all the right looks and the right words and offered lots of new consciousness theories, fabulous books to read, and fascinating insights. Then I did some business with him, and the time came for him to pay me. He turned out to be all talk and no walk. I heard a plethora[14] of reasonable excuses, including in-depth descriptions of the big break around the corner. In six months of work, I saw less than a hundred bucks. When I confronted him, he raised both eyebrows and tried to convince me that I'd heard him wrong, that he'd made no commitment to me. A simple investigation into his past revealed a crowded graveyard of disenchanted former friends.

Ignoring the Plain Facts

12   In the sixties, the Catholic Church in Massachusetts began hearing complaints that Father James Porter was sexually molesting children. Rather than relieving him of his duties, the ecclesiastical[15] authorities simply moved him from one parish to another between 1960 and 1967, actually providing him with a fresh supply of unsuspecting families and innocent children to abuse. After treatment in 1967 for pedophilia[16], he went back to work, this time in Minnesota. The new diocese[17] was aware of Father Porter's obsession with children, but they needed priests and recklessly believed treatment had cured him. More children were abused until he was relieved of his duties a year later. By his own admission, Porter may have abused as many as a hundred children.

13   Ignoring the facts may not in and of itself be a form of lying, but consider the context[18] of this situation. If a lie is *a false action done with the intent to deceive*, then the Catholic Church's conscious covering for Porter created irreparable consequences. The church became a coperpetrator[19] with Porter.

12. **Pittance:** a small amount

13. **Facades:** masks

14. **Plethora:** excess

15. **Ecclesiastical:** relating to a church

16. **Pedophilia:** sexual abuse of children

17. **Diocese:** a district of churches under the guidance of a bishop

18. **Context:** surrounding situation

19. **Coperpetrator:** the helper of a person who commits an action

Stereotypes and Clichés

14   Stereotype and cliché serve a purpose as a form of shorthand. Our need for vast amounts of information in nanoseconds[20] has made the stereotype vital to modern communication. Unfortunately, it often shuts down original thinking, giving those hungry for truth a candy bar of misinformation instead of a balanced meal. The stereotype explains a situation with just enough truth to seem unquestionable.

15   All the *isms*—racism, sexism, ageism, et al.—are founded on and fueled by the stereotype and the cliché, which are lies of exaggeration, omission, and ignorance. They are always dangerous. They take a single tree and make it a landscape. They destroy curiosity. They close minds and separate people. The single mother on welfare is assumed to be cheating. Any black male could tell you how much of his identity is obliterated[21] daily by stereotypes. Fat people, ugly people, beautiful people, old people, large-breasted women, short men, the mentally ill, and the homeless all could tell you how much more they are like us than we want to think. I once admitted to a group of people that I had a mouth like a truck driver. Much to my surprise, a man stood up and said, "I'm a truck driver, and I never cuss." Needless to say, I was humbled.

Out-and-Out Lies

16   Of all the ways to lie, I like this one the best, probably because I get tired of trying to figure out the real meanings behind things. At least I can trust the bald-faced lie. I once asked my five-year-old nephew, "Who broke the fence?" (I had seen him do it.) He answered, "The murderers." Who could argue?

17   At least when this sort of lie is told it can be easily confronted. As the person who is lied to, I know where I stand. The bald-faced lie doesn't toy with my perceptions—it argues with them. It doesn't try to refashion reality; it tries to refute[22] it. *Read my lips* . . . No sleight[23] of hand. No guessing. If this were the only form of lying, there would be no such thing as floating anxiety or the adult-children of alcoholics movement.

18   These are only a few of the ways we lie. Or are lied to. As I said earlier, it's not easy to entirely eliminate lies from our lives. No matter how pious[24] we may try to be, we will still embellish[25], hedge, and omit to lubricate the daily machinery of living. But there is a world of difference between telling functional lies and living a lie. Martin Buber once said, "The lie is the spirit committing treason against itself." Our acceptance of lies becomes a cultural cancer that eventually shrouds[26] and reorders reality until moral garbage becomes as invisible to us as water is to a fish.

20. **Nanoseconds:** billionths of a second

21. **Obliterated:** wiped out

22. **Refute:** to deny
23. **Sleight:** a skillful trick

24. **Pious:** religious
25. **Embellish:** to decorate

26. **Shrouds:** covers; conceals

19   How much do we tolerate before we become sick and tired of being sick and tired? When will we stand up and declare our *right* to trust? When do we stop accepting that the real truth is in the fine print? Whose lips do we read this year when we vote for president? When will we stop being so reticent[27] about making judgments? When do we stop turning over our personal power and responsibility to liars?

20   Maybe if I don't tell the bank the check's in the mail I'll be less tolerant of the lies told to me every day. A country song I once heard said it all for me: "You've got to stand for something or you'll fall for anything."

27. **Reticent:** reserved; silent; reluctant

CHECK COMPREHENSION

Make sure you can answer the following questions:

1. What are Ericsson's purpose and main idea?

2. What's the difference between telling a functional lie and living a lie?

3. What is the danger of a white lie?

4. How is racism (or sexism) a lie?

5. Why does the author like out-and-out lies?

MAKE INFERENCES

Would the author agree or disagree with the following statements? Explain your answer.

1. If the majority of people behave a certain way, then that behavior is acceptable.

2. If an idea or statement cannot be traced back to a specific individual, it isn't a lie.

3. If you fail to tell information that you know, you are lying.

WRITE TO IMPROVE READING Summarize

Use your answers to the preceding Check Comprehension questions, the guidelines from Chapter 6, and your annotations to write a summary of Ericsson's essay. Remember that your summary will include the main point and major supporting details, written in your own words.

Explore Grammar: Parallel Structure

In paragraph 3, Ericsson says, "We exaggerate, we minimize, we avoid confrontation, we spare people's feelings, we conveniently forget, we keep secrets, we justify lying to the big-guy institutions." What do the underlined phrases have in common? In a list, all the words must have the same grammatical structure. This is called **parallel structure**. In this case, each item in the list contains the subject "we" and a verb in the present tense.

For more information on parallel structure, see Chapter 23.

PRACTICE

Find at least two other sentences in Ericsson's essay that contain lists with parallel structure. What grammatical structure do the items in each list share?

Understand Strategies Used in Classification: Consistent Structure

Ericsson uses a consistent structure for each category of lie she presents: she develops the category and shows a problem or danger with this type of lie. Identify each of these elements in each section of her essay:

Type of Lie	Strategy for providing details: definition, description, illustration	The problem or danger with this lie
"The White Lie"		
"Facades"		
"Ignoring the Plain Facts"		
"Stereotypes and Clichés"		
"Out-and-Out Lies"		

PRACTICE   **P/Q Assignment**

Look carefully now at the final three paragraphs of the essay. Which sentence best captures her thesis? Paraphrase that thesis here: _____

_____

_____

Now think critically: How does the organization of each category support her thesis? Explain.

RESPOND IN WRITING

1. Ericsson uses a definition in her introduction (para. 6): "a false statement or action especially made with the intent to deceive." Using this definition of *lie*, answer the following questions: What is the difference between *being wrong or confused about something* and *lying*? Do you think all categories of lies as given by Ericsson meet this definition of lying from *Webster's Dictionary*? If not, explain your concerns.

2. Ericsson says, "Our acceptance of lies becomes a cultural cancer that eventually shrouds and reorders reality until moral garbage becomes as invisible to us as water is to a fish" (201). Review the context of this quote in paragraph 18. Discuss what it means with your classmates. Then, in a paragraph, paraphrase this quote without looking back at the original. Be sure to cite your paraphrase accurately. (See Chapter 6 for a review of paraphrasing.) Once you have written your paraphrase, complete the paragraph by providing your own response. Do you agree with Ericsson? Why or why not?

3. Ericsson says, "It is an act of subtle arrogance for anyone to decide what is best for someone else" (199). This quote comes from the category of "white lies." Reread this section carefully. Discuss what it means with your classmates. Then, in a paragraph, paraphrase this quote without looking back at the original. Be sure to cite your paraphrase accurately. Once you have written your paraphrase, complete your paragraph by providing your own response. Do you agree with Ericsson? Why or why not?

Professional Essay: "The Dog Ate My Flash Drive, and Other Tales of Woe," Carolyn Foster Segal

Preview

1. Skim the essay title, the category headings in bold, and the information about the author. What does Segal classify in this essay? What is her purpose? For whom did she write this essay?

2. Have you ever given a teacher an excuse for not doing or turning in your work? What was it? Was it honest? How did your teacher respond?

3. Create a guiding question for this essay.

Read and annotate the essay carefully, using the Guidelines for Reading and Annotating Classification on page 194.

Carolyn Foster Segal

The Dog Ate My Flash Drive, and Other Tales of Woe

Carolyn Foster Segal is Professor Emerita of English at Cedar Crest College in Pennsylvania and a lecturer at Muhlenberg College. This article originally appeared in the *Chronicle of Higher Education*.
PHOTO BY KATIE MCMUTRIE, COURTESY OF CAROLYN FOSTER SEGAL

1   Taped to the door of my office is a cartoon that features a cat explaining to his feline[1] teacher, "The dog ate my homework." It is intended as a gently humorous reminder to my students that I will not accept excuses for late work, and it, like the lengthy warning on my syllabus, has had absolutely no effect. With a show of energy and creativity that would be admirable if applied to the (missing) assignments in question, my students persist, week after week, semester after semester, year after year, in offering excuses about why their work is not ready. Those reasons fall into several broad categories: the family, the best friend, the evils of dorm life, the evils of technology, and the totally bizarre.

2   **The Family.** The death of the grandfather/grandmother is, of course, the grandmother of all excuses. What heartless teacher would dare to question a student's grief or veracity[2]? What heartless student would lie, wishing death on a revered family member, just to avoid a deadline? Creative students may win extra extensions (and days off) with a little careful planning and fuller plot development, as in the sequence of "My grandfather/grandmother is sick"; "Now my grandfather/grandmother is in the hospital"; and finally, "We could all see it coming—my grandfather/grandmother is dead."

3   Another favorite excuse is "the family emergency," which (always) goes like this: "There was an emergency at home, and I had to help my family." It's a lovely sentiment[3], one that conjures[4] up images of Louisa May Alcott's[5] little women rushing off with baskets of food and copies of *Pilgrim's Progress*, but I do not understand why anyone would turn to my most irresponsible students in times of trouble.

1. **Feline:** catlike

2. **Veracity:** truthfulness

3. **Sentiment:** expression of feeling
4. **Conjures:** summons or creates
5. **Louisa May Alcott:** nineteenth-century American author best known for her novel *Little Women*

4   **The Best Friend**. This heartwarming concern for others extends beyond the family to friends, as in, "My best friend was up all night and I had to (a) stay up with her in the dorm, (b) drive her to the hospital, or (c) drive to her college because (1) her boyfriend broke up with her, (2) she was throwing up blood [no one catches a cold anymore; everyone throws up blood], or (3) her grandfather/grandmother died."

6. **Adjunct:** part-time instructor

7. **Motifs:** patterns

5   At one private university where I worked as an adjunct[6], I heard an interesting spin that incorporated the motifs[7] of both best friend and dead relative: "My best friend's mother killed herself." One has to admire the cleverness here: A mysterious woman in the prime of her life has allegedly committed suicide, and no professor can prove otherwise! And I admit I was moved, until finally I had to point out to my students that it was amazing how the simple act of my assigning a topic for a paper seemed to drive large numbers of otherwise happy and healthy middle-aged women to their deaths. I was careful to make that point during an off week, during which no deaths were reported.

6   **The Evils of Dorm Life.** These stories are usually fairly predictable; almost always feature the evil roommate or hallmate, with my student in the role of the innocent victim; and can be summed up as follows: My roommate, who is a horrible person, likes to party, and I, who am a good person, cannot concentrate on my work when he or she is partying. Variations include stories about the two people next door who were running around and crying loudly last night because (a) one of them had boyfriend/girlfriend problems; (b) one of them was throwing up blood; or (c) someone, somewhere, died. A friend of mine in graduate school had a student who claimed that his roommate attacked him with a hammer. That, in fact, was a true story; it came out in court when the bad roommate was tried for killing his grandfather.

7   **The Evils of Technology.** The computer age has revolutionized the student story, inspiring almost as many new excuses as it has Internet businesses. Here are just a few electronically enhanced explanations:

> The computer wouldn't let me save my work.
>
> The printer wouldn't print.
>
> The printer wouldn't print this disk.
>
> The printer wouldn't give me time to proofread.
>
> The printer made a black line run through all my words, and I know you can't read this, but do you still want it, or wait, here, take my disk. File name? I don't know what you mean.
>
> I swear I attached it.
>
> It's my roommate's computer, and she usually helps me, but she had to go to the hospital because she was throwing up blood.

I did write to the newsgroup, but all my messages came back to me.

I just found out that all my other newsgroup messages came up under a different name. I just want you to know that its really me who wrote all those messages, you can tel which ones our mine because I didnt use the spelcheck! But it was yours truely :) Anyway, just in case you missed those messages or dont belief its my writing, I'll repeat what I sad: I thought the last movie we watched in clas was boring.

8   **The Totally Bizarre.** I call the first story "The Pennsylvania Chain Saw Episode." A commuter student called to explain why she had missed my morning class. She had gotten up early so that she would be wide awake for class. Having a bit of extra time, she walked outside to see her neighbor, who was cutting some wood. She called out to him, and he waved back to her with the saw. Wouldn't you know it, the safety catch wasn't on or was broken, and the blade flew right out of the saw and across his lawn and over her fence and across her yard and severed a tendon in her right hand. So she was calling me from the hospital, where she was waiting for surgery. Luckily, she reassured me, she had remembered to bring her paper and a stamped envelope (in a plastic bag, to avoid bloodstains) along with her in the ambulance, and a nurse was mailing everything to me even as we spoke.

9   That wasn't her first absence. In fact, this student had missed most of the class meetings, and I had already recommended that she withdraw from the course. Now I suggested again that it might be best if she dropped the class. I didn't harp on the absences (what if even some of this story were true?). I did mention that she would need time to recuperate and that making up so much missed work might be difficult. "Oh, no," she said, "I can't drop this course. I had been planning to go on to medical school and become a surgeon, but since I won't be able to operate because of my accident, I'll have to major in English, and this course is more important than ever to me." She did come to the next class, wearing—as evidence of her recent trauma—a bedraggled[8] Ace bandage on her left hand.

8. **Bedraggled:** messy; untidy

10   You may be thinking that nothing could top that excuse, but in fact I have one more story, provided by the same student, who sent me a letter to explain why her final assignment would be late. While recuperating from her surgery, she had begun corresponding on the Internet with a man who lived in Germany. After a one-week, whirlwind Web romance, they had agreed to meet in Rome, to rendezvous[9] (her phrase) at the papal[10] Easter Mass. Regrettably, the time of her flight made it impossible for her to attend class, but she trusted that I—just this once—would accept late work if the pope wrote a note.

9. **Rendezvous:** to meet

10. **Papal:** relating to the pope of the Roman Catholic Church

1. What are the five categories of excuses that Segal introduces?

2. Does Segal accept excuses for late work?

3. What is Segal's main point?

MAKE INFERENCES

Based on your reading of the essay, determine whether the following statements are true or false.

1. Segal believes that most of her students are telling the truth when they present an excuse for missed work.

2. Segal holds high expectations for her students.

3. Segal rejects most of the excuses she receives.

WRITE TO IMPROVE READING   **Summarize**

Using the guidelines from Chapter 6 and your annotations, write a summary of Segal's essay. Remember that your summary will include the main point and major supporting details, written in your own words.

Build Vocabulary: Tone

Look at the following quotations from the essay. Review the meaning of any words you are unsure of. Then, consider the choice of words that Segal has made. What is her tone (her attitude toward her topic)? What words or phrases in particular has she chosen that help communicate her tone? Are we as readers meant to take her words literally or as exaggerated for effect?

PRACTICE

1. What heartless teacher would dare to question a student's grief or veracity? What heartless student would lie, wishing death on a revered family member, just to avoid a deadline? (para. 2)

2. I do not understand why anyone would turn to my most irresponsible students in times of trouble. (para. 3)

3. It was amazing how the simple act of my assigning a topic for a paper seemed to drive large numbers of otherwise happy and healthy middle-aged women to their deaths. (para. 6)

Understand Strategies Used in Classification: A Thesis Statement That Establishes the Essay's Structure

Segal states her thesis directly at the end of the first paragraph. Look at the structure of that sentence:

> Those reasons fall into several broad categories: the family, the best friend, the evils of dorm life, the evils of technology, and the totally bizarre.

Segal uses a pattern that is common in classification. She begins with a general statement about the topic followed by a colon (:) and a list. Look carefully at her sentence:

1. Segal does not have to list the categories. She could have ended the sentence after the word "categories." (*Those reasons fall into several broad categories.*) This illustrates an important rule for using colons: always use a complete thought before a colon. If you have only part of a sentence at the beginning, you cannot use a colon.

   For more on colons, see Chapter 31.

2. The words in her list have the same grammatical structure; each one is a noun. We can tell that each category is a noun because of the word "the" in each one.

   For more on nouns, see Chapter 15.

3. The categories in her list are separated with commas.

PRACTICE

Look at the sample paragraphs and essays in this chapter. Can you find another topic sentence or thesis statement that uses Segal's pattern?

WRITE TO IMPROVE READING   Summarize

Segal's pattern can also be useful when writing a summary. For example, suppose you wanted to write a summary of Lorenza Mattazi's paragraph (pp. 194–195). You might begin your summary this way:

> In her paragraph entitled "All My Music," Lorenza Mattazi classifies three types of music that she loves: opera, rock, and rap.

1. Using Segal's pattern, write a one-sentence summary of Beth Trimmer's essay, "Birth Order."

2. Using Segal's pattern, write a one-sentence summary of Ericsson's essay, "The Ways We Lie."

1. Write a Paragraph: Can you think of a category that Segal has not included? Write a paragraph that defines and illustrates another category of excuses.

2. Write a Summary and Response Paragraph: Select one of Segal's categories, such as "The Totally Bizarre" or "The Family." Write a 1-to-2-sentence summary of this section of her essay. Then, to complete your paragraph, find at least two examples of excuses that fit this category by asking your classmates or friends. Explain the examples and show how they fit into Segal's category.

3. Segal does not define the word *excuse* in her essay. Draft a paragraph that introduces and defines *excuse*. Does your definition make sense with all of her categories? Why or why not?

Extend and Connect: Write Your Own Classification

1. Both Ericsson and Segal address dishonest behaviors. Another type of dishonesty is cheating. Write an essay in which you classify types of cheating, thinking about an audience of first-year students. What do those students need to know about the many types of cheating?

2. Do you think Segal's excuses might form another category of lies, or should they be included in one or more of the categories that Ericsson has already presented? Explain.

3. Working with your classmates, study different types of assignments given by instructors in different classes. What organizing principle (other than the classes themselves) could you use to classify the types of assignments students may be given in college? Write a classification essay that categorizes the types of assignments for the purpose of helping students understand how to be successful with each type.

CHECKLIST

Writing a Classification

Prewrite > Draft > Revise > Edit

NARROW AND EXPLORE YOUR TOPIC (see Chapter 2)

☐ Make the topic more specific.

☐ Use prewriting techniques to get ideas about your narrow topic.

Prewrite > Draft > Revise > Edit

DRAFT A TOPIC SENTENCE OR THESIS STATEMENT (see Chapter 4)

☐ State your topic and your organizing principle/categories.

SUPPORT YOUR POINT (see Chapter 4)

☐ Find definitions, descriptions, or examples for each category.

WRITE A FULL DRAFT (see Chapter 4)

☐ Make a plan that puts the categories in logical order.

☐ Include the topic sentence (paragraph), an introduction and a thesis (essay), and all the supporting categories, with details.

☐ Add a concluding sentence or concluding paragraph.

Prewrite > Draft > Revise > Edit

REVISE YOUR DRAFT (see Chapter 5)

☐ Make sure you have covered the Four Basics of Good Classification.

☐ Make sure your readers have all the information they need to clearly see the differences between categories.

☐ Make sure you have included transitions to move readers smoothly from one event to the next.

Prewrite > Draft > Revise > Edit

EDIT YOUR REVISED DRAFT (see Chapter 5)

☐ Correct mistakes in grammar, spelling, punctuation, and word usage.

☐ Make sure your document is formatted correctly.

11

Comparison and Contrast:
Texts That Show Similarity and Difference

Understand What Comparison and Contrast Are

Comparison is writing that shows the similarities among subjects—people, ideas, situations, or items; **contrast** shows the differences. In conversation, people often use the word *compare* to mean either compare or contrast, but as you work through this chapter, the terms will be separated.

Compare	=	Similarities

Contrast	=	Differences

Four Basics of Good Comparison and Contrast

1. It uses subjects that have enough in common to be compared/contrasted in a useful way.

2. It serves a purpose—to help readers make a decision, to help them understand the subjects, or to show your understanding of the subjects.

3. It presents several important, parallel points of comparison/contrast.

4. It arranges points in a logical order.

In the following paragraph, written for a biology course, the numbers and colors correspond to the Four Basics of Good Comparison and Contrast.

1 Although frogs and toads are closely related, **2** they differ in appearance, in habitat, and in behavior. **3** The first major difference is in the creatures' physical characteristics. Whereas most frogs have smooth, slimy skin that helps them move through water, toads tend to have rough, bumpy skin suited to drier surroundings. Also, whereas frogs have long, muscular hind legs that help them leap away from predators or toward food, most toads have shorter legs and, therefore, less ability to move quickly. Another physical characteristic of frogs and toads is their bulging eyes, which help them see in different directions. This ability is important, because neither creature can turn its head to look for food or spot a predator. However, frogs' eyes may protrude more than toads'. The second major difference between frogs and toads is their choice of habitat. Frogs tend to live in or near ponds, lakes, or other sources of water. In contrast, toads live mostly in drier areas, such as gardens, forests, and fields. But, like frogs, they lay their eggs in water. The third major difference between frogs and toads concerns their behavior. Whereas frogs may be active during the day or at night, most toads keep a low profile until nighttime. Some biologists believe that it is nature's way of making up for toads' inability to escape from danger as quickly as frogs can. At night, toads are less likely to be spotted by predators. Finally, although both frogs and toads tend to live by themselves, toads, unlike frogs, may form groups while they are hibernating. Both creatures can teach us a lot about how animals adapt to their environments, and studying them is a lot of fun.

4 Points arranged in logical order.

Many situations require you to understand similarities and differences.

College	In a pharmacy course, you compare and contrast the side effects of two drugs prescribed for the same illness.
Work	You are asked to contrast this year's sales with last year's.
Everyday life	At the supermarket, you contrast brands of the same food to decide which to buy.

In college, writing assignments may include the words *compare and contrast,* but they might also use phrases such as *discuss similarities and differences, how is X like* (or *unlike*) *Y?,* or *what do X and Y have in common?* Also, assignments may use only the word *compare.*

Comparison and Contrast in the Classroom: Reviewing for a Test

Paulo is taking an introductory biology class. He is reviewing for a test on the different macromolecules found in living things, which include proteins, carbohydrates, lipids, and nucleic acids. A friend who took the class in a previous semester gave Paulo some advice: prepare to compare and contrast carbohydrates and proteins.

Paulo was confused. Nothing in his notes mentioned comparisons or contrasts, and the textbook had only one paragraph about each type of macromolecule. Paulo began to think about what his friend said, and he remembered the Four Basics of Good Comparison and Contrast from his English class. Carbohydrates and proteins are important to living things, but they function in different ways. Paulo began to look for points of comparison and contrast—in other words, the areas in which the molecules are similar, and the areas in which they are different. As he skimmed each paragraph from the text, he saw one area of comparison (similarity) and three areas of contrast (difference).

Paulo organized his information into a chart:

Name of Macromolecule	Polymers	Monomers	Function	Synthesis and Digestion Reactions
Carbohydrates	1. Simple (i.e., sucrose) 2. Complex (i.e., starch)	Monosaccharides	Serve as energy source for cells Store energy in plants	Dehydration and hydrolysis
Proteins	1. Structural (i.e., tubulins) 2. Functional (i.e., enzymes)	Amino acids	Provide structure to the cell Catalyze chemical reactions	Dehydration and hydrolysis

By arranging his notes to show the points of difference between each type of molecule, Paulo felt confident he could answer his exam question: compare and contrast carbohydrates and proteins.

APPLY WHAT YOU HAVE LEARNED

1. Explore your textbook. In chapters 7 through 13 of this textbook, there are charts titled "Paragraph vs. Essays" (see page 218 in this chapter, for example). The abbreviation "vs." (for "versus") often indicates a comparison or contrast. Do these charts show similarities, differences, or both? Can you find another example of a comparison/contrast chart in this textbook?

2. Explore graphic organizers. Many textbooks use charts or diagrams, also called "graphic organizers," to illustrate concepts for students. Do

an Internet search to find examples of common graphic organizers used for comparison and contrast (such as T-diagrams or Venn diagrams). Then see if you can find examples of these graphic organizers in one of your textbooks. How can the graphic organizer help you understand the material more effectively? Explain.

Main Point in Comparison and Contrast

The main point in comparison and contrast should state the subjects being compared or contrasted, and it should reflect the writer's purpose: to help readers make a decision or understand the subjects better. To help you identify a main point, complete the following sentence:

The writer compared/contrasted these subjects to show that . . .

If you are writing a comparison/contrast, complete the following sentence to discover your main point:

I want my readers to _____ after reading my comparison/contrast.

Here is an example of a topic sentence for a paragraph:

Subjects + Main point = Topic sentence

Compared with conventional cars, hybrids show less mechanical wear over time.

[Purpose: to help readers understand mechanical differences between conventional cars and hybrids.]

Remember that the topic for an essay can be a little broader than one for a paragraph.

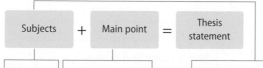

Subjects + Main point = Thesis statement

A hybrid car is a better choice than a conventional car, even one with low gas mileage.

[Purpose: to help readers decide which type of car to buy.]

Whereas the topic sentence focuses on the mechanical advantages of hybrid cars, the thesis statement sets up a broader discussion of these cars' benefits.

| PRACTICE 1 | Identify Parts of a Comparison and Contrast Main Point |

For each of the following topic sentences, identify the subjects and the main idea.

1. My two daughters have completely different personalities.

2. U.S. military involvement in Vietnam and Iraq shared several significant features.

3. Grocery stores in wealthy suburbs are much better than those in poor inner-city neighborhoods.

4. Wal-Mart and Target really are not that different in terms of merchandise quality, business practices, and effect on local economies.

Support in Comparison and Contrast

The paragraph and essay models on pages 218–219 use the topic sentence (paragraph) and thesis statement (essay) from the Main Point in Comparison and Contrast section in this chapter. Both models include the **support** used in all comparison and contrast writing: points of comparison/contrast backed up by details. In the essay model, however, the points of comparison/contrast are topic sentences for individual paragraphs.

The support in a comparison and contrast essay shows how the two subjects are the same or different. When you are reading a comparison and contrast essay, it may help you understand the support more effectively if you create a list with two columns, showing parallel points of comparison or contrast. Consider the chart below, based on the sample paragraph from page 213:

Frogs	Toads
Differences in Appearance	
Skin is smoother and slimier	Skin is rough and bumpy
Back legs are long and muscular	Legs are shorter
Frogs' eyes stick out	Toads' eyes don't stick out as far
Differences in Habitat	
Live in or near water	Live in drier areas (fields, forests, gardens)

Frogs	Toads
Differences in Behavior	
Active day and night	Active mainly at night
Live alone	Live alone but may get into a group during hibernation

PRACTICE 2   **Identify Support in a Comparison and Contrast Essay**

Use the essay on page 219 to create a chart showing the major differences between conventional cars and hybrid cars.

Hybrid Cars	Conventional Cars
Advantage 1:	
Details:	Details:
Advantage 2:	
Details:	Details:
Advantage 3:	
Details:	Details:

The same strategy (making a chart) can also be used to find support when you are prewriting for comparison/contrast. Here is one student's prewriting, based on the following topic sentence:

The two credit cards I am considering offer different financial terms.

Big Card	Mega Card
no annual fee	$35 annual fee
$1 fee per cash advance	$1.50 fee per cash advance
30 days before interest charges begin	25 days before interest charges begin
15.5% finance charge	17.9% finance charge

Paragraphs vs. Essays in Comparison and Contrast

For more on the important features of comparison and contrast, see the Four Basics of Good Comparison and Contrast on page 212.

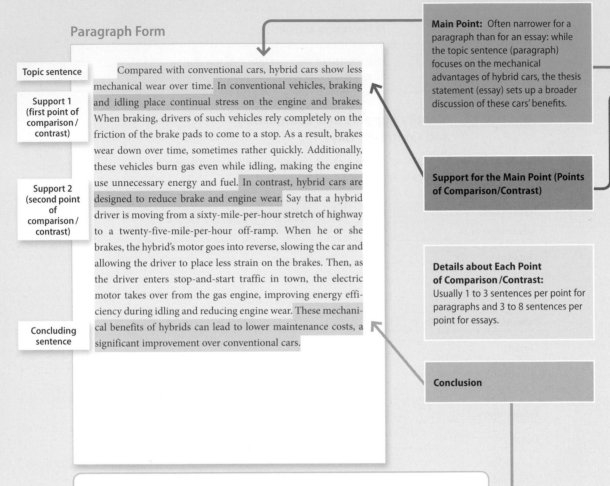

Paragraph Form

Topic sentence

Support 1 (first point of comparison / contrast)

Support 2 (second point of comparison / contrast)

Concluding sentence

Compared with conventional cars, hybrid cars show less mechanical wear over time. In conventional vehicles, braking and idling place continual stress on the engine and brakes. When braking, drivers of such vehicles rely completely on the friction of the brake pads to come to a stop. As a result, brakes wear down over time, sometimes rather quickly. Additionally, these vehicles burn gas even while idling, making the engine use unnecessary energy and fuel. In contrast, hybrid cars are designed to reduce brake and engine wear. Say that a hybrid driver is moving from a sixty-mile-per-hour stretch of highway to a twenty-five-mile-per-hour off-ramp. When he or she brakes, the hybrid's motor goes into reverse, slowing the car and allowing the driver to place less strain on the brakes. Then, as the driver enters stop-and-start traffic in town, the electric motor takes over from the gas engine, improving energy efficiency during idling and reducing engine wear. These mechanical benefits of hybrids can lead to lower maintenance costs, a significant improvement over conventional cars.

Main Point: Often narrower for a paragraph than for an essay: while the topic sentence (paragraph) focuses on the mechanical advantages of hybrid cars, the thesis statement (essay) sets up a broader discussion of these cars' benefits.

Support for the Main Point (Points of Comparison/Contrast)

Details about Each Point of Comparison /Contrast: Usually 1 to 3 sentences per point for paragraphs and 3 to 8 sentences per point for essays.

Conclusion

Think Critically As You Write Comparison and Contrast

Ask Yourself

- Have I provided all the information needed to fulfill my purpose: to help readers make a decision or to understand the subjects being compared or contrasted? (This information includes all the important similarities or differences between the subjects, as well as details about these similarities or differences.)
- If my information about similarities or differences feels "thin," might consulting outside sources help me find new details? (For more on finding and evaluating sources, see pp. 309–317.)

Essay Form

1

They are too expensive. For the last two years, while trying to keep my dying 1999 Che[vy] **Thesis statement** road, these words have popped into my head every time I have thought about purchasing a hybrid car. But now that I have done some research, I am finally convinced: A hybrid car is a better choice than a conventional car, even one with low gas mileage.

The first advantage of hybrid cars over conventional cars is that buyers can get tax breaks and other hybrid-specific benefits. Although federal [cred]its for hybrid purchasers expired in 201[ ], **Topic sentence 1 (first point of comparison/contrast)** states, including Colorado, Louisiana, [ ] and New Mexico, continue to offer such credits. Also, in Arizona, Florida, and several other states, hybrid drivers are allowed to use the less congested high-occupancy vehicle (HOV) lanes even if the driver is the only person on board. Additional benefits for hybrid drivers include longer warranties than those offered for conventional cars and, in some states and cities, rebates, reduced licensing fees, and free parking. None of these benefits are offered to drivers of conventional cars.

2

The second advantage of hybrid cars over conventional cars is that they save money over the long term. In addition to using less fuel, hybrid[s] less mechanical wear over time, reducing maint[enance] costs. When braking, drivers of conventional c[ars] completely on the friction of the brake pads to come to a stop. As a result, brakes wear down over time, sometimes rather quickly. Additionally, these vehicles burn gas even while idling, making the engine use un[neces]sary energy and fuel. In contrast, when hybrid [drivers] hit the brakes, the car's motor goes into reverse, [slow]ing the car and allowing the driver to place less strain on the brakes. Then, as the driver enters stop-and-start traffic in town, the electric motor takes over from the gas engine, improving energy efficiency during idling and reducing engine wear.

Topic sentence 2 (second point of comparison/contrast)

Topic sentence 3 (third point of comparison/contrast)

The most important benefit of hybrid cars over conventional cars is that they have a lower impact on the environment. Experts estimate that each gallon of gas burned by conventional motor vehicles produces 28 pounds of carbon dioxide (CO_2), a greenhouse gas that is a major contributor to global warming. Because

3

hybrid cars use about half as much gas as conventional vehicles, they reduce pollution and greenhouse gases by at least 50 percent. Some experts estimate that they reduce such emissions by as much as 80 percent. The National Resources Defense Council says that if hybrid vehicles are widely adopted, annual reductions in emissions could reach 450 million metric tons by the year 2050. This reduction would be equal to taking 82.5 million cars off the road.

Concluding paragraph

Although hybrid cars are more expensive than conventional cars, they are well worth it. From an economic standpoint, they save on fuel and maintenance costs. But, to me, the best reasons for buying a hybrid are ethical: By switching to such a vehicle, I will help reduce my toll on the environment. So goodbye, 1999 Chevy, and hello, Toyota Prius!

PRACTICE 3   **Find Points of Comparison or Contrast and Write Main Ideas**

Each of the following items lists some points of comparison or contrast. Fill in the blanks with additional points. Then, write a topic sentence for your list. The first one has been done for you.

Example: Contrast hair lengths

Long hair	**Short hair**
takes a long time to dry	dries quickly
can be worn a lot of ways	*only one way to wear it*
does not need to be cut often	needs to be cut every five weeks
gets tangled, needs brushing	*low maintenance*

Topic Sentence: *Short and long hairstyles offer different options for busy college students.*

1.   Contrast sports

Basketball	**Soccer**
baskets = points	goals = points
_____	ball is kicked
_____	_____

Topic Sentence: _____

_____

_____

2.   Compare sports

Basketball	**Soccer**
team sport	team sport
_____	_____
_____	_____

Topic Sentence: _____

_____

_____

Organization in Comparison and Contrast

Comparison/contrast can be organized in one of two ways: A **point-by-point** organization presents one point of comparison or contrast between the subjects and then moves to the next point. (See the essay model on p. 219.) A **whole-to-whole** organization presents all the points of comparison or contrast for one subject and then all the points for the next subject. (See the paragraph model on p. 218.) Consider which organization will best explain the similarities or differences to your readers. Whichever organization you choose, stay with it throughout your writing.

> **PRACTICE 4** **Recognize Patterns of Organization in Comparison and Contrast**

1. Is the sample paragraph about frogs and toads (p. 213) organized point-by-point or whole-to-whole? How do you know?

2. Is the sample student paragraph (p. 225) organized point-by-point or whole-to-whole? How do you know?

3. Is the paragraph on coffeehouses in Practice 6 (pp. 223–224) organized point-by-point or whole-to-whole? How do you know?

> **PRACTICE 5** **Organize Comparison and Contrast Essays**

The first outline that follows is for a comparison paper using a whole-to-whole organization. Reorganize the ideas and create a new outline (outline 2) using a point-by-point organization. The first blank in outline 2 has been filled in for you.

The third outline is for a contrast paper using a point-by-point organization. Reorganize the ideas and create a new outline (outline 4) using a whole-to-whole organization. The first blank in outline 4 has been filled in for you.

1. Comparison paper using whole-to-whole organization

   Main point: My daughter is a lot like I was at her age.

   a. Me

      Not interested in school

      Good at sports

      Hard on myself

   b. My daughter

      Does well in school but doesn't study much or do more than the minimum

      Plays in a different sport each season

      When she thinks she has made a mistake, she gets upset with herself

2. Comparison paper using point-by-point organization

   Main point: My daughter is a lot like I was at her age.

   a. Interest in school

   Me: _Not interested in school_ _____

   My daughter: _____

   b. _____

   Me: _____

   My daughter: _____

   c. _____

   Me: _____

   My daughter: _____

3. Contrast paper using point-by-point organization

   Main point: My new computer is a great improvement over my old one.

   a. Weight and portability

   New computer: _small and light_ _____

   Old computer: _heavy, not portable_ _____

   b. _Speed_ _____

   New computer: _fast_ _____

   Old computer: _slow_ _____

   c. _Cost_ _____

   New computer: _inexpensive_ _____

   Old computer: _expensive_ _____

4. Contrast paper using whole-to-whole organization

   Main point: My new computer is a great improvement over my old one.

   a. New computer

   small and light _____

   _____

   _____

   b. Old computer

   _____

   _____

   _____

Comparison/contrast is often organized by **order of importance**, meaning that the most important point is saved for last. This strategy is used in the essay model on page 219.

Transitions in comparison/contrast move readers from one subject to another and from one point of comparison or contrast to the next.

For more information on using and punctuating these transitions, see Chapters 17 and 24.

Common Transitions in Comparison and Contrast

	Adjective + Noun	Conjunctive Adverbials	Subordinating Conjunctions	Prepositions
Comparison	one similarity another similarity both subjects	similarly likewise in the same way	just as	like similar to
Contrast	one difference another difference the most important difference	on the other hand in contrast however	while although whereas	unlike different from

PRACTICE 6   **Use Transitions in Comparison and Contrast**

Read the paragraph that follows, and fill in the blanks with transitions. You are not limited to the ones listed in the preceding box.

Modern coffee shops share many similarities with the coffeehouses that opened hundreds of years ago in the Middle East and Europe. _____ is that the coffeehouses of history, like modern cafés, were popular places to socialize. In sixteenth-century Constantinople (now Istanbul, Turkey) and in seventeenth- and eighteenth-century London, customers shared stories, information, and opinions about current events, politics, and personal matters. The knowledge shared at London coffee-houses led customers to call these places "Penny Universities," a penny being the price of admission. _____ is that the old coffee-houses, like today's coffee shops, were often places of business. However, although most of today's coffee-shop customers work quietly on their laptops, customers of the old shops openly, and sometimes loudly, discussed business and sealed deals. In fact, for more than seventy years, traders for the London Stock Exchange operated out of coffeehouses.

_____ similarity between the old coffeehouses and modern coffee shops is that they both increased the demand for coffee and places to drink it. In 1652, a former servant from western Turkey opened the first coffeehouse in London. As a result of its popularity, many more coffeehouses soon sprouted up all over the city, and within a hundred years there were more than 500 coffeehouses in London. _____ , in recent years the popularity of Starbucks, and its shops, spread rapidly throughout the United States.

Read and Analyze Comparison and Contrast

Student Comparison/Contrast Paragraph: "Eyeglasses vs. Laser Surgery: Benefits and Drawbacks," Said Ibrahim

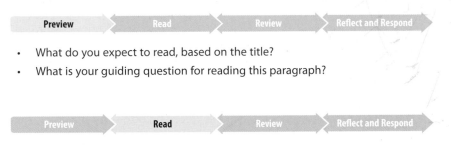

- What do you expect to read, based on the title?
- What is your guiding question for reading this paragraph?

Preview > **Read** > Review > Reflect and Respond

Guidelines for Reading and Annotating Comparison and Contrast

Read and annotate this paragraph using these guidelines:

1. Pay attention to vocabulary using marginal notes, context clues, or a dictionary.

2. Find the main point and underline it. Remember that the main point shows the writer's purpose for comparing or contrasting the two subjects. Try to identify the writer's purpose: is the author showing that one subject is better than the other, or is the writer trying to help the readers understand the subjects more fully?

3. Identify supporting details and organizational strategies. Number the points of comparison or contrast, circle the transitions, and determine whether the writer has organized the paragraph point-by-point or whole-to-whole.

4. Ask questions and make connections. Remember to connect the points of comparison/contrast to your own experiences and other things you have read.

Said Ibrahim

Eyeglasses vs. Laser Surgery: Benefits and Drawbacks

1   Although both eyeglasses and laser[1] surgery can address vision problems successfully, each approach has particular benefits and drawbacks. Whereas one pair of eyeglasses is reasonably[2] priced in comparison with laser surgery, eyeglass prescriptions often change over time, requiring regular lens replacements. As a result, over the wearer's lifetime, costs of eyeglasses can exceed $15,000. On the positive side, an accurate lens prescription results in clear vision with few or no side effects. Furthermore, glasses of just the right shape or color can be a great fashion accent. In contrast to eyeglasses, laser vision correction often has to be done only once. Consequently, although the costs average $2,500 per eye, the patient can save thousands of dollars over the following years. On the downside, some recipients of laser surgery report difficulties seeing at night, dry eyes, or infections. Fortunately, these problems are fairly rare. The final advantage of laser surgery applies to those who are happy to forgo[3] the fashion benefits of eyeglasses. Most laser-surgery patients no longer have to wear any glasses other than sunglasses until later in life. At that point, they may need reading glasses. All in all, we are fortunate to live in a time when there are many good options for vision correction. Choosing the right one is a matter of carefully weighing the pros and cons of each approach.

1. **Laser:** a concentrated beam of light; in this case it is used to reshape part of the eye

2. **Reasonably:** not excessively

3. **Forgo:** go without

| Preview | Read | Review | Reflect and Respond |

Review your reading. Make sure you can answer these questions:

1. What are Ibrahim's main point and purpose in this paragraph?
2. How has he organized the paragraph? How do you know?
3. Does the paragraph illustrate the Four Basics of Good Comparison and Contrast? Explain.

| Preview | Read | Review | Reflect and Respond |

1. What specific details help Ibrahim develop the points of contrast? Has he provided enough details to make the points of contrast clear to the reader? Explain.
2. Based on the reading, which of the two options for correcting vision would you be more likely to choose? Why?

Student Comparison/Contrast Essay: "A Whiff of Memory,"
Rui Dai

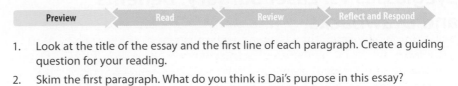

1. Look at the title of the essay and the first line of each paragraph. Create a guiding question for your reading.

2. Skim the first paragraph. What do you think is Dai's purpose in this essay?

3. Is there a smell that brings a memory to your mind?

Read and annotate this essay using the Guidelines for Reading and Annotating Comparison and Contrast on page 224.

Rui Dai

A Whiff of Memory

1. **Etiquette:** rules about how to behave

2. **Habituate to:** to get used to

3. **Idiosyncratic:** peculiar or unique to one place, individual, or thing

4. **Musk:** a strong scent

5. **Endogenous:** coming from within

1   There are many things that distinguish China's street etiquette[1] from the U.S. equivalent: For example, China forbids honking except in the most extreme cases. In the United States, there are no car horns to habituate to[2], nor are there so many people with so many voices. However, what is most distinctive about China is its smell.

2   Simply put, China smells different than America. It is a weird and completely overwhelming phenomenon that seems wholly inexplicable in scientific terms. How can one country smell different from another? China and the United States are both vast countries with obviously different, idiosyncratic[3] odors in separate regions of each. The American Northeast smells of the sea, and the Midwest, dry cornfields. What is so distinctive between the two that, without opening my eyes, I can tell which country is which? Let me explain. The smell of China carries a distinctive musk[4] that is the combination of age and non-ammonia cleaning supplies. America, on the other hand, smells clean—literally, and not necessarily in a good way. Cleaning detergents are used almost ubiquitously in America, while relatively rare in China. In the States, the complex chemical combinations in cleaning agents destroy almost any endogenous[5] smell of the environment, leaving only a hint of pine or lavender, or whatever oil extract the manufacturer had dropped into the mixture.

3   In every grocery store in America there is always an entire row of cleaning supplies, each with bottles of 409 or Scrubbing Bubbles lined neatly on steel shelves. In China, there are no comparable brands; there

is classic soap and there is liquid soap: no ammonia in sight. Such a difference in cleaning protocol[6] has a dramatic effect on the resulting odor of each country.

4   The reason why the difference in odor between the two countries is so distinctive and apparent is because olfaction[7] evokes strong emotional memories. Biologically, the olfactory system is one of the few senses in the human body that has a direct connection to the part of the brain that is in charge of emotional memories, the amygdala. The olfactory system's mitral cells and olfactory receptor neurons help send information about scents to the amygdala. This is the reason why the smell of cinnamon evokes more memories and emotions than just the sight of cinnamon. It also elicits memories of Christmas morning or the cinnamon rolls after a Thanksgiving dinner. In comparison, few other sensory faculties call to mind a similar distinctive memory. Hearing, for example, does not evoke as powerful memories as olfaction, or else, every single time we heard something we would be reliving the past.

5   To me, America smells like driving alone down a road really fast with the wind in your hair; it is freedom. China smells like getting breakfast with my grandmother at dawn in the street market just as it is beginning to bustle; it is nostalgia. As a Chinese American, it is always difficult to distinguish between which part of my heritage is which. I have always wondered what I would have been like if I stayed with my grandmother and had gotten breakfast with her everyday at the street market. Would I still be as argumentative as I am today? Or would I be more pliable?

6   The distinction between my identity as both Chinese and American is even harder now that I am on a service project in China. I alternate sporadically[8] as needed between my personalities as a Duke student and another Chinese pedestrian on the street. I converse normally with the rest of my service group as I would on Duke's campus, but the moment I turn to speak to a native or to translate something from English to Chinese, I become one of the more than 1.3 billion people who populate China.

7   Right now, the unique scent of China is correlated[9] with a set of childhood memories. Once in a while, under the influence of a particular familiar waft of odor, memories of my childhood will rush me back in time. But memory is malleable[10]. And soon, new memories will become associated with the scents of old, for better or for worse. I hope it will be for the better.

6. **Protocol:** a specific system for how to proceed

7. **Olfaction:** the act of smelling or the sense of smell

8. **Sporadically:** appearing or happening irregularly or occasionally

9. **Correlated:** closely connected

10. **Malleable:** flexible; easily changed

| Preview | Read | Review | Reflect and Respond |

Review your reading. Make sure you can answer these questions:

1. What is the answer to your guiding question?

2. Does Dai's main point address only the differences between China and the United States? Explain.

3. If you had to choose a different title for this essay, what would you choose?

4. Write to Improve Reading: Using your annotations, write a summary of the essay. Make sure that the summary captures the main point and the major supporting ideas in your own words. Use strong descriptive verbs in each sentence (see p. 94).

Preview > Read > Review > **Reflect and Respond**

1. Does the writer use point-by-point or whole-by-whole organization?

2. Make Inferences: Which smell does the author prefer, the smell of China or the smell of the United States?

3. Why is smell so closely connected to our memories? Why does the writer explain the biological reason for the power of smell?

4. The writer uses the contrasting smells of the United States and China to explain something about herself. What does she show her readers about her identity?

Reading/Writing Workbook: Comparison and Contrast

Professional Essay: "The Ugly Truth about Beauty," Dave Barry

Preview

1. Skim the title, the author information, and the first three paragraphs. What will be compared and contrasted in this essay?

2. What do you think the author's purpose might be?

3. In the first three paragraphs, Barry addresses his reader with second-person pronouns (*you*). To whom is he speaking? How do you know?

4. What is your guiding question for this reading?

Read and annotate this essay carefully, following the Guidelines for Reading and Annotating Comparison and Contrast on page 224.

Dave Barry

The Ugly Truth about Beauty

Born in 1947 in Armonk, New York, Dave Barry earned a B.A. from Haverford College. He then worked for several years as a newspaper reporter and a lecturer on business writing before discovering his talent as a humor columnist. The columns he wrote for the *Miami Herald* from 1983 to 2004 have been collected in numerous books. Barry's observations on American life won him the Pulitzer Prize for Commentary in 1988. In "The Ugly Truth about Beauty," first published in the *Miami Herald* in 1998, Barry compares and contrasts men's and women's beauty routines. The essay humorously highlights differences in the ways that men and women view themselves.

© WALTER MCBRIDE/CORBIS

1   If you're a man, at some point a woman will ask you how she looks.

2   "How do I look?" she'll ask.

3   You must be careful how you answer this question. The best technique is to form an honest yet sensitive opinion, then collapse on the floor with some kind of fatal seizure. Trust me, this is the easiest way out. Because you will never come up with the right answer.

4   The problem is that women generally do not think of their looks in the same way that men do. Most men form an opinion of how they look in the seventh grade, and they stick to it for the rest of their lives. Some men form the opinion that they are irresistible stud muffins, and they do not change this opinion even when their faces sag and their noses bloat to the size of eggplants and their eyebrows grow together to form what appears to be a giant forehead-dwelling tropical caterpillar.

5   Most men, I believe, think of themselves as average-looking. Men will think this even if their faces cause heart failure in cattle at a range of 300 yards. Being average does not bother them; average is fine for men. This is why men never ask anybody how they look. Their primary form of beauty care is to shave themselves, which is essentially the same form of beauty care that they give to their lawns. If, at the end of his four-minute daily beauty regimen[1], a man has managed to wipe most of the shaving cream out of his hair and is not bleeding too badly, he feels that he has done all he can, so he stops thinking about his appearance and devotes his mind to more critical issues, such as the Super Bowl.

1. **Regimen:** a routine

6   Women do not look at themselves this way. If I had to express, in three words, what most women think about their appearance, those words would be:

"not good enough." No matter how attractive a woman may appear to others, when she looks at herself in the mirror, she thinks, "woof." She thinks that at any moment a municipal animal-control officer is going to throw a net over her and haul her off to the shelter.

7   Why do women have such low self-esteem? There are many complex psychological and societal reasons, by which I mean "Barbie." Girls grow up playing with a doll proportioned such that, if it were human, it would be seven feet tall and weigh 81 pounds, of which 53 pounds would be bosoms. This is a difficult appearance standard to live up to, especially when you contrast it with the standard set for little boys by their dolls . . . excuse me, by their action figures. Most of the action figures that my son played with when he was little were hideous looking. For example, he was fond of an action figure (part of the He-Man series) called "Buzz-Off," who was part human, part flying insect. Buzz-Off was not a looker. But he was extremely self-confident. You could not imagine Buzz-Off saying to the other action figures, "Do you think these wings make my hips look big?"

8   But women grow up thinking they need to look like Barbie, which for most women is impossible, although there is a multibillion-dollar beauty industry devoted to convincing women that they must try. I once saw an Oprah show wherein supermodel Cindy Crawford dispensed makeup tips to the studio audience. Cindy had all these middle-aged women apply beauty products to their faces; she stressed how important it was to apply them in a certain way, using the tips of their fingers. All the women dutifully did this, even though it was obvious to any sane observer that no matter how carefully they applied these products, they would never look remotely like Cindy Crawford, who is some kind of genetic mutation.

9   I'm not saying that men are superior. I'm just saying that you're not going to get a group of middle-aged men to sit in a room and apply cosmetics to themselves under the instruction of Brad Pitt, in hopes of looking more like him. Men would realize that this task was pointless and demeaning[2]. They would find some way to bolster their self-esteem that did not require looking like Brad Pitt. They would say to Brad, "Oh YEAH? Well what do you know about LAWN CARE, pretty boy?"

2. **Demeaning:** degrading; lowering one's character

10   Of course many women will argue that the reason they become obsessed with trying to look like Cindy Crawford is that men, being as shallow as a drop of spit, WANT women to look that way. To which I have two responses:

1. Hey, just because WE'RE idiots, that does not mean YOU have to be; and
2. Men don't even notice 97 percent of the beauty efforts you make anyway. Take fingernails. The average woman spends 5,000 hours per year

worrying about her fingernails; I have never once, in more than 40 years of listening to men talk about women, heard a man say, "She has a nice set of fingernails!" Many men would not notice if a woman had upward of four hands.

11   Anyway, to get back to my original point: If you're a man, and a woman asks you how she looks, you're in big trouble. Obviously, you can't say she looks bad. But you also can't say that she looks great, because she'll think you're lying, because she has spent countless hours, with the help of the multibillion-dollar beauty industry, obsessing about the differences between herself and Cindy Crawford. Also, she suspects that you're not qualified to judge anybody's appearance. This is because you have shaving cream in your hair.

CHECK COMPREHENSION

1. What is Barry contrasting?

2. What are the points of contrast Barry presents?

3. How has he organized the essay?

4. In paragraphs 8 and 9, Barry uses different details to emphasize the differences between men and women. What are the specific examples used to make the point in those paragraphs?

MAKE INFERENCES

Would Barry agree or disagree with the following statements? Explain your answer.

1. Men and women have different emotional responses to most situations.

2. Toys help shape a child's perception of himself or herself.

3. Women shouldn't be so concerned with their looks.

WRITE TO IMPROVE READING   Summarize

Using the guidelines from Chapter 6 and your annotations, write a summary of Barry's essay. Remember that your summary will include the main point and major support (points of contrast), written in your own words.

Understand Strategies Used in Some Comparison and Contrast: A Tone of Comic Exaggeration

Tone is the attitude of the author toward the subject he is writing about. Tone also helps a reader know how to interpret what a writer says. It is important for a reader to understand a writer's tone. Writers have several techniques for creating tone, including word choice and **exaggeration**.

Dave Barry is known for writing with humor and exaggeration, even when the topic he addresses is serious. For example, in paragraph 3 of "The Ugly Truth about Beauty," Barry says that a man who is asked how a woman looks must form "an honest yet sensitive opinion, then collapse on the floor with some kind of fatal seizure." Obviously, Barry does not really expect his readers to resort to medical emergencies in response to a woman's question about her appearance. His exaggeration allows him to emphasize his point: because men and women think differently about their appearances, it is very difficult for a man to answer the question appropriately.

> **PRACTICE**   P/Q Assignment

> 1. Find two additional examples of humor in Barry's essay. Quote these examples (see Chapter 8, p. 152), and cite them appropriately. Use these quotations in a paragraph that answers this question: how does Barry use humor to help make his point?

> 2. Is Barry's representation of women (or men) fair and accurate? Find a **generalization** (general statement) that Barry makes about women (or men). Quote and cite that generalization accurately, and explain your response to it.

Know P/Q: Using Quotes inside Quotes

Look at the following quote from Barry's essay:

> No matter how attractive a woman may appear to others, when she looks at herself in the mirror, she thinks, "woof."

For more information on using quotation marks, see Chapter 30.

When the material you are quoting includes quotation marks, use single quotation marks where the original has double quotation marks, as in the following example:

> Barry says, "No matter how attractive a woman may appear to others, when she looks at herself in the mirror, she thinks, 'woof'" (229).

RESPOND IN WRITING

1. Barry addresses the differences between men and women in relation to physical appearance. What is another area in which men and women behave in different ways? Write an essay in which you explore these gender-based differences.

2. Choose a male (or female) role model, hero, or superstar from today and one from twenty-five years ago. Are the expectations similar or different? Compare and/or contrast the concept of role model then and now.

3. In paragraph 7, Barry emphasizes the differences between male and female approaches to beauty by focusing on toys. Write a paragraph or an essay in which you answer the following questions: Why does Barry focus on toys? Do his specific examples help him make his point? Why or why not? Would his point have worked as well if he had chosen a superhero action figure such as Captain America, Superman, or Spider-Man? Explain your answer.

Professional Essay: "The Myth of the Latin Woman: I Just Met a Girl Named Maria," Judith Ortiz Cofer

Preview

1. Skim the title, the author information, and the first three paragraphs. What will be compared and contrasted in this essay?

2. What do you think the author's purpose might be?

3. What kind of myths do you think Cofer refers to in the title? Explain.

4. Who do you think is the audience for this piece? (Hint: Think carefully about the title. To whom is Cofer speaking?)

5. What will be your guiding question for this reading?

Read and annotate this essay carefully, following the Guidelines for Reading and Annotating Comparison and Contrast on page 224.

Judith Ortiz Cofer

The Myth of the Latin Woman: I Just Met a Girl Named Maria

Judith Ortiz Cofer is a Puerto Rican author and the Regents' and Franklin Professor of English and Creative Writing at the University of Georgia, where she has taught since 1984. She earned a B.A. in English from Augusta College and an M.A. in English from Florida Atlantic University. In 2007, she was awarded an honorary doctorate in human letters from Lehman University in New York City. Cofer's works span across literary genres, including books of poetry, novels, autobiographical writing, and collections of short stories and essays. Her work has appeared in numerous literary journals, and it is often anthologized and included in textbooks.

1. **Tenor:** the highest range of the adult male voice

2. **Rendition:** a performance

3. **"Maria":** a song from *West Side Story* about one of the main Puerto Rican characters

4. **West Side Story:** a 1957 Broadway musical, made into a film in 1961

5. **Latina:** a female Latin American living in the United States

6. **Rita Moreno:** a Puerto Rican actress who played in *West Side Story*

7. **Microcosm:** a world in miniature

8. **Casas:** Spanish for "houses"

9. **Bodega:** Spanish for "small grocery store"

10. **Surveillance:** a watch kept over a person or group of people

11. **Flashy:** showy

1   On a bus to London from Oxford University, where I was earning some graduate credits one summer, a young man, obviously fresh from a pub, approached my seat. With both hands over his heart, he went down on his knees in the aisle and broke into an Irish tenor's[1] rendition[2] of "Maria"[3] from *West Side Story*[4]. I was not amused. "Maria" had followed me to London, reminding me of a prime fact of my life: You can leave the island of Puerto Rico, master the English language, and travel as far as you can, but if you're a Latina[5], especially one who so clearly belongs to Rita Moreno's[6] gene pool, the island travels with you.

2   Growing up in New Jersey and wanting most of all to belong, I lived in two completely different worlds. My parents designed our life as a microcosm[7] of their casas[8] on the island—we spoke Spanish, ate Puerto Rican food bought at the bodega[9], and practiced strict Catholicism complete with Sunday mass in Spanish.

3   I was kept under tight surveillance[10] by my parents, since my virtue and modesty were, by their cultural equation, the same as their honor. As teenagers, my friends and I were lectured constantly on how to behave as proper senoritas. But it was a conflicting message we received, since our Puerto Rican mothers also encouraged us to look and act like women by dressing us in clothes our Anglo schoolmates and their mothers found too "mature" and flashy[11]. I often felt humiliated when I appeared at an American friend's birthday party wearing a dress more suitable for a semiformal. At Puerto Rican festivities, neither the music nor the colors we wore could be too loud.

4   I remember Career Day in high school, when our teachers told us to come dressed as if for a job interview. That morning, I agonized[12] in front of my closet, trying to figure out what a "career girl" would wear, because the only model I had was Marlo Thomas[13] on TV. To me and my Puerto Rican girlfriends, dressing up meant wearing our mothers' ornate[14] jewelry and clothing.

5   At school that day, the teachers assailed[15] us for wearing "everything at once"—meaning too much jewelry and too many accessories. And it was painfully obvious that the other students in their tailored skirts and silk blouses thought we were hopeless and vulgar[16]. The way they looked at us was a taste of the cultural clash that awaited us in the real world, where prospective[17] employers and men on the street would often misinterpret our tight skirts and bright colors as a come-on[18].

6   It is custom, not chromosomes[19], that leads us to choose scarlet over pale pink. Our mothers had grown up on a tropical island where the natural environment was a riot of primary colors, where showing your skin was one way to keep cool as well as to look sexy. On the island, women felt free to dress and move provocatively[20] since they were protected by the traditions and laws of a Spanish Catholic system of morality and machismo[21], the main rule of which was, "You may look at my sister, but if you touch her, I will kill you." The extended family and church structure provided them with a circle of safety on the island; if a man "wronged" a girl, everyone would close in to save her family honor.

7   Off-island, signals often get mixed. When a Puerto Rican girl who is dressed in her idea of what is attractive meets a man from mainstream[22] culture who has been trained to react to certain types of clothing as a sexual signal, a clash is likely to take place. She is seen as a Hot Tamale, a sexual firebrand[23]. I learned this lesson at my first formal dance when my date leaned over and painfully planted a sloppy, overeager kiss on my mouth. When I didn't respond with sufficient passion, he said in a resentful tone, "I thought you Latin girls were supposed to mature early." It was the first time I would feel like a fruit or vegetable—I was supposed to ripen, not just grow into womanhood like other girls.

8   These stereotypes[24], though rarer, still surface in my life. I recently stayed at a classy metropolitan hotel. After having dinner with a friend, I was returning to my room when a middle-aged man in a tuxedo stepped directly into my path. With his champagne glass extended toward me, he exclaimed, "*Evita*[25]!"

9   Blocking my way, he bellowed the song "Don't Cry for Me, Argentina." Playing to the gathering crowd, he began to sing loudly, a ditty[26] to the tune of "La

12. **Agonized:** worried

13. **Marlo Thomas:** an American actress who played a modern single woman on the television show *That Girl*, which ran from 1966 to 1971

14. **Ornate:** decorated with complex patterns

15. **Assailed:** attacked

16. **Vulgar:** common; crude; lacking in good taste

17. **Prospective:** likely to become; expected

18. **Come-on:** flirting

19. **Chromosomes:** materials that carry genes or biological traits from parent to child

20. **Provocatively:** in a way that causes a response or calls forth feelings, thoughts, or actions

21. **Machismo:** a strong or exaggerated sense of manliness or power

22. **Mainstream:** what is considered to be normal

23. **Firebrand:** a person who is passionate about a particular cause

24. **Stereotypes:** conventional and oversimplified ideas, opinions, or images

25. *Evita:* a musical and film about Eva Perón, Argentina's first lady from 1946 to 1952

26. **Ditty:** a short, simple song

27. **Exploits:** bold and daring actions
28. **Gonorrhea:** a sexually transmitted disease
29. **Regaled:** entertained

Bamba"—except the lyrics were about a girl named Maria whose exploits[27] all rhymed with her name and gonorrhea[28].

10   I knew that this same man—probably a corporate executive, even worldly by most standards—would never have regaled[29] a white woman with a dirty song in public. But to him, I was just a character in his universe of "others," all cartoons.

11   Still, I am one of the lucky ones. There are thousands of Latinas without the privilege of the education that my parents gave me. For them, every day is a struggle against the misconceptions[30] perpetuated[31] by the myth of the Latina as a whore, domestic worker, or criminal.

30. **Misconceptions:** false opinions based on lack of understanding
31. **Perpetuated:** preserved
32. **Pervasive:** widespread

12   Rather than fight these pervasive[32] stereotypes, I try to replace them with a more interesting set of realities. I travel around the United States reading from my books of poetry and my novel. With the stories I tell, the dreams and fears I examine in my work, I try to get my audience past the particulars of my skin color, my accent, or my clothes.

33. **Fervently:** passionately
34. **Omnipotent:** all-powerful

13   I once wrote a poem in which I called Latinas "God's brown daughters." It is really a prayer of sorts, for communication and respect. In it, Latin women pray "in Spanish to an Anglo God with a Jewish heritage," and they are "fervently[33] hoping that if not omnipotent[34], at least He be bilingual."

CHECK COMPREHENSION

1. What is the writer's main point?

2. What is she contrasting in this essay?

3. Why does she describe people singing to her?

4. What is the writer's conclusion?

5. What is the stereotype that the author says she had to confront?

MAKE INFERENCES

Determine if the following statements are true or false, based on your understanding of the essay.

1. Cofer's parents were stricter than the parents of her friends.

2. The Catholic church was an important part of Cofer's childhood and culture.

3. Cofer resents the way Latina women are presented in American movies and musicals.

WRITE TO IMPROVE READING　　Summarize

Using your answers to these questions and your annotations, write a summary of this essay, following the guidelines from Chapter 6.

Explore Grammar: Commas

Pay attention to the commas in the following sentence from Cofer's essay:

It is custom, not chromosomes, that leads us to choose scarlet over pale pink.

In this sentence, the words "not chromosomes" interrupt the sentence and help Cofer emphasize her point. Because these words interrupt the sentence, they are set off with commas. Marking interruptions with commas is just one basic use of commas.

PRACTICE

Find two additional examples of commas marking interruptions in Cofer's essay.

For additional information about commas, see Chapter 28.

Understand Strategies Used in Comparison and Contrast: Details

Like Amy Tan (Chapter 7), Judith Ortiz Cofer struggled growing up because her family's traditional culture was different from the culture around her. She uses specific details about clothing, food, and habits to emphasize these differences.

PRACTICE

1. Go back through the reading and place checkmarks on the details that show how Cofer's childhood was different from the culture around her.

2. In some cases, the details involve words that are borrowed from Spanish, including *casas*, *bodega*, and *machismo*. What does the use of these words add to the essay?

3. In other instances, Cofer refers to the musicals *West Side Story* and *Evita*. Why does she mention these works? Are you familiar with the music or story of either production? If so, what does your experience add to your understanding of the essay?

RESPOND IN WRITING

1. How does Cofer suggest she will respond to stereotypes? Do you think her response can make a difference? Explain.

2. Cofer is writing about stereotypes of Latinas. Where do these images and ideas come from? How do they distort reality?

3. According to Cofer, she has a privilege that many other Latinas do not. What is her privilege, and what does this advantage allow her to do?

4. P/Q Assignment: In a paragraph, compare or contrast the stereotype of Latinas as presented in Cofer's essay with the presentation of Latinas on a television program or movie you have seen. Are Latinas presented in the way Cofer describes, or differently? Be sure to quote or paraphrase Cofer (and cite your reference accurately).

Extend and Connect: Write Your Own Comparison and Contrast

1. Write about a time when people have misunderstood you. Contrast the misunderstanding with the reality of the situation, and try to understand the source of the mistake.

2. Cofer focuses primarily on misunderstandings or myths about Latinas, but there are many other stereotypes in our culture as well. Choose and describe a common stereotype that you think is mistaken; then, compare and contrast that stereotypical image or idea with a more accurate portrait or reality.

3. In his essay, Dave Barry suggests that toy manufacturers help promote unrealistic ideals of female beauty. Do you think toys can also perpetuate or promote the sorts of stereotypes described by Cofer in her essay? Explain your answer in an essay.

4. Both Rui Dai and Judith Ortiz Cofer contrast different cultures. Like Amy Tan (Chapter 7), these authors discuss how the differences between cultures have affected their lives. If you have lived in two places or in two cultures, what differences have you seen? How have those differences affected your life? Explain your answer in a comparison/contrast essay.

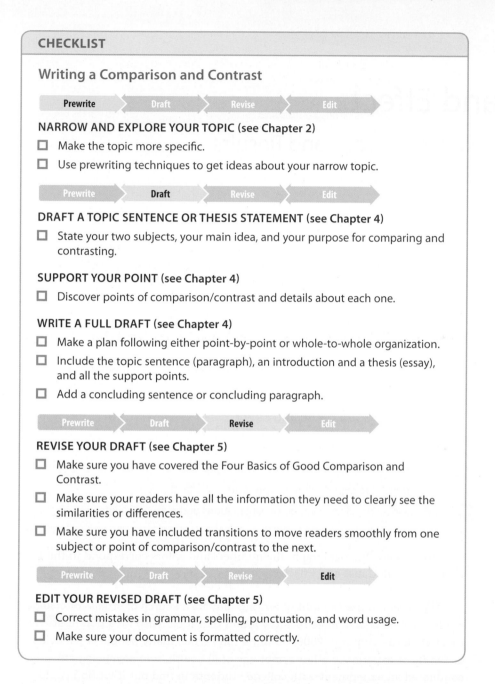

CHECKLIST

Writing a Comparison and Contrast

Prewrite › Draft › Revise › Edit

NARROW AND EXPLORE YOUR TOPIC (see Chapter 2)
☐ Make the topic more specific.
☐ Use prewriting techniques to get ideas about your narrow topic.

Prewrite › **Draft** › Revise › Edit

DRAFT A TOPIC SENTENCE OR THESIS STATEMENT (see Chapter 4)
☐ State your two subjects, your main idea, and your purpose for comparing and contrasting.

SUPPORT YOUR POINT (see Chapter 4)
☐ Discover points of comparison/contrast and details about each one.

WRITE A FULL DRAFT (see Chapter 4)
☐ Make a plan following either point-by-point or whole-to-whole organization.
☐ Include the topic sentence (paragraph), an introduction and a thesis (essay), and all the support points.
☐ Add a concluding sentence or concluding paragraph.

Prewrite › Draft › **Revise** › Edit

REVISE YOUR DRAFT (see Chapter 5)
☐ Make sure you have covered the Four Basics of Good Comparison and Contrast.
☐ Make sure your readers have all the information they need to clearly see the similarities or differences.
☐ Make sure you have included transitions to move readers smoothly from one subject or point of comparison/contrast to the next.

Prewrite › Draft › Revise › **Edit**

EDIT YOUR REVISED DRAFT (see Chapter 5)
☐ Correct mistakes in grammar, spelling, punctuation, and word usage.
☐ Make sure your document is formatted correctly.

12

Cause and Effect:

Texts That Explain Reasons and Results

Understand What Cause and Effect Are

A **cause** is what made an event happen. An **effect** is what happens as a result of the event.

Four Basics of Good Cause and Effect

1 The main point reflects the writer's purpose: to explain causes, effects, or both.

2 If the purpose is to explain causes, the writing presents real causes.

3 If the purpose is to explain effects, it presents real effects.

4 It gives readers detailed examples or explanations of the causes or effects.

In the following paragraph, the numbers and colors correspond to the Four Basics of Good Cause and Effect.

1 Although the thought of writing may be a source of stress for college students, researchers have recently found that it can also be a potent stress reliever. In the winter of 2008, during a time when many people catch colds or the flu or experience other symptoms of ill health, two psychologists conducted an experiment with college students to find out if writing could have positive effects on their minds and/or their bodies. After gathering a large group of college students, a mix of ages, genders, and backgrounds, the psychologists explained the task. The students were asked to write for

only 2 minutes, on two consecutive days, about their choice of three different kinds of experiences: a traumatic experience, a positive experience, or a neutral experience (something routine that happened). The psychologists did not give more detailed directions about the kinds of experiences, rather just a bad one, a good one, or one neither good nor bad. A month after collecting the students' writing, the psychologists interviewed each of the students and asked them to report any symptoms of ill health, such as colds, flu, headaches, or lack of sleep. **3** What the psychologists found was quite surprising. **4** Those students who had written about emotionally charged topics, either traumatic or positive, all reported that they had been in excellent health, avoiding the various illnesses that had been circulating in the college and the larger community. The students who had chosen to write about routine, day-to-day things that didn't matter to them reported the ill health effects that were typical of the season, such as colds, flu, poor sleep, and coughing. From these findings, the two psychologists reported that writing about things that are important to people actually has a positive effect on their health. Their experiment suggests the value to people of regularly recording their reactions to experiences, in a journal of some sort. If writing can keep you well, it is worth a good try. The mind–body connection continues to be studied because clearly each affects the other.

When you are reading for causes and effects or writing about them, make sure that you do not confuse something that happened before an event with a real cause or something that happened after an event with a real effect. For example, if you have pizza on Monday and get the flu on Tuesday, eating the pizza is not the cause of the flu just because it happened before you got the flu, nor is the flu the effect of eating pizza. You just happened to get the flu the next day.

You can use cause and effect in many situations:

College	In a nutrition course, you are asked to identify the consequences (effects) of poor nutrition.
Work	Sales are down in your group, and you have to explain the cause.
Everyday life	You explain to your child why a certain behavior is not acceptable by warning him or her about the negative effects of that behavior.

In college, assignments might include the words *discuss the causes* (or *effects*) *of,* but they might also use phrases such as *explain the results of, discuss the impact of,* or *how did X affect Y*? In all these cases, use the strategies discussed in this chapter.

Cause and Effect in the Classroom: Using Diagrams to Show a Chain of Events

In Chapter 1, we met Jackie. In Jackie's Student Development class, the instructor asked the students to consider the **chain of events** that led to a failure in their lives. Jackie decided to write about her failure in her first college English class. She had learned the Four Basics of Good Cause and Effect analysis, so she brainstormed the following list of causes for her failure.

CAUSES OF MY F GRADE:

missed classes

not enough time spent on assignments (no editing or proofreading)

late assignments

didn't understand assignments

Jackie wanted to show that she had made mistakes in her class, and that was why she failed. She knew all of her reasons were real causes, but she did not know how to show a chain of events. She took the assignment to her English teacher,

First — • I was behind on bills due to unexpected medical issues.

So — • My boss offered to help me out by giving me lots of overtime with extra pay.

Then — • I started to miss class because of the overtime; I was either scheduled to work or just exhausted.

So — • I didn't understand the assignments I missed, so I turned them in without spending much time on them.

As a result — • I got some really low grades.

So — • I got very discouraged.

Then — • I decided to skip some assignments.

Then — • My grades hit rock bottom.

So — • I quit going to class.

In the end — • I failed.

who explained that a "chain of events" is a series of cause and effect relationships. The effect of one initial event causes the next event to happen, which in turn causes the next step in the chain. After talking with her teacher, Jackie realized that she could make a diagram like the one on page 242 to help her show the chain of events.

The diagram helped Jackie understand the "chain of events": each effect became a cause that led to another effect. The causes weren't just separate events; each problem could be traced back to her original decision to work overtime in order to pay her medical bills.

> **APPLY WHAT YOU HAVE LEARNED**
>
> Using Jackie's diagram as a model, consider what chain of events might lead a struggling student to become more successful.

Main Point in Cause and Effect

The **main point** introduces causes, effects, or both. To help you discover your main point, complete the following sentence:

(The topic) causes (or caused) . . .
(The topic) results in (or resulted in) . . .

Here is an example of a topic sentence for a paragraph:

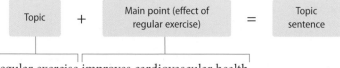

Regular exercise improves cardiovascular health.

Remember that the main point for an essay can be a little broader than one for a paragraph.

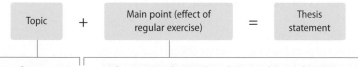

Regular exercise provides more physical and mental benefits than any medication could offer.

Whereas the topic sentence focuses on just one major benefit of regular exercise, the thesis statement considers multiple benefits.

Paragraphs vs. Essays in Cause and Effect

For more on the important features of cause and effect, see the Four Basics of Good Cause and Effect on page 240.

Paragraph Form

Topic sentence

Support 1 (cause 1 or effect 1)

Support 2 (cause 2 or effect 2)

Support 3 (cause 3 or effect 3)

Concluding sentence

Regular exercise improves cardiovascular health. One benefit of exercise is that it strengthens the heart. Like any other muscle, the heart becomes stronger with use, and is able to pump blood through the body more efficiently. The result can be lower blood pressure, reducing the risk of heart disease. Another benefit of exercise is that it lessens the toll that excessive weight can take on the heart. In seriously overweight individuals, the strain of carrying extra pounds can cause the heart to enlarge, interfering with its ability to pump blood. By losing weight through exercise and dietary changes, people can reduce the burden on their hearts and also their cardiovascular risk. The most important cardiovascular benefit of exercise is that it lowers the risk of heart disease. As previously noted, exercise can reduce blood pressure and strain on the heart, both risk factors for heart attack, stroke, and heart failure. In addition, it can lower levels of "bad" cholesterol while raising levels of "good" cholesterol. Controlling bad cholesterol is important because when there is too much of this substance in the blood, it can build up on artery walls, causing reduced blood flow. Regular and vigorous aerobic exercise is the best way to reap these cardiovascular benefits, but even a brisk walk a few times a week is better than no activity at all.

Main Point: Often narrower for a paragraph than for an essay: while the topic sentence (paragraph) focuses on just one major benefit of exercise, the thesis statement (essay) considers multiple benefits.

Support for the Main Point (Statements of Cause or Effect)

Detailed Explanations or Examples of Cause/Effect Statements: Usually 1 to 3 sentences per statement for paragraphs and 3 to 8 sentences per statement for essays.

Conclusion

Think Critically As You Write Cause and Effect

Ask Yourself

- Have I examined a variety of possible causes and/or effects related to my topic? (If not, research them, and consider revising your main point and support based on what you learn. For more on finding and evaluating outside sources, see Chapter 14.)

- Am I certain that my causes are real causes and my effects real effects?

244

1

Most people know how hard it is to start and stick with an exercise program. However, there is a good reason to build a significant amount of **Thesis statement** activity into every week: Regular exercise provides more physical and mental benefits than any medication could offer.

First, exercise helps people achieve and maintain a healthy weight. A nutritious diet that is no **Topic sentence 1 (cause 1 or effect 1)** in calories has a greater effect on weight los ercise does. However, regular exercise—ideally, interspersed throughout the day—can make an important contribution. For instance, people trying to lose weight might walk to work or to other destinations instead of driving. Or, they might take the stairs to their office instead of the elevator. If they g the at the end of the day, so much the better. Ad **Topic sentence 2 (cause 2 or effect 2)** these efforts can make a difference.

Second, exercise boosts mood and energy levels. For example, exercise causes the body to release endorphins, chemicals that give us a sense of well-being, even happiness. Accordingly, exercise can help reduce stress and combat depression. In addition, because

2

exercise can make people look and feel more fit, it can improve their self-esteem. Finally, by improving strength and endurance, exercise gives indi **Topic sentence 3 (cause 3 or effect 3)** more energy to go about their lives.

The most important benefit of exercise is that it can help prevent disease. For example, exercise can improve the body's use of insulin and, as noted earlier, help people maintain a healthy weight. Therefore, it can help prevent or control diabetes. Additionally, exercise can lower the risk of heart attacks, strokes, and heart failure. For instance, exercise strengthens the heart muscle, helping it pump blood more efficiently and reducing high blood pressure, a heart disease risk factor. Also, exercise can lower levels of "bad" cholesterol while raising levels of "good" cholesterol. Controlling levels of bad cholesterol is important because when there is too much of this substance in the blood, it can build up in the walls of arteries, possibly blocking blood flow. Finally, some research suggests that regular exercise can reduce the risk of certain cancers, including breast, colon, and lung cancer.

3

In my own life, exercise has made a huge difference. Before starting a regular exercise program, I was close to needing prescription medications to lower my blood pressure and cholesterol. Thanks to regular **Concluding paragraph** physical activity, however, both my blood pressure and cholesterol levels are now in the normal range, and I have never felt better. Every bit of time spent at the gym or exchanging a ride in an elevator for a walk up the stairs has been well worth it.

PRACTICE 1 **Identify the Main Point in Cause and Effect**

1. The topic sentence in the sample paragraph on pages 240–241 is high-lighted in green. Identify:

   a. The topic: _____

   b. The main idea: _____

   c. Is the focus here on causes or effects? _____

2. Find the main point in the sample paragraph on page 244. Identify:

   a. The topic: _____

   b. The main idea: _____

   c. Is the focus here on causes or effects? _____

3. Find the main point in the essay by Tyler Dashner on pages 252–256. Identify:

   a. The topic: _____

   b. The main idea: _____

   _____

   c. Is the focus here on causes or effects? _____

Support in Cause and Effect

The paragraph and essay models on pages 244–245 use the topic sentence (paragraph) and thesis statement (essay) from the Main Point in Cause and Effect section of this chapter. Both models include the **support** used in all cause/effect writing: statements of cause or effect backed up by detailed explanations or examples. In the essay model, however, the major support points (statements of cause/effect) are topic sentences for individual paragraphs.

PRACTICE 2 **Recognize Support and Details**

The topic sentence has been double underlined in the following paragraph. Study the paragraph and underline and number (1, 2, 3, etc.) the major supporting details.

   Between weeks 11 and 12 of the semester, a strange phenomenon happens across our community college campus: the "third quarter drop out." During these weeks, as many as ten percent of the students who had been regularly attending disappear. What happens? <u><u>There are three</u></u>

primary causes for the attendance slump. One powerful reason for a student to stop coming to class is discouragement . The mid-terms are finished, and if a student's grade is not good at this point, there may be little chance to improve the overall grade in the course. If the deadline to drop the course has already passed, the student may see no reason to continue without a chance for success. In addition, pressures of life, family, job, and finances may become overwhelming to a student. Some students may stop attending class to pick up extra overtime pay at work, while others become stressed due to illness or lack of transportation to and from class. Finally, and perhaps most importantly, many students do not know how to get the help they need to finish the class, even though resources are available. For example, many colleges provide carpool services for students with transportation issues, while others will work with students to handle financial issues through payment plans. Many colleges make tutoring and writing centers available to students without charge, but students may not know how to find these services on their own. While no one program or service will stop the attendance drop, instructors and college personnel can work with students to identify issues early and direct them to the help that they need.

PRACTICE 3   Giving Examples and Details

Write down two causes or two effects for two of the three topics listed below. Then give an example or detail that explains each cause or effect.

Example:

Topic: Bankruptcy

> **Cause 1:** _Overspending_
>
> > **Example / Detail:** _bought a leather jacket I liked and charged it_
>
> **Cause 2:** _Poor budgeting_
>
> > **Example / Detail:** _not tracking monthly expenses versus income_

1.   Topic: A fire in someone's home

    Cause / Effect 1: _____

        Example / Detail: _____

    Cause / Effect 2: _____

        Example / Detail: _____

    2.   Topic: An A in this course

        Cause / Effect 1: _____

            Example / Detail: _____

        Cause / Effect 2: _____

            Example / Detail: _____

    3.   Topic: A car accident

        Cause / Effect 1: _____

            Example / Detail: _____

Organization in Cause and Effect

Cause and effect can be organized in a variety of ways, depending on your purpose.

Main Point	Purpose	Organization
The "Occupy" protests of 2011 brought attention to the economic difficulties faced by low- and middle-income citizens.	to explain the effects of the protests	order of importance, saving the most important effect for last
A desire to remain at a protest site for an extended period led "Occupy" protesters to create miniature towns, with food service, libraries, and more.	to describe the places where protesters camped out	space order
The "Occupy" protests in New York City inspired other protests throughout the country.	to describe the spread of the protest movement over time	time order

Note: If you are explaining both causes and effects, you would present the causes first and the effects later.

    Use **transitions** to move readers smoothly from one cause to another, or from one effect to another, or from causes to effects. Because cause and effect can use any method of organization depending on your purpose, the following list shows just a few of the transitions you might use.

Common Transitions in Cause and Effect

	Conjunctive Adverbials	Subordinating Conjunctions	Adjective + Noun	Prepositions
Cause		because since	one cause a primary cause the most important cause a serious cause	because of due to
Effect	therefore as a result consequently		one effect a primary effect the most important effect a serious effect a long-term or short-term effect	

For more information on using and punctuating these transitions, see Chapters 17 and 24.

PRACTICE 4   **Use Transitions in Cause and Effect**

Read the paragraph that follows, and fill in the blanks with transitions. You are not limited to the ones in the preceding box.

Recently, neuroscientists, who have long been skeptical about meditation, confirmed that it has numerous positive outcomes. _____ is that people who meditate can maintain their focus and attention longer than people who do not. This ability to stay "on task" was demonstrated among students who had been practicing meditation for several weeks. They reported more effective studying and learning because they were able to pay attention. _____ positive outcome is the ability to relax on command. Many people lead busy, stressful lives with multiple pressures on them—family responsibilities, work duties, financial worries, and uncertainties about the future. While meditating, people learned how to reduce their heart rates and blood pressure so that they could relax more easily in all kinds of situations. _____ outcome is a thickening of the brain's cortex. Meditators' cortexes were uniformly thicker than nonmeditators'. Because the cortex enables memorization and the production of new ideas, this last outcome is especially exciting, particularly in fighting Alzheimer's disease and other dementias.

Read and Analyze Cause and Effect

Student Cause and Effect Paragraph: "A Difficult Decision with a Positive Outcome," Caitlyn Prokop

Preview	Read	Review	Reflect and Respond

- Read the title and the first sentence. Will this essay address causes, effects, or both? How do you know?
- What are some difficult decisions you have made?

Preview	**Read**	Review	Reflect and Respond

Guidelines for Reading and Annotating Cause and Effect

Read and annotate this paragraph using these guidelines:

1. Pay attention to vocabulary using marginal notes, context clues, or a dictionary.
2. Find the main point and underline it. Remember that the main point shows the writer's purpose (to show causes or effects).
3. Identify supporting details and organizational strategies. Number the causes or effects, and determine whether these are organized chronologically or by order of importance.
4. Ask questions and make connections. Remember to connect the causes or effects to your own experiences and other things you have read.

Caitlin Prokop

A Difficult Decision with a Positive Outcome

1   When my mother made the decision to move back to New York, I made the choice to move in with my dad so that I could finish high school. This decision affected me in a positive way because I graduated with my friends, built a better relationship with my father, and had the chance to go to college without leaving home. Graduating with my friends was very important to me because I have known most of them since we were in kindergarten. It was a journey through childhood that we had shared, and I wanted to finish it with them. Accomplishing the goal of graduating from high school with my close friends, those who accompanied[1] me through school, made me a stronger and more confident person. Another good outcome of my difficult decision was the relationship I built with my dad. We never saw eye to eye when I lived with both of my parents. For example, we stopped talking for five months

1. **Accompany:** to be with; to go with

because I always sided against him with my mom. Living together for the past five years has made us closer, and I cherish[2] that closeness we have developed. Every Thursday is our day, a day when we talk to each other about what is going on in our lives, so that we will never again have a distant relationship. A third good outcome of my decision is that I can go to Brevard Community College, which is right down the street. In high school, I had thought that I would want to go away to college, but then I realized that I would miss my home. By staying here, I have the opportunity to attend a wonderful college that is preparing me for transferring to a four-year college and finding a good career. I have done some research and believe I would like to become a police officer, a nurse, or a teacher. Through the school, I can do volunteer work in each of these areas. Right now, I am leaning toward becoming a teacher, based on my volunteer work in a kindergarten class. There, I can explore what grades I want to teach. In every way, I believe that my difficult decision was the right one, giving me many opportunities that I would not have had if I had moved to a new and unfamiliar place.

2. **Cherish:** to value highly

Preview >	Read >	**Review** >	Reflect and Respond >

Review your reading. Make sure you can answer these questions:

1. What are Prokop's main point and purpose in this paragraph?
2. How has she organized the paragraph? How do you know?
3. Does the paragraph illustrate the Four Basics of Good Cause and Effect? Explain.

Preview >	Read >	Review >	**Reflect and Respond**

1. Has Prokop provided enough details for a reader to understand the results of her decision? Explain.
2. Have you ever made a difficult decision that turned out to be a good one? Explain. When and how did you recognize the positive effects?

Student Cause and Effect Essay: "A Look at Academic Dishonesty," Tyler Dashner

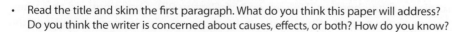

Preview	Read >	Review >	Reflect and Respond >

- Read the title and skim the first paragraph. What do you think this paper will address? Do you think the writer is concerned about causes, effects, or both? How do you know?
- How would you define "academic dishonesty"? Do you think your instructors and friends work from the same definition?
- How common do you think academic dishonesty is?

Preview ▸ **Read** ▸ Review ▸ Reflect and Respond

Read and annotate this essay using the Guidelines for Reading and Annotating Cause and Effect on page 250.

Tyler Dashner

A Look at Academic Dishonesty

1   I was thinking up topics for this paper when I stepped into one of my other classes. Another student asked me for an answer on a take home quiz we had been assigned. I politely said that it was a quiz and I was not comfortable sharing my answers. Everyone in the class gave me a funny look, as if I was the bad guy for not helping this other student. In my mind, breaking the "Academic Honesty Pledge" was not something I was willing to do. Judging from the response of almost every other student in the room though, I began to wonder how the average student felt about this topic.

2   I began asking myself some basic questions on academic honesty. I had never given it a large amount of thought. Would I cheat if given the opportunity? Would I not cheat due to morals and ethics? To be totally honest I came to a very arrogant conclusion: I don't cheat because I know I can do better work than the students around me; cheating would lower my grade, not raise it. When it comes to critical writing, there is a wealth of information available from writers who are much more experienced and more articulate[1] than I. What keeps me from plagiarizing these expert writers?

3   "Academic dishonesty involves, but is not limited to, one of the following: giving or receiving, offering or soliciting unauthorized assistance on any exam or assignment; plagiarism or collusion[2]" (LFCC Student Handbook). This is Lord Fairfax Community College's official description of academic dishonesty and the definition I will be using in my paper when referring to cheating or academic dishonesty.

4   While doing research on this topic, I noticed an obvious pattern. A large majority of academics conducting research on this topic felt that teachers create an environment that either encourages or discourages cheating. If a teacher is honest with his or her students (e.g., sticking to the syllabus and grading fairly), this promotes a trusting environment and has been shown to discourage cheating (Hulsart and McCarthy 93). I have noticed this phenomenon for myself. When I have professors who are engaging and positive and have a clear syllabus that they stick to, I find that doing the work for the class comes easily. When the professor is constantly behind on the syllabus and puts down students, I always have trouble staying motivated to put forth one hundred percent effort in the class.

1. **Articulate:** to express something in a way that can be clearly heard and understood
2. **Collusion:** secret co-operation for an illegal or dishonest purpose

5   It isn't just the atmosphere in the classroom that propagates[3] the mentality to cheat; "[s]ocial norms theory says that people tend to maintain behavior consistent with peer descriptive norms[4], and that overestimating the frequency that one's peers engage in a behavior can lead to increases in that behavior" (Hard, Conway, and Moran 1059). This theory involves the idea that perception is reality. If students think everyone is cheating, then they will be more inclined to cheat themselves in order to keep up academically with their peers. This makes it incredibly difficult for educators to address cheating. If they discourage it, students will think everyone is doing it, so they should too. If they do nothing about it, students will feel they can cheat without repercussions[5].

6   This perception of cheating was exemplified[6] by a Scanlon and Neumann study that found that eight percent of students admitted to cutting and pasting directly from sources, whereas fifty percent of students felt that other students were doing this behavior (380). Clearly students believe that cheating is more prevalent[7] than it really is. This cycle, if left unchecked, should be spiraling out of control, but it's clearly not. Researchers say that the Internet is making it easier to cheat, but the number of students cheating has remained fairly constant from the 1980s to the 1990s (Scanlon and Neumann 381–82). Still, students with a propensity[8] to cheat will cheat by any means available to them (Witherspoon, Maldonado, and Lacey 82).

7   Zwagerman asks his fellow academics to address plagiarism differently. He feels that professors are concerned only with catching cheaters and punishing them. Plagiarism is a result of students who see their futures dependent on their grades and, out of fear, cheat to ensure they get good grades. Zwagerman says that a poor student will cheat poorly and get caught, but a good student will cheat better and most likely not get caught. In the end, the grade is the same. Academia's call to arms[9] against plagiarism hurts students and faculty by destroying any trust between them. Teachers should educate their students about plagiarism instead of threatening them (Zwagerman).

8   After thinking all of this over and doing research on the subject, I began to realize just how complex the issue truly is. I came up with a series of questions that I wanted to see how students at LFCC would answer. I surveyed thirty students randomly in the cafeteria of the school and some in various classes of mine. I asked them a series of questions:

1. On a scale of 1 to 10, 1 being solely for a degree and 10 being solely for an education, how would you rate your reason for attending Lord Fairfax Community College?
2. On a scale of 1 to 10, 1 being my professors grade fairly and 10 being my professors have no rhyme or reason to their grading, how would you rate your professors' grading standards at Lord Fairfax Community College?

3. **Propagates:** to make something known to many people
4. **Descriptive norms:** people's perceptions of what is commonly done in specific situations

5. **Repercussions:** something usually bad or unpleasant that happens as a result of an action and that usually affects people for a long time
6. **Exemplified:** to be a very good example of something
7. **Prevalent:** common or widespread

8. **Propensity:** a strong natural tendency to do something

9. **Call to arms:** a summons, invitation, or appeal to undertake a particular course of action

3. On a scale of 1 to 10, 1 being my professors always follow their syllabus and 10 being my professors never follow their syllabus, how would you rate your professors on how well they follow their syllabus at Lord Fairfax Community College?

4. On a scale of 1 to 10, 1 being my professors set a clear standard for assignments and 10 being my professors are very ambiguous[10] about what they want from their students, how would you rate your professors' expectations on assignments at Lord Fairfax Community College?

5. Knowing that you would not get caught and that you would receive a better grade on an assignment or a test, would you cheat in some way (e.g., plagiarize or copy off another student)?

10. **Ambiguous:** able to be understood in more than one way; having more than one possible meaning

9   I then spoke with them afterward to clarify[11] their results and to gain further insight into how these issues affected them. Of the students I surveyed, they were all surprisingly upfront about these issues. This was due to the fact that I assured each student that no professor would ever see their surveys and I would destroy them after completing this assignment. Without these assurances, I feared that students would be apprehensive[12] about giving me the candid responses I would need to legitimize my data.

11. **Clarify:** to make something easier to understand

10   I would have liked to have been able to ask more in-depth questions, but I felt that a shorter survey would get a better sampling of the average college student, instead of just getting the more motivated students (i.e., the "good" students), thus skewing the results. Students in the cafeteria did not always have the time to fill out a lengthy survey, especially those students that had procrastinated[13] and were desperately trying to finish an assignment for an upcoming class (i.e., the "bad" students).

12. **Apprehensive:** afraid that something bad or unpleasant is going to happen

11   I added up the numbers the students provided for each question and averaged them. I used this to give me an idea of how the average student felt about these topics. I also tabulated[14] how the response to each of the first four questions affected the answer to the final question. I feel that both sets of data were necessary to determine the mind-set of a student when confronted with the option of cheating.

13. **Procrastinated:** to be slow or late about doing something that should be done

12   The first question's average was 2. I felt this question was important because I wanted to know what effect a student's reason for attending college had on his or her propensity to cheat. I also was curious to see if students at LFCC were interested in an education at all. From talking to students, I came to the conclusion that an education was a means to an end. Students need a degree in order to get the job they want, and in most career fields a large majority of the information they need to know is gained from on-the-job training.

14. **Tabulated:** to arrange information in an organized way so that it can be studied, recorded, etc.

13   The second question's average was 5. From interactions I had with the participants after the survey I have determined this was because students felt that about half of their professors graded fairly and half did not grade fairly. Also from their feedback I determined this to be

the most discouraging thing for students when it came to their college experience.

14   The third question's average was 3. Students felt that their professors almost always followed their syllabuses. If professors needed to make adjustments they would either amend the syllabus, making the new syllabus available on Blackboard, or they would clarify the changes in class. Students did mention that this would be frustrating if it happened to them. Judging from these results I determined that the instructors at LFCC do a good job of issuing syllabuses and keeping to the schedule they lay out at the beginning of the semester.

15   The fourth question's average was 6. Most students responded to this question with the complaint that teachers at LFCC purposely make the assignments and tests at the beginning of the semester hard or ambiguous in order to "weed out" the students who won't be taking the class seriously and who will eventually drop it. This could be frustrating to these students, but the professors usually had extra credit and/or an abundance of points throughout the semester to compensate[15] for this initial bad grade on an assignment or test. The feelings on this subject were split pretty evenly; some students felt this was unfair, while others understood the rationale and adapted to their professors' individual teaching styles.

15. **Compensate:** to provide something good as a balance against something bad or undesirable

16   The fifth and final question I left as a simple yes/no question. Only seven people answered yes and twenty-seven answered no. Interestingly, the students that answered yes to this question were also more critical of their professors in the previous questions, while the students that answered no were either equally as critical or far less critical of their professors. This can be explained because for some students, an ethical code keeps them from cheating, regardless of the professor's behavior. I also believe that there is some margin for error on the final question due to students' apprehension about admitting to a random person that they are willing to cheat.

17   Judging from these results, my data confirms what other researchers have been saying. The way a professor conducts a class has an impact on a student's propensity to cheat. Although there is no way to keep every student from cheating, by exercising the same respect toward students as is expected from them in return, professors can mitigate[16] the amount of dishonest behavior among their students. Professors can also inform their students that cheating will not be tolerated and ensure that all students have read the academic dishonesty guidelines.

16. **Mitigate:** to make something less severe, harmful, or painful

18   From my research it is obvious that administrators at LFCC understand this research and have implemented most of the recommendations made by the research I read. I now understand why on the first day of class every one of my professors has the same routine of going over the syllabus and ensuring each student understands all of the school policies toward academic dishonesty. These simple steps clearly mitigate the amount of students who cheat without degrading students by treating them all like cheaters.

Works Cited

Hard, Stephen F., James M. Conway, and Antonia C. Moran. "Faculty and College Student Beliefs about the Frequency of Student Academic Misconduct." *Journal of Higher Education* 77.6 (2006): 1058–**80**. Web. 29 Sep. 2012.

Hulsart, Robyn, and Victoria McCarthy. "Utilizing a Culture of Trust to Promote Academic Integrity." *Journal of Continuing Higher Education* 59 (2011): 92–96. Web. 29 Sep. 2012.

Scanlon, Patrick M., and David R. Neumann. "Internet Plagiarism among College Students." *Journal of College Student Development* 43.3 (2002): 374–85. Web. 29 Sep. 2012.

"Student Handbook." *LFCC.edu*. Lord Fairfax Community College, Web. 1 Jan 2012. <http://www.lfcc.edu/files/documents/current-students/college-catalog/2010-11/Student-Handbook.pdf>

Witherspoon, Michelle, Nancy Maldonado, and Candace H. Lacey. "Undergraduates and Academic Dishonesty." *International Journal of Business and Social Science* 3.1 (2012): 76–86. Web. 29 Sep. 2012.

Zwagerman, Sean. "The Scarlet P: Plagiarism, Panopticism, and the Rhetoric of Academic Integrity." *College Composition and Communication* 59.4 (2008): 676–710. Web. 29 Sep. 2012.

Preview   Read   **Review**   Reflect and Respond

Review your reading. Make sure you can answer the following questions:

1. What is Dashner's main point?
2. What are the causes of academic dishonesty, according to the paper?
3. What evidence does Dashner provide for the causes he mentions?
4. Does the paper demonstrate the Four Basics of Good Cause and Effect? Explain.

Now, using your annotations, write a summary of Dashner's essay, following the guidelines from Chapter 6.

Preview   Read   Review   **Reflect and Respond**

1. In this paper, the writer begins by referring to scholarly sources, but he also cites the results of an informal survey he conducted on his campus. How do the questions he asked in his survey relate to the scholarly research he mentions? Would the paper have been as effective if he had left out the informal survey? Explain.
2. Does he provide enough evidence for the causes he presents? Explain.
3. Do you think he left out any possible causes of academic dishonesty? Explain.
4. Are there situations in which cheating might be justified? Explain.
5. Craft a survey similar to Dashner's to investigate attitudes and habits of cheating on your campus. Report your results in a paragraph or an essay that describes either the causes or the effects of cheating.

Reading/Writing Workbook: Cause and Effect

Professional Essay: "Yes, Money Can Buy Happiness,"
John Tierney

Preview

1. Skim the title, the information about the author, and the first paragraph. What is the rhetorical context (audience, purpose, and topic) for this essay?

2. Does this essay address causes, effects, or both? How do you know?

3. Create a guiding question for your reading, based on your previewing.

Read and annotate this essay carefully, following the Guidelines for Reading and Annotating Cause and Effect on page 250.

John Tierney

Yes, Money Can Buy Happiness

A well-known columnist for the *New York Times* since 1990, John Tierney has an extensive background in news writing. After graduating with a degree in American studies from Yale University, Tierney reported for a series of publications, including the *Bergen Record,* the *Washington Star,* and *Science* magazine. He then worked for several years as a freelance writer, reporting on six continents and publishing articles in more than fifteen national newspapers and magazines. His book, *Willpower: Rediscovering the Greatest Human Strength,* written with Roy Baumeister, was named one of Amazon's Best Books of 2011.

1   Yes, money can buy happiness, but probably not in the way you imagined. Spending it on yourself may not do much for your spirits, but spending it on others will make you happier, according to a report from a team of social psychologists in the new issue of *Science.*

2   The researchers confirmed[1] the joys of giving in three separate ways. First, by surveying a national sample of more than 600 Americans, they found that spending more on gifts and charity correlated[2] with greater happiness, whereas spending more money on oneself did not. Second, by tracking sixteen workers before and after they received profit-sharing bonuses, the researchers found that the workers who gave more of the money to others ended up happier than the ones who spent more of it on themselves. In fact, how the bonus was spent was a better predictor of happiness than the size of the bonus.

1. **Confirmed:** showed that something was true or actual

2. **Correlated:** is related or connected to something else

3   The final bit of evidence came from an experiment in which forty-six students were given either $5 or $20 to spend by the end of the day. The ones who were instructed to spend the money on others—they bought toys for siblings, treated friends to meals, and made donations to the homeless—were happier at the end of the day than the ones who were instructed to spend the money on themselves.

4   "These experimental results," the researchers conclude, "provide direct support for our causal argument that spending money on others promotes happiness more than spending money on oneself." The social psychologists—Elizabeth Dunn and Lara Aknin of the University of British Columbia, Vancouver, and Michael Norton of Harvard Business School—also conclude that "how people choose to spend their money is at least as important as how much money they make."

5   I asked Dr. Dunn if she had any advice for readers on how much to spend on others. Her reply was, "I think even minor changes in spending habits can make a difference. In our experiment with college students, we found that spending just $5 prosocially[3] had a substantial[4] effect on happiness at the end of the day. But I wouldn't say that there's some fixed amount that everyone should spend on others. Rather, the best bet might be for people to think about whether they can push themselves to devote just a little more of their money to helping others."

6   But why wouldn't people be doing that already? Because most people don't realize the personal benefits of charity, according to Dr. Dunn and her colleagues. When the researchers surveyed another group of students, they found that most of the respondents predicted that personal spending would make them happier than spending the money on other people.

7   Perhaps that will change as word of these experiments circulates—although that prospect raises another question, which I put to Dr. Dunn: If people started giving away money chiefly in the hope of making themselves happier, as opposed to wanting to help others, would they still derive[5] the same happiness from it?

8   "This is a fascinating question," she replied. "I certainly hope that telling people about the emotional benefits of prosocial spending doesn't completely erase these benefits; I would hate to be responsible for the downfall[6] of joyful prosocial behavior."

9   Do you have any theories on the joys of giving? Any reports of your own experiments? Or any questions you'd like to ask the researchers? Dr. Dunn, in keeping with the results of her experiments, has generously offered to provide some answers free of charge.

---

3. **Prosocially:** for the benefit or good of someone else
4. **Substantial:** large

5. **Derive:** receive from a source

6. **Downfall:** decline or end of something

CHECK COMPREHENSION

1. What is Tierney's main point?

2. What evidence does he provide for his point?

3. What question does Tierney raise about the main point at the end of his essay?

MAKE INFERENCES

Use clues and information from the reading to answer the following questions:

1. Who is Tierney's audience? What does he expect his audience to believe about money and happiness?

2. Does Tierney believe he has answered all of the readers' questions about money and happiness?

3. What would Tierney recommend that his readers do to improve their happiness?

WRITE TO IMPROVE READING   Summarize

Use your notes and annotations to summarize this essay, following the guidelines in Chapter 6.

Explore Grammar: Use By-Modifiers Correctly

For more on modifiers, see Chapter 22.

Look at the following sentences from Tierney's essay:

First, **by surveying a national sample of more than 600 Americans,** they found that spending more on gifts and charity correlated with greater happiness…

Second, **by tracking workers before and after they received profit-sharing bonuses,** the researchers found that the workers who gave more of the money to others ended up happier…

The bold part of each sentence is a modifier; it explains how the subject of the sentence completed the action of the sentence. Notice each sentence has a subject and a verb. The modifier helps clarify the meaning of the sentence, but it does not replace the subject or the verb. When you begin a sentence with a "by" modifier, be sure not to omit the subject of the sentence. Be sure to put a comma after the modifier.

Incorrect	By studying the notes several days before the test can improve your score.
Correct	By studying the notes several days before the test, a student can improve his or her score.
Incorrect	By giving money to charitable organizations can save on taxes.
Correct	By giving money to charitable organizations, taxpayers can save on taxes they owe.

Know P/Q: How to Use Quotations

In his essay, Tierney quotes experts, a strategy you have seen several times in other readings. You have already learned how to introduce a quote with a signal phrase (see p. 152). Tierney's essay illustrates a variation on this basic pattern.

VARIATION 1: MOVE THE SIGNAL PHRASE

In paragraph 4, Tierney quotes three researchers. Notice where he puts the signal phrase:

> "These experimental results," ***the researchers conclude,*** "provide direct support for our causal argument that spending money on others promotes happiness more than spending money on oneself."

For more information on quotation marks, punctuation, and capital letters, see Chapters 30–32.

- What happens to capital letters when the signal phrase interrupts a complete quote?
- How are commas used when the signal phrase interrupts a complete quote?
- What happens to the flow or rhythm of a sentence when a signal phrase interrupts a complete quote? (Read it out loud.)
- Could the signal phrase occur in a different place in the sentence? Why or why not?

PRACTICE   **Moving the Signal Phrase**

Rewrite each of the following quotes, moving the signal phrase to a different part of the sentence each time. Check your punctuation carefully, and read your sentence aloud. Which version is better, the original or the revision?

1. According to Tierney, "The final bit of evidence came from an experiment in which forty-six students were given either $5 or $20 to spend by the end of the day" (258).

2. Tierney asks, "But why wouldn't people be doing that already?" (258).

3. John Tierney claims, "Yes, money can buy happiness, but probably not in the way you imagined" (258).

RESPOND IN WRITING

1. The scientist in the article says she hopes that people will "think about whether they can push themselves to devote just a little more of their money to helping others." Will this article change your attitude about charity or cause you to alter your behavior in any way? Write a paragraph explaining your answer.

2. Tierney's article explores "the emotional benefits of prosocial spending." Have you ever experienced these benefits? Write an essay to explore an experience in which you spent money on or helped others. Did the action cause the effects that scientists found in their studies?

Professional Essay: "Are Your Genes to Blame?" Steven Pinker

Preview

- Skim the title and the first line of each paragraph. What can you learn about the rhetorical context (audience, purpose, and topic) for this essay?
- Look at paragraph 9. Is this essay about causes, effects, or both? How do you know?
- Create a guiding question for your reading of this essay.

Read and annotate this essay carefully, following the Guidelines for Reading and Annotating Cause and Effect on page 250.

Steven Pinker

Are Your Genes to Blame?

Steven Pinker (b. 1954) is an experimental psychologist, language researcher, and cognitive scientist who writes about science and language for publications such as the *New York Times*, *TIME*, and *The New Republic*. He has written several books, including *How the Mind Works* (1997) and *The Better Angels of Our Nature* (2011), and is considered one of the most influential thinkers of our time. Pinker teaches psychology at Harvard University. PHOTO BY © DAVID LEVENSON/GETTY IMAGES

1   Study after study has shown that genes can affect behavior and mental life. Identical twins separated at birth (who share their genes but not their environment) are similar in their intellectual talents, their personality traits (such

1. **Introversion:** a personality trait often characterized by shyness and a preference for not being in the company of others

2. **Conscientiousness:** attention to what is right and wrong; following one's conscience in a careful and consistent way

3. **Antagonism:** a clear and obvious hostility between people or groups

4. **Incessantly:** constantly, without stopping

5. **Heritable:** can be passed down genetically from one generation to another

6. **Susceptibility:** an ability to be affected by something, such as a disease

7. **Maladies:** illnesses or disorders

8. **Brave New World:** title of a book published in 1932 by Aldous Huxley that describes a fictional world in which reproduction, social order, and economics are managed and tightly controlled by the state

9. **Genome:** a full set of human chromosomes containing all genetic material passed from one generation to the next

10. **Genophobe:** a person who is afraid of genes, genetics, and genetic research

11. **Erode:** reduce or wear away

12. **Paradox:** a statement that contradicts itself; a situation in which two opposites are true at the same time

as introversion[1], conscientiousness[2], and antagonism[3]), their average level of lifelong happiness, and personal quirks such as giggling incessantly[4] or flushing the toilet both before and after using it. Identical twins (who share all their genes) are more similar than fraternal twins (who share half their genes). And biological siblings (who share half their genes) are more similar than adopted siblings (who share none of their genes). It's not only personality and intelligence that are partly heritable[5], but susceptibility[6] to psychological maladies[7] such as schizophrenia, obsessive-compulsive disorder, and major depression.

2   The discovery that genes have something to do with behavior came as a shock in an era in which people thought that the mind of a newborn was a blank slate and that anyone could do anything if only they strove hard enough. And it continues to set off alarm bells. Many people worry about a Brave New World[8] in which parents or governments will try to re-engineer human nature. Others see genes as a threat to free will and personal responsibility, citing headlines such as "Man's genes made him kill, his lawyers claim." Behavioral geneticists are sometimes picketed, censored, or compared to Nazis.

3   With increasing knowledge of how the genome[9] works, many beliefs about ourselves will indeed have to be rethought. But the worst fears of the genophobes[10] are misplaced. It is easy to exaggerate the significance of behavioral genetics for our lives.

4   For one thing, genes cannot pull the strings of behavior directly. Behavior is caused by the activity of the brain, and the most the genes can do is affect its wiring, its size and shape, and its sensitivity to hormones and other molecules. Among the brain circuits laid down by the genes are ones that reflect on memories, current circumstance, and the anticipated consequences of various courses of action and that select behavior accordingly, in an intricate and not entirely predictable way. These circuits are what we call "free will," and providing them with information about the likely consequences of behavioral options is what we call "holding people responsible." All normal people have this circuitry, and that is why the existence of genes with effects on behavior should not be allowed to erode[11] responsibility in the legal system or in everyday life.

5   Don't count on any single gene with a large behavioral effect being identified any time soon. Behavioral genetics has uncovered a paradox[12]. Studies that measure similarities among twins and adoptees reliably show strong effects of sharing many genes (such as half a genome, or all of one). The outcome is so reliable that behavioral geneticists now speak of the First Law of their field: that all behavioral traits are partly heritable.

6   But studies that try to isolate a single gene for a behavioral trait have been fickle[13]; many of putative[14] genes-for-X have not held up in replications[15]. Genes must exert their effects by acting together in complex combinations. A rough analogy[16]: a computer program can have a trait, such as being easy to use, without necessarily having a single magical programming instruction that makes any program easy to use when added and any program hard to use when omitted.

7   So psychological engineering is more remote than the futurologists[17] would have you believe. Though musical talent may be partly heritable, there is probably no single gene for musical talent that ambitious parents can have implanted into their unborn children. It might take hundreds or thousands of the right genes, with a different combination needed for each child.

8   Finally, the fact that genes matter doesn't mean that other things don't matter. Some of these causes are obvious. There are no genes for speaking English or for being a Presbyterian (though there may be sets of genes for verbal skill and religiosity). These depend entirely on one's culture. Others are less obvious, such as germs, accidents, chance encounters in life, and random events in the development of the brain in utero[18].

9   And still other environmental factors may not be acting as we think they do. It's easy to assume that the variation in behavior that is not caused by genes must be caused by parents. But it's been surprisingly hard to demonstrate any long-term effects of growing up in a particular family within a culture. Identical twins reared together are similar, but they are not literally identical: one may be more anxious than the other, one may be gay and the other straight. This shows that genes are not everything—but since these twins grow up in the same family, it also shows that what isn't explained by genes isn't explained by family influences either. Similarly, children need to hear English to acquire it. But if their parents are immigrants, they end up with the accent of their peers, not their parents.

10   Though the effects of genes may be easy to overestimate, they are also easy to underestimate. Many failed utopias[19] of the twentieth century dreamed of nurturing a "new man" free of selfishness, family ties, and individual differences. Some psychotherapists promise what they cannot deliver, such as transforming a shy person into a bold one or a sad sack into a barrel of monkeys.

11   None of this means that social and personal improvement are a waste of time. Even if each of us is born with a range of temperament and talent, we can try to reach the best point in that range. And even if we have a nature, part of that nature is an open-ended ingenuity[20] that can think up possible solutions to our problems. Using our genes as an excuse for fatalism[21] is unwise. But so is pretending that they don't matter at all.

13. **Fickle:** not consistent, likely to change

14. **Putative:** supposed

15. **Replications:** studies that repeat previous similar experiments in order to verify the outcomes

16. **Analogy:** a comparison used to illustrate a concept or situation

17. **Futurologist:** a person who thinks about or makes predictions about the future

18. **In utero:** in the uterus; before birth

19. **Utopia:** a perfect society or an attempt to create such a society

20. **Ingenuity:** cleverness

21. **Fatalism:** the belief that a person cannot change his or her nature or circumstances because everything is determined by fate

CHECK COMPREHENSION

1. What is the main idea of this essay?

2. Why are people afraid of research discussing behavior and genetics? (See paragraph 2)

3. What are three reasons we should not be afraid of researching genetics and behavior? (See paragraphs 4, 5, and 8)

4. What other factors influence behavior? (See paragraph 9)

5. What is a rational response to the influence of genetics on behavior and ability, according to Pinker? (See paragraph 11)

WRITE TO IMPROVE READING   Summarize

Using your annotations, write a summary of Pinker's essay, making sure that you address the answers to the Check Comprehension questions above.

MAKE INFERENCES

Based on your understanding of the essay, what would Pinker say to the following students?

1. Bethany: "I am destined to fail math; after all, my parents weren't good math students, and I inherited their lousy math skills."

2. Darrin: "I would love to play professional football, but I'm 5'4" and I weigh only 160 pounds. I guess football isn't a career option that is open to me."

Know P/Q: How to Use Partial Quotations

We have learned how to quote a complete sentence and how to vary the structure of a quote by moving the signal phrase (see p. 260). Another way to use a quotation is to quote only *part* of a sentence.

VARIATION 2: QUOTE ONLY PART OF THE ORIGINAL SENTENCE

Let's look at an example. One student responded to a question about this article by writing this sentence:

Pinker explains that the genes we inherit from our parents "cannot pull the strings of behavior directly" (262).

Notice how this sentence is different from other examples you have seen:

- Only part of the original sentence is quoted (and the quoted part is not a complete sentence).
- The quoted part is not introduced by a signal phrase. Instead, it fits into the structure of the whole sentence.
- The first letter of the first word in the quote is not capitalized.

Quoting only part of a sentence—or a phrase—is another way to use quoted material in your own writing. Take a look at one more example:

Steven Pinker describes two fears concerning behavioral genetics: society's ability to "re-engineer human nature" and the potential of using genes as an excuse for crimes and other forms of bad behavior (262).

Here, only three words are copied from the original essay; the rest of the sentence is actually a paraphrase. But since the ideas and some specific words are borrowed from Pinker's essay, we still include a citation.

PRACTICE   **Using Partial Quotations**

Answer each of the following questions. In each answer, be sure to quote part of a sentence from Pinker's essay. Cite your quote properly. The first one has been done for you.

Example: What do studies of twins separated at birth tell us?

Answer: *Pinker explains that identical twins who are not raised in the same home show how genes can affect intelligence, personality, happiness and even "personal quirks such as giggling incessantly or flushing the toilet both before and after using it" (261).*

1. How do genes affect behavior? (para. 4)

2. How does Pinker view "free will"? (para. 4)

3. Can science give us a single gene connected to a single behavior? (para. 6)

4. What sorts of abilities or behaviors are determined by culture instead of genes? (para. 7)

5. Are family environment and genetics the only factors that influence behavior? (para. 8)

6. What is a reasonable attitude towards our genetic inheritance? (para. 10)

Build Vocabulary: Prefixes

Many English words include a **prefix**, one or more letters added to the beginning of the word that can change the meaning of the word. Recognizing common prefixes, such as *pre-*, can help you understand new vocabulary.

Look at the following words that begin with the prefix *pre-*: What do you think *pre-* means?

*pre*fix, *pre*view, *pre*pay, *pre*caution, *pre*historic, *pre*dict

Identify the prefix in each of the following words from Pinker's article. What does each prefix mean?

Word	Prefix	Meaning of Prefix
introversion (related words are introvert, introverted, and introspection)		
re-engineer, rethink		
misplaced		
uncovered, unborn, unwise		
transforming		
implanted		

Understanding Strategies Used in Cause and Effect: Nouns and Verbs

Steven Pinker uses both nouns and verbs to describe the effects of our genes on our behavior. Look at the following sentence from paragraph 4:

Behavior is caused by the activity of the brain, and the most genes can do is <u>affect</u> its wiring, its size and shape, and its sensitivity to hormones and other molecules.

Is the underlined word a noun or a verb? How do you know? Now look at this sentence, from paragraph 6:

Genes must exert their <u>effects</u> by acting together in complex combinations.

Is the underlined word a noun or a verb? How do you know?

Based on these sentences, how would you explain the difference between **affect** and **effect**? Can you find additional examples in Pinker's essay to support your answer?

Understanding Strategies Used in Cause and Effect: Transition Words

Steven Pinker provides his readers with clues that will help them follow his discussion of genetics and behavior. Those clues include clear transition words. For example, at the end of paragraph 2, he suggests that we should not be too worried about genetic influence, and he introduces his first supporting reason in paragraph 4: "for one thing." Using transition words helps readers follow a complicated explanation of causes and effects.

Skim Pinker's article and circle the transition words you find. What does each word signal to the reader? Use your answers to complete the following chart. The first one has been done for you.

Word	Paragraph	Signal
But	6	Contrast

RESPOND IN WRITING

1. Pinker suggests that some of our behavioral and personality traits are inherited genetically, but others may not be. What is one trait that you believe you inherited from your parents genetically? What is one trait that you do not believe you inherited from your parents? Describe these two traits and explain why you believe you did (or did not) inherit each trait genetically.

2. In paragraph 5, the writer suggests that behavioral genetics presents us with a paradox. What is a paradox? What is the paradox that Pinker describes in paragraphs 5 and 6? Explain this paradox in your own words, making sure that you cite Pinker's ideas accurately.

3. Pinker provides an analogy in paragraph 6: genetic traits may be like a computer program. Write a paragraph explaining this analogy in your own words, making sure to cite your paraphrase accurately. Can you use another analogy to illustrate the same point?

4. In paragraph 4, Pinker defines both "free will" and "holding people responsible" in terms of circuits within our brains. How would you define these concepts? Explain your answer in a paragraph.

Extend and Connect: Write Your Own Cause and Effect Essay

1. In paragraph 2, Pinker describes society's fears about the science of behavioral genetics. What might cause someone to be afraid of science and scientific research? Explore your answer in an essay.

2. While genetic inheritance does impose some limits on a person's abilities, according to Pinker, that should not stop people from trying to improve themselves and make changes for the better. What can cause a person to make a significant change in behavior? What can prevent a person from making such a change? Explore these questions in an essay, referring to Pinker and at least one other essay in the text for support.

3. Tierney's essay explains how giving money to others can make us happy. What else can cause happiness? Explore the causes of happiness, using Tierney's essay and at least one other essay in the book.

CHECKLIST

Writing a Cause and Effect Essay

Prewrite > Draft > Revise > Edit

NARROW AND EXPLORE YOUR TOPIC (see Chapter 2)

☐ Make the topic more specific.

☐ Use prewriting techniques to get ideas about your narrow topic.

Prewrite > **Draft** > Revise > Edit

DRAFT A TOPIC SENTENCE OR THESIS STATEMENT (see Chapter 4)

☐ Determine your purpose: do you want to analyze causes, effects, or both?

SUPPORT YOUR POINT (see Chapter 4)

☐ Prewrite to find causes (or effects), and make sure that each one is a real cause (or effect).

☐ Choose the most significant causes or effects.

☐ Discover details, definitions, and examples to support the causes or effects.

WRITE A FULL DRAFT (see Chapter 4)

☐ Make a plan that arranges the causes and effects logically.

☐ Include the topic sentence (paragraph), an introduction and a thesis (essay), and all the support points.

☐ Add a concluding sentence or concluding paragraph.

Prewrite > Draft > **Revise** > Edit

REVISE YOUR DRAFT (see Chapter 5)

☐ Make sure you have covered the Four Basics of Good Cause and Effect.

☐ Get feedback from your peers.

☐ Make sure all your causes and/or effects are directly related to the topic.

☐ Make sure you have included transitions to move readers smoothly from one cause/effect to the next.

Prewrite > Draft > Revise > **Edit**

EDIT YOUR REVISED DRAFT (see Chapter 5)

☐ Correct mistakes in grammar, spelling, punctuation, and word usage.

☐ Make sure your draft is formatted correctly.

13

Argument:
Texts That Persuade

Understand What Argument Is

Argument is writing that takes a position on an issue and gives supporting evidence to persuade someone else to accept, or at least consider, the position. Argument is also used to convince someone to take (or not take) an action.

Four Basics of Good Argument

1	It takes a strong and definite position.
2	It gives good reasons and supporting evidence to defend the position.
3	It considers opposing views.
4	It has enthusiasm and energy from start to finish.

In the following paragraph, the numbers and colors correspond to the Four Basics of Good Argument.

4 Argument is enthusiastic and energetic.

1 Even though I write this blog post on an 88-degree day, I am truly glad that I stopped using my air conditioner, and I urge you to follow my lead. **2** For one thing, going without air conditioning can save a significant amount of money. Last summer, this strategy cut my electricity costs by nearly $2,000, and I am on my way to achieving even higher savings this summer. For another thing, living without air conditioning reduces humans' effect on the environment. Agricultural researcher Stan Cox estimates that air conditioning creates 300 million tons of carbon dioxide (CO_2) emissions each year. This amount, he says, is the equivalent of every U.S. household buying an additional car and driving it 7,000 miles annually. Because CO_2 is one of the greenhouse gases responsible for trapping heat in our atmosphere, reducing CO_2 emissions is essential to curbing climate change. The final reason for going without air conditioning is that it is actually pretty comfortable. The key to staying cool is keeping the blinds down on south-facing windows during the day. It is also a good idea to open windows throughout the home for cross ventilation while turning on ceiling fans to improve air circulation. **3** Although some people argue that using fans is just as bad as switching on the air conditioner, fans use far less electricity. In closing, let me make you a promise: The sooner you give up air conditioning, the sooner you will get comfortable with the change—and the sooner you and the planet will reap the rewards.

4 Argument is enthusiastic and energetic.

Reading an argument critically and writing an argument effectively are two of the most useful skills you can develop.

College	You read arguments supporting different interpretations of history and determine which is more effective.
	You write an argument for or against makeup exams for students who do not do well the first time.
Work	You listen to presentations from different contractors to determine which offers the best solution for your office needs.
	You need to leave work an hour early one day a week for twelve weeks to take a course, and you persuade your boss to allow you to do so.
Everyday life	You read a community group's petition to change traffic patterns in front of the public schools, and you decide whether or not to support the petition.
	You try to negotiate a better price on an item you want to buy.

In college, reading and writing assignments may include questions or statements such as the following:

Do you agree or disagree with _____ ?

Evaluate the evidence in _____ .

Defend (or refute) the position that _____ .

Is _____ fair, just, and reasonable?

Explain and evaluate reasons for _____ .

Argument in the Classroom: Commenting Effectively on Discussion Boards

Chase is taking a student development class online. A major component of the course is the online discussion board. Each week, the instructor posts a question about a college policy or requirement for the students to discuss. Students are required to submit an initial response to the question as well as two responses to the comments of others. Chase received low grades on the first two discussion boards, with the following comment from his instructor: "Go back and look at the instructions for posting and commenting, Chase. While you are meeting the minimum posting requirements, you are not contributing to an effective and reasonable class discussion. In fact, your posts often shut down discussion rather than build it up."

At first, Chase was frustrated by the comments from his teacher. But he decided to review the instructions again. As he did so, he recognized the Four Basics of Good Argument:

Student Development 100: Instructions for Discussion Board Posts	Four Basics of Good Argument
1. Each post is at least three sentences long.	1. Strong and definite position
2. Each post considers the ideas of the others in the class respectfully and carefully.	2. Good reasons and supporting evidence
3. Each post provides a supporting quote, example, or statistic.	3. Consideration of opposing views
4. The post may contradict, extend, complicate, support, or raise key questions about other posts, but the position must be clear.	4. Enthusiasm and energy
5. The post should be written in college-level English.	
6. The post should reflect a student's interest and engagement in the class discussion.	

Chase then considered a post from a classmate and his initial response to it:

Tasha: I think the service learning requirement is a great idea, for a couple of reasons. First, a lot of us learn best by doing. If we can find a project that relates to what we are learning in the classroom, I think we will learn better. I want to be a kindergarten

> teacher, so volunteering at a school makes sense. Plus, we get to know the people in the community better, and isn't that what "community college" is all about?
>
> (Reply) **Chase**: I just think it's a dumb idea. I have enough to do without doing more hours. You are wrong.

Chase had the three required sentences and a definite position, but his response lacked support and respect for the opposing point of view. When he showed the response to his friend Jordan, Jordan said, "All I see here is a guy who didn't want to do this assignment, so he wrote something off the top of his head." "In other words," replied Chase, "it tells Professor Landon that I don't care. I guess I see why she didn't give me much credit."

Chase decided to revise his response, to see what Professor Landon would say. Here is what he wrote:

> (Reply) **Chase**: Tasha, I can see your point about practical experience. But I don't think it always makes sense. For example, are there always service projects related to our courses? What about someone doing history or biology? Couldn't we make service learning an option for the classes where it makes sense? I guess I just don't like the idea of requiring it for everyone. Some people, like me, already work 30 hours a week in addition to class. I get to meet a lot of the community through work, and I don't think I need to do extra service to get to meet the community.

APPLY WHAT YOU HAVE LEARNED

1. Does Chase's second response illustrate the Four Basics of Good Argument? Explain.

2. If you were Chase's instructor, how would you respond to the second version of his post?

3. With your classmates, draft a set of "Guidelines for Class Discussion" based on the Four Basics of Good Argument. Then, conduct a discussion on a reading from this chapter with your classmates. How can following the Four Basics of Good Argument improve class discussion? Explain.

Main Point in Argument

The main point in argument is the position the writer takes on the **issue** (or **topic**). When you are identifying or drafting a main point for an argument, start by using a "should" or "should not" sentence:

Main point in argument   College football players should/should not be paid.

In an argument, the topic sentence (paragraph) or thesis statement (essay) usually includes the **issue** or **topic** and the **writer's position** on that topic. Here is an example of a topic sentence for a paragraph:

Our company should make regular contributions to local food banks.

Remember that the main point for an essay can be a little broader than one for a paragraph.

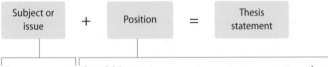

Our company should become more active in supporting charities.

Whereas the topic sentence focuses on just one type of charitable organization, the thesis statement sets up a discussion of different ways to help different charities.

> **PRACTICE 1**   **Identify Main Parts of the Main Idea in Argument**

1. Identify the subject/issue and the position for the sample paragraph on pages 270–271:

2. Identify the subject/issue and the position for the essay by Jason Yilmaz on pages 288–289:

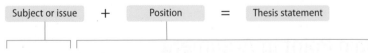

3. Identify the subject/issue and the position for the essay by Shari Beck on pages 289–290:

Subject or issue   +   Position   =   Thesis statement

PRACTICE 2   Write a Statement of Your Position

Write a statement of your position for each item.

Example:

Issue: Prisoners' rights

Position statement: _Prisoners should not have more rights and_
privileges than law-abiding citizens.

1. Issue: Lab testing on animals

   Position statement: _____

   _____

   _____

2. Issue: Use of cell phones while driving

   Position statement: _____

   _____

   _____

3. Issue: Athletes' salaries

   Position statement: _____

   _____

   _____

4. Issue: Treadmill desks

   Position statement: _____

   _____

   _____

5. Issue: Organic farming

   Position statement: _____

   _____

   _____

Paragraphs vs. Essays in Argument

For more on the important features of argument, see the Four Basics of Good Argument on page 270.

Paragraph Form

Topic sentence

Support 1 (reason 1)

Support 2 (reason 2)

Support 3 (reason 3)

Concluding sentence

Our company should make regular contributions to local food banks. The first reason for making these contributions is that, as a food wholesaler, we have the resources to do so. Often, we find that we have a surplus of certain items, such as canned goods and pasta, and it would be a waste not to donate this food to organizations that need it so desperately. We could also donate food that is safe to consume but that we cannot sell to stores or institutions. These items include market-testing products from manufacturers and goods with torn labels. Second, these contributions will improve our image among clients. All other things being equal, grocers, schools, hospitals, and other institutions will be more likely to purchase food from a wholesaler that gives something back to the community than one focused on its financial interests alone. The most important reason for making these contributions is to help our company become a better corporate citizen. Especially in challenging economic times, many people see corporations as heartless, and motivated by profits alone. It is important to show not only clients but also the wider community that we are one of the "good guys." That is, we are willing to do what is right, not only within our organization but also in society. Although some question the need for a donation program, arguing that it would take too much time to organize, the good that will come from the program will far exceed the effort devoted to it.

Main Point: Often narrower for a paragraph than for an essay: while the topic sentence (paragraph) focuses on just one type of charitable organization, the thesis statement (essay) sets up a discussion of different ways to help different charities.

Support for the Main Point (Reasons for the Writer's Position)

Evidence to Back Up Each Reason: Usually 1 to 3 sentences per reason for paragraphs and 3 to 8 sentences per reason for essays.

Conclusion

Think Critically As You Write Argument

Ask Yourself

- Have I questioned the assumptions behind my main point?
- Have I looked for evidence to respond to these questions and to develop support for my argument? (For more on finding and evaluating outside sources, see pp. 309–317.)
- Have I tested this evidence before including it in my paper? (For more on testing evidence, see p. 282.)

1

At the last executive meeting, we discussed several possible ways to improve our company's marketing and advertising and to increase employee morale. Since attending the meeting, I have become convinced [**Thesis statement**] effort would help in those areas and more: Our company should become more active in supporting charities.

[**Topic sentence 1 (reason 1)**] First, giving time and money to community organizations is a good way to promote our organization. This approach has worked well for several competitors. For example, Lanse Industries is well known for sponsoring Little League teams throughout the city. Its name is on the back of each uniform, and banners promoting Lanse's new products appear on the ball fields. Lanse gets free promotion of these efforts through articles in the local papers, and according to one company source quoted in the *Hillsburg Gazette,* Lanse's good works in the community have boosted its sales by 5 to 10 percent. Another competitor, Great Deals, has employees serve meals at soup kitchens over the holidays and at least once during the spring or summer. It, too, has gotten great publicity from these efforts, including a spot on a local TV news

2

show. It is time for our company to start reaping these kinds of benefits.

[**Topic sentence 2 (reason 2)**] Second, activities like group volunteering help employees feel more connected to one another and to their community. Kay Rodriguez, a manager at Great Deals and a good friend of mine, organized the company's group volunteering efforts at the soup kitchens, and she cannot say enough good things about the results. Aside from providing meals to the needy, the volunteering has boosted the morale of Great Deals employees because they understand that they are supporting an important cause in their community. Kay has also noticed that as employees work together at the soup kitchens, they form closer bonds. She says, "Some of these people work on different floors and rarely get to see each other during the work week. Or they just do not have time to talk. But while they work together on the volunteering, I see real connections forming." I know that some members of our executive committee might think it would be too time-consuming to organize companywide volunteering efforts. Kay assures me, however, that this is not

3

the case and that the rewards of such efforts far exceed the costs in time.

[**Topic sentence 3 (reason 3)**] The most important reason for supporting charities is that it is the right thing to do. As a successful business that depends on the local community for a large share of revenue and employees, I believe we owe that community something in return. If our home city does not thrive, how can we? By giving time and money to local organizations, we provide a real service to people, and we present our company as a good and caring neighbor instead of a faceless corporation that could not care less if local citizens went hungry, had trash and graffiti in their parks, or couldn't afford sports teams for their kids. We could make our community proud to have us around.

[**Concluding paragraph**] I realize that our main goal is to run a profitable and growing business. I do not believe, however, that this aim must exclude doing good in the community. In fact, I see these two goals moving side-by-side, and hand-in-hand. When companies give back to local citizens, their businesses benefit, the community benefits, and everyone is pleased by the results.

Support in Argument

The paragraph and essay models on pages 276–277 use the topic sentence (paragraph) and thesis statement (essay) from the Main Point in Argument section of this chapter. Both models include the **support** used in all argument writing: the reasons for the writer's position backed up by evidence. In the essay model, however, the major support points (or reasons) are topic sentences for individual paragraphs.

Recognizing and writing strong support for an argument requires critical thinking. We learned in Chapter 1 that critical thinking is a careful and reasoned approach to making decisions, solving problems, and understanding complex issues. Let's look more closely at critical thinking for reading and writing arguments.

Four Basics of Critical Thinking

1   Be alert to assumptions made by you and others.

2   Question those assumptions.

3   Consider and connect various points of view, even those different from your own.

4   Do not rush to conclusions; instead, remain patient with yourself and others, and keep an open mind.

Jess, a college student working on sharpening her reading and writing skills, applied these four basics while working on an argument paper for her English class. She got an idea for the paper while waiting to start her shift at a local restaurant. On the TV over the restaurant's bar, a political commentator and a doctor were debating whether a tax on soda and other sugary drinks would help reduce obesity.

Jess was in favor of just about any reasonable approach to fighting obesity, although she wasn't sure that a tax on soda and other sugary beverages would work. Even the doctor seemed a little unsure.

After finishing her shift, Jess thought about the issue some more, and she began to see how the pros of such a tax might outweigh the cons, but she decided to sleep on the issue before coming to any final conclusions. Here is the working main point she wrote down in her notebook before going to bed.

MAIN POINT   *Taxing sugary drinks might be a good way to reduce obesity.*

Questioning Assumptions to Build Evidence

The next morning, Jess used a key critical-thinking strategy to explore her main point in more depth. Specifically, she tried to identify some of the **assumptions** (unquestioned ideas or opinions) behind her main point. She wrote them down on one-half of a sheet of notebook paper. Next, she questioned each of her assumptions, trying to put herself in the shoes of someone opposed to beverage taxes. She wrote these questions on the other half of the notebook paper.

ASSUMPTIONS BEHIND MAIN POINT	QUESTIONS ABOUT ASSUMPTIONS
Sugary drinks, like soda, energy drinks, and sweetened tea, can make people fat.	But why target sugary drinks instead of other junk food? Aren't french fries just as bad for the waistline as soda is?
Taxes on sugary drinks would make people less likely to buy these beverages.	Really? It's easy for me to say that this tax would work because I'm not a big fan of these drinks. But if they taxed coffee, the taxes would have to be pretty big to break my four-cup-a-day habit.
The tax revenues would benefit the public.	How much difference would they really make?

To answer these questions, Jess turned to some sources recommended by a college librarian later that day. She also drew on information she found through a Google search, and on a few of her own experiences and observations. In doing so, she gathered the following four types of evidence used most often in support of arguments.

- Facts: Statements or observations that can be proved. One type of fact is statistics, or real numbers taken from carefully designed studies of the issue. Be sure to check the context and source of any statistical data. For example, if a source says that 75 percent of college students surveyed support a tax on soda, you need to know how many students were surveyed and where those students came from.

- Examples: Specific information or experiences that support a position. Examples can come from a writer's reading and research, or they may be drawn from the writer's own life.

- Expert Opinions: The opinions of people considered knowledgeable about a topic because of their credentials (education, work, experience, or research). It is important to investigate expert opinions carefully. For example, an economics professor might be very knowledgeable about the possible benefits and drawbacks of beverage taxes. He or she probably wouldn't be the best source of information on the health effects of soda.

- Predictions: Forecasts of the possible outcomes of events or actions. These forecasts should be the informed or educated views of experts, not the best guesses of nonexperts.

PRACTICE 3   **Identify Types of Evidence**

Jess revised and expanded her original questions as she followed the fourth basic of critical thinking: keeping an open mind. The following chart shows the evidence that Jess pulled together to address her assumptions and her questions about them. Determine which kind of evidence Jess found: fact, example, expert opinion, or prediction. The first one has been done for you.

Assumptions/Questions to Investigate	Evidence in Response
To what degree do sugary drinks contribute to obesity?	**Example: According to the Centers for Disease Control and Prevention, about half of all Americans get a major portion of their daily calories from sweetened beverages.** Type of evidence: *fact* _____ 1. In the *Journal of Pediatrics*, Robert Murray reported that one-fourth of U.S. teenagers drink as many as four cans of soda or fruit drinks a day, each one containing about 150 calories. That translates to a total of 600 calories a day, the equivalent of an additional meal. Type of evidence: _____ 2. Dr. Richard Adamson, senior scientific consultant for the American Beverage Association, says, "Blaming one specific product or ingredient as the root cause of obesity defies common sense. Instead, there are many contributing factors, including regular physical activity." Type of evidence: _____
Do sugary drinks deserve to be targeted more than other dietary factors that can contribute to obesity?	3. My brother, his wife, and their three kids are all big soda drinkers, and they are all overweight. They also eat lots of junk food, however, so it is hard to tell how much the soda is to blame for their weight. Type of evidence: _____ 4. The Center for Science in the Public Interest says that sugary beverages are more likely to cause weight gain than solid foods are. After eating solid food, people tend to reduce their consumption of other calorie sources. Unlike solid foods, however, sugary beverages do not make people feel full.

Assumptions/Questions to Investigate	Evidence in Response
	Therefore, they may add on calories to satisfy their hunger. Type of evidence: _____
To what degree would taxes on sugary drinks discourage people from buying these beverages and reduce obesity?	5. Several researchers say that the taxes would have to be pretty significant to affect consumer behavior. The average national tax on a 12-ounce bottle of soda is five cents, and that has not provided enough discouragement. Type of evidence: _____ 6. In the *New England Journal of Medicine*, Kelly D. Brownell says that a penny-per-ounce tax on sugary beverages could reduce consumption of these beverages by more than 10 percent. Type of evidence: _____
Would the taxes have any other benefits?	7. Kelly D. Brownell says that by reducing the consumption of sugary beverages, the taxes could help cut public expenditures on obesity. Each year, about $79 billion goes toward the health-care costs of overweight and obese individuals. Approximately half of these costs are paid by taxpayers. Type of evidence: _____ 8. Brownell also believes that the tax revenues could/should be used for programs to prevent childhood obesity. Type of evidence: _____

In the process of investigating her assumptions, Jess not only gathered good support; she also encountered some opposing views (one of the Four Basics of Good Argument). One of the opposing views, from Dr. Richard Adamson of the American Beverage Association, gave her a little pause. Because he represents the interests of the beverage industry, he might not offer a completely balanced opinion on the health effects of sweetened drinks, but Jess decided that as long as she mentioned his affiliation with the beverage industry, his point might be worth including in her paper.

In reviewing her evidence, Jess also referred to the following tips from her instructor.

Addressing Audience and Testing Evidence

- Consider your audience's view of the issue. Are audience members likely to agree with you, to be uncommitted, or to be hostile? Then, make sure your evidence would be convincing to a typical member of your audience.

- Reread your evidence from an opponent's perspective, looking for ways to knock it down. Anticipate your opponent's objections, and include evidence to answer them.

- Do not overgeneralize. Statements about what everyone else does or what always happens are easy to disprove. It is better to use facts (including statistics), specific examples, expert opinions, and informed predictions.

- Make sure you have considered every important angle of the issue.

- Reread the evidence to make sure it provides good support for your position. Also, the evidence must be relevant to your argument.

PRACTICE 4   **Consider the Audience**

Jess needed to consider her audience. What questions would her audience ask, and would they find her evidence convincing? Select one of the following target audiences. Determine what objections they would have to the tax on sugary sodas. Would the evidence Jess has gathered address their concerns? Why or why not?

1. Parents of children and teens

   Objections to the tax:

   Response to the evidence:

2. Soda company employees

   Objections to the tax:

   Response to the evidence:

3. College students

   Objections to the tax:

   Response to the evidence:

4. Restaurant owners

   Objections to the tax:

   Response to the evidence:

| PRACTICE 5 | **Review the Evidence** |

For each of the following positions, one piece of evidence is weak: it does not support the position. Circle the letter of the weak evidence, and, in the space provided, state why it is weak.

Example:

Position: Advertisements should not use skinny models.

Reason: Skinny should not be promoted as ideal.

    a.   Three friends of mine became anorexic trying to get skinny.

    b.   Everyone knows that most people are not that thin.

    c.   A survey of girls shows that they think that they should be as thin as models.

    d.   People can endanger their health trying to fit the skinny "ideal" promoted in advertisements.

Not strong evidence because *"everyone knows" is not strong*

evidence; everyone obviously doesn't know that.

  1. Position: People who own guns should not be allowed to keep them at home.

      Reason: It is dangerous to keep a gun in the house.

    a.   Guns can go off by accident.

    b.   Keeping guns at home has been found to increase the risk of home suicides and adolescent suicides.

    c.   Just last week, a story in the newspaper told about a man who, in a fit of rage, took his gun out of the drawer and shot his wife.

    d.   Guns can be purchased easily.

      Not strong evidence because _____

      _____

  2. Position: Schoolchildren in the United States should go to school all year.

      Reason: Year-round schooling promotes better learning.

    a.   All my friends have agreed that we would like to end the long summer break.

b. A survey of teachers across the country showed that children's learning improved when they had multiple shorter vacations rather than entire summers off.

c. Many children are bored and restless after three weeks of vacation and would be better off returning to school.

d. Test scores improved when a school system in Colorado went to year-round school sessions.

Not strong evidence because _____

_____

3. Position: The "three strikes and you're out" law that forces judges to send people to jail after three convictions should be revised.

Reason: Basing decisions about sentencing on numbers alone is neither reasonable nor fair.

a. A week ago, a man who stole a slice of pizza was sentenced to eight to ten years in prison because it was his third conviction.

b. The law makes prison overcrowding even worse.

c. Judges always give the longest sentence possible anyway.

d. The law too often results in people getting major prison sentences for minor crimes.

Not strong evidence because _____

_____

After Jess reviewed her evidence, she decided to refine her initial position.

REVISED MAIN POINT   To help address the obesity crisis, states should place significant taxes on sugary beverages.

Notice that Jess got rid of the "might" wording that had been part of her original main point. Having done some research, she now believes strongly that the taxes are a good idea—as long as they are high enough to make a significant dent in consumption.

Before writing her paper, Jess created a rough outline stating her main point and her major support points—the reasons for the position expressed in her main point. The reasons are based on the evidence Jess gathered.

Jess's rough outline

> **Main point:** To help address the obesity crisis, states should place significant taxes on sugary beverages.
>
> **Support/reasons:**
>
> I. Sugary drinks are a major contributor to obesity.
>
> II. As long as they are significant, taxes on these drinks could reduce consumption.
>
> III. The taxes could fund programs targeting childhood obesity.

Organization in Argument

Most arguments are organized by **order of importance**, starting with the least important evidence and saving the most convincing reason and evidence for last.

Use **transitions** to move your readers smoothly from one supporting reason to another. Here are some of the transitions you might use in your argument.

For more information on using and punctuating these transitions, see Chapters 17 and 24.

Common Transitions in Argument

Conjunctive Adverbials	Adjectives and Nouns	Verbs
above all	one/another fact	remember that
also	the more/most important reason	note that
especially		
for example	the first (second, third) point	
in addition		
in fact		
in particular		
in the first place		
moreover		
nevertheless		

Jess used order of importance to organize her argument in favor of taxes on sugary drinks, which follows. You will notice that Jess did not incorporate all the evidence from the chart on page 280–281. Instead, she chose the evidence she believed offered the strongest support for her main point. She also included an opposing view. As you read the draft of her essay below, pay attention to the transition words she used. (The transitions have been highlighted in bold.)

To help address the obesity crisis, states should place significant taxes on sugary beverages, such as soda, sweetened tea and fruit juices, and energy drinks. These drinks are a good target for taxation because they are a major contributor to obesity. According to the Centers for Disease Control and Prevention, about half of all Americans get a major portion of their daily calories from sweetened beverages. **In addition**, the *Journal of Pediatrics* reports that one-fourth of U.S. teenagers get as many as 600 calories a day from soda or fruit drinks. This consumption is the equivalent of an additional meal. **Another reason to tax sugary drinks is that** such taxation could reduce consumption. However, it is important that these taxes be significant, because taxes of just a few additional pennies per can or bottle probably wouldn't deter consumers. According to Kelly D. Brownell, director of the Rudd Center for Food Policy and Obesity, a penny-per-ounce tax on sugary beverages could cut consumption of these beverages by more than 10 percent. It could also reduce the estimated $79 billion of taxpayer money spent each year on health care for overweight and obese individuals. **The most important reason to tax sugary drinks is that** the money from such taxes could be used to prevent future cases of obesity. As Brownell notes, the taxes could fund antiobesity programs aimed at educating children about healthy diets and encouraging them to exercise. Some people who are opposed to taxing sugary beverages, such as Dr. Richard Adamson of the American Beverage Association, argue that it is unfair to blame one product for our expanding waistlines. It is true that overconsumption of soda and other sweetened beverages is just one cause of obesity. Nevertheless, targeting this one cause could play a vital, lasting role in a larger campaign to bring this major health crisis under control.

PRACTICE 6 **Use Transitions in Argument**

The following argument essay encourages students to get involved in service work during college. It was written by Jorge Roque, an Iraq War veteran and Miami-Dade College student who is vice president of a service fraternity. After reading Roque's essay, fill in the blanks with transitions. You are not limited to the ones listed in the box on page 285.

_____

_____ you meet many new people and form a new and larger network of friends and colleagues. You also learn new skills, like organization, project management, communication, teamwork, and public speaking. The practical experience I have now is more than I could have gotten from a class, and I have met people who want to help me in my career.

_____

_____ you help other people and learn about them. You feel as if you have something valuable to give. You also feel part of something larger than yourself. So often, students are not connected to meaningful communities and work, and service helps you while you help others.

_____ service work makes you feel better about yourself and your abilities. What I am doing is important and real, and I feel better than I ever have because of my service involvement. If you get involved with community service of any kind, you will become addicted to it. You get more than you could ever give.

Read and Analyze Argument

These two student essays argue about the wisdom of using social media, like Facebook and Twitter, as educational aids in college.

Preview	Read	Review	Reflect and Respond

- Before you begin reading, think about your own experiences with social media and education. Have you ever used social media as part of your high school or college classrooms? What happened?
- Skim the titles of both essays. What do the titles tell you about the position taken by each writer?
- Create a guiding question for your reading.

Preview ➤ Read ➤ Review ➤ Reflect and Respond

Guidelines for Reading and Annotating Argument

Read and annotate the essays using these guidelines:

1. Pay attention to vocabulary using marginal notes, context clues, or a dictionary.

2. Find the main point and double underline it. Remember that the main point shows the writer's topic or issue and his or her position on that issue.

3. Underline reasons for the writer's position, and identify the evidence that the writer uses to support the reasons. Determine whether the evidence consists of facts, examples, expert opinions, or predictions, and test the evidence: is it accurate, fair, relevant, and complete?

4. Ask questions and make connections. Connect the author's reasons to your own experience, and determine which reasons are the most effective for you.

Student Argument Essay: "Yes" to Social Media in Education

Jason Yilmaz

A Learning Tool Whose Time Has Come

1. **Incorporate:** to add; to bring into

2. **Objection:** an argument against something

3. **Distractions:** things that draw attention away from something else

4. **Engage:** to become involved in

1   Efforts to incorporate[1] social media into courses at our college have drawn several complaints. A major objection[2] is that Facebook and Twitter are distractions[3] that have no place in the classroom. Based on my own experiences, I must completely disagree. Social media, when used intelligently, will get students more involved with their courses and help them be more successful in college.

2   In the first place, social media can help students engage[4] deeply with academic subjects. For example, in a sociology class that I took in high school, the instructor encouraged students to use Twitter in a research assignment. This assignment called for us to record, over one week, the number of times we observed students of different races and ethnic groups interacting outside of the classroom. Each of us made observations in the lunchroom, in the courtyard where students liked to hang out between classes, and in other public areas. We tweeted our findings as we did our research, and in the end, we brought them together to write a group report. The Twitter exchanges gave each of us new ideas and insights. Also, the whole process helped us understand what a research team does in the real world.

3   In the second place, social media are a good way for students to get help and support outside of class. As a commuter student with a job, it is hard for me to get to my instructors' office hours, let alone meet with

other students. Therefore, I would value Facebook groups that would let me post questions about assignments and other homework and get responses from instructors and other students. Also, I would be able to form online study groups with classmates.

4   Finally, social networking can make students feel more confident and connected. In the sociology course where I used Twitter, I found that other students valued and respected the information that I shared, just as I valued their contributions. Also, all of us felt like we were "in this together"—an uncommon experience in most classrooms. I have heard that feeling connected to other students and to the larger college community can make people less likely to drop out, and I believe it.

5   New things often scare people, and the use of social media in education is no exception. However, I would hate to see fears about social media get in the way of efforts to make students more engaged with and successful in college. We owe it to students to overcome such fears.

Student Argument Essay: "No" to Social Media in Education

Shari Beck

A Classroom Distraction—and Worse

1   Last week, I saw the campus newspaper's story about new efforts to incorporate Twitter, Facebook, and other social media into courses. What did I think about these efforts? To get my answer, I only had to lower the newspaper. Across the table from me was my fourteen-year-old son, whom I'd just told, for the third time, to go upstairs and do his homework. Instead, he was still under the spell[1] of his phone, thumbs flying as he continued to text a friend about who knows what.

1. **Spell:** a state of being enchanted or fascinated by something

2   As you might have guessed already, my answer to my own question is this: Making social media part of a college education is a terrible idea, for a whole lot of reasons.

3   One reason is the distraction factor, illustrated by my phone-addicted son. I am confident that he is not the only person incapable of turning his full attention to any subject when the competition is an incoming or outgoing text message, or anything happening on a computer screen. Supporters of the college's social-media initiative[2] say that students will benefit from discussing course material on Facebook or Twitter. I am concerned, however, that such discussions—when and if they ever take place—would quickly go off-topic, turning into social exchanges. Also, participants' attention could easily wander to other links and news flashes.

2. **Initiative:** a program or process

3. **Compromise:** to inter-fere with

4. **Savvy:** knowledge-able or sophisticated

5. **Plagiarism:** using other people's words as your own

4   Another reason I am opposed to social media in education is that students' postings on Facebook or Twitter might compromise[3] their pri-vacy. I am not confident that all teachers will educate students about the importance of limiting the personal information that they make available in public forums. Tech-savvy[4] students probably know how to maximize their privacy settings, but I doubt that all students do.

5   My biggest concern is that students will use social media to cheat. According to proponents of the social-media initiative, one of the big-gest educational advantages of Facebook and Twitter is that students can exchange information and form study groups. But it is also possible that they will share answers to homework or test questions or take credit for information posted or tweeted by others. They may not real-ize that such information theft is plagiarism[5]—something that could cause them to fail a course, or worse. In responding to a 2011 survey by the Pew Research Center, 55 percent of college presidents said that student plagiarism had increased over the previous ten years. Of those who reported this increase, 89 percent said computers and the Inter-net played "a major role." It would be a shame to make this growing problem even worse through programs like the college's social-media initiative.

6   From where I sit—once again, across the table from my phone-distracted son—the disadvantages of this initiative far outweigh the ben-efits. I plan to send an e-mail opposing it to the Student Affairs Office. First, though, I'm taking my son's phone away for the night.

> Preview   Read   **Review**   Reflect and Respond

Review your reading. Make sure you can answer these questions:

1.   What is each writer's main point?

2.   What are the reasons that each writer gives for his or her position?

Following the guidelines from Chapter 6, write a summary of each essay.

> Preview   Read   Review   **Reflect and Respond**

1.   Using the guidelines on page 282, test the evidence used by each writer. What is the weakest evidence each writer presents? Why?

2.   What additional reasons or evidence could each writer include to strengthen his or her argument? Explain.

3.   Write a response to either essay. First summarize the argument that the writer has presented, and then explain your reasons for supporting or opposing the argument.

Reading/Writing Workbook: Argument

Professional Essay: "Start Snitching," Bill Maxwell

Preview

- Skim the information about the author, the title, and the first paragraph. What is the rhetorical context (audience, topic, and purpose) for this essay?
- What does the word *snitch* suggest to you? What are the connotations of this word?
- Based on your previewing, create a guiding question for your reading of this essay.

Read and annotate this essay carefully, following the Guidelines for Reading and Annotating Argument on page 288.

Bill Maxwell

Start Snitching

 Bill Maxwell is an internationally syndicated columnist and editorial writer for the *Tampa Bay Times* (formerly the *St. Petersburg Times*) in Florida. After receiving a B.A. from Bethune-Cookman College, he went on to earn a master's and a doctoral degree from the University of Chicago before he began teaching in 1973. His diverse background as an educator and a writer is evident in the many publications for which he has written, including the *Fort Pierce Tribune*, the *Gainesville Sun*, and the *Tampa Bay Times*. He wrote the essay "Start Snitching" in September 2007 for the *Times* in response to the deaths of several black men from the community. © MICHELLE GRAY PHOTOGRAPHY/STPETESPHOTOS.COM

1   Cedric "C. J." Mills. Isaiah Brooks. Tedric Maynor. Felicia Hines. Vinson Phillips. Kurt Anthony Bryant. Amuel Murph. Alfonso Williams. These names are forever inscribed[1] on my private "Wall of Black Death." My wall contains the names of black people killed by other black people, along with those believed to have been killed by fellow blacks, in the Tampa Bay area since May. I will update the roster[2] as soon as new deaths are reported. More are sure to follow. I do not have answers as to how to stop blacks from killing their brethren[3]. But I do have an answer for catching some, if not all, of these murderers. Snitch.

2   Nationwide, too many blacks refuse to help the police identify, find, and arrest killers in their communities. To enjoy a decent quality of life in their communities, blacks must begin to help the police. Studies show that homicides[4], especially unsolved homicides, destabilize[5] low-income communities. Needless

1. **Inscribed:** listed; written

2. **Roster:** a list of people
3. **Brethren:** brothers; men within the same race, nationality, or group
4. **Homicides:** murders
5. **Destabilize:** to make unsteady or cause something to fail

6. **Amenities:** comforts, conveniences, or pleasures
7. **Wary:** cautious

to say, many of the nation's black communities have individuals and families with low incomes. Businesses that can provide jobs for unemployed residents and provide the amenities[6] that other areas take for granted are wary[7] of locating in black communities where homicide rates are high.

3   A recent *St. Petersburg Times* article reported that a group of Tampa black residents have organized an effort to stop the "don't snitch" culture that permits killers to remain free. Many of the organizers are related in some way to a youngster killed by a fellow black. Consider this sobering portrait of blacks and homicide and other serious crimes from a recent U.S. Bureau of Justice Statistics report: Although blacks comprised only 13 percent of the population in 2005, they were victims of about 49 percent of all homicides. The bureau estimated that 16,400 murders occurred in the United States in 2005. Of that number, 8,000 victims were black, 93 percent of those victims were killed by other blacks, and 77 percent of those murders involved firearms. Most black victims were between ages 17 and 29.

4   Many people, including police officials I have spoken with, say that fear prevents most blacks from snitching. I agree that some residents remain silent out of fear, but I suspect that the fear factor receives too much weight. I have come to believe that an untold number of blacks have grown as insensitive to black-on-black murders as they have to other black-on-black crimes. For one thing, the high number of homicides in their communities has made many blacks inured[8] to all but the most sensational killings that receive a lot of press.

8. **Inured:** accustomed to or used to

9. **Predominantly:** mainly

5   "I expect somebody to shoot somebody every week around here," a St. Petersburg woman who lives in a predominantly[9] black neighborhood said a few weeks ago when I asked if she had known a man who had been killed recently. "I don't go near my windows at night. They shoot guns around here all the time. I don't pay attention when they say somebody got shot. I just try to make sure it won't be me one of these days."

10. **Sociologist:** a person who studies the origin, development, and other aspects of human society
11. **Syndrome:** a disorder or an illness
12. **Internalized:** made something part of your core beliefs or attitudes
13. **Perpetuating:** continuing
14. **Apparent:** obvious
15. **Brace:** to prepare for

6   I am not a sociologist[10], but I suspect that many blacks in high-crime communities have all the symptoms of the abused person syndrome[11]: We have been cruel toward one another for so long we have internalized[12] the belief that such cruelty is normal. Those of us who have internalized the cruelty think nothing of treating other blacks likewise, thus perpetuating[13] the cycle without apparent[14] end. Each day I open the newspaper and switch on TV news, I brace[15] myself for yet another murder. With each killing, I feel sadness, regret, helplessness, anger, and shame—shame of being associated with such people in any way.

7   Because I regularly write about this issue, I receive a lot of hate mail from both whites and blacks. White letter-writers remind me that blacks are "animals" and "cause all of America's social problems." Black letter-writers see me as the "enemy of the people" and a "sell-out" because I condemn blacks for killing one

another without taking into account the nation's history of racism. To whites, I have nothing to say. To blacks, I have one message: We need to start snitching. Only we can stop black-on-black murders. Until then, I will be adding names to the Wall of Black Death.

CHECK COMPREHENSION

1. What is Maxwell's position about snitching?

2. What are his major reasons?

3. What evidence does he provide for his reasons?

MAKE INFERENCES

Use your understanding of the reading to answer the following questions:

1. Does Maxwell expect more black deaths to occur?

2. How does Maxwell expect readers to respond to his argument? Does he expect readers of different races to react the same way?

WRITE TO IMPROVE READING   Summarize

Using the guidelines from Chapter 6, write a summary of this essay. Make sure your summary contains the answers to the Check Comprehension questions above.

Know P/Q: How to Make Sure That Quotations Are Clear

In a college English class, students were asked to quote an idea from Maxwell's essay and respond to it. Look at the beginning of these two student responses:

Isaac's answer
Bill Maxwell says that many black people are so used to violence that it doesn't affect them very much. In fact, he says, "I don't pay attention when they say somebody got shot" (292).

Desiree's answer
According to Maxwell and some police officers he talked to "say that fear prevents most blacks from snitching" (292).

These responses illustrate two possible problems you may encounter when you are quoting: an unclear/incorrect speaker and confusing sentence structure with partial quotes.

THE UNCLEAR/INACCURATE SPEAKER

Isaac's answer tells a reader that Bill Maxwell said the words that are in quotation marks. But this is not accurate. If you look carefully at paragraph 5 of the essay, you will find that a woman from St. Petersburg made this comment. Maxwell interviewed this woman and reported her comments in his essay. When you are writing with a source, you must make sure that you correctly identify the person speaking, especially when the essay you are writing about contains many quotes from other speakers. If you don't identify the speaker correctly, you may *misrepresent* your source; in other words, you may make the source say something that it doesn't say, or something that the author might not even agree with.

Isaac can correct this problem simply by identifying the actual speaker:

> Bill Maxwell says that many black people are so used to violence that it doesn't affect them very much. In fact, <u>a woman he interviewed for the article commented,</u> "I don't pay attention when they say somebody got shot" (292).

CONFUSING SENTENCE STRUCTURE

Desiree's answer has a different problem: confusing sentence structure. Desiree has chosen to quote only part of a sentence, beginning with the verb "say." That verb, however, does not have a subject in Desiree's sentence. Look at the sentence again carefully:

> [According to Maxwell and some police officers he talked to] "<u>say</u> that fear prevents most blacks from snitching" (292).

For more on subjects, see Chapter 15.

"According to" is a preposition. "Maxwell and some police officers he talked to" are the objects of the preposition. Because these words are the objects of the preposition, they cannot also be a subject for "say." Therefore, the sentence is missing a subject, making the structure confusing for a reader. When you incorporate part of a quote, you must make sure that the structure of the words you quote fits grammatically and logically with your sentence.

Desiree can correct her sentence in several ways:

> According to Maxwell, many people "say that fear prevents most blacks from snitching" (292).

> Maxwell talked to some people who "say that fear prevents most blacks from snitching" (292).

> According to the people Maxwell interviewed, "fear prevents most blacks from snitching" (292).

Notice that all of Desiree's corrections have a clear structure: the reader knows *who* believes that fear stops people from reporting crime.

PRACTICE 7   **Make Sure Quotations Are Clear**

Each of the following partial quotations is problematic. Identify the problem (incorrect speaker or confusing structure), and rewrite the quotation correctly.

1. Bill Maxwell suggests that people who want "to enjoy a decent quality of life in their communities, blacks must begin to help the police" (291).

   a.   Problem: _____

   b.   Revision: _____

   _____

2. Bill Maxwell explains how common violence is, since people "shoot guns around here all the time" (292).

   a.   Problem: _____

   b.   Revision: _____

   _____

3. Bill Maxwell wants to change the culture of "many blacks in high-crime communities have all the symptoms of the abused person syndrome" (292).

   a.   Problem: _____

   b.   Revision: _____

   _____

4. Bill Maxwell argues that "residents remain silent out of fear" (292).

   a.   Problem: _____

   b.   Revision: _____

   _____

5. Bill Maxwell admits he is the "enemy of the people" and a "sell-out" (293).

   a.   Problem: _____

   b.   Revision: _____

   _____

Understand Strategies Used in Argument: Counterarguments and Rebuttals

Look at the following quote from Maxwell's essay: "I agree that some residents remain silent out of fear, but I suspect that the fear factor receives too much weight" (292). In the first part of this sentence, Maxwell acknowledges the value of an idea that he does not fully support ("residents remain silent out of fear"). In the second part, Maxwell clarifies his own position ("the fear factor receives too much weight"). When we acknowledge the ideas of the "other side," we are addressing **counterarguments**. When we show our response to those counterarguments, we are **rebutting** the other side. A **rebuttal** is our response to someone who offers a different perspective. Many arguments use a "counterargument-rebuttal" pattern:

$\left\{\begin{array}{l} \text{I agree that} \\ \text{I admit that} \\ \text{Opponents say that} \\ \text{It's true/It's possible that} \\ \text{Some people suggest that} \end{array}\right\}$ + Counterargument

$\left\{\begin{array}{l} \text{, but} \\ \text{; however,} \end{array}\right\}$ + Rebuttal or response

You will see an example of the same strategy in Alexandra Natapoff's essay (see pp. 298–301):

Counterargument

{Critics of the T-shirts tend} to dismiss the "stop snitching" sentiment as pro-criminal and antisocial, a subcultural

Rebuttal

expression of misplaced loyalty. {But} the T-shirts should be heeded as evidence of a failed public policy.

> **PRACTICE 8**   **Identify Counterarguments and Rebuttals**

Look back at the essays by Yilmaz (p. 288) and Beck (p. 289). Identify one example of the counterargument and rebuttal strategy in each essay.

> **PRACTICE 9**   **Write a Counterargument and Rebuttal**

For each following topic and position, think of a counterargument that an opponent might suggest. Use a signal phrase to introduce the counterargument. Then, write a rebuttal. Highlight your rebuttal, and circle the word that you used to introduce it. The first one has been done for you.

Example:

Topic/Position: Colleges should be able to ban certain kinds of words in the classroom.

Some might say that banning racial, ethnic, or gender-based slurs and epithets is a limit on our freedom of speech, (but) I think that those kinds of names intimidate and interfere with learning—and everyone has a right to learn.

1. Topic/Position: Students should not be required to take standardized tests for placement in college English and math classes.

   _____

   _____

   _____

2. Topic/Position: To encourage recycling, people who put aluminum cans or plastic bottles in the trash should be fined.

   _____

   _____

   _____

RESPOND IN WRITING

1. Write a paragraph that answers the following questions: Why does Maxwell open his essay with the list of names? Do you find the introduction effective? Why or why not?

2. Write a paragraph explaining how the quotation in paragraph 5 supports Maxwell's argument. Summarize his argument in your paragraph.

3. Choose one of your revised quotations from Practice 7. Write a paragraph that includes the quote and your response to it. Do you agree with Maxwell? Why or why not?

4. How does Maxwell address his critics? Find and quote an example of how Maxwell addresses those who disagree with him. Be sure to cite your example accurately. Do you think he treats his opponents with respect? Why or why not? Explain your answer in a paragraph.

Professional Essay: "Bait and Snitch: The High Cost of Snitching for Law Enforcement," Alexandra Natapoff

Preview

- Skim the title, the information about the author, and the first paragraph. What is the rhetorical context for this essay (audience, purpose, and topic)?
- How do you respond to Natapoff's credentials? Explain.
- Predict what Natapoff's position will be.
- Create a guiding question for your reading.

Read and annotate this essay following the Guidelines for Reading and Annotating Argument on page 288.

Alexandra Natapoff

Bait and Snitch: The High Cost of Snitching for Law Enforcement

Alexandra Natapoff is a law professor at Loyola Law School in Los Angeles, California, where she teaches criminal law and criminal procedure. She graduated cum laude with a B.A. from Yale University and earned her J.D. with distinction at Stanford Law School. Before becoming a professor, Natapoff worked as an assistant federal public defender in Baltimore, Maryland; while there, she founded the Urban Law & Advocacy Project. As a scholar and writer, Natapoff is interested in the criminal justice system, as well as race and the law and administrative law. Her book, *Snitching: Criminal Informants and the Erosion of American Justice,* was published in 2009. COURTESY OF ALEXANDRA NATAPOFF. REPRODUCED BY PERMISSION.

1. **Ominous:** threatening

2. **Controversy:** an argument; a conflict of opinion

3. **Dust-up:** a fight

4. **Counterculture:** opposed to established culture

5. **Entrepreneurs:** people who start or manage businesses

6. **Insidious:** dangerous while appearing harmless

1   From Baltimore to Boston to New York; in Pittsburgh, Denver, and Milwaukee, kids are sporting the ominous[1] fashion statement, "Stop Snitchin," prompting local fear, outrage, and fierce arguments over crime. Several trials have been disrupted by the T-shirts; some witnesses refuse to testify. With cameo appearances in the growing controversy[2] by NBA star Carmelo Anthony of the Denver Nuggets and the rapper Lil Kim, snitching is making urban culture headlines.

2   The "Stop Snitchin'" T-shirt drama looks, at first, like a dust-up[3] over a simple counterculture[4] message launched by some urban criminal entrepreneurs[5]; that friends don't snitch on friends. But it is, in fact, a symptom of a more insidious[6] reality that has largely escaped public notice.

3   For the last 20 years, state and federal governments have been creating criminal snitches and setting them loose in poor, high-crime communities. The backlash[7] against snitches reflects a growing national recognition that snitching is dangerous public policy—producing bad information, endangering innocent people, letting dangerous criminals off the hook, compromising the integrity[8] of police work, and inciting[9] violence and distrust in socially vulnerable[10] neighborhoods.

4   The heart of the snitching problem lies in the secret deals that police and prosecutors make with criminals. In investigating drug offenses, police and prosecutors rely heavily—and sometimes exclusively—on criminals willing to trade information about other criminals in exchange for leniency[11]. Many snitches avoid arrest altogether, thus continuing to use and deal drugs and commit other crimes in their neighborhoods, while providing information to the police. As drug dockets[12] swell and police and prosecutors become increasingly dependent on snitches, high-crime communities are filling up with these active criminals who will turn in friends, family, and neighbors in order to "work off" their own crimes.

5   Critics of the T-shirts tend to dismiss the "stop snitching" sentiment as pro-criminal and antisocial, a subcultural expression of misplaced loyalty. But the T-shirts should be heeded[13] as evidence of a failed public policy. Snitching is an entrenched[14] law-enforcement practice that has become pervasive[15] due to its crucial role in the war on drugs. This practice is favored not only by police and prosecutors, but by legislatures: Mandatory[16] minimum sentences and restrictions on judges make snitching one of the only means for defendants to negotiate in the face of rigid and drastic[17] sentences. But the policy has turned out to be a double-edged sword[18]. Nearly every drug offense involves a snitch, and snitching is increasingly displacing more traditional police work, such as undercover operations and independent investigation.

6   According to some agents and prosecutors, snitching is also slowly crippling law enforcement: "Informers are running today's drug investigations, not the agents," says veteran DEA [Drug Enforcement Administration] agent Celerino Castillo. "Agents have become so dependent on informers that the agents are at their mercy."

7   The government's traditional justification for creating criminal snitches—"we-need-to-flip-little-fishes-to-get-to-the-Big-Fish"—is at best an ideal and mostly the remnant[19] of one. Today, the government lets all sorts of criminals, both big and little, trade information to escape punishment for nearly every kind of crime, and often the snitches are more dangerous than the targets.

7. **Backlash:** a strong or sudden violent reaction toward something

8. **Integrity:** morality, honesty, and legality

9. **Inciting:** urging on; encouraging

10. **Vulnerable:** easily harmed

11. **Leniency:** mildness; softness; tolerance

12. **Dockets:** lists of legal cases to be tried

13. **Heeded:** paid attention to

14. **Entrenched:** deeply dug in; secure

15. **Pervasive:** widespread

16. **Mandatory:** required

17. **Drastic:** extreme

18. **Double-edged sword:** something that can have both good and bad consequences

19. **Remnant:** a piece or part of

20. **Through the looking glass:** a place or situation where things happen in a way that is the opposite of expectations

21. **Incarcerate:** to put in jail

22. **Concoct:** to make up or invent

23. **Incentive:** a reason to do something

24. **Fabricating:** making up or inventing

25. **Attributing:** giving credit to someone

26. **Fiascos:** complete failures

27. **Devastating:** overwhelming; destructive

28. **Ironically:** in a way that goes against expectations or a desired outcome

8   Snitching thus puts us right through the looking glass[20]: Criminals direct police investigations while avoiding arrest and punishment. Nevertheless, snitching is ever more popular with law enforcement: It is easier to "flip" defendants and turn them into snitches than it is to fight over their cases. For a criminal system that has more cases than it can prosecute, and more defendants than it can incarcerate[21], snitching has become a convenient case-management tool for an institution that has bitten off more than it can chew.

9   And while the government's snitching policy has gone mostly unchallenged, it is both damaging to the justice system and socially expensive. Snitches are famously unreliable: A 2004 study by the Northwestern University Law School's Center on Wrongful Convictions reveals that 46 percent of wrongful death penalty convictions are due to snitch misinformation—making snitches the leading cause of wrongful conviction in capital cases. Jailhouse snitches routinely concoct[22] information; the system gives them every incentive[23] to do so. Los Angeles snitch Leslie White infamously avoided punishment for his crimes for years by fabricating[24] confessions and attributing[25] them to his cellmates.

10   Snitches also undermine law-enforcement legitimacy—police who rely on and protect their informants are often perceived as favoring criminals. In a growing number of public fiascos[26], snitches actually invent crimes and criminals in order to provide the government with the information it demands. In Dallas, for example, in the so-called "fake drug scandal," paid informants set up innocent Mexican immigrants with fake drugs (gypsum) while police falsified drug field tests in order to inflate their drug-bust statistics.

11   Finally, as the T-shirt controversy illustrates, snitching worsens crime, violence, and distrust in some of the nation's most socially vulnerable communities. In the poorest neighborhoods, vast numbers of young people are in contact with the criminal justice system. Nearly every family contains someone who is in prison, under supervision, or has a criminal record. In these communities, the law-enforcement policy of pressuring everyone to snitch can have the devastating[27] effect of tearing families and social networks apart. Ironically[28], these are the communities most in need of positive role models, strong social institutions, and good police-community relations. Snitching undermines these important goals by setting criminals loose, creating distrust, and compromising police integrity.

12   The "Stop Snitchin'" T-shirts have drawn local fire for their perceived threat to law-abiding citizens who call the police. But in the outrage over that perceived threat, the larger message of the shirts has been missed: Government policies that favor criminal snitching harm the communities most in need of law-enforcement protection.

13   While snitching will never be abolished[29], the practice could be substantially improved, mostly by lifting the veil of secrecy that shields law-enforcement practices from public scrutiny. As things stand, police and prosecutors can cut a deal with a criminal; turn him into a snitch or cut him loose; forgive his crimes or resurrect them later; release him into the community; or decide to pick him up. They do all this at their discretion, without legal rules, in complete secrecy, with no judicial or public accountability. As a result, we have no idea whether snitching even reduces crime or actually increases it, and we can only guess at the collateral harms it imposes on high-crime communities.

29. **Abolished:** ended

14   The government should reveal snitching's real costs, including data on how many snitches are released into high-crime neighborhoods and what sorts of snitch crimes are forgiven. The government should also be required to establish the concrete benefit of a policy that releases some criminals to catch others, by accounting for how much crime actually gets stopped or solved by snitch information. Only then can we rationally evaluate how much government-sponsored snitching makes sense. Until we can know the real value of snitching, the T-shirts remain an important reminder that this particular cure for crime may be as bad as the disease.

CHECK COMPREHENSION

1. What is Natapoff's position about snitching?

2. What are her major reasons?

3. What evidence does she provide for her reasons?

MAKE INFERENCES

1. Which of the following best describes Natapoff's intended audience? Why?

    a. criminals

    b. potential snitches

    c. government officials

    d. law enforcement officers

    e. general citizens

2. Do you think Natapoff would be likely to purchase a "Stop Snitchin'" T-shirt?

WRITE TO IMPROVE READING   Summarize

Using the guidelines from Chapter 6, write a summary of this essay. Before you begin, make sure that you can answer the Check Comprehension questions above. Include the answers to the questions in your written summary.

Build Vocabulary: Word Choice

Natapoff relies on carefully selected words to help her audience understand her point. Consider the following pairs of words. The first word appears in the essay, while the second is a synonym that Natapoff does not use. In each pair, discuss the differences in the connotations of the words. Why is Natapoff's choice effective?

Natapoff's Word	Synonym
insidious	dangerous
concoct	make up
fiasco	failure
drastic	extreme or severe
devastating	harmful

Understand Strategies Used in Argument: Using Qualifiers to Avoid Logical Fallacies

Look at the following section from Natapoff's essay. Pay attention to the words that are underlined.

> <u>Nearly</u> every drug offense involves a snitch, and snitching is <u>increasingly</u> displacing more traditional police work, such as undercover operations and independent investigation.

What would happen if these words were removed? In an argument, writers must avoid making generalizations that are too strong and cannot be supported. To do that, we add words like "nearly," "many," "increasingly," "often," or "usually" (instead of "all" or "always"). In addition, we can add words like "may," "can," and "could." These words soften the meaning of a statement.

PRACTICE

Find additional examples of words that soften statements in paragraphs 7 and 11.

RESPOND IN WRITING

1. Do you find Natapoff's evidence against snitching convincing? Explain.

2. Natapoff begins and ends her essay with a discussion of a t-shirt campaign to "stop snitching." What are the advantages and disadvantages of using t-shirts to make an argument? Explain.

3. In paragraph 9, Natapoff uses statistics to support her position. What is the topic sentence in paragraph 9? What statistics does she use to support this reason? Are her statistics effective? Explain.

4. In paragraph 10, Natapoff argues that the practice of snitching has created "public fiascos." How does she support this claim?

5. What does Natapoff ask for in her conclusion? Do you think her suggestions are reasonable? Explain.

Extend and Connect: Write Your Own Argument

1. Do you think that Maxwell and Natapoff define *snitch* in exactly the same way? Write an essay in which you compare and contrast the implied definition of *snitch* in the two essays.

2. The immediate focus of Natapoff's essay is the role of snitching in law enforcement, but the figure of the "snitch," "rat," informant, or even "tattletale" has almost always been one that many people dislike. Why do you think this is the case, even if such informants and snitches can help bring criminals to justice or perhaps stop bad things from happening? Write a paragraph or an essay that addresses these issues.

3. Do you see any areas of common ground in the arguments of Natapoff and Maxwell? Write a paragraph in which you discuss the common ground as a place to begin a reasonable discussion of the issue of snitching to stop crime.

4. Write a response that opposes or complicates either Natapoff's or Maxwell's conclusions. Be sure to explain your reasons carefully, and make sure that you accurately and fairly represent the other side.

CHECKLIST

Writing an Argument

Prewrite > Draft > Revise > Edit

NARROW AND EXPLORE YOUR TOPIC (see Chapter 2)

☐ Make the topic more specific.

☐ Use prewriting techniques to get ideas about your narrow topic.

Prewrite > **Draft** > Revise > Edit

DRAFT A TOPIC SENTENCE OR THESIS STATEMENT (see Chapter 4)

☐ Determine your position.

SUPPORT YOUR POINT (see Chapter 4)

☐ Prewrite to discover reasons for your position. If you are struggling, try one of the following tips:

1. *Imagine yourself arguing your position with someone who disagrees.*
2. *Imagine that your whole grade rests on persuading your instructor to agree with you.*
3. *Imagine how this issue could affect you or your family personally.*
4. *Imagine that you are representing a large group of people who care about the issue. It is up to you to win their case.*

☐ Choose the most significant reasons and evidence to support your position.

☐ Test your evidence.

☐ Make sure to consider the opposing point of view.

WRITE A FULL DRAFT (see Chapter 4)

☐ Make a plan that arranges the reasons logically.

☐ Include the topic sentence (paragraph), an introduction and a thesis (essay), and all the supporting points.

☐ Add a concluding sentence or concluding paragraph.

Prewrite > Draft > **Revise** > Edit

REVISE YOUR DRAFT (see Chapter 5)

☐ Make sure you have covered the Four Basics of Good Argument.

☐ Get feedback from your peers.

☐ Make sure you have included transitions to move readers smoothly from one reason to the next. →

CHECKLIST

Writing an Argument

Prewrite > Draft > Revise > **Edit**

EDIT YOUR REVISED DRAFT (see Chapter 5)

☐ Correct mistakes in grammar, spelling, punctuation, and word usage.

☐ Make sure your draft is formatted correctly.

14

Research:

Texts That Explore a Question and Synthesize Information

Understand What Research Is

In all areas of your life, and especially in college, you will do **research**—research is looking for information so that you can understand an issue or make an informed decision. Here are some situations in which you might use research skills:

College	In a criminal justice course, you are asked to explore whether or not the death penalty deters crime.
Work	You are asked to research a major office product that your company wants to purchase.
Everyday life	Your child's doctor has prescribed a certain medication, and you would like more information about it.

In your college courses, a research project requires that you use both reading and writing skills: you must read and understand source information carefully so that you can make a point, support it, and present it clearly to your readers. This chapter explores the process of writing a college research essay.

Four Basics of Good Research

1. Research is a process that begins with a question.
2. Research finds answers in relevant and appropriate sources.
3. Research uses source information fairly and honestly.
4. Research synthesizes (connects and combines) information from sources to support a thesis.

You learned in Chapter 1 that reading and writing are processes; in other words, they move through a series of steps that take time. Research also takes time. It cannot be started and completed successfully in a day or two. To make sure you allow enough time, make a schedule and stick to it. The first step in creating a strong working schedule is to review the requirements for your project, including the following:

Sample essay schedule

Assignment: (Write out what your instructor has assigned.) _____

_____

Number of outside sources required: _____

Length (if specified): _____

Draft due date: _____

Final due date: _____

My general topic: _____

Use these requirements to sketch a plan for your research process. Here is a sample checklist that you can follow:

Do by	Step
_____	Choose a topic.
_____	Find and evaluate sources; decide which ones to use.
_____	Take notes, keeping publication information for each source.
_____	Write a working thesis statement by answering a research question.
_____	Review all notes; choose the best support for your working thesis.
_____	Make an outline that includes your thesis statement and support.
_____	Write a draft, including a title.
_____	Revise the draft.
_____	Prepare a list of Works Cited using the correct form of documentation.
_____	Edit the revised draft.
_____	Submit the final copy.

Many of the steps in this process should be familiar to you; good research is built on the steps of the reading and writing processes you have been learning about in this book.

Begin with a Question: Choosing a Topic to Research

Your instructor may assign a research paper topic or may want you to think of your own topic. If you are free to choose your own topic, find a subject that interests you and that you would like to explore. Ask yourself questions such as the following:

1. What is going on in my own life that I want to know more about?

2. What do I daydream about? What frightens me? What inspires or encourages me?

3. What am I interested in doing in the future, either personally or professionally?

4. What famous person or people interest me?

5. What current issue do I care about?

Here are some current topics you might want to research:

Alternative energy sources	Jobs of the future
Behavior disorders	Music/musical groups
A career you are interested in	Obesity in the United States
Education issues	Online dating services
Environmental issues	Privacy and the Internet
Gay/lesbian marriage	Travel
Health/medical issues	Violence in the media
Immigration trends/policies	Volunteer opportunities

Whether you choose a topic or are assigned a specific one, you can do some prewriting activities (see Chapter 2) to help you narrow and refine your topic before you begin to do research. As you prewrite, you should develop a **guiding research question**, which is often a variation of "What do I want to find out about my topic?" This question will help direct and focus your research. In other words, a guiding research question gives you a **purpose** for the processes of finding, evaluating, and reading source information.

The following is a guiding research question used by Dara Riesler, who chose the topic of dogs trained to help war veterans suffering from post-traumatic stress disorder (PTSD). (To learn how Dara answered this question, see her research paper on pp. 326–330).

GUIDING RESEARCH QUESTION	*What benefits do service dogs provide to veterans suffering from PTSD?*

PRACTICE 1	**Write a Research Question**

Select one of the topics listed on page 308. Complete at least two prewriting activities (see Chapter 2), and then write a guiding research question for the topic you selected.

Find Appropriate Sources

The second basic of good research tells us that research requires appropriate sources to answer the guiding research question. With both the Internet and libraries available to you, finding information is not a problem. However, knowing how to find appropriate sources—those that are relevant, timely, and reliable—can be a challenge. The following strategies will help you.

Consult a Reference Librarian

Reference librarians are essential resources in helping you find appropriate information in both print and electronic forms. They will save you time and possible frustration in your search for relevant material.

If your library allows, schedule an appointment with a librarian. Before your appointment, write down some questions to ask, such as the following. Begin your conversation by telling the librarian your research topic.

Questions for the librarian

- How do I use an online catalog? What information will the library's catalog give me?

- Can I access the library catalog and article databases from home or other locations?

- What other reference tools would you recommend as a good starting place for research on my topic?

- Once I identify a source that might be useful, how do I find it?

- Can you recommend an Internet search engine that will help me find information on my topic? Can you also recommend some useful keywords?

- Does the college have access to a research database, such as *EBSCO*, *InfoTrac*, or *LexisNexis*?

- How can I tell whether a Web site is reliable?

- I have already found some articles related to my topic. Can you suggest some other places to look for sources?

- I have found good online sources, but how can I find some good print sources on my topic?

Use the Online Catalog

Most libraries now list their holdings online rather than in a card catalog. You can search by keyword, title, author, subject, publication data, and call number. Online catalog help is usually easy to find (generally on the screen or in a Help menu) and easy to follow. If you are just beginning your research, use the keyword search.

Dara Riesler, who wrote the research essay that appears later in this chapter, searched the library's online catalog using the keywords "service dogs and veterans." Here is one source she found:

Author:	Montalván, Luis Carlos
Additional contributors:	Witter, Bret
Title:	Until Tuesday: A Wounded Warrior and the Golden Retriever Who Saved Him
Published:	New York - Hyperion
Location:	Main Library
Call number:	HV1569.6.M56 2011
Status:	Available
Physical description:	xi, 252 p. : ill. ; 22 cm.
Contents:	The story of how a trained service dog has helped a traumatized Iraq War veteran live a better life.

A **call number** is an identification number that helps you locate a book in the library. Once you find the book you are looking for, browse the nearby shelves, where you may find other sources related to your topic. If the book is available only at another library, ask a librarian to have the book sent to your library, or request it at your library's Web site (interlibrary loan). Although these requests may take a few days, you should have enough time to request a relevant book if you have planned your research schedule carefully.

Look at Your Library's Web Site

Most libraries have a Web site that can help researchers find useful information. The home page may have links to electronic research sources that the library subscribes to and that are free to library users. These databases are usually reliable and legitimate sources of information. The library home page may also list the library's hours, provide search tools, and offer research tips and other valuable information.

Use the Internet

This section will offer some basics on finding what you need on the Internet. To start, visit sites that categorize information on the Web, such as the Internet Public Library at **www.ipl.org**.

Some Internet sites charge fees for information (such as archived newspaper or magazine articles). Before using any of these sources, check to see whether they are available free through your library's databases.

USE YOUR LIBRARY'S ONLINE DATABASES AND OTHER REFERENCE MATERIALS

Magazines, journals, and newspapers are called **periodicals**. Periodical indexes help you locate information published in these sources. Online periodical indexes are called **periodical databases** and often include the full text of magazine, journal, or newspaper articles. Libraries often subscribe to these online services. Here are some of the most popular periodical indexes and databases:

EBSCO	*LexisNexis*
InfoTrac	*NewsBank*
JSTOR	*ProQuest*

USE SEARCH ENGINES AND KEYWORD SEARCHES

Google (**www.google.com**) is the most commonly used search engine. Others include Yahoo! at **www.yahoo.com**, **www.duckduckgo.com**, and **www.bing.com**.

To use a search engine, type in keywords related to your subject. Adding more specific keywords or phrases and using an Advanced Search option may narrow the number of entries (called **hits**) you have to sift through to find relevant information. Adding additional search terms can narrow a search even more. (With many search engines, you get the best results by enclosing phrases in quotation marks.)

When you discover a Web site to which you might want to return, save the Web address so that you do not have to remember it each time you want to go to the site. Different browsers have different ways of saving Web addresses; use the Bookmarks menu in Google Chrome, Safari, or Firefox, or the Favorites menu in Microsoft Internet Explorer.

OTHER HELPFUL ONLINE RESEARCH SITES

Go to the following sites for tutorials on research processes and for other research advice. To access these sites, type their names and sponsors into a search engine.

- **The Bedford Research Room** (from Bedford/St. Martin's). This site provides advice on finding and evaluating sources and on writing research papers.
- **Citing Electronic Information** (from the Internet Public Library). This site contains links to various sources that explain how to document information found online.
- **Evaluating Web Sites** (from Cornell University). This site lists ways to evaluate Internet sources. Your own college library may have a similar Web site.

Interview People

Personal interviews can be excellent sources of information. Before interviewing anyone, however, plan carefully. First, consider what kind of person to interview. Do you want information from an expert on the subject or from someone directly affected by the issue? The person should be knowledgeable about the subject and have firsthand experience. When you have decided whom to interview, schedule an appointment.

Next, prepare a list of five to ten **open-ended questions**, such as "What do you think of the proposal to build a new library?" **Closed questions**, such as "Are you in favor of building a new library?" will only lead to simple yes/no responses. Yes/no responses are more appropriate for a **survey**, in which you interview a larger number of people to get a representative sample of opinions. (For an example of a survey in a student research paper, see Tyler Dashner's essay in Chapter 12, pp. 252–256.)

At the time of the interview, record the person's full name and qualifications and the date. Listen carefully to the responses to your questions and ask follow-up questions. Write down important ideas. If you plan to use any of the person's exact words, put them in quotation marks in your notes so that you can identify direct quotations later.

For more on using direct quotations, see Chapter 30.

Using a small recorder during the interview can be helpful. If you want to do so, make sure that you first ask the person for permission.

Evaluate Sources

Whether you are doing research for a college course, for a work assignment, or for personal reasons, make sure the sources you use are reliable. Reliable sources present accurate, up-to-date information written by authors with appropriate credentials for the subject matter. Research materials found in a college library (books, journals, and newspapers, for example) are generally considered reliable sources.

Materials found on the Internet must be approached with more caution. When you are doing research on the Internet, try to determine each source's purpose. A Web site set up solely to provide information might be more reliable than an online product advertisement. A keyword search on "how to lose weight," for example, would point a researcher to thousands of sites; the two shown on pages 314–315 are just samples. Which site do you think contains more reliable information?

Here are some questions you can ask to evaluate a source. If you answer "no" to any of these questions, do not use the source.

Questions for evaluating a print or electronic source

- Is the source reliable? It should be a well-known magazine or publisher or from a reputable Web site. (For Web sites, also consider the Internet address extension; see the box below for guidance.)

- Is the author qualified to write reliably about the subject? If there is no biographical information, do an online search using the author's name to learn more about the author's qualifications.

- Do you know who sponsored the publication or Web site? Be aware of the sponsor's motives (for example, to market a product).

- Does the author provide adequate support for key points, and does he or she cite the sources of this support?

Guide to Internet Address Extensions

Extension	Sponsor of site	How reliable?
.com	A commercial or business organization	Varies. Consider whether you have heard of the organization, and be sure to read its home page or "About us" link carefully.
.edu	An educational institution	Reliable, but may include materials of varying quality.
.gov	A government agency	Reliable.
.net	A commercial organization	Varies. See the advice for ".com" extensions.
.org	A nonprofit organization	Generally reliable, although each volunteer or professional group promotes its own interests.

> **PRACTICE 2**   Evaluate Sources
>
> Use the questions for evaluating a print or electronic source to evaluate
> the following two sites. Discuss which site is more appropriate for a college
> research essay. Be sure to state your reasons clearly.

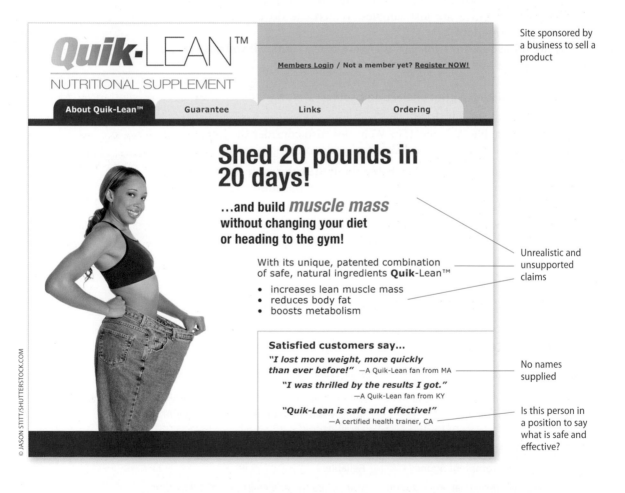

Site sponsored by a business to sell a product

Unrealistic and unsupported claims

No names supplied

Is this person in a position to say what is safe and effective?

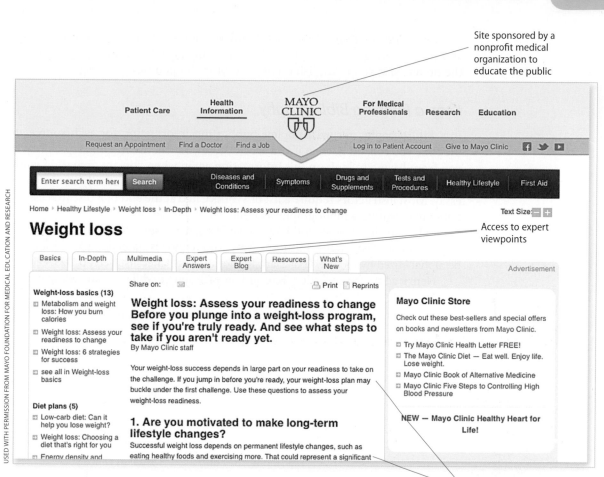

Site sponsored by a nonprofit medical organization to educate the public

Access to expert viewpoints

Realistic information

Use Sources Fairly and Honestly: Avoid Plagiarism

Plagiarism is passing off someone else's ideas and information as your own. Turning in a paper written by someone else, whether it is from the Internet or from a friend or family member who gives you permission, is deliberate plagiarism. Sometimes, however, students plagiarize by mistake because the notes they have taken do not indicate which ideas are theirs and which were taken from outside sources. As you find sources for your research project, you must be careful to read and take notes accurately. You have already learned some key strategies for good note taking in previous chapters: annotate carefully; paraphrase key ideas in your own words; and summarize what you read, with references to the author in each sentence. You have also learned how to use a signal phrase and a citation for paraphrases and quotes that you include in your writing. If you apply these same strategies to your research project, you will be less likely to plagiarize unintentionally. In this section, you will learn additional strategies that will help you avoid plagiarism.

Note: This section's advice on recording source information, and on citing and documenting sources, reflects Modern Language Association (MLA) style, the preferred style for English classes and other humanities courses.

Keep a Running Bibliography

In a **bibliography**, record complete publication information for each source at the time you consult it, even if you are not sure you will use it. This step will save you from having to look up this information again when you are preparing your list of **Works Cited**, which includes all the sources that you actually use in your essay. Most instructors require a list of Works Cited at the end of a research essay. Some may require a bibliography as well.

In both bibliographies and Works Cited lists, make sure to alphabetize sources by the authors' last names. In most cases, if no author is named, a source should be alphabetized by its title. (For Dara Riesler's Works Cited list, see pp. 329–330.)

Here is a list of information to record for each source while you are taking notes.

Books	Articles	Web sites
Author name(s)	Author name(s)	Author name(s) (if any)
Title and subtitle	Title of article	Title of page or site
Publisher and location of publisher	Page number(s) (for print sources)	Date of publication or latest update (if available)
Year of publication	Title of magazine, journal, or newspaper	Name of sponsoring organization
	Year, month, day of publication (2012 Jan. 4)	Date on which you accessed the source
	Main address for Web-based articles (for example, www.nytimes.com)	Optional: Web address in angle brackets (< />)

Students have different methods for organizing research notes. Choose any method that works for you, making sure that you organize and record your work carefully.

METHOD 1: PRINT AND WRITE

In this note-taking strategy, make print copies of all potential source material. Write the full bibliographic information (see above) on the back of the printed copies, and staple the copies or sort them into labeled folders. Annotate directly on the source material, and write a summary of the entire article (or of a section of the article) either on the back of the printed copy or on another sheet of paper. Keep the summary with the original source.

METHOD 2: DEDICATED NOTEBOOK OR NOTECARDS

Dedicate a notebook or notecards to the research project. Rather than copying an entire source, annotate main ideas and supporting details on the cards or in the notebook. Use notes to summarize the source, and copy bibliographic information into the notebook (or on a separate card). If you use this method, be sure to pay attention to what you are writing: if you copy main ideas or supporting details, be sure to use quotation marks. If you decide to paraphrase, make sure that you avoid a cut-and-paste paraphrase (see page 95). With both quotes and paraphrases, you must make a note of page numbers.

METHOD 3: ONLINE NOTES

Some students prefer to organize notes in an online file or a note-taking app available for iPads or other devices. Record annotations, quotes, paraphrases, and summaries in the online file, along with bibliographic information. As with Method 2, be careful to make notes clear: quotes should be marked with quotation marks, paraphrases should be carefully worded to avoid accidental plagiarism, and both quotes and summaries should include page numbers. Include links to online sources in your notes, so that you can go back to verify information if needed.

Notice that all three methods have one feature in common: they require you to *read and respond in writing* to the sources *before* you include them in the research paper itself. One of the most common mistakes students make (especially when they have not planned the research process well) is to find sources, use sources, and write the paper at the same time. Taking notes, summarizing, and responding to each individual source (before writing the paper) is an essential step in the research process.

Synthesize Information to Support a Thesis

Once you have gathered enough information, you can begin to **synthesize** your sources to form an answer to your research question. To synthesize means to combine or put together, drawing information from different places to create a unified idea. Dara Riesler, for example, asked about the benefits of using service dogs to help war veterans with PTSD. After exploring her sources, Dara drafted this thesis for her paper: "As the benefits of service dogs become clearer, and as more PTSD sufferers return from the wars in Iraq and Afghanistan, demand for these helpful and caring pets is growing; in fact, at the present time, demand far exceeds supply."

One strategy for planning a research paper draft is a chart. Look again at Dara's thesis:

> As the benefits of service dogs become clearer, and as more PTSD sufferers return from the wars in Iraq and Afghanistan, demand for these helpful and caring pets is growing; in fact, at the present time, demand far exceeds supply.

There are three important components to her thesis: background/examples of PTSD, benefits of using service dogs, and problems in supplying service dogs. To prepare for her draft, Dara can *organize her information* according to these three areas:

Source	Background and Examples	Benefits of Using Service Dogs	Challenges to Supplying Service Dogs
Albrecht, Brian	Example of Margaux Vair		
Bavley, Alan		Reports of study on 39 PTSD sufferers with service dogs	
Caprioli, Jennifer	Example of Ken Costich	Help with panic attacks and medication Statistics on the effectiveness of dogs as treatment for PTSD	Statistics from agencies that place dogs with veterans Expense of training
Dreazen, Yochi			Facts about keeping up with demand Facts about expense of training
Esnayra and Love		Constant companionship	
"Franken-Isakson Service Dogs for Veterans Act…"			Government effort to fund more dogs for veterans
Lorber, Janie	Example of Jacob Hyde		Statistics about numbers of dogs placed
Montalván and Witter			Information about what is required for training a service dog

(continued)

Source	Background and Examples	Benefits of Using Service Dogs	Challenges to Supplying Service Dogs
Peters, Sharon			Veterans Dog Training Therapy Act
U.S. Dept. of Veterans Affairs, "PTSD and Problems with Alcohol Use"	Background on PTSD		
U.S. Dept. of Veterans Affairs, "Treatment of PTSD"	Background on treatments for PTSD other than service dogs		
U.S. Dept. of Veterans Affairs, "What Are the Symptoms of PTSD?"	Definition of PTSD and background on problems		
U.S. Dept. of Veterans Affairs, "What Is PTSD?"	Background information		
Williams, Carol	Background: PTSD and suicide		

With her sources organized into these three sections, Dara could make a plan for her paper and write a draft.

Cite and Document Your Sources

You need not only to document your sources at the end of your research essay in a Works Cited list, but also to include in-text citations of sources as you use them in the essay. No one can remember the specifics of correct citation and documentation, so be sure to refer to this section or a reference that your instructor directs you to. Include all the correct information, and pay attention to where punctuation marks such as commas, periods, and quotation marks should go.

There are several different systems of documentation. Most English instructors prefer the Modern Language Association (MLA) system, which is used in this chapter. When you are writing a research paper in another course, you may be required to use another system.

Use In-Text Citations within Your Essay

You have already learned about using in-text citations with a signal (introductory) phrase and a page number in parentheses. The strategy you have been practicing is most commonly used for citing books and periodicals (magazines, newspapers, and academic journals). For Web sites and other electronic sources, you typically will not be able to include page numbers, although you can note any paragraph, chapter, or part numbers used in place of page numbers.

When you refer to the author (or authors) in an introductory phrase, write just the relevant page number(s), if available, in parentheses at the end of the quotation.

> **Direct Quotation:** In an article by Alan Bavley, veteran and PTSD sufferer Chris Kornkven was quoted as saying the following about service dogs he had observed: "They seemed like they would be really helpful, particularly for individuals living alone" (5).

> **Paraphrase:** In an article by Alan Bavley, veteran and PTSD sufferer Chris Kornkven expressed the belief that service dogs would be especially beneficial to vets who live by themselves (5).

When you do not refer to the author(s) in an introductory phrase, write the author's name followed by the page number(s), if available, at the end of the quotation. If an author is not named, use the title of the source.

> **Direct Quotation:** "Today's all-volunteer military is far smaller than past draftee-fed forces, requiring troops to be repeatedly recycled through combat zones" (*Issues in Peace and Conflict Studies* 395).

> **Paraphrase:** Because the current wars are not supported by a draft, military forces are smaller than in past wars, and troops are being deployed multiple times (*Issues in Peace and Conflict Studies* 395).

The following section shows you how to include an in-text citation for various kinds of sources, inserting the citation after the material you have used. For a direct quotation, insert the citation after the end quote and before the period ending the sentence.

Note: The following formats are for print sources. To cite a Web source, use page numbers if available; if not, use a paragraph number instead. If there are no paragraphs, cite the author, the title of the part of the Web site, or the site sponsor.

The series of dots (called ellipses) in the following examples indicate that words have been left out. Two examples are provided for each citation: (1) The author is named in an introductory phrase, with the page or paragraph number in parentheses. (2) The author's name and page or paragraph number appear in parentheses.

ONE AUTHOR

As David Shipler states, ". . ." (16).

The number of people who work and fall below the poverty line has increased dramatically (Shipler 16).

TWO OR THREE AUTHORS   Use all authors' last names.

Quigley and Morrison found that . . . (243).

Banks and credit card companies are charging many more fees . . . (Quigley and Morrison 243).

FOUR OR MORE AUTHORS   Use the first author's last name and the words *et al.* (*et al.* means "and others").

According to Sen et al., . . . (659).

The overuse of antibiotics can result in . . . (Sen et al. 659).

GROUP, CORPORATION, OR GOVERNMENT AGENCY   Use the name of the group, corporation, or government agency. The source can be abbreviated in the parentheses, as shown in the second example.

The Texas Parks and Wildlife Department offers guidelines for landscaping . . . (26).

Texas has more native plants than any other . . . (Texas Parks and Wildlife Dept. 26).

AUTHOR NOT NAMED   Use article title in quotations, shortened if it is a long title.

In the article "Texas Wildscapes," . . . (7).

Many areas of Texas are filled with drought-tolerant native . . . ("Texas Wild-scapes" 7).

ENCYCLOPEDIA OR OTHER REFERENCE WORK   Use the name of the entry you are using as a source.

In its entry on xeriscaping, the *Landscape Encyclopedia* claims that . . . ("Xeriscaping").

Xeriscaping is often used in . . . ("Xeriscaping").

WORK IN AN ANTHOLOGY   Use the name of the author(s) of the piece you are using as a source.

As Rich Chiappone believes, . . . (200).

Fly-fishing is as much a spiritual . . . (Chiappone 200).

INTERVIEW, E-MAIL, SPEECH   Use the name of the speaker or person interviewed, or of the author of the e-mail.

> As University of Texas Vice President of Student Affairs Juan Gonzalez said in an interview . . .

> Students have many resources available to . . . (Gonzalez).

Use a Works Cited List at the End of Your Essay

Following are model Works Cited entries for major types of sources. At the end of your paper, you will need to include an entry for each source you cite in the body of the paper.

BOOKS

Book with one author

Author, last name first   Full title

All lines after first line of entry are indented.

Anker, Susan. *Real Writing: Paragraphs and Essays for College, Work, and Everyday Life*. 6th ed. Boston: Bedford/St. Martin's, 2013. Print.

Edition number   Place of publication   Publisher   Publication date

Book with two or three authors

Baumeister, Roy F., and John Tierney. *Willpower: Rediscovering the Greatest Human Strength*. New York: Penguin, 2011. Print.

Hudson, Valerie M., Bonnie Ballif-Spanvill, Mary Caprioli, and Chad F. Emmett. *Sex and World Peace*. New York: Columbia UP, 2012. Print.

Book with four or more authors   *Et al.* means "and others."

McKay, John P., et al. *A History of World Societies*. 9th ed. Boston: Bedford/St. Martin's, 2012. Print.

Book with an editor

Price, Steven D., ed. *The Best Advice Ever Given: Life Lessons for Success in the Real World*. Guilford: Lyons Press, 2006. Print.

Work in an anthology

Vowell, Sarah. "Shooting Dad." *50 Essays: A Portable Anthology*. 3rd ed. Ed. Samuel Cohen. Boston: Bedford/St. Martin's, 2011. 412–19. Print.

Encyclopedia article

"Metaphor." *The Columbia Encyclopedia*. 6th ed. 2000. Print.

PERIODICALS

Magazine article

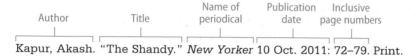

Kapur, Akash. "The Shandy." *New Yorker* 10 Oct. 2011: 72–79. Print.

Newspaper article

Oliveira, Rebeca. "The Art of Storytelling Is Alive and Well." *Jamaica Plain Gazette* 7 Oct. 2011: 10–11. Print.

Editorial in a magazine or newspaper

Escobar, Veronica. "All Quiet on the Southern Front." Opinion. *New York Times* 6 Oct. 2011: A27. Print.

ELECTRONIC SOURCES

Electronic sources include Web sites; databases or subscription services such as *ERIC*, *InfoTrac*, *LexisNexis*, and *ProQuest*; and electronic communications such as e-mail. Because electronic sources change often, always note the date you accessed or read the source as well as the date on which the source was posted or updated online, if this information is available. If no date is available, write "n.d."

An entire Web site

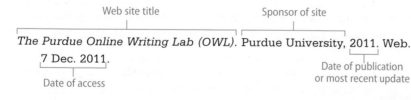

The Purdue Online Writing Lab (OWL). Purdue University, 2011. Web. 7 Dec. 2011.

Part of a larger Web site

"How to Evaluate Sources: Introduction." *The Bedford Research Room*. Bedford / St. Martin's, n.d. Web. 7 Jan. 2012.

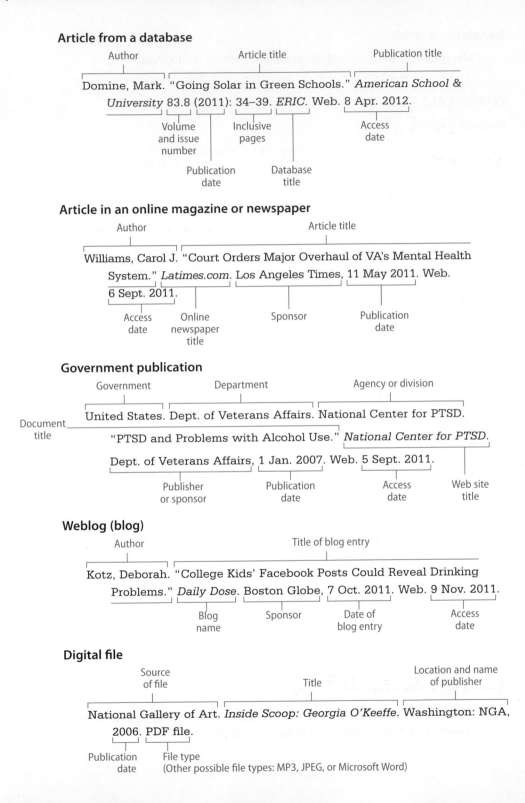

Article from a database

Author — Domine, Mark.
Article title — "Going Solar in Green Schools."
Publication title — *American School & University*
Volume and issue number — 83.8
Publication date — (2011):
Inclusive pages — 34–39.
Database title — *ERIC.* Web.
Access date — 8 Apr. 2012.

Article in an online magazine or newspaper

Author — Williams, Carol J.
Article title — "Court Orders Major Overhaul of VA's Mental Health System."
Online newspaper title — *Latimes.com.*
Sponsor — Los Angeles Times,
Publication date — 11 May 2011. Web.
Access date — 6 Sept. 2011.

Government publication

Government — United States.
Department — Dept. of Veterans Affairs.
Agency or division — National Center for PTSD.
Document title — "PTSD and Problems with Alcohol Use."
Web site title — *National Center for PTSD.*
Publisher or sponsor — Dept. of Veterans Affairs,
Publication date — 1 Jan. 2007. Web.
Access date — 5 Sept. 2011.

Weblog (blog)

Author — Kotz, Deborah.
Title of blog entry — "College Kids' Facebook Posts Could Reveal Drinking Problems."
Blog name — *Daily Dose.*
Sponsor — Boston Globe,
Date of blog entry — 7 Oct. 2011. Web.
Access date — 9 Nov. 2011.

Digital file

Source of file — National Gallery of Art.
Title — *Inside Scoop: Georgia O'Keeffe.*
Location and name of publisher — Washington: NGA,
Publication date — 2006.
File type — PDF file.
(Other possible file types: MP3, JPEG, or Microsoft Word)

E-mail

Sender's name   Subject line   Recipient's name

Bustin, Martha. "Note on Research Essays." Message to Susan Anker.
    4 Apr. 2012. E-mail.

Date of message

MULTIMEDIA

Film

Title   Director   Major performers

Midnight in Paris. Dir. Woody Allen. Perf. Owen Wilson, Kathy Bates,
    Adrien Brody, Marion Cotillard, and Rachel McAdams. Sony,
    2011. Film.

Release date   Distributor

Film on DVD

Campion, Jane, dir. *Bright Star.* Perf. Abbie Cornish, Ben Whishaw, and
    Paul Schneider. Apparition, 2009. DVD.

Television and radio

"Dogs Decoded." *Nova.* PBS. 12 Oct. 2011. Television.

Podcast online

"Hidden Costs of Energy." Narr. Ann Merchant. *Sounds of Science.*
    National Academies, 29 Jan. 2010. Web. 13 Dec. 2011.

Recording

Jay-Z and Kanye West. "Made in America." *Watch the Throne.* Roc-A-
    Fella, 2011. CD.

Personal interview

Hain, Carla. Personal interview. 5 Sept. 2011.

Student Research Essay

Here is Dara Riesler's research essay, with annotations pointing out standard
characteristics of content, documentation, and formatting.

Riesler 1

Dara Riesler

Professor Gomes

English 99

4 October 2011

Service Dogs Help Heal the Mental Wounds of War

Whenever Ken Costich, a former army colonel, is on the edge
of a panic attack, his dog, Bandit, senses it immediately, nuzzling
Costich until he feels calm again (Caprioli). Across the country,
another dog, Maya, is also looking out for her owner, veteran Jacob
Hyde. When Hyde, feeling nervous in a crowd, gives the command
"block," Maya stands between him and other people, easing Hyde's
fears (Lorber). Elsewhere, Mush, a Siberian husky, is helping her
owner, Margaux Vair, get out and meet people—something Vair had
avoided since returning from her service in Iraq (Albrecht). "Because
[Mush] is a Husky and very pretty, everybody wants to pet her," Vair
says. "What's happening is that people are coming up and talking to
me, and it's helping with my confidence."

Bandit, Maya, and Mush—specially trained service dogs—are
making a significant difference in the lives of their owners, all of
whom suffer from post-traumatic stress disorder (PTSD) as a result
of military service. As the benefits of service dogs become clearer,
and as more PTSD sufferers return from the wars in Iraq and
Afghanistan, demand for these helpful and caring pets is growing; in
fact, at the present time, demand far exceeds supply.

PTSD, as defined by the United States Department of Veterans
Affairs (VA), is an anxiety disorder that can result from a traumatic
experience, such as personal injury in combat or witnessing the deaths
or injuries of others. According to the VA, symptoms of the condition
include flashbacks of the trauma or nightmares about it. PTSD
sufferers may also have difficulty forming or maintaining relationships
with others. Additionally, some of them are constantly "keyed up" and
"on the lookout for danger," as if they are still in a war zone ("What
Are the Symptoms of PTSD?"). According to the RAND Corporation,
a nonprofit research group, an estimated 300,000 veterans from the
wars in Afghanistan and Iraq suffer from PTSD or major depression. In
attempts to escape or to numb the effects of PTSD, sufferers may turn

---

Annotations (left margin):

½" margin between top of page and header

Student's last name and page number on top of each page

Identification of student, professor, course, and date

Title centered

Introduction

Indirect and direct quotations with in-text citations

Thesis statement

Topic sentence

Titles used for in-text citations of sources without authors

Riesler 2

to alcohol or drugs, possibly leading to addiction ("PTSD and Problems with Alcohol Use"). Worse, they may decide to end their lives, as an estimated 6,500 veterans do each year (Williams).

 A variety of treatments are available to veterans with PTSD. They include one-on-one discussions with a therapist, group therapy, and medicines—usually antidepressants—that address the symptoms of the condition ("Treatment of PTSD"). The use of service dogs as an additional therapy for PTSD is a relatively new practice. According to researchers Joan Esnayra and Craig Love, a key benefit of these dogs is that they are constant companions to PTSD sufferers, helping them go about their daily lives and directly addressing their symptoms. For example, service dogs may be trained to alert easily startled veterans that someone is approaching, to scan surroundings for possible threats, or to turn on the lights and wake up veterans suffering from nightmares (Esnayra and Love). These pets can also soothe veterans experiencing panic attacks and remind their owners when it is time to take medications (Caprioli).

 Some veterans, however, find that their dog companions outshine medication as a PTSD treatment. "This dog [did] more for me in three weeks than any medication," says Ken Costich (qtd. in Caprioli; see fig. 1). Alicia Miller, an Army veteran who cofounded an organization that donates and trains service dogs for vets, agrees. "Medication works 50 percent of the time," says Miller, who also experiences symptoms of PTSD. "Talk therapy, alone, works 30 percent of the time, and dogs work 84.5 percent of the time" (qtd. in Caprioli).

 In a recent study, Esnayra and Love found that among 39 PTSD

Fig. 1. Ken Costich and his service dog, Bandit (Caprioli).

PHOTO BY JENNIFER CAPRIOLI/COURTESY OF U.S. ARMY

Annotations (right margin):

Titles used for in-text citations of sources without authors

Topic sentence

Indirect quotations with in-text citations

Topic sentence

Source quoted within another source

Riesler 3

sufferers paired with service dogs, 82% reported fewer PTSD symptoms (Bavley 5). In addition, 40% reported that they were able to reduce their use of medications. Recognizing that more research into the effectiveness of service-dog therapy is needed, the United States Department of Defense is funding a $300,000 study on this topic (Bavley 5). Esnayra and Love are conducting the research.

Topic sentence — Although service-dog therapy has many benefits, organizations that train these dogs have trouble keeping up with the demand created by the thousands of veterans who have returned from Iraq or Afghanistan with PTSD (Dreazen). Training is time-consuming and demanding; the dogs are taught to respond to as many as 150 commands and to notice subtle changes in vets—such as a quickening pulse—that signal emotional distress (Montalván and Witter 4). During a two-year period that ended in the spring of 2010, Puppies Behind Bars, a program in which prisoners train service dogs, placed 23 dogs with veterans suffering from PTSD (Lorber). Other nonprofit training organizations report similar, or lower, numbers of vet-ready dogs (Caprioli). Given the labor-intensive training, these numbers are understandable; however, the need remains.

Topic sentence — Another challenge is the expense of the training, which in the case of many nonprofit organizations, like Puppies Behind Bars, is paid for by donations, not by the veterans (Caprioli; Dreazen). At Puppies Behind Bars, $26,000 is needed to train each dog. Other training organizations report similar expenses.

Topic sentence — Some lawmakers are taking steps to meet vets' growing need for helper dogs. In 2009, President Obama signed into law the Service Dogs for Veterans Act, which was sponsored by Senator Al Franken and Senator Johnny Isakson. According to Franken's office, this legislation matches at least 200 veterans with VA-funded service dogs, and it requires that at least 50% of these vets suffer mainly from mental-health problems, as opposed to physical disabilities. It also calls for a study of the participating veterans to learn more about the therapeutic and economic benefits of service dogs. Additionally, in January 2011, the Veterans Dog Training Therapy Act was introduced in the U.S. House of Representatives.

Riesler 4

Under this legislation, vets with PTSD would be taught how to train
service dogs which, in turn, would be used by other vets (Peters).

With luck, and with the continuing efforts of legislators and
concerned citizens, more helper dogs will find homes with veterans,
providing not only valued service but also lasting friendship. As Army
veteran Luis Carlos Montalván says of his service dog, Tuesday: "We
are bonded, dog and man, in a way able-bodied people can never
understand, because they will never experience anything like it. As
long as Tuesday is alive, he will be with me. Neither of us will ever
be alone. We will never be without companionship" (Montalván and
Witter 6).

— Conclusion

Works Cited

Albrecht, Brian. "Psychiatric Service Dogs Aid Northeast Ohio
    Veterans." *Cleveland.com*. Cleveland.com, 13 July 2011. Web.
    8 Sept. 2014.

— Article from online news site

Bavley, Alan. "PTSD Treatment Goes to the Dogs: DOD Research
    Pairs Soldiers with K-9s." *Stars and Stripes* 10 Sept. 2009,
    Mideast ed.: 5. Print.

— Article from print newspaper

Caprioli, Jennifer M. "Dogs Go the Distance: Program Provides
    Service to Veterans with PTSD." *www.army.mil: The Official
    Homepage of the United States Army*. United States Army,
    4 Mar. 2010. Web. 8 Sept. 2014.

— Part of larger Web site

Dreazen, Yochi J. " 'Sit! Stay! Snuggle!': An Iraq Vet Finds His Dog
    Tuesday." *Wsj.com*. Wall Street Journal, 11 July 2009. Web.
    9 Sept. 2014.

— Article from online newspaper

Esnayra, Joan, and Craig Love. "A Survey of Mental Health Patients
    Utilizing Psychiatric Service Dogs." *PSD Lifestyle*. Psychiatric
    Service Dog Society, 2008. Web. 8 Sept. 2014.

"Franken-Isakson Service Dogs for Veterans Act Passes Senate." *Al
    Franken: U.S. Senator for Minnesota*. Al Franken: U.S. Senator
    for Minnesota, 24 July 2009. Web. 7 Sept. 2014.

— Parts of larger Web sites

"Invisible Wounds: Mental Health and Cognitive Care Needs of
    America's Returning Veterans." *RAND Corporation*. RAND
    Corporation, 2008. Web. 7 Sept. 2014.

Riesler 5

Lorber, Janie. "For the Battle-Scarred, Comfort at Leash's End."
    Nytimes.com. New York Times, 3 Apr. 2010. Web. 8 Sept.
    2014.

Montalván, Luis Carlos, and Bret Witter. *Until Tuesday: A Wounded
    Warrior and the Golden Retriever Who Saved Him*. New York:
    Hyperion, 2011. Print.

Peters, Sharon L. "Man's Best Friend Could Soon Be Veteran's Best
    Medicine." *Usatoday.com*. USA Today, 19 Jan. 2011. Web. 7
    Sept. 2014.

United States. Dept. of Veterans Affairs. National Center for PTSD.
    "PTSD and Problems with Alcohol Use." *National Center for
    PTSD*. Dept. of Veterans Affairs, 1 Jan. 2007. Web. 5 Sept. 2014.

---. ---. National Center for PTSD. "Treatment of PTSD." *National
    Center for PTSD*. Dept. of Veterans Affairs, 1 Jan. 2007. Web.
    5 Sept. 2014.

---. ---. National Center for PTSD. "What Are the Symptoms of
    PTSD?" *National Center for PTSD*. Dept. of Veterans Affairs,
    1 Jan. 2007. Web. 5 Sept. 2014.

---. ---. National Center for PTSD. "What Is PTSD?" *National Center
    for PTSD*. Dept. of Veterans Affairs, 1 Jan. 2007. Web. 5 Sept.
    2014.

Williams, Carol J. "Court Orders Major Overhaul of VA's Mental
    Health System." *Latimes.com*. Los Angeles Times, 11 May 2011.
    Web. 6 Sept. 2014.

Article from online newspaper

Book with two authors

Article from online newspaper

Online government publications. **Note:** Three hyphens used in place of government and department names in each entry after the first

Article from online newspaper

Reading/Writing Workbook: The Research Essay

Professional Essay: "The Designer Player," Rodrigo Villagomez

Preview

- Read the title of the essay, the information about the author, and the first paragraph. What is the purpose and thesis of the essay?

- This essay is an argument. What other strategies do you expect the writer to use, based on the first paragraph?

- Create a guiding question for your reading.

Read and Annotate this essay carefully, using the guidelines for Reading and Annotating Argument on page 288. As you read, pay special attention to when and how Villagomez uses sources in this essay.

Rodrigo Villagomez

The Designer Player

Rodrigo Villagomez is a blogger, podcaster, and social-media journalist. Born in 1976, he graduated from high school in Stockton, California, in 1994, joined the U.S. Army as a musician, and served ten years in Afghanistan and Korea as well as stateside. In 2005, Villagomez returned to Stockton to pursue a career in sports broadcasting. He worked for Citadel Broadcasting, where he held various positions ranging from promotions assistant to producer to on-air talent. At the same time, he attended San Joaquin Delta College and reported on campus sports for the college's newspaper, radio station, and television network. Villagomez earned degrees in liberal arts and sciences (A.A., 2007) and communications (A.A., 2009). He is currently the owner of, and a play-by-play announcer for, Valley Sports Network, an online broadcast service that covers high school and semiprofessional sports in the San Joaquin Valley.

PHOTO BY ANJELICA MARIE GAMEZ, COURTESY OF RODRIGO VILLAGOMEZ

1   Baseball is a multibillion-dollar entertainment industry. The modern age of American sports has seen to it that we no longer look at baseball as just "America's pastime." We must now see it as another corporation striving to produce a product that will be consumed by the populace[1]. It is a corporation that produces the reluctant hero, a man who begrudgingly[2] accepts the title "role model." These players are under intense pressure to be continually on top of their game. They are driven by relentless fans to achieve greater levels of strength and

1. **Populace:** ordinary people in a society
2. **Begrudgingly:** reluctantly

prowess. Because of this pressure, more professional baseball players are turning to performance-enhancing drugs, specifically steroids, to aid them in their quest for greatness. Many believe that these drugs decrease the integrity of the players and ultimately the game itself. But if it were not for the small percentage of players who have recently been found to use steroids, baseball would not be enjoying the success it does today. We should be thanking these players for keeping the game popular.

3. **Clinical:** objective and scientific

2   Let's first look at the clinical[3] definition of a steroid. A steroid is "any group of organic compounds belonging to the general class of biochemical called lipids, which are easily soluble in organic solvents and slightly soluble in water" (Dempsey). The sportswriter Dayn Perry explains that steroids build muscle mass and that the physical conditioning of players, combined with the ingestion[4] of the hormone testosterone, accelerates the muscle building. There are a million other supplements out there designed to do the same thing, so why the big fuss over steroids?

4. **Ingestion:** taking into the body; eating

3   Most people have a problem with steroids because of the speed with which users obtain results. But it is not the drug alone that causes enhanced play.

4   In fact, by using steroids, a batter could be hurting his swing. Being big and bulky and able to hit the ball out of the park is great, but not being able to move those humongous arms around quickly enough to hit a 90 mph fastball is counterproductive[5]. To be a better hitter, the player must combine an over-the-top workout schedule with the drugs. If it were possible to become the world's greatest baseball player by simply using steroids and doing nothing else, don't you think that everyone would be doing so?

5. **Counterproductive:** unhelpful; preventing the achievement of a goal

5   The main opponents against the use of steroids are those who say that using is an attack on baseball's integrity. Every player who takes the drug damages the credibility[6] of the sport, and this is unfair to those who choose not to partake.

6. **Credibility:** the quality of being trustworthy; believability

6   These opponents should wake up. Long before the media brought the issue of steroids to the forefront, the drugs were being injected, rubbed, or swallowed in locker rooms. In his tell-all book *Juiced,* Jose Canseco claims that many of his fellow teammates joined him in using steroids and that he personally injected most of them, beginning as early as 1985 (4). In 2002, Ken Caminiti, a retired third baseman and National League MVP, told *Sports Illustrated,* "It's no secret what's going on in baseball. At least half the guys are using. They talk about it. They joke about it with each other" (qtd. in Verducci). In reality, the so-called integrity of the game has been lost for years. Pitchers have always found ways to doctor the ball so that their pitches have extra movement. Batters have used lighter or corked bats to achieve a faster swing. Pete Rose was caught betting on his team while he was a manager. Baseball has not been a fair game for years.

7   Another of the major arguments of those opposed to using steroids is the health risk factor. Steroid use has been linked to liver, prostate, and even testicular cancers as well as to heart disease. According to epidemiologist Charles Yesalis, however, "We know steroids can be used with a reasonable measure of safety. We know this because they're used in medicine all the time, just not to enhance body image or improve athletic performance" (qtd. in Perry).

8   Steroids are also used in the treatment of breast cancer. In response to the fear of long-term effects from the continued use of steroids, Yesalis has this to say: "We've had thousands upon thousands [of long-term studies] done on tobacco, cocaine, you name it . . . but for as much as you see and hear about anabolic steroids, [we] haven't taken that step" (qtd. in Perry). The truth is that we hear all the time from modern medicine that we can get cancer in ways we never thought about. Remember when standing in front of the microwave could give us cancer? Or now we hear that talking on a cell phone might be damaging to our health. Living is unhealthy. We all do things that are not good for our bodies, be it smoking or drinking or whatever. These players are no more ruining their bodies than those people who have to have a smoke break every thirty minutes; in fact, using a natural hormone to increase muscle mass is arguably healthier.

9   Baseball fans love home runs. Ever since the days of Babe Ruth, the loyal fan has loved to see the sheer beauty of a baseball leaving the stadium. The home run is a display of strength; it is poetry in motion. So is it any wonder that players continually strive to increase the power of their swing? Nobody wants to be known just as the one who could consistently get on base or the one with the stellar[7] batting average. They all want to be the one who gets noticed by both the press and the fans for home runs. Without the ever-present chance that sluggers can take it deep when they step up to the plate, the game might get a little boring. In fact baseball itself has been making changes in the game to help encourage home-run production: Many ballparks have changed the dimensions of their outfields, moving the fences in to make it easier to hit the ball out. Just look at steroids as a baseball player's attempt at trying to move the wall in a little closer.

7. **Stellar:** outstanding; excellent

10   The recent batch of steroid allegations[8] is not the first case of performance-enhancing drugs in baseball causing a stir. During the 1998 season Mark McGwire broke Roger Maris's long-standing record of sixty-one home runs in a single season. This new record could not have come at a better time for baseball, as most fans still held on to disappointing memories of the 1994 players' strike and a season cut short. McGwire's assault on the record revitalized[9] the game and gave people a reason to watch again. That joy was carried into the very next season, when both McGwire and Sammy Sosa embarked on a head-to-head battle to break McGwire's record. After the excitement died down, controversy ignited

8. **Allegations:** accusations or statements that have not been proved

9. **Revitalized:** gave new life to something

10. **Vilification:** process of speaking negatively about something and giving it a bad name

when accusations were made that McGwire was taking androstendione, a substance equal to the over-the-counter supplement hydroxycut. Most fans did not care whether Mark McGwire was hitting his home runs with help or not. We just loved the excitement of it all—until the vilification[10] of the supplement he used forced us to feel guilty for enjoying the show.

11   Above all, we must remember baseball is a game. It is intended for the entertainment of the crowd. There are of course fanatics (like myself) who hang on every swing and every throw, but most are casual fans who watch their favorite team when possible. Arguing over the integrity of a product meant for entertainment is futile[11]. We as a society should not look to baseball to produce our perfect example of humanity. These people put themselves on stage every night in order to show us things we are not capable of, things that we want to do but can't. For three hours or so we get to escape into a world that is filled with strength and agility[12]. Does it matter how our modern-day gladiators[13] achieve their greatness? I certainly think not. Fans should not be let down because their favorite players used steroids to make them watch. They should thank them.

12   Without those players, there might not even be a game to watch.

11. **Futile:** useless or time-wasting; impossible to accomplish

12. **Agility:** the ability to move easily and quickly

13. **Gladiators:** competitors in ancient Rome who fought animals or each other, often to the death, to entertain crowds

Works Cited

Canseco, Jose. *Juiced: Wild Times, Rampant 'Roids, Smash Hits, and How Baseball Got Big.* New York: HarperCollins, 2005. Print.

Dempsey, Mary E. "Steroid." *AccessScience.* McGraw-Hill, 2010. Web. 14 Feb. 2014.

Perry, Dayn. "The Problem of Steroid Use in Major League Baseball Is Exaggerated." *Opposing Viewpoints Resource Center.* Thomson Gale, 2005. Web. 15 Feb. 2014.

Verducci, Tom. "Totally Juiced." *Sports Illustrated* 3 June 2002: 34+. *MasterFILE Premier.* Web. 17 Feb. 2014.

CHECK COMPREHENSION

1. What is the main point?

2. How does Villagomez support his point?

3. What three counterarguments does he refer to?

4. How does he rebut each of these counterarguments?

MAKE INFERENCES

Do you think that Roderigo Villagomez would agree or disagree with the following statements? Explain.

1. Using science to improve sports equipment (bats, sneakers, gloves, etc.) is a good idea.
2. Americans view athletes in an appropriate way.
3. It's OK to cheat in sports.

WRITE TO IMPROVE READING   Summarize

Following the guidelines from Chapter 6, summarize this essay. Before you begin, make sure you can answer the Check Comprehension questions on the preceding page, and include the answers in your summary.

Know P/Q: Using Paraphrase and Quotation in the Research Essay

To understand how Villagomez has used research in his essay, use a highlighter to mark each sentence of the essay that comes from a source. As you highlight the source-based parts of the essay, consider how source material is introduced and marked. Is it clear in each case?

Here is an excerpt from one of Villagomez's sources, which he mentions in paragraph 2. Read the selection carefully, and then answer the questions that follow.

> There are more than 600 different types of steroids, but it's testosterone, the male sex hormone, that's most relevant to athletics. Testosterone has an androgenic, or masculinizing, function and an anabolic, or tissue-building, function. It's the second set of effects that attracts athletes, who take testosterone to increase their muscle mass and strength and decrease their body fat. When testosterone is combined with a rigorous weight-training regimen, spectacular gains in size and power can result. The allure is obvious, but there are risks as well.
>
> —excerpt from Dayn Perry's article "The Problem of Steroid Use in Major League Baseball Is Exaggerated"

> **PRACTICE**

1. How does Villagomez introduce this source in paragraph 2?

2. Does Villagomez summarize, paraphrase, or quote the source? How do you know?

3. Look at the Works Cited list at the end of Villagomez's essay. What type of source is this? Why doesn't Villagomez cite a page number for this source?

Here is another excerpt from the same source. Read the source carefully, and then answer the questions that follow.

Health effects

Anecdotal accounts of harrowing side effects are not hard to find—everything from "'roid rage" to sketchy rumors of a female East German swimmer forced to undergo a sex change operation because of the irreversible effects of excess testosterone. But there are problems with the research that undergirds many of these claims. The media give the impression that there's something inevitably Faustian about taking anabolics—that gains in the present will undoubtedly exact a price in the future. Christopher Caldwell, writing recently in the *Wall Street Journal*, proclaimed, "Doctors are unanimous that [anabolic steroids] increase the risk of heart disease, and of liver, kidney, prostate, and testicular cancer."

This is false. "We know steroids can be used with a reasonable measure of safety," says Charles Yesalis, a Penn State epidemiologist, steroid researcher for more than 25 years, and author of the 1998 book *The Steroids Game*. "We know this because they're used in medicine all the time, just not to enhance body image or improve athletic performance." Yesalis notes that steroids were first used for medical purposes in the 1930s, some three decades before the current exacting standards of the Food and Drug Administration (FDA) were in place. . . .

One reason the health effects of steroids are so uncertain is a dearth of research. In the almost 65 years that anabolic steroids have been in our midst, there has not been a single epidemiological study of the effects of long-term use. Instead, Yesalis explains, concerns about extended usage are extrapolated from what's known about short-term effects. The problem is that those

▶

short-term research projects are often case studies, which Yesalis calls the "lowest life form of scientific studies." Case studies often draw conclusions from a single test subject and are especially prone to correlative errors.

"We've had thousands upon thousands [of long-term studies] done on tobacco, cocaine, you name it," Yesalis complains. "But for as much as you see and hear about anabolic steroids, they haven't even taken that step."

—excerpt from Dayn Perry's article "The Problem of Steroid Use in Major League Baseball Is Exaggerated"

PRACTICE

1. How is this source introduced in paragraph 7?

2. Is Villagomez's use of the source in paragraph 7 a summary, a paraphrase, or a quote? How do you know?

3. This article was written by Dayn Perry, but the speaker in this case is an expert, Charles Yesalis. Does Villagomez make the source of the information about steroids clear?

4. How are the references to this article cited?

Consider Audience and Source Selection

In Chapter 13, you learned that you must consider your audience when you are writing an argument and developing evidence in support of your argument.

PRACTICE

1. Who is the intended audience for Villagomez's essay? How do you know?

2. Villagomez uses four sources. Two of the sources (Canseco and Verducci) focus on eyewitness testimony from current and former baseball players. One source (Dempsey) defines the term *steroid* in scientific terms. The other source (Perry) suggests that society has overreacted to the use of steroids in sports.

   a. Which of these sources most clearly supports Villagomez's position? Why?

   b. Why are the other sources useful in Villagomez's argument? Explain.

    c. Does Villagomez need another source that includes counterarguments? Why or why not?

    d. Given the audience you identified in question 1 above, are the sources used adequate and effective for the argument Villagomez is making? Explain.

RESPOND IN WRITING

1. Which of Villagomez's arguments supporting steroids in sports do you find most convincing? Explain.

2. Which of his arguments seems the most problematic to you? Write a rebuttal to his argument.

3. Select your answer to either #1 or #2 above, and expand your answer by including an additional source. Be sure to cite your source accurately.

Extend and Connect: Write Your Own Research Paper

1. What questions does Villagomez's essay raise in your mind? Write a researched response to this essay, using one of your questions to guide your research.

2. Do a library or Internet search to find additional source material on this topic. Find three sources that are relevant and reliable. Summarize each source, and explain what each source can contribute to the debate described in Villagomez's essay.

3. Select one of Villagomez's sources. Find the entire source and read it. Summarize the source, and write a response to it.

4. Villagomez mentions that one concern about steroids in baseball is harm to the "integrity of the game." Could steroid use be considered a form of lying? Write an answer to this question, connecting the ideas in Villagomez's essay to those in Stephanie Ericsson's essay "The Ways We Lie" (pp. 198–202). Be sure to cite both authors accurately.

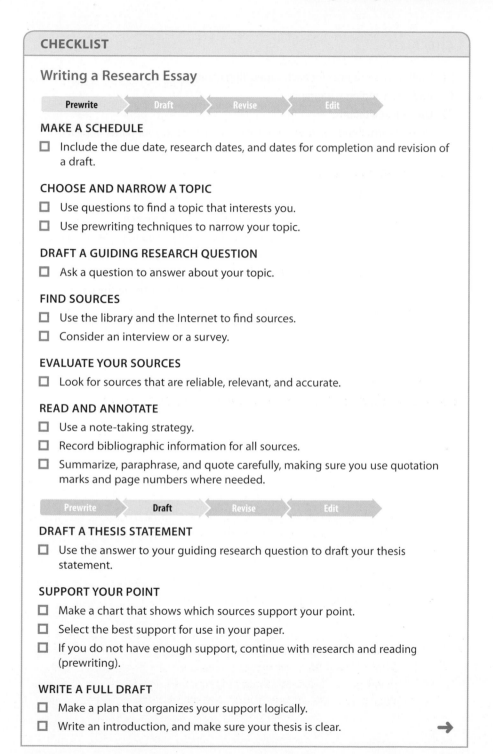

CHECKLIST

Writing a Research Essay

Prewrite › Draft › Revise › Edit

MAKE A SCHEDULE

☐ Include the due date, research dates, and dates for completion and revision of a draft.

CHOOSE AND NARROW A TOPIC

☐ Use questions to find a topic that interests you.

☐ Use prewriting techniques to narrow your topic.

DRAFT A GUIDING RESEARCH QUESTION

☐ Ask a question to answer about your topic.

FIND SOURCES

☐ Use the library and the Internet to find sources.

☐ Consider an interview or a survey.

EVALUATE YOUR SOURCES

☐ Look for sources that are reliable, relevant, and accurate.

READ AND ANNOTATE

☐ Use a note-taking strategy.

☐ Record bibliographic information for all sources.

☐ Summarize, paraphrase, and quote carefully, making sure you use quotation marks and page numbers where needed.

Prewrite › **Draft** › Revise › Edit

DRAFT A THESIS STATEMENT

☐ Use the answer to your guiding research question to draft your thesis statement.

SUPPORT YOUR POINT

☐ Make a chart that shows which sources support your point.

☐ Select the best support for use in your paper.

☐ If you do not have enough support, continue with research and reading (prewriting).

WRITE A FULL DRAFT

☐ Make a plan that organizes your support logically.

☐ Write an introduction, and make sure your thesis is clear.   →

CHECKLIST

- ☐ Draft topic sentences for each supporting paragraph.
- ☐ Add a concluding paragraph.
- ☐ Use in-text citations.
- ☐ Draft a Works Cited list. Make sure each source used in your paper appears in the alphabetized Works Cited list.

Prewrite ⟩ Draft ⟩ **Revise** ⟩ Edit

REVISE YOUR DRAFT

- ☐ Make sure you have covered the Four Basics of Good Research.
- ☐ Make sure your readers have all the information they need to understand the support.
- ☐ Make sure you have included transitions.
- ☐ Make sure readers can identify where source material is used in the paper.

Prewrite ⟩ Draft ⟩ Revise ⟩ **Edit**

EDIT YOUR REVISED DRAFT

- ☐ Correct mistakes in grammar, spelling, punctuation, and word usage.
- ☐ Make sure your draft is formatted correctly.

Part 3
The Four Most Serious Errors

15

The Basic Sentence:

An Overview

The Four Most Serious Errors

This part of the book focuses first on four grammar errors that people most often notice.

The Four Most Serious Errors

1. Fragments (Chapter 16)

2. Run-ons (Chapter 17)

3. Problems with subject-verb agreement (Chapter 18)

4. Problems with verb form and tense (Chapter 19)

If you can edit your writing to correct these four errors, your grades will improve.

This chapter reviews the basic sentence elements that you will need to understand to find and fix the four most serious errors. Knowledge of basic sentence structure will also help you analyze and understand what you read.

e Log in to **macmillanhighered .com/rrw** and look for LearningCurve > Parts of Speech: Nouns and Pronouns; Parts of Speech: Verbs, Adjectives, and Adverbs; and Parts of Speech: Prepositions and Conjunctions

The Parts of Speech

There are seven basic parts of speech:

1. **Noun:** names a person, place, thing, or idea. A <u>noun phrase</u> is a group of words that includes a **noun**, or a word that functions as a noun, and any surrounding article and modifiers.

e Log in to **macmillanhighered .com/rrw** and look for Additional Grammar Exercises > Identifying Parts of Speech

For information on making nouns plural, see Chapter 27.

For **Christmas** I prayed for this blond-haired **boy**, **Robert**, and a slim new American **nose** (Tan, 117).

2. **Pronoun:** replaces a noun in a sentence. *He, she, it, we,* and *they* are pronouns.

   He was not Chinese, but as white as Mary in the manger (Tan, 117).

For more on verbs, see Chapter 19.

3. **Verb:** tells what action the subject does or links a subject to another word that describes it.

   For Christmas I **prayed** for this blond-haired boy, Robert, and a slim new American nose (Tan, 117).

   [The verb *prayed* tells us what the subject—*I*—did].

   He **was** not Chinese, but as white as Mary in the manger (Tan, 117).

   [The verb *was* links the subject, *he*, to the describing word *Chinese*. In this case, the link is negative.]

4. **Adjective:** describes a noun or a pronoun.

   For Christmas I prayed for this **blond-haired** boy, Robert, and a **slim new American** nose (Tan, 117).

   [The adjective *blond-haired* describes the noun *boy*, while the adjectives *slim, new,* and *American* describe the noun *nose*.]

For more on adjectives and adverbs, see Chapter 21.

5. **Adverb:** describes an adjective, a verb, or another adverb. Adverbs often end in *-ly*.

   I discovered that telling the truth all the time is **nearly** impossible (Ericsson, 200).

   [The adverb *nearly* describes the adjective *impossible*.]

   . . . they needed priests and **recklessly** believed treatment had cured him (Ericsson, 200).

   [The adverb *recklessly* describes the verb *believed*.]

6. **Preposition:** connects a noun, pronoun, or verb with information about it. *Across, around, at, in, of, on,* and *out* are examples of common prepositions. See page 347 for a list of additional prepositions.

   He was not Chinese, but as white as Mary **in** the manger (Tan, 117).

   [The preposition *in* connects a noun, *Mary*, with a place, *the manger*.]

7. **Conjunction:** connects words to each other. The most common conjunctions are the seven coordinating conjunctions. You can memorize these easily using the word **FANBOYS**: *for, and, nor, but, or, yet, so.*

For more on coordinating conjunctions, see Chapter 24.

. . . they needed priests **and** recklessly believed treatment had cured him (Ericsson, 200).

PRACTICE 1   **Using the Parts of Speech**

Fill in each blank with the part of speech indicated.

Example: More and more wild animals are coming into towns and cities, making life ___*challenging*___ (adjective) for them and humans.

1.   Two _____ (adjective) hawks built a _____ (noun) on the

     roof _____ (preposition) a city apartment building.

2.   The female laid _____ (noun) there, and _____ (pronoun)

     hatched a few days later, releasing four _____ (adverb) noisy

     chicks.

3.   Some of the building's residents _____ (verb) about the

     hawks, _____ (conjunction) others loved to stand _____ (prepo-

     sition) the street from the birds and watch _____ (pronoun).

4.   Because of the complaints, the _____ (noun) was removed,

     _____ (conjunction) the people who liked the hawks got _____

     (adverb) upset.

5.   The supporters _____ (preposition) the birds eventually won, and

     the hawks were allowed to _____ (verb) to rebuild their _____

     (noun).

The Basic Sentence

A sentence is the basic unit of written communication. A sentence must contain at least one independent clause. A **clause** is a group of words with a subject and a verb. A clause is **independent** if it is complete; in other words, it doesn't depend on any other sentences to make sense. To make sure that each sentence contains an independent clause, writers look for three required elements: a subject, a verb, and completeness. Let's look at each of these elements separately.

Log in to **macmillanhighered .com/rrw** and look for Additional Grammar Exercises > Identifying Subjects

Subjects

The **subject** of a sentence (or of a clause) is the person, place, or thing that the sentence is about. The subject of a sentence is usually a noun or a pronoun. For a list of common pronouns, see page 434.

To find the subject, ask yourself: **Whom or what is the sentence about?**

Note: In all of the sample sentences throughout the rest of this chapter, the subject has been underlined once, while the verb has been underlined twice.

Person as Subject	Kissinger asked an aide to produce a report (Mali, 42).

[*Whom* is the sentence about? Kissinger]

Thing as Subject	The kitchen was littered with appalling mounds of raw food (Tan, 117).

[*What* is the sentence about? the kitchen]

A **compound subject** consists of two or more subjects joined by *and, or,* or *nor.*

Two subjects	Kelli and Kate love animals of all kinds.
Several subjects	The baby, the cats, and the dog play well together.

The subject of a sentence is *never* in a **prepositional phrase**, a word group that begins with a preposition and ends with a noun or pronoun, called the **object of a preposition**.

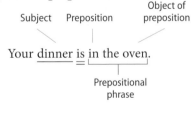

Preposition	Object	Prepositional phrase
from	the bakery	from the bakery
to	the next corner	to the next corner
under	the table	under the table

🌐 Language note: *In* and *on* can be tricky prepositions for people whose native language is not English. Keep these definitions and examples in mind:

in = inside of (in the box, in the classroom); on a nonspecific day in a month, season, or year (in September, in spring, in 2014); for any time within a limited period of time (in three weeks, in two years, in six days); indicating a general location (in the United States, in London)

on = resting on top of something (on the table, on my head); indicating a more specific location (on this side of the street, on the next page, on Elm Avenue); on a specific day (on December 25, on Thursday)

For more information on how to use prepositions, see Chapter 25.

Common Prepositions

about	before	for	on	until
above	behind	from	out	up
across	below	in	outside	upon
after	beneath	inside	over	with
against	beside	into	past	within
along	between	like	since	without
among	by	near	through	
around	down	next to	to	
at	during	of	toward	
because of	except	off	under	

See if you can identify the subject of the following sentence.

One of my best friends races cars.

Although you might think that the word *friends* is the subject, it isn't. *One* is the subject. The word *friends* cannot be the subject because it is in the prepositional phrase *of my best friends*. When you are looking for the subject of a sentence, cross out the prepositional phrase.

Prepositional phrase crossed out

One ~~of the students~~ won the science prize.

The rules ~~about the dress code~~ are specific.

Language note: The example sentences use the word *the* before each noun (*the students, the science prize, the rules, the dress code*). *The, a,* and *an* are called **articles**. Articles are noun markers; they always introduce nouns or noun phrases. If you have trouble deciding which article to use with which noun, see Chapter 25.

e Log in to **macmillanhighered .com/rrw** and look for Additional Grammar Exercises > Identifying Verbs

Verbs

Every sentence has a **main verb**, the word or words that tell what the subject does or that link the subject to another word or group of words that describes it. There are three types of verbs: action verbs, linking verbs, and auxiliary (helping) verbs.

ACTION VERBS

An **action verb** tells what action the subject performs.

To find the main action verb(s) in a sentence, ask yourself: **What action does the subject perform?**

Subject   Action verbs

So he sheepishly took it back and revised it (Mali, 42).

LINKING VERBS

A **linking verb** connects (links) the subject to another word or group of words that describes the subject. Linking verbs show no action. The most common linking verb is *be* (*am, is, are,* and so on). Other linking verbs, such as *seem* and *become,* can usually be replaced by a form of the verb *be,* and the sentence will still make sense.

To find linking verbs, ask yourself: **What word joins the subject and the words that describe the subject?**

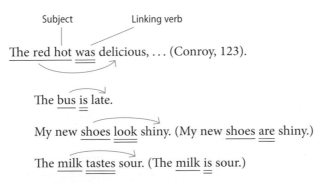

Subject   Linking verb

The red hot was delicious, . . . (Conroy, 123).

The bus is late.

My new shoes look shiny. (My new shoes are shiny.)

The milk tastes sour. (The milk is sour.)

Some words can be used as either action verbs or linking verbs, depending on how the verb is used in a particular sentence.

Action verb   Justine smelled the flowers.

Linking verb   The flowers smelled wonderful.

Common Linking Verbs

Forms of *be*	Forms of *seem* and *become*	Forms of sense verbs
am	seem, seems, seemed	look, looks, looked
are	become, becomes, became	appear, appears, appeared
is		smell, smells, smelled
was		taste, tastes, tasted
were		feel, feels, felt

Language note: The linking verb *be* and its other forms cannot be left out of sentences in English.

Incorrect   Sergio not here today.

Correct   Sergio is not here today.

AUXILIARY (HELPING) VERBS

An **auxiliary verb** or **helping verb** joins the main verb in a sentence to form the complete verb. The helping verb is often a form of the verb *be*, *have*, or *do*. A sentence may have more than one helping verb along with the main verb.

Common Helping Verbs

Forms of *be*	Forms of *have*	Forms of *do*	Other
am	have	do	can
are	has	does	could
been	had	did	may
being			might
is			must
was			should
were			will
			would

Helping verb	+	Main verb	=	Complete verb

The complete verbs in the following sentences have been double-underlined:

Yes, money <u>can buy</u> happiness, but probably not in the way you <u>imagined</u>. Spending it <u>on yourself may</u> not <u>do</u> much for your spirits, but spending it on others <u>will make</u> you happier, according to a report from a team of social psychologists in the new issue of *Science* (Tierney, 257).

Before you begin Practice 2, look at these examples to see how action, linking, and helping verbs are different.

Action verb   Kara <u>graduated</u> last year.

[The verb *graduated* is an action that Kara performed.]

Linking verb   Kara <u>is</u> a graduate.

[The verb *is* links Kara to the word that describes her: *graduate*. No action is performed.]

Helping verb   Kara <u>is graduating</u> next spring.

[The helping verb *is* joins the main verb *graduating* to make the complete verb *is graduating*, which tells what action the subject is taking.]

PRACTICE 2   **Identifying the Verb (Action, Linking, or Helping Verb + Main Verb)**

In the following sentences, underline each subject and double-underline each verb. Then, identify each verb as an action verb, a linking verb, or a helping verb + a main verb.

Helping verb + main verb
Example: Bowling <u>was created</u> a long time ago.

1. The ancient Egyptians invented bowling.

2. Dutch settlers were responsible for bowling's introduction to North America.

3. They bowled outdoors on fields of grass.

4. One area in New York City is called Bowling Green because the Dutch bowled there in the 1600s.

5. The first indoor bowling alley in the United States opened in 1840 in

New York.

Completeness

A sentence (or an independent clause) is complete when it makes sense by itself, without additional words. An incomplete thought will leave readers confused, and wondering what is going on.

Incomplete thought	because my alarm did not go off
Complete thought	I was late because my alarm did not go off.
Incomplete thought	the people who won the lottery
Complete thought	The people who won the lottery were old.

To determine whether a thought is complete, ask yourself: **Do I have to ask a question to understand?**

Incomplete thought	in my wallet

[You would have to ask a question to understand, so it is not a complete thought.]

Complete thought	My ticket is in my wallet.

Six Basic English Sentence Patterns

In English, there are six basic sentence patterns, some of which you have just worked through in this chapter. Although there are other patterns, they build on these six.

1. Subject-Verb (S-V). This pattern is the most basic one.

   Musicians practice.

2. Subject-Linking Verb-Noun (S-LV-N)

    My <u>students</u> <u>are</u> musicians.

3. Subject-Linking Verb-Adjective (S-LV-ADJ)

    My <u>students</u> <u>are</u> talented.

4. Subject-Verb-Adverb

    <u>They</u> <u>practice</u> regularly.

5. Subject-Verb-Direct Object (S-V-DO). A direct object directly receives the action of the verb.

    <u>Students</u> <u>write</u> essays. [The essays are written.]

6. Subject-Verb-Direct Object-Indirect Object (S-V-DO-IO). An indirect object does not directly receive the action of the verb.

    <u>Students</u> <u>give</u> essays to the instructor. [The essays are given, not the instructor.]

    This pattern can also have the indirect object before the direct object.

    <u>Students</u> <u>give</u> the instructor essays.

    Language note: Some verbs occur only in specific patterns in English. For example, the verb *eat* can occur in patterns 1, 4, and 5:

    The <u>athletes</u> <u>ate</u>.
    The <u>athletes</u> <u>ate</u> quickly.
    The <u>athletes</u> <u>ate</u> their postgame steak dinner quickly.

    The verb *devour*, however, occurs only in pattern 5:

    | **Wrong** | The <u>athletes</u> <u>devoured</u>. |
    | **Wrong** | The <u>athletes</u> <u>devoured</u> quickly. |
    | **Correct** | The <u>athletes</u> <u>devoured</u> their postgame steak dinner quickly. |

Students whose first language is not English may have difficulty knowing which pattern to use with which verb. An ESL (English as a second language) dictionary provides information about sentence patterns along with the definitions of verbs.

PRACTICE 3 **Identifying Basic Sentence Patterns**

Identify the subject, complete verb, and sentence pattern for each of the following sentences, adapted from Carolyn Foster Segal's essay "The Dog Ate My Flash Drive, and Other Tales of Woe" (Chapter 10). Remember to cross out any prepositional phrases before you identify the subject.

Example: The dog ate my flash drive.

Subject: _the dog_

Complete verb: _ate_

Pattern: _S-V-DO_

1. The death of the grandfather/grandmother is, of course, the grandmother of all excuses.

   Subject: _____

   Complete verb: _____

   Pattern: _____

2. Creative students may win extra extensions (and days off) with a little
   careful planning and fuller plot development.

   Subject: _____

   Complete verb: _____

   Pattern: _____

3. Her grandfather/grandmother died.

   Subject: _____

   Complete verb: _____

   Pattern: _____

4. These stories are usually fairly predictable.

   Subject: _____

   Complete verb: _____

   Pattern: _____

5. The computer has revolutionized the study story.

   Subject: _____

   Complete verb: _____

   Pattern: _____

6. The printer wouldn't print.

   Subject: _____

   Complete verb: _____

   Pattern: _____

7. A nurse was mailing everything to me.

Subject: _____

Complete verb: _____

Pattern: _____

8. This course is more important than ever to me.

Subject: _____

Complete verb: _____

Pattern: _____

PRACTICE 4   **Identifying Complete Sentences**

In this essay, underline the subject of each sentence, and double-underline the verb. Correct five incomplete thoughts.

1 Space travel fascinates my grandpa Bill. 2 He watches every space movie at least a dozen times. 3 Before 1996, he never even thought about the moon, Mars, or beyond. 4 He was too old to be an astronaut. 5 Now, however, he is on board a satellite. 6 It analyzes particles in the atmosphere. 7 He has the company of millions of other people. 8 And me, too. 9 Truthfully, only our names travel to Mars or beyond. 10 We are happy with that.

11 In 1996, the Planetary Society flew the names of members into space. 12 Using the Mars *Pathfinder*. 13 At first, individuals signed a paper. 14 Then, Planetary Society members put the signatures into electronic form. 15 Now, people submit names on the Internet. 16 By filling out a form. 17 The names go on a microchip. 18 One spacecraft to the moon had more than a million names on board. 19 Some people have placed their names on a spacecraft going past Pluto and out of our solar system. 20 Their names are on a CD.   21 Which could survive for billions of years.

22 Grandpa and I feel good about our journey into space. 23 In a way, we will travel to places only dreamed about. 24 After signing up, we received colorful certificates to print out. 25 To tell about our mission. 26 My certificate hangs on my wall. 27 My grandpa and I travel proudly into space.

Chapter Review

1. List the seven parts of speech, and give an example of each one:

   _____

   _____

   _____

2. What are three things that a sentence must have?

   _____

3. A _____ is the person, place, or thing that a sentence is about.

4. A prepositional phrase is _____

   _____

5. Add a prepositional phrase to each of the following sentences:

   I bought a hat _____ to wear to the party.

   The exhausted runner walked _____.

6. An action verb tells _____. Write a sentence with

   an action verb: _____

7. A linking verb _____

   _____. Write a sentence with a linking verb: _____

   _____

8. An auxiliary verb (helping verb) _____

   _____.

Chapter Test

Circle the correct choice for each of the following items.

1. Identify the underlined part of speech in this sentence.

   Devon <u>walks</u> so fast that I can never keep up with him.

   a.   Noun   b.   Verb   c.   Preposition   d.   Adjective

2. Identify the underlined part of speech in this sentence.

   In spring, the trees around our house are a <u>beautiful</u> shade of green.

   a. Adjective   b. Adverb   c. Preposition   d. Verb

3. Identify the underlined part of speech in this sentence.

   <u>Shopping</u> is Jerimiah's favorite hobby.

   a. Noun   b. Verb   c. Adjective   d. Adverb

4. Identify the type of verb in this sentence.

   The baby always <u>seems</u> tired after lunch.

   a. Action verb   b. Linking verb   c. Helping verb

5. Choose the item that is a complete sentence.

   a. Driving to the store.

   b. Driving to the store, I saw Rick jogging.

   c. Driving to the grocery store last Wednesday.

16

Fragments:
Incomplete Sentences

Understand What Fragments Are

Log in to **macmillanhighered .com/rrw** and look for LearningCurve > Fragments

A **fragment** is a group of words that is punctuated like a sentence but is missing one of the three required elements of an independent clause: a subject, a verb, or completeness. Like its name suggests, a fragment is a piece of a sentence but cannot be a sentence by itself. (In the examples that follow, subjects are underlined, and verbs are double-underlined.)

Sentence	I was hungry, so I ate some cold pizza and drank a soda.
Fragment	I was hungry, so I ate some cold pizza. *And drank a soda.*

[*And drank a soda* contains a verb (*drank*) but no subject.]

Language note: Remember that any group of words that ends with a period should include an **independent clause**: a subject, a verb, and a complete thought. As a quick review, a subject is the person, place, or thing that a sentence is about. A verb tells what the subject does, links the subject to another word that describes it, or helps another verb form a complete verb.

The terms *independent clause, subject, verb,* and *completeness* were introduced in Chapter 15.

Language and Writing

Log in to **macmillanhighered .com/rrw** and look for Additional Grammar Exercises > Identifying Complete Thoughts

You might be wondering why a fragment is considered a major sentence error. After all, in ordinary conversations, people can use fragments without causing any problems:

Mallory: Why didn't you do the homework assignment?

Ben: Because I didn't understand it.　[By itself, this group of words is a fragment. It is not a complete thought.]

Mallory: You could have asked me for help.

Ben: Nah—didn't want to. I can figure it out later.　[By itself, the first group of words is a fragment; it does not contain a subject.]

The standards for college and professional writing, however, are different from the rules we follow in conversations. Fragments may confuse a reader, and they may suggest to a reader that the writer is careless or sloppy. In fact, academic readers may not take a piece of writing seriously if it contains fragments and other major sentence mistakes.

In Chapter 13, you met Chase, who was struggling with discussion board posts in his online class. Early in the semester, Chase was asked to comment on a class reading about learning styles. Here is what he wrote:

> **Chase:** I'm the last kind, kinesthetic. Because I like to move. To do things with my hands when Im trying to learn stuff. Most of my teachers don't do anything kinesthetic in their classes. We just sit there. Being bored. I feel like I am in a cage sometimes. Or back in high school.

Chase thought he would get a good grade on this assignment; after all, he had more than twice the number of required sentences. Unfortunately, there are four fragments in his post. When Professor Landon pointed out Chase's mistakes, she reminded him how important the discussion board was to the class: "You've got to show me you take it seriously, Chase."

Log in to **macmillanhighered .com/rrw** and look for Additional Grammar Exercises > Correcting Various Fragments

Find and Correct Fragments

To find fragments in your own writing, look for the five trouble spots in this chapter. They often signal fragments.

When you find a fragment in your own writing, you can usually correct it in one of two ways.

Basic ways to correct a fragment

- Add what is missing (a subject, a verb, or both).
- Attach the fragment to the sentence before or after it.

Finding and fixing fragments: Fragments that start with prepositions	**Find**
	I did not work on improving my grammar. (In) high school.
	1. **Circle** any preposition at the beginning of a word group.
	2. *Ask:* Does the word group have a subject? No. Does it have a verb? No. Underline the subject, and double-underline any verb.
	3. *Ask:* Does the word group express a complete thought? No.
	4. If the word group is missing a subject or verb or does not express a complete thought, it is a fragment. *This word group is a fragment.*
	Fix
	$\overset{in}{}$
	I did not work on improving my grammar. ~~In~~ high school.
	5. **Correct** the fragment by joining it to the sentence before or after it.

PRACTICE 1   **Finding Fragments**

Find and underline four fragments in Chase's discussion board post on page 358.

1. Fragments That Start with Prepositions

Whenever a preposition starts what you think is a sentence, check for a subject, a verb, and a complete thought. If the group of words is missing any of these three elements, it is a fragment.

> **Fragment**   I pounded as hard as I could. *Against the door.*
>
> [*Against the door* lacks both a subject and a verb.]

Correct a fragment that starts with a preposition by connecting it to the sentence either before or after it. If you connect such a fragment to the sentence after it, put a comma after the fragment to join it to the next sentence.

2. Fragments That Start with Dependent Words

A **dependent word** is the first word in a **dependent clause**. A dependent clause has a subject and a verb, like all clauses do. But a dependent clause can never express a complete thought by itself; it depends on another clause (an independent clause) to make sense. When writers begin a sentence with a dependent

e Log in to **macmillanhighered .com/rrw** and look for Additional Grammar Exercises > Correcting Fragments that Start with Prepositions

Common Prepositions

about	before	for	on	until
above	behind	from	out	up
across	below	in	outside	upon
after	beneath	inside	over	with
against	beside	into	past	within
along	between	like	since	without
among	by	near	through	
around	down	next to	to	
at	during	of	toward	
because of	except	off	under	

clause, they must always attach that clause to an independent clause. Otherwise, they will have a fragment.

Sentence with a Dependent Word   In anger-therapy sessions with Doris Wilde Helmering, <u>he</u> <u>learned</u> that such <u>outbursts</u> <u>accomplish</u> nothing (Hales, 149).

[The word *that* is a dependent word that introduces a dependent clause. If we put a period after the word **learned**, what happens? *That such outbursts accomplish nothing.* This sentence is a fragment. It is a dependent clause which is not attached to an independent clause.]

Whenever you see a dependent word at the beginning of what you think is a sentence, check for a subject, a verb, and another clause (a complete thought).

Writing Note: In Chapters 7–13, you learned about using transition words in writing. One type of transition is a **subordinating conjunction**. Subordinating conjunctions are dependent words (see the chart on p. 361). Be careful when you are creating transitions in your writing: if you use a subordinating conjunction, you must make sure there is also an independent clause so that your sentence is complete.

Fragment   *Since I moved.* <u>I</u> <u>have eaten</u> out every day.

[*Since I moved* has a subject (*I*) and a verb (*moved*), but it does not express a complete thought.]

Corrected   Since I moved, <u>I</u> <u>have eaten</u> out every day.

Dependent Words		
after	although	as/as if/as though
as long as	as soon as	because
before	even if/even though	if/if only
now that	once	since
so that	though	unless
until	who/whom/whose	whether
that	while	when/whenever
which/whichever		where/wherever

When a word group starts with *who, whose,* or *which,* it is not a complete sentence unless it is a question.

Fragment	That <u>woman</u> <u>is</u> the police officer. *Who gave me a ticket last week.*
Question	*<u>Who</u> <u>gave</u> you a ticket last week?*
Fragment	<u>He</u> <u>is</u> the goalie. *Whose team is so bad.*
Question	*<u>Whose</u> team <u>are</u> <u>you</u> on?*
Fragment	<u>Sherlene</u> <u>went</u> to the HiHo Club. *Which does not serve alcohol.*
Question	*<u>Which</u> <u>club</u> <u>serves</u> alcohol?*

Correct a fragment that starts with a dependent word by connecting it to the sentence before or after it. If you join a dependent clause to the sentence after it, put a comma after the dependent clause.

> **PRACTICE 2** **Correcting Fragments That Start with Prepositions or Dependent Words**

Read the following paragraph, and circle the ten fragments that start with prepositions or dependent words. Then, correct the fragments.

Staying focused at an office job can be difficult. Because of these jobs' many distractions. After making just a few changes. Workers will find that they are less distracted and more productive. A good first step is to clear away clutter, such as old paperwork. From the desk. Once the workspace is cleared. It is helpful to make a list of the most important tasks for the day. It is best for workers to do brain-demanding tasks when they are at their best. Which is often the start of the day. Workers can take on simpler tasks, like filing. When they are feeling less energetic. While they are doing something especially challenging. Workers might want to disconnect themselves from e-mail and turn off their cell phones. Although it is tempting to answer e-mails and phone calls immediately. They are among the worst workplace distractions. Some people set up a special electronic folder. For personal e-mails. They check this folder only while they are on break or between tasks. Finally, it is important for workers to remember the importance of breaks. Which recharge the mind and improve its focus.

Finding and fixing fragments:

Fragments that start with dependent words

Find

(Because) research <u>takes</u> a lot of time. Students should make a schedule to follow during the process.

1. **Circle** any dependent words at the beginning of a word group.

2. *Ask*: Does the word group beginning with a dependent word have a subject? *Yes.* Does it have a verb? *Yes.* **Underline** the subject, and **double-underline** any verb.

3. *Ask*: Does the word group express a complete thought? *No.*

4. If the word group is missing a subject or verb or does not express a complete thought, it is a fragment. *This word group is a fragment.*

Fix

, students
Because research takes a lot of time. ~~Students~~ should make a schedule to follow during the process. ^

5. **Correct** the fragment by joining it to the sentence before or after it. Add a comma if the dependent clause comes first.

---

3. Fragments That Start with -ing Verb Forms

An *-ing* verb form is the form of a verb that ends in *–ing: walking, writing, running.* Sometimes, an *-ing* verb form is used at the beginning of a complete sentence.

Sentence   <u>Writing</u> <u><u>takes</u></u> a lot of practice.

[The -*ing* verb form *Writing* is the subject; *takes* is the verb. The sentence is a complete thought. In this sentence, *Writing* is a **gerund**; in other words, it is the -*ing* form of the verb used as a noun. We know that *writing* is used as a noun here, because we can replace it with a pronoun: *Is writing hard? Yes,* ***it*** *takes a lot of practice.*]

Sometimes, an -*ing* verb form introduces a fragment. Whenever an -*ing* verb form starts what you think is a sentence, stop and check for a subject, a verb, and a complete thought.

Fragment   I worked as hard as I could. Hoping to get a good grade.

[*Hoping to get a good grade* does not have a subject or a complete verb, and it does not express a complete thought.]

Correct a fragment that starts with an -*ing* verb form either by adding whatever sentence elements are missing (usually a subject and a helping verb) or by connecting the fragment to the sentence before or after it. You will usually need to put a comma before or after the fragment to join it to the complete sentence.

Finding and fixing fragments:

Fragments that start with -*ing* verb forms

Find

I ran as hard as I could. (Hoping) to get there on time.

1. **Circle** any -*ing* verb form that begins a word group.

2. *Ask*: Does the word group have a subject? No. Does it have a verb? No. (Note: *to* + a verb form is an infinitive and can never be the main verb in a sentence—see p. 364). Underline any subject, and double-underline any verb.

3. *Ask*: Does the word group express a complete thought? No.

4. If the word group is missing a subject or verb or does not express a complete thought, it is a fragment. *This is a fragment.*

Fix

, *hoping*
I ran as hard as I could./ ~~Hoping~~ to get there on time.
^ I *was hoping*
I ran as hard as I could. ~~Hoping~~ to get there on time.
^

5. **Correct** the fragment by joining it to the sentence before or after it. If you put the word group with the –*ing* verb form first, add a comma after it. **Alternative:** Add the missing sentence elements.

> **PRACTICE 3** **Correcting Fragments That Start with -*ing* Verb Forms**

Circle any -*ing* verb that appears at the beginning of a word group in the paragraph. Then, read the word group to see if it has a subject and a verb and expresses a complete thought. Not *all* the word groups that start with an -*ing* verb are fragments, so read carefully. In the space provided, record the numbers of the word groups that are fragments. Then, correct each fragment either by adding the missing sentence elements or by connecting it to the sentence before or after it.

Which word groups are fragments? _____

1 People sometimes travel long distances in unusual ways trying to set new world records. 2 Walking is one unusual way to set records. 3 In 1931, Plennie Wingo set out on an ambitious journey. 4 Walking backward around the world. 5 Wearing sunglasses with rearview mirrors, he started his trip early one morning. 6 After eight thousand miles, Wingo's journey was interrupted by a war in Pakistan. 7 Ending his ambitious journey. 8 Hans Mullikan spent more than two years in the late 1970s traveling to the White House by crawling from Texas to Washington, D.C. 9 Taking time out to earn money as a logger and a Baptist minister. 10 Alvin Straight, suffering from poor eyesight, traveled across the Midwest on a lawn mower. 11 Looking for his long-lost brother.

e Log in to **macmillanhighered.com/rrw** and look for Additional Grammar Exercises > Correcting Fragments that Start with To and a Verb

4. *Fragments That Start with* To *and a Verb*

When a word group begins with *to* and a verb (called the **infinitive** form of the verb), you need to make sure it is not a fragment.

Fragment   Each day, I check freecycle.org. *To see if it has anything I need.*

Corrected   Each day, I check freecycle.org to see if it has anything I need.

If a word group begins with *to* and a verb (an infinitive), it must have another verb; if it doesn't, it is not a complete sentence. Whenever you see a word group that begins with an infinitive, first check to see if there is another verb. If there is no other verb, the word group is a fragment.

Finding and fixing fragments:

Fragments that start with *to* and a verb

Find

Cheri got underneath the car. [To change] the oil.

1. **Circle** any infinitives that start a word group.

2. *Ask*: Does the word group have a subject? No. Does it have a verb? No. (Remember that an infinitive can never be a complete verb in a sentence). Underline any subject, and double underline any verb.

3. *Ask*: Does the word group express a complete thought? No.

4. If the sentence is missing a subject or verb or does not express a complete thought, it is a fragment. *This word group is a fragment.*

Fix

                   to
Cheri got underneath the car. ~~To~~ change the oil.
                      ^
To change the oil,
Cheri got underneath the car. ~~To change the oil.~~
   ^
                         She needed to
Cheri got underneath the car. ~~To~~ change the oil.
                         ^

5. **Correct** the fragment by joining it to the sentence before or after it. If you put the infinitive first, add a comma after it. **Alternative:** Add the missing sentence elements.

Sentence   To run a complete marathon was my goal.

[*To run* is the subject; *was* is the verb.]

Fragment   Cheri got underneath the car. *To change the oil.*

[No other verb appears in the word group that begins with *to change*.]

To correct a fragment that starts with *to* and a verb, join it to the sentence before or after it, or add the missing sentence elements.

> **PRACTICE 4**   **Correcting Fragments That Start with Infinitives**
>
> Circle any *to*-plus-verb combination that appears at the beginning of a word group in the paragraph. Then, read the word group to see if it has a subject and a verb and expresses a complete thought. Not *all* the word groups that start with *to* and a verb are fragments, so read carefully. In the space provided, record the numbers of the word groups that are fragments.

Then, correct each fragment either by adding the missing sentence elements or by connecting it to the sentence before or after it.

Which word groups are fragments? _____

1 For people older than twenty-five, each hour spent watching TV lowers life expectancy by nearly twenty-two minutes. 2 This finding is the result of Australian researchers' efforts. 3 To investigate the health effects of TV viewing. 4 To put it another way, watching an hour of television is about the same as smoking two cigarettes. 5 The problem is that most people are inactive while watching TV. 6 They are not doing anything, like walking or playing sports. 7 To strengthen their heart and maintain a healthy weight. 8 Fortunately, it is possible. 9 To counteract some of TV's negative health effects. 10 To increase their life expectancy by three years. 11 People need to exercise just fifteen minutes a day. 12 To accomplish this goal, they might exchange a ride in an elevator for a climb up the stairs. 13 Or they might walk around the block during a lunch break at work.

5. Fragments That Are Examples or Explanations

As you edit your writing, pay special attention to groups of words that are examples or explanations of information you presented in the previous sentence. They may be fragments.

Fragment	More and more people are reporting food allergies. *For example, allergies to nuts or milk.*
Fragment	My body reacts to wheat-containing foods. *Such as bread or pasta.*

[*For example, allergies to nuts or milk* and *Such as bread or pasta* are not complete thoughts.]

This last type of fragment is harder to recognize because there is no single word or kind of word to look for. The following words may signal a fragment, but fragments that are examples or explanations do not always start with these words.

especially	for example	like	such as

When a group of words gives an example or explanation connected to the previous sentence, stop to check it for a subject, a verb, and a complete thought.

Fragment	<u>I</u> <u>have found</u> great things at freecycle.org. *Like a nearly new computer.*
Fragment	<u>Freecycle.org</u> <u>is</u> a good site. *Especially for household items.*
Fragment	<u>It</u> <u>lists</u> many gently used appliances. *Such as DVD players.*

[*Like a nearly new computer, Especially for household items,* and *Such as DVD players* are not complete thoughts.]

Correct a fragment that starts with an example or explanation by connecting it to the sentence before or after it. Sometimes, you can add whatever sentence elements are missing (a subject, a verb, or both) instead. When you connect the fragment to a sentence, you may need to change some punctuation. For example, fragments that are examples are often set off by a comma.

Finding and fixing fragments:

Fragments that are examples or explanations

Find

Freecycle.com recycles usable items. (Such as clothing.)

1. **Circle** the word group that is an example or explanation.

2. *Ask*: Does the word group have a subject, a verb, and a complete thought? No.

3. If the word group is missing a subject or verb or does not express a complete thought, it is a fragment. *This word group is a fragment.*

Fix

Freecycle.org recycles usable items, ~~Such~~ *such* as clothing.

I should list some things on freecycle.org. The sweaters I never wear, *could keep others warm.*

4. **Correct** the fragment by joining it to the sentences before or after it or by adding the missing sentence elements.

PRACTICE 5   Correcting Fragments That Are Examples or Explanations

Circle word groups that are examples or explanations. Then, read the word group to see if it has a subject and verb and expresses a complete thought. In the space provided, record the numbers of the word groups that are fragments. Then, correct each fragment either by adding the missing sentence elements or by connecting it to the sentence before or after it.

Which word groups are fragments? _____

1 Being a smart consumer can be difficult. 2 Especially when making a major purchase. 3 At car dealerships, for example, important information is often in small type. 4 Like finance charges or preparation charges. 5 Advertisements also put negative information in small type. 6 Such as a drug's side effects. 7 Credit-card offers often use tiny, hard-to-read print for the terms of the card. 8 Like interest charges and late fees, which can really add up. 9 Phone service charges can also be hidden in small print. 10 Like limits on text messaging and other functions. 11 Especially now, as businesses try to make it seem as if you are getting a good deal, it is important to read any offer carefully.

EDIT FOR FRAGMENTS

Use the chart on page 372, "Finding and fixing fragments," to help you complete the practice exercise in this section and edit your own writing.

PRACTICE 6   Editing for Fragments

Find and correct eight fragments in the following paragraph.

1 In her essay, "Why Are We So Angry?," Dianne Hales describes the growing trend in our country toward violent anger over relatively unimportant things. 2 For example, anger about minor traffic delays or having to wait in a fast-food restaurant. 3 Hales also gives readers advice for addressing anger problems. 4 Although I have not dealt with the kinds of dangerous anger that Hales describes. 5 I do sometimes get irritated or impatient. 6 Especially when I am tired. 7 For this reason, I can appreciate

one particular piece of advice. 8 That Hales gives in this essay. 9 She encourages readers to check themselves for "early signs of exhaustion or overload" (149). 10 I know that my irritation skyrockets to levels that are not at all appropriate when I am extremely tired. 11 Which basically means after a twelve-hour shift at work. 12 I need to plan carefully on those days so that I can relax and unwind as soon as I can. 13 For example, letting my husband take care of dinner on those days. 14 Or making sure I have finished my homework early on those days. 15 If I just think ahead a little bit. 16 I can reduce my stress levels and avoid the kinds of angry outbursts that Hales describes.

Chapter Review

1. A sentence (or independent clause) is a group of words that has three elements: _____ , _____ , and _____ .

2. A _____ is a group of words that is punctuated like a complete sentence but is only a piece of one. It lacks a _____ , a _____ , or a _____

   _____ .

3. What are five trouble spots that signal possible fragments?

   _____

   _____

   _____

   _____

   _____

4. What are two basic ways to correct a fragment?

   _____

   _____

Chapter Test

Circle the correct choice for each of the following items. For help, refer to the chart on page 372, "Finding and Fixing Fragments."

1. If an underlined portion of this word group is incorrect, select the revision that fixes it. If the word group is correct as written, choose d.

   Natalie did not go on our bike trip. Because she could not ride a bike.
   <u>　　　　　　　　A　　　　　　B　　　　　　　　　　　　C</u>

   a. go. On   c. ride; a
   b. trip because   d. No change is necessary.

2. Choose the item that has no errors.

   a. Since Gary is the most experienced hiker here, he should lead the way.
   b. Since Gary is the most experienced hiker here. He should lead the way.
   c. Since Gary is the most experienced hiker here; he should lead the way.

3. If an underlined portion of this passage is incorrect, select the revision that fixes it. If the passage is correct as written, choose d.

   Planting fragrant flowers will attract wildlife. Such as butterflies.
   <u>　　　A　　　　　　　B　　　　　　　　C</u>

   a. When planting   c. wildlife, such
   b. flowers; will   d. No change is necessary.

4. Choose the item that has no errors.

   a. To get to the concert hall; take exit 5 and drive for three miles.
   b. To get to the concert hall. Take exit 5 and drive for three miles.
   c. To get to the concert hall, take exit 5 and drive for three miles.

5. If an underlined portion of this passage is incorrect, select the revision that fixes it. If the passage is correct as written, choose d.

   Buying many unnecessary groceries. Can result in wasted food
   <u>　　　　　　　　　　A　　　　　　　B</u>

   and wasted money.
   <u>　　　C</u>

   a. groceries can   c. : wasted money.
   b. : in wasted food   d. No change is necessary.

6. If an underlined portion of this passage is incorrect, select the revision that fixes it. If the passage is correct as written, choose d.

Some scientists <u>predict that</u> people will <u>soon take</u> vacuation
     A   B
<u>cruises. Into space.</u>
         C

a. predict, that   c. cruises into
b. soon; take   d. No change is necessary.

7. Choose the item that has no errors.

a. Walking for ten miles after her car broke down. Pearl became tired and frustrated.

b. Walking for ten miles after her car broke down; Pearl became tired and frustrated.

c. Walking for ten miles after her car broke down, Pearl became tired and frustrated.

8. Choose the item that has no errors.

a. Many people find it hard. To concentrate during stressful times.

b. Many people find it hard to concentrate during stressful times.

c. Many people find it hard, to concentrate during stressful times.

9. If an underlined portion of this sentence is incorrect, select the revision that fixes it. If the sentence is correct as written, choose d.

<u>Growing suspicious,</u> the secret <u>agent discovered</u> a tiny recording
        A   B
device <u>inside a flower vase.</u>
             C

a. Growing, suspicious   c. inside, a flower vase.
b. agent. Discovered   d. No change is necessary.

10. If an underlined portion of this passage is incorrect, select the revision that fixes it. If the passage is correct as written, choose d.

<u>Early in their training,</u> <u>doctors learn</u> that there is a fine
        A   B
<u>line. Between</u> life and death.
        C

a. Early, in   c. line between
b. doctors. Learn   d. No change is necessary.

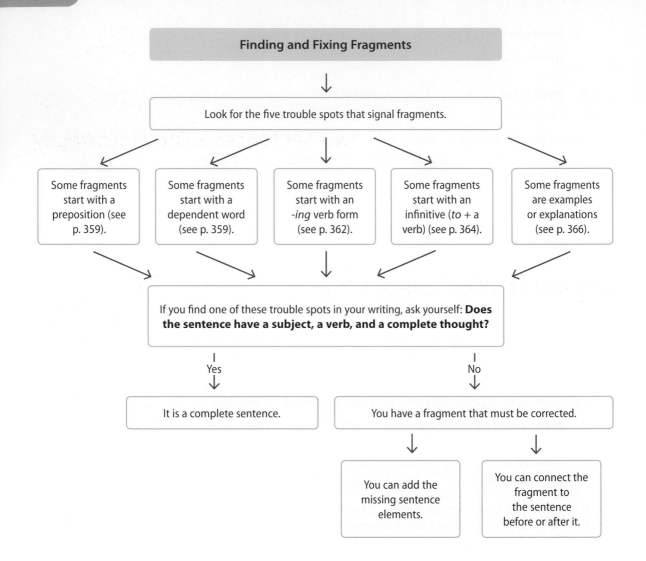

Finding and Fixing Fragments

Look for the five trouble spots that signal fragments.

| Some fragments start with a preposition (see p. 359). | Some fragments start with a dependent word (see p. 359). | Some fragments start with an *-ing* verb form (see p. 362). | Some fragments start with an infinitive (*to* + a verb) (see p. 364). | Some fragments are examples or explanations (see p. 366). |

If you find one of these trouble spots in your writing, ask yourself: **Does the sentence have a subject, a verb, and a complete thought?**

Yes → It is a complete sentence.

No → You have a fragment that must be corrected.

You can add the missing sentence elements.

You can connect the fragment to the sentence before or after it.

17

Run-Ons:

Two Sentences Joined Incorrectly

Understand What Run-Ons Are

ⓔ Log in to **macmillanhighered .com/rrw** and look for LearningCurve > Run-On Sentences

In Chapter 15, you learned that a sentence must contain at least one **independent clause**, or a group of words with a subject and a verb that expresses a complete thought. Sometimes, a sentence can contain two independent clauses that are joined together.

Sentences with two independent clauses

(Note: Each independent clause is in brackets. Subjects are underlined, and verbs are double-underlined.)

[The college offers financial aid], and [it encourages students to apply].

[Nearly every drug offense involves a snitch], and [snitching is increasingly displacing more traditional police work, such as undercover operations and independent investigation] (Natapoff, 299).

[I once tried going a whole week without telling a lie], and [it was paralyzing] (Ericsson, 199).

A **run-on** is two independent clauses joined incorrectly as one sentence. There are two kinds of run-ons: fused sentences and comma splices.

A **fused sentence** is two complete sentences joined without a coordinating conjunction or any punctuation.

	Independent clause	Independent clause
Fused sentence	Exercise is important	it has many benefits.

No punctuation

A **comma splice** is two complete sentences joined only by a comma.

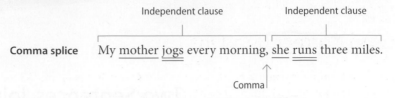

When you join two independent clauses (sentences), you must use proper punctuation.

Corrections   Exercise is important, and it has many benefits.

My mother jogs every morning; she runs three miles.

In the Real World, Why Is It Important to Correct Run-Ons?

People outside the English classroom notice run-ons and consider them major mistakes.

Situation: Naomi is applying to a special program for returning students at Cambridge College. Here is one of the essay questions on the application, followed by a paragraph from Naomi's answer.

Statement of purpose: In two hundred words or less, describe your intellectual and professional goals and how a Cambridge College education will assist you in achieving them.

> For many years, I did not take control of my life, I just drifted without any goals. I realized one day as I met with my daughter's guidance counselor that I hoped my daughter would not turn out like me. From that moment, I decided to do something to help myself and others. I set a goal of becoming a teacher. To begin on that path, I took a math course at night school, then I took another in science. I passed both courses with hard work, I know I can do well in the Cambridge College program. I am committed to the professional goal I finally found it has given new purpose to my whole life.

There are four run-ons in Naomi's paragraph. While the content of the paragraph shows important qualities of Naomi's character, the writing looks sloppy and careless. In other words, the quality of writing says something about Naomi; it gives readers an impression of her that is not necessarily favorable. Taking the time to find and correct run-ons will help your readers form a more favorable impression of you as a careful writer and thinker.

Find and Correct Run-Ons

To find run-on sentences when you edit your own writing, focus on one sentence at a time, looking for fused sentences and comma splices.

e Log in to **macmillanhighered .com/rrw** and look for Additional Grammar Exercises > Correcting Various Run-Ons

> **PRACTICE 1**   **Finding Run-Ons**
>
> Find and underline the four run-ons in Naomi's writing on page 374.

Once you have found a fused sentence or a comma splice, there are five ways to correct it. Each of the methods represents a **sentence pattern** that you can use to improve your writing.

How To Correct Run-Ons

Strategy	Example	Pattern IC = independent clause DC = dependent clause ca = conjunctive adverb cc = coordinating conjunction sc = subordinating conjunction S = subject V = verb
Add a period.	*He* I saw the man. he did not see me.	IC. IC. (S + V. S + V.)
Add a semicolon.	I saw the man; he did not see me.	IC; IC. (S + V; S + V.)
Add a semicolon, a conjunctive adverb, and a comma.	*however,* I saw the man; he did not see me.	IC; ca, IC. (S + V; ca, S + V.)
Add a comma and a coordinating conjunction.	*but* I saw the man, he did not see me.	IC, cc IC. (S + V, cc S + V.)
Add a subordinating conjunction (dependent word).	*when* The man did not see me I saw him. *When* I saw the man, he did not see me.	IC DC. DC, IC. (S + V + sc + S + V.) (sc + S + V, S + V.)

Notice that the corrections are the same for both fused sentences and comma splices. Some students mistakenly believe that they can correct a fused sentence by adding a comma. What happens if you add a comma to a fused sentence?

Fused   I saw the man he saw me.
sentence

If you answered that adding a comma creates a comma splice, you are correct.

Comma splice   I saw the man, he saw me.

Adding a comma does not correct the fused sentence; you must use one of the five strategies listed in the chart on page 375. Let's look at these strategies in more detail.

Add a Period

You can correct run-ons by adding a period to make two separate sentences. After adding the period, capitalize the letter that begins the new sentence. Reread your two sentences to make sure they each contain a subject, a verb, and a complete thought.

PATTERN 1: IC. IC.

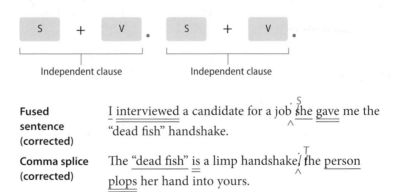

Fused   I interviewed a candidate for a job she gave me the
sentence   "dead fish" handshake.
(corrected)

Comma splice   The "dead fish" is a limp handshake the person
(corrected)   plops her hand into yours.

Add a Semicolon

A second way to correct run-ons is to use a semicolon (;) to join the two sentences. Use a semicolon only when the two independent clauses express closely related ideas. Also, remember that a semicolon only works between independent clauses; if you cannot correct the sentence by adding a period, you cannot correct it with a semicolon, either.

PATTERN 2: IC; IC.

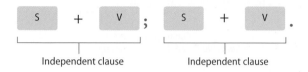

Independent clause   Independent clause

Pattern 2 is an example of **coordination**: using two independent clauses in a single sentence. For more information on coordination, see Chapter 24.

Do not capitalize the word that follows a semicolon unless it is the name of a specific person, place, or thing that is usually capitalized—for example, Melissa, Baltimore, or Waffle House.

Fused sentence (corrected)	Slouching creates a terrible impression it makes a person seem uninterested, bored, or lacking in self-confidence.
Comma splice (corrected)	It is important in an interview to hold your head up; it is just as important to sit up straight.

Add a Semicolon, a Conjunctive Adverbial, and a Comma

A third way to correct run-ons is to add a semicolon followed by a **conjunctive adverbial** and a comma. In Chapters 7–13, you learned that a conjunctive adverbial can be used as a transitional expression in writing. Pay attention to the punctuation required for conjunctive adverbials when you use them to correct run-ons.

PATTERN 3: IC; ca, IC.

Like Pattern 2, Pattern 3 is an example of coordination: a sentence that contains two independent clauses.

Independent clause   Conjunctive adverbial   Independent clause

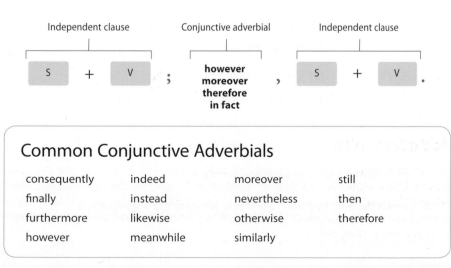

Common Conjunctive Adverbials

consequently	indeed	moreover	still
finally	instead	nevertheless	then
furthermore	likewise	otherwise	therefore
however	meanwhile	similarly	

Comma splice   I stopped by the market, it was closed.

Fused sentence   Sharon is a neighbor she is my friend.

                                   Conjunctive
                      Semicolon   adverbial   Comma

Comma splice (corrected)   I stopped by the market; however, it was closed.

                                  Conjunctive
                    Semicolon   adverbial   Comma

Fused sentence (corrected)   Sharon is a neighbor; moreover, she is my friend.

Finding and fixing run-ons:

Adding a period; a semicolon; or a semicolon, a conjunctive adverbial, and a comma

Find

Few people know the history of many popular holidays

Valentine's Day is one of these holidays.

1. To see if there are two independent clauses in a sentence, **underline** the subjects, and **double-underline** the verbs.

2. *Ask:* If the sentence has two independent clauses, are they separated by either a period or a semicolon? *No. The sentence is a run-on.*

Fix

Few people know the history of many popular holidays.
                                                        ^

Valentine's Day is one of these holidays.

Few people know the history of many popular holidays;
                                                        ^

Valentine's Day is one of these holidays.

                                                        indeed,

Few people know the history of many popular holidays;
                                                        ^ ^

Valentine's Day is one of these holidays.

3. **Correct** the error by adding a period; a semicolon; or a semicolon, a conjunctive adverbial, and a comma.

> **PRACTICE 2** **Correcting Run-Ons by Adding a Period or a Semicolon**

For each of the following items, indicate in the space to the left whether it is a fused sentence ("FS") or a comma splice ("CS"). Then, correct the error by adding a period or a semicolon. Capitalize the letters as necessary to make two sentences.

Example: ___FS___ Being a farmer can mean dealing with all types of challenges; one of the biggest ones comes from the sky.

_CS_ 1. Farmers have been trying to keep hungry birds out of their crops for centuries, the first scarecrow was invented for this reason.

_CS_ 2. Some farmers have used a variety of chemicals, other farmers have tried noise, such as small cannons.

_FS_ 3. Recently, a group of berry farmers tried something new they brought in bigger birds called falcons.

_FS_ 4. Small birds such as starlings love munching on berries each year they destroy thousands of dollars' worth of farmers' berry crops.

_CS_ 5. Because these starlings are frightened of falcons, they fly away when they see these birds of prey in the fields, they need to get to where they feel safe.

Add a Comma and a Coordinating Conjunction

A fourth way to correct run-ons is to add a comma and a coordinating conjunction. A coordinating conjunction is one of these seven words: *and, but, for, nor, or, yet, so.* Some people remember the coordinating conjunctions by thinking of **FANBOYS**: *for, and, nor, but, or, yet, so.*

To correct a fused sentence this way, add a comma and a coordinating conjunction. A comma splice already has a comma, so just add a coordinating conjunction that makes sense in the sentence. As the name *coordinating conjunction* suggests, when you connect two independent clauses using this pattern, you are using coordination.

e Log in to **macmillanhighered.com/rrw** and look for Additional Grammar Exercises > Correcting a Run-On by Adding a Comma and a Conjunction

PATTERN 4: IC, cc IC.

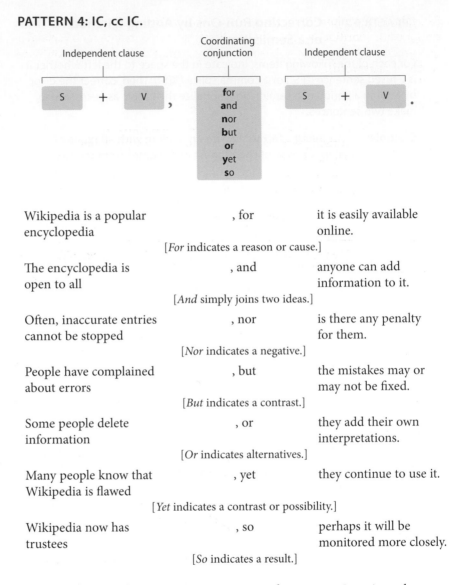

| Wikipedia is a popular encyclopedia | , for | it is easily available online. |

[*For* indicates a reason or cause.]

| The encyclopedia is open to all | , and | anyone can add information to it. |

[*And* simply joins two ideas.]

| Often, inaccurate entries cannot be stopped | , nor | is there any penalty for them. |

[*Nor* indicates a negative.]

| People have complained about errors | , but | the mistakes may or may not be fixed. |

[*But* indicates a contrast.]

| Some people delete information | , or | they add their own interpretations. |

[*Or* indicates alternatives.]

| Many people know that Wikipedia is flawed | , yet | they continue to use it. |

[*Yet* indicates a contrast or possibility.]

| Wikipedia now has trustees | , so | perhaps it will be monitored more closely. |

[*So* indicates a result.]

Be careful to choose an appropriate coordinating conjunction when you are correcting a run-on.

Fused sentence	Nekeisha was qualified for the job she hurt her chances by mumbling.
Illogical correction	Nekeisha was qualified for the job, and she hurt her chances by mumbling.
Logical correction	Nekeisha was qualified for the job, but she hurt her chances by mumbling.

Coordinating conjunctions are used to connect two independent clauses. We cannot use a coordinating conjunction between an independent clause and a **dependent clause** (a group of words that begins with a subordinating conjunction or dependent word).

Incorrect

Dependent clause

Although we warned Min-li to wear a seatbelt, **but** she never did.

Independent clause

Correct

Independent clause   Independent clause

We warned Min-li to wear a seatbelt, **but** she never did.

Finding and fixing run-ons:

Using a comma and/or a coordinating conjunction

Find

Foods <u>differ</u> from place to place your favorite <u>treat</u> <u>might disgust</u> someone from another culture.

1. To see if there are two independent clauses in a sentence, **underline** the subjects, and **double-underline** the verbs.

2. *Ask:* If the sentence has two independent clauses, are they separated by either a period or a semicolon? *No. The sentence is a run-on.*

Fix

, and

Foods differ from place to place ^ your favorite treat might disgust someone from another culture.

3. **Correct** a fused sentence by adding a comma and a coordinating conjunction between the two independent clauses. Correct a comma splice by adding just a coordinating conjunction.

> **PRACTICE 3**   **Correcting Run-Ons by Adding a Comma and/or a Coordinating Conjunction**

Correct each of the following run-ons by adding a comma, if necessary, and an appropriate coordinating conjunction. First, underline the subjects and double-underline the verbs.

Example: Most Americans do not like the idea of eating certain kinds of

and
food, most of us would probably reject horse meat.

1. In most cultures, popular foods depend on availability and tradition, *so* people tend to eat old familiar favorites.

2. Sushi shocked many Americans thirty years ago, *but* today some young people in the United States have grown up eating raw fish.

3. In many societies, certain foods are allowed to age *for* this process adds flavor.

4. Icelanders bury eggs in the ground to rot for months, *yet* these aged eggs are considered a special treat.

5. As an American, you might not like such eggs *and* the thought of eating them might even revolt you.

Add a Dependent Word

A fifth way to correct run-ons is to make one of the complete sentences a dependent clause by adding a **dependent word** (a subordinating conjunction or a relative pronoun), such as *after, because, before, even though, if, that, though,* or *which.* (For a complete list of dependent words, see page 361.) A dependent word shows the relationship between the two clauses. We can turn one of the independent clauses into a dependent clause when it is less important than the other clause or explains it in some way.

> When *I get to the train station*, I will call Josh.

The italicized clause is dependent (or subordinate) because it explains when the most important idea in the sentence—calling Josh—will happen. It begins with the dependent word *when.*

Because a dependent clause is not a complete sentence (because it does not express a complete thought), it can be joined to an independent clause without creating a run-on. When the dependent clause is the first clause in a sentence, it is followed by a comma. When the dependent clause is the second clause in the sentence, you usually do not need to separate the clauses with a comma (unless the dependent clause shows contrast).

Two sentences

Halloween <u>was</u> originally a religious holiday. <u>People</u> <u>worshipped</u> the saints.

Dependent clause: no comma needed

Halloween <u>was</u> originally a religious holiday *when* <u>people</u> <u>worshipped</u> the saints.

Dependent clause showing contrast: comma needed

Many <u>holidays</u> <u>have</u> religious origins, *though some <u>celebrations</u> <u>have moved</u> away from their religious roots.*

PATTERN 5, OPTION 1: IC DC.

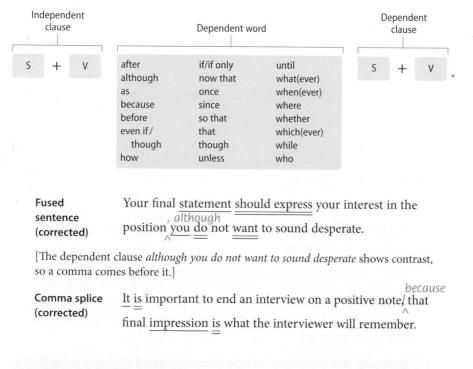

| Fused sentence (corrected) | Your final <u>statement</u> <u>should express</u> your interest in the *, although* position you <u>do</u> not <u>want</u> to sound desperate. |

[The dependent clause *although you do not want to sound desperate* shows contrast, so a comma comes before it.]

| Comma splice (corrected) | *because* <u>It</u> <u>is</u> important to end an interview on a positive note that final <u>impression</u> <u>is</u> what the interviewer will remember. |

PATTERN 5, OPTION 2: DC, IC.

Fused sentence (corrected)	*When the* ~~The~~ interviewer stands , the candidate should shake his or her hand firmly.
Comma splice (corrected)	*After the* ~~The~~ interview is over, the candidate should stand and smile politely.

Finding and fixing run-ons:

Making a dependent clause

Find

Alzheimer's disease is a heartbreaking illness, it causes a steady decrease in brain capacity.

1. To see if there are two independent clauses in a sentence, **underline** the subjects, and **double-underline** the verbs.

2. *Ask:* If the sentence has two independent clauses, are they separated by a period, a semicolon, or a comma and a coordinating conjunction? *No. The sentence is a run-on.*

Fix

because
Alzheimer's disease is a heartbreaking illness, it causes a steady decrease in brain capacity.

3. If one part of the sentence is less important than the other, or if you want to make it so, add a dependent word to the less important part.

PRACTICE 4   **Correcting Run-Ons by Adding a Dependent Word**

Correct run-ons by adding a dependent word to make a dependent clause. First, underline the subjects, and double-underline the verbs. Although these run-ons can be corrected in different ways, in this exercise correct them by adding dependent words. You may want to refer to the graphic on page 383.

When many
Example: ~~Many~~ soldiers returned from Iraq and Afghanistan missing arms or legs, demand for better artificial limbs increased.

Before
1. Computer chips were widely used artificial limbs remained largely unchanged for decades.

Because.

2. Computer chips now control many artificial limbs, these limbs have more capabilities than the ones of the past.

While.

3. The i-LIMB artificial hand picks up electrical signals from nearby arm muscles the amputee can move individual fingers of the hand.

Before.

4. Lighter-weight materials were introduced artificial limbs were not as easy to move as they are today.   *because*

5. Now, the C-Leg artificial leg is popular it is lightweight, flexible, and technically advanced.

Special Considerations: Two Situations That Cause Run-Ons

The Word Then

Many run-ons are caused by the word *then*. You can use *then* to join two independent clauses, but you must use correct punctuation when you do (Patterns 1–4). Otherwise, you will have a run-on sentence. Many writers use a comma alone to connect independent clauses with *then*. Unfortunately, this makes a comma splice.

Comma splice   I picked up my laundry, then I went home.

Examples of correcting this error using Patterns 1, 2, 4, and 5 are illustrated below.

. T
I picked up my laundry, then I went home.

;
I picked up my laundry, then I went home.

and
I picked up my laundry, then I went home.

before
I picked up my laundry, ~~then~~ I went home.

[dependent word *before* added to make a dependent clause]

Introducing a Quotation

In Chapters 7–14, you learned that you can include a reference to another writer's words in your own writing. When you introduce a quote with a signal phrase, the signal phrase is followed by a comma.

Amy Tan <u>says</u>, "For Christmas I prayed for this blond-haired boy, Robert, and a slim new American nose" (117).

The introductory phrase has a subject (*Amy Tan*) and a verb (*says*), but it is not an independent clause (a complete thought). We can also introduce a quote with an independent clause.

Amy Tan <u>explains</u> that she was unhappy with her Chinese appearance: "For Christmas I prayed for this blond-haired boy, Robert, and a slim new American nose" (117).

In this sentence, an independent clause explains what a reader will find in the quote that follows. The reader is prompted to look for evidence that Tan was not happy with the fact that she looked Chinese.

Be careful when you introduce a quote with an independent clause. If you join an independent clause to a quote with a comma alone, you create a comma splice.

Comma splice   Amy Tan explains that she was unhappy with her Chinese appearance, "For Christmas I prayed for this blond-haired boy, Robert, and a slim new American nose" (117).

This kind of comma splice is usually corrected with a colon rather than with one of the patterns listed in this chapter. For more on colons, see Chapter 31.

Edit for Run-Ons

Use the chart on page 390, "Finding and Fixing Run-Ons," to help you complete the practice exercise in this section and edit your own writing.

> **PRACTICE 5**   **Editing Run-Ons in a P/Q Assignment**
>
> The following paraphrase/quote assignment contains five run-on sentences. Find and correct each one.

1 In her essay "The Ways We Lie," Stephanie Ericsson discusses types of lies, and she argues that each type carries negative consequences, even if the lie seems innocent or common. 2 One of the types of lies she discusses is stereotype or cliché this is of course when someone judges someone else without getting to know that person fully. 3 I understand

Ericsson's point when she calls a stereotype a lie; after all, stereotypes do a lot of damage. 4 My brother, for example, is a high school dropout.

5 People always assume that he is not intelligent or that he won't under-stand instructions. 6 The truth is that he is much smarter than the average high school graduate he dropped out because of peer pressure and social problems, not academic issues. 7 I agree with Ericsson when she points out just how bad stereotypes are, "They are always dangerous" (201). 8 On the other hand, I am not sure that a stereotype is a lie. 9 When a person forms an opinion without enough information, I don't think that person intends to mislead anyone; he is just being stupid. 10 Stereotyping proves a person is not thinking, it doesn't mean a person is deceptive.

Chapter Review

1. A sentence can also be called an _____ .

2. A _____ is two complete sentences joined without any punctuation.

3. A _____ is two complete sentences joined by only a comma.

4. What are the five ways to correct run-ons?

   _____

   _____

   _____

   _____

   _____

5. What word in the middle of a sentence may signal a run-on? _____

6. What are the seven coordinating conjunctions? _____

Chapter Test

Circle the correct choice for each of the following items. For help, refer to the "Finding and Fixing Run-Ons" chart on page 390.

1. Choose the item that has no errors.

   a. Please fill this prescription for me, it is for my allergies.

   b. Please fill this prescription for me. It is for my allergies.

   c. Please fill this prescription for me it is for my allergies.

2. If an underlined portion of this sentence is incorrect, select the revision that fixes it. If the sentence is correct as written, choose d.

   Harlan is busy <u>now ask</u> <u>him if</u> he can do his <u>report next</u> week.
                                                     A   B   C

   a. now, so ask

   b. him, if

   c. report; next

   d. No change is necessary.

3. Choose the item that has no errors.

   a. You cut all the onion slices to the same thickness, they will finish cooking at the same time.

   b. You cut all the onion slices to the same thickness they will finish cooking at the same time.

   c. If you cut all the onion slices to the same thickness, they will finish cooking at the same time.

4. Choose the correct answer to fill in the blank.

   I have told Jervis several times not to tease the baby _____ he never listens.

   a. ,

   b. , but

   c. No additional word or punctuation is necessary.

5. Choose the item that has no errors.

   a. I am in no hurry to get a book I order it online.

   b. I am in no hurry to get a book, I order it online.

   c. When I am in no hurry to get a book, I order it online.

6. If an underlined portion of this sentence is incorrect, select the revision that fixes it. If the sentence is correct as written, choose d.

   Many people think a tomato is a <u>vegetable it</u> is <u>really a</u> fruit.
                             A   B   C

   a. Many, people

   b. vegetable; it

   c. really; a

   d. No change is necessary.

7. Choose the item that has no errors.

   a. Although air conditioning makes hot days more comfortable, it will increase your energy bills.

   b. Air conditioning makes hot days more comfortable it will increase your energy bills.

   c. Air conditioning makes hot days more comfortable, it will increase your energy bills.

8. If an underlined portion of this sentence is incorrect, select the revision that fixes it. If the sentence is correct as written, choose d.

   In northern Europe, bodies that are thousands of years <u>old have</u> been

   **   A**

   found in <u>swamps, some</u> bodies are so well preserved that they <u>look like</u>

   **   B   C**

   sleeping people.

   a. old, have   c. look, like

   b. swamps. Some   d. No change is necessary.

9. Choose the item that has no errors.

   a. Do not be shy about opening doors for strangers, courtesy is always appreciated.

   b. Do not be shy about opening doors for strangers; courtesy is always appreciated.

   c. Do not be shy about opening doors for strangers courtesy is always appreciated.

10. Choose the correct answer to fill in the blank.

   You can ride with me to work _____ you can take the train.

   a. , or   c. No additional word or punctuation
                                              is necessary.
   b. if

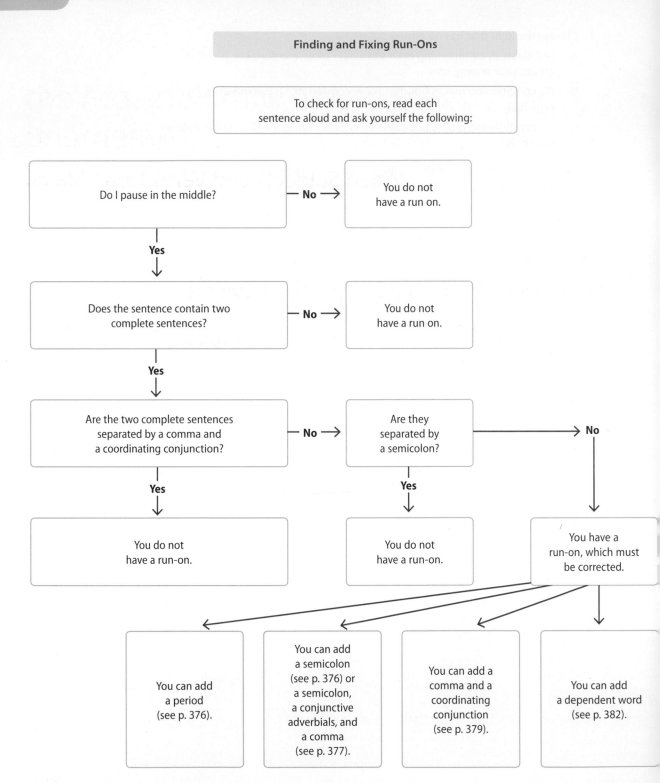

Finding and Fixing Run-Ons

To check for run-ons, read each
sentence aloud and ask yourself the following:

Do I pause in the middle? — **No** → You do not have a run on.

↓ **Yes**

Does the sentence contain two complete sentences? — **No** → You do not have a run on.

↓ **Yes**

Are the two complete sentences separated by a comma and a coordinating conjunction? — **No** → Are they separated by a semicolon? → **No**

↓ **Yes** (left)   ↓ **Yes** (middle)

You do not have a run-on.   You do not have a run-on.   You have a run-on, which must be corrected.

You can add a period (see p. 376).

You can add a semicolon (see p. 376) or a semicolon, a conjunctive adverbials, and a comma (see p. 377).

You can add a comma and a coordinating conjunction (see p. 379).

You can add a dependent word (see p. 382).

18

Problems with Subject-Verb Agreement:

When Subjects and Verbs Don't Match

Understand What Subject-Verb Agreement Is

e Log in to
**macmillanhighered
.com/rrw** and look
for LearningCurve >
Subject-Verb Agreement

In any sentence, the **subject and the verb must match—or agree**—in number. If the subject is singular (one person, place, or thing), the verb must also be singular. If the subject is plural (more than one), the verb must also be plural.

Singular	The skydiver jumps out of the airplane.
Plural	The skydivers jump out of the airplane.

   Regular verbs (with forms that follow standard English patterns) have two forms in the present tense: one that ends in *-s* and one that has no ending. The third-person subjects—*he, she, it*—and singular nouns always use the form that ends in *-s*. First-person subjects (*I*), second-person subjects (*you*), and plural subjects use the form with no ending.

Regular Verbs, Present Tense

	Singular		Plural
First person	I walk.	no -s	We walk.
Second person	You walk.		You walk.
Third person	He (she, it) walks.	all end in -s	They walk.
	Joe walks.		Joe and Alice walk.
	The student walks.		The students walk.

e Log in to **macmillanhighered .com/rrw** and look for Additional Grammar Exercises > Correcting Various Subject-Verb Agreement Problems

In the Real World, Why Is It Important to Correct Errors in Subject-Verb Agreement?

People outside the English classroom notice subject-verb agreement errors and consider them major mistakes. In Chapter 8, you met Jason, who was writing a résumé as part of his student development class. Jason later wanted to use his résumé to apply for a job as a landscaping intern at his college. The application process required a cover letter. Look at Jason's first draft:

> I am applying for the landscaping intern position. I have been working for three years at A and G Landscaping Company. This company, which is highly respected, handle lawn care needs for several businesses and commercial properties in our community. When I began at the company, I was a crew member assigned to a residential team, but since then, I have risen to be a crew manager. Crew managers makes sure that the client are satisfied with the level of service. The members of my crew has given me excellent reviews. As a result, my boss continues to give me new responsibilities. I am confident that I am ready to extend my training in a new way at the college. The experience of working with new crew members at the college will help me take another step toward my dream: owning my own landscaping company.

There are four significant subject-verb agreement errors in this application letter. If Jason submits the letter without editing it carefully for these sorts of mistakes, he is much less likely to get the job. Although his resume clearly shows he has experience and leadership potential, carelessness on his application tells the employer that he may rush through jobs without taking time to review his work. Writing, like landscaping and many other professions, requires attention to detail. Jason can demonstrate his attention to detail by checking his written work more carefully.

e Log in to **macmillanhighered .com/rrw** and look for Additional Grammar Exercises > Correcting Subject-Verb Agreement Problems with the Verbs Be, Have, and Do

Find and Correct Errors in Subject-Verb Agreement

To find problems with subject-verb agreement in your own writing, look for five trouble spots that often signal these problems.

1. The Verb Is a Form of Be, Have, or Do

The verbs *be*, *have*, and *do* do not follow the rules for forming singular and plural forms; they are **irregular verbs**.

Forms of the Verb *Be*

Present tense	Singular	Plural
First person	I am	we are
Second person	you are	you are
Third person	she, he, it is	they are
	the student is	the students are

Past tense		
First person	I was	we were
Second person	you were	you were
Third person	she, he, it was	they were
	the student was	the students were

Forms of the Verb *Have,* Present Tense

	Singular	Plural
First person	I have	we have
Second person	you have	you have
Third person	she, he, it has	they have
	the student has	the students have

Forms of the Verb *Do,* Present Tense

	Singular	Plural
First person	I do	we do
Second person	you do	you do
Third person	she, he, it does	they do
	the student does	the students do

These verbs cause problems for writers who in conversation use the same form in all cases: *He do the cleaning; they do the cleaning.* People also sometimes use the word *be* instead of the correct form of *be*: *She be on vacation.*

In college and at work, use the correct forms of the verbs *be*, *have*, and *do* as shown in the preceeding charts.

> *are*
> They ~~is~~ sick today.

> *has*
> Joan ~~have~~ the best jewelry.

> *does*
> Carlos ~~do~~ the laundry every Wednesday.

Finding and fixing problems with subject-verb agreement:

Making subjects and verbs agree when the verb is *be*, *have*, or *do*

Find

> I (am / is / are) a true believer in naps.

1. **Underline** the subject.

2. *Ask:* Is the subject in the first (*I*), second (*you*), or third person (*he / she*)? *First person.*

3. *Ask:* Is the subject singular or plural? *Singular.*

Fix

> I (am / is / are) a true believer in naps.

4. **Choose** the verb by matching it to the form of the subject (first person, singular).

PRACTICE 1 **Identifying Problems with Subject-Verb Agreement**

Find and underline the four problems with subject-verb agreement in Jason's cover letter on page 392.

2. Words Come between the Subject and the Verb

When the subject and verb are not directly next to each other, it is more difficult to find them to make sure they agree. Most often, either a prepositional phrase or a dependent clause comes between the subject and the verb.

PREPOSITIONAL PHRASE BETWEEN THE SUBJECT AND THE VERB

A *prepositional phrase* starts with a preposition and ends with a noun or pronoun: I took my bag *of books* and threw it *across the room*.

The subject of a sentence is never in a prepositional phrase. When you are looking for the subject of a sentence, you can cross out any prepositional phrases.

On the downside, some recipients of laser surgery (report / reports) difficulties seeing at night, dry eyes, or infections. (from Said Ibrahim)

Log in to **macmillanhighered .com/rrw** and look for Additional Grammar Exercises > Correcting Subject-Verb Agreement Problems when the Subject and Verb are Separated by a Prepositional Phrase

Finding and fixing problems with subject-verb agreement:
Making subjects and verbs agree when they are separated by a prepositional phrase

Find

Learners with dyslexia (face / faces) many challenges.

1. **Underline** the subject.
2. **Cross out** any prepositional phrase that follows the subject.
3. *Ask:* Is the subject singular or plural? *Plural.*

Fix

Learners with dyslexia (face / faces) many challenges.

4. **Choose** the form of the verb that matches the subject.

PRACTICE 2 **Making Subjects and Verbs Agree When They Are Separated by a Prepositional Phrase**

In each of the following sentences, cross out the prepositional phrase between the subject and the verb, and circle the correct form of the verb. Remember that the subject of a sentence is never in a prepositional phrase.

Example: Tomatoes from the supermarket (is / are) often tasteless.

1. Experts in agriculture and plant science (identifies / identify) several reasons for flavorless tomatoes.

2. First, many commercial growers in the United States (chooses / choose) crop yield over taste.

3. Specially engineered breeds of tomatoes (produces / produce) many more bushels per planting than traditional breeds do.

4. Unfortunately, the tomatoes inside each bushel (tastes / taste) nothing like their sweet, juicy homegrown relatives.

5. Growing conditions at commercial farms also (contributes / contribute) to the problem.

e Log in to **macmillanhighered .com/rrw** and look for Additional Grammar Exercises > Correcting Subject-Verb Agreement Problems when the Subject and Verb are Separated by a Dependent Clause

DEPENDENT CLAUSE BETWEEN THE SUBJECT AND THE VERB

A *dependent clause* has a subject and a verb, but it does not express a complete thought. When a dependent clause comes between the subject and the verb, it usually starts with the word *who, whose, whom, that,* or *which.*

The subject of a sentence is never in a dependent clause. When you are looking for the subject of a sentence, you can cross out any dependent clauses.

The cell phones and pagers ~~that were supposed to make our lives easier~~ (has / <u>have</u>) put us on call 24/7/365 (Hales, 148).

Finding and fixing problems with subject-verb agreement:

Making subjects and verbs agree when they are separated by a dependent clause

Find

The security <u>systems</u> ~~that shopping sites on the Internet provide~~ (is / are) surprisingly effective.

1. **Underline** the subject.

2. **Cross out** any dependent clause that follows the subject. (Look for the words *who, whose, whom, that,* and *which* because they can signal such a clause.)

3. *Ask:* Is the subject singular or plural? *Plural.*

Fix

The security systems that shopping sites on the Internet provide (is / are) surprisingly effective.

4. **Choose** the form of the verb that matches the subject.

PRACTICE 3   **Making Subjects and Verbs Agree When They Are Separated by a Dependent Clause**

In each of the following sentences, cross out any dependent clauses. Then, correct any problems with subject-verb agreement. If the subject and the verb agree, write "OK" next to the sentence.

Example: My cousins ~~who immigrated to this country from~~ Ecuador
have
~~has~~ jobs in a fast-food restaurant.

1. The restaurant ~~that hired my cousins~~ are not treating them fairly. *is*

2. People ~~who work in the kitchen~~ has to report to work at 7:00 a.m. *have*

3. The boss ~~who supervises the morning shift~~ tells the workers not to punch in until 9:00 a.m.

4. The benefits ~~that full-time workers earn~~ have not been offered to my cousins.

5. Ramón, ~~whose hand was injured slicing potatoes,~~ need to have physical therapy. *needs*

3. *The Sentence Has a Compound Subject*

A **compound subject** is two (or more) subjects joined by *and, or,* or *nor*.

And/Or Rule: If two subjects are joined by *and,* use a plural verb. If two subjects are joined by *or* (or *nor*), they are considered separate, and the verb should agree with whatever subject it is closer to.

e Log in to
macmillanhighered
.com/rrw and look for
Additional Grammar
Exercises > Correcting
Subject-Verb Agreement
Problems with
Compound Subjects

Plural subject = Plural verb

The teacher *and* her aide grade all the exams.

Subject *or* Singular subject = Singular verb

Either the teacher *or* her aide grades all the exams.

Subject *or* Plural subject = Plural verb

The teacher *or* her aides grade all the exams.

Subject *nor* Plural subject = Plural verb

Neither the teacher *nor* her aides grade all the exams.

Finding and fixing problems with subject-verb agreement:	**Find**
Making subjects and verbs agree in a sentence with a compound subject	Watermelon or cantaloupe (makes / make) a delicious and healthy snack.

1. **Underline** the subjects.

2. **Circle** the word between the subjects.

3. *Ask:* Does that word join the subjects to make them plural or keep them separate? *It keeps them separate.*

4. *Ask:* Is the subject that is closer to the verb singular or plural? *Singular.*

Fix

Watermelon or cantaloupe (makes / make) a delicious and healthy snack.

5. **Choose** the verb form that agrees with the subject that is closer to the verb.

PRACTICE 4   **Choosing the Correct Verb in a Sentence with a Compound Subject**

In each of the following sentences, underline the word (*and* or *or*) that joins the parts of the compound subject. Then, circle the correct form of the verb.

Example: My mother and my sister (has / have) asked a nutritionist for advice on a healthy diet.

1. A tomato and a watermelon (shares / share) more than just red-colored flesh.

2. A cooked tomato or a slice of watermelon (contains / contain) a nutrient called lycopene that seems to protect the human body from some diseases.

3. Fruits and vegetables (is / are) an important part of a healthy diet, most experts agree.

4. Nutrition experts and dietitians (believes / believe) that eating a variety of colors of fruits and vegetables is best for human health.

5. Collard greens or spinach (provides / provide) vitamins, iron, and protection from blindness to those who eat them.

4. The Subject Is an Indefinite Pronoun ·

An **indefinite pronoun** replaces a general person, place, or thing or a general group of people, places, or things. Indefinite pronouns are often singular, although there are some exceptions, as shown in the chart below.

e Log in to **macmillanhighered .com/rrw** and look for Additional Grammar Exercises > Correcting Subject-Verb Agreement Problems when the Subject is an Indefinite Pronoun

Singular	Everyone wants the semester to end.
Plural	Many want the semester to end.
Singular	Either of the meals is good.

Often, an indefinite pronoun is followed by a prepositional phrase or dependent clause. Remember that the verb of a sentence must agree with the subject of the sentence, and the subject of a sentence is *never in a prepositional phrase or dependent clause*. To choose the correct verb, cross out the prepositional phrase or dependent clause.

Everyone in all the classes (want / wants) the term to end.

Several who have to take the math exam (is / are) studying together.

Indefinite Pronouns

Always Singular			**May Be Singular or Plural**
another	everybody	no one	all
anybody	everyone	nothing	any
anyone	everything	one (of)	none
anything	much	somebody	some
each (of)*	neither (of)*	someone	
either (of)*	nobody	something	

*When one of these words is the subject, mentally replace it with the word *one*. *One* is singular and takes a singular verb.

Finding and fixing problems with subject-verb agreement:

Making subjects and verbs agree when the subject is an indefinite pronoun

Find

One of my best friends (lives / live) in California.

1. **Underline** the subject.

2. **Cross out** any prepositional phrase or dependent clause that follows the subjects.

3. *Ask:* Is the subject singular or plural? *Singular.*

Fix

One of my best friends (lives / live) in California.

4. **Choose** the verb form that agrees with the subject.

PRACTICE 5   **Choosing the Correct Verb When the Subject Is an Indefinite Pronoun**

In each of the following sentences, cross out any prepositional phrase or dependent clause that comes between the subject and the verb. Then, underline the subject, and circle the correct verb.

Example: One of the strangest human experiences (results / result) from the "small-world" phenomenon.

1. Everyone (remembers / remember) an example of a "small-world" phenomenon.

2. Someone whom you have just met (tells / tell) you a story.

3. During the story, one of you (realizes / realize) that you are connected somehow.

4. One of your friends (lives / live) next door to the person.

5. Someone in your family (knows / know) someone in the person's family.

5. *The Verb Comes before the Subject*

In most sentences, the subject comes before the verb. Two kinds of sentences often reverse the usual subject-verb order: (1) questions and (2) sentences that begin with *here* or *there*. In these two types of sentences, check carefully for errors in subject-verb agreement.

Log in to **macmillanhighered .com/rrw** and look for Additional Grammar Exercises > Correcting Subject-Verb Agreement Problems when the Verb Comes before the Subject

QUESTIONS

In questions, the verb or part of the verb comes before the subject. To find the subject and verb, you can turn the question around as if you were going to answer it.

> What would Robert think of our shabby Chinese Christmas (Tan, 117)?
> Why are manhole covers round (Adams, 114)?

> **Language note:** For reference charts showing how to form questions, see pages 516–521 in Chapter 25.

Note: Sometimes the verb appears before the subject even in sentences that are *not* questions.

> Most inspiring of all were her speeches on freedom.

SENTENCES THAT BEGIN WITH *HERE* OR *THERE*

When a sentence begins with *here* or *there*, the subject often follows the verb. Sometimes, you can turn the sentence around to find the subject and verb.

> Here is your copy of the study guide. / Your copy of the study guide is here.
> There are four copies on the desk. / Four copies are on the desk.

Notice the subjects (underlined once) and the verbs (underlined twice) in the following sentences from Gail Godwin's essay "The Watcher at the Gates."

> There are various ways to outsmart, pacify, or coexist with your Watcher. Here are some I have tried, or my writer friends have tried, with success.

Finding and fixing problems with subject-verb agreement:

Making subjects and verbs agree when the verb comes before the subject

Find

What classes (is / are) the professor teaching?

There (is / are) two good classes in the music department.

1. If the sentence is a question, **turn the question into a statement**: *The professor (is/are) teaching the classes.*

2. If the sentence begins with *here* or *there*, **turn it around**: *Two good classes (is/are) in the music department.*

3. **Identify** the subject in each of the two new sentences. *It is "professor" in the first sentence and "classes" in the second.*

4. *Ask:* Is the subject singular or plural? *"Professor" is singular; "classes" is plural.*

Fix

What classes ((is)/ are) the professor teaching?

There (is / (are)) two good classes in the music department.

5. **Choose** the form of the verb in each sentence that matches the subject.

| PRACTICE 6 | **Correcting a Sentence When the Verb Comes before the Subject** |

Correct any problems with subject-verb agreement in the following sentences. If a sentence is already correct, write "OK" next to it.

does

Example: What electives ~~do~~ the school offer?

1. What are the best reason to study music?

2. There is several good reasons.

3. There is evidence that music helps students with math.

4. What is your favorite musical instrument?

5. Here is a guitar, a saxophone, and a piano.

🌐 **Language note:** When the complete verb in a sentence contains a modal auxiliary verb (*can, could, should, would, may, might, must,* or *will*), there is no -*s* at the end of the modal verb or the main verb of the sentence.

Incorrect	My teacher cans speak four languages.
Incorrect	My teachers can speaks four languages.
Correct	My teacher can speak four languages.

Subject-Verb Agreement in Partial Quotations

The Reading/Writing Workbook section in Chapter 12 introduces the skill of quoting only part of a sentence. When you choose to include a partial quote in your writing, pay attention to subject-verb agreement.

Incorrect	Stephanie Ericsson says that a stereotype—such as the idea that all truck drivers use foul language—"take a single tree and make it a landscape" (201).
Correct	Stephanie Ericsson says that stereotypes—such as the idea that all truck drivers use foul language—"take a single tree and make it a landscape" (201).
Correct	Stephanie Ericsson says that a stereotype—such as the idea that all truck drivers use foul language—can "take a single tree and make it a landscape" (201).

Edit for Subject-Verb Agreement

Use the chart on page 407, "Finding and Fixing Problems with Subject-Verb Agreement," to help you complete the practice exercise in this section and edit your own writing.

> **PRACTICE 7** **Editing for Subject-Verb Agreement in a P/Q Assignment**
>
> Find and correct ten fragments in the following P/Q paragraph.

1 In his essay "A Learning Tool Whose Time Has Come," Jason Yilmaz argues we should use social media in the classroom because such online interaction "make students feel more confident and connected" (289).

2 This argument makes sense; after all, each one of the students in this class have talked about the ways the discussion board helps the class understand the material and feel more empowered to express opinions. 3 On the other hand, Shari Beck raises a legitimate concern in her essay "A Classroom Distraction—and Worse." 4 Beck, who is a mom to young teenagers, say she does not want to see social network platforms in a class because "students' postings on Facebook or Twitter might compromise their privacy" (290). 5 There is several choices that students and teachers can make to receive the benefits of social networks while reducing the privacy problems. 6 For example, our English course use the BlackBoard platform, and only students who are registered in the class gets to see what is posted there. 7 Teachers and assistants with administrative control of the site sets the rules and the guidelines. 8 But if a student group wants to avoid the oversight of a teacher, it cans create a private Facebook group. 9 Only members of the group can see the content on the site. 10 Unfortunately, a private group without the presence of teachers make cheating easier, as Shari Beck points out in her essay. 11 If a site is created by the students and for the students, the teacher cannot controls what happens on the site. 12 Maybe the best solution is for the teacher to offer a private but dynamic media platform for students so that students won't see a need to create a separate discussion space.

| PRACTICE 8 | **Editing Jason's Cover Letter** |

Look back at Jason's cover letter on page 392. You may have already underlined the subject-verb agreement errors; if not, do so now. Next, using what you have learned in this chapter, correct each error.

Chapter Review

1. The _____ and the _____ in a sentence must agree (match) in terms of number. They must both be _____, or they must both be plural.

2. Five trouble spots can cause errors in subject-verb agreement:

   1. when the verb is a form of _____, _____, or _____

   2. when a _____ or a _____ comes between the subject and the verb

   3. when the sentence has a _____ subject joined by *and, or,* or *nor*

   4. when the subject is an _____ pronoun

   5. when the _____ comes _____ the subject

Chapter Test

Circle the correct choice for each of the following items. For help, refer to the "Finding and Fixing Problems with Subject-Verb Agreement" chart on page 407.

1. If an underlined portion of this sentence is incorrect, select the revision that fixes it. If the sentence is correct as written, choose d.

   There is only certain times when you can call to get technical
   $\quad\quad$ A $\qquad\qquad\qquad\qquad$ B $\qquad$ C

   support for this computer.

   a. There are $\qquad\qquad$ c. getting

   b. you could $\qquad\qquad$ d. No change is necessary.

2. Choose the correct word to fill in the blank.

   Dana's dog Bernard _____ just a puppy, but he moves so slowly that he seems old.

   a. be $\qquad\qquad\qquad$ c. being

   b. am $\qquad\qquad\qquad$ d. is

3. If an underlined portion of this sentence is incorrect, select the revision that fixes it. If the sentence is correct as written, choose d.

   The umpire was not happy to see that everyone were watching
   $\quad\quad$ A $\qquad\qquad\qquad\qquad\qquad$ B

   him argue with the baseball player.
   $\qquad$ C

   a. umpire were $\qquad\qquad$ c. argues with

   b. everyone was $\qquad\qquad$ d. No change is necessary.

4. Choose the correct word to fill in the blank.

    The woman who rented us our kayaks _____ now paddling her own kayak down the river.

    a.   are   b.   be   c.   is

5. Choose the item that has no errors.

    a.   Alex and Dane likes to travel now that they have retired from their jobs.

    b.   Alex and Dane liking to travel now that they have retired from their jobs.

    c.   Alex and Dane like to travel now that they have retired from their jobs.

6. Choose the correct word to fill in the blank.

    The builders of this house _____ used the best materials they could find.

    a.   have   b.   having   c.   has

7. Choose the correct word to fill in the blank.

    The calm before hurricanes _____ most people with anxiety.

    a.   fill   b.   filling   c.   fills

8. Choose the item that has no errors.

    a.   Sheryl and her sons go to the beach whenever they can find the time.

    b.   Sheryl and her sons goes to the beach whenever they can find the time.

    c.   Sheryl and her sons is going to the beach whenever they can find the time.

9. Choose the correct word to fill in the blank.

    Where _____ the children's wet swimsuits?

    a.   are   b.   is   c.   be

10. If an underlined portion of this sentence is incorrect, select the revision that fixes it. If the sentence is correct as written, choose d.

    Anybody who <u>can speak</u> several languages <u>are</u> in great demand to
             A   B
    <u>work</u> for the government, especially in foreign embassies.
       C

    a.   could   c.   working

    b.   is   d.   No change is necessary.

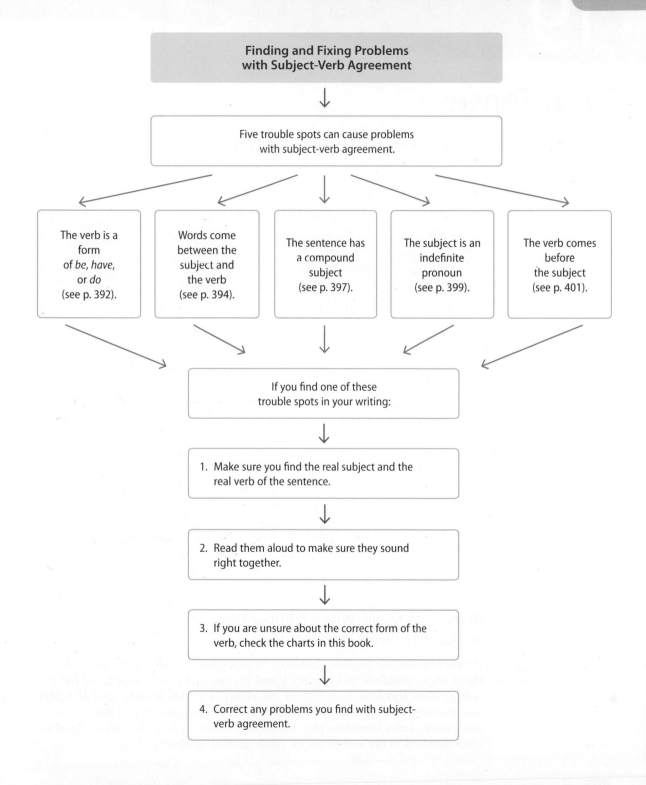

Finding and Fixing Problems with Subject-Verb Agreement

↓

Five trouble spots can cause problems with subject-verb agreement.

The verb is a form of *be*, *have*, or *do* (see p. 392).

Words come between the subject and the verb (see p. 394).

The sentence has a compound subject (see p. 397).

The subject is an indefinite pronoun (see p. 399).

The verb comes before the subject (see p. 401).

If you find one of these trouble spots in your writing:

↓

1. Make sure you find the real subject and the real verb of the sentence.

↓

2. Read them aloud to make sure they sound right together.

↓

3. If you are unsure about the correct form of the verb, check the charts in this book.

↓

4. Correct any problems you find with subject-verb agreement.

19

Verb Tense:

Using Verbs to Express Different Times

Understand What Verb Tense Is

Verb tense tells *when* an action happened: in the past, in the present, or in the future. Verbs change their **base form** or use the helping verbs *have, be,* or *will* to indicate different tenses.

Present	Women <u>fly</u> off the handle just as often as men, . . . (Hales, 148).
Past	After the game, <u>my father</u> <u>drove</u> my Uncle Willie and me to a place called Superdawg to get a red hot (Conroy, 123).
Future	I <u>will update</u> the roster as soon as new deaths are reported (Maxwell, 291).

In the Real World, Why Is It Important to Use the Correct Verb Tense?

People outside the English classroom notice errors in verb tense and consider them major mistakes. In Chapters 1 and 12, you met Jackie, who failed her first college class and later wrote about the chain of events leading to that failure. The second part of Jackie's student development class assignment was to use the analysis of causes to make a plan for success. Here is part of Jackie's draft, which she submitted to her instructor for some general feedback.

Since I had failed my first English class two years ago, I have realize that college success is an investment. Yes, I could make more money by working full-time, but then I would not earn my degree. As Mr. Holloway saying in class, "If we stop learning, we are stuck." I need a plan for success so that I won't be stuck. First, I need to attend class, and I done that regularly since last fall. In fact, I keep perfect attendance since last October. Second, I must spend more time studying than I done two years ago. Third, I must ask for help when I don't understand. I still working part-time each week, but I have promise myself that I will go to the tutoring center at least one hour a week. I have a plan, and I know I will make it this time.

Jackie's instructor, Mr. Holloway, wrote these comments on her draft:

Jackie, I think you have a good plan, and you have shown that you are following the plan by giving me a rough draft to look at. Your paragraph has some problems with grammar, especially verbs. If you don't address these problems, your paper is not going to succeed. I have two suggestions for you: first, read your paragraph out loud slowly. See if you can hear any of the mistakes. Second, take your draft to the tutoring center this week, since I know you are going there! ☺

Using Verbs Correctly

This section will teach you about verb tenses and give you practice with using them. You should also pay attention to the verb tenses in your reading. Select paragraphs from your reading, circle the verbs, and think about the way the tenses are used. You can also read the paragraph out loud, focusing on pronouncing and hearing yourself say the verb forms correctly.

> **PRACTICE 1**   **Identifying Verb Errors**
>
> Find and underline the eight verb errors in Jackie's draft.

Regular Verbs

Most verbs in English are **regular verbs** that follow standard rules about what endings to use to express time.

Log in to **macmillanhighered .com/rrw** and look for Additional Grammar Exercises > Using the Correct Verb Form for Regular Verbs in the Present Tense

PRESENT-TENSE ENDINGS: -S AND NO ENDING

The **present tense** is used for actions that are happening at the same time that they are being written about (the present) and for things that happen all the time. Present-tense regular verbs either end in -s or have no ending added.

-s ending	no ending
jumps	jump
walks	walk
lives	live

For more information on making subjects and verbs match in the present tense, see Chapter 18.

Use the -s ending when the subject is *he, she, it,* or the name of one person or thing. Use no ending for all other subjects.

Do not confuse the simple present tense with the present progressive (or continuous) tense, which combines the present tense of the verb *be* with the -*ing* form of the verb to describe actions in progress right now. The -*ing* form of a verb cannot be used as the main verb in a sentence without a form of the verb *be*.

Incorrect	I studying in the library.
Simple present	I study in the library every Saturday.
Present progressive	I am studying in the library right now.

Language note: Some languages do not use progressive tenses. If you have trouble using progressive tenses, see Chapter 25.

Usage note: Signal verb phrases (see Chapter 7) are written in the present tense.

Incorrect	Stephanie Ericsson said, "When someone lies, someone loses" (199).
Correct	Stephanie Ericsson says, "When someone lies, someone loses" (199).

e Log in to
**macmillanhighered
.com/rrw** and look for
Additional Grammar
Exercises > Using the
Correct Verb Form for
Regular Verbs in the Past
Tense

PRACTICE 2   Using Present-Tense Regular Verbs Correctly

In each of the following sentences, first underline the subject, and then circle the correct verb form.

Example: I (tries /(try) to keep to my budget.

1. My classes (requires / require) much of my time these days.

2. In addition to attending school, I (works / work) twenty hours a week in the college library.

3. The other employees (agrees / agree) that the work atmosphere is pleasant.

4. Sometimes, we even (manages / manage) to do homework at the library.

5. The job (pays / pay) a fairly low wage, however.

ONE REGULAR PAST-TENSE ENDING: -ED

The simple **past tense** is used for actions that have already happened; they were completed in the past.

An *-ed* ending is needed for all regular verbs in the past tense.

	Present tense	**Past tense**
First person	I avoid her.	I avoid**ed** her.
Second person	You help me.	You help**ed** me.
Third person	He walks quickly.	He walk**ed** quickly.

PRACTICE 3   Using the Past Tense of Regular Verbs Correctly

In each of the following sentences, fill in the correct past-tense forms of the verbs in parentheses.

1 Last winter, I _____ (*display*) the clear signs of a cold.
2 I _____ (*sneeze*) often, and I _____ (*develop*) a sore throat.
3 The congestion in my nose and throat _____ (*annoy*) me, and
it _____ (*seem*) that blowing my nose was useless. 4 However, I
_____ (*visit*) with my friends and _____ (*attend*) classes at college. 5 I _____ (*assume*) that I could not give anyone else my cold
once I showed the symptoms. 6 Unfortunately, many people _____

(*join*) me in my misery because of my ignorance. 7 Later, I _____ (*learn*) that I _____ (*remain*) contagious for several days after I first showed symptoms. 8 My doctor _____ (*explain*) to me that I _____ (*start*) spreading my cold about one day after I became infected with it. 9 However, after my symptoms _____ (*disappear*), I _____ (*pass*) on my cold to others for up to three days more. 10 I _____ (*want*) to apologize to everyone I had infected, but I also _____ (*realize*) that others had given me their colds as well.

ONE REGULAR PAST PARTICIPLE ENDING: *-ED*

The **past participle** is a verb form that is used with the auxiliary verb *have* to form the perfect tenses (for more on the perfect tenses, see pp. 419–423). The past participle is also used with a form of the verb *be* to show the passive voice (see p. 423). For all regular verbs, the past participle form has an *-ed* ending, just as the simple past tense does.

Past tense	Past participle
My kids watched cartoons.	They have watched cartoons before.
George visited his cousins.	He has visited them every year.

PRACTICE 4 **Using the Past Participle of Regular Verbs Correctly**

In each of the following sentences, underline the helping verb (a form of *have*), and fill in the correct form of the verb in parentheses.

**Example: Because of pressure to keep up with others, families have
____started___ (*start*) to give fancier and fancier birthday parties.**

1. We have all _____ (*receive*) invitations to simple birthday parties where children played games and had cake, but those days are gone.

2. Kids' birthday parties have _____ (*turn*) into complicated and expensive events.

3. Price tags for some of these parties have _____ (*climb*) to $1,000 or more.

4. By the time she had finished planning her daughter's birthday, one mother had _____ (*devote*) hundreds of dollars to the event.

5. She discovered that she had _____ (*hand*) out $50 for a club-house rental, $200 for a cotton-candy maker, and $300 for an actor dressed as Woody from *Toy Story*.

Irregular Verbs

Irregular verbs do not follow the simple rules of regular verbs, which have just two present-tense endings (*-s* or *-es*) and two past-tense endings (*-d* or *-ed*). The past tense and past participle of irregular verbs involve a change in spelling, although some irregular verbs, such as *cost*, *hit*, and *put*, do not change their spelling. The most common irregular verbs are *be* and *have* (see p. 416). As you write and edit, refer to the chart on pages 413–416 to make sure you have the correct form of irregular verbs.

Note: What is called "present tense" in the chart below is often called the "base form of the verb." This is the form of the verb you will find in a dictionary entry.

e Log in to **macmillanhighered .com/rrw** and look for Additional Grammar Exercises > Using the Correct Verb Form for Irregular Verbs in the Past Tense

Irregular Verbs

Present tense (base form of verb)	Past tense	Past participle (used with helping verb)
be (am /are /is)	was /were	been
become	became	become
begin	began	begun
bite	bit	bitten
blow	blew	blown
break	broke	broken
bring	brought	brought
build	built	built
buy	bought	bought
catch	caught	caught
choose	chose	chosen
come	came	come
cost	cost	cost

Present tense (base form of verb)	Past tense	Past participle (used with helping verb)
dive	dived, dove	dived
do	did	done
draw	drew	drawn
drink	drank	drunk
drive	drove	driven
eat	ate	eaten
fall	fell	fallen
feed	fed	fed
feel	felt	felt
fight	fought	fought
find	found	found
fly	flew	flown
forget	forgot	forgotten
get	got	gotten
give	gave	given
go	went	gone
grow	grew	grown
have/has	had	had
hear	heard	heard
hide	hid	hidden
hit	hit	hit
hold	held	held
hurt	hurt	hurt
keep	kept	kept
know	knew	known
lay	laid	laid
lead	led	led
leave	left	left
let	let	let
lie	lay	lain

Present tense (base form of verb)	Past tense	Past participle (used with helping verb)
light	lit	lit
lose	lost	lost
make	made	made
mean	meant	meant
meet	met	met
pay	paid	paid
put	put	put
quit	quit	quit
read	read	read
ride	rode	ridden
ring	rang	rung
rise	rose	risen
run	ran	run
say	said	said
see	saw	seen
seek	sought	sought
sell	sold	sold
send	sent	sent
shake	shook	shaken
show	showed	shown
shrink	shrank	shrunk
shut	shut	shut
sing	sang	sung
sink	sank	sunk
sit	sat	sat
sleep	slept	slept
speak	spoke	spoken
spend	spent	spent
stand	stood	stood
steal	stole	stolen

Present tense (base form of verb)	Past tense	Past participle (used with helping verb)
stick	stuck	stuck
sting	stung	stung
strike	struck	struck, stricken
swim	swam	swum
take	took	taken
teach	taught	taught
tear	tore	torn
tell	told	told
think	thought	thought
throw	threw	thrown
understand	understood	understood
wake	woke	woken
wear	wore	worn
win	won	won
write	wrote	written

e Log in to **macmillanhighered .com/rrw** and look for Additional Grammar Exercises > Using the Correct Verb Forms for Be and Have in the Present Tense

PRESENT TENSE OF *BE* AND *HAVE*

The present tense of the verbs *be* and *have* is very irregular, as shown in the following chart.

Present Tense of *Be* and *Have*

Be		Have	
I am	we are	I have	we have
you are	you are	you have	you have
he, she, it is	they are	he, she, it has	they have
the editor is	the editors are		
Beth is	Beth and Christina are		

PRACTICE 5   **Using *Be* and *Have* in the Present Tense**

In each of the following sentences, fill in the correct present-tense form of the verb indicated in parentheses.

Example: Because of my university's internship program, I ___am___ (*be*) able to receive academic credit for my summer job.

1. I __have__ (*have*) a job lined up with a company that provides private security to many local businesses and residential developments.

2. The company __has__ (*have*) a good record of keeping its clients safe from crime.

3. The company __is__ (*be*) part of a fast-growing industry.

4. Many people no longer __have__ (*have*) faith in the ability of the police to protect them.

5. People with lots of money __are__ (*be*) willing to pay for their own protection.

PAST TENSE OF *BE*

The past tense of the verb *be* is tricky because it has two different forms: *was* and *were*.

Past Tense of *Be*

	Singular	Plural
First person	I was	we were
Second person	you were	you were
Third person	she, he, it was	they were
	the student was	the students were

PRACTICE 6   **Using Irregular Verbs in the Past Tense**

In the following paragraph, replace any incorrect present-tense verbs with the correct past tense of the verb. If you are unsure of the past-tense forms of irregular verbs, refer to the chart on pages 413–416.

1 For years, Homer and Langley Collyer are [were] known for their strange living conditions. 2 Neighbors who passed by the brothers' New York City townhouse see [saw] huge piles of trash through the windows. 3 At night, Langley roamed the streets in search of more junk. 4 In March 1947, an anonymous caller tells [told] the police that someone had died in the Collyers' home. 5 In response, officers break [broke] through a second-floor window and tunneled through mounds of newspapers, old umbrellas, and other junk. 6 Eventually, they find [found] the body of Homer Collyer, who seemed to have [had] died of starvation. 7 But where was Langley? 8 In efforts to locate [located] him, workers spend days removing trash from the house—more than one hundred tons' worth in total. 9 They bring [brought] a strange variety of items to the curb, including medical equipment, bowling balls, fourteen pianos, and the frame of a Model T car. 10 In early April, a worker finally discovered Langley's body. 11 It lies [lay] just 10 feet from where Homer had been found. 12 Apparently, Langley died while bringing food to his disabled brother. 13 As he tunneled ahead, a pile of trash falls [fell] on him and crushed him. 14 This trash was part of a booby trap that Langley had created to stop intruders. 15 Not long after the brothers' deaths, the city demolished their former home. 16 In 1965, community leaders do [did] something that might have surprised Homer and Langley: Where the trash-filled home once stands [stood], workers created a neat and peaceful park. 17 In the 1990s, this green space becomes [became] the Collyer Brothers Park.

For irregular verbs, the past participle is often different from the past tense.

	Past tense	Past participle
Regular verb	I walked home.	I have walked home before.
Irregular verb	I drove home.	I have driven home before.

There are no simple rules that can tell you what the past participle form of a verb will be. Until you are familiar with past participles, use the chart on pages 413–416 to determine the correct form.

> **PRACTICE 7**   **Using the Past Participle of Irregular Verbs**
>
> In each of the following sentences, fill in the correct form of the helping verb *have* and the correct past participle form of the verb in parentheses. If you do not know the correct form, find the word in the chart on pages 413–416.
>
> **Example: Even though she has passed her seventy-fourth birthday,**
> **Ernestine Shepherd ___*has become*___ (*become*) a star in the fitness world.**
>
> 1. In 2010, recognizing the work Shepherd __had done__(*do*) to build
>
>   her muscles, the *Guinness Book of World Records* named her the oldest
>
>   female bodybuilder.
>
> 2. Since then, Shepherd __has told__ (*tell*) many fans the story of her
>
>   success.
>
> 3. She and her sister started working out in their fifties because
>
>   they __had grown__(*grow*) tired of carrying extra pounds.
>
> 4. Tragically, Shepherd's sister died soon afterward; nevertheless, by the
>
>   end of a long mourning period, Shepherd __had made__ (*make*) an
>
>   even stronger commitment to staying in shape.
>
> 5. From that time on, she __has kept__ (*keep*) a busy workout schedule.

Perfect Tenses and Past Participles

A past participle by itself cannot be the main verb of a sentence. When a past participle is combined with a form of the helping verb *have*, they form the present perfect or past perfect tense.

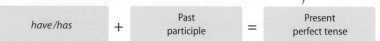

| *have/has* | + | Past participle | = | Present perfect tense |

The **present perfect tense** is used to describe two kinds of action:

1. Actions that began in the past and continue (or are expected to continue) into the present

2. Actions that occurred at an unknown time before the present

Log in to **macmillanhighered .com/rrw** and look for Additional Grammar Exercises > Using the Correct Verb Forms for the Past Participles of Regular and Irregular Verbs

Present tense of   Past participle
have (helping verb)

Present perfect tense   My car has stalled several times recently.

[This sentence says that the stalling began in the past and may continue into the present.]

Past tense   My car stalled.

[This sentence says that the car stalled once and that it's over.]

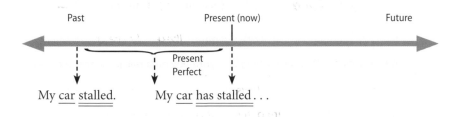

Past   Present (now)   Future

Present
Perfect

My car stalled.   My car has stalled . . .

Present   I have read all seven books in the Harry Potter series.
perfect tense

[This sentence says that some time before now the speaker read the books, but that time is not specified.]

Past tense   I read *Harry Potter and the Order of the Phoenix* three years ago.

[This sentence describes an action that was completed at a specific time before now.]

📧 Log in to **macmillanhighered .com/rrw** and look for Additional Grammar Exercises > Using the Present Perfect Tense

Present Perfect Tense

	Singular	**Plural**
First person	I have laughed.	We have laughed.
Second person	You have laughed.	You have laughed.
Third person	She /he /it has laughed.	They have laughed.
	The baby has laughed.	The babies have laughed.

🌐 **Language note:** The words *since* and *for* often signal that the present perfect is required. We do not use simple present or present progressive to describe actions that began in the past and continue into the present.

| Incorrect | I drive since 1987. | I am living here for three years. |
| Correct | I have driven since 1987. | I have lived here for three years. |

PRACTICE 8 **Using the Present Perfect Tense**

In each of the following sentences, circle the correct verb tense.

Example: For many years now, the laws of most states (allowed / have allowed) only doctors to write prescriptions for patients.

1. In the past few years, a number of states (began / have begun) to allow physician assistants and nurse practitioners to write prescriptions.

2. Before the changes in the laws, physician assistants and nurse practitioners (saw / have seen) patients with common illnesses.

3. However, if the patients (needed / have needed) a prescription, a doctor had to write it.

4. Many doctors (said / have said) that the changes are a good idea.

5. Physician assistants and nurse practitioners (spent / have spent) years in training by the time they get their licenses.

| had | + | Past participle | = | Past perfect tense |

Use *had* plus the past participle to make the **past perfect tense**. The past perfect tense is used for an action that began in the past and ended before some other past action.

had (helping verb)   Past participle

Past perfect tense   My car had stalled several times before I called the mechanic.

[This sentence says that both the *stalling* and *calling the mechanic* happened in the past but that the stalling happened before the calling.]

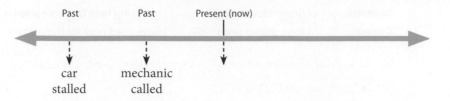

Past   Past   Present (now)

car   mechanic
stalled   called

🌐 **Language note:** The past perfect is used only to emphasize that one action happened before another. It should not be used for events that occurred at the same time as each other or for the main events in a story.

Incorrect   Yesterday, I had seen my teacher. She told me about the quiz next week.

Correct   Yesterday, I saw my teacher. She told me about the quiz next week.

Notice the way Pat Conroy uses the past perfect in his essay "Chili Cheese Dogs, My Father, and Me."

> On that occasion, when my family had finished the meal, my mother lit six candles on a cupcake she had made, and Stanny, Papa Jack, my mother, and my sister Carol sang "Happy Birthday" as I blushed with pleasure and surprise.

The main event in this story is the moment that the family sang to Conroy. Conroy uses past perfect only for the two actions that happened before the main event of the story: the ending of the meal and the baking of the cupcake.

PRACTICE 9   **Using the Past Perfect Tense**

In each of the following sentences, circle the correct verb tense.

Example: When musician Ray Charles was born in September 1930, the Great Depression already (caused / had caused) many Americans to lose hope.

🅔 Log in to **macmillanhighered .com/rrw** and look for Additional Grammar Exercises > Using the Past Perfect Tense

1. His family (was / had been) poor even before the Great Depression started.

2. Until he was four years old, Ray (enjoyed / had enjoyed) normal vision.

3. However, by the time he was seven, he (became / had become) totally blind.

4. When he (tripped / had tripped) over furniture and asked for his mother's help, often she just watched him and remained silent.

5. In this way, she (encouraged / had encouraged) him to learn how to help himself get back up.

Passive Voice and Past Participles

e Log in to **macmillanhighered .com/rrw** and look for LearningCurve > Active and Passive Voice

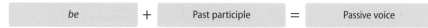

| be | + | Past participle | = | Passive voice |

A sentence that is written in the **passive voice** has a subject that does not perform an action. Instead, the subject is acted upon. To create the passive voice, combine a form of the verb *be* with a past participle.

Look at these passive sentences from Judith Ortiz Cofer's essay "Don't Misread My Signals."

e Log in to **macmillanhighered .com/rrw** and look for Additional Grammar Exercises >Identifying Active and Passive Voice

Passive voice	I was kept under tight surveillance by my parents, since my virtue and modesty were, by their cultural equation, the same as their honor. [In this sentence, the subject (I) is not doing the action. Instead, the subject is receiving the action of surveillance from the parents.]
Passive voice	As teenagers, my friends and I were lectured constantly on how to behave as proper senoritas. [The subject (my friends and I) is not giving the lecture; instead, the subject is receiving the lecture from someone else.]

| | Form of *be* (helping verb) | Past participle |

Passive The newspaper was thrown onto the porch.

[The subject (newspaper) did not throw itself onto the porch. Some unidentified person threw the newspaper.]

Writers use the passive voice when no one specific performed an action, when they do not know who performed the action, or when they want to emphasize the receiver of the action. In Cofer's example, the emphasis is on Cofer and her friends, who were receiving the surveillance and lectures of the adults in their community.

Writers generally do not use passive voice when they know who performed the action or when they want to emphasize the action itself. Instead, they use the active voice, which means the subject performs the action. Notice how Cofer uses the active voice in these sentences:

Active voice	<u>My parents</u> <u><u>designed</u></u> our life as a microcosm of their casas on the island.
	[Here, the subject (parents) performs the action of designing.]
Active voice	At school that day, <u>the teachers</u> <u><u>assailed</u></u> us for wearing "everything at once"—meaning too much jewelry and too many accessories.
	[Here, the subject (teachers) performs the action of assailing.]

Finding and fixing verb-tense errors:

Changing from passive to active voice

Find

1. **Underline** the subject, and **double-underline** the verb (in this case, a form of *be* with a past participle).

2. **Circle** any word or words that describe who or what performed the action in the sentence.

   The <u>game</u> <u><u>was turned</u></u> around by ⟨Jo Cortez's touchdown pass⟩.

Fix

3. Make the circled words the subject of the sentence, and delete the word *by*.

   Jo Cortez's touchdown pass
   The game was turned around. ~~by Jo Cortez's touchdown pass.~~
   ^   ^

4. Change the verb from a past-participle form, using the correct tense.

   Jo Cortez's touchdown pass
   The game ~~was~~ turned around. ~~by Jo Cortez's touchdown pass.~~
   ^   ^

5. Move the former subject so that it receives the action.

   Jo Cortez's touchdown pass turned the game
   ~~The game was turned~~ around. ~~by Jo Cortez's touchdown pass.~~
   ^   ^   ^

   Note: If you do not have specific information on who or what performed the action, you might use a general word like *someone* or *people*.

   Someone left flowers
   ~~Flowers were left~~ on my desk.
   ^

| PRACTICE 10 | **Changing the Passive Voice to the Active Voice** |

Rewrite the following sentences, changing them from the passive voice to the active voice.

The legislature cut funding

Example: **Funding** for animal shelters ~~was cut by the legislature.~~
          ^

1. Some shelters were going to be closed by the owners.

2. What would become of the animals was unknown.

3. A campaign was started by animal lovers.

4. Interviews were given by the owners and volunteers at shelters.

5. The animals were filmed by news teams.

Consistency of Verb Tense

Consistency of verb tense means that all actions in a sentence that happen (or happened) at the same time are in the same tense. If all the actions happen in the present or happen all the time, use the present tense for all verbs in the sentence. If all the actions happened in the past, use the past tense for all verbs.

e Log in to **macmillanhighered .com/rrw** and look for Additional Grammar Exercises > Correcting Problems with Consistency of Verb Tense

| | Past tense | Present tense |
| | \| | \| |

Inconsistent   The <u>movie</u> <u>started</u> just as <u>we</u> <u>take</u> our seats.

[The actions both happened at the same time, but *started* is in the past tense, and *take* is in the present tense.]

| | Past tense | Past tense |
| | \| | \| |

Consistent,   The <u>movie</u> <u>started</u> just as <u>we</u> <u>took</u> our seats.
past tense

[The actions *started* and *took* both happened in the past, and both are in the past tense.]

Use different tenses only when you are referring to different times.

My <u>daughter</u> <u>hated</u> math as a child, but now <u>she</u> <u>loves</u> it.

[The sentence uses two different tenses because the first verb (*hated*) refers to a past condition, whereas the second verb (*loves*) refers to a present one.]

> **PRACTICE 11**   **Using Consistent Verb Tense**

In each of the following sentences, double-underline the verbs, and correct any unnecessary shifts in verb tense. Write the correct form of the verb in the blank space provided.

Example: ___*have*___ **Although some people dream of having their picture taken by a famous photographer, not many had the chance.**

1. _____ Now, special stores in malls take magazine-quality photographs of anyone who wanted one.

2. _____ The founder of one business got the idea when she hear friends complaining about how bad they looked in family photographs.

3. _____ She decide to open a business to take studio-style photographs that did not cost a lot of money.

4. _____ Her first store included special lighting and offers different sets, such as colored backgrounds and outdoor scenes.

5. _____ Now, her stores even have makeup studios for people who wanted a special look for their pictures.

Edit for Verb Problems

Use the chart on page 430, "Finding and Fixing Verb-Tense Errors," to help you complete the practice exercises in this section and edit your own writing.

> **PRACTICE 12**   **Editing Verb Problems in a P/Q Assignment**

In the following paragraph, find and correct twelve problems with verb tense, verb form, and subject-verb agreement.

1 In her essay "Your Brain on Fiction," Annie Murphy Paul explains that brain scans can show "what happens in our heads when we read a detailed description, an evocative metaphor, or an emotional exchange between characters" (44). 2 I think I understand what she talking about, because this experience has happen to me. 3 When I had read *Harry Potter and the*

Chamber of Secrets, for example, I cried when Hermione was bully by Draco and the other Slytherin students. 4 Based on the research that Paul describes in her essay, my reaction makes sense. 5 My brain can't distinguished between "reading about an experience and encountering it in real life," as Paul explains (45). 6 When it come to my feelings, I will put myself in the place of the characters. 7 My negative reaction to the bully characters is so strong that it carry over into real life. 8 Just a few weeks ago, I meet a new coworker who just happened to look like the bully character, Draco, in the Harry Potter movies. 9 Even though I had never saw this man before, I had a strong negative reaction. 10 I felt defensive and angry before he even had spoke to me. 11 After we talking for a while, I realized this man is not a bully at all. 12 Reading Annie Paul's essay helped me understand why I feeled the way I did.

> **PRACTICE 13**   **Editing Jackie's Paragraph**
>
> Look back at Jackie's paragraph on page 409. You may have already underlined the verb errors; if not, do so now. Next, correct each error, using what you have learned in this chapter.

Chapter Review

1. Verb _____ indicates when the action in a sentence happens (past, present, or future).

2. What are the two present-tense endings for regular verbs?

   _____

3. How do regular verbs in the past tense end? _____

4. The past participle is used with a _____ verb.

5. Verbs that do not follow the regular pattern for verbs are called _____.

6. An action that started in the past but might continue into the present uses the _____.

7. An action that happened in the past before something else that happened in the past uses the _____.

Chapter Test

Circle the correct choice for each of the following items. For help, refer to the "Finding and Fixing Verb-Tense Errors" chart on page 430.

1. If an underlined portion of this sentence is incorrect, select the revision that fixes it. If the sentence is correct as written, choose d.

   It has <u>became</u> difficult to tell whether Trisha <u>is</u> tired of her work or
         A   B

   <u>tired</u> of her boss.
     C

   a. become   c. tiring

   b. be   d. No change is necessary.

2. Choose the item that has no errors.

   a. By the time we arrived, Michelle already gave her recital.

   b. By the time we arrived, Michelle had already given her recital.

   c. By the time we arrived, Michelle has already given her recital.

3. If an underlined portion of this sentence is incorrect, select the revision that fixes it. If the sentence is correct as written, choose d.

   I <u>likes</u> Manuel's new car, but I <u>wish</u> he wouldn't park it in my
         A   B

   space when he <u>comes</u> home from work.
                 C

   a. like   c. came

   b. wishing   d. No change is necessary.

4. Choose the item that has no errors.

   a. Patrick has such a bad memory that he has to write down everything he is supposed to do.

   b. Patrick had such a bad memory that he has to write down everything he is supposed to do.

   c. Patrick had such a bad memory that he having to write down everything he is supposed to do.

5. Choose the correct word(s) to fill in the blank.

   For many years, Steven _____ the manual typewriter his grandfather had given to him.

   a. keeped   b. kept   c. was keeping

6. Choose the item that has no errors.
   a. I have be cutting back on the amount of coffee I drink.
   b. I has been cutting back on the amount of coffee I drink.
   c. I have been cutting back on the amount of coffee I drink.

7. Choose the correct word(s) to fill in the blank.

   We had intended to visit Marina's parents while we _____ in town, but we did not have time.

   a. was   b. had were   c. were

8. Choose the correct word(s) to fill in the blank.

   Each family _____ a dish and brought it to our knitting club's annual dinner.

   a. prepares   b. prepared   c. have prepared

9. If an underlined portion of this sentence is incorrect, select the revision that fixes it. If the sentence is correct as written, choose d.

   The boy jumped out of the way just before the car is about to hit him.
   A, B, C

   a. jumping   c. hitted
   b. was   d. No change is necessary.

10. Choose the correct word to fill in the blank.

    Who has _____ the train to New York before?

    a. taken   b. take   c. taked

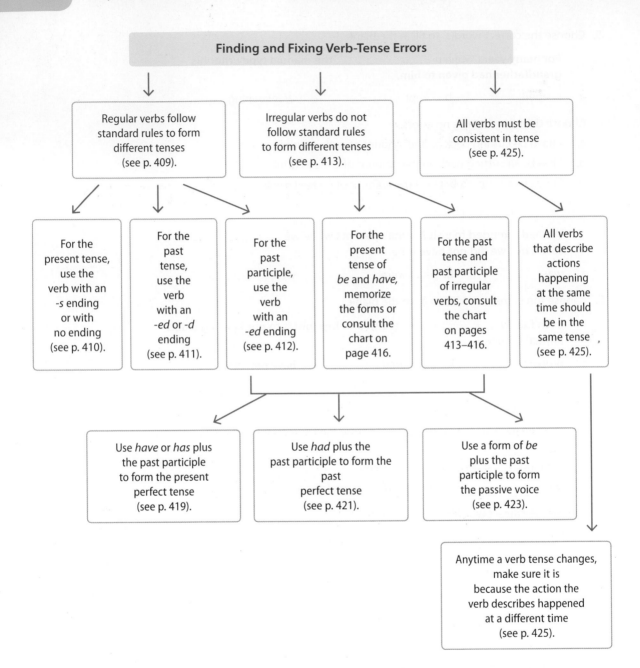

Finding and Fixing Verb-Tense Errors

Regular verbs follow standard rules to form different tenses (see p. 409).

Irregular verbs do not follow standard rules to form different tenses (see p. 413).

All verbs must be consistent in tense (see p. 425).

For the present tense, use the verb with an -s ending or with no ending (see p. 410).

For the past tense, use the verb with an -ed or -d ending (see p. 411).

For the past participle, use the verb with an -ed ending (see p. 412).

For the present tense of *be* and *have,* memorize the forms or consult the chart on page 416.

For the past tense and past participle of irregular verbs, consult the chart on pages 413–416.

All verbs that describe actions happening at the same time should be in the same tense (see p. 425).

Use *have* or *has* plus the past participle to form the present perfect tense (see p. 419).

Use *had* plus the past participle to form the past perfect tense (see p. 421).

Use a form of *be* plus the past participle to form the passive voice (see p. 423).

Anytime a verb tense changes, make sure it is because the action the verb describes happened at a different time (see p. 425).

Part 4
Other Grammar Concerns

20

Pronouns:
Using Substitutes for Nouns

Understand What Pronouns Are

A **pronoun** is used in place of a noun or another pronoun mentioned earlier. Pronouns enable you to avoid repeating those nouns or other pronouns.

> Sheryl got into ~~Sheryl's~~ *her* car.
> I like Mario. ~~Mario~~ *He*^ is a good dancer.

The noun or pronoun that a pronoun replaces is called the **antecedent**. In most cases, a pronoun refers to a specific antecedent nearby.

Antecedent

I picked up my new glasses. They are cool.

Pronoun replacing antecedent

Using Pronouns Correctly

Identify Pronouns

Before you practice finding and correcting common pronoun errors, it is helpful to practice identifying pronouns.

Log in to **macmillanhighered .com/rrw** and look for LearningCurve > Pronouns

Log in to **macmillanhighered .com/rrw** and look for Additional Grammar Exercises > Identifying Pronouns

Common Pronouns

Personal pronouns	Possessive pronouns	Indefinite pronouns	
I	my	all	much
me	mine	any	neither (of)
you	your/yours	anybody	nobody
she/he	her/hers/his	anyone	none (of)
her/him	her/hers/his	anything	no one
it	its	both	nothing
we	our/ours	each (of)	one (of)
us	our/ours	either (of)	some
they	their/theirs	everybody	somebody
them	their/theirs	everyone	someone
		everything	something
		few (of)	

Pronouns are also an important part of the reading process. If you do not match pronouns and their antecedents accurately, you may misunderstand what you are reading. Identifying pronouns and their antecedents can help you improve both your reading and your writing skills.

| PRACTICE 1 | **Identifying Pronouns**

In each of the following sentences, circle the pronoun, underline the noun it refers to, and draw an arrow from the pronoun to the noun.

Example: **People** can have a hard time seeing stars at night if they live in or near a big city.

1. As writers solve development problems, they often have to consider questions of *dimension* (Murray, 88).

2. Keep your Watcher in shape and he'll have less time to keep you from shaping (Godwin, 68).

3. Rather than fight these pervasive stereotypes, I try to replace them with a more interesting set of realities (Ortiz Cofer, 235).

4. In fact, this student had missed most of the class meetings, and I had already recommended that she withdraw from the course. (Foster Segal, 207)

5. Now a graduating senior, Trevino, 22, realizes she got bum advice. (Levine-Finley, 177)

6. For the last 20 years, state and federal governments have been creating criminal snitches and setting them loose in poor, high-crime communities. (Natapoff, 299)

7. If you're a man, at some point a woman will ask you how she looks. (Barry, 229)

8. The video watchers were later given a concentration test in which they were asked to identify the color in which words were displayed. (Parker-Pope, 173)

9. In fact, there are several reasons, including the fact that a round lid can't fall into the hole the way a square one can and the fact that it can be rolled. (Adams, 144)

10. My relatives licked their chopsticks and reached across the table, dipping them into the dozen or so plates of food. (Tan, 118)

Check for Pronoun Agreement

A pronoun must agree with (match) the noun or pronoun it refers to in number. It must be either singular (one) or plural (more than one).

If a pronoun is singular, it must also match the noun or pronoun it refers to in gender (*he, she,* or *it*).

Consistent   Magda sold *her* old television set.

[*Her* agrees with *Magda* because both are singular and feminine.]

Consistent   The Wilsons sold *their* old television set.

[*Their* agrees with *the Wilsons* because both are plural.]

Watch out for singular generic nouns. If a noun is singular, the pronoun that refers to it must be singular as well.

Inconsistent   Any student can tell you what *their* least favorite course is.

[*Student* is singular, but the pronoun *their* is plural.]

Consistent   Any student can tell you what *his* or *her* least favorite course is.

[*Student* is singular, and so are the pronouns *his* and *her*.]

To avoid using the awkward phrase *his or her*, make the subject plural when you can.

Consistent   Most students can tell you what *their* least favorite course is.

Two types of words often cause errors in pronoun agreement: indefinite pronouns and collective nouns.

INDEFINITE PRONOUNS

An **indefinite pronoun** does not refer to a specific person, place, or thing: It is general. Indefinite pronouns often take singular verbs. Whenever a pronoun refers to an indefinite pronoun, check for agreement.

Log in to **macmillanhighered.com/rrw** and look for Additional Grammar Exercises > Using Indefinite Pronouns

The monks got up at dawn. Everybody had ~~their~~ his chores for the day.

Indefinite Pronouns

Always singular			May be plural or singular
another	everyone	nothing	all
anybody/anyone	everything	one (of)	any
anything	much	somebody	none
each (of)	neither (of)	someone	some
either (of)	nobody	something	
everybody	no one		

Note: Many people object to the use of only the masculine pronoun *he* when referring to a singular indefinite pronoun, such as *everyone*. Although grammatically correct, using the masculine form alone to refer to an indefinite pronoun is considered sexist. Here are two ways to avoid this problem:

1. Use *his or her*.

   Someone posted *his or her* e-mail address to the Web site.

2. Change the sentence so that the pronoun refers to a plural noun or pronoun.

Some students posted *their* e-mail addresses to the Web site.

PRACTICE 2   **Using Indefinite Pronouns**

Circle the correct pronoun or group of words in parentheses.

1 Anyone who wants to start (their / his or her) own business had better be prepared to work hard. 2 One may find, for example, that (his or her / their) work is never done. 3 Something is always waiting, with (its / their) own peculiar demands. 4 Nothing gets done on (their / its) own. 5 Anybody who expects to have more freedom now that (he or she no longer works / they no longer work) for a boss may be disappointed. 6 After all, when you work as an employee for a company, someone above you makes decisions as (they see / he or she sees) fit. 7 When you are your own boss, no one else places (themselves / himself or herself) in the position of final responsibility.

8 Somebody starting a business may also be surprised by how much tax (they / he or she) must pay. 9 Each employee at a company pays only about half as much toward social security as what (they / he or she) would pay if self-employed. 10 Neither medical nor dental coverage can be obtained as inexpensively as (it / they) can when a person is an employee at a corporation.

COLLECTIVE NOUNS

A **collective noun** names a group that acts as a single unit.

e Log in to **macmillanhighered .com/rrw** and look for Additional Grammar Exercises > Using Collective Nouns and Pronouns

Common Collective Nouns

audience	company	group
class	crowd	jury
college	family	society
committee	government	team

Collective nouns are usually singular, so when you use a pronoun to refer to a collective noun, it is also usually singular.

The team had ~~their~~ *its* sixth consecutive win of the season.

If the people in a group are acting as individuals, however, the noun is plural and should be used with a plural pronoun.

The class brought *their* papers to read.

Finding and fixing pronoun problems:

Using collective nouns and pronouns

Find

The <u>committee</u> changed (its / their) meeting time.

1. **Underline** any collective nouns.

2. *Ask:* Is the collective noun singular (a group acting as a single unit) or plural (people in a group acting as individuals)? *Singular.*

Fix

The committee changed ((its) / their) meeting time.

3. **Choose** the pronoun that agrees with the subject.

PRACTICE 3   **Using Collective Nouns and Pronouns**

Fill in the correct pronoun (*it, its,* or *their*) in each of the following sentences.

Example: The Vidocq Society is known for _its_ unusual approach to investigating unsolved murders, or "cold cases."

1. The Philadelphia-based club got _its_ name from Eugène François Vidocq, a French detective who also worked on unsolved crimes.

2. A police department with a cold case may find that _its_ can benefit from the Vidocq Society's services.

3. During the society's monthly meetings, a team of crime investigators, psychologists, scientists, and others bring ___their___ varied skills to such cases.

4. When guests with knowledge about a case speak to the society, the audience gives ___its___ full attention to the information.

5. A group of police officers who worked a particular murder case might describe ___their___ original findings in detailed presentations.

Make Pronoun Reference Clear

In an **ambiguous pronoun reference**, the pronoun could refer to more than one noun.

Ambiguous   Enrico told Jim that *he* needed a better resume.

[Did Enrico tell Jim that Enrico himself needed a better resume? Or did Enrico tell Jim that Jim needed a better resume?]

Edited   Enrico advised Jim to revise his resume.

Ambiguous   I put the glass on the shelf, even though *it* was dirty.

[Was the glass dirty? Or was the shelf dirty?]

Edited   I put the dirty glass on the shelf.

In a **vague pronoun reference**, the pronoun does not refer clearly to any particular person, place, or thing. To correct a vague pronoun reference, use a more specific noun instead of the pronoun.

Vague   When Tom got to the clinic, *they* told him it was closed.

[Who told Tom the clinic was closed?]

Edited   When Tom got to the clinic, the nurse told him it was closed.

Vague   Before I finished printing my report, *it* ran out of paper.

[What ran out of paper?]

Edited   Before I finished printing my report, the printer ran out of paper.

Finding and fixing pronoun problems:

Avoiding ambiguous or vague pronoun references

Find

The <u>cashier</u> said that (they) were out of milk.

1. **Underline** the subject.

2. **Circle** the pronoun.

3. *Ask:* Who or what does the pronoun refer to? *No one. "They" does not refer to "cashier."*

Fix

The cashier said that ~~they were~~ out of milk.
the store was
^

4. **Correct** the pronoun reference by revising the sentence to make the pronoun more specific.

PRACTICE 4   **Avoiding Ambiguous or Vague Pronoun References**

Edit each sentence to eliminate ambiguous or vague pronoun references. Some sentences may be revised in more than one way.

Example: I am always looking for good advice on controlling my weight,
experts
but they have provided little help.
^

1. My doctor referred me to a physical therapist, and ~~she~~ said that I
   my doctor /
   needed to exercise more.

2. I joined a <u>workout</u> group and did exercises with the members, but ~~it~~ did
   workout
   not solve my problem.

3. I tried a lower-fat diet along with the exercising, but ~~it~~ did not really
   diet
   work either.

4. ~~They used to~~ say that eliminating carbohydrates is the easiest way to
   People
   lose weight.

5. Therefore, I started eating fats again and stopped consuming carbs,
   but ~~this~~ was not a permanent solution.
   eating fats
   these

In a **repetitious pronoun reference**, the pronoun repeats a reference to a noun rather than replacing the noun.

The nurse at the clinic ~~he~~ told Tom that it was closed.

The newspaper ~~it~~ says that the new diet therapy is promising.

Finding and fixing pronoun problems:

Avoiding repetitious pronoun references

Find

Television advertising ⌐it⌐ sometimes has a negative influence on young viewers.

1. **Underline** the subject, and **double-underline** the verb.

2. **Circle** any pronouns in the sentence.

3. *Ask:* What noun does the pronoun refer to? *Advertising.*

4. *Ask:* Do the noun and the pronoun that refers to it share the same verb? *Yes.* Does the pronoun just repeat the noun rather than replace it? *Yes.* If the answer to one or both questions is yes, the pronoun is repetitious.

Fix

Television advertising ~~it~~ sometimes has a negative influence on young viewers.

5. **Correct** the sentence by crossing out the repetitious pronoun.

PRACTICE 5   **Avoiding Repetitious Pronoun References**

Correct any repetitious pronoun references in the following sentences.

Example: Car commercials ~~they~~ want viewers to believe that buying a certain brand of car will bring happiness.

1. Young people ~~they~~ sometimes take advertisements too literally.

2. ~~In~~ a beer advertisement, ~~it~~ might suggest that drinking alcohol makes people more attractive and popular.

3. People who see or hear an advertisement ~~they~~ have to think about the message.

4. Parents should help ~~their~~ children understand why advertisements ~~they~~ do not show the real world.

5. A recent study, ~~it~~ said that parents can help kids overcome the influence of advertising.

Use the Right Type of Pronoun

Three important types of pronouns are subject pronouns, object pronouns, and possessive pronouns. Notice their uses in the following sentences:

Object pronoun Subject pronoun

The dog barked at *him,* and *he* laughed.

Possessive pronoun

As Josh walked out, *his* phone started ringing.

Pronoun Types

	Subject	Object	Possessive
First-person singular/plural	I/we	me/us	my, mine/ our, ours
Second-person singular/plural	you/you	you/you	your, yours/ your, yours
Third-person singular	he, she, it	him, her, it	his, her, hers, its
	who	whom	whose
Third-person plural	they	them	their, theirs
	who	whom	whose

Language note: Notice that pronouns have gender (*he/she, him/her, his/her/hers*). The pronoun must agree with the gender of the noun it refers to.

Incorrect	Carolyn went to see *his* boyfriend.
Correct	Carolyn went to see *her* boyfriend.

Also, notice that English has different forms for subject and object pronouns, as shown in the previous chart.

Read the following sentence, and replace the underlined nouns with pronouns. Notice that the pronouns are all different.

When Andreas made an A on <u>Andreas's</u> final exam, <u>Andreas</u> was proud of

himself, and the teacher congratulated <u>Andreas</u>.

SUBJECT PRONOUNS

Subject pronouns serve as the subject of a verb.

You live next door to a coffee shop.
I opened the door too quickly.

OBJECT PRONOUNS

Object pronouns either receive the action of a verb or are part of a prepositional phrase.

| Object of the verb | Jay gave *me* his watch. |
| Object of the preposition | Jay gave his watch to *me*. |

POSSESSIVE PRONOUNS

Possessive pronouns show ownership.

Dave is *my* uncle.

OTHER TYPES OF PRONOUNS

Intensive pronouns emphasize a noun or another pronoun. **Reflexive pronouns** are used when the performer of an action is also the receiver of the action. Both types of pronouns end in *-self* or *-selves*.

| Reflexive | He taught *himself* how to play the guitar. |
| Intensive | The club members *themselves* have offered to support the initiative. |

Relative pronouns refer to a noun already mentioned, and introduce a group of words that describe this noun (*who, whom, whose, which, that*).

Tomatoes, *which* are popular worldwide, were first grown in South America.

Interrogative pronouns are used to begin questions (*who, whom, whose, which, what*).

What did the senator say at the meeting?

Demonstrative pronouns specify which noun is being referred to (*this, these, that, those*).

Use *this* simple budgeting app, not *that* complicated one.

Reciprocal pronouns refer to individuals when the antecedent is plural (*each other, one another*).

My friend and I could not see *one another* in the crowd.

Three trouble spots make it difficult to know what type of pronoun to use: compound subjects and objects; comparisons; and sentences that need *who* or *whom*.

PRONOUNS USED WITH COMPOUND SUBJECTS AND OBJECTS

A **compound subject** has more than one subject joined by *and* or *or*. A **compound object** has more than one object joined by *and* or *or*.

Finding and fixing pronoun problems:

Using pronouns in compound constructions

Find

My friend and me talk at least once a week.

1. **Underline** the subject, **double-underline** the verb, and **circle** any object or objects.

2. *Ask:* Does the sentence have a compound subject or object? *Yes—"friend and me" is a compound subject.*

3. *Ask:* Do the nouns in the compound construction share a verb? *Yes—"talk."*

4. **Cross out** one of the subjects so that only the pronoun remains.

5. *Ask:* Does the sentence sound correct with just the pronoun as the subject? *No.*

Fix

My friend and ~~me~~ talk at least once a week.
   I

6. **Correct** the sentence by replacing the incorrect pronoun with the correct one.

Compound subject	Chandler and *I* worked on the project.

Compound object	My boss gave the assignment to Chandler and *me*.

To decide what type of pronoun to use in a compound construction, try leaving out the other part of the compound and the *and* or *or*. Then, say the sentence aloud to yourself.

e Log in to **macmillanhighered .com/rrw** and look for Additional Grammar Exercises > Using the Right Type of Pronoun with Compound Subjects and Objects

Compound subject

~~Joan and~~ (me / I) went to the movies last night.

[Think: *I* went to the movies last night.]

Compound object

The car was headed right for ~~Tom and~~ (she / her).

[Think: The car was headed right for *her*.]

If a pronoun is part of a compound object in a prepositional phrase, use an object pronoun.

Compound object

I will keep that information just between you and (I / me).

[*Between you and me* is a prepositional phrase, so an object pronoun, *me*, is required.]

PRACTICE 6   **Editing Pronouns in Compound Constructions**

Correct any pronoun errors in the following sentences. If a sentence is correct, write a "C" next to it.

Example: Marie Curie made several major contributions to science, but
                                she
                in 1898, ~~her~~ and her husband, Pierre Curie, announced their
                                ^
                greatest achievement: the discovery of radium.

1. Before this discovery, Marie and Pierre understood that certain sub-
                                                      they
   stances gave off rays of energy, but ~~them~~ and other scientists were just

   beginning to learn why and how.
                                                               them
2. Eventually, the Curies made a discovery that intrigued <u>they</u> and, soon

   afterward, hundreds of other researchers.

3. Two previously unknown elements, radium and polonium, were responsible for the extra radioactivity; fascinated by this finding, Marie began thinking about the consequences of the work that she and her husband had done.

4. As ~~them~~ *they* and other researchers were to discover, radium was especially valuable because it could be used in X-rays and for other medical purposes.

5. Marie was deeply moved when, in 1903, the scientific community honored ~~she~~ *her* and Pierre with the Nobel Prize in physics.

Log in to macmillanhighered .com/rrw and look for Additional Grammar Exercises > Using the Right Type of Pronoun in Comparisons

PRONOUNS USED IN COMPARISONS

Using the right type of pronoun in comparisons is particularly important because using the wrong type changes the meaning of the sentence. Editing comparisons can be tricky because they often imply (suggest the presence of) words that are not actually included in the sentence.

Bob trusts Donna more than *I*.

[This sentence means that Bob trusts Donna more than I trust her. The implied words are *trust her*.]

Bob trusts Donna more than *me*.

[This sentence means that Bob trusts Donna more than he trusts me. The implied words are *he trusts*.]

Finding and fixing pronoun problems:

Using pronouns in comparisons

Find

The other band attracts a bigger audience (than) us on Friday nights.

1. **Circle** the word that indicates a comparison.

2. *Ask:* What word or words that would come after the comparison word are implied but missing from the sentence? "Do."

3. *Ask:* If you add the missing word or words, does the pronoun make sense? No.

Fix

                                                              we (do)
The other band attracts a bigger audience than ~~us~~ on Friday nights.
                                                               ^

4. **Correct** the sentence by replacing the incorrect pronoun with the correct one.

To decide whether to use a subject pronoun or an object pronoun in a comparison, try adding the implied words and saying the sentence aloud.

The registrar is much more efficient than (us / we).

[Think: The registrar is much more efficient than *we are*.]

Susan rides her bicycle more than (he / him).

[Think: Susan rides her bicycle more than *he does*.]

> **PRACTICE 7**   **Editing Pronouns in Comparisons**
>
> Correct any pronoun errors in the following sentences. If a sentence is correct, write a "C" next to it.
>
> Example: **The camping trip we planned did not seem dangerous to Hannah, so she was not as nervous about it as me.**
>
> 1. In addition, I was nowhere near as well equipped for camping as her.
>
> 2. In the store, Hannah rather than me did all the talking.
>
> 3. At the campground, I could see that some of the other camping groups were not as prepared as we.
>
> 4. The park ranger chatted with the other campers more than we.
>
> 5. He seemed to believe that we were more experienced than them.

CHOOSING BETWEEN *WHO* AND *WHOM*

Who is always a subject; *whom* is always an object. If a pronoun performs an action, use the subject form *who*. If a pronoun does not perform an action, use the object form *whom*.

> **who = subject**   I would like to know *who* delivered this package.
>
> **whom = object**   He told me to *whom* I should report.

In sentences other than questions, when the pronoun (*who* or *whom*) is followed by a verb, use *who*. When the pronoun (*who* or *whom*) is followed by a noun or pronoun, use *whom*.

The pianist (who / whom) played was excellent.

[The pronoun is followed by the verb *played*. Use *who*.]

e Log in to **macmillanhighered .com/rrw** and look for Additional Grammar Exercises > Choosing Between Who and Whom

The pianist (who / whom) I saw was excellent.

[The pronoun is followed by another pronoun: *I*. Use *whom*.]

PRACTICE 8   Choosing between *Who* and *Whom*

In each sentence, circle the correct word: *who* or *whom*.

Example: Police officers (who / whom) want to solve a crime—or prevent one—are now relying more than ever on technology.

1. Face-recognition software is supposed to identify possible criminals (who / whom) cameras have photographed in public places.

2. Use of such software, which compares security-camera images with photos from a criminal database, can help law enforcement officials determine (who / whom) they want to question about a crime.

3. Police will try to detain any person (who / whom) is identified by the software as a criminal.

4. Police know that the software will single out some innocent people (who / whom) resemble criminals.

5. However, police and nervous Americans are hopeful that this method can help identify terrorists (who / whom) appear in airports or other locations.

Make Pronouns Consistent in Person

e Log in to **macmillanhighered .com/rrw** and look for Additional Grammar Exercises > Making Pronouns Consistent in Person

Person is the point of view a writer uses—the perspective from which he or she writes. Pronouns may be in first person (*I* or *we*), second person (*you*), or third person (*he, she,* or *it*). (See the chart on p. 442.)

Inconsistent	As soon as *a shopper* walks into the store, *you* can tell it is a weird place.

[The sentence starts with the third person (*a shopper*) but shifts to the second person (*you*).]

Consistent, singular	As soon as a *shopper* walks into the store, *he* or *she* can tell it is a weird place.
Consistent, plural	As soon as *shoppers* walk into the store, *they* can tell it is a weird place.

Finding and fixing pronoun problems:

Making pronouns consistent in person

Find

I had the correct answer, but to win the tickets (you) had to be the ninth caller.

1. **Underline** all the subject nouns and pronouns in the sentence.
2. **Circle** any pronouns that refer to another subject noun or pronoun in the sentence.
3. *Ask:* Is the subject noun or pronoun that the circled pronoun refers to in the first (*I* or *we*), second (*you*), or third person (*he, she,* or *it*)? *First person.*
4. *Ask:* What person is the circled pronoun in? *Second.*

Fix

I had the correct answer, but to win the tickets you had to be the ninth caller.

5. **Correct** the sentence by changing the pronoun to be consistent with the noun or pronoun it refers to.

PRACTICE 9   Making Pronouns Consistent in Person

In the following sentences, correct the shifts in person. There may be more than one way to correct some sentences.

Example: **Many college students have access to a writing center**
                    they
                where ~~you~~ can get tutoring.

1. A writing tutor must know ~~your~~ way around college writing

   assignments.

2. I have gone to the writing center at my school because sometimes ~~you~~

   need a second pair of eyes to look over a paper.

3. Students signing up for tutoring at the writing center may not be in

   ~~your~~ first semester of college.

4. Even a graduate student may need help with ~~your~~ writing at times.

5. The writing-center tutor is careful not to correct ~~their~~ students' papers.

Edit for Pronoun Problems

Use the chart on page 454, "Finding and Fixing Pronoun Problems," to help you complete the practice exercise in this section and edit your own writing.

PRACTICE 10 **Editing Paragraphs for Pronoun Problems**

Find and correct seven errors in pronoun use in the following paragraphs.

1 Ask anyone who has moved to a city, and they will tell you: At first, life can feel pretty lonely. 2 Fortunately, it is possible to make friends just about anywhere. 3 One good strategy is to get involved in a group that interests you, such as a sports team or arts club. 4 In many cases, a local baseball team or theater group will open their arms to new talent. 5 Joining in on practices, games, or performances is a great way to build friendships with others whom have interests like yours. 6 Also, most community organizations are always in need of volunteers. 7 It is a great way to form new friendships while doing something positive for society.

8 Getting a pet or gardening, it is another great way to meet new people. 9 In many cities, you can walk down the street for a long time and never be greeted by another person. 10 If you are walking a dog, though, it is likely that others will say hello. 11 Some may even stop to talk with you and pet your dog. 12 Also, gardeners tend to draw other gardeners. 13 If you are planting flowers and other flower growers stop by to chat, them and you will have plenty to talk about.

14 To sum up, newcomers to any city do not have to spend all their nights alone in front of the TV. 15 You have plenty of opportunities to get out and feel more connected.

Chapter Review

1. Pronouns replace _____ or other _____ in a sentence.

2. A pronoun must agree with (match) the noun or pronoun it replaces in

   _____ and _____ .

3. In an _____ pronoun reference, the pronoun could refer to more than

   one noun.

4. Subject pronouns serve as the subject of a verb. Write a sentence using a sub-

   ject pronoun. _____

   _____

5. What are two other types of pronouns? _____

   _____

6. What are three trouble spots in pronoun use?

   _____

   _____

   _____

Chapter Test

Circle the correct choice for each of the following items. For help, refer to the "Finding and Fixing Pronoun Problems" chart on page 454.

1. Choose the item that has no errors.

   a.   When he skis, Jim never falls down as much as me.

   b.   When he skis, Jim never falls down as much as I.

   c.   When he skis, Jim never falls down as much as mine.

2. Choose the correct word(s) to fill in the blank.

   Everyone hopes that the jury will deliver _____ verdict by the end of this week.

   a.   his or her   b.   their   c.   its

3. If an underlined portion of this sentence is incorrect, select the revision that fixes it. If the sentence is correct as written, choose d.

> **She is the one who Jake always calls whenever he wants a favor.**
>   A   B   C

   a. Her   c. him
   b. whom   d. No change is necessary

4. If an underlined portion of this sentence is incorrect, select the revision that fixes it. If the sentence is correct as written, choose d.

> **Somebody has left their camera here, and we do not know to whom**
>   A   B   C
> **it belongs.**

   a. his or her   c. who
   b. us   d. No change is necessary

5. Choose the item that has no errors.
   a. Becky told Lydia that she needed to help clean up after the party.
   b. Becky told Lydia to help clean up after the party.
   c. Becky told Lydia that she needed to help clean up after it.

6. Choose the item that has no errors.
   a. When I applied for the tour operator job, I was told that you needed a special certificate.
   b. When I applied for the tour operator job, you were told that you needed a special certificate.
   c. When I applied for the tour operator job, I was told that I needed a special certificate.

7. Choose the correct word(s) to fill in the blank.

> **Nicole's _____ must be lonely because he barks all the time.**

   a. dog he   b. dog him   c. dog

8. Choose the correct words to fill in the blank.

> **The other players in my soccer club like me because _____ agree on the importance of teamwork.**

   a. they and I   b. them and me   c. them and I

9. If an underlined portion of this sentence is incorrect, select the revision that
    fixes it. If the sentence is correct as written, choose d.

    > I think that <u>my next-door</u> neighbor has mice in <u>him house</u> because
    >   A   B
    >
    > he keeps asking me to <u>lend him</u> my cat.
    >   C

    a. me next-door   c. lend he

    b. his house   d. No change is necessary.

10. Choose the item that has no errors.

    a. Any lifeguard can tell you about a scary experience they have had on the
        job.

    b. Any lifeguard can tell you about a scary experience her have had on the job.

    c. Most lifeguards can tell you about a scary experience they have had on the
        job.

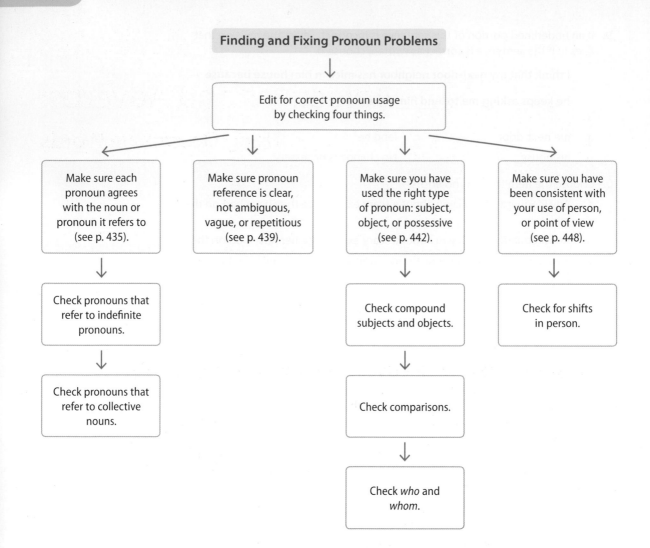

Finding and Fixing Pronoun Problems

Edit for correct pronoun usage by checking four things.

Make sure each pronoun agrees with the noun or pronoun it refers to (see p. 435).

Make sure pronoun reference is clear, not ambiguous, vague, or repetitious (see p. 439).

Make sure you have used the right type of pronoun: subject, object, or possessive (see p. 442).

Make sure you have been consistent with your use of person, or point of view (see p. 448).

Check pronouns that refer to indefinite pronouns.

Check pronouns that refer to collective nouns.

Check compound subjects and objects.

Check comparisons.

Check *who* and *whom*.

Check for shifts in person.

21

Adjectives and Adverbs:

Using Descriptive Words

Understand What Adjectives and Adverbs Are

Adjectives describe or modify nouns (words that name people, places, things, or ideas) and pronouns (words that replace nouns). They add information about *what kind, which one,* or *how many.*

Consider the following sentences from Amy Tan's narrative "Fish Cheeks." In each sentence, the adjectives are in italics, and the nouns which these adjectives describe are underlined.

> The kitchen was littered with *appalling* <u>mounds</u> of *raw* <u>food</u>: A *slimy* <u>rock cod</u> with *bulging* <u>eyes</u> that pleaded not to be thrown into a pan of *hot* <u>oil</u>. Tofu, which looked like *stacked* <u>wedges</u> of *rubbery white* <u>sponges</u>. A bowl soaking *dried* <u>fungus</u> back to life.

> **Language note:** In English, adjectives do not indicate whether the words they describe are singular or plural.

> **Incorrect**   The three babies are *adorables*.
>
> [The adjective *adorables* should not end in -s.]
>
> **Correct**   The three babies are *adorable*.

Adverbs describe or modify verbs (words that tell what happens in a sentence), adjectives, or other adverbs. They add information about *how, how much, when, where, why,* or *to what extent.*

Log in to **macmillanhighered .com/rrw** and look for LearningCurve > Adjectives and Adverbs; Additional Grammar Exercises > Choosing Between Adjectives and Adverbs

Look at the following sentences from Stephanie Ericsson's "The Ways We Lie." The adverbs are underlined.

I discovered that telling the truth all the time is <u>nearly</u> impossible.

As I said <u>earlier</u>, it's not easy to <u>entirely</u> eliminate lies from our lives.

The new diocese was aware of Father Porter's obsession with children, but they needed priests and <u>recklessly</u> believed treatment had cured him.

Adjectives usually come before the words they modify; adverbs come before or after. You can use more than one adjective or adverb to modify a word.

> **Language note:** The *-ed* and *-ing* forms of verbs (known as participles) can be used as adjectives. Common examples include *bored/boring*, *interested/interesting*, and *excited/exciting*. Sometimes, these forms are confused for each other. Usually, the *-ed* form describes a person's reaction, while the *-ing* form describes the thing that causes the reaction.

Incorrect	Some students are boring in their grammar classes.
Correct	Some students are bored in their grammar classes.
Correct	Grammar classes can be very boring for students.
	Some students find their grammar classes boring.

Using Adjectives and Adverbs Correctly

Choosing between Adjectives and Adverbs

Many adverbs are formed by adding *-ly* to the end of an adjective.

Adjective	**Adverb**
She received a *quick* answer.	Her sister answered *quickly*.
Our *new* neighbors just got married.	The couple is *newly* married.
That is an *honest* answer.	Please answer *honestly*.

To decide whether to use an adjective or an adverb, find the word being described. If that word is a noun or pronoun, use an adjective. If it is a verb, an adjective, or another adverb, use an adverb.

> **PRACTICE 1**   **Choosing between Adjectives and Adverbs**

In each sentence, underline the word that is being described or modified. Then, circle the correct word in parentheses.

Example: People are (common /(commonly)) <u>aware</u> that smoking causes health risks.

1. Many smokers are (stubborn / stubbornly) about refusing to quit.

2. Others who are thinking about quitting may decide (sudden / suddenly) that the damage from smoking has already been done.

3. In such cases, the (typical / typically) smoker sees no reason to stop.

4. The news about secondhand smoke may have made some smokers stop (quick / quickly) to save the health of their families.

5. Research now shows that pet lovers who smoke can have a (terrible / terribly) effect on their cats.

Using Adjectives and Adverbs in Comparisons

To compare two people, places, or things, use the **comparative** form of adjectives or adverbs. Comparisons often use the word *than*.

> Carol ran *faster* than I did.
> Johan is *more intelligent* than his sister.

To compare three or more people, places, or things, use the **superlative** form of adjectives or adverbs.

> Carol ran the *fastest* of all the women runners.
> Johan is the *most intelligent* of the five children.

If an adjective or adverb is short (one syllable), add the endings *-er* to form the comparative and *-est* to form the superlative. Also use this pattern for adjectives that end in *-y* (but change the *-y* to *-i* before adding *-er* or *-est*).

For all other adjectives and adverbs, add the word *more* to make the comparative and the word *most* to make the superlative.

e Log in to
macmillanhighered
.com/rrw and look for
Additional Grammar
Exercises > Using
Comparatives and
Superlatives

Forming Comparatives and Superlatives

Adjective or adverb	Comparative	Superlative
Adjectives and adverbs of one syllable		
tall	taller	tallest
fast	faster	fastest
Adjectives ending in -y		
happy	happier	happiest
silly	sillier	silliest
Other adjectives and adverbs		
graceful	more graceful	most graceful
gracefully	more gracefully	most gracefully
intelligent	more intelligent	most intelligent
intelligently	more intelligently	most intelligently

Use either an ending (*-er* or *-est*) or an extra word (*more* or *most*) to form a comparative or superlative—not both at once.

David Ortiz is the ~~most~~ greatest designated hitter in the team's history.

PRACTICE 2   **Using Adjectives and Adverbs in Comparisons**

In the space provided in each sentence, write the correct form of the adjective or adverb in parentheses. You may need to add *more* or *most* to some adjectives and adverbs.

Example: It was one of the ___scariest___ (scary) experiences of my life.

1. I was driving along Route 17 and was _____ (relaxed) than I

   ought to have been.

2. Knowing it was a busy highway, I was _____ (careful) than

   usual to make sure my cell phone was ready in case of an accident.

3. I had run the cord for the phone's earbud over my armrest, where it would be in the _____ (easy) place to reach if the phone rang.

4. I was in the _____ (heavy) traffic of my drive when the cell phone rang.

5. I saw that the earbud was _____ (hard) to reach than before because the cord had fallen between the front seats of the car.

Using Good, Well, Bad, and Badly

Four common adjectives and adverbs have irregular forms: *good, well, bad,* and *badly.*

e Log in to **macmillanhighered .com/rrw** and look for Additional Grammar Exercises > Using Good, Well, and Badly; Using Comparative and Superlative Forms of Good and Bad

Forming Irregular Comparatives and Superlatives

	Comparative	Superlative
Adjective		
good	better	best
bad	worse	worst
Adverb		
well	better	best
badly	worse	worst

People often get confused about whether to use *good* or *well*. *Good* is an adjective, so use it to describe a noun or pronoun. *Well* is an adverb, so use it to describe a verb or an adjective.

Adjective   She has a *good* job.

Adverb   He works *well* with his colleagues.

Well can also be an adjective to describe someone's health: I am not *well* today.

> **PRACTICE 3**   Using *Good* and *Well*

Complete each sentence by circling the correct word in parentheses. Underline the word that *good* or *well* modifies.

Example: A (good)/ well) <u>pediatrician</u> spends as much time talking with parents as he or she does examining patients.

1. The ability to communicate (good / well) is something that many parents look for in a pediatrician.

2. With a firstborn child, parents see a doctor's visit as a (good / well) chance to ask questions.

3. Parents can become worried when their infant does not feel (good / well) because the child cannot say what the problem is.

4. Doctors today have (good / well) diagnostic tools, however.

5. An otoscope helps a doctor see (good / well) when he or she looks into a patient's ear.

> **PRACTICE 4**   Using Comparative and Superlative Forms of *Good* and *Bad*

Complete each sentence by circling the correct comparative or superlative form of *good* or *bad* in parentheses.

Example: One of the (worse /(worst) outcomes of heavy drinking is severe impairment of mental and physical functioning.

1. Research has shown that if a man and a woman drink the same amount of alcohol, the woman may experience (worse / worst) effects.

2. The (better / best) explanation for this difference concerns the physical differences between women and men.

3. Men are (better / best) at processing alcohol because they have a higher proportion of water in their bodies than women do, and this higher water content helps lower the concentration of alcohol in men's blood.

4. Also, because of additional physical differences between women and men, the same amount of alcohol may have a (worse / worst) effect on women's livers.

5. The (worse / worst) effect of heavy drinking on the liver is cirrhosis, in which normal liver cells are replaced with scar tissue.

Edit for Adjective and Adverb Problems

Use the chart on page 464, "Editing for Correct Usage of Adjectives and Adverbs," to help you complete the practice exercise in this section and edit your own writing.

> **PRACTICE 5**   **Editing Paragraphs for Correct Adjectives and Adverbs**
>
> Find and correct seven adjective and adverb errors in the following paragraphs.

1 Every day, many people log on to play one of the popularest computer games of all time, *World of Warcraft*. 2 This multiplayer game was first introduced by Blizzard Entertainment in 1994 and has grown quick ever since. 3 More than 11 million players participate in the game every month, according to the recentest figures.

4 Computer game experts call *World of Warcraft* a "massively multiplayer online role-playing game," or MMORPG for short. 5 Players of this game select a realm in which to play. 6 They choose from among four differently realms. 7 Each realm has its own set of rules and even its own language. 8 Players also choose if they want to be members of the Alliance or the Horde, which are groups that oppose each other. 9 Each side tends to think that it is gooder than the other one.

10 In *World of Warcraft*, questing is one of the funnest activities. 11 Questing players undertake special missions or tasks to earn experience and gold. 12 The goal is to trade these earnings for better skills and

equipment. 13 Players must proceed careful to stay in the game and increase their overall power and abilities.

Chapter Review

1. Adjectives modify _____ and _____ .

2. Adverbs modify _____ , _____ , or _____ .

3. Many adverbs are formed by adding an _____ ending to an adjective.

4. The comparative form of an adjective or adverb is used to compare how many people, places, things, or ideas? _____

5. The superlative form of an adjective or adverb is used to compare how many people, places, things, or ideas? _____

6. What four words have irregular comparative and superlative forms?

_____

Chapter Test

Circle the correct choice for each of the following items. For help, refer to the "Editing for Correct Usage of Adjectives and Adverbs" chart on page 464.

1. Choose the correct word to fill in the blank.

    We performed _____ in the debate, so we will have to be better prepared next time.

    a.   bad   b.   worse   c.   badly

2. If an underlined portion of this sentence is incorrect, select the revision that fixes it. If the sentence is correct as written, choose d.

    After the beautiful wedding, the groom danced happy down the
    <u>A</u>   <u>B</u>
    church's stone steps.
    <u>C</u>

    a.   beautifully   c.   stonily

    b.   happily   d.   No change is necessary.

3. Choose the item that has no errors.

    a.   Sarah's foot is healing well, and she is making a good recovery.

    b.   Sarah's foot is healing good, and she is making a good recovery.

    c.   Sarah's foot is healing good, and she is making a well recovery.

4. Choose the correct word(s) to fill in the blank.

    With Kenneth's wild imagination, he is a _____ choice than Conor for writing the play's script.

    a.   gooder   b.   better   c.   more good

5. If an underlined portion of this sentence is incorrect, select the revision that fixes it. If the sentence is correct as written, choose d.

    When asked about the <u>thoughtfulest</u> person I know, I immediately
                               A

    gave the name of my <u>best</u> friend, who is <u>kind</u> to everyone.
                        B   *C*

    a.   most thoughtful   c.   kindest

    b.   bestest   d.   No change is necessary.

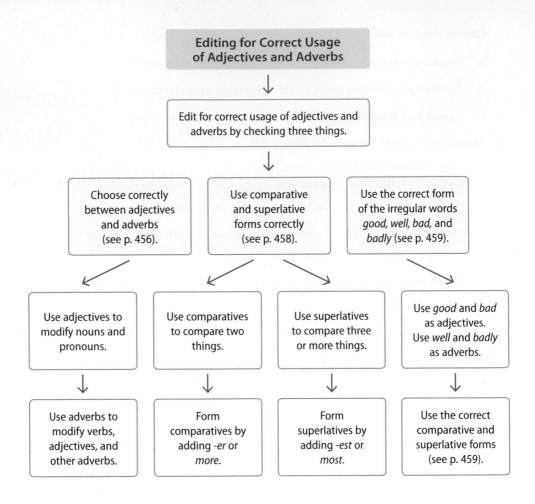

Editing for Correct Usage of Adjectives and Adverbs

↓

Edit for correct usage of adjectives and adverbs by checking three things.

↓

Choose correctly between adjectives and adverbs (see p. 456).

Use comparative and superlative forms correctly (see p. 458).

Use the correct form of the irregular words *good, well, bad,* and *badly* (see p. 459).

Use adjectives to modify nouns and pronouns.

Use comparatives to compare two things.

Use superlatives to compare three or more things.

Use *good* and *bad* as adjectives. Use *well* and *badly* as adverbs.

↓ ↓ ↓ ↓

Use adverbs to modify verbs, adjectives, and other adverbs.

Form comparatives by adding *-er* or *more.*

Form superlatives by adding *-est* or *most.*

Use the correct comparative and superlative forms (see p. 459).

22

Misplaced and Dangling Modifiers:
Avoiding Confusing Descriptions

Understand What Misplaced Modifiers Are

A **modifier** is a word or word group that describes another word or word group in a sentence. Experienced writers choose and place modifiers in a sentence carefully so that readers will understand what they are reading. Look at the following short paragraph from Donald Murray's essay "The Maker's Eye." The modifiers are marked with brackets.

> [The first] thing [writers look for in their drafts] is information. They know that [a good] piece [of writing] is built from [specific, accurate, and interesting] information. The writer must have an abundance [of information] [from which] to construct [a readable] piece [of writing].

A modifier should be near the word or words that it modifies; otherwise, the sentence can be confusing or, in some cases, unintentionally funny. A **misplaced modifier** describes the wrong word or words because it is in the wrong place in a sentence.

To correct a misplaced modifier, place the modifier as close as possible to the word or words it modifies, often directly before it.

Wearing my bathrobe,
I went outside to chat with the neighbor. ~~wearing my bathrobe.~~
 ^

e Log in to **macmillanhighered .com/rrw** and look for Additional Grammar Exercises > Correcting Misplaced Modifiers

Four constructions often lead to misplaced modifiers.

1. **Modifiers such as *only, almost, hardly, nearly,* and *just.*** These words need to be immediately before — not just close to — the words or phrases they modify.

   I ~~only~~ found two old photos in the drawer.
   only

   [The intended meaning is that just two photos were in the drawer.]

   Joanne ~~almost~~ ate the whole cake.
   almost

   [Joanne actually ate; she did not "almost" eat.]

   Thomas ~~nearly~~ spent two hours waiting for the bus.
   nearly

   [Thomas spent close to two hours waiting; he did not "nearly" spend them.]

2. **Modifiers that are prepositional phrases.**

   The cashier found money on the floor. ~~from the cash register.~~
   from the cash register

   Jen served punch to the seniors. ~~in plastic cups.~~
   in plastic cups

3. **Modifiers that start with *-ing* verbs.**

   Darlene started the car. ~~using jumper cables.~~
   Using jumper cables,

   [The car was not using jumper cables; Darlene was.]

   Javier climbed the mountain. ~~wearing flip-flops.~~
   Wearing flip-flops,

   [The mountain was not wearing flip-flops; Javier was.]

4. **Modifier clauses that start with *who, whose, that,* or *which.***

   Joel found the computer virus attached to an e-mail message. ~~that was infecting my hard drive.~~
   that was infecting my hard drive

   [The e-mail did not infect the hard drive; the virus did.]

   The baby on the bus ~~who was crying~~ had curly hair.
   who was crying

   [The bus was not crying; the baby was.]

Correcting Misplaced Modifiers

> **PRACTICE 1**   **Correcting Misplaced Modifiers**
>
> Find and correct misplaced modifiers in the following sentences.
>
> Example: **I write things in my blog that I used to** ~~**only**~~ *only* **tell my best friends.**

1. I used to write about all kinds of personal things and private observations in a diary.

2. Now, I nearly write the same things in my blog.

3. Any story might show up in my blog that is entertaining.

4. The video I was making was definitely something I wanted to write about in my blog of my cousin Tim's birthday.

5. I had invited to the birthday party my loudest, wildest friends wanting the video to be funny.

Understand What Dangling Modifiers Are

A **dangling modifier** "dangles" because the word or word group it modifies is not in the sentence. Dangling modifiers usually appear at the beginning of a sentence and seem to modify the noun or pronoun that immediately follows them, but they are really modifying another word or group of words.

> **Dangling**   *Rushing to class,* the books fell out of my bag.
>
> [The books were not rushing to class.]
>
> **Clear**   *Rushing to class,* I dropped my books.

There are two basic ways to correct dangling modifiers. Use the one that makes more sense. One way is to add the word being modified immediately after the opening modifier so that the connection between the two is clear.

Trying to eat a hot dog, *I* ~~my bike~~ swerved *on my bike*.

Another way is to add the word being modified in the opening modifier itself.

While I was trying
~~Trying~~ to eat a hot dog, my bike swerved.

ⓔ Log in to **macmillanhighered .com/rrw** and look for Additional Grammar Exercises > Correcting Dangling Modifiers

Correcting Dangling Modifiers

PRACTICE 2 Correcting Dangling Modifiers

Find and correct any dangling modifiers in the following sentences. If a sentence is correct, write a "C" next to it. It may be necessary to add new words or ideas to some sentences.

Because I had invited
Example: ~~Inviting~~ my whole family to dinner, the kitchen was filled with
     ^
all kinds of food.

1. Preparing a big family dinner, the oven suddenly stopped working.

2. In a panic, we searched for Carmen, who can solve any problem.

3. Trying to help, the kitchen was crowded.

4. Looking into the oven, the turkey was not done.

5. Discouraged, the dinner was about to be canceled.

Edit for Misplaced and Dangling Modifiers

Use the chart on page 472, "Editing for Misplaced and Dangling Modifiers," to help you complete the practice exercise in this section and edit your own writing.

PRACTICE 3 Editing Paragraphs for Misplaced and Dangling Modifiers

Find and correct any misplaced or dangling modifiers in the following paragraphs.

1 Carrying overfilled backpacks is a common habit, but not necessarily a good one. 2 Bulging with books, water bottles, and sports equipment and weighing an average of 14 to 18 pounds, students' backs can gradually become damaged. 3 Because they have to plan ahead for the whole day and often need books, extra clothes, and on-the-go meals, backpacks get heavier and heavier. 4 An increasing number of doctors, primarily physical therapists, are seeing young people with chronic back problems.

5 Researchers have recently invented a new type of backpack from the University of Pennsylvania and the Marine Biological Laboratory.

6 Designed with springs, the backpack moves up and down as a person walks. 7 This new backpack creates energy, which is then collected and transferred to an electrical generator. 8 Experiencing relief from the wear and tear on muscles, the springs make the pack more comfortable.

9 What is the purpose of the electricity generated by these new backpacks? 10 Needing electricity for their night-vision goggles, the backpacks could solve a problem for soldiers. 11 Soldiers could benefit from such an efficient energy source to power their global positioning systems and other electronic gear. 12 Instead of being battery operated, the soldiers could use the special backpacks and would not have to carry additional batteries. 13 For the average student, these backpacks might one day provide convenient energy for video games, television, and music players, all at the same time. 14 Designed with this technology, kids would just have to look both ways before crossing the street.

Chapter Review

1. _____ are words or word groups that describe other words in a sentence.

2. A _____ describes the incorrect word or word group because it is in the wrong place in a sentence.

3. When an opening modifier does not modify any word in the sentence, it is a _____.

4. Which four constructions often lead to misplaced modifiers?

_____

_____

_____

_____

Chapter Test

Circle the correct choice for each of the following items. For help, refer to the "Editing for Misplaced and Dangling Modifiers" chart on page 472.

1. If an underlined portion of this sentence is incorrect, select the revision that fixes it. If the sentence is correct as written, choose d.

   Annoyed by the flashing cameras, the limousine drove the celebrity
       A   B
   away from the crowd in front of the restaurant.
                                         C

   a. Annoying

   b. the celebrity got into the limousine, which drove

   c. the restaurant in front of

   d. No change is necessary.

2. Choose the item that has no errors.

   a. The thief found the code in the bank clerk's desk for the alarm system.

   b. The thief found the code for the alarm system in the bank clerk's desk.

   c. For the alarm system, the thief found the code in the bank clerk's desk.

3. If an underlined portion of this sentence is incorrect, select the revision that fixes it. If the sentence is correct as written, choose d.

   Talking on his cell phone, his shopping cart rolled over my foot.
       A   B   C

   a. Talking and concentrating too much

   b. his cell phones

   c. he rolled his shopping cart

   d. No change is necessary.

4. If an underlined portion of this sentence is incorrect, select the revision that
   fixes it. If the sentence is correct as written, choose d.

   I <u>only bought</u> two <u>tickets to the game</u>, so one <u>of the three of us</u>
        A   B   C

   cannot go.

   a. bought only

   b. to go to the game

   c. of the us three of

   d. No change is necessary.

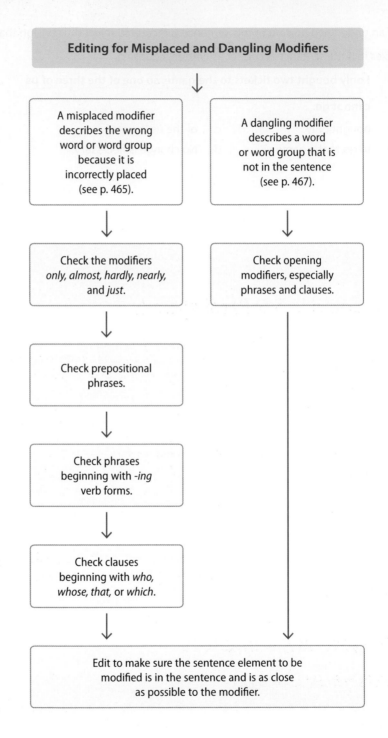

Editing for Misplaced and Dangling Modifiers

A misplaced modifier describes the wrong word or word group because it is incorrectly placed (see p. 465).

A dangling modifier describes a word or word group that is not in the sentence (see p. 467).

Check the modifiers *only, almost, hardly, nearly,* and *just.*

Check opening modifiers, especially phrases and clauses.

Check prepositional phrases.

Check phrases beginning with *-ing* verb forms.

Check clauses beginning with *who, whose, that,* or *which.*

Edit to make sure the sentence element to be modified is in the sentence and is as close as possible to the modifier.

23

Parallelism:
Balancing Ideas

Understand What Parallelism Is

Log in to **macmillanhighered .com/rrw** and look for LearningCurve > Parallelism

Parallelism in writing means that similar parts in a sentence have the same structure: the parts are balanced. Look at the following sentences from Dianne Hales's essay "Why Are We So Angry?" What do the underlined parts in each sentence have in common?

> "Everyone everywhere seems to be hotter under the collar these days," observes Sybil Evans, a conflict-resolution expert in New York City who singles out three primary culprits: <u>time</u>, <u>technology</u>, and <u>tension</u>.

> We <u>rely on computers that crash</u>, <u>drive on roads that gridlock</u>, <u>place calls to machines that put us on endless hold</u>.

> "The people who react by <u>hitting</u>, <u>kicking</u>, <u>screaming</u>, and <u>swearing</u> just feel more angry."

In each case, the parts that are underlined share a similar grammatical structure: nouns are grouped with nouns, verbs with verbs, and gerunds (the *-ing* form of a verb used as a noun) with gerunds.

Writing Parallel Sentences

Parallelism in Pairs and Lists

When two or more items in a series are joined by *and* or *or*, use a similar form for each item.

473

e Log in to
macmillanhighered
.com/rrw and look for
Additional Grammar
Exercises > Correcting
Errors in Parallelism

Not parallel	The professor assigned <u>readings</u>, <u>practices to do</u>, and <u>a paper</u>.
Parallel	The professor assigned <u>readings</u>, <u>practices</u>, and <u>a paper</u>.
Not parallel	The story was <u>in the newspaper</u>, <u>on the radio</u>, and <u>the television</u>.

[*In the newspaper* and *on the radio* are prepositional phrases. *The television* is not.]

Parallel	The story was <u>in the newspaper</u>, <u>on the radio</u>, and <u>on the television</u>.

PRACTICE 1   Using Parallelism in Pairs and Lists

In each sentence, underline the parts of the sentence that should be parallel. Then, edit the sentence to make it parallel.

Example: Coyotes roam the <u>western mountains</u>, <u>the central plains</u>,
~~and~~ <u>~~they are in the~~ suburbs</u> ~~of the East Coast of the~~
~~United States.~~   *suburbs.*

1. Wild predators, such as wolves, are vanishing because people hunt
   them and are taking over their land.

2. Coyotes are surviving and they do well in the modern United States.

3. The success of the coyote is due to its varied diet and adapting easily.

4. Coyotes are sometimes vegetarians, sometimes scavengers, and sometimes they hunt.

5. Today, they are spreading and populate the East Coast for the first time.

Parallelism in Comparisons

Comparisons often use the word *than* or *as*. When you edit for parallelism, make sure the items on either side of those words have parallel structures.

Not parallel	<u>Taking the bus</u> downtown is as fast as <u>the drive</u> there.
Parallel	<u>Taking the bus</u> downtown is as fast as <u>driving</u> there.

Not parallel	To admit a mistake is better than denying it.
Parallel	To admit a mistake is better than to deny it.
	Admitting a mistake is better than denying it.

Sometimes you need to add or delete a word or two to make the parts of a sentence parallel.

Not parallel	A tour package is less expensive than arranging every travel detail yourself.
Parallel, word added	*Buying* a tour package is less expensive than arranging every travel detail yourself.
Not parallel	The sale price of the shoes is as low as paying half of the regular price.
Parallel, words added	The sale price of the shoes is as low as half of the regular price.

PRACTICE 2   Using Parallelism in Comparisons

In each sentence, underline the parts of the sentence that should be parallel. Then, edit the sentence to make it parallel.

Example: Leasing a new car may be less expensive than ~~to buy~~ one.
                                                                    buying

1. Car dealers often require less money down for leasing a car than for the purchase of one.

2. The monthly payments for a leased car may be as low as paying for a loan.

3. You should check the terms of leasing to make sure they are as favorable as to buy.

4. You may find that to lease is a safer bet than buying.

5. You will be making less of a financial commitment by leasing a car than to own it.

Parallelism with Certain Paired Words

Certain paired words, called **correlative conjunctions**, link two equal elements and show the relationship between them. Here are the paired words:

both . . . and   neither . . . nor   rather . . . than

either . . . or   not only . . . but also

Make sure the items joined by these paired words are parallel.

Not parallel   Bruce wants *both* <u>freedom</u> *and* <u>to be wealthy</u>.

[*Both* is used with *and*, but the items joined by them are not parallel.]

Parallel   Bruce wants *both* <u>freedom</u> *and* <u>wealth</u>.

Parallel   Bruce wants *both* <u>to have freedom</u> *and* <u>to be wealthy</u>.

Not parallel   He can *neither* <u>fail the course</u> and <u>quitting his job</u> is also impossible.

Parallel   He can *neither* <u>fail the course</u> *nor* <u>quit his job</u>.

PRACTICE 3   Using Parallelism with Certain Paired Words

In each sentence, circle the paired words, and underline the parts of the sentence that should be parallel. Then, edit the sentence to make it parallel. You may need to change one of the paired elements to make the sentence parallel.

Example: A cell phone can be (either) a lifesaver (or) ~~it can be annoying.~~ *an annoyance*

1. Twenty years ago, most people neither had cell phones nor did they want them.

2. Today, cell phones are not only used by people of all ages but also are carried everywhere.

3. Cell phones are not universally popular: Some commuters would rather ban cell phones on buses and trains than being forced to listen to other people's conversations.

4. No one denies that a cell phone can be both useful and convenience is a factor.

5. A motorist stranded on a deserted road would rather have a cell phone than to walk to the nearest gas station.

Edit for Parallelism Problems

Use the chart on page 480, "Editing for Parallelism," to help you complete the practice exercise in this section and edit your own writing.

> **PRACTICE 4**   **Editing Paragraphs for Parallelism Problems**
>
> Find and correct five parallelism errors in the following paragraphs.
>
> 1 On a mountainous island between Norway and the North Pole is a special underground vault. 2 It contains neither gold and other currency. 3 Instead, it is full of a different kind of treasure: seeds. 4 They are being saved for the future in case something happens to the plants that people need to grow for food.
>
> 5 The vault has the capacity to hold 4.5 million types of seed samples. 6 Each sample contains an average of five hundred seeds, which means that up to 2.25 billion seeds can be stored in the vault. 7 To store them is better than planting them. 8 Stored, they are preserved for future genera-tions to plant. 9 On the first day that the vault's storage program began, 268,000 different seeds were deposited, put into sealed packages, and collecting into sealed boxes. 10 Some of the seeds were for maize (corn), while others were for rice, wheat, and barley.
>
> 11 Although some people call it the "Doomsday Vault," many others see it as a type of insurance policy against starvation in the case of a terrible natural disaster. 12 The vault's location keeps it safe from floods, earth-quakes, and storming. 13 Carefully storing these seeds not only will help ensure people will have food to eat plus make sure important crops never go extinct.

Chapter Review

1. Parallelism in writing means that _____

_____ .

2. In what three situations do problems with parallelism most often occur?

_____

3. What are two pairs of correlative conjunctions? _____

_____

4. Write two sentences using parallelism.

_____

_____

Chapter Test

Circle the correct choice for each of the following items. For help, refer to the "Editing for Parallelism" chart on page 480.

1. If an underlined portion of this sentence is incorrect, select the revision that fixes it. If the sentence is correct as written, choose d.

   For our home renovation, we are planning to <u>expand the kitchen,</u>
   <u>A</u>

   <u>retile the bathroom,</u> and <u>we also want to add a bedroom.</u>
   B   **C**

   a. add space to the kitchen   c. add a bedroom
   b. replace the tile in the   d. No change is necessary.
      bathroom

2. Choose the correct word(s) to fill in the blank.

   In my personal ad, I said that I like taking long walks on the beach,

   dining over candlelight, and _____ sculptures with a

   chain saw.

   a. to carve   b. carving   c. carved

3. If an underlined portion of this sentence is incorrect, select the revision that fixes it. If the sentence is correct as written, choose d.

    To get her elbow back into shape, she wants exercising and not
    ⎯⎯⎯
    A   B

    to take pills.
    ⎯⎯⎯⎯⎯
    C

    a. To getting   c. taking pills
    b. to do exercises   d. No change is necessary.

4. Choose the correct word(s) to fill in the blank.

    I have learned that ⎯⎯⎯⎯⎯⎯⎯ a pet is better than buying one from a pet store.

    a. adopting   b. have adopted   c. to adopt

5. Choose the correct words to fill in the blank.

    You can travel by car, by plane, or ⎯⎯⎯⎯⎯⎯⎯ .

    a. boating is fine   b. by boat   c. on boat

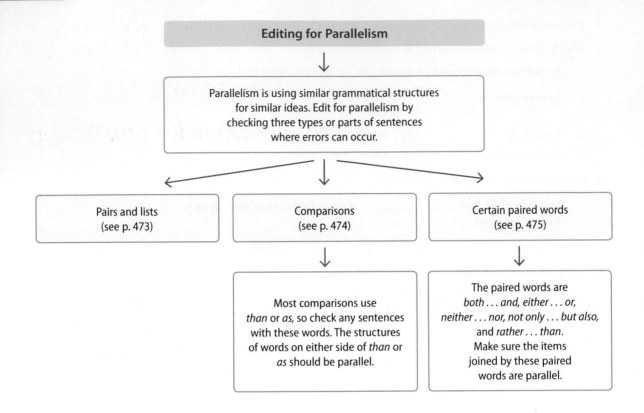

24

Sentence Variety:

Finding a Rhythm for Your Writing

Understand What Sentence Variety Is

Sentence variety means using different sentence patterns and lengths to give your writing rhythm and flow. In his essay "The Maker's Eye," Donald Murray explains how writers revise and edit for sentence variety:

e Log in to **macmillanhighered .com/rrw** and look for LearningCurve > Coordination and Subordination

> Writers often read aloud at this stage of the editing process, muttering or whispering to themselves, calling on the ear's experience with language. Does this sound right—or that? Writers edit, shifting back and forth from eye to page to ear to page. . . .
>
> The maker's eye moves back and forth from word to phrase to sentence to paragraph to sentence to phrase to word. The maker's eye sees the need for variety and balance, for a firmer structure, for a more appropriate form.

You can apply Murray's technique to the following paragraph. Read it aloud, and ask yourself these questions: Does it sound right? Does it flow, or is it choppy? Is there variety and balance in the style of the sentences?

With short, simple sentences

Many people do not realize how important their speaking voice and style are. Speaking style can make a difference, particularly in a job interview. What you say is important. How you say it is nearly as important. Your speaking voice creates an impression. Mumbling is a bad way of speaking. It makes the speaker appear sloppy and lacking in confidence. Mumbling also makes it difficult for the interviewer to hear what is being said. Talking too fast is another bad speech behavior. The speaker runs his or her ideas together. The interviewer cannot follow them or distinguish what is important. A third common bad speech behavior concerns verbal "tics." Verbal tics are empty filler phrases like "um," "like," and "you know." Practice for an interview. Sit up straight. Look the person to whom you are speaking directly in the eye. Speak up. Slow down. One good way to find out how you sound is to leave yourself a voice-mail message. If you sound bad to yourself, you need practice speaking aloud. Do not let poor speech behavior interfere with creating a good impression.

Now compare the first version with the one that follows. Do you see a difference? Do you hear a difference?

With sentence variety

Many people do not realize how important their speaking voice and style are, particularly in a job interview. What you say is important, but how you say it is nearly as important in creating a good impression. Mumbling is a bad way of speaking. Not only does it make the speaker appear sloppy and lacking in confidence, but mumbling also makes it difficult for the interviewer to hear what is being said. Talking too fast is another bad speech behavior. The speaker runs his or her ideas together, and the interviewer cannot follow them or distinguish what is important. A third common bad speech behavior is called verbal "tics," empty filler expressions such as "um," "like," and "you know." When you practice for an interview, sit up straight, look the person to whom you are speaking directly in the eye, speak up, and slow down. One good way to find out how you sound is to leave yourself a voice-mail message. If you sound bad to yourself, you need practice speaking aloud. Do not let poor speech behavior interfere with creating a good impression.

Creating Sentence Variety

Most writers tend to write short sentences that start with the subject, so this chapter will focus on techniques for lengthening sentences and changing sentence openers. As you learn about these techniques, look for examples in the essays that you have read. Make a note of the ways in which other writers have used these techniques to keep their writing varied and balanced.

Join Ideas Together to Lengthen Sentences: Coordination

Coordination means joining two (or more) independent clauses together to form a compound sentence. In Chapter 17, you learned three methods of joining independent clauses correctly.

PATTERN 1: ADD A COMMA AND A COORDINATING CONJUNCTION (IC, cc IC.)

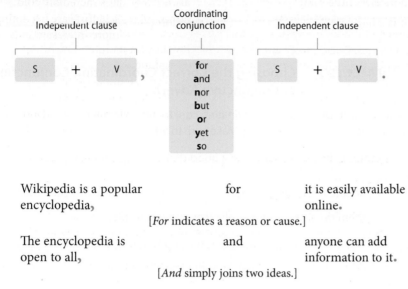

Wikipedia is a popular encyclopedia,   for   it is easily available online.

[*For* indicates a reason or cause.]

The encyclopedia is open to all,   and   anyone can add information to it.

[*And* simply joins two ideas.]

PATTERN 2: ADD A SEMICOLON (IC; IC.)

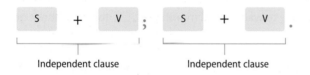

Cindy had all these middle-aged women apply beauty products to their faces; she stressed how important it was to apply them in a certain way, using the tips of their fingers (Barry, 230).

PATTERN 3: ADD A SEMICOLON, A CONJUNCTIVE ADVERB, AND A COMMA (IC; ca, IC.)

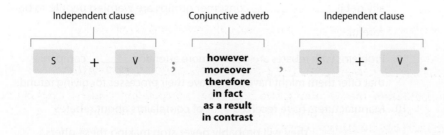

Antarctica is largely unexplored;	as a result,	it is unpopulated.
It receives little rain;	also,	it is incredibly cold.
It is a huge area;	therefore,	scientists are becoming more interested in it.

PRACTICE 1 Choosing the Correct Coordinating Conjunction or Conjunctive Adverb

Fill in each blank with a coordinating conjunction or conjunctive adverb that makes sense in the sentence. Make sure to add the correct punctuation.

Example: Rebates sound like a good deal ___, *but*___ they rarely are.

1. Rebate offers are common _____ you have probably seen many of them on packages for appliances and electronics.

2. These offers may promise to return hundreds of dollars to consumers _____ many people apply for them.

3. Applicants hope to get a lot of money back soon _____ they are often disappointed.

4. They might have to wait several months _____ they might not get their rebate at all.

5. Rebate applications are not short _____ are they easy to fill out.

6. One applicant compared completing a rebate form to filling out tax forms _____ he spent more than an hour on the process.

7. Manufacturers sometimes use rebates to move unpopular products off the shelves _____ they can replace these products with newer goods.

8. Only about 10 to 30 percent of people who apply for a rebate eventually get it _____ consumer groups are warning people to be careful.

9. Problems with rebates are getting more attention _____ companies that offer them might have to improve their processes for giving refunds.

10. Manufacturers have received a lot of complaints about rebates _____ they will probably never stop making these offers.

Join Ideas Together: Subordination

Subordination means joining ideas together by making one of the ideas a dependent or subordinate clause. You learned in Chapter 17 that a dependent clause begins with a dependent word such as *because, after, although, who,* or *when.*

SUBORDINATION, OPTION 1: IC DC.

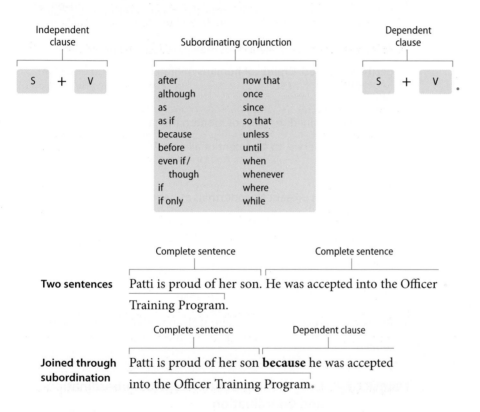

SUBORDINATION, OPTION 2: DC, IC.

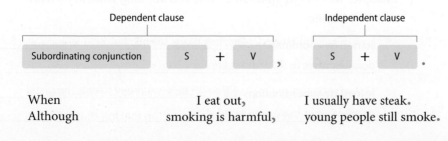

> **PRACTICE 2**   **Combining Sentences Using Subordination**

Combine each pair of sentences into a single sentence by adding an appropriate subordinating conjunction either between (Option 1) or at the beginning of the two sentences (Option 2). Use a subordinating conjunction that makes sense with the two sentences, and add commas where necessary.

Example: *If someone*
          Someone told you that you share DNA with humans'
                                                        , you
          extinct relatives, the Neanderthals. You might be surprised.

1. In fact, scientists have found that mating between humans and Neanderthals occurred. Groups of humans migrated north and east from Africa.

2. Scientists examined the DNA of modern humans. They made a startling discovery: 1 to 4 percent of all non-Africans' DNA is Neanderthal DNA.

3. Old illustrations present Neanderthals as bent over and primitive looking. It may be hard to believe that humans would want to mate with them.

4. However, a Neanderthal man got a good shave and a nice set of clothes. He might pass for a modern man.

5. Researchers are learning more about Neanderthals. Many mysteries remain.

> **PRACTICE 3**   **Lengthening Sentences with Subordination and Coordination**

Join each of the following sentence pairs in two ways, first by coordination and then by subordination.

Example: Rick has many talents. He is still deciding what to do with his life.

Joined by coordination: *Rick has many talents, but he is still deciding what to do with his life.*

Joined by subordination: *Although Rick has many talents, he is still deciding what to do with his life.*

1. Rick rides a unicycle. He can juggle four oranges.

   Joined by coordination: _____

   _____

   Joined by subordination: _____

   _____

2. A trapeze school opened in our town. Rick signed up immediately.

   Joined by coordination: _____

   _____

   Joined by subordination: _____

   _____

3. Rick is now at the top of his class. He worked hard practicing trapeze
   routines.

   Joined by coordination: _____

   _____

   Joined by subordination: _____

   _____

4. Rick asks me for career advice. I try to be encouraging.

   Joined by coordination: _____

   _____

   Joined by subordination: _____

   _____

5. He does not want to join the circus. He could study entertainment
   management.

   Joined by coordination: _____

   _____

   Joined by subordination: _____

   _____

Other Ways to Join Ideas

Join Ideas Using an -ing Verb

One way to combine sentences is to add *-ing* to the verb in the less important of the two sentences and to delete the subject, creating a phrase.

Two sentences	A pecan roll from our bakery is not a health food. It contains 800 calories.
Joined with *-ing* **verb form**	*Containing* 800 calories, a pecan roll from our bakery is not a health food.

You can add the *-ing* phrase to the beginning or the end of the other sentence, depending on what makes more sense.

The fat content is also high. ^{equaling}~~It equals~~ the fat in a huge country breakfast.

If you add the *-ing* phrase to the beginning of a sentence, you will usually need to put a comma after it. If you add the phrase to the end of a sentence, you will usually need to put a comma before it. A comma should *not* be used only when the *-ing* phrase is essential to the meaning of the sentence.

Two sentences	Experts examined the effects of exercise on arthritis patients. The experts found that walking, jogging, or swimming could reduce pain.
Joined without commas	Experts examining the effects of exercise on arthritis patients found that walking, jogging, or swimming could reduce pain.

[The phrase *examining the effects of exercise on arthritis patients* is essential to the meaning of the sentence.]

If you put a phrase starting with an *-ing* verb at the beginning of a sentence, be sure the word that the phrase modifies follows immediately. Otherwise, you will create a dangling modifier.

Two sentences	I ran through the rain. My raincoat got all wet.
Dangling modifier	Running through the rain, my raincoat got all wet.
Edited	Running through the rain, I got my raincoat all wet.

PRACTICE 4   **Joining Ideas Using an *-ing* Verb**

Combine each pair of sentences into a single sentence by using an *-ing* verb. Add or delete words as necessary.

Example: Some people read faces amazingly well. They interpret

interpreting

nonverbal cues that other people miss.

1. A recent study tested children's abilities to interpret facial expressions. The study made headlines.

2. Physically abused children participated in the study. They saw photographs of faces changing from one expression to another.

3. The children told researchers what emotion was most obvious in each face. The children chose among fear, anger, sadness, happiness, and other emotions.

4. The study also included nonabused children. They served as a control group for comparison with the other children.

5. All the children in the study were equally good at identifying most emotions. They all responded similarly to happiness or fear.

Join Ideas Using a Past Participle

Another way to combine sentences is to use a past participle (often, a verb ending in *-ed*) to turn the less important of the two sentences into a phrase.

Two sentences	Henry VIII was a powerful English king. He is *remembered* for his many wives.
Joined with a past participle	*Remembered* for his many wives, Henry VIII was a powerful English king.

Past participles of irregular verbs do not end in *-ed*; they take different forms.

Two sentences	Tim Treadwell was *eaten* by a grizzly bear. He showed that wild animals are unpredictable.
Joined with a past participle	*Eaten* by a grizzly bear, Tim Treadwell showed that wild animals are unpredictable.

Notice that sentences can be joined this way when one of them has a form of *be* along with a past participle (*is remembered* in the first Henry VIII example and *was eaten* in the first Tim Treadwell example).

To combine sentences this way, delete the subject and the *be* form from the sentence that has the *be* form and the past participle. You now have a phrase that can be added to the beginning or the end of the other sentence, depending on what makes more sense.

| | *be* | Past | | Pronoun changed |
| Subject | form | participle | | to a noun |

D , *Henry VIII*
~~Henry VIII was~~ determined to divorce one of his wives. ~~He~~ created the Church of England because Catholicism does not allow divorce.

If you add a phrase that begins with a past participle to the beginning of a sentence, put a comma after it. If you add the phrase to the end of the sentence, put a comma before it.

PRACTICE 5 **Joining Ideas Using a Past Participle**

Combine each pair of sentences into a single sentence by using a past participle.

Forced
Example: ~~The oil company was forced~~ to take the local women's
,the oil
objections seriously. ~~The~~ company had to close for ten days
during their protest.

1. The women of southern Nigeria were angered by British colonial rule in 1929. They organized a protest.

2. Nigeria is now one of the top ten oil-producing countries. The nation is covered with pipelines and oil wells.

3. The oil is pumped by American and other foreign oil companies. The oil often ends up in wealthy Western economies.

4. The money from the oil seldom reaches Nigeria's local people. The cash is stolen by corrupt rulers in many cases.

5. The Nigerian countryside is polluted by the oil industry. The land then becomes a wasteland.

Join Ideas Using an Appositive

An **appositive** is a noun or noun phrase that renames a noun or pronoun. Appositives can be used to combine two sentences into one.

Two sentences	Brussels sprouts can be roasted for a delicious flavor. They are a commonly disliked food.
Joined with an appositive	Brussels sprouts, a commonly disliked food, can be roasted for a delicious flavor.

[The phrase *a commonly disliked food* renames the noun *Brussels sprouts*.]

Notice that the sentence that renames the noun was turned into a noun phrase by dropping the subject and the verb (*They* and *are*). Also, commas set off the appositive.

PRACTICE 6   Joining Ideas Using an Appositive

Combine each pair of sentences into a single sentence by using an appositive. Be sure to use a comma or commas to set off the appositive.

Example: Levi's jeans have looked the same for well over a century. *, perhaps the most famous work clothes in the world,* ~~They are perhaps the most famous work clothes in the world.~~

1. Jacob Davis was a Russian immigrant working in Reno, Nevada. He was the inventor of Levi's jeans.

2. Davis came up with an invention that made work clothes last longer. The invention was the riveted seam.

3. Davis bought denim from a wholesaler. The wholesaler was Levi Strauss.

4. In 1870, he offered to sell the rights to his invention to Levi Strauss for the price of the patent. Patents then cost about $70.

5. Davis joined the firm in 1873 and supervised the final development of its product. The product was the famous Levi's jeans.

Join Ideas Using an Adjective Clause

An **adjective clause** is a group of words with a subject and a verb that describes a noun. An adjective clause often begins with the word *who, which,* or *that,* and it can be used to combine two sentences into one.

Two sentences	Lauren has won many basketball awards. She is captain of her college team.
Joined with an adjective clause	Lauren, *who is captain of her college team,* has won many basketball awards.

To join sentences this way, use *who, which,* or *that* to replace the subject in a sentence that describes a noun in the other sentence. You now have an adjective clause that you can move so that it follows the noun it describes. The sentence with the more important idea (the one you want to emphasize) should become the main clause. The less important idea should be in the adjective clause.

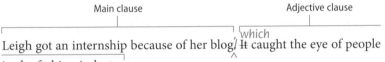

Leigh got an internship because of her blog. It caught the eye of people in the fashion industry.

[The more important idea here is that Leigh got an internship because of her blog. The less important idea is that the blog caught the eye of people in the fashion industry.]

Note: If an adjective clause can be taken out of a sentence without completely changing the meaning of the sentence, put commas around it.

Lauren, *who is captain of her college team,* has won many basketball awards.

[The phrase *who is captain of her college team* adds information about Lauren, but it is not essential.]

If an adjective clause is an essential part of a sentence, do not put commas around it.

Lauren is an award-winning basketball player who overcame childhood cancer.

[*Who overcame childhood cancer* is an essential part of this sentence.]

| PRACTICE 7 | **Joining Ideas Using an Adjective Clause** |

Combine each pair of sentences into a single sentence by using an adjective clause beginning with *who, which,* or *that.*

Example: My friend Erin had her first child last June. ~~She has been~~
                    , who has been going to college for the past three years,
                                      ^
~~going to college for the past three years.~~

1. While Erin goes to classes, her baby boy stays at a day-care center. The day-care center costs Erin about $100 a week.

2. Twice when her son was ill, Erin had to miss her geology lab. The lab is an important part of her grade for that course.

3. Occasionally, Erin's parents come up and watch the baby while Erin is studying. They live about 70 miles away.

4. Sometimes Erin feels discouraged by the extra costs. The costs have come from having a child.

5. She believes that some of her professors are not very sympathetic. These professors are the ones who have never been parents themselves.

6. Erin understands that she must take responsibility for both her child and her education. She wants to be a good mother and a good student.

7. Her grades have suffered somewhat since she had her son. They were once straight A's.

8. Erin wants to graduate with honors. She hopes to go to graduate school someday.

9. Her son is more important than an A in geology. He is the most important thing to her.

10. Erin still expects to have a high grade point average. She has simply given up expecting to be perfect.

Strategies for Changing Sentence Openers

In addition to combining or lengthening sentences to achieve rhythm and variety, you may also consider changing how you begin a sentence. Most student writers follow a basic pattern, beginning each sentence with a subject. In this section, we will explore other ways to begin a sentence.

Start Some Sentences with Adverbs

Adverbs are words that describe verbs, adjectives, or other adverbs; they often end with *-ly*. As long as the meaning is clear, adverbs can be placed at the beginning of a sentence instead of in the middle. Adverbs at the beginning of a sentence are usually followed by a comma.

Adverb in middle	Stories about haunted houses *frequently* surface at Halloween.
Adverb at beginning	*Frequently*, stories about haunted houses surface at Halloween.
Adverb in middle	These stories *often* focus on ship captains lost at sea.
Adverb at beginning	*Often*, these stories focus on ship captains lost at sea.

Start Some Sentences with Prepositions or Infinitives

You may also begin a sentence with a prepositional phrase or an infinitive.

Prepositional phrase at the end	John and his team celebrated *after their final match*.
Prepositional phrase at the beginning	*After their final match*, John and his team celebrated.
Infinitive phrase at the end	Carolyn signed up for a math class *to help her daughter with algebra homework*.
Infinitive phrase at the beginning	*To help her daughter with algebra homework*, Carolyn signed up for a math class.

Notice that when you begin a sentence with a prepositional phrase or an infinitive, the phrase is usually followed by a comma.

> **PRACTICE 8**   **Starting Sentences with Prepositional Phrases or Infinitives**
>
> Practice changing sentence structure by moving the prepositional phrase or the infinitive phrase to the beginning of each sentence. Pay attention to punctuation.
>
> **Example:** *To help reduce the amount of vehicle traffic in the city,* **Washington, D.C., began a public bicycle-sharing program.** ~~to help reduce the amount of vehicle traffic in the city.~~

1. The idea has been popular in Europe for years.

2. Citizens must pay $7 a day, $25 a month, or $75 a year to join the program in Washington.

3. They have access to more than one thousand bikes for that fee.

4. They must return the bikes to a local station after each use.

5. A number of stations are located in Washington, D.C., and Arlington, Virginia, to make sure all riders can have convenient access to the bicycles.

6. Cycling has become much more popular throughout the United States in recent years.

7. People are turning to bicycles to save money on fuel costs.

Edit for Sentence Variety

Use the chart on page 499, "Editing for Sentence Variety," to help you complete the practice exercise in this section and edit your own writing.

> **PRACTICE 9**   **Editing Sentences for Sentence Variety**
>
> Create sentence variety in the following paragraphs by joining at least two sentences in each of the paragraphs. Use several of the techniques covered in this chapter. More than one correct answer is possible.
>
> 1 Few people would associate the famous English poet and playwright William Shakespeare with prison. 2 However, Shakespeare has taken on an

important role in the lives of certain inmates. 3 They are serving time at the Luther Luckett Correctional Complex in Kentucky. 4 These inmates were brought together by the Shakespeare Behind Bars program. 5 They spend nine months preparing for a performance of one of the great writer's plays.

6 Recently, prisoners at Luckett performed *The Merchant of Venice.* 7 It is one of Shakespeare's most popular plays. 8 Many of the actors identified with Shylock. 9 He is a moneylender who is discriminated against because he is Jewish. 10 When a rival asks Shylock for a loan to help a friend, Shylock drives a hard bargain. 11 He demands a pound of the rival's flesh if the loan is not repaid. 12 One inmate shared his views of this play with a newspaper reporter. 13 The inmate said, "It deals with race. It deals with discrimination. It deals with gambling, debt, cutting people. It deals with it all. And we were all living that someway, somehow."

Chapter Review

1. Having sentence variety means _____

   _____ .

2. If you tend to write short, similar-sounding sentences, what five techniques should you try? _____

   _____

   _____

3. What are three patterns for joining ideas through coordination? _____

   _____

   _____

4. What is subordination? _____

   _____

5. An _____ is a noun or noun phrase that renames a noun.

6. An _____ clause often starts with *who,* _____, or _____. It describes a noun or pronoun.

7. Use commas around an adjective clause when the information in it is (essential / not essential) to the meaning of the sentence.

Chapter Test

For each of the following sentence pairs, choose the answer that joins the sentences logically using one of the strategies in this chapter. For help, refer to the "Editing for Sentence Variety" chart on page 499.

1. Luis straightened his tie. He waited to be called in for his job interview.
   a. Straightened his tie, Luis waited to be called in for his job interview.
   b. Straightening his tie, Luis waited to be called in for his job interview.

2. _____ the candidate stepped up to the podium, a group of protesters began to shout criticisms of her.
   a. So that   b. As if   c. As

3. My niece is a star softball player. She loves to watch baseball on TV.
   a. My niece, a star softball player, loves to watch baseball on TV.
   b. Starring as a softball player, my niece loves to watch baseball on TV.

4. _____ you are sure that the lightning has stopped, don't let the kids get back into the pool.
   a. Until   b. Before   c. As if

5. The lawyer believed passionately in his client's innocence. He convinced the jury to come to a verdict of not guilty.
   a. The lawyer, who believed passionately in his client's innocence, convinced the jury to come to a verdict of not guilty.
   b. The lawyer believed passionately in his client's innocence, yet he convinced the jury to come to a verdict of not guilty.

6. Matt speaks out against glorifying college sports _____ he himself is the star of our football team.
   a. until   b. even though   c. unless

7. I did not like the teacher's criticism of my paper; _____ I must admit that everything she said was right.

   a. as a result,   b. in addition,   c. still,

8. Jenna is the best speaker in the class, _____ she will give the graduation speech.

   a. or   b. so   c. yet

9. There were now neat rows of suburban homes _____ there had once been orange groves.

   a. where   b. as if   c. before

10. _____ we bought a snowblower, my son has not complained about having to shovel after storms.

   a. Since   b. Where   c. Unless

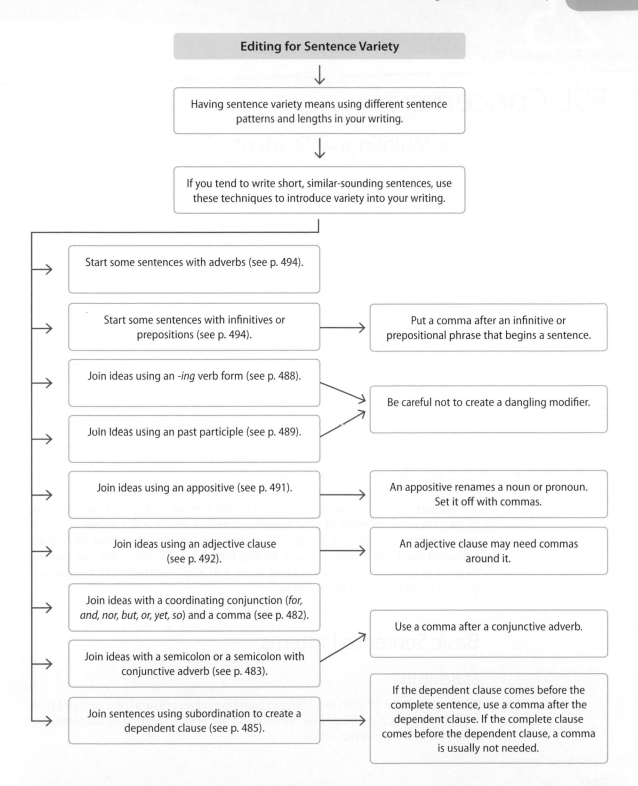

Editing for Sentence Variety

Having sentence variety means using different sentence patterns and lengths in your writing.

If you tend to write short, similar-sounding sentences, use these techniques to introduce variety into your writing.

Start some sentences with adverbs (see p. 494).

Start some sentences with infinitives or prepositions (see p. 494).

Put a comma after an infinitive or prepositional phrase that begins a sentence.

Join ideas using an *-ing* verb form (see p. 488).

Be careful not to create a dangling modifier.

Join Ideas using an past participle (see p. 489).

Join ideas using an appositive (see p. 491).

An appositive renames a noun or pronoun. Set it off with commas.

Join ideas using an adjective clause (see p. 492).

An adjective clause may need commas around it.

Join ideas with a coordinating conjunction (*for, and, nor, but, or, yet, so*) and a comma (see p. 482).

Use a comma after a conjunctive adverb.

Join ideas with a semicolon or a semicolon with conjunctive adverb (see p. 483).

Join sentences using subordination to create a dependent clause (see p. 485).

If the dependent clause comes before the complete sentence, use a comma after the dependent clause. If the complete clause comes before the dependent clause, a comma is usually not needed.

25

ESL Concerns:

Trouble Spots for Multilingual Students

e Log in to **macmillanhighered .com/rrw** and look for LearningCurve > Sentence Structures for Multilingual Writers

The English you use in casual conversations is not always the same as the formal, academic English you are expected to use in college and work situations, especially in writing. Students whose first language is not English may encounter special challenges in writing academic English. This chapter will help you understand and overcome those challenges.

Grammar information does not apply to all situations; instead, the grammatical structure depends on the specific words you use. In these cases, you need to pay attention to **word choice**, because different words will require different grammatical structures. A good ESL dictionary contains this kind of **lexical information**. Lexical information tells you how a specific word can and cannot be used in sentences. As you read and write, you may want to keep a vocabulary list that includes lexical information.

Basic Sentence Patterns

Statements

Every sentence in English must have at least one subject (S) and one verb (V) that together express a complete idea. The subject *performs* the action of the sentence, while the verb *names* the action.

```
 S        V
 |        |
```
The pitcher throws.

All other sentence patterns build on this basic structure. For example, you can add a prepositional phrase to the subject and verb. In standard English, the prepositional phrase often follows the subject and verb.

```
 S     V   Prepositional phrase
 |     |    ┌───────┴───────┐
```
Lilah went to the movies.

One common pattern is the subject-verb-direct object (S-V-DO) pattern. The **direct object** (DO) is the person or thing that directly receives the action of the verb.

```
 S        V         DO
 |        |          |
```
The pitcher throws the ball.

An **indirect object** does not receive the action of the verb directly. The indirect object explains to whom or for whom the subject does the action.

```
 S       V    IO    DO
 |       |    |      |
```
The pitcher throws me the ball.

Note: Not every verb can occur in every pattern. For example, the verbs *give* and *throw* have two patterns:

S + V + IO + DO
The teacher gives the students extra credit.
The pitcher throws me the ball.

S + V + DO + *to* + IO
The teacher gives extra credit to the students.
The pitcher throws the ball to me.

The verb *explain*, however, occurs only in the second pattern:

Incorrect   The teacher explains us the grammar rules.

Correct   The teacher explains the grammar rules to us.

The verbs *ask* and *cost*, in contrast, occur only in the first pattern:

Incorrect	The <u>students</u> <u>ask</u> questions to the teacher.
	The new <u>car</u> <u>cost</u> a lot of money to me.
Correct	The <u>students</u> <u>ask</u> the teacher questions.
	The new <u>car</u> <u>cost</u> me a lot of money.

Use a dictionary to help you understand which patterns to use when you are writing.

> **PRACTICE 1**   **Sentence Patterns**

Label the subject (S), verb (V), direct object (DO), and indirect object (IO), if any, in the following two sentences.

1. John sent the letter.

2. John sent Beth the letter.

> **PRACTICE 2**   **Using Correct Word Order**

Read each of the sentences that follow. If the sentence is correct, write "C" in the blank to the left of it. If it is incorrect, write "I"; then, rewrite the sentence using correct word order.

Example: __I__ **My friend to me gave a present.**

      Revision: *My friend gave me a present.*_____

_____ 1. Presents I like very much.

    Revision: _____

_____ 2. To parties I go often.

    Revision: _____

_____ 3. To parties, I always bring a present.

    Revision: _____

_____ 4. At my parties, people bring me presents, too.

    Revision: _____

_____ 5.   Always write to them a thank-you note.

Revision: _____

Negatives

No matter which sentence pattern you use, you can form a negative by adding the word *not* after the auxiliary (helping) verb. If a sentence does not have a helping verb, make the verb negative by adding a form of the helping verb *do* and the word *not*.

Sentence	Dina can sing.
	cannot
Negative	Dina ~~no can~~ sing.
Sentence	The store sells cigarettes.
	does not
Negative	The store ~~no sells~~ cigarettes.
Sentence	Bruce will call.
	not
Negative	Bruce ~~no~~ will call.
Sentence	Caroline walked.
	not
Negative	Caroline ~~no~~ did walk.

Common Helping Verbs

Forms of *Be*	Forms of *Have*	Forms of *Do*	Other Verbs
am	have	do	can
are	has	does	could
is	had	did	may
been			might
being			must
was			should
were			will
			would

You must include an auxiliary verb with the negative *not*.

Incorrect	The store *not sell* cigarettes.
Correct	The store *does not sell* cigarettes.

[*Does*, a form of the helping verb *do*, must come before *not*.]

Correct	The store *is not selling* cigarettes.

[*Is*, a form of *be*, must come before *not*.]

Use only one negative word per sentence; double negatives are not used in standard English.

Incorrect (negative subject and negative verb)	No students aren't finished with the tests.
Incorrect (negative object and negative verb)	Shane does not have no ride.
Incorrect (two negatives in a verb)	John has not never seen a snow storm.
Correct	No students are finished with the tests. The students are not finished with the tests.
Correct	Shane does not have a ride. Shane has no ride.
Correct	John has never seen a snow storm. John has not ever seen a snow storm.

Common Negative Words

never	nobody	no one
no	none	nowhere

When forming a negative in the simple past tense, use the past tense of the helping verb *do*.

| *did* | + | *not* | + | Base verb without *-ed* ending | = | Negative past tense |

Sentence   I *talked* to Jairo last night.

[*Talked* is the past tense.]

Negative   I *did not* talk to Jairo last night.

[Notice that *talk* in this sentence does not have an *-ed* ending because the helping verb *did* conveys the past tense.]

PRACTICE 3   **Forming Negatives**

Rewrite the sentences to make them negative.

Example: Hassan's son is talking now.
                                          not

1. He can say several words.

2. Hassan remembers when his daughter started talking.

3. He thinks it was at the same age.

4. His daughter was an early speaker.

5. Hassan expects his son to be a talkative adult.

Questions

To turn a statement into a question, move the helping verb so that it comes before the subject. Add a question mark (**?**) in place of the period at the end of the statement.

Statement   Johan *can go* tonight.

Question   *Can* Johan *go* tonight?

If the only verb in the statement is a form of *be*, it should be moved before the subject.

Statement   Jamie *is* at work.

Question   *Is* Jamie at work?

If the statement does not contain a helping verb or a form of *be,* add a form of *do* and put it before the subject. Be sure to end the question with a question mark.

Statement	Norah sings in the choir.	Tyrone goes to college.
Question	*Does* Norah sing in the choir?	*Does* Tyrone go to college?
Statement	The building burned.	The plate broke.
Question	*Did* the building burn?	*Did* the plate break?

Notice that the verb changed once the helping verb *did* was added. *Do* is used with *I, you, we,* and *they. Does* is used with *he, she,* and *it.*

| Examples | *Do* [I / you / we / they] practice every day? |
| | *Does* [he / she / it] sound terrible? |

PRACTICE 4   **Forming Questions**

Rewrite the sentences to make them into questions.

Example: *Does* Brad knows how to cook?

1. He makes dinner every night for his family.

2. He goes to the grocery store once a week.

3. He uses coupons to save money.

4. Brad saves a lot of money using coupons.

There Is *and* There Are

English sentences often include *there is* or *there are* to indicate the existence of something.

There is a man at the door.

[You could also say, *A man is at the door.*]

There are many men in the class.

[You could also say, *Many men are in the class.*]

When a sentence includes the words *there is* or *there are*, the verb (*is*, *are*) comes before the noun it goes with (which is actually the subject of the sentence). The verb must agree with the noun in number. For example, the first sentence in the preceding example uses the singular verb *is* to agree with the singular noun *man*, and the second sentence uses the plural verb *are* to agree with the plural noun *men*.

In questions, *is* or *are* comes before *there*.

Statements	*There is* plenty to eat.
	There are some things to do.
Questions	*Is there* plenty to eat?
	Are there some things to do?

PRACTICE 5   **Using *There Is* and *There Are***

In each of the following sentences, fill in the blank with *there is* or *there are*, using the correct word order for any questions.

Example: Although my parents are busy constantly, they say that
        __there is__ **always more that can be done.**

1. Every morning, _____ flowers to water and weeds to pull.

2. Later in the day, _____ more chores, like mowing the lawn or cleaning out the garage.

3. I always ask, " _____ anything I can do?"

4. They are too polite to say that _____ work that they need help with.

5. If _____ more productive parents in the world, I would be surprised.

Pronouns

Pronouns replace nouns or other pronouns in a sentence so that you do not have to repeat them. There are three types of pronouns: subject pronouns, object pronouns, and possessive pronouns.

SUBJECT PRONOUNS serve as the subject of the verb (and remember that every English sentence *must* have a subject).

He
Rob is my cousin. R̶o̶b̶ lives next to me.

OBJECT PRONOUNS receive the action of the verb or are part of a prepositional phrase.

Rob asked *me* for a favor.

[The object pronoun *me* receives the action of the verb *asked*.]

Rob lives next door *to me*.

[*To me* is the prepositional phrase; *me* is the object pronoun.]

POSSESSIVE PRONOUNS show ownership.

Rob is *my* cousin.

Use the chart below to check which type of pronoun to use.

The singular pronouns *he/she, him/her,* and *his/hers* show gender. *He, him,* and *his* are masculine pronouns; *she, her,* and *hers* are feminine.

Here are some examples of common pronoun errors, with corrections.

Confusing Subject and Object Pronouns

Use a subject pronoun for the word that *performs* the action of the verb, and use an object pronoun for the word that *receives* the action.

Pronoun Types

Subject		Object		Possessive	
Singular	**Plural**	**Singular**	**Plural**	**Singular**	**Plural**
I	we	me	us	my / mine	our / ours
you	you	you	you	your / yours	your / yours
he / she / it	they	him / her / it	them	his / her / hers / its	their/theirs
Relative Pronouns					
who, which, that					

Tashia is a good student. ~~Her~~ *She* gets all A's.

[The pronoun performs the action *gets*, so it should be the subject pronoun, *she*.]

Tomas gave the keys to ~~she~~ *her*. Banh gave the coat to ~~he~~ *him*.

[The pronoun receives the action of *gave*, so it should be the object pronoun, *her* or *him*.]

Confusing Gender

Use masculine pronouns to replace masculine nouns, and use feminine pronouns to replace feminine nouns.

Nick is sick. ~~She~~ *He* has the flu.

[*Nick* is a masculine noun, so the pronoun must be masculine.]

The jacket belongs to Jane. Give it to ~~him~~ *her*.

[*Jane* is feminine, so the pronoun must be feminine.]

Leaving Out a Pronoun

Some sentences use the pronoun *it* as the subject or object. Do not leave *it* out of the sentence.

~~Is~~ *It is* a holiday today.

Maria will bring the food. ~~Will~~ *It will* be delicious.

I tried calamari last night and liked *it* very much.

Using a Pronoun to Repeat a Subject

A pronoun *replaces* a noun, so do not use both a subject noun and a pronoun.

My father ~~he~~ is very strict.

[*Father* is the subject noun, so the sentence should not also have the subject pronoun *he*.]

The bus ~~it~~ was late.

[*Bus* is the subject noun, so the sentence should not also have the subject pronoun *it*.]

Using Relative Pronouns

The words *who, which,* and *that* are **relative pronouns**. Use relative pronouns in a clause that gives more information about the subject.

- Use *who* to refer to a person or people.
  The <u>man</u> *who* lives next door <u>plays</u> piano.
- Use *which* or *that* to refer to nonliving things.
  The <u>plant</u>, *which* was a gift, <u>died</u>.
  The <u>phone</u> *that* I bought last week <u>is</u> broken.

e Log in to **macmillanhighered .com/rrw** and look for LearningCurve > Verbs for Multilingual Writers

Verbs

Verbs have different tenses to show when something happened: in the past, present, or future.

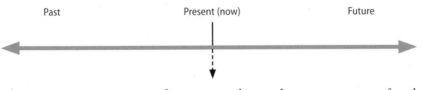

This section contains time lines, examples, and common errors for the simple and perfect tenses; coverage of progressive tenses; and more. See Chapter 19 for full coverage of the simple and perfect tenses, as well as practice exercises.

The Simple Tenses

SIMPLE PRESENT

Use the **simple present** to describe situations that exist now, including facts, habits, schedules, and preferences.

I like pizza.

<u>I</u> / <u>You</u> / <u>We</u> / <u>They</u> <u>like</u> pizza.
<u>She</u> / <u>He</u> <u>likes</u> pizza.

The third-person singular (*she/he*) of regular verbs ends in *-s* or *-es*.

SIMPLE PAST

Use the **simple past** to describe situations that began and ended in the past.

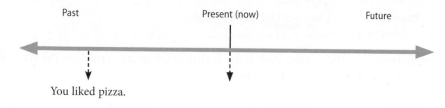

I / You / She / He / We / They **liked** pizza.

For regular verbs, the simple past is formed by adding either *-d* or *-ed* to the verb. For the past forms of irregular verbs, see the chart on pages 413–416.

SIMPLE FUTURE

Use the **simple future** to describe situations that will happen in the future. It is easier to form than the past tense. Use this formula for forming the future tense.

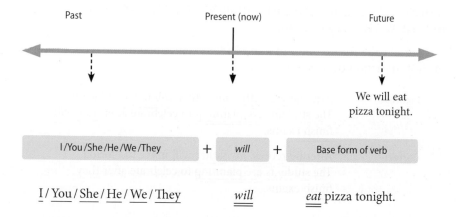

I / You / She / He / We / They   *will*   *eat* pizza tonight.

COMMON ERRORS IN USING SIMPLE TENSES

Following are some common errors in using simple tenses.

Simple present. Forgetting to add *-s* or *-es* to verbs that go with third-person singular subjects (*she / he / it*):

Incorrect	She know the manager.
Correct	She knows the manager.

Simple past. Forgetting to add *-d* or *-ed* to regular verbs:

Incorrect	Gina work late last night.
Correct	Gina work**ed** late last night.

Forgetting to use the correct past-tense forms of irregular verbs (see the chart of irregular verb forms on pp. 413–416):

Incorrect	Gerard speaked to her about the problem.
Correct	Gerard **spoke** to her about the problem.

Forgetting to use the base verb without an ending for negative sentences:

Incorrect	She does not wants money for helping.
Correct	She does not **want** money for helping.

USING THE FUTURE TENSE IN A DEPENDENT CLAUSE THAT BEGINS WITH A TIME WORD

Do not use the future tense in a dependent clause beginning with a time word, even if the action occurs in the future.

Incorrect	After he will retire, my father will move to Florida. The students are planning to celebrate after they will finish exams.
Correct	After he retires, my father will move to Florida. The students are planning to celebrate after they finish exams.

Common Time Words (Subordinating Conjunctions)

after	before	while
as soon as	when	

The Perfect Tenses

PRESENT PERFECT

Use the **present perfect** to describe situations that started in the past and either continue into the present or were completed at some unknown time in the past.

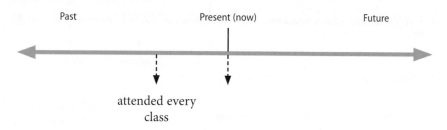

To form the present perfect tense, use this formula:

Subject	+	*has/have*	+	Past participle of base verb

She / He	*has*	*attended* every class.
I / We / They	*have*	*attended* every class.

Notice that *I / We / They* use *have* and that *She / He* use *has*.

PAST PERFECT

Use the **past perfect** to describe situations that began and ended before some other situation happened.

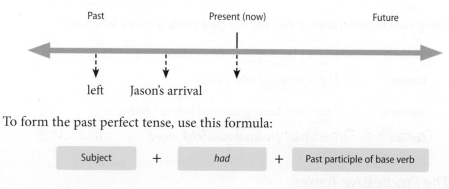

To form the past perfect tense, use this formula:

Subject	+	*had*	+	Past participle of base verb

I / You / She / He / We / They	*had*	*left* before Jason arrived.

FUTURE PERFECT

Use the **future perfect** to describe situations that begin and end before another situation begins.

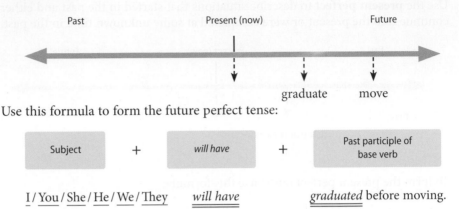

Use this formula to form the future perfect tense:

Subject	+	*will have*	+	Past participle of base verb

I / You / She / He / We / They   *will have*   *graduated* before moving.

COMMON ERRORS IN FORMING THE PERFECT TENSE

Using *had* instead of *has* or *have* for the present perfect:

Incorrect   We **had** lived here since 2003.

Correct   We **have** lived here since 2003.

Forgetting to use past participles (with *-d* or *-ed* endings for regular verbs):

Incorrect   She has attend every class.

Correct   She has attend**ed** every class.

Using *been* between *have* or *has* and the past participle of a base verb:

Incorrect   I have **been** attended every class.

Correct   I have attended every class.

Incorrect   I will have **been** graduated before I move.

Correct   I will have graduated before I move.

The Progressive Tenses

The **progressive tense** is used to describe ongoing actions in the present, past, or future. Following are some common errors in using the present progressive tense.

Forgetting to add *-ing* to the verb:

Incorrect	I am type now.
	She / he is not type now.
Correct	I am typ**ing** now.
	She / he is not typ**ing** now.

Forgetting to include a form of *be* (*am* / *is* / *are*):

Incorrect	He typing now.
	They typing now.
Correct	He **is** typing now.
	They **are** typing now.

Forgetting to use a form of *be* (*am* / *is* / *are*) to start questions:

Incorrect	They typing now?
Correct	**Are** they typing now?

Note: Some English verbs do not generally occur in the progressive tense. These verbs are nonaction verbs; they usually describe states, possession, or opinion.

Incorrect	My mother is owning a house at the beach.
	I am needing a haircut.
Correct	My mother owns a house at the beach.
	I need a haircut.

Common Nonaction Verbs

believe	own	prefer
like	possess	seem
need		

The following charts show how to use the present, past, and future progressive tenses in regular statements, negative statements, and questions.

THE PROGRESSIVE TENSES

Tense	

Present progressive

Timeline: a situation that is happening now but started in the past

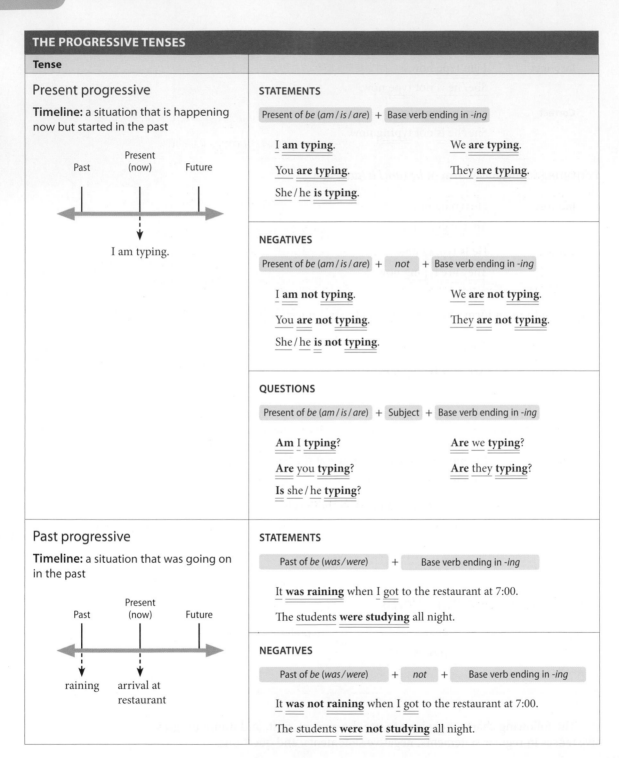

I am typing.

STATEMENTS

Present of *be* (*am* / *is* / *are*) + Base verb ending in *-ing*

I **am typing**.   We **are typing**.

You **are typing**.   They **are typing**.

She / he **is typing**.

NEGATIVES

Present of *be* (*am* / *is* / *are*) + *not* + Base verb ending in *-ing*

I **am not typing**.   We **are not typing**.

You **are not typing**.   They **are not typing**.

She / he **is not typing**.

QUESTIONS

Present of *be* (*am* / *is* / *are*) + Subject + Base verb ending in *-ing*

Am I **typing**?   **Are** we **typing**?

Are you **typing**?   **Are** they **typing**?

Is she / he **typing**?

Past progressive

Timeline: a situation that was going on in the past

STATEMENTS

Past of *be* (*was* / *were*) + Base verb ending in *-ing*

It **was raining** when I got to the restaurant at 7:00.

The students **were studying** all night.

NEGATIVES

Past of *be* (*was* / *were*) + *not* + Base verb ending in *-ing*

It **was not raining** when I got to the restaurant at 7:00.

The students **were not studying** all night.

Tense	
	QUESTIONS Past of *be* (*was/were*) + Subject + Base verb ending in *-ing* **Was** it **raining** when I got to the restaurant at 7:00? **Were** the students **studying** all night?

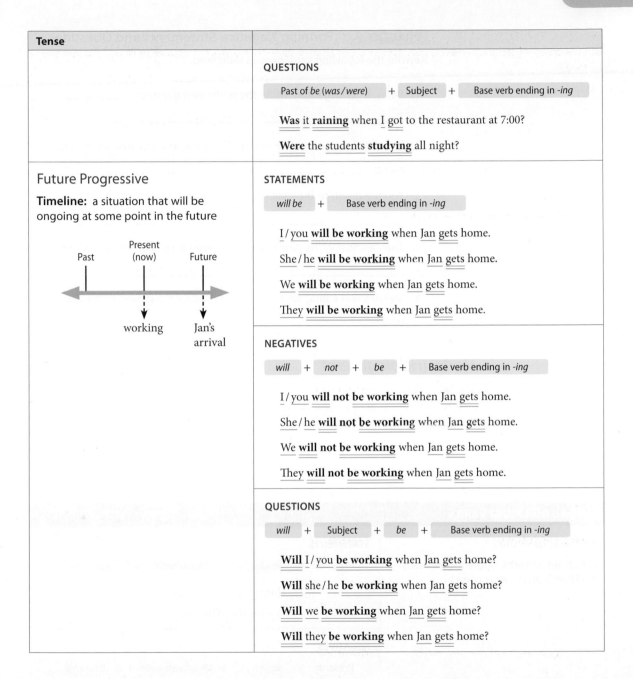

Future Progressive

Timeline: a situation that will be ongoing at some point in the future

Past — Present (now) — Future

working — Jan's arrival

STATEMENTS

will be + Base verb ending in *-ing*

I / you **will be working** when Jan gets home.

She / he **will be working** when Jan gets home.

We **will be working** when Jan gets home.

They **will be working** when Jan gets home.

NEGATIVES

will + *not* + *be* + Base verb ending in *-ing*

I / you **will not be working** when Jan gets home.

She / he **will not be working** when Jan gets home.

We **will not be working** when Jan gets home.

They **will not be working** when Jan gets home.

QUESTIONS

will + Subject + *be* + Base verb ending in *-ing*

Will I / you **be working** when Jan gets home?

Will she / he **be working** when Jan gets home?

Will we **be working** when Jan gets home?

Will they **be working** when Jan gets home?

> PRACTICE 6   **Forming Negative Statements and Questions**
>
> Rewrite the following sentences as indicated.

1. Betsy is golfing today. *Make the sentence a question:* _____
   _____

2. It was snowing when we got up. *Make the sentence a negative state-*
   ment: _____

3. You are going to the mall. *Make the sentence a question:* _____
   _____

4. They are losing the game. *Make the sentence a negative statement:*
   _____

5. Meriam was eating when you arrived. *Make the sentence into a ques-*
   tion: _____

Modal (Helping) Verbs

Modal verbs (or modal auxiliary verbs) are helping verbs that express the writer's attitude about an action. You do not have to learn too many modal verbs—just the eight in the chart that follows.

MODAL (HELPING) VERBS	

General formulas
 	
For all modal verbs. (More modal verbs are shown on the next page.)
	STATEMENTS
	
	Present: Subject + Modal verb + Base verb
	
	            Dumbo can fly.
	
	Past: Forms vary—see the following.
	
	NEGATIVES
	
	Present: Subject + Modal verb + *not* + Base verb
	
	            Dumbo cannot fly.
	
	Past: Forms vary—see the following.

	QUESTIONS
	Present: [Modal verb] + [Subject] + [Base verb]
	Can Dumbo fly?
	Past: Forms vary—see the following.
Can Means *ability*	**STATEMENTS** **Present:** Beth **can** work fast. **Past:** Beth **could** work fast.
	NEGATIVES **Present:** Beth **can**not work fast. **Past:** Beth **could** not work fast.
	QUESTIONS **Present: Can** Beth work fast? **Past: Could** Beth work fast?
Could Means *possibility*. It can also be the past tense of *can*.	**STATEMENTS** **Present:** Beth **could** work quickly if she had more time. **Past:** Beth **could** have worked quickly if she had had more time.
	NEGATIVES *Can* is used for present negatives. (See above.) **Past:** Beth **could** not have worked quickly.
	QUESTIONS **Present: Could** Beth work quickly? **Past: Could** Beth have worked quickly?
May Means *permission* For past-tense forms, see *might*.	**STATEMENTS** **Present:** You **may** borrow my car.
	NEGATIVES **Present:** You **may** not borrow my car. ➡

	QUESTIONS **Present:** <u>May</u> I <u>borrow</u> your car?
## Might Means *possibility*. It can also be the past tense of *may*.	STATEMENTS **Present** (with *be*): Lou **might** be asleep. **Past** (with *have* + past participle of *be*): Lou **might** have been asleep. **Future:** Lou **might** sleep.
	NEGATIVES **Present** (with *be*): Lou **might** not be asleep. **Past** (with *have* + past participle of *be*): Lou **might** not have been asleep. **Future:** Lou **might** not sleep.
	QUESTIONS *Might* in questions is very formal and not often used.
## Must Means *necessary*	STATEMENTS **Present:** We **must** try. **Past** (with *have* + past participle of base verb): We **must** have tried. **Past** (with *had* + *to* + base verb): We **had to** try.
	NEGATIVES **Present:** We **must** not try. **Past** (with *have* + past participle of base verb): We **must** not have tried.
	QUESTIONS **Present:** <u>Must</u> we <u>try</u>? Past-tense questions with *must* are unusual.
## Should Means *duty* or *expectation*	STATEMENTS **Present:** They **should** call. **Past** (with *have* + past participle of base verb): They **should** have called.

	NEGATIVES
	Present: They **should** not call.
	Past (with *have* + past participle of base verb): They **should** not have called.
	QUESTIONS
	Present: **Should** they call?
	Past (with *have* + past participle of base verb): **Should** they have called?
Will Means *intend to* (future) For past-tense forms, see *would*.	STATEMENTS
	Future: I **will** succeed.
	NEGATIVES
	Future: I **will** not succeed.
	QUESTIONS
	Future: **Will** I succeed?
Would Means *prefer* or is used to start a future request. It can also be the past tense of *will*.	STATEMENTS
	Present: I **would** like to travel.
	Past (with *have* + past participle of base verb): I **would** have traveled if I had had the money.
	NEGATIVES
	Present: I **would** not like to travel.
	Past (with *have* + past participle of base verb): I **would** not have traveled if it had not been for you.
	QUESTIONS
	Present: **Would** you like to travel?
	Or to start a request: **Would** you help me?
	Past (with *have* + past participle of base verb): **Would** you have traveled with me if I had asked you?

COMMON ERRORS WITH MODAL VERBS

Following are some common errors in using modal verbs.

Using more than one helping verb:

Incorrect	They **will can** help.
Correct	They **will** help. [future intention]
	They **can** help. [are able to]

Using *to* between the modal verb and the main (base) verb:

Incorrect	Emilio **might to** come with us.
Correct	Emilio **might** come with us.

Using *must* instead of *had to* to form the past tense:

Incorrect	She **must** work yesterday.
Correct	She **had to** work yesterday.

Forgetting to change *can* to *could* to form the past negative:

Incorrect	Last night, I **can**not sleep.
Correct	Last night, I **could** not sleep.

Forgetting to use *have* with *could/should/would* to form the past tense:

Incorrect	Tara **should** called last night.
Correct	Tara **should have** called last night.

Using *will* instead of *would* to express a preference in the present tense:

Incorrect	I **will** like to travel.
Correct	I **would** like to travel.

Using -s on verbs that follow modals:

Incorrect	John can speaks French.
Correct	John can speak French.

PRACTICE 7   Using Modal Verbs

Fill in the appropriate modal verbs in the sentences below.

Example: Lilly __would__ like to help the homeless.

1. What _____ she do?

2. First, she _____ find out what programs exist in her community.

3. For example, there _____ be a chapter of Habitat for Humanity.

4. Religious organizations _____ have started soup kitchens.

5. If she _____ find anything in her community, she should contact a national organization, such as the National Coalition for the Homeless.

PRACTICE 8   Using Correct Tense

Fill in each blank with the correct form of the verb in parentheses, adding helping verbs as needed. Refer to the verb charts if you need help.

Example: __Have__ you __heard__ (hear) of volcano boarding?

1 In a November 5, 2002, article in *National Geographic Today*, Zoltan Istvan _____ (report) on a new sport: volcano boarding. 2 Istvan first _____ (get) the idea in 1995, when he _____ (sail) past Mt. Yasur, an active volcano on an island off the coast of Australia. 3 For centuries, Mt. Yasur _____ (have) the reputation of being a dangerous volcano. 4 For example, it regularly _____ (spit) out lava bombs. 5 These large molten rocks _____ often _____ (strike) visitors on the head.

6 There is a village at the base of Mt. Yasur. 7 When Istvan arrived with his snowboard, the villagers _____ not _____ (know) what to think.

8 He _____ (make) his way to the volcano, _____ (hike) up the highest peak, and rode his board all the way down. 9 After he _____ (reach) the bottom, Istvan admitted that volcano boarding is more difficult than snowboarding. 10 Luckily, no lava bombs _____ (fall) from the sky, although the volcano _____ (erupt) seconds before his descent. 11 Istvan hopes that this new sport _____ (become) popular with snowboarders around the world.

Gerunds and Infinitives

A **gerund** is a verb form that ends in *-ing* and acts as a noun. An **infinitive** is a verb form that is preceded by the word *to*. Gerunds and infinitives cannot be the main verbs in sentences; each sentence must have another word that is the main verb.

Gerund   Mike loves **swimming**.

[*Loves* is the main verb, and *swimming* is a gerund.]

Infinitive   Mike loves **to run**.

[*Loves* is the main verb, and *to run* is an infinitive.]

Note: How do you decide whether to use a gerund or an infinitive after the main verb in a sentence? The decision depends on the main verb. A good ESL dictionary will include information about using gerunds and infinitives, or you may refer to the charts on pages 524–525.

Verbs That Can Be Followed by Either a Gerund or an Infinitive

begin	hate	remember	try
continue	like	start	
forget	love	stop	

Sometimes, using a gerund or an infinitive after one of these verbs results in the same meaning.

Gerund   Joan likes **playing** the piano.

Infinitive   Joan likes **to play** the piano.

Other times, however, the meaning changes depending on whether you use a gerund or an infinitive.

Infinitive   <u>Carla</u> <u>stopped</u> **helping** me.

[This wording means Carla no longer helps me.]

Gerund   <u>Carla</u> <u>stopped</u> **to help** me.

[This wording means Carla stopped what she was doing and helped me.]

Verbs That Are Followed by a Gerund

admit	discuss	keep	risk
avoid	enjoy	miss	suggest
consider	finish	practice	
deny	imagine	quit	

The <u>politician</u> <u>risked</u> losing her supporters.
<u>Sophia</u> <u>considered</u> quitting her job.

Verbs That Are Followed by an Infinitive

agree	decide	need	refuse
ask	expect	offer	want
beg	fail	plan	
choose	hope	pretend	
claim	manage	promise	

<u>Aunt Sally</u> <u>wants</u> to help.
<u>Cal</u> <u>hopes</u> to become a millionaire.

Do not use the base form of a verb when you need a gerund or an infinitive.

Incorrect base form (used as subject)	Swim is my favorite activity.
Correct gerund form (used as subject)	Swimming is my favorite activity.
Incorrect base form (following the main verb)	I need stop at the store.
Correct infinitive form (following the main verb)	I need to stop at the store.

Incorrect base form (following the main verb)	My instructor enjoys tell jokes.
Correct gerund form (following the main verb)	My instructor enjoys telling jokes.

> **PRACTICE 9**   **Using Gerunds and Infinitives**
>
> Read the paragraphs, and fill in the blanks with either a gerund or an infinitive as appropriate.
>
> **Example: If you want __*to be*__ (be) an actor, be aware that the profession is not all fun and glamour.**

1 When you were a child, did you pretend _____ (be) famous people? 2 Did you imagine _____ (play) roles in movies or on television? 3 Do you like _____ (take) part in plays? 4 If so, you might want _____ (make) a career out of acting.

5 Be aware of some drawbacks, however. 6 If you hate _____ (work) with others, acting may not be the career for you. 7 Also, if you do not enjoy _____ (repeat) the same lines over and over, you will find acting dull. 8 You must practice _____ (speak) lines to memorize them. 9 Despite these drawbacks, you will gain nothing if you refuse _____ (try). 10 Anyone who hopes _____ (become) an actor has a chance at succeeding through hard work and determination.

e Log in to **macmillanhighered.com/rrw** and look for LearningCurve > Articles and Nouns for Multilingual Writers

Articles

Articles announce a noun. English uses only three articles—*a*, *an*, and *the*—and the same articles are used for both masculine and feminine nouns.

Definite and Indefinite Articles

The is a **definite article** and is used before a specific person, place, or thing. *A* and *an* are **indefinite articles** and are used with a person, place, or thing whose specific identity is not known.

Definite article   *The* car crashed into the building.

[A specific car crashed into the building.]

Indefinite article   *A* car crashed into the building.

[Some car—we don't know which one exactly—crashed into the building.]

When the word following the article begins with a vowel (*a, e, i, o, u*), use *an* instead of *a*.

An **o**ld car crashed into the building.

Note: Pay attention to words that begin with *u*. When the *u* is pronounced like the consonant *y*, use the article *a*:

My mother works at a university.

When the *u* sounds like a vowel, use the article *an*:

Do you need an umbrella?

Refer to the dictionary if you are not sure how to pronounce the *u* at the beginning of a word.

To use the correct article, you need to know what count and noncount nouns are.

Count and Noncount Nouns

Count nouns name things that can be counted, and they can be made plural, usually by adding *-s* or *-es*. **Noncount nouns** name things that cannot be counted, and they are usually singular. They cannot be made plural.

Count noun / singular   I got a **ticket** for the concert.

Count noun / plural   I got two **tickets** for the concert.

Noncount noun   The Internet has all kinds of **information**.

[You would not say, *The Internet has all kinds of informations*.]

Note: The following is a brief list of several count and noncount nouns. All English nouns are either count or noncount. Most ESL dictionaries include this information in entries for nouns.

Count	Noncount	
apple / apples	beauty	milk
chair / chairs	flour	money
dollar / dollars	furniture	postage
letter / letters	grass	poverty
smile / smiles	grief	rain
tree / trees	happiness	rice
	health	salt
	homework	sand
	honey	spaghetti
	information	sunlight
	jewelry	thunder
	mail	wealth

Use the chart that follows to determine when to use *a, an, the,* or no article.

Articles with Count and Noncount Nouns

Count nouns Singular	Article used
Specific	*the*
	I want to read **the book** on taxes that you recommended.
	[The sentence refers to one particular book: the one that was recommended.]
	I cannot stay in **the sun** very long.
	[There is only one sun.]
Not specific	*a* or *an*
	I want to read **a book** on taxes.
	[It could be any book on taxes.]
Plural	
Specific	*the*
	I enjoyed **the books** that we read.
	[The sentence refers to a particular group of books: the ones that we read.]

Not specific	no article or *some*
	I usually enjoy books.
	[The sentence refers to books in general.]
	She found some books.
	[I do not know which books she found.]

Noncount nouns	Article used
Singular	

Specific	*the*
	I put away the food that we bought.
	[The sentence refers to particular food: the food that we bought.]
Not specific	no article or *some*
	There is food all over the kitchen.
	[The reader does not know what food the sentence refers to.]
	Give some food to the neighbors.
	[The sentence refers to an indefinite quantity of food.]

PRACTICE 10   **Using Articles Correctly**

Fill in the correct article (*a, an,* or *the*) in each of the following sentences. If no article is needed, write "no article."

Example: Children who go to __*no article*__ preschool have several advantages over those who do not.

1. First, _____ good preschool will help students learn about letters and numbers.

2. These skills can make _____ big difference when preschoolers move on to kindergarten.

3. Research shows that _____ prereading and math skills of children who have attended preschool are stronger than those of kids who have not.

4. Additionally, preschoolers learn everyday information, such as _____ names of the days of the week.

5. But _____ biggest advantage of preschool is that it teaches social skills.

e Log in to **macmillanhighered .com/rrw** and look for LearningCurve > Prepositions for Multilingual Students

Prepositions

A **preposition** is a word (such as *of, above, between,* or *about*) that connects a noun, pronoun, or verb with information about it. The correct preposition to use is often determined by common practice rather than by the preposition's actual meaning.

Prepositions after Adjectives

Adjectives are often followed by prepositions. Here are some common examples.

afraid of	full of	scared of
ashamed of	happy about	sorry about/sorry for
aware of	interested in	tired of
confused by	proud of	
excited about	responsible for	

Peri is afraid ~~to~~ walking alone.
                    ^of

We are happy ~~of~~ Dino's promotion.
                  ^about

Note: It is not obvious which preposition occurs with which adjective. Check an ESL dictionary to make sure you are using the correct preposition with an adjective.

Prepositions after Verbs

Many verbs consist of a verb plus a preposition. In ESL dictionaries, these verbs are called **phrasal verbs**. The meaning of the combination is not usually the meaning that the verb and the preposition would each have on their own. Often, the meaning of the verb changes completely depending on which preposition is used with it.

You must **take out** the trash.   [*take out* = bring to a different location]

You must **take in** the exciting sights of New York City.   [*take in* = observe]

Here are a few common verb/preposition combinations.

call in (telephone)	You can *call in* your order.
call off (cancel)	They *called off* the party.
call on (ask for a response)	The teacher always *calls on* me.
drop in (visit)	*Drop in* the next time you are around.
drop off (leave behind)	Juan will *drop off* the car for service.
drop out (quit)	Many students *drop out* of school.
fight against (combat)	He tried to *fight against* the proposal.
fight for (defend)	We will *fight for* our rights.
fill out (complete)	Please *fill out* the form.
fill up (make full)	Do not *fill up* with junk food.
find out (discover)	Did you *find out* the answer?
give up (forfeit)	Do not *give up* your chance to succeed.
go by (visit, pass by)	I may *go by* the store on my way home.
go over (review)	Please *go over* your notes before the test.
grow up (mature)	All children *grow up*.
hand in (submit)	Please *hand in* your homework.
lock up (secure)	*Lock up* the apartment before leaving.
look up (check)	*Look up* the meaning in the dictionary.
pick out (choose)	*Pick out* a good apple.
pick up (take or collect)	Please *pick up* some drinks.
put off (postpone)	Do not *put off* starting your paper.
sign in (register)	*Sign in* when you arrive.
sign out (borrow)	You can *sign out* a book from the library.
sign up (register)	I want to *sign up* for the contest.
think about (consider)	Simon *thinks about* moving.
turn in (submit)	Please *turn in* your homework.

Separable vs. Inseparable Phrasal Verbs

Some verb/preposition pairs can be separated by an object.

Correct (verb + preposition not separated)   I had to fill out a form.

Correct (verb + preposition separated)   I had to fill a form out.

Other verb/preposition pairs cannot be separated by an object.

Correct (verb + preposition not separated)   We need to go over your notes.

Incorrect (verb + preposition separated)   We need to go your notes over.

Note: Use an ESL dictionary to identify the meaning of phrasal verbs and to determine whether the verb and preposition are separable or inseparable.

PRACTICE 11   **Editing Paragraphs for Preposition Problems**

Edit the following paragraphs to make sure the correct prepositions are used.

Example: At some point, many people think ~~out~~ ^{about} having a more flexible work schedule.

1 If they are responsible in child care, they might want to get home from work earlier than usual. 2 Or they might be interested on having one workday a week free for studying or other activities. 3 Employees shouldn't be afraid to asking a supervisor about the possibility of a flexible schedule. 4 For instance, the supervisor might be very willing to allow the employee to do 40 hours of work in four days instead of five days. 5 Or a worker who wants to leave a little earlier than usual might give out half of a lunch hour to do so.

6 The wide use of computers also allows for flexibility. 7 For example, busy parents might use their laptops to work from home a day or two a week. 8 They can stay in touch with the office by e-mailing supervisors or coworkers, or they might call on.

9 Often, employers who allow more flexibility find in that they benefit, too. 10 Workers are happy on having more control over their own time; therefore, they are less stressed out and more productive than they would have been on a fixed schedule.

Chapter Review

1. What is a pronoun? _____

   What are the three types of pronouns in English? _____

   _____

2. Rewrite this sentence in the simple past and the simple future:

   Melinda picks flowers every morning.

   Past: _____

   Future: _____

3. Rewrite this sentence so that it uses the perfect tense correctly:

   They have call an ambulance. _____

4. Using the progressive tenses, first rewrite this sentence as a question; then, re-write the question in the past tense and in the future tense:

   Chris is learning Spanish.

   Question: _____

   Past: _____

   Future: _____

5. Rewrite these sentences so that they use the modal verb correctly:

   Jennifer should to help her mother. _____

   Yesterday, I cannot work. _____

6. What is a gerund? _____

   Write a sentence with a gerund in it. _____

   _____

7. What is an infinitive? _____

   Write a sentence with an infinitive in it. _____

   _____

8. Give an example of a count noun. _____ Give an example of a non-

   count noun. _____

9. What is a preposition? _____

   _____

   Write a sentence using a preposition. _____

   _____

Chapter Test

Circle the correct choice for each of the following items.

1. Choose the correct word(s) to fill in the blank.

   You need _____ me if you have a problem.

   a. telling   b. to tell   c. told

2. Choose the sentence that has no errors.

   a. I have been written to my congressman three times, but I have never heard back from him.

   b. I have been writing to my congressman three times, but I have never heard back from him.

   c. I have written to my congressman three times, but I have never heard back from him.

3. Choose the sentence that has no errors.

   a. I walked five miles yesterday.

   b. I walk five miles yesterday.

   c. I walking five miles yesterday.

4. Choose the correct word(s) to fill in the blank.

   In January, they _____ to vacation in Florida.

   a. going   b. is going   c. are going

5. If an underlined portion of this sentence is incorrect, select the revision that fixes it. If the sentence is correct as written, choose d.

    Pasquale might to get a Job at his father's construction business.
    $\qquad\qquad$ A $\qquad\qquad\qquad$ B $\qquad\qquad$ C

    a.   might
    b.   on
    c.   constructing
    d.   No change is necessary

6. Choose the correct word to fill in the blank.

    Elena tells the funniest jokes. _____ always makes me laugh.

    a.   Her
    b.   Him
    c.   She

7. Choose the sentence that is in the correct order.

    a.   One pound of chocolate I ate last week.
    b.   I ate one pound of chocolate last week.
    c.   Chocolate one pound I ate last week.

8. If an underlined portion of this sentence is incorrect, select the revision that fixes it. If the sentence is correct as written, choose d.

    The healths of our employees is very important.
    $\quad$ A $\quad$ B $\qquad\qquad\qquad\quad$ C

    a.   A
    b.   health
    c.   were
    d.   No change is necessary

9. Choose the sentence that has no errors.

    a.   Was it snowing when you got to the mountain?
    b.   Snowing it was when you got to the mountain?
    c.   When you got to the mountain, snowing it was?

10. Choose the correct word to fill in the blank.

    Because it rained, we called _____ the picnic.

    a.   on
    b.   in
    c.   off

Part 5
Word Use

26

Vocabulary and Word Choice:

Finding the Right Word

Understanding the Importance of Building Vocabulary and Choosing Words Carefully

In conversation, you show much of your meaning through facial expressions, tone of voice, and gestures. In reading and writing, however, you have only the words on the page to help you understand a point or make a point, so you need to expand your vocabulary and choose your words carefully. Writers who use vague or inappropriate words may confuse their readers; readers who do not recognize specific words used by a writer may not understand what they are reading.

Four strategies will help you build your vocabulary for reading and writing: recognizing context clues, understanding word parts, using a dictionary, and using a thesaurus.

Context Clues

When you are reading, you may encounter a word you do not know. Some readings may include definitions for new words in footnotes, but sometimes you can discover what the word means without using the footnotes or a dictionary. Instead, you can use clues in the context around the word to find the meaning. Consider the following paragraph from Stephanie Ericsson's essay "The Ways We Lie":

> We all put up facades to one degree or another. When I put on a suit to go to see a client, I feel as though I am putting on another face, obeying the expectation that serious businesspeople wear suits rather than sweatpants. But I'm a writer. Normally, I get up, get the kid off to school, and sit at my computer in my pajamas until four in the afternoon. When I answer the phone, the caller thinks I'm wearing a suit (although the UPS man knows better).

Log in to **macmillanhighered** **.com/rrw** and look for LearningCurve > Word Choice and Appropriate Language

A reader who does not know the word *facade* can guess the meaning of the word by looking at the next sentence, where Ericsson mentions "putting on another face." A facade is a mask, or a "false front." Ericsson gives her reader clues to the definition of this term through her description and examples. Good readers make a habit of using context clues to guess the meanings of new words.

Word Parts

Another strategy readers and writers use to acquire new vocabulary is understanding word parts. Many words in English can be divided into recognizable parts: a root, which provides the basic meaning of the word, and either a prefix or a suffix. A prefix is added at the beginning of a word and changes the meaning of the word (see Chapter 12). A suffix is added to the end of a word and can change either the meaning or the part of speech of the word (see Chapter 7).

You may already know some common roots, such as *bene* (good), *bio* (life), or *scope* (seeing). You find these roots in words like *beneficial*, *biology*, and *microscope*. You may also recognize common prefixes such as *un-* (not) and *pre-* (before) and suffixes such as *-tion* (a noun suffix) and *-ly* (an adverb suffix). Understanding word parts can help you understand new words you encounter.

Dictionary

Dictionaries give you all kinds of useful information about words: spelling, division of words into syllables, pronunciation, parts of speech, other forms of words, definitions, and examples of use. Following is a sample dictionary entry.

Spelling and end-of-line division   Pronunciation   Parts of speech   Other forms

Definitions

Example of use

con • crete (kon´krēt, kong´-, kon-krēt´), *adj., n., v.* **-cret • ed,** **-cret • ing,** *adj.* **1.** constituting an actual thing or instance; real; perceptible; substantial: *concrete proof.* **2.** pertaining to or concerned with realities or actual instances rather than abstractions; particular as opposed to general: *concrete proposals.* **3.** referring to an actual substance or thing, as opposed to an abstract quality: The words *cat, water,* and *teacher* are concrete, whereas the words *truth, excellence,* and *adulthood* are abstract.

—*Random House Webster's College Dictionary*

TIPS FOR USING A DICTIONARY WHEN YOU ARE READING

Use a dictionary when you are reading and make vocabulary a part of your annotating process. (For more information on how to annotate, see Chapter 3.)

- Don't always use the first definition given for a word; look to see what makes the most sense in the context.
- Make a quick note of the meaning and part of speech in your annotations.
- Develop a system for reviewing and using vocabulary that you encounter while reading.
  - Consider keeping a vocabulary journal or an online list of new words.
  - Note the definition, the part of speech, and the sentence and source where you found the word.
  - Create a sentence of your own using the word.
  - Look for ways to incorporate new vocabulary into your own writing.

Thesaurus

A thesaurus gives **synonyms** (words that have the same meaning) for the word you look up. Use a thesaurus when you cannot find the right word for what you mean. Be careful, however, to choose a word that has the precise meaning you intend. Following is a sample thesaurus entry.

> **Concrete**, *adj.* 1. Particular, specific, single, certain, special, unique, sole, peculiar, individual, separate, isolated, distinct, exact, precise, direct, strict, minute; definite, plain, evident, obvious; pointed, emphasized; restrictive, limiting, limited, well-defined, clear-cut, fixed, finite; determining, conclusive, decided.
>
> —J. I. Rodale, *The Synonym Finder*

Avoiding Four Common Word-Choice Problems

Four common problems with word choice may make it hard for readers to understand your point.

Vague and Abstract Words

Vague and abstract words are too general. They do not give your readers a clear idea of what you mean. Here are some common vague and abstract words.

e Log in to
macmillanhighered
.com/rrw and look for
Additional Grammar
Exercises > Using the
Right Word

Vague and Abstract Words

a lot	cute	nice	stuff
amazing	dumb	OK (okay)	terrible
awesome	good	old	thing
bad	great	pretty	very
beautiful	happy	sad	whatever
big	huge	small	young

When you see one of these words or another general word in your writing, replace it with a concrete or more specific word or description. A **concrete** word names something that can be seen, heard, felt, tasted, or smelled. A **specific** word names a particular person or quality. Compare these two sentences:

Vague and abstract   An old man crossed the street.

Concrete and specific   An eighty-seven-year-old priest stumbled along Main Street.

The first version is too general to be interesting. The second version creates a clear, strong image. Some words are so vague that it is best to avoid them altogether.

For more information on
recognizing concrete and
specific terms in reading,
see Chapter 7, page 125,
and Chapter 8, pages
145–146.

Vague and abstract   It is awesome.

[This sentence is neither concrete nor specific.]

PRACTICE 1   **Avoiding Vague and Abstract Words**

In the following sentences, underline any words that are vague or abstract. Then, edit each sentence by replacing the vague or abstract words with concrete, specific ones. You may invent details or base them on brief online research into physician assistant careers.

Example: It would be cool to be a physician assistant (PA). _It would be_
rewarding to be a physician assistant (PA).

1. I am drawn to this career because it would let me do neat things for

    others. _____

    _____

2. I know that becoming a PA would require tons of work. _____

    _____

3. Also, each day in the classroom or clinic would be long. _____

    _____

4. Furthermore, I would have to be able to tolerate some rough sights.

    _____

    _____

5. However, I would learn a lot. _____

    _____

Slang

Slang, informal and casual language, should be used only in informal situations. Avoid it when you write, especially for college classes or at work. Use language that is appropriate for your audience and purpose.

Slang	Edited
S'all good.	Everything is going well.
Dawg, I don't deserve this grade.	Professor, I don't deserve this grade.

PRACTICE 2   Avoiding Slang

In the following sentences, underline any slang words. Then, edit each sentence by replacing the slang with language appropriate for a formal audience and purpose. Imagine that you are writing to a boss where you work.

Example: Yo, Randy, I need to talk at you for a minute.
(Hello)   (to)

1. That reference letter you wrote for me was really awesome sweet.

2. I am grateful because the one my English instructor did for me sucked.

3. She said that I thought I was all that, but that is not true.

4. I would be down with doing a favor for you in return if you need it.

5. Maybe you and I could hang sometime one of these weekends?

Wordy Language

People sometimes use too many words to express their ideas. They may think that using more words will make them sound smart, but too many words can weaken a writer's point.

Wordy	I am not interested *at this point in time.*
Edited	I am not interested now.

[The phrase *at this point in time* uses five words to express what could be said in one word: *now.*]

Common Wordy Expressions

Wordy	Edited
As a result of	Because
Due to the fact that	Because
In spite of the fact that	Although
It is my opinion that	I think (*or just make the point*)
In the event that	If
The fact of the matter is that	(*Just state the point.*)
A great number of	Many
At that time	Then
In this day and age	Now
At this point in time	Now
In this paper I will show that	(*Just make the point; do not announce it.*)
Utilize	Use

PRACTICE 3   **Avoiding Wordy Language**

In the following sentences, underline the wordy or repetitive language. Then, edit each sentence to make it more concise. Some sentences may contain more than one wordy phrase.

Example: Sugar substitutes are a popular diet choice for people
                                                                                    reduce
        of all ages when they are searching for ways to cut down
                                              each day   ^
        on all the calories they ingest on a daily basis.
                                          ^

1. It is a well-known fact that dieting is difficult for most people.

2. Due to the fact that people are trying to cut calories, sugar substitutes are used in sodas, snacks, and other products.

3. The fact of the matter is that these substitutes provide a sweet taste, but without the calories of sugar or honey.

4. A great number of researchers have stated at this time that such substitutes are not necessarily safe or healthy to use in large quantities.

5. Some of the current experts on the matter are of the opinion that sugar substitutes can cause cancer, allergies, and other serious health problems.

Clichés

Clichés are phrases used so often that people no longer pay attention to them. To get your point across and to get your readers' attention, replace clichés with fresh and specific language.

Clichés	Edited
I cannot *make ends meet*.	I do not have enough money to live on.
My uncle *worked his way up the corporate ladder*.	My uncle started as a shipping clerk but ended up as a regional vice president.
This roll is as *hard as a rock*.	This roll is so hard I could bounce it.

Common Clichés

as big as a house	few and far between	spoiled brat
as light as a feather	hell on earth	starting from scratch
better late than never	last but not least	sweating blood/bullets
break the ice	no way on earth	too little, too late
crystal clear	110 percent	24/7
a drop in the bucket	playing with fire	work like a dog
easier said than done		

> **PRACTICE 4**   **Avoiding Clichés**

In the following sentences, underline the clichés. Then, edit each sentence by replacing the clichés with fresh and specific language.

Example: Riding a bicycle 100 miles a day can be ~~hell on earth~~ unless
you are willing to ~~give 110 percent~~.

excruciating
work extremely hard

1. You have to persuade yourself to sweat blood and work like a dog for up to ten hours.

2. There's no way on earth you can do it without extensive training.

3. Staying on your bike until the bitter end, of course, is easier said than done.

4. It is important to keep the fire in your belly and keep your goal of finishing the race crystal clear in your mind.

5. No matter how long it takes you to cross the finish line, remind yourself that it's better late than never.

A final note: Language that favors one gender over another or that assumes that only one gender performs a certain role is called *sexist*. Such language should be avoided.

Sexist   A doctor should politely answer *his* patients' questions.

[Not all doctors are male, as suggested by the pronoun *his*.]

Revised   A doctor should politely answer *his or her* patients' questions. *Doctors* should politely answer *their* patients' questions.

[The first revision changes *his* to *his or her* to avoid sexism. The second revision changes the subject to a plural noun (*Doctors*) so that a genderless pronoun (*their*) can be used. Usually, it is preferable to avoid *his or her*.]

Edit for Word Choice

Use the chart on page 549, "Editing for Word Choice," to help you complete the practice exercise in this section and edit your own writing.

PRACTICE 5   **Editing Paragraphs for Word Choice**

Find and edit six examples of vague or abstract language, slang, wordy language, or clichés in the following paragraphs.

1 Imagine spending almost two weeks living in the coolest home in the world. 2 That is what scientist Lloyd Godson did when he lived at the bottom of a lake in Australia for thirteen days. 3 While there is no way on earth I would want to do that, it sure sounds fascinating.

4 Godson's home was an 8-by-11-foot-long yellow steel box that he dubbed the BioSUB. 5 His air supply came from the algae plants growing inside the BioSUB. 6 Divers brought him food, water, and other junk through a manhole built in the bottom of his underwater home. 7 To keep busy, he rode on an exercise bicycle, which created electricity for him to recharge his laptop and run the lights for his plants. 8 He used his computer to talk to students all over the world and to watch movies.

9 Godson paid for this experiment with money he had won in the "Live Your Dream" contest. 10 At this point in time, I have to say that for most people, the BioSUB home would be less appealing than a regular, above-ground room, apartment, or house. 11 Indeed, by the time his two weeks were over, Godson was ready to come up, feel the sunshine and wind on his face again, and "smell the roses."

Chapter Review

1. What are four strategies you can use to build your vocabulary? _____

    _____

2. What are four common word-choice problems? _____

    _____

3. Replace vague and abstract words with _____ and _____ words.

4. When is it appropriate to use slang in college writing or in writing at work?

_____

5. Give two examples of wordy expressions. _____

_____

Chapter Test

For each of the following items, choose the word(s) or sentence that is specific and appropriate for a formal (academic or work) audience.

1. Choose the item that uses words most effectively.
    a. My dorm is just an OK place to study.
    b. My dorm is so noisy and full of activity that it is difficult to study there.
    c. My dorm is not where I go when I want to study.

2. Choose the best words to fill in the blank.

    I am afraid that all your hard work did not _____.
    a. solve our problem   b. do the trick   c. do it for us

3. Choose the best word(s) to fill in the blank.

    Kevin was extremely _____ about his new job.
    a. juiced   b. pumped   c. enthusiastic

4. Choose the item that uses words most effectively.
    a. I like that thing Nikki does whenever she scores a goal.
    b. I like the way Nikki goes nuts whenever she scores a goal.
    c. I like the way Nikki does a backflip whenever she scores a goal.

5. Choose the item that uses words most effectively.
    a. In the event that you are ever in River City, stop by to see me.
    b. If you are ever in River City, stop by to see me.
    c. If by chance you are ever in River City, stop by to see me.

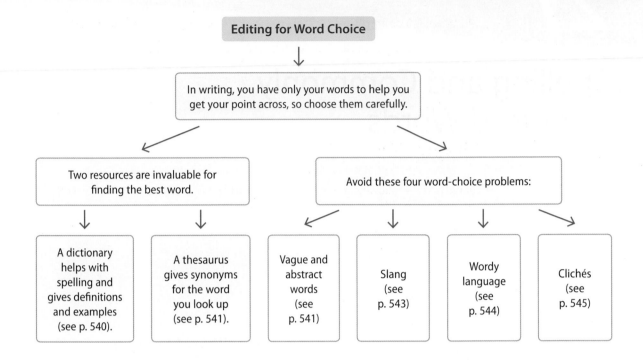

27

Spelling and Commonly Confused Words

Finding and Correcting Spelling Mistakes

Spelling is a challenge for many people, including some who are extremely intelligent. Unfortunately, spelling errors are easy for readers to spot, and those mistakes make a bad impression. Good writers learn strategies for finding and correcting spelling mistakes and avoiding commonly misspelled and confused words. This chapter introduces some of these techniques.

Use a Dictionary

When proofreading your papers, consult a dictionary whenever you are unsure about the spelling of a word. *Checking a dictionary is the single most important thing you can do to improve your spelling.*

Use a Spell Checker—with Caution

Use a **spell checker** after you have completed a piece of writing but before you print it out. This word-processing tool finds and highlights a word that may be misspelled, suggests other spellings, and gives you the opportunity to change the spelling of the word.

However, you should never rely on a spell checker to do your editing for you. Because a spell checker ignores anything that it recognizes as a word, it will not help you find words that are misused or misspelled words that are also words.

For example, a spell checker will not recognize an error if you make a mistake with any of the commonly confused words listed later in this chapter, such as *to, two,* and *too*.

Use Proofreading Techniques

Use some of the following proofreading techniques to focus on the spelling of one word at a time. Try them all. Then, decide which ones work best for you.

- Print out your paper before proofreading. (Many writers find it easier to detect errors on paper than on a computer screen.)
- Put a piece of paper under the line that you are reading.
- Proofread your paper backward, one word at a time.
- Print out a version of your paper that looks noticcably different: Make the words larger, make the margins larger, triple-space the lines, or make all these changes.
- Read your paper aloud. This strategy will help you if you tend to leave words out.
- Have someone else read your paper aloud. You may hear where you have used a word wrong or left a word out.

Make a Personal Spelling List

Set aside a section of your course notebook or learning journal for your spelling list. Every time you edit a paper, write down the words that you misspelled. Every couple of weeks, go back to your spelling list to see if your problem words have changed. Are you misspelling fewer words in each paper?

For each word on your list, create a memory aid or silly phrase to help you remember the correct spelling. For example, if you often misspell *a lot*, you could remember that "*a lot* is a lot of words."

Strategies for Becoming a Better Speller

Here are three good strategies for becoming a better speller.

Master Commonly Confused Words

The last part of this chapter covers twenty-seven sets of words that are commonly confused because they sound similar, such as *write* and *right*. Mastering this list will help you avoid many spelling mistakes.

Learn Six Spelling Rules

If you can remember the following six rules, you can correct many of the spelling errors in your writing.

First, here is a quick review of vowels and consonants.

Vowels:	*a, e, i, o,* and *u*
Consonants:	*b, c, d, f, g, h, j, k, l, m, n, p, q, r, s, t, v, w, x,* and *z*

e Log in to **macmillanhighered .com/rrw** and look for Additional Grammar Exercises > Using the Six Spelling Rules

The letter *y* can be either a vowel or a consonant. It is a vowel when it sounds like the *y* in *fly* or *hungry.* It is a consonant when it sounds like the *y* in *yellow.*

Rule 1. "*I* before *e,* except after *c.* Or when sounded like *a,* as in *neighbor* or *weigh.*"

Many people repeat this rhyme to themselves as they decide whether a word is spelled with an *ie* or an *ei.*

pie**ce** (*i* before *e*)

re**ce**ive (except after *c*)

eight (sounds like *a*)

Exceptions: *either, neither, foreign, height, seize, society, their, weird*

Rule 2. **Drop the final *e*** when adding an ending that begins with a vowel.

hop**e** + ing = hoping

imagin**e** + ation = imagination

Keep the final *e* when adding an ending that begins with a consonant.

achiev**e** + ment = achievement

definit**e** + ly = definitely

Exceptions: *argument, awful, judgment, simply, truly,* and others

Rule 3. When adding an ending to a word that ends in *y,* **change the *y* to *i*** when a consonant comes before the *y.*

lone**ly** + est = loneliest   apolo**gy** + ize = apologize happy + er = happier   likely + hood = likelihood

Do not change the *y* when a vowel comes before the *y*.

boy + ish = boyish   survey + or = surveyor

pay + ment = payment   buy + er = buyer

Exceptions:

1. When adding *-ing* to a word ending in *y*, always keep the *y*, even if a consonant comes before it: study + ing = studying.

2. Other exceptions include *daily, dryer, said*, and *paid*.

Rule 4. When adding an ending that starts with a vowel to a one-syllable word, follow these rules.

Double the final consonant only if the word ends with a consonant-vowel-consonant.

trap + ed = trapped   knit + ed = knitted

drip + ed = dripped   fat + er = fatter

Do not double the final consonant if the word ends with some other combination.

Vowel-vowel-consonant	Vowel-consonant-consonant
clean + est = cleanest	slick + er = slicker
poor + er = poorer	teach + er = teacher
clear + ed = cleared	last + ed = lasted

Rule 5. When adding an ending that starts with a vowel to a word with two or more syllables, follow these rules.

Double the final consonant only if the word ends with a consonant-vowel-consonant and the stress is on the last syllable.

submit + ing = submitting

prefer + ed = preferred

Do not double the final consonant in other cases.

understand + ing = understanding

offer + ed = offered

Rule 6. Add -s to most nouns to form the plural, including words that end in *o* preceded by a vowel.

Most words	Words that end in vowel plus *o*
book + **s** = book**s**	vid**eo** + **s** = video**s**
college + **s** = college**s**	ster**eo** + **s** = stereo**s**

Add -*es* to words that end in *o* preceded by a consonant and words that end in *s, sh, ch,* or *x.*

Words that end in consonant plus *o*	Words that end in *s, sh, ch,* or *x*
pota**to** + **es** = potato**es**	clas**s** + **es** = class**es**
he**ro** + **es** = hero**es**	pus**h** + **es** = push**es**
	ben**ch** + **es** = bench**es**
	fa**x** + **es** = fax**es**

Exceptions When Forming Plurals

A **compound noun** is formed when two nouns are joined, with a hyphen (*in-law*), a space (*life vest*), or no space (*keyboard, stockpile*). Plurals of compound nouns are generally formed by adding an -*s* to the end of the last noun (*in-laws, life vests*) or to the end of the combined word (*keyboards, stockpiles*). Some hyphenated compound words such as *mother-in-law* or *hole-in-one* form plurals by adding an -*s* to the chief word (*mothers-in-law, holes-in-one*).

Some words form plurals in different ways, as in the list on the next page.

Different Types of Plurals

Singular	Plural	Singular	Plural
analysis	analyses	loaf	loaves
bacterium	bacteria	louse	lice
bison	bison	man	men
cactus	cacti	medium	media
calf	calves	mouse	mice
child	children	phenomenon	phenomena
deer	deer	roof	roofs
die	dice	sheep	sheep
focus	foci	shelf	shelves
foot	feet	thief	thieves
goose	geese	tooth	teeth
half	halves	vertebra	vertebrae
hoof	hooves	wife	wives
knife	knives	wolf	wolves
leaf	leaves	woman	women

Consult a List of Commonly Misspelled Words

Use a list like the one below as an easy reference to check your spelling.

One Hundred Commonly Misspelled Words

absence	convenient	harass	receive
achieve	cruelty	height	recognize
across	daughter	humorous	recommend
aisle	definite	illegal	restaurant
a lot	describe	immediately	rhythm
already	develop	independent	roommate
analyze	dictionary	interest	schedule
answer	different	jewelry	scissors
appetite	disappoint	judgment	secretary
argument	dollar	knowledge	separate
athlete	eighth	license	sincerely
awful	embarrass	lightning	sophomore
basically	environment	loneliness	succeed
beautiful	especially	marriage	successful
beginning	exaggerate	meant	surprise
believe	excellent/excellence	muscle	truly
business	exercise	necessary	until
calendar	fascinate	ninety	usually
career	February	noticeable	vacuum
category	finally	occasion	valuable
chief	foreign	perform	vegetable
column	friend	physically	weight
coming	government	prejudice	weird
commitment	grief	probably	writing
conscious	guidance	psychology	written

Using Commonly Confused Words Correctly

Study the different meanings and spellings of these twenty-seven sets of commonly confused words. Complete the sentence after each set of words, filling in each blank with the correct word.

A / AN / AND

a: used before a word that begins with a consonant sound

> *A* friend of mine just won the lottery.

an: used before a word that begins with a vowel sound

> *An* old friend of mine just won the lottery.

and: used to join two words

> My friend *and* I went out to celebrate.

A friend *and* I ate at *an* Italian restaurant.

Other lottery winners were _____ algebra teacher _____ bowling team.

ACCEPT / EXCEPT

accept: to agree to receive or admit (verb)

> I will *accept* the job offer.

except: but, other than

> All the stores are closed *except* the Quik-Stop.

I *accept* all the job conditions *except* the low pay.

Do not _____ gifts from clients _____ those who are also personal friends.

ADVICE / ADVISE

advice: opinion (noun)

> I would like your *advice* before I make a decision.

advise: to give an opinion (verb)

> Please *advise* me what to do.

Please *advise* me what to do; you always give me good *advice*.

If you do not like my _____ , please _____ me how to proceed.

AFFECT / EFFECT

affect: to make an impact on, to change something (verb)

> The whole city was *affected* by the hurricane.

effect: a result (noun)

> What *effect* will the hurricane have on the local economy?

Although the storm will have many negative *effects*, it will not *affect* the price of food.

The _____ of the disaster will _____ many people.

ARE / OUR

are: a form of the verb *be*

> The workers *are* about to go on strike.

our: a pronoun showing ownership

> The children played on *our* porch.

My relatives *are* staying at *our* house.

_____ new neighbors _____ moving in today.

BY / BUY / BYE

by: next to, before, or past

> Meet me *by* the entrance.
>
> Make sure the bill is paid *by* the fifteenth of the month.
>
> The motorcycle raced *by* me.

buy: to purchase (verb)

> I would like to *buy* a new laptop.

bye: an informal way to say *goodbye*

> "Bye, Grandma!"

Terence heard his wife say "*Bye*" as he ran out to go *buy* milk at the convenience store *by* the highway.

I said " _____ " from the window as we drove _____ our friends, who were

standing next to the house I wanted to _____ .

CONSCIENCE / CONSCIOUS

conscience: a personal sense of right and wrong (noun)

> Jake's *conscience* would not allow him to cheat.

conscious: awake, aware (adjective)

> The coma patient is now *conscious*.
>
> I am *conscious* that it is getting late.

The judge was *conscious* that the accused had acted according to his *conscience* even though he had broken the law.

The man said that he was not _____ that what he had done was illegal,

or his _____ would not have let him do it.

FINE / FIND

fine: of high quality (adjective); feeling well (adjective); a penalty for breaking a law (noun)

> This jackct is made of *fine* leather.
>
> After a day in bed, Jacob felt *fine*.
>
> The *fine* for exceeding the speed limit is $50.

find: to locate, to discover (verb)

> Did Clara *find* her glasses?

I *find* gardening to be a *fine* pastime.

Were you able to _____ a place to store your _____ jewelry?

ITS / IT'S

its: a pronoun showing ownership

> The dog chased *its* tail.

it's: a contraction of the words *it is*

> *It's* about time you got here.

It's very hard for a dog to keep *its* teeth clean.

_____ no surprise that the college raised _____ tuition.

KNEW / NEW / KNOW / NO

knew: understood; recognized (past tense of the verb *know*)

> I *knew* the answer, but I could not think of it.

new: unused, recent, or just introduced (adjective)

> The building has a *new* security code.

know: to understand; to have knowledge of (verb)

> I *know* how to bake bread.

no: used to form a negative

I have *no* idea what the answer is.

I never *knew* how much a *new* car costs.

The _____ teacher _____ many of her students already.

There is _____ way Tom could _____ where Celia is hiding.

I _____ that there is _____ cake left.

LOOSE / LOSE

loose: baggy; relaxed; not fixed in place (adjective)

In hot weather, people tend to wear *loose* clothing.

lose: to misplace; to forfeit possession of (verb)

Every summer, I *lose* about three pairs of sunglasses.

If the ring is too *loose* on your finger, you might *lose* it.

I _____ my patience with the _____ rules on Wall Street.

MIND / MINE

mind: to object to (verb); the thinking or feeling part of one's brain (noun)

Toby does not *mind* if I borrow his tool chest.

Estela has a good *mind,* but often she does not use it.

mine: belonging to me (pronoun); a source of ore and minerals (noun)

That coat is *mine.*

My uncle worked in a coal *mine* in West Virginia.

That writing problem of *mine* was on my *mind.*

If you do not _____ , the gloves you just took are _____ .

OF / HAVE

of: coming from; caused by; part of a group; made from (preposition)

The leader *of* the band played bass guitar.

have: to possess (verb; also used as a helping verb)

I *have* one more course to take before I graduate.

I should *have* started studying earlier.

The president *of* the company should *have* resigned.

Sidney could _____ been one _____ the winners.

Note: Do not use *of* after *would*, *should*, *could*, and *might*. Use *have* after those words (*would have*, *should have*).

PASSED / PAST

passed: went by or went ahead (past tense of the verb *pass*)

> We *passed* the hospital on the way to the airport.

past: time that has gone by (noun); gone by, over, just beyond (preposition)

> In the *past*, I was able to stay up all night and not be tired.

> I drove *past* the burning warehouse.

This *past* school year, I *passed* all my exams.

Trish _____ me as we ran _____ the one-mile marker.

PEACE / PIECE

peace: no disagreement; calm

> Could you quiet down and give me a little *peace*?

piece: a part of something larger

> May I have a *piece* of that pie?

The feuding families found *peace* after they sold the *piece* of land.

To keep the _____ , give your sister a _____ of candy.

PRINCIPAL / PRINCIPLE

principal: main (adjective); head of a school or leader of an organization (noun)

> Brush fires are the *principal* risk in the hills of California.

> Ms. Edwards is the *principal* of Memorial Elementary School.

> Corinne is a *principal* in the management consulting firm.

principle: a standard of beliefs or behaviors (noun)

> Although tempted, she held on to her moral *principles*.

The *principal* questioned the delinquent student's *principles*.

The _____ problem is that you want me to act against my _____ .

QUIET / QUITE / QUIT

quiet: soft in sound; not noisy (adjective)

> The library was *quiet*.

quite: completely; very (adverb)

> After cleaning all the windows, Alex was *quite* tired.

quit: to stop (verb)

She *quit* her job.

After the band *quit* playing, the hall was *quite* quiet.

If you would _____ shouting and be _____ , you would find that the scenery is _____ pleasant.

RIGHT / WRITE

right: correct; in a direction opposite from left (adjective)

> You definitely made the *right* choice.

> When you get to the stoplight, make a *right* turn.

write: to put words on paper (verb)

> Will you *write* your phone number for me?

Please *write* the *right* answer in the space provided.

You were _____ to _____ to the senator.

SET / SIT

set: a collection of something (noun); to place an object somewhere (verb)

> Paul has a complete *set* of Johnny Cash records.

> Please *set* the package on the table.

sit: to rest in a chair or other seatlike surface; to be located in a particular place

> I need to *sit* on the sofa for a few minutes.

> The shed *sits* between the house and the garden.

If I *sit* down now, I will not have time to *set* the plants outside.

Before you _____ on that chair, _____ the magazines on the floor.

SUPPOSE / SUPPOSED

suppose: to imagine or assume to be true

> I *suppose* you would like something to eat.

> *Suppose* you won a million dollars.

supposed: past tense of *suppose*; intended

> Karen *supposed* Thomas was late because of traffic.

I *suppose* you know that Rita was *supposed* to be home by 6:30.

I _____ you want to leave soon because we are _____ to arrive before the guests.

THAN / THEN

than: a word used to compare two or more people, places, or things

It is colder inside *than* outside.

then: at a certain time; next in time

I got out of the car and *then* realized the keys were still in it.

Clara ran more miles *than* she ever had before, and *then* she collapsed.

Back _____ , I smoked more _____ three packs a day.

THEIR / THERE / THEY'RE

their: a pronoun showing ownership

I borrowed *their* clippers to trim the hedges.

there: a word indicating location or existence

Just put the keys *there* on the desk.

There are too many lawyers.

they're: a contraction of the words *they are*

They're about to leave.

There is a car in *their* driveway, which indicates that *they're* home.

_____ beach house is empty except for the one week that _____ vacationing _____ .

THOUGH / THROUGH / THREW

though: however; nevertheless; in spite of (conjunction)

Though he is short, he plays great basketball.

through: finished with (adjective); from one side to the other (preposition)

I am *through* arguing with you.

The baseball went right *through* the window.

threw: hurled; tossed (past tense of the verb *throw*)

She *threw* the basketball.

Even *though* it was illegal, she *threw* the empty cup *through* the window onto the road.

_____ she did not really believe it would bring good luck, Jan _____ a penny _____ the air into the fountain.

TO / TOO / TWO

to: a word indicating a direction or movement (preposition); part of the infinitive form of a verb

Please give the message *to* Sharon.

It is easier *to* ask for forgiveness than *to* get permission.

too: also; more than enough; very (adverb)

I am tired *too*.

Dan ate *too* much and felt sick.

That dream was *too* real.

two: the number between one and three (noun)

The lab had only *two* computers.

They went *to* a restaurant and ordered *too* much food for *two* people.

When Marty went _____ pay for his meal, the cashier charged him _____ times, which was _____ bad.

USE / USED

use: to employ or put into service (verb)

How do you plan to *use* that blueprint?

used: past tense of the verb *use*. *Used to* can indicate a past fact or state, or it can mean "familiar with."

He *used* his lunch hour to do errands.

He *used* to go for a walk during his lunch hour.

She *used* to be a chef, so she knows how to *use* all kinds of kitchen gadgets.

She is also *used* to improvising in the kitchen.

Tom _____ the prize money to buy a boat; his family hoped he would _____ the money for his education, but Tom was _____ to getting his way.

WHO'S / WHOSE

who's: a contraction of the words *who is*

Who's at the door?

whose: a pronoun showing ownership

> *Whose* car is parked outside?

Who's the person *whose* car sank in the river?

The student _____ name is first on the list is the one _____ in charge.

YOUR / YOU'RE

your: a pronoun showing ownership

> Did you bring *your* wallet?

you're: a contraction of the words *you are*

> *You're* not telling me the whole story.

You're going to have *your* third exam tomorrow.

_____ teacher says that _____ good with numbers.

> **PRACTICE 1** **Editing Paragraphs for Commonly Confused Words**

Edit the following paragraphs to correct eighteen errors in word use.

1 More and more women are purchasing handguns, against the advise of law enforcement officers. 2 Few of these women are criminals or plan to commit crimes. 3 They no the risks of guns, and they except those risks. 4 They buy weapons primarily because their tired of feeling like victims. 5 They do not want to contribute too the violence in are society, but they also realize that women are the victims of violent attacks far to often. 6 Many women loose they're lives because they cannot fight off there attackers. 7 Some women have made a conscience decision to arm themselves for protection.

8 But does buying a gun make things worse rather then better? 9 Having a gun in you're house makes it three times more likely that someone will be killed there—and that someone is just as likely to be you or one of your children as a criminal. 10 Most young children cannot tell the difference between a real gun and a toy gun when they fine one. 11 Every

year, their are tragic examples of children who accidentally shoot and even kill other youngsters while they are playing with guns. 12 A mother who's children are injured while playing with her gun will never again think that a gun provides piece of mind. 13 Reducing the violence in are society may be a better solution.

Chapter Review

1. What are two important tools for finding and correcting spelling mistakes?

   _____

   _____

2. What three strategies can you use to become a better speller?

   _____

   _____

Chapter Test

In each sentence, fill in the blank with the correctly spelled word.

1. Your joining us for dinner is a pleasant _____ .
   a. suprise   b. surprize   c. surprise

2. When can I expect to _____ the package?
   a. recieve   b. receive   c. reeceive

3. The solar technology program is _____ many new students.
   a. admiting   b. admitting   c. addmitting

4. Colin's roommate is _____ weird.
   a. definately   b. definitely   c. definitly

5. After my doctor diagnosed my injury, she _____ me to a physical therapist.
   a. refered   b. reffered   c. referred

6. We will have to go in _____ cars.
   a. separate   b. seperate   c. sepurate

7. I have not seen her since _____ grade.

    a. eith   b. eigth   c. eighth

8. The date is circled on the _____ .

    a. callender   b. calendar   c. calander

9. Dana got her _____ last week.

    a. lisense   b. liscence   c. license

10. That ring is _____ .

    a. valuble   b. valuable   c. valueble

Part 6
Punctuation and Capitalization

Part 6
Punctuation and
Capitalization

28

Commas ,

Understand What Commas Do

e Log in to
macmillanhighered
.com/rrw and look
for LearningCurve >
Commas

Commas (,) are punctuation marks that help readers understand a sentence. Read aloud the following three sentences. How does the use of commas change the meaning?

No comma	When you call Sarah I will start cooking.
One comma	When you call Sarah, I will start cooking.
Two commas	When you call, Sarah, I will start cooking.

To get your intended meaning across to your readers, it is important that you understand when and how to use commas.

Using Commas Correctly

Commas between Items in a Series

Use commas to separate the items in a series (three or more items), including the last item in the series, which usually has *and* before it.

item , item , item , and item .

To get from South Dakota to Texas, we will drive through *Nebraska, Kansas,* and *Oklahoma.*

We can *sleep in the car, stay in a motel,* or *camp outside.*

As I drive, I see many beautiful sights, such as *mountains, plains,* and *prairies.*

Note: Writers do not always use a comma before the final item in a series. In college writing, however, it is best to include it.

Commas between Coordinate Adjectives

Coordinate adjectives are two or more adjectives that independently modify the same noun and are separated by commas.

> Conor ordered a *big, fat, greasy* burger.
> The diner food was *cheap, unhealthy,* and *delicious.*

Do *not* use a comma between the final adjective and the noun it describes.

| Incorrect | Joelle wore a *long, clingy, red,* dress. |
| Correct | Joelle wore a *long, clingy, red* dress. |

Cumulative adjectives describe the same noun but are not separated by commas because they form a unit that describes the noun. You can identify cumulative adjectives because separating them by *and* does not make any sense.

> The store is having its *last storewide clearance* sale.

[Putting *and* between *last* and *storewide* and between *storewide* and *clearance* would make an odd sentence: The store is having its *last* and *storewide* and *clearance* sale. The adjectives in the sentence are cumulative adjectives and should not be separated by commas.]

In summary:

- **Do** use commas to separate two or more **coordinate adjectives**.
- **Do not** use commas to separate **cumulative adjectives**.

PRACTICE 1   **Using Commas in Series and with Adjectives**

Edit the following sentences by underlining the items in the series and adding commas where they are needed. If a sentence is already correct, put a "C" next to it.

Example: In 1935, the U.S. government hired writers, teachers, historians, and others to work for the Federal Writers' Project (FWP).

1. The FWP was part of an effort to create jobs during the long, devastating economic crisis known as the Great Depression.

2. Many famous writers, such as John Cheever, Ralph Ellison, and Zora Neale Hurston, joined the FWP.

3. The FWP's Folklore Unit dedicated itself to interviewing ordinary Americans, writing down their stories, and bringing together this information so that it could be shared with the public.

4. Folklore Unit workers were able to collect not only life stories but also songs, folktales, and superstitions.

C 5. The director of the Folklore Unit hoped that by publishing this information, the FWP might make Americans more accepting of fellow citizens whose experiences, beliefs, and interests were different from their own.

Commas in Compound Sentences

A **compound sentence** contains two complete sentences joined by a coordinating conjunction: *and, but, for, nor, or, so, yet.* Use a comma before the joining word to separate the two complete sentences.

e Log in to **macmillanhighered .com/rrw** and look for Additional Grammar Exercises > Using Commas in Compound Sentences

| Sentence | , | and, but, for, nor, or, so, yet | Sentence | . |

I called my best friend, and she agreed to drive me to work.

I asked my best friend to drive me to work, but she was busy.

I can take the bus to work, or I can call another friend.

Language note: A comma alone cannot separate two sentences in English. Doing so creates a run-on (see Chapter 17).

> **PRACTICE 2**   **Using Commas in Compound Sentences**

Edit the following compound sentences by adding commas where they are needed. If a sentence is already correct, put a "C" next to it.

Example: Marika wanted to get a college education, but her husband did not like the idea.

1. Marika's hospital volunteer work had convinced her to become a physical therapist, but she needed a college degree to qualify.

2. Deciding to apply to college was difficult for her, so she was excited when she was admitted.

3. She had chosen the college carefully, for it had an excellent program in physical therapy.

4. Marika knew that the courses would be difficult, but she had not expected her husband to oppose her plan.

5. They had been married for twelve years, and he was surprised that she wanted a career.

Editing for correct comma usage:

Using commas in compound sentences

Find

Many college <u>students</u> are the first in their families to go to college (and) these students' <u>relatives</u> are proud of them.

1. To determine if the sentence is compound, **underline** the subjects, and **double-underline** the verbs.

2. *Ask:* Is the sentence compound? *Yes.*

3. **Circle** the word that joins them.

Edit

Many college students are the first in their families to go to college, and these students' relatives are proud of them.

4. **Put a comma** before the word that joins the two sentences.

Commas after Introductory Words

Log in to **macmillanhighered .com/rrw** and look for Additional Grammar Exercises > Using Commas after Introductory Word Groups

Use a comma after an introductory word, phrase, or clause. The comma lets your readers know when the main part of the sentence is starting.

> [Introductory word or word group] **,** [Main part of sentence] .

Introductory word	*Yesterday,* I went to the game.
Introductory phrase	*By the way,* I do not have a babysitter for tomorrow.
Introductory clause	*While I waited outside,* Susan went backstage.

PRACTICE 3   **Using Commas after Introductory Word Groups**

In each item, underline the introductory word or word group. Then, add a comma where it is needed. If a sentence is already correct, put a "C" next to it.

Example: **In the 1960s, John Mackey became famous for his speed and strength as a tight end for the Baltimore Colts football team.**

1. In his later years, the National Football League Hall-of-Famer was in the news for another reason: he suffered from dementia possibly linked to the head blows he received on the football field.

C 2. According to medical experts, repeated concussions can severely damage the brain over time, and they are especially harmful to young people, whose brains are still developing.

3. Based on these warnings and on stories like John Mackey's, athletic associations, coaches, and parents of young athletes are taking new precautions.

4. For example, more football coaches are teaching players to tackle and block with their heads up, reducing the chance that they will receive a blow to the top of the head.

5. Also, when players show signs of a concussion—such as dizziness, nausea, or confusion—more coaches are taking them out of the game.

Commas around Appositives and Interrupters

An **appositive** comes directly before or after a noun or pronoun and renames it.

> Lily, *a senior*, will take her nursing exam this summer.
> The prices are outrageous at Beans, *the local coffee shop*.

An **interrupter** is an aside or transition that interrupts the flow of a sentence and does not affect its meaning.

> My sister, *incidentally*, has good reasons for being late.
> Her child had a fever, *for example*.

e Log in to **macmillanhighered .com/rrw** and look for Additional Grammar Exercises > Using Commas to Set Off Appositives and Interrupters

Putting commas around appositives and interrupters tells readers that these elements give extra information but are not essential to the meaning of a sentence. If an appositive or interrupter is in the middle of a sentence, set it off with a pair of commas, one before and one after. If an appositive or interrupter comes at the beginning or end of a sentence, separate it from the rest of the sentence with one comma.

By the way, your proposal has been accepted.

Your proposal, *by the way,* has been accepted.

Your proposal has been accepted, *by the way.*

Note: Sometimes, an appositive is essential to the meaning of a sentence. When a sentence would not have the same meaning without the appositive, the appositive should not be set off with commas.

The actor *Leonardo DiCaprio* has never won an Oscar.

[The sentence *The actor has never won an Oscar* does not have the same meaning.]

Editing for correct comma usage:

Using commas to set off appositives and interrupters

Find

Tamara my sister-in-law moved in with us last week.

1. **Underline** the subject.

2. **Underline** any appositive (which renames the subject) or interrupter (which interrupts the flow of the sentence).

3. *Ask:* Is the appositive or interrupter essential to the meaning of the sentence? No.

Edit

Tamara, my sister-in-law, moved in with us last week.

4. If it is not essential, **set it off with commas.**

| PRACTICE 4 | Using Commas to Set Off Appositives and Interrupters |

Underline all the appositives and interrupters in the following sentences. Then, use commas to set them off.

Example: Harry, an attentive student, could not hear his teacher because the radiator in the classroom made a constant rattling.

1. Some rooms, in fact, are full of echoes, dead zones, and mechanical noises that make it hard for students to hear.

2. The American Speech-Language-Hearing Association, experts on how noise levels affect learning abilities, has set guidelines for how much noise in a classroom is too much.

3. The association recommends that background noise, the constant whirring or whining sounds made by radiators, lights, and other machines, be no more than 35 decibels.

4. That level, 35 decibels, is about as loud as a whispering voice fifteen feet away.

5. One study found a level of 65 decibels, the volume of a vacuum cleaner, in a number of classrooms around the country.

Commas around Adjective Clauses

An **adjective clause** is a group of words that begins with *who, which,* or *that*; has a subject and a verb; and describes a noun right before it in a sentence.

If an adjective clause can be taken out of a sentence without completely changing the meaning of the sentence, put commas around the clause.

Lily, *who is my cousin,* will take her nursing exam this summer.

Beans, *which is the local coffee shop,* charges outrageous prices.

I complained to Mr. Kranz, *who is the shop's manager.*

If an adjective clause is essential to the meaning of a sentence, do not put commas around it. You can tell whether a clause is essential by taking it out and seeing if the meaning of the sentence changes significantly, as it would if you took the clauses out of the following examples.

The only grocery store *that sold good bread* went out of business.

Students *who do internships* often improve their hiring potential.

Salesclerks *who sell liquor to minors* are breaking the law.

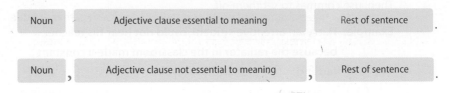

Editing for correct comma usage:
Using commas to set off adjective clauses

Find

The woman who had octuplets received much publicity.

1. **Underline** any adjective clause (a word group that begins with *who, which,* or *that*).

2. **Read** the sentence without this clause.

3. *Ask:* Does the meaning change significantly without the clause? *Yes.*

Edit

The woman who had octuplets received much publicity.

4. If the meaning *does* change, as in this case, **do not put in commas**. (Add commas only if the meaning *does not* change.)

PRACTICE 5   **Using Commas to Set Off Adjective Clauses**

Underline the adjective clauses in the following sentences. Then, put commas around these clauses where they are needed. Remember that if an adjective clause is essential to the meaning of a sentence, commas are not necessary. If a sentence is already correct, put a "C" next to it.

Example: Daniel Kish, who has been blind since the age of one, has changed many people's ideas about what blind people can and cannot do.

1. Kish, who runs the organization World Access for the Blind, regularly rides his bike down busy streets and goes on long hikes.

2. His system for "seeing" his surroundings, which is known as echolocation, uses sound waves to create mental pictures of buildings, cars, trees, and other objects.

3. As Kish bikes around his neighborhood, or hikes to sites that are deep in the wilderness, he clicks his tongue and listens to the echoes.

4. The echoes, which differ depending on the distance and physical features of nearby objects, allow him to map his surroundings in his mind.

5. This mental map, which he constantly revises as he moves ahead, helps him avoid running into cars, trees, and other obstacles.

Other Uses for Commas

COMMAS WITH QUOTATION MARKS

Quotation marks are used to show that you are repeating exactly what someone said. Use commas to set off the words inside quotation marks from the rest of the sentence.

Log in to **macmillanhighered .com/rrw** and look for Additional Grammar Exercises > Using Commas in Other Situations

> "Let me see your license," demanded the police officer.
> "Did you realize," she asked, "that you were going 80 miles per hour?"
> I exclaimed, "No!"

Notice that a comma never comes directly after a quotation mark.

When quotations are not attributed to a particular person, commas may not be necessary.

> "Pretty is as pretty does" never made sense to me.

COMMAS IN ADDRESSES

Use commas to separate the elements of an address included in a sentence. However, do not use a comma before a zip code.

> My address is 2512 Windermere Street, Jackson, Mississippi 40720.

If a sentence continues after a city-state combination or after a street address, put a comma after the state or the address.

I moved here from Detroit, Michigan, when I was eighteen.

I've lived at 24 Heener Street, Madison, since 1989.

COMMAS IN DATES

Separate the day from the year with a comma when including a date in a sentence. If you give just the month and year, do not separate them with a comma.

My daughter was born on November 8, 2004.

The next conference is in August 2014.

If a sentence continues after the date, put a comma after the date.

On April 21, 2013, the contract will expire.

COMMAS WITH NAMES

Put a comma after (and sometimes before) the name of someone being addressed directly.

Don, I want you to come look at this.

Unfortunately, Marie, you need to finish the report by next week.

COMMAS WITH *YES* OR *NO*

Put a comma after the word *yes* or *no* in response to a question.

Yes, I believe that you are right.

> **PRACTICE 6**   **Using Commas in Other Ways**
>
> Edit the following sentences by adding commas where they are needed. If a sentence is already correct, put a "C" next to it.
>
> **Example: On August 12, 2011, beachfront property was badly damaged by a fast-moving storm.**
>
> 1. Some homeowners were still waiting to settle their claims with their insurance companies in January 2012.
>
> 2. Rob McGregor of 31 Hudson Street, Wesleyville, is one of those homeowners.
>
> 3. Asked if he was losing patience, McGregor replied, "Yes I sure am."

4. "I've really had it up to here," McGregor said.

5. His wife said "Rob don't go mouthing off to any reporters."

Edit for Commas

PRACTICE 7   **Editing Paragraphs for Commas**

Edit the following paragraphs by adding commas where they are needed.

1 By the end of 2011, communities in California Texas Washington and several other states had banned the use of plastic bags. 2 One grocery store chain Whole Foods Market was an early leader in restricting the use of these bags. 3 As of April 22 2008 Whole Foods stopped asking customers if they wanted paper bags or plastic bags. 4 The store which cares about environmental issues now offers only paper bags made from recycled paper.

5 The president of Whole Foods stated "We estimate we will keep 100 million new plastic grocery bags out of our environment between Earth Day and the end of this year." 6 The company also sells cloth bags, hoping to encourage shoppers to bring their own reusable bags with them when they go shopping.

7 Experts believe that plastic bags do a great deal of damage to the environment. 8 They clog drains harm wildlife and take up an enormous amount of space in the nation's landfills. 9 According to the experts it takes more than a thousand years for a plastic bag to break down, and Americans use 100 billion of them every single year.

Chapter Review

1. A comma (,) is a _____ that helps readers understand a sentence.

2. How do you use commas in these three situations?

   In a series of items, _____

   _____.

In a compound sentence, _____

_____ .

With introductory words, _____

_____ .

3. An appositive comes before or after a noun or pronoun and _____

_____ .

4. An interrupter is an _____ that interrupts the flow of a sentence.

5. Put commas around an adjective clause when it is _____ to the
meaning of a sentence.

Chapter Test

Circle the correct choice for each of the following items.

1. If an underlined portion of this sentence is incorrect, select the revision that
   fixes it. If the sentence is correct as written, choose d.

   > The company <u>owners, for</u> your <u>information are</u> planning to inspect
   > $\qquad$ A $\qquad$ B
   >
   > our <u>department this</u> afternoon.
   > $\qquad$ C

   a. owners for   c. department, this
   b. information, are   d. No change is necessary.

2. Choose the item that has no errors.
   a. I used to hate parties but now I like to socialize with others.
   b. I used to hate parties, but now I like to socialize with others.
   c. I used to hate parties, but, now I like to socialize with others.

3. Choose the item that has no errors.
   a. If you do not file your income tax forms by April 15, 2015 you could face
       penalties.
   b. If you do not file your income tax forms by April 15, 2015, you could face
       penalties.
   c. If you do not file your income tax forms by April 15 2015 you could face
       penalties.

4. If an underlined portion of this sentence is incorrect, select the revision that fixes it. If the sentence is correct as written, choose d.

   Henry's <u>favorite hobbies</u> <u>are watching birds,</u> collecting <u>stamps, and</u>
               A   B   C
   fixing up old cars.

   a. favorite, hobbies   c. stamps and

   b. are watching, birds   d. No change is necessary.

5. Choose the item that has no errors.

   a. Roger, who teaches dance at a local studio, will be my partner for the ballroom competition.

   b. Roger who teaches dance at a local studio will be my partner for the ballroom competition.

   c. Roger who teaches dance at a local studio, will be my partner for the ballroom competition.

6. If an underlined portion of this sentence is incorrect, select the revision that fixes it. If the sentence is correct as written, choose d.

   Feeling <u>adventurous, Alexia</u> <u>tasted the</u> guava, <u>mango and</u> passion
                        A   B   C
   fruit.

   a. adventurous Alexia   c. mango, and

   b. tasted, the   d. No change is necessary.

7. Choose the item that has no errors.

   a. I discovered that Lansing, Michigan was the hometown of four people at the party.

   b. I discovered that Lansing Michigan, was the hometown of four people at the party.

   c. I discovered that Lansing, Michigan, was the hometown of four people at the party.

8. If an underlined portion of this sentence is incorrect, select the revision that fixes it. If the sentence is correct as written, choose d.

   Just to be <u>different I</u> <u>decided to</u> wear a top <u>hat to</u> all my classes
                          A   B   C
   today.

   a. different, I   c. hat, to

   b. decided, to   d. No change is necessary.

9. Choose the item that has no errors.

   a. "If you follow my instructions precisely" said the manager, "I will consider you for a promotion."

   b. "If you follow my instructions precisely," said the manager "I will consider you for a promotion."

   c. "If you follow my instructions precisely," said the manager, "I will consider you for a promotion."

10. If an underlined portion of this sentence is incorrect, select the revision that fixes it. If the sentence is correct as written, choose d.

   No Bob, I cannot <u>swim, paddle</u> a <u>kayak, or</u> steer a sailboat.
         _A_   _B_   _C_

   a. No, Bob,   c. kayak or

   b. swim paddle   d. No change is necessary.

Apostrophes '

Understand What Apostrophes Do

An **apostrophe** (') is a punctuation mark that either shows ownership (*Susan's*) or indicates that a letter has been intentionally left out to form a contraction (*I'm, that's, they're*).

Log in to **macmillanhighered.com/rrw** and look for LearningCurve > Apostrophes

Using Apostrophes Correctly

Apostrophes to Show Ownership

Add -*'s* to a singular noun to show ownership even if the noun already ends in -*s*.

Log in to **macmillanhighered.com/rrw** and look for Additional Grammar Exercises > Using Apostrophes to Show Ownership

> *Karen's* apartment is on the South Side.
>
> *James's* roommate is looking for him.

If a noun is plural and ends in -*s*, just add an apostrophe. If it is plural but does not end in -*s*, add -*'s*.

> My *books'* covers are falling off.
>
> [more than one book]
>
> The *twins'* father was building them a playhouse.
>
> [more than one twin]
>
> The *children's* toys were broken.
>
> The *men's* locker room is being painted.

The placement of an apostrophe makes a difference in meaning.

> My *sister's* six children are at my house for the weekend.
>
> [one sister who has six children]

My *sisters'* six children are at my house for the weekend.

[two or more sisters who together have six children]

Do not use an apostrophe to form the plural of a noun.

Gina went camping with her *sister/s* and their children.

All the *highway/s* to the airport are under construction.

Do not use an apostrophe with a possessive pronoun. These pronouns already show ownership (possession).

Is that bag *your/s*?   No, it is *our/s*.

Possessive Pronouns

my	his	its	their
mine	her	our	theirs
your	hers	ours	whose
yours			

The single most common error with apostrophes and pronouns is confusing *its* (a possessive pronoun) with *it's* (a contraction meaning "it is"). Whenever you write *it's*, test correctness by replacing it with *it is* and reading the sentence aloud to hear if it makes sense. (For more on *its/it's*, see p. 559.)

> **PRACTICE 1**   **Using Apostrophes to Show Ownership**
>
> Edit the following sentences by adding -'s or an apostrophe alone to show ownership and by crossing out any incorrect use of an apostrophe or -'s.
>
> **Example: Not long ago, my cousins resume was looking thin because he was young and had not held many job/s.**

1. Also, his previous jobs as a welders assistant and a line cook did not relate to what he most wanted to do: landscaping.

2. He had some contacts in the landscaping business: two friends sisters were landscapers, and another friends father managed the grounds at a golf course.

3. But my cousin couldn't get jobs through these contacts because he had no experience working on a landscapers crew or with a professional gardener.

4. To build up the right kind of skills, he spent six month's of last year volunteering at a community garden.

5. Under the guidance of the community gardens most expert member, my cousin learned about soil drainage, composting, and chemical-free pest control.

Apostrophes in Contractions

A **contraction** is formed by joining two words and leaving out one or more of the letters. When writing a contraction, put an apostrophe where the letter or letters have been left out.

Tip Ask your instructor if contractions are acceptable in papers.

Common Contractions

aren't = are not
can't = cannot
couldn't = could not
didn't = did not
don't = do not
he'd = he would, he had
he'll = he will
he's = he is, he has
I'd = I would, I had
I'll = I will
I'm = I am
I've = I have
isn't = is not
it's = it is, it has
let's = let us
she'd = she would, she had

she'll = she will
she's = she is, she has
there's = there is
they'd = they would, they had
they'll = they will
they're = they are
they've = they have
who'd = who would, who had
who'll = who will
who's = who is, who has
won't = will not
wouldn't = would not
you'd = you would, you had
you'll = you will
you're = you are
you've = you have

She's on her way. = *She is* on her way.
I'll see you there. = *I will* see you there.

Be sure to put the apostrophe in the correct place.

It *doesn't* really matter.

Tip To shorten the full year to only the final two numbers, replace the first two numbers: the year 2015 becomes '15.

PRACTICE 2 **Using Apostrophes in Contractions**

Read each sentence carefully, looking for any words that have missing letters. Edit these words by adding apostrophes where needed and crossing out incorrectly used apostrophes.

Example: Although we observe personal space boundaries in our daily lives, they're not something we spend much time thinking about.

1. You'll notice right away if a stranger leans over and talks to you so that his face is practically touching yours.

2. Perhaps you'd accept this kind of behavior from a family member.

3. There isn't one single acceptable boundary we'd use in all situations.

4. An elevator has its own rules: don't stand right next to a person if there is open space.

5. With strangers, we're likely to keep a personal space of four to twelve feet.

Apostrophes with Letters, Numbers, and Time

Use -'s to make letters and numbers plural. The apostrophe prevents confusion or misreading.

In Scrabble games, there are more *e's* than any other letter.
In women's shoes, size *8's* are more common than size *10's*.

Use an apostrophe or -'s in certain expressions in which time nouns are treated as if they possess something.

She took four *weeks'* maternity leave after the baby was born.
This *year's* graduating class is huge.

Edit for Apostrophes

PRACTICE 3 **Editing Paragraphs for Apostrophes**

Edit the following paragraphs by adding two apostrophes where needed and crossing out five incorrectly used apostrophes.

1 Have you noticed many honeybee's when you go outside? 2 If not, it isn't surprising. 3 For reasons that scientists still don't quite understand, these bees have been disappearing all across the country. 4 This mass disappearance is a problem because bees are an important part of growing a wide variety of flowers, fruits, vegetables, and nuts as they spread pollen from one place to another.

5 In the last year, more than one-third, or billions, of the honeybees in the United States have disappeared. 6 As a consequence, farmers have been forced either to buy or to rent beehives for their crops. 7 Typically, people who are in the bee business ship hives to farmers fields by truck. 8 The hives often have to travel hundreds of miles.

9 Scientist's have been trying to find out what happened to the once-thriving bee population. 10 They suspect that either a disease or chemicals harmed the honeybee's.

Chapter Review

1. An apostrophe (') is a punctuation mark that either shows _____ or indicates that a letter or letters have been intentionally left out to form a _____ .

2. To show ownership, add _____ to a singular noun, even if the noun already ends in -s. For a plural noun, add an _____ alone if the noun ends in -s; add _____ if the noun does not end in -s.

3. Do not use an apostrophe with a _____ pronoun.

4. Do not confuse *its* and *it's*. *Its* shows _____ ; *it's* is a _____ meaning "it is."

5. A _____ is formed by joining two words and leaving out one or more of the letters.

Chapter Test

Circle the correct choice for each of the following items.

1. If an underlined portion of this sentence is incorrect, select the revision that fixes it. If the sentence is correct as written, choose d.

   I've always believed that its a crime to use software that you
   <u>A</u>   <u>B</u>

   haven't paid for.
   <u>C</u>

   a. Ive   c. havent

   b. it's   d. No change is necessary.

2. Choose the item that has no errors.

   a. The thieves boldness made them a lot of money, but it eventually landed them in jail.

   b. The thieves's boldness made them a lot of money, but it eventually landed them in jail.

   c. The thieves' boldness made them a lot of money, but it eventually landed them in jail.

3. Choose the item that has no errors.

   a. By playing that slot machine, your throwing away money.

   b. By playing that slot machine, you're throwing away money.

   c. By playing that slot machine, youre' throwing away money.

4. If an underlined portion of this sentence is incorrect, select the revision that fixes it. If the sentence is correct as written, choose d.

   The house is now Renee's, but she'll regret having an address with
                    <u>A</u>   <u>B</u>

   five 3s in it.
       <u>C</u>

   a. Renees   c. 3's

   b. sh'ell   d. No change is necessary.

5. Choose the item that has no errors.

   a. Her eighteen months' service overseas has somehow made her seem older.

   b. Her eighteen month's service overseas has somehow made her seem older.

   c. Her eighteen months service overseas has somehow made her seem older.

30

Quotation Marks " "

Understand What Quotation Marks Do

Quotation marks (" ") always appear in pairs. Quotation marks have two common uses in college writing:

- They are used with **direct quotations**, which exactly repeat, word for word, what someone said or wrote. (*Nick said, "You should take the downtown bus."*)
- They are used to set off **titles**. (*My favorite song is "Sophisticated Lady."*)

Using Quotation Marks Correctly

Quotation Marks for Direct Quotations

When you write a direct quotation, use quotation marks around the quoted words. Quotation marks tell readers that the words used are exactly what was said or written.

> "I do not know what she means," I said to my friend Lina.
>
> Lina asked, "Do you think we should ask a question?"
>
> "Excuse me, Professor Soames," I called out, "but could you explain that again?"
>
> "Yes," said Professor Soames. "Let me make sure you all understand."
>
> After further explanation, Professor Soames asked, "Are there any other questions?"

Tip For practice and examples of using quotes from readings, see the Reading/Writing Workbooks in Chapters 7–13.

e Log in to **macmillanhighered .com/rrw** and look for Additional Grammar Exercises > Using Quotation Marks for Direct Quotations and Certain Titles

When you are writing a paper that uses outside sources, use quotation marks to indicate where you quote the exact words of a source.

> We all need to become more conscientious recyclers. A recent editorial in the *Bolton Common* reported, "When recycling volunteers spot-checked bags that were supposed to contain only newspaper, they found a collection of nonrecyclable items such as plastic candy wrappers, aluminum foil, and birthday cards."

When quoting, writers usually use words that identify who is speaking, such as *I said to my friend Lina* in the first example on the previous page. The identifying words can come after the quoted words (as in that first example), before them (second example), or in the middle of them (third example). Here are some guidelines for capitalization and punctuation.

Guidelines for capitalization and punctuation

- Capitalize the first letter in a complete sentence that is being quoted, even if it comes after some identifying words (the second example on p. 591).
- Do not capitalize the first letter in a quotation if it is not the first word in a complete sentence (*but* in the third example).
- If it is a complete sentence and it is clear who the speaker is, a quotation can stand on its own (the second sentence in the fourth example).
- Identifying words must be attached to a quotation; they cannot be a sentence on their own.
- Use commas to separate any identifying words from quoted words in the same sentence.
- Always put quotation marks after commas and periods. Put quotation marks after question marks and exclamation points if they are part of the quoted sentence.

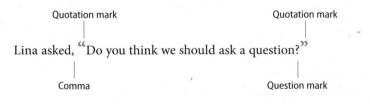

- If a question mark or an exclamation point is part of your own sentence, put it after the quotation mark.

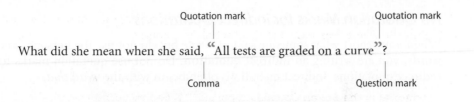

Quotation mark   Quotation mark

What did she mean when she said, "All tests are graded on a curve"?

Comma   Question mark

SETTING OFF A QUOTATION WITHIN ANOTHER QUOTATION

Sometimes, when you quote someone directly, part of what that person said quotes words that someone else said or wrote. Put single quotation marks (' ') around the quotation within a quotation so that readers understand who said what.

> The student handbook says, "Students must be given the opportunity to make up work missed for legitimate reasons."

> Terry told his instructor, "I am sorry I missed the exam, but that is not a reason to fail me for the term. Our student handbook says, 'Students must be given the opportunity to make up work missed for legitimate reasons,' and I have a good reason."

PRACTICE 1   Punctuating Direct Quotations

Edit the following sentences by adding quotation marks and commas where needed.

Example: A radio journalist asked a nurse at a critical-care facility, "Do you believe that the medical community needlessly prolongs the life of the terminally ill?

1. If I could answer that question quickly the nurse replied I would deserve an honorary degree in ethics.

2. She added But I see it as the greatest dilemma we face today.

3. How would you describe that dilemma? the reporter asked the nurse.

4. The nurse said It is a choice of when to use our amazing medical technology and when not to.

5. The reporter asked So there are times when you would favor letting patients die on their own?

No Quotation Marks for Indirect Quotations

e Log in to **macmillanhighered .com/rrw** and look for Additional Grammar Exercises > Punctuating Direct and Indirect Quotations

When you report what someone said or wrote but do not use the person's exact words, you are writing an **indirect quotation**. Do not use quotation marks for indirect quotations. Indirect quotations often begin with the word *that*.

Indirect quotation	Direct quotation
Sam said that there was a fire downtown.	Sam said, "There was a fire downtown."
The police told us to move along.	"Move along," directed the police.
Tara told me that she is graduating.	Tara said, "I am graduating."

PRACTICE 2 **Punctuating Direct and Indirect Quotations**

Edit the following sentences by adding quotation marks where needed and crossing out quotation marks that are used incorrectly. If a sentence is already correct, put a "C" next to it.

Example: Three days before her apartment was robbed, Jocelyn told a friend, "I worry about the safety of this building."

1. Have you complained to the landlord yet? her friend asked.

2. Not yet, Jocelyn replied, although I know I should.

C 3. Jocelyn phoned the landlord and asked him to install a more secure lock on the front door.

4. The landlord said that he believed that the lock was fine the way it was.

5. When Jocelyn phoned the landlord after the burglary, she said, I know this burglary would not have happened if that lock had been installed.

e Log in to **macmillanhighered .com/rrw** and look for Additional Grammar Exercises > Using Quotation Marks for Titles

Quotation Marks for Certain Titles

When you refer to a short work such as a magazine or newspaper article, a chapter in a book, a short story, an essay, a song, or a poem, put quotation marks around the title of the work.

Newspaper article	"Volunteers Honored for Service"
Short story	"The Awakening"
Essay	"Why Are We So Angry?"

Usually, titles of longer works, such as novels, books, magazines, newspapers, movies, television programs, and CDs, are italicized. The titles of sacred books such as the Bible or the Koran are neither italicized nor surrounded by quotation marks.

Book	*The Good Earth*
Newspaper	*Washington Post*

[Do not italicize or capitalize the word *the* before the name of a newspaper or magazine, even if it is part of the title: I saw that article in the *New York Times*. But do capitalize *The* when it is the first word in titles of books, movies, and other sources.]

If you are writing a paper with many outside sources, your instructor will probably refer you to a particular system of citing sources. Follow that system's guidelines when you use titles in your paper. (The Modern Language Association [MLA] system of documentation is explained in Chapter 14.)

Note: Do not enclose the title of a paragraph or an essay that you have written in quotation marks when it appears at the beginning of your paper. Do not italicize it either.

Edit for Quotation Marks

> **PRACTICE 4**   **Editing Paragraphs for Quotation Marks**

Edit the following paragraphs by adding twelve sets of quotation marks where needed and crossing out the two sets of incorrectly used quotation marks. Correct any errors in punctuation.

1 When Ruiz first came into my office, he told me that he was a poor student. 2 I asked, What makes you think that?

3 Ruiz answered, I have always gotten bad grades, and I do not know how to get any better. 4 He shook his head. 5 I have just about given up.

6 I told him that there were some resources on campus he could use and that we could work together to help him.

7 "What kind of things are you talking about?" asked Ruiz. 8 What exactly will I learn?

9 I said, There are plenty of programs to help you. 10 You really have no excuse to fail.

11 Can you be a little more specific? he asked.

12 Certainly, I said. 13 I told him about the survival skills program.

14 I also pulled out folders on study skills, such as managing time, improving memory, taking notes, and having a positive attitude. 15 Take a look at these, I said.

16 Ruiz said, No, I am not interested in that. 17 And I do not have time.

18 I replied, "That is your decision, Ruiz, but remember that education is one of the few things that people are willing to pay for and not get."

19 I paused and then added, It sounds to me like you are wasting the money you spent on tuition. 20 Why not try to get what you paid for?

21 Ruiz thought for a moment, while he looked out the window, and finally told me that he would try.

22 Good, I said. 23 I am glad to hear it.

Chapter Review

1. Quotation marks look like _____ . They always appear in (pairs / threes).

2. A direct quotation exactly _____ what someone (or some outside source) said or wrote. (Use / Do not use) quotation marks around direct quotations.

3. An indirect quotation _____

    _____.

    (Use / Do not use) quotation marks with indirect quotations.

4. To set off a quotation within a quotation, use _____.

5. Put quotation marks around the titles of short works such as (give four examples) _____

   _____.

6. For longer works such as magazines, novels, books, newspapers, and so on, _____ the titles.

Chapter Test

Circle the correct choice for each of the following items.

1. If an underlined portion of this sentence is incorrect, select the revision that fixes it. If the sentence is correct as written, choose d.

   Do you think that <u>she</u> was serious when she <u>said, "Leave the</u>

   A   B

   building <u>immediately?"</u>

   C

   a. "she"   c. immediately"?
   b. said "Leave   d. No change is necessary.

2. Choose the item that has no errors.
   a. "You need to strengthen that knee," Dr. Wheeler warned, "so be sure to do all your exercises".
   b. "You need to strengthen that knee," Dr. Wheeler warned, so be sure to do all your exercises.
   c. "You need to strengthen that knee," Dr. Wheeler warned, "so be sure to do all your exercises."

3. Choose the item that has no errors.
   a. Eric pointed at an article titled 'New Alternative Fuel in Your Backyard.'
   b. Eric pointed at an article titled New Alternative Fuel in Your Backyard.
   c. Eric pointed at an article titled "New Alternative Fuel in Your Backyard."

4. If an underlined portion of this sentence is incorrect, select the revision that fixes it. If the sentence is correct as written, choose d.

       The man said, "I'm sorry, <u>officer, but</u> did I hear you correctly

                                            A

       when you <u>said, "Drive into that</u> <u>ditch</u>'?"

                            B   C

   a.   officer, "but   c.   ditch'"?

   b.   said, 'Drive   d.   No change is necessary.

5. Choose the item that has no errors.

   a.   Rachel told the security guard that she needed to enter the building for official business.

   b.   Rachel told the security guard that "she needed to enter the building for official business."

   c.   Rachel told the security guard that she "needed to enter the building for official business."

31

Other Punctuation

Understand What Punctuation Does

Punctuation helps readers understand your writing. If you use punctuation incorrectly, you send readers a confusing—or, even worse, a wrong—message. This chapter covers five punctuation marks that people sometimes use incorrectly because they are not quite sure what these marks are supposed to do.

Using Other Punctuation Correctly

Semicolon ;

SEMICOLONS TO JOIN CLOSELY RELATED SENTENCES

Use a **semicolon** to join two closely related sentences into one sentence.

> In an interview, hold your head up and do not slouch; it is important to look alert.

> Make good eye contact; looking down is not appropriate in an interview.

> Language note: Using a comma instead of semicolon to join two sentences creates a run-on (see Chapter 17).

SEMICOLONS WHEN ITEMS IN A LIST CONTAIN COMMAS

Use semicolons to separate items in a list that itself contains commas. Otherwise, it is difficult for readers to tell where one item ends and another begins.

For dinner, Bob ate an order of onion rings; a 16-ounce steak; a baked potato with sour cream, bacon bits, and cheese; a green salad; and a huge bowl of ice cream with fudge sauce.

Because one item, *a baked potato with sour cream, bacon bits, and cheese,* contains its own commas, all items need to be separated by semicolons.

Colon :

COLONS BEFORE LISTS

Use a **colon** after an independent clause to introduce a list. An independent clause contains a subject, a verb, and a complete thought. It can stand on its own as a sentence.

The software conference fair featured a vast array of products: financial-management applications, games, educational CDs, college-application programs, and so on.

COLONS BEFORE EXPLANATIONS OR EXAMPLES

Use a colon after an independent clause to let readers know that you are about to provide an explanation or example of what you just wrote.

The conference was overwhelming: too much hype about too many things.

One of the most common misuses of colons is to use them after a phrase instead of an independent clause. Watch out especially for colons following the phrases *such as* and *for example.*

Incorrect	Tonya enjoys sports that are sometimes dangerous. For example: white-water rafting, wilderness skiing, rock climbing, and motorcycle racing.
Correct	Tonya enjoys sports that are sometimes dangerous: white-water rafting, wilderness skiing, rock climbing, and motorcycle racing.
Incorrect	Jeff has many interests. They are: bicycle racing, sculpting, and building musical instruments.
Correct	Jeff has many interests: bicycle racing, sculpting, and building musical instruments.

COLONS IN BUSINESS CORRESPONDENCE AND BEFORE SUBTITLES

Use a colon after a greeting (called a *salutation*) in a business letter and after the standard heading lines at the beginning of a memorandum.

> Dear Mr. Hernandez:
>
> To: Pat Toney
> From: Susan Anker

Colons should also be used before subtitles—for example, "Running a Marathon: The Five Most Important Tips."

Parentheses ( )

Use **parentheses** to set off information that is not essential to the meaning of a sentence. Parentheses are always used in pairs and should be used sparingly.

> My grandfather's most successful invention (and also his first) was the electric blanket.
>
> When he died (at the age of ninety-six), he had more than 150 patents registered.

Dash —

Dashes can be used like parentheses to set off additional information, particularly information that you want to emphasize. Make a dash by writing or typing two hyphens together. Do not put extra spaces around a dash.

> The final exam—worth 25 percent of your total grade—will be next Thursday.

A dash can also indicate a pause, much like a comma does.

> My uncle went on long fishing trips—without my aunt and cousins.

Hyphen -

HYPHENS TO JOIN WORDS THAT FORM A SINGLE DESCRIPTION

Writers often join two or more words that together form a single description of a person, place, or thing. To join the words, use a **hyphen**.

> Being a stockbroker is a high-risk career.
>
> Jill is a lovely three-year-old girl.

When writing out two-word numbers from twenty-one to ninety-nine, put a hyphen between the two words.

Seventy-five people participated in the demonstration.

HYPHENS TO DIVIDE A WORD AT THE END OF A LINE

Use a hyphen to divide a word when part of the word must continue on the next line.

Critics accused the tobacco industry of increasing the amounts of nicotine in cigarettes to encourage addiction and boost sales.

Tip Most word-processing programs automatically put an entire word on the next line rather than hyphenating it. When you write by hand, however, you need to hyphenate correctly.

If you are not sure where to break a word, look it up in a dictionary. The word's main entry will show you where you can break the word: dic • tio • nary. If you still are not confident that you are putting the hyphen in the correct place, do not break the word; write it all on the next line.

Edit for Other Punctuation Marks

PRACTICE 1   **Editing Paragraphs for Other Punctuation Marks**

Edit the following paragraphs by adding semicolons, colons, parentheses, dashes, and hyphens when needed. In some places, more than one type of punctuation may be acceptable.

1 When John Wood was on a backpacking trip to Nepal in 1998, he discovered something he had not expected only a few books in the nation's schools. 2 He knew that if the students did not have the materials they needed, it would be much harder for them to learn. 3 They did not need high tech supplies as much as they needed old fashioned books. 4 Wood decided that he would find a way to get those books.

5 Two years later, Wood founded Room to Read, an organization dedicated to shipping books to students who needed them. 6 Since then, the group has donated more than three million books. 7 One of Wood's first shipments was carried to students on the back of a yak. 8 Many others arrived in a Cathay Pacific Airlines plane.

9 Along with the books, Room to Read has also built almost three hundred schools and has opened five thousand libraries. 10 Different companies donate books to the organization Scholastic, Inc., recently sent 400,000 books to Wood's group. 11 Money to fund all these efforts comes through various fund-raisers read-a-thons, auctions, and coin drives.

Chapter Review

1. Semicolons (;) can be used to _____
   and to _____.

2. Colons (:) can be used in what three ways? _____
   _____
   _____
   _____

3. A colon used in a sentence must always follow an _____.

4. Parentheses ( ) set off information that is _____ to a sentence.

5. _____ also set off information in a sentence, usually information that you want to emphasize.

6. Hyphens (-) can be used to join two or more words that together _____ and to _____ a word at the end of a line.

Chapter Test

Circle the correct choice for each of the following items.

1. Choose the item that has no errors.
   a. Our car trip took us through Pittsburgh, Pennsylvania, Wheeling, West Virginia, and Bristol, Tennessee.
   b. Our car trip took us through Pittsburgh, Pennsylvania; Wheeling, West Virginia; and Bristol, Tennessee.
   c. Our car trip took us through Pittsburgh; Pennsylvania, Wheeling; West Virginia, and Bristol; Tennessee.

2. If an underlined portion of this sentence is incorrect, select the revision that fixes it. If the sentence is correct as written, choose d.

> Gary's dog (a seventeen-year-old easily won first prize in the
>   A
>
> Elderly Dog Show; she had the shiniest coat and the most
>   B   C
>
> youthful step.

   a.   (a seventeen-year-old)   c.   coat: and

   b.   Show-she   d.   No change is necessary.

3. Choose the item that has no errors.

   a.   As our computer specialist, you have three tasks: fixing malfunctioning computers, teaching people to use their computers, and not making any problem worse.

   b.   As our computer specialist: you have three tasks, fixing malfunctioning computers, teaching people to use their computers, and not making any problem worse.

   c.   As our computer specialist, you have three tasks: fixing malfunctioning computers, teaching people to use their computers (and not making any problem worse).

4. Choose the item that has no errors.

   a.   Is there such a thing as a low-stress-job?

   b.   Is there such a thing as a low-stress job?

   c.   Is there such a thing as a low stress-job?

5. If an underlined portion of this sentence is incorrect, select the revision that fixes it. If the sentence is correct as written, choose d.

> You will have five and only five minutes to leave the office before the
>   A   B   C
>
> alarm sounds.

   a.   five—and only five—   c.   before; the

   b.   to: leave   d.   No change is necessary.

32

Capitalization:

Using Capital Letters

Understand the Three Rules of Capitalization

e Log in to
macmillanhighered
.com/rrw and look for
LearningCurve >
Capitalization >
Additional Grammar
Exercises > Capitalizing

Capital letters (A, B, C) are generally bigger than lowercase letters (a, b, c), and they may have a different form. To avoid the most common errors of capitalization, follow these three rules:

Capitalize the first letter

- of every new sentence;
- in names of specific people, places, dates, and things (also known as proper nouns); and
- of important words in titles.

Using Capitalization Correctly

Capitalization of Sentences

Capitalize the first letter of each new sentence, including the first word of a direct quotation.

> The superintendent was surprised.
> He asked, "What is going on here?"

Capitalization of Names of Specific People, Places, Dates, and Things

The general rule is to capitalize the first letter in names of specific people, places, dates, and things. Do not capitalize a generic (common) name such as *college* as opposed to the specific name: *Carroll State College*. Look at the examples for each group.

PEOPLE

Capitalize the first letter in names of specific people and in titles used with names of specific people.

Specific	Not specific
Jean Heaton	my neighbor
Professor Fitzgerald	your math professor
Dr. Cornog	the doctor
Aunt Pat, Mother	my aunt, your mother

The name of a family member is capitalized when the family member is being addressed directly: Happy Birthday, *Mother*. In other instances, do not capitalize: It is my *mother's* birthday.

The word *president* is not capitalized unless it comes directly before a name as part of that person's title: *President* Barack Obama.

PLACES

Capitalize the first letter in names of specific buildings, streets, cities, states, regions, and countries.

Specific	Not specific
Bolton Town Hall	the town hall
Arlington Street	our street
Dearborn Heights	my hometown
Arizona	this state
the South	the southern region
Spain	that country

Do not capitalize directions in a sentence.

Drive *south* for five blocks.

DATES

Capitalize the first letter in the names of days, months, and holidays. Do not capitalize the names of the seasons (winter, spring, summer, fall).

Specific	Not specific
Wednesday	tomorrow
June 25	summer
Thanksgiving	my birthday

Language note: Some languages, such as Spanish, French, and Italian, do not capitalize days, months, and languages. In English, such words must be capitalized.

Incorrect	I study russian every monday, wednesday, and friday from january through may.
Correct	I study *Russian* every *Monday*, *Wednesday*, and *Friday* from *January* through *May*.

ORGANIZATIONS, COMPANIES, AND GROUPS

Specific	Not specific
Taft Community College	my college
Microsoft	that software company
Alcoholics Anonymous	the self-help group

LANGUAGES, NATIONALITIES, AND RELIGIONS

Specific	Not specific
English, Greek, Spanish	my first language
Christianity, Buddhism	your religion

The names of languages should be capitalized even if you aren't referring to a specific course.

I am taking psychology and *Spanish*.

COURSES

Specific	Not specific
Composition 101	a writing course
Introduction to Psychology	my psychology course

COMMERCIAL PRODUCTS

Specific	Not specific
Diet Pepsi	a diet cola
Skippy peanut butter	peanut butter

Capitalization of Titles

Tip For more on punctuating titles, see pages 594–595. For a list of common prepositions, see page 347.

When you write the title of a book, movie, television program, magazine, newspaper, article, story, song, paper, poem, and so on, capitalize the first word and all important words. The only words that do not need to be capitalized (unless they are the first word) are *the, a, an,* coordinating conjunctions (*and, but, for, nor, or, so, yet*), and prepositions.

> *I Love Lucy* was a long-running television program.
>
> Both *USA Today* and the *New York Times* are popular newspapers.
>
> "Once More to the Lake" is one of Chuck's favorite essays.

Chapter Review

1. Capitalize the _____ of every new sentence.

2. Capitalize the first letter in names of specific _____ , _____ , _____ , and _____ .

3. Capitalize the first word and all _____ in titles.

Chapter Test

Circle the correct choice for each of the following items.

1. Choose the item that has no errors.
   a. My daughter's school, Spitzer High School, no longer sells pepsi and other sodas in its vending machines.
   b. My daughter's school, Spitzer high school, no longer sells pepsi and other sodas in its vending machines.
   c. My daughter's school, Spitzer High School, no longer sells Pepsi and other sodas in its vending machines.

2. If an underlined portion of this sentence is incorrect, select the revision that fixes it. If the sentence is correct as written, choose d.

   Will our company **President** speak at the **annual meeting**, or will
   　　　　　　　　　 A 　　　　　　　　　　　　 B

   Dr. Anders?
   　 C

   a. president   c. doctor Anders
   b. Annual Meeting   d. No change is necessary.

3. Choose the item that has no errors.
   a. Which Library do you go to, Hill Library or Barry Township Library?
   b. Which library do you go to, Hill Library or Barry Township Library?
   c. Which library do you go to, Hill library or Barry Township library?

4. If an underlined portion of this sentence is incorrect, select the revision that fixes it. If the sentence is correct as written, choose d.

   In my **english 99** class **last summer**, we read some interesting
   　　　　　　 A 　　　　　　 B

   essays by famous authors.
   　　　　　　 C

   a. English 99   c. Famous Authors
   b. last Summer   d. No change is necessary.

5. If an underlined portion of this sentence is incorrect, select the revision that fixes it. If the sentence is correct as written, choose d.

   Of the states in the **East,** one can travel the farthest **North** in **Maine.**
   　　　　　　　　　　 A 　　　　　　　　　　　　　　　 B 　　 C

   a. east   c. maine
   b. north   d. No change is necessary.

1

Editing Review Test 1

The Four Most Serious Errors (Chapters 15–19)

Directions: Each of the underlined word groups contains one or more errors. As you locate and identify each error, write its item number on the appropriate line below. Then, edit the underlined word groups to correct the errors. If you need help, turn back to the chapters indicated.

2 fragments _____   2 verb problems _____

2 run-ons _____   4 subject-verb agreement errors _____

1 Every time you step outside, you are under attack. 2 Which you may not know what is hitting you, but the attack is truly happening. 3 Invisible storms of sky dust rain down on you all the time. 4 It does not matter if the sun is shining and the sky are bright blue. 5 The dust is still there.

6 Sky dust consist of bug parts, specks of hair, pollen, and even tiny chunks of comets. 7 According to experts, 6 million pounds of space dust settle on the earth's surface every year. 8 You will never notice it, scientists, however, are collecting it in order to learn more about weather patterns and pollution. 9 Using sophisticated equipment like high-tech planes and sterile filters to collect dust samples.

10 Dan Murray, a geologist at the University of Rhode Island, has began a new project that invites students and teachers to help collect samples of cosmic dust. 11 Murray says that collecting the dust particles are quite simple. 12 It starts with a researcher setting up a small, inflatable swimming pool. 13 Next, this investigator leaves the pool out in the open for 48 hours. 14 Finally, the researcher uses a special type of tape to pick up whatever have settled over time. 15 The tape is put into a beaker of water to dissolve a microscope is used to analyze what comes off the tape. 16 The information finded there will help scientists predict insect seasons, measure meteor showers, or even catch signs of global warming.

Editing Review Test 2

The Four Most Serious Errors (Chapters 15–19)
Other Grammar Concerns (Chapters 20–25)

Directions: Each of the underlined word groups contains one or more errors. As you locate and identify each error, write its item number on the appropriate line below. Then, edit the underlined word groups to correct the errors. If you need help, turn back to the chapters indicated.

2 fragments _____   1 run-on _____

1 subject-verb agreement error _____   1 pronoun error _____

1 misplaced/dangling modifier _____   2 coordination/subordination errors _____

1 use of inappropriately informal or casual
language _____

1 Early on May 1, 2011, Sohaib Athar, an IT consultant in Pakistan, was surprised to hear helicopters flying over his house. 2 Soon, he sent a Twitter message about it: "Helicopter hovering above Abbottabad at 1 AM (is a rare event)." 3 He continued to tweet about what he was hearing for the next half hour, attracting many Twitter followers.

4 Because he didn't know it at the time, Athar became the first person to publicize the raid in which Osama bin Laden was captured and killed. 5 For this reason, Athar also became one of the most famous of a growing number of so-called citizen journalists. 6 Unlike most traditional news gatherers, citizen journalists aren't trained in journalism. 7 They follow events and trends that interest them, but they send their observations to others through Facebook, Twitter, and other social media.

8 Certain media critics argue, however, that if someone tweets about something newsworthy, they don't necessarily deserve to be called a journalist. 9 That is the view of Dan Miller, a reporter who had the following reaction to Athar's famous reports: "Wondering on Twitter why there are helicopters flying around your neighborhood isn't journalism." 10 According to Miller, traditional media, not Athar, got the 411 about bin Laden's capture out to the whole world. 11 Not to just some Twitter followers.

→

Editing Review Test 2, continued

12 Others say that Athar provided a more valuable service. 13 For example, he communicated with people who were following him and tried to answer their questions, he sought out other sources of information and shared them. 14 Also, tried to analyze what he observed himself and what he learned from other sources.

15 Whether or not Athar deserves to be called a journalist, one thing is clear: More people is feeling driven to tweet, text, or blog from their particular corners of the world.

Editing Review Test 3

The Four Most Serious Errors (Chapters 15–19)
Other Grammar Concerns (Chapters 20–25)
Word Use (Chapters 26–27)

3

Directions: Each of the underlined word groups contains one or more errors. As you locate and identify each error, write its item number on the appropriate line below. Then, edit the underlined word groups to correct the errors. If you need help, turn back to the chapters indicated.

1 run-on _____   1 verb problem _____

1 word-choice error _____   2 pronoun errors _____

1 adjective error _____   1 spelling error _____

1 subject-verb agreement error _____   1 misplaced/dangling modifier _____

2 commonly confused word errors _____

1 How do you celebrate the New Year? 2 Some people watch television on New Year's Eve so that he can see the glittering ball drop in New York's Times Square. 3 Others invite friends and family over to celebrate with special foods or fireworks.

4 The New Year are celebrated all over the world in a variety of ways. 5 For example, in Australia, people spent the day in fun, outdoor activities, such as picnics, trips to the beach, and rodeos. 6 After all, it is summertime there in January. 7 In Spain, people eat a dozen grapes at midnight. 8 They eat one each time the clock chimes because she believe that it will bring good luck for the New Year. 9 The people of Denmark have the unusualest tradition. 10 On New Year's Eve, they throw old dishes at the doors of their friends' homes. 11 If you find a lot of broken junk in front of your house in the morning, you are well-liked. 12 Wearing all new clothes is the way many Koreans celebrate the start of the New Year. 13 In Germany, people leave food on there plates, this practice is meant to ensure that their kitchens will be full of food for the coming New Year.

14 Not all countries celebrate the New Year on January 1. 15 Setting off firecrackers, the holiday is celebrated later by the Chinese people. 16 The date of the Chinese New Year ➡

Editing Review Test 3, continued

depends on the lunar calander and usually falls somewhere between January 21 and February 20.
17 The Chinese often have a big parade with colorful floats of dancing dragons. 18 The mythical
creatures are supposed to be cymbals of wealth and long life.

Editing Review Test 4

The Four Most Serious Errors (Chapters 15–19)
Other Grammar Concerns (Chapters 20–25)
Word Use (Chapters 26–27)
Punctuation and Capitalization (Chapters 28–32)

Directions: Each of the underlined word groups contains one or more errors. As you locate and identify each error, write its item number on the appropriate line below. Then, edit the underlined word groups to correct the errors. If you need help, turn back to the chapters indicated.

1 run-on _____   1 verb problem _____

1 apostrophe error _____   1 pronoun error _____

1 adverb error _____   1 quotation mark error _____

1 subject-verb agreement error _____   1 capitalization error _____

1 comma error _____   1 semicolon error _____

1 In response to the ongoing economic crisis, more high schools are teaching financial literacy: how to create a budget, save money, and stay out of debt. 2 Although most experts agree that teaching these skills is a good idea, some recommend that such education begin more earlier—even in preschool. 3 This way, young people have more time to learn good habit's, save money, and plan for their financial future.

4 The Moonjar is one Tool for teaching children good money skills. 5 It consists of three tin boxes; each of which is labeled "spend," "save," or "share." 6 Children are encouraged to divide allowances or gifts of money equally among the boxes. 7 As the weeks pass by, they watch their savings grow, helping them see the benefits of saving money over time, they also learn discipline about spending. 8 For example a child who is shopping with a parent might ask for a pack of candy or a small toy. 9 The parent can reply, "Do you have enough money in your spend box"?10 Exchanges like that one help the child understand the consequences of financial decisions; if they spend money on one item now, less money will be available for other purchases in the future.

→

Editing Review Test 4, continued

11 <u>Mary Ryan Karges, who is in charge of sales for Moonjar LLC, recommend that financial skills be emphasized as much as other basic skills taught to young children.</u> 12 She says, "If we teach save, spend, share with the same vigor that we teach stop, look, listen, we won't run into so many financial problems." 13 <u>Once children have seed the benefits of good financial choices, they are on their way to a better future.</u>

Editing Review Test 5
The Four Most Serious Errors (Chapters 15–19)
Other Grammar Concerns (Chapters 20–25)
Word Use (Chapters 26–27)
Punctuation and Capitalization (Chapters 28–32)

5

Directions: Each of the underlined word groups contains one or more errors. As you locate and identify each error, write its item number on the appropriate line below. Then, edit the underlined word groups to correct the errors. If you need help, turn back to the chapters indicated.

1 run-on _____   1 semicolon error _____

1 pronoun error _____   1 verb problem _____

1 comma error _____   1 adverb error _____

1 apostrophe error _____   1 spelling error _____

1 use of inappropriately informal or casual   1 parallelism error _____

language _____   1 hyphen error _____

1 capitalization error _____

   1 If it seems as though places in the United States are more crowded lately; it might be
because the country's population recently hit 300 million. 2 The nation has the third-largest
population in the world. 3 Only China and India have more people. 4 Experts belief that by 2043
there will be 400 million people in the United States.

   5 The country is growing rapidly because people are having more babies more people are
moving to the United States. 6 The northeast is the most populated area within the country.
7 It took fifty two years for the country's population to go from 100 million to 200 million. 8 It
took only thirty-nine years to rise from 200 million to its current 300 million. 9 If experts statistics
are correct, it will take even less time for the population of the United States to reach 400 million.

   10 Some people worry that the United States is growing too quick. 11 Researchers predict
some super scary possibilitys. 12 They state that if the population grows too large, it will stress
available land, deplete water resources, and it can increase air pollution. 13 Its concerns are valid
ones; in the meantime, the population just keeps growing. 14 Although this country is large
future generations may be squeezed in more tightly than the present generation can imagine.

Acknowledgments

Susan Adams, "The Weirdest Job Interview Questions and How to Handle Them." From *Forbes,* June 16, 2011. Copyright © 2011 by Forbes. All rights reserved. Used by permission and protected by the Copyright Laws of the United States. The printing, copying, redistribution, or retransmission of this Content without express written permission is prohibited.

Dave Barry, "The Ugly Truth about Beauty" (originally titled "Beauty and the Beast"). First appeared in *The Miami Herald*, February 1, 1998. Reprinted by permission of the author.

Judith Ortiz Cofer, "The Myth of the Latin Woman: I Just Met a Girl Named Maria," from *The Latin Deli: Prose and Poetry*. Copyright © 1993 by Judith Ortiz Cofer. Reprinted by permission of the University of Georgia Press.

Patrick Conroy, "Chili Cheese Dogs, My Father, and Me." Copyright © 2004 by Pat Conroy. First appeared in *Parade*, November 14, 2004. Reprinted by permission of Marly Rusoff & Associates, Inc.

Barbara DeMarco-Barrett, "Set Your Writing Free: Use This Technique to Spark Creativity and Loosen Your Inhibitions," from *Pen On Fire: A Busy Woman's Guide to Igniting the Writer Within*. Copyright © 2004 by Barbara DeMarco-Barrett. Reprinted by permission of the Houghton Mifflin Harcourt Publishing Company.

George Dorrill, "Reading: A Personal History." First appeared in *The Voice*, January/February 2003. Reprinted by permission of the National Writing Project (NWP).

Stephanie Ericsson, "The Ways We Lie." Copyright © 1992 by Stephanie Ericsson. First appeared in *The Utne Reader*, November/December 1992. Reprinted by permission of Dunham Literary as agent for the author.

Gail Godwin, "The Watcher at the Gates," from *The New York Times*, January 9, 1977. Copyright © 1977 by The New York Times. All rights reserved. Used by permission and protected by the Copyright Laws of the United States. The printing, copying, redistribution, or retransmission of this Content without express written permission is prohibited.

Dianne Hales, "Why Are We So Angry?" Copyright © 2001 by Dianne Hales. First appeared in *Parade*, September 2, 2001. Reprinted by permission.

Samantha Levine-Finley, "Isn't It Time You Hit The Books?" First appeared in U.S. News and World Report's *America's Best Colleges 2008*, Aug. 17, 2007. Reprinted by permission.

Taylor Mali, "Making Kids Work Hard," from *What Teachers Make: In Praise of the Greatest Job in the World*. Copyright © 2012 by Taylor Mali. Reprinted by permission of G.P. Putnam's Sons, a division of Penguin Group (USA) LLC.

Bill Maxwell, "Start Snitching." First appeared in *Tampa Bay Times*, September 30, 2007. Reprinted by permission of the author.

Donald M. Murray, "The Maker's Eye," from *The Writer*. Copyright © 1973 by Donald Murray. Reprinted by permission of The Rosenberg Group on behalf of the author's estate.

Alexandra Natapoff, "Bait and Snitch: The High Cost of Snitching for Law Enforcement." First appeared in *Slate*, December 12, 2005. Reprinted by permission of the author.

Tara Parker-Pope, "How to Boost Your Willpower," from *The New York Times*, December 6, 2007. Copyright © 2007 by The New York Times. All rights reserved. Used by permission and protected by the Copyright Laws of the United States. The printing, copying, redistribution, or retransmission of this Content without express written permission is prohibited.

Annie Murphy Paul, "Your Brain on Fiction," from *The New York Times*, March 18, 2012. Copyright © 2012 by The New York Times. All rights reserved. Used by permission and protected by the Copyright Laws of the United States. The printing, copying, redistribution, or retransmission of this Content without express written permission is prohibited.

Dayn Perry. "The Problem of Steroid Use in Major League Baseball Is Exaggerated" (originally titled "Pumped Up Hysteria"). First appeared in *Reason*, January 2003. Reprinted by permission.

Steven Pinker, "Are Your Genes to Blame?" from *Time,* January 20, 2003. Copyright © 2003 by Time Inc. All rights reserved. Reprinted/Translated from TIME and published with permission of Time Inc. Reproduction in any manner in any language in whole or in part without written permission is prohibited.

Carolyn Foster Segal, "The Dog Ate My Flash Drive, and other Tales of Woe" (originally titled "The Dog Ate My Disk, and other Tales of Woe"). First appeared in *The Chronicle Review*, August 11, 2000. Reprinted by permission of the author.

Amy Tan, "Fish Cheeks." Copyright © 1987 by Amy Tan. First appeared in *Seventeen Magazine*, December 1987. Reprinted by permission of the author and the Sandra Dijkstra Literary Agency.

John Tierney, "Yes, Money Can Buy Happiness," from *The New York Times*, April 16, 2008. Copyright © 2008 by The New York Times. All rights reserved. Used by permission and protected by the Copyright Laws of the United States. The printing, copying, redistribution, or retransmission of this Content without express written permission is prohibited.

Rodrigo Villagomez, "The Designer Player." First appeared in *Delta Winds: A Magazine of Student Essays*, a Publication of San Joaquin Delta College, 2006. Reprinted by permission of the author and *Delta Winds*.

Index

Inside LaunchPad Solo for *Real Reading and Writing*

LearningCurve Activities

Active and Passive Voice

Apostrophes

Coordination and Subordination

Capitalization

Commas

Critical Reading

Fragments

Multilingual—Articles and Types of Nouns

Multilingual—Prepositions

Multilingual—Sentence Structure

Multilingual—Verbs

Parallelism

Parts of Speech—Nouns and Pronouns

Parts of Speech—Verbs, Adjectives, and Adverbs

Parts of Speech—Prepositions and Conjunctions

Pronoun Agreement and Pronoun Reference

Run-On Sentences

Subject-Verb Agreement

Verb Tenses

Vocabulary

Word Choice and Appropriate Language

Additional Grammar Exercises

Chapter 15: The Basic Sentence: An Overview

Chapter 16: Fragments: Incomplete Sentences

Chapter 17: Run-Ons: Two Sentences Joined Incorrectly

Chapter 18: Problems with Subject-Verb Agreement: When Subjects and Verbs Don't Match

Chapter 19: Verb Tense: Using Verbs To Express Different Times

Chapter 20: Pronouns: Using Substitutes for Nouns

Chapter 21: Adjectives and Adverbs: Using Descriptive Words

Chapter 22: Misplaced and Dangling Modifiers: Avoiding Confusing Descriptions

Chapter 23: Parallelism: Balancing Ideas

Chapter 26: Vocabulary and Word Choice: Finding the Right Word

Chapter 27: Spelling and Commonly Confused Words

Chapter 28: Commas

Chapter 29: Apostrophes

Chapter 30: Quotation Marks

Chapter 32: Capitalization: Using Capital Letters